IDAHO
A CLIMBING GUIDE

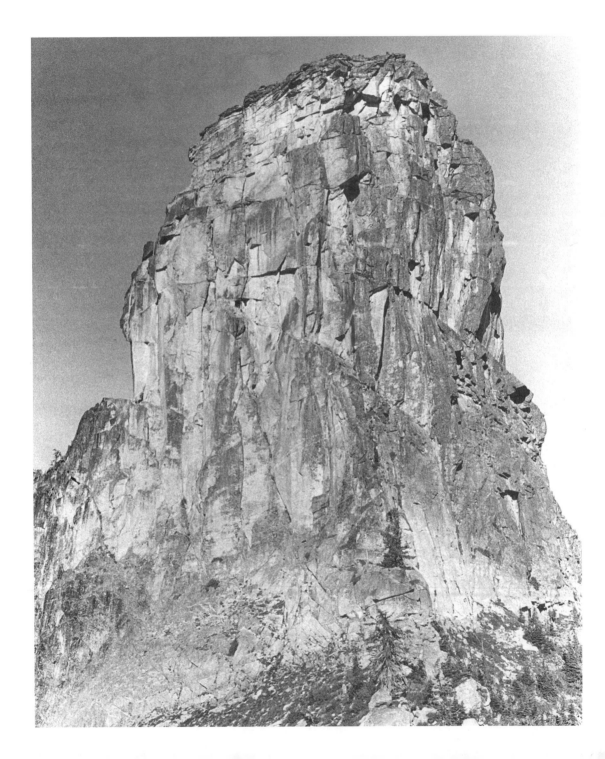

IDAHO
A CLIMBING GUIDE

CLIMBS, SCRAMBLES, AND HIKES

[ORIGINALLY TITLED *EXPLORING IDAHO'S MOUNTAINS*]

TOM LOPEZ

THE MOUNTAINEERS BOOKS

Published by
The Mountaineers Books
1001 SW Klickitat Way, Suite 201
Seattle, WA 98134

© 2000 by Tom Lopez

First edition, 1990 (originally titled *Exploring Idaho's Mountains*). Second edition: first printing 2000, second printing 2011

Manufactured in the United States of America

Managing Editor: Kathleen Cubley
Editor: Brenda Pittsley
Designer: Ani Rucki
Maps: Moore Creative Designs
Book layout: Hargrave Designs
Photo enhancement: Red Shoe Design
All photographs by the author unless otherwise noted

Cover photograph: *Mount Heyburn and the Elephant's Perch from Saddleback Lakes (from left to right: the West Pinnacle, the west summit, the east summit, and, in the foreground, the Elephant's Perch's face), Sawtooth Mountains.* ©Tom Lopez

Frontispiece: *Chimney Rock—the lightening rod of the Selkirks*

Library of Congress Cataloging-in-Publication Data
Lopez, Tom, 1951–
    Idaho, a climbing guide : climbs, scrambles, and hikes / Tom Lopez.— 2nd ed.
        p.   cm.
    Rev. ed. of: Exploring Idaho's mountains. c1990.
    Includes bibliographical references (p.   ) and index.
    ISBN 0-89886-608-1 (pbk.)
    1. Mountaineering—Idaho—Guidebooks. 2. Idaho—Guidebooks. I. Lopez, Tom, 1951– Exploring Idaho's mountains.
II. Title.
    GV199.42.I2 L67 2000
    796.52'2'09796—dc21
                                00-08234
                                CIP

Printed on recycled paper
ISBN (paperback): 978-0-89886-608-7
ISBN (ebook): 978-1-59485-310-4

CONTENTS

ACKNOWLEDGMENTS

It is now well over twenty years since I started the initial research for my first book, *Exploring Idaho's Mountains*, and ten years since the first edition was published. *Idaho: A Climbing Guide* represents an evolution of the first book. Like the first, the second would not exist without the help and input of many people. First, everyone listed in the acknowledgments for *Exploring Idaho's Mountains* are also contributors to this book. Next, the staff at The Mountaineers Books, especially Kathleen Cubley, are responsible for taking a manuscript, photos, and maps and turning the pieces into the book before you.

Dana Hanson, a.k.a. Dana Lopez, my former wife and climbing partner for seventeen of the last twenty years, shared the exploration of Idaho with me. She was a major contributor to this book and the first book.

Author Randall Green provided photos and route information from his 1987 book *Idaho Rock* and reviewed the Selkirk chapter. Randall's generosity was motivated by his desire to serve the climbing community. Roger Jansson, area supervisor for the Priest Lake State Forest, and his staff also reviewed the Selkirk chapter and provided valuable insights. Chris Paulson of Bonners Ferry reviewed the Selkirk, Purcell, and Cabinet chapters and provided valuable updates for trail and road access entries. He also provided photos. Bruce Dreher provided information and photos for the Gospel Hump area.

Rick Baugher of Idaho Falls made so many contributions to this book that I hardly know where to start recounting them. I have given him two bylines in the text and referenced his name in many places. He reviewed and contributed extensively to the eastern Idaho section, as well as to several southern Idaho chapters. His knowledge of eastern Idaho's topography and mountain history is unsurpassed—he was the source for almost all of the historical material contained herein related to the United States Geological Survey (USGS) and other early explorers. His contributions to this book are priceless.

The route descriptions, comments, and photos provided by Lyman Dye formed the foundation of my original Sawtooth chapter. Lyman graciously allowed me to use his material again. Reid Dowdle of Hailey is the guru of Idaho's big wall climbers. He reviewed the Sawtooth chapter and provided route descriptions, photos, and corrections. His efforts helped expand and improve the Sawtooth chapter. Kirk Bachman of Sawtooth Mountain Guides also reviewed and contributed to a total rewrite of the Sawtooth chapter. Gary Estep provided valuable information on Sawtooth cross-country routes. Evelio Echevarria shared his experiences in Idaho's mountains from the 1950s, as well as his photographs.

Sheldon Bluestein, the dean of Idaho hiking guidebook authors, generously provided me with a selection of his Northern Idaho photos. His photos document areas of Idaho that few people ever see. Thank him at www.hikeidaho.com.

Terry Maley, author of *Exploring Idaho Geology*, provided professional editing for the original geology section. Mark Mollner of the National Weather Service edited the original weather section. Alan Virta, archivist for the Robert Limbert Collection at the Boise State University Library, assisted my review of Limbert's documents and photographs.

Basil Service has joined me on many climbs over the last fifteen years and provided valuable information that was included in the original book. This time around, he contributed to the Mountaineering History section.

Ron Watters, another Idaho author, reviewed a number of chapters and shared information relating to his climbs and the efforts of other Pocatello area climbers. Bob Boyles, of Boise, shared his climbing experiences and helped to straighten out the complicated route history on Borah's north face. He also contributed photographs. Bob Moseley of Boise provided route information and photos documenting climbs on the north faces of several Lost River Range peaks. Greg Parker of Boise provided valuable route information covering the Sawtooths and the Boise Mountains.

Doug Colwell of the American Alpine Club contributed his knowledge and encouraged others to provide additional route information.

Debbie Bloom acted as a part-time editor and typist and a full-time promoter. Many times during the winter of 1998–99 when I was overwhelmed with the task before me, she stepped in and kept the project on track.

Finally, my thanks go out to the United States Forest Service and its employees. Over the last twenty years I have learned much from their "on the ground" knowledge. They provided detailed information on road and trail conditions, anonymously authored brochures, updated maps, and built and maintained trails.

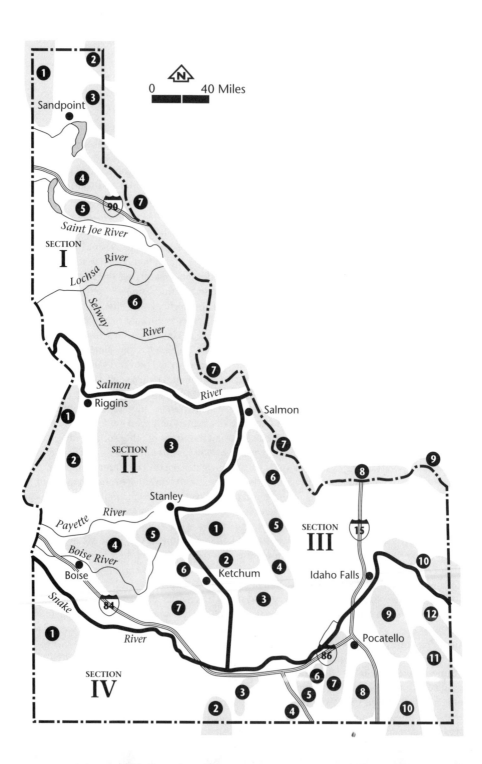

SECTION I

Sandpoint

Saint Joe River

Lochsa River

Selway River

SECTION II

Salmon River

Riggins

Salmon

Stanley

Payette River

Boise River

Boise

Ketchum

SECTION III

Idaho Falls

Pocatello

Snake River

SECTION IV

0   40 Miles

N

A WORD ABOUT SAFETY

Safety is an important concern in all outdoor activities. No guidebook can alert you to every hazard or anticipate the limitations of every reader. Therefore, the descriptions of roads, trails, routes, and natural features in this book are not representations that a particular place or excursion will be safe for your party. When you follow any of the routes described in this book, you assume responsibility for your own safety. Under normal conditions, such excursions require the usual attention to traffic, road and trail conditions, weather, terrain, the capabilities of your party, and other factors. A route that is safe in good weather or for a highly conditioned, properly equipped climber may be completely unsafe for someone else or under adverse conditions. Keeping informed of current conditions and exercising common sense are the keys to a safe, enjoyable outing.

You can minimize your risks by being knowledgeable, prepared, and alert. There is insufficient space in this book for a general discussion on climbing, but there are a number of good books and training courses on the subject, and you should take advantage of them to increase your knowledge. Just as important, you should always be aware of your own limitations and existing conditions when and where you are climbing. If conditions are dangerous or if you are not prepared to deal with them safely, change your plans. It is better to have wasted a few hours or days than to be the subject of a bad fall or rescue.

Climb safely and have fun!

—*The Mountaineers Books*

KEY TO MAP SYMBOLS

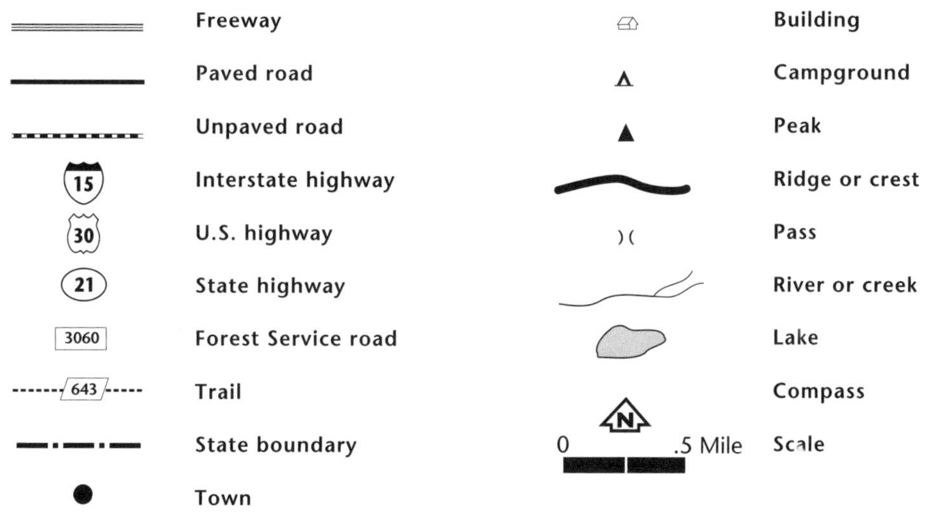

═══════	Freeway		⌂	Building
───────	Paved road		Λ	Campground
▪▪▪▪▪▪▪	Unpaved road		▲	Peak
(15)	Interstate highway		〰	Ridge or crest
(30)	U.S. highway		) (	Pass
(21)	State highway		⟋	River or creek
3060	Forest Service road		⬭	Lake
----/ 643 /----	Trail		△N	Compass
▪–▪–▪–	State boundary		0 .5 Mile	Scale
●	Town			

9

Idaho Batholith granite: the summit of Needles Peak

INTRODUCTION

For those who enjoy climbing mountains, the opportunities are unlimited in Idaho. This guidebook is an idea book and a starting point for mountaineers, hikers, and explorers. In the ten years since *Exploring Idaho's Mountains* (the first edition of this book) was published, Idaho's population has skyrocketed. Boise has become a city, and Coeur d'Alene has been transformed into a major resort destination. Surprisingly, this growth has had a positive effect and has not seriously degraded Idaho's environment. Increased recreation use has lead to major improvements in access roads and trails. While there are many different political battles still to be fought, recreationists are now an irresistible force demanding wise use of the mountains.

The climbs listed in this guidebook represent a multitude of climbing opportunities throughout the state. They range from extremely difficult technical ascents far from roads and trails to short trail walks. This book includes more than a hundred new peaks and hundreds of new routes. Nevertheless, a lot of Idaho is still *terra incognita*. The adventurous will find that Idaho is far from "climbed out"—there is still room to explore, still time to create your own climbing history.

Mountaineers will find no shortage of challenging routes on granite, basalt, and limestone. The Bighorn Crags, Lost River Range, Sawtooths, Selkirks, Seven Devils, and a host of individual peaks scattered throughout Idaho's remaining mountain ranges provide high quality Class 5 and Class 6 climbing opportunities. Many other peaks not suitable for technical climbing (because of rotten rock) offer exceptionally good Class 3 and Class 4 climbing on exposed ridges and incredible broken walls.

"Scramblers" will find at least a thousand Idaho peaks well suited to those who want to explore the sky. The variety of nontechnical routes is staggering. "Peak baggers," those who climb to collect summits, will find a wealth of ideas to stimulate their psyches, starting with Idaho's nine 12,000-foot summits and perhaps ending with the highest peak in each Idaho mountain range. No one has come close to climbing all of Idaho's 10,000-foot peaks.

Hikers will discover that many of Idaho's mountain summits can be reached by trail and that many of Idaho's most "chic" hiking destinations are not listed in hiking guidebooks. Trails lead to more than a hundred Idaho summits, ranging

from the craggy 7,009-foot Scotchman Peak in the Cabinet Mountains and the nearly 10,000-foot Trinity Mountain in the Boise Mountains to tiny Three Tree Butte (3,330 feet) in the Hoodoo Mountains.

"A GEOGRAPHIC MONSTROSITY"

Captains Meriwether Lewis and William Clark were the first white men to enter Idaho, crossing over the Beaverhead Range from Montana at Lemhi Pass in 1805. Unbeknownst to them as they enjoyed the view to the west, the lands that lay ahead would one day become the state of Idaho. The two explorers soon discovered that the land that stretched before them was the most mountainous land they would cross on their journey to the west coast. Idaho is a virtual sea of mountains.

More than 65 percent of the state's 83,557 square miles consists of mountain terrain. Elevations range from 12,662 feet on Mount Borah in the Lost River Range to only 736 feet above sea level at Lewiston. The land is up and down, with few truly level acres anywhere. More than four hundred summits reach above 10,000 feet, and valley-to-summit elevation differences exceed 8,000 feet in the Seven Devils Mountains and are often greater than 4,000 feet, even when maximum elevations do not exceed 8,000 feet. The predominance of mountains is Idaho's most consistent characteristic and the factor that prevents the state from developing into a homogeneous community. Thanks to its formidable mountain barriers, Idaho has always consisted of parts—north, west, east, and south.

The difficulty of Idaho's terrain is underscored by the fact that until 1920 not even a dirt road connected northern and southern Idaho; and it was not until 1938 that U.S. Highway 95 was completely paved its entire length. The first attempt to define and catalog Idaho's geologic features and geographic parts took place in the 1930s. This depression-era effort resulted in *The Idaho Encyclopedia*, which was compiled by the Federal Writers' Project of the Works Progress Administration. In those days, the writers were without high-quality maps and few people were familiar with a state that was almost entirely a roadless wilderness. Idaho's diversity and regionalism proved to be nemeses for the writers. They said of the state:

Idaho is a geographic monstrosity. Its shape and size were determined with no regard to what they should have been, but as a leftover area after the limits had been fixed in the states around it. In consequence, of all States in the Union, it has perhaps the least geographic logic and integrity within its borders.

Its long narrow panhandle is bounded on the north by Canada, on the west by Washington and on the east by Montana. The Bitterroot Range between it and Montana is a natural and logical boundary, and so is Canada on the north, but the western limit was fixed arbitrarily. South of the Salmon River, the state is bounded on the west by Oregon, with the Snake River serving as a natural boundary for more than half the distance. On the south are Nevada and Utah, with no natural demarcation between Idaho and those States. On the east is Wyoming, with a high mountain range as a logical division. Montana is on the north and northeast with the Bitterroot Range of the Continental Divide logically separating the two states.

Today, with the aid of an extensive road system and high-quality topographic maps, we know much more about the land that the writers of *The Idaho Encyclopedia* found a "geographic monstrosity." There is much still to be discovered about Idaho's mountains. Yet after twenty-five years of trying to climb every peak, I still have a long "to-do" list. Climb Idaho and you will not be disappointed.

MOUNTAINEERING HISTORY

Today mountaineers often think of mountaineering history in terms of first ascents. No doubt, this emphasis on first ascents originates from our innate desire for immortality and fame. Yet, in the past, the idea of a "first ascent" paled in importance to other motivations. Native Americans, explorers, trappers, prospectors, and settlers were the first humans to visit the summits of many Idaho peaks. Since these early "mountaineers" were motivated by utilitarian goals, they left little documentation recording their ascents. Thus, the true beginnings of Idaho mountaineering are, for the most part, undocumented. For example, Native Americans traversed the Clearwater and Salmon River Mountains extensively as part of their everyday lives. Their trails crossed many summits listed in this guide, but we know next to nothing of their adventures. Other Native American tribes used summits in the Beaverhead Mountains for vision quests. We know of their pilgrimages only by the small stone piles, remnants of their quests, found on a few remote peaks. Likewise, Lewis and Clark were sent across the Beaverhead, Bitterroot, and Clearwater Ranges in 1805 by a government anxious to understand the Louisiana Purchase. Although they wrote extensively of their travels, they left no accounts of ascents

Idaho's highest cabin was built by miners on the north end of Big Windy Peak. Sheep Mountain and Gilmore Peak are in the background. (Photo by Rick Baugher)

of Idaho peaks. Motivated by economics, trappers followed Lewis and Clark into the mountains and prospectors afflicted with gold fever relentlessly crossed and recrossed mountains and ridges all over the state. They marked their claims, often high up on a mountainside, but left nothing on the summits that they no doubt crossed.

It was not until the twentieth century that Idahoans had enough time on their hands to climb as a recreational pursuit. As exploits in the Alps and Himalayas were published, local climbers began to emulate the great climbers by forging new routes up Idaho's peaks. Since at least the beginning of the 1900s, each generation has produced groups of dedicated climbers who have made first ascents throughout the state. While these ascents were undoubtedly important to these climbers, few recorded their exploits and we know little of their accomplishments. Occasionally, we earn a glimpse into their lives when we discover an old, overlooked register buried at the bottom of a summit cairn. Therefore, when this book credits someone with a first ascent of a peak with a Class 1, 2, or 3 route to its summit, it is likely that someone else made an earlier ascent of the peak. The following is a thumbnail sketch of Idaho's mountaineering history, filled with unfortunate, but unavoidable gaps.

1800–1920

Trappers and Adventurers

The Lewis and Clark Corps of Discovery traversed the Beaverhead, Bitterroot, and Clearwater Ranges in 1805 and 1806 crossing high divides and following Native American trails. It is likely that the Corps of Discovery crossed a few summits during their journey. One of Corps' members, Sargent Patrick Gass, left us one comment on Idaho's mountains. He noted that the Bitterroot and Clearwaters were "the most terrible mountains I ever beheld." After Lewis and Clark, trappers, adventures, and prospectors began to trickle into Idaho. Only minimal documentation of the exploits of these people remains. One remaining account, perhaps the earliest written account of an ascent of an Idaho peak, was recorded by Warren A. Ferris in his book *Life in the Rocky Mountains* (Western Literary Messenger, 1844). The following is his account of climbing Pyramid Peak in the Beaverhead Mountains.

The sides of the mountains were very steep, and were covered with green or fallen pines, of which the latter were so interlocked with each other, and so numerous, that we were continually forced to leap our horses over them, and were frequently compelled to retrace our steps and seek some other passage. Here, an avalanche of huge rocks, trees and snows had been precipitated from the summit, and the sharp fragments left in the route, if slightly

disturbed, would immediately resume their headlong course downward.

Suddenly we came to the brink of some frightful ravine. Here we again turned, and followed the sharp edge of a very narrow ridge with yawning caverns almost beneath our feet on either side. Continuing our progress we reached a small cover above the regions of pine, surrounded by a naked wall of rock, which forms the base of the huge pyramids that constitute in general the summits of the Rocky Mountains.

With great difficulty we succeeded in gaining the top of the wall between two peaks, and halted beside a vast bank of snow from which little rills were trickling sources of the Missouri and Columbia. From this height, we surveyed the bottoms bordering Salmon River on the one side and the more extensive and fertile valley of the Wisdom River [Big Hole Valley] on the other.

After a cool draught from a rivulet, we commenced our descent which was by far more rapid and dangerous than our ascent, though infinitely less difficult.

Settlers crossing the Oregon Trail followed the trappers and prospectors. Some stopped short of Oregon and settled in Idaho. As Idaho developed, more folks were drawn or assigned to the state and occasionally, during their duties, a recorded ascent has come down to us. For example, in 1879 Captain Reuben F. Bernard and the U.S. Army troops under his command pursued a band of Sheepeater Indians over the summit of Sleeping Deer Mountain in the Salmon River Mountains, forcing a first recorded ascent by the Native Americans.

The Pioneering Alpine Surveyors

by Rick Baugher

Upon reaching the top of an Idaho summit you might find a benchmark (or an iron boundary marker if the peak is along Idaho's eastern border). On some peaks you might be fortunate enough to find a large rock cairn or a wooden tripod (a triangulation signal) left there many years before and occasionally you may find spent flares and battery casings from the 1950s. These artifacts were left by government surveyors who worked for the United States Geologic Survey (USGS) or the Coast and Geodetic Survey (CGS), or private surveyors who were hired by the General Land Office (GLO). Today, most mountaineers plan their trips with the aid of 7-½ minute USGS quadrangles (quad) maps that are staples for exploration from Florida to Alaska. The surveyors who collected the data that ultimately led to the development of these high-quality maps wrote perhaps the most important chapter in Idaho's mountaineering history: a chapter filled with exploration, first recorded ascents, and public service.

The earliest United States government surveyors were interested in the easiest land and water routes through Idaho. After Lewis and Clark, John C. Fremont's 1843 expedition was the next government expedition to pass through Idaho. Fremont's topographer/artist, Charles Preuss, made the first recognizable sketch of an Idaho mountain: Saddle Mountain in the Lemhi Range. Next, in 1855, John Mullan surveyed potential railroad routes across northern Idaho and in the process recorded three major traverses in the Clearwater and Coeur d'Alene Mountains. Government efforts were put on hold until after the Civil War.

After the Civil War, the federal government organized four famous survey crews to map the great American West. These surveys, which operated independently of each other, were headed by F. V. Hayden, J. W. Powell, Clarence King, and G. M. Wheeler. In 1879, the four groups were combined into a new agency: the United States Geologic Survey. (The Hayden survey group was originally known as the U.S. Geologic Survey of the Territories.)

During the field seasons of 1871–1872 and 1877–1878, topographers of the United States Geological Survey of the Territories under Hayden extensively explored southeastern Idaho. Surveyors Orestes St. John, Allen D. Wilson, Henry Gannett, and Gustavaus Bechler made more than thirty ascents and established triangulation stations on each of these summits. Triangulation is the process surveyors used to link known and unknown points together in the mapping process. It is not an easy process, since in the late 1800s it involved lugging more than forty pounds of equipment to a mountain summit. The information these men collected led to the creation of the first accurate maps of Idaho. Peaks used as triangulation stations by Hayden's surveyors included Oxford and Elkhorn in the Bannock Range, Sherman Peak in the Bear River Range and Meade Peak in the Peale Mountains, Caribou Mountain in the Caribou Range, and Sawtelle Peak in the Centennial Mountains.

During this same period, Alonzo V. Richards contracted with the General Land Office to survey the Idaho-Wyoming border and he no doubt crossed a summit or two during the survey. The Wheeler Survey, which focused on the Great Basin, also entered Idaho in 1877 and Fred Clark recorded the first ascent of a 10,000-foot Idaho summit, Cache Peak in the Albion Range. The peak was surveyed in 1877 at 10,451 feet (the current elevation is listed at 10,339 feet).

In 1889, the USGS sent a team of topographers to central Idaho. This crew, headed by William Griswold who was assisted by Edmund T. Perkins, established the first baseline in Idaho and set many triangulation stations that in turn

allowed the completion of Idaho's first topographic maps. These maps covered the area around Sun Valley. By the time they had completed their work, they had climbed Smoky Dome in the Soldier Mountains, Snowyside Peak in the Sawtooths, and Galena and Easely Peaks in the Boulders. Their highest ascent was Hyndman Peak in the Pioneer Mountains, which was probably not a first ascent. They measured the peak at 12,078 feet, and for the next 35 years Hyndman would be incorrectly recognized as Idaho's highest summit.

In 1897, the Department of Interior assigned USGS Topographer Joseph B. Lippincott to mark the boundaries of the newly created Bitterroot Forest Reserve. After completing his field work, Lippincott published a reconnaissance map and named several peaks including one triangulation station he called XIII, indicating that he probably climbed at least twelve other summits. Although his records are sketchy, we know he climbed 8,267-foot Graves Peak, now in the Selway-Bitterroot Wilderness, where he took one of the earliest, if not the earliest, photos from the top of an Idaho mountain.

Between 1897 and 1906, the entire Idaho/Montana border was surveyed. From 1897 to 1899, the northern 72 miles, a straight-line shot over rugged mountains, was surveyed by a USGS crew under the direction of E. T. Perkins and D. L. Reaburn. During their travels they climbed rugged Scotchman Peak and reported that they had climbed more than 50,000 vertical feet. Further south Howard B. Carpenter, under a GLO contract, surveyed the southern end of Idaho's eastern border from 1904 to 1906. Carpenter began in the north at the point where Perkins and Reaburn had stopped and surveyed south for 650 miles. Over the next three years, he planted iron mile markers the entire distance. Many of these mile markers are still in place today. Carpenter and his crew undoubtedly climbed every summit along the border and many had to be first ascents. Eighteenmile Peak, at 11,141 feet the highest point on the Continental Divide in the northern Rocky Mountains, was the crew's high point. The cost of the survey: $65,000.

The early 1900s also found the USGS busy in Idaho's interior. In the northern panhandle, Charles F. Urquhart and Clarence L. Nelson lead the crews that assembled the first northern Idaho topographic maps. George T. Hawkins surveyed the western mountains and Albert Pike and Herbert H. Hodgson continued the mapping of southeastern Idaho. This work continued to fill more of the blank spots but left most of central Idaho untouched. From a mountaineering viewpoint, central Idaho would turn out to be the most interesting venue for the USGS' mountaineering surveyors.

Officially designated as a USGS topographical engineer,

Howard Carpenter mile marker on top of Monument Peak in the northern Beaverheads (Photo by Rick Baugher)

Thomas M. Bannon was also a self-taught mountaineer. Although his name is not widely known in mountaineering circles, during his surveying career from 1889 to 1917 he climbed nearly one thousand summits in the American West. More than two hundred of these summits were in Idaho. Bannon's cryptic reports, supplemented by the rock cairns, wooden triangulation signals, chiseled cross-reference marks, and brass benchmarks that he left behind tell his fascinating story. More than one hundred of his Idaho ascents were probably first ascents. These climbs included many of Idaho's highest and most famous peaks, including Mount Borah (which he called Beauty), Leatherman Peak, and Invisible Mountain in the Lost River Range; Diamond Peak (which he called Thumb), Bell Mountain (Bannon's Finger), Lem Peak, and May Mountain (Bannon's Hi Peak) in the Lemhi Range; Standhope Peak and Smiley Mountain in the Pioneers; Castle Peak in the White Clouds; and Mount McGuire in the Salmon

River country. Bannon's death at 48 cut short an incredibly active life.

Another government agency, the Coast and Geodetic Survey under Carey V. Hodgson occupied several southern Idaho summits in 1915 while setting up a land-line net to the Pacific Ocean. A land-line net was used to link various independent surveys into a unified database. Unlike Bannon and his contemporaries, the CGS crews relied on trucks rather than horses to haul their gear whenever possible. Aerial reconnaissance was also used by the CGS crews. One other interesting point, unlike the USGS, the CGS worked at night and is responsible for flare and battery remnants found on many Idaho summits. Although the pioneering days were fading, much of Idaho was still unmapped and surveying activity continues right up to the present.

1920–1935

The Outdoorsmen Take Over

As Idaho's frontier stabilized, outdoorsmen such as Robert Limbert turned to Idaho's mountains for purely aesthetic pursuits. In 1926, Limbert published an article in the Idaho Statesman titled "Trailing Through the Land of Tomorrow."

T.M. Bannon (Courtesy United States Geologic Survey)

It is the earliest written account known of recreational climbing in Idaho.

The article, which recounts Limbert's 158-day pack trip through the Boise and Sawtooth Mountains, includes an account of his climb of Snowyside Peak in the Sawtooths with a party consisting of John Ewald, F. S. Barber, and Ted Williams. According to Limbert, Ewald, an Idaho native, had climbed many of Idaho's peaks by the mid-1920s. Although Limbert's article fails to provide exact details of these climbers' accomplishments, it is clear that the locals were "peak bagging" long before the outside world knew much about the state.

In 1927, in a second article in the *Statesman,* "The Crown of the Sawtooths," Limbert provided a detailed route description of Snowyside Peak's main ridges, including the Class 4 North Ridge.

Bob "Two Gun" Limbert, a.k.a. "The Man from the Sawtooths," was a naturalist, explorer, guide, humorist, author, photographer, mountaineer, poet, painter, trick-shot artist, taxidermist, sculptor, big game hunter, and a bird and animal imitator. Limbert knew central Idaho perhaps better than any of his contemporaries and, unlike others, wrote about what he saw on his many journeys throughout the state. He spent a great deal of his short life (he died at 48) promoting Idaho's scenic attractions and is credited with inspiring President Calvin Coolidge to create the Craters of the Moon National Monument.

After his success with President Coolidge, Limbert turned his attention to the Sawtooths, where he constructed the Redfish Lake Lodge below Mount Heyburn and extensively explored and photographed the range. Limbert did not fill the stereotype of a true mountaineer, but he was the prototype for the Idaho mountaineer—part woodsman, part explorer, and part thrill-seeker. Although Two Gun Bob was probably the first person to reach the top of several Idaho peaks, we will never know the full extent of his Idaho ramblings.

Who Lives Next to the Highest Peak?

Despite T. M. Bannon's 1912 ascent of Idaho's highest summit, he did not realize that it was higher than Griswold and Perkins' measurement of Hyndman Peak. In fact, it would take another sixteen years before Mount Borah was recognized as Idaho's highest summit. Although Hyndman Peak was popularly proclaimed Idaho's highest summit, not everyone was happy with this situation. In the early 1920s, the Idaho Statesman ran an article that proclaimed Hyndman Peak Idaho's highest peak and, soon after, the paper received

Self-portrait, Robert Limbert (Courtesy Robert Limbert Collection, Boise State University Library)

protests declaring Patterson Peak in the White Cloud Peaks as the highest. The protesters even pinned a height of 13,000 feet on their choice. The fact was that in the early 1920s, determining which peak was Idaho's highest was not a top priority for the USGS. In fact, the discovery that Borah is Idaho's highest peak was inadvertent.

In 1929, Lee Morrison of the USGS was conducting a mapping survey of the terrain west of Challis, Idaho, when he trained his instruments to the east on a far-off group of unnamed peaks that seemed a little bit too high to him. His calculations put the height of the highest peak at 12,655 feet. Soon after, the *Statesman* declared "Unnamed Peaks in Pahsimeroi Range Steal Hyndman's Glory." The unnamed peak quickly became a celebrity attracting the public's interest and raising demands that it deserved a name. A year after Morrison's discovery, the peak was named for Idaho's late Senator, William E. Borah, who served in the U.S. Senate for thirty-four years.

Most of what we know of Mount Borah's early history is due to the efforts of Robert Fulton, a free-spirited author, ranch hand, and explorer who published two articles about the peak. Fulton, along with Ray Odle, placed the first register on the summit in 1930. Their climb was probably the first ascent made after the peak was declared Idaho's highest. In his 1935 article in the *Statesman,* Fulton, surprisingly unaware of T. M. Bannon's 1912 ascent, stated that, before Borah's height was established, at least three people had summited. These were Clyde Jennings of Twin Falls, Norman Wilson from California, and Will Bascom of Mackay. In 1938, Fulton published the first climbing guide to Mount Borah in the magazine *Seeing Idaho.* By that year, more than thirty people had signed their names in the summit register and Fulton had climbed the peak three times.

1930–1945

Modern mountaineering finally arrived in Idaho in 1934, the year that experienced mountaineers first tested and conquered several of the state's most demanding peaks. In northern Idaho, Chimney Rock, dubbed Idaho's "lightning rod," was first climbed by mountaineers from the Seattle area. Farther south, the Sawtooths saw the first visit of dedicated East Coast mountaineers Robert and Miriam Underhill. After the 1934 climbing season, Idaho would no longer be a sanctuary for local climbers and "the word" slowly began to trickle out.

Chimney Rock

Chimney Rock is a fantastic granite shaft that sits square on top of the Selkirk Crest, east of Priest Lake. It is so close to Spokane, it is difficult to believe that the first recorded attempt of its tiny summit was not made until 1933. Nonetheless, the growing contingent of U.S. mountaineers remained oblivious to Chimney Rock's fine lines and the first attempt was left to a local, Byron Ward, and his friend John Carey. Ward and Carey's first attempt was valiant, inadequately equipped, and almost successful. Nearly at the top of the west face, the two finally turned back in foul weather. After a winter to think about their missed success, the pair returned to the rock in 1934 supplemented by experienced Seattle climbers Mart Chamberlain and Fred Thieme and completed the route on the west face. The exploits of Ward and Carey are retold in some detail in Ron Klimko's 1972 article in *Off Belay* (See December 1972, p. 446).

The Easterners and the Woodsman

In 1934, when Boston mountaineers Robert and Miriam Underhill came to the Stanley Basin, the Sawtooths were well-known for their spectacular scenery, but were still unknown to mountaineers. Unlike Bob Limbert, John Ewald, and other local climbers, the Underhills were established "cutting edge" climbers. Robert had established difficult routes in the Tetons and climbed in the Alps and Himalayas. Miriam was not far behind Robert in skill and determination. While climbing in the Tetons, Robert heard stories of the Sawtooths and set out to confirm rumors of "sharp granite peaks." When the husband-and-wife team arrived in Stanley, they hooked up with local rancher Dave Williams, a superb woodsman who knew the Sawtooth backcountry well, having spent many years hunting goats along the ridges and guiding fishermen into the high lakes. The Underhills contributed technical expertise, Williams, the woodsman's knowledge, and the perfect Idaho climbing team went to work.

With Williams proclaiming "You folks pick out the mountain you want to climb, and . . . I'll take you to it," the climbers wandered up their first canyon and set their eyes on Snowyside Peak. When they reached the top, they discovered others had preceded them, but whatever disappointment this revelation might have caused was probably eased by the summit view, which was filled with dozens of stunning and probably unclimbed summits. As Miriam Underhill explained, "It was from the top of Snowyside that we first discovered Red Finger Peak, (known today as the North Raker) quite far to the northwest, but so striking in its vertical lines that we set our hearts on it at once." While few peaks were difficult enough to turn the Underhills back, the smooth walls of Red Finger were too much for them. Recognizing the peak would not be surmounted without some form of direct aid, they scampered up the lower south peak and planned their next climb.

Mountaineers were introduced to the Sawtooths by an article published by Miriam in *Appalachia* titled "Leading a Cat by Its Tail." Apparently their first Sawtooth fling left the Underhills with an appetite for more Sawtooth climbing and, not surprisingly, the article, while enthusiastic, was not too informative as it recounted the couple's 1934 experiences in the Sawtooths. With the outside world unaware of the many first ascents still available in the Sawtooths, 1935 saw the Underhills return and again team up with Williams. This second time around, they climbed everything that was within their abilities. During their two climbing seasons in the Sawtooths they racked up an impressive list of nearly twenty first ascents, including the difficult, crumbling west summit of Mount Heyburn, Mount Regan, Williams Peak, and Thompson Peak. More importantly, Robert published a second 1935 article in *Appalachia* entitled "The Sawtooth Mountains of Idaho," which lured many mountaineers to the Sawtooths over the next twenty years.

Heaven and Hell

During the late 1930s and early 1940s, a solitary man named A. H. Marshall was making climbing history in the Seven Devils Mountains by undertaking many lonely expeditions in what was then extremely remote country. Marshall, who may have been the first person to reach the highest point in each of the forty-eight contiguous states, was a true Idaho mountaineer who enjoyed the approach as much as the climb. As the editor of the Mazama Journal explained:

Since few men are willing to live solely on dates, peanuts and dehydrated soup for days at a time, carry heavy packs for miles through wild mountain terrain, go a whole day without water, sleep out in snow storms, ford foaming mountain torrents and tackle unscaled cliffs miles from any sign of civilization, he has seldom had companions on his journeys into the wilderness.

Marshall's Seven Devils exploits were published in the 1947 *Mazama Journal,* Vol. 29, No. 13. When Marshall began his explorations in 1934, the Seven Devils country was not only difficult, it was also roadless—and his journeys to the alpine summits began 7,000 feet below, along the desert-like shores of the Salmon River. Despite the arduous nature of trips into the high country, between 1934 and 1943 Marshall recorded the first ascents of almost all of the major Seven Devils summits. Today, Marshall's solo routes, which often verged on Class 5, are among the most rewarding climbs found in Idaho—a little wilderness, a little rotten rock, a little exposure, and a little history. Like the Underhills' Sawtooth articles, Marshall's article would eventually bring well-equipped and highly skilled climbers to the Seven Devils.

The Railroad Tycoon and the Count

adapted from an article by Basil Service

During the Depression-era years of the mid-1930s, an idea grew in the mind of a young, wealthy, railroad baron who had visited Europe's grand mountain resorts. This idea would eventually transform central Idaho's mountain culture forever. The man was Averell Harriman, chairman of the board of the Union Pacific Railroad from 1932 to 1946 and later ambassador to the Soviet Union and Great Britain, and Secretary of Commerce. Convinced that America needed a destination ski resort (served by his railroad), he became committed to developing a resort that would surpass the European resorts.

Harriman's first step in the process was the retention of a European acquaintance, Count Felix Schaffgotsch, to scour the American West in search of a new Saint Moritz. The Count was evidently a perfectionist because after his initial journeys through Colorado, Wyoming, Utah, and California he rejected locations that are now considered some of America's premier ski resorts. In fact, the Count's initial findings were so discouraging that Harriman began to wonder if America's West was suitable for an elegant resort.

Finally, the Count was taken to a little mining and sheep-raising center in central Idaho named Ketchum. There, in the dead of a winter (and in a good snow year), the Count found his conception of perfection. He reported that the Ketchum area "contained more delightful features than any other place he had seen in the U.S., Switzerland, or Austria for a winter sports center." Harriman was especially pleased because his railroad already had a spur line leading to the town. In 1936, the railroad started construction of Sun Valley, an innovative resort that would produce the world's first chairlifts and bring countless celebrities to Idaho's backcountry.

Harriman's commitment to the European tradition also led to the importation of European ski guides and the construction of high mountain ski huts in the Pioneer and Smoky Mountains. These huts, Pioneer Cabin built in 1937 and Owl Creek Cabin built in 1940, brought "European Ski Mountaineering" to Idaho. Pioneer Cabin still sits on an incredibly picturesque, high saddle directly south of Handwerk Peak. The Owl Creek Cabin was destroyed by an avalanche in 1952.

The European Guides

The following information was contributed by Basil Service

Reaching the small, two-room Pioneer Cabin today after a strenuous spring ski ascent or summer hike, it is easy to appreciate how resort skiing and the concept of luxury has changed over the years. Physically, the cabins were nothing more than rustic bivouacs that Harriman knew needed additional luxuries to satisfy his chosen clienteles' expectations. To meet these expectations, he provided a chef and two ski-patrol boys to act as porters and European guides for each foray to the cabins. This lessened the pain of the all-day ski approach from Trail Creek Cabin, crossing twenty-four avalanche runs to get there.

One of the first guides engaged by Sun Valley was a young Bavarian painter and former Dartmouth College ski coach, Florian Haemmerle. He and fellow guides Victor Gottschalk and Andy Henning enjoyed a paradise, guiding clients into the cabins, skiing remote slopes and making winter ascents of many of the surrounding peaks until World War II erupted, ending their idyllic lifestyle. The war's effect on the community that had quickly evolved around the resort was devastating.

Henning, after serving in the highly-decorated U.S. Army 10th Mountain Division, returned to Sun Valley and in 1948 published *A Sun Valley Ski Guide,* still the best reference on the subject for those few fortunate persons who own a copy. Haemmerle, who also served in the 10th Mountain Division, returned and named several nearby peaks after some of his fallen comrades-in-arms. Salzburger Spitzel was named in honor of deceased guides Max Hauser, Hans Hauser, and Franz Epp; Handwerk Peak for Ted Handwerk, a waiter at the Ram Bar; Duncan Peak for Captain Jonathan Duncan, former manager of the lodge; and Bromaghin Peak for Captain Ralph Bromaghin, a Sun Valley ski instructor.

1945–1970

World War II changed everything in America. After the social upheaval caused by the war, people appreciated life and sought to enjoy it. More people attended college. Service men who had shared their memories of home with comrades from all over the country inspired greater travel across the states. Provincialism gave way to cosmopolitanism and new frontiers were born. In short, Americans began to discover America.

Idaho, like the rest of the country, was liberated, invaded by visitors, and integrated into the new world. Idaho's mountains were considered virgin territory by climbers who were determined to push climbing standards to new levels. Still, local Idaho climbers were making headway in their routinely quiet manner. An article in the *Idaho Statesman* in 1948 by Jack Anderson, titled "Here's a Club for You to Join, But it's a Rough Organization," suggested that by the end of the 1940s most, if not all, of the named, highly visible Idaho peaks had been climbed. Also of note in the article was a reference to a climbing fatality on Leatherman Peak. Although no details were provided, this was probably Idaho's first mountaineering fatality.

Corn and Potatoes

The Iowa Mountaineers were among the first outsiders to arrive in Idaho after World War II. They were enticed to the Sawtooths by the Underhill articles. Their leader, John Ebert, bolstered by guides, and combining skill, group organization, and a "let's do it" attitude, set out to explore and conquer the Sawtooth granite. Led by various guides, including Paul Petzoldt, these flatlanders would continue to make Sawtooth history for the next twenty-five years. They racked up a set of impressive first ascents and named many Sawtooth peaks. Among the Iowa Mountaineers, first ascents in the 1940s were Chockstone Peak, The Goat Perch, Redfish Peak, Mount Carter, Schwartz Pinnacle, Mount Bush, Mount Ebert, Mount Iowa, and Warbonnet Peak.

Perhaps the finest accomplishment of the Iowa Mountaineers was their 1947 ascent of Warbonnet Peak, a granite spire with a long-standing reputation for invincibility. The difficulty of the peak was first noted in the 1920s by Arval Anderson of the USGS, who conducted the initial survey of the range. Interestingly, the Underhills never mentioned this peak and it was not until after the war, more than twenty years after Anderson named the peak, that Bob Merriam, John Speck, Cal Wilcox, Bruce Adams, Cole Fisher, and Paul Petzoldt climbed the peak by its northwest face.

The 1960s began with the Iowa Mountaineers making the first ascent of a large, twin-humped peak in the Sawtooths, then known as Saddleback Peak or Sawtooth Dome. Although the peak is close to both Redfish Lake and many of the Iowan's earlier climbs, its Yosemite-like walls were bypassed in favor of other sharper peaks. Despite its size, the mountain has no walk-up route and its west and east faces are arguably Idaho's finest and most difficult granite walls. The Iowa Mountaineers pioneered the original route up the Class 4 northwest shoulder and left the great west and east walls to others.

Yes, Beckey Climbed Here

Those others were Fred Beckey, Steve Marts, and Herb Swedlund, who climbed the 1,200-foot west face in 1963 using fixed ropes, 110 pitons, and five bolts. Their climb was perhaps the most technically difficult Idaho route yet climbed. Fred Beckey, probably the most prolific climber of all time, arrived on the Sawtooth scene in the late 1940s. Over the next twenty-five years, driven by an intense desire to record first ascents, Beckey, along with many partners, pitoned and bolted his way up the range's most treacherous spires. Beckey's exploits are recorded in various volumes of the *American Alpine Journal.*

Also making stops in the Sawtooths in the 1940s were the Harvard Mountaineers, Dartmouth Mountaineers, and Seattle Mountaineers. Among the accomplishments of these diverse groups were the first ascent of Mount Heyburn's westernmost summit, the West Pinnacle (called unclimbable by the Underhills); the Grand Aiguille by Joe Hieb, Wes Grande, Graham Matthews, and Ralph Widrig; Splinter Tower by Jack Schwabland and Art Hoblen; the Thimble by Fred Beckey and Harry King; and Big Baron Spire and El Pima by Fred Beckey,

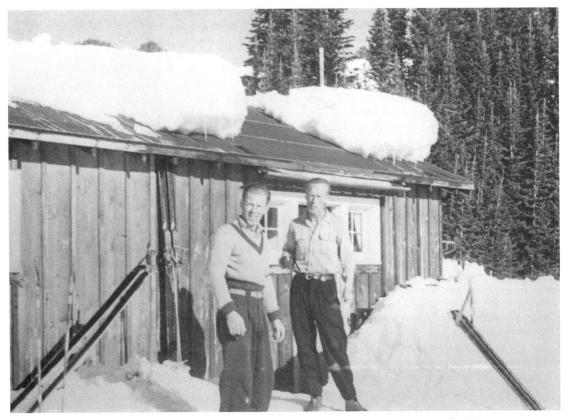

Victor Gottschalk and unidentified client at Pioneer cabin (Photo by Andy Henning, courtesy Basil Service Collection)

Pete Schoening, and Jack Schwabland. Finally, Beckey and Schoening bagged the North Raker via a difficult Class 6 route on the spire's north face.

The Bighorn Crags

While many mountaineers knew of the Selkirks and Sawtooths, few climbers had ventured beyond these spots. This changed in the mid 1950s when Lincoln Hales and Pete Schoening, two northwest-based mountaineers, discovered the Bighorn Crags in a remote corner of the Salmon River Mountains. Although Hales' brief article in the 1955 edition of the *Mountaineers Journal,* titled "Climbing the Big Horn Crags of Idaho," raised more questions than it answered, the pair were clearly the first to test the Crags' granite. Hales and Schoening made several first ascents, including their climb of shark-tooth-shaped, misnamed Knuckle Peak, the major climbing prize in the Crags. Hales' article served as a stimulus for Idaho's mountaineers to travel to the Crags. Beginning in

1957, a group of climbers centered in Idaho Falls formed the Idaho Alpine Club and adopted the Bighorn Crags as their climbing gym. These climbers, including Bill Echo, Dean Millsap, and Bob Hammer, knocked off all but one of the major rock formations that dot the Bighorn Crags and made many ascents throughout eastern Idaho.

The Lost River Range: Beyond Mount Borah

From the time of Bannon's first ascent of Mount Borah until the 1960s, little climbing took place in Idaho's highest mountain range, the Lost River Range. Spurred on by the successful 1963 American Mount Everest Expedition, climbers began to venture into these formidable mountains. Lyman Dye, a native of Ucon, Idaho, who learned to climb in the nearby Tetons, turned his attention to his home state in the early 1960s. He quickly established himself as one of Idaho's premier climbers, started a guide service in the Sawtooths in the 1970s and placed many imposing routes in eastern Idaho.

Dye's routes on the broken rock of the Lost River and Lemhi Ranges defy gravity and have seldom been repeated. Among his accomplishments are the first ascents of Diamond Peak's west face, Mount McCaleb's east face, Mount Borah's east face, and Bell Mountain's north face. Only those who have climbed in the Lost River and Lemhi Ranges can appreciate the beauty and difficulty of these climbs.

Louis Stur

In 1951, Louis Stur came to Sun Valley to visit, fell in love with Idaho and his wife Gail, and never left. The Hungarian immigrant was destined to become the most prolific climber among the European guides who worked at Sun Valley. Stur, with Jim Ball, occasionally with Fred Beckey, and often with Jerry Fuller, raised the standards of Idaho mountaineering as he explored every nook and cranny of the Sawtooths and established classic routes on many peaks. He pioneered three routes on Warbonnet: the south face in 1957 with Ring, Bennet, and Franke; the west ridge in 1958 with Jerry Fuller; and the east face in 1960. Stur specialized in climbing Warbonnet Peak and Mount Heyburn, both of which he ringed with new routes. He and his companions often found lines of attack that others had missed.

Mount Heyburn, a conglomeration of spectacular shattered towers, attracted climbers to its slopes at least as early as the 1920s, when the east summit was probably first climbed. After making the first ascent of the higher west peak, Robert Underhill described the peak's granite as "some of the worst stuff I have ever seen." Although many had tested the notoriously rotten granite, in 1958 none of the established routes were considered enjoyable and getting to the top was strictly a "because it's there" proposition. Stur, along with Jim Ball and Jerry Fuller, changed the mountain's reputation when they discovered an untried chimney on the peak's west face, which now bears Stur's name. Of moderate difficulty, the route avoided the "ball-bearing" granite encountered on other Heyburn routes by following a classic line grooved in solid granite for its entire distance.

Stur was as much a legend for his generosity as he was for his climbing exploits. One of the many beneficiaries of Stur's generosity and love for the mountains was Dr. Evellio Echeverria. Echeverria, on a personal quest to explore the world, arrived in Sun Valley from Chile in 1953 and took a job as a waiter. Stur quickly invited him into his climbing circle and the two shared many adventures over the next three years. Climber after climber discovered that no matter how busy Stur was at the lodge, he would always take time to answer a climbing question or point out the best route on a peak.

John Koppes on Borah Peak in 1954 (Photo by E.V. Echeverria)

Louis Stur died from a fall in 1989 at age 64 while exploring a chimney on Baron Peak in the Sawtooth backcountry.

Following A. H. Marshall's Trail

In 1963, a Mazama Club outing led by Don Eastman arrived in the Seven Devils hoping to follow in A. H. Marshall's footsteps. In the process of retracing Marshall's steps, they added a new chapter to the range's climbing history by establishing new routes on several peaks and by making the first ascents of the North Imp and the Devils Tooth. Their success was documented in two articles in the *Mazama Journal*, "We Climbed Nine of the Seven Devils" by Don Eastman and "North Tower of Devil's Tooth—First Ascent" by Jim Angell.

Chimney Rock, the Sequels

In 1958, twenty-five years after the first ascent, Ed Cooper and Don Bergman placed a second route on Chimney Rock when they climbed its northeast face. Cooper returned in 1961, this time with Dave Hiser, to climb a new route on the east face. In 1968 Fred Beckey and Jerry Fuller climbed the peak's South Nose. In the 1970s and 80s the rock's popularity increased geometrically and dozens of new routes were placed on its faces. Among the most active of the many climbers on Chimney Rock during this period were Chris Kopczynski, John Roskelley, Dane Burns, G. Oka, R. Bergner, W. Parks and T. Nephew, and Randall Green.

The Sawtooth Tradition, the Next Generation

The opening of Lyman Dye's guide service began the next chapter in the development of the Sawtooth mountaineering tradition. Following the course set by the post-war climbers, Dye's guide service promoted clean climbing and exploration. Along the way, Dye guided many groups, including the Mazamas and the Iowa Mountaineers. Both on his own and while leading his clients, Dye discovered new ways up many Sawtooth summits and set the stage for the less-than-experienced mountaineer to challenge the range. His first ascents are detailed throughout the Sawtooth chapter. Unlike many climbers who focused on small sections of the range, Dye climbed throughout the range and published articles detailing the available climbing opportunities. He was responsible for

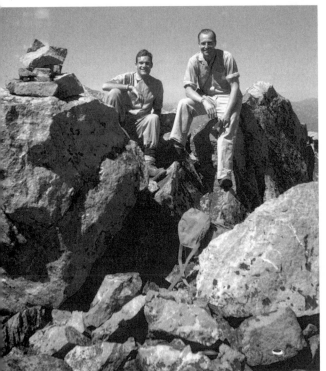

Louis Stur and Freddi Haemisaeger on top of Horstmann Peak in 1955 (Photo by E.V. Echeverria)

raising climbing standards to new levels and for paving the way for the next generation of climbers.

1970–1990

The period from 1970 through 1990 is less documented than one might expect. At least two factors contributed to this lack of documentation. First, the growing popularity of rock climbing and sport climbing lessened the emphasis on peaks, spires, and alpine walls to a certain extent. Second, many of the climbers who moved to Idaho during this period felt compelled to keep the unspoiled terrain of Idaho a secret. As the Eagles rock 'n' roll hit put it "call some place paradise, kiss it goodbye."

In fact, many of these climbers are still reluctant to talk about their accomplishments. This philosophy hid many spectacular climbing achievements. For example, in 1971 Harrison Hilbert and Geraldine Grady made the first ascent of Borah's treacherous north face across hard black ice and only reported their success to friends in Pocatello. Hilbert made at least two other early ascents on the face.

Another little known adventure took place in December of 1971 when Ron Watters, Jeff Elphanson, Steve Shafer, Harrison Hilbert, Jim Hokum, and Ike Gayfield decided to make the first winter ascent of Castle Peak. In 1971, the American Smelting and Refining Company (ASARCO) was beginning development of a huge open pit mining operation on Castle Peak's lower slopes. Watters and his companions realized that the mine would be an environmental catastrophe. The political forces at work teetered back and forth between miners and their supporters and environmentalists. Cecil Andrus' successful 1970 gubernatorial campaign was attributed to his strong opposition to the mine. Watters, who was active in the Greater Sawtooth-White Cloud Preservation Counsel, divided his time in 1971 between White Cloud exploration and political action work opposing the mine.

As a climber and a protector of the White Clouds, Watters could not resist the invitation to join a winter expedition to one of Idaho's most impressive peaks. Deep snow impeded the group's progress, but after two days they arrived at the base of the peak. Watters' account of the climb continues:

ASARCO had built cabins at the base of the peak, which housed their summer crews. In Idaho, it has long been a wilderness tradition that remote cabins are left open in the winter and that passersby are welcome to use them as long as they are cleaned and fresh kindling is left for the next person. ASARCO probably had no idea of this tradition, but had nevertheless left one cabin open—which we, in time-honored fashion, used.

A storm moved in that night, and we holed up in the cabin for another day. Finally, on the fourth day, the skies started clearing and we skied up to the unnamed lake just northwest of the peak and established a high camp. The fifth day dawned clear and bitter cold.

The deep snow and cold made the ascent arduous. Most of the party carried skies almost to the summit. Ike and I, both members of the Idaho State Track Team, were new to skiing, felt more secure on foot and left our skis midway up. That turned out to be a big mistake.

I was so tired from the steep incline and waist-deep snow that when I reached the summit, I had to remind myself to look around. The summit of Castle Peak overlooks an incomparable tableau of the unmatched landscape of central Idaho—a view that had been part of my motivation to make the climb—but I only had the energy to make a quick, forced survey and then begin the descent.

On the descent, night fell, as did the temperature, and my inexperience on skis compounded an already physically trying day. Below me, the siren call of the cabin was too much to resist, and long before I reached high camp, my companions had pulled down the tents and were deadheading for the ASARCO cabin.

During the bitter cold day, Ike and Jim's feet had suffered frost bite. Once their feet thawed at the cabin, we knew that skiing out would cause more damage. The next morning, Harrison, Steve, and Jeff skied out to hire a helicopter to airlift the three remaining climbers out. Just before dark, the helicopter arrived along with the Blaine County Sheriff, leaving only room for two climbers. Since the sheriff wasn't planning on walking out in his cowboy boots, I waved my friends off and spent the night alone in the cabin, a bit chagrined that I had been denied the splendid ride out. Yet, the ski out the next day more than made up for it. It was all downhill, and the snow soft, light, and cold.

Jim and Ike, who was the first African American to make a winter ascent of an Idaho peak, both recovered. Ike and Ron started Pocatello's first mountaineering store, Mountain Folk. Ron continued to develop his skiing and other outdoor skills, eventually becoming the director of the Idaho State University Outdoor Program and a prolific author on outdoor subjects.

Across the state in Boise, Lou and Frank Florence opened Boise's first specialized mountaineering shop, Sawtooth Mountaineering. Florence, a strong climber who made the first winter ascent of Borah via the standard route in 1973, also offered professional climbing instruction to locals. As a result, Frank was responsible for inspiring a generation of Boise climbers. Table Rock, which is a small butte behind Boise, was graced by a rock quarry that Florence used as a climbers' classroom. He and his students were also among the first to climb at the Black Cliffs near Lucky Peak Reservoir. They placed many of the routes rediscovered and rechristened by climbers in the 1990s.

In 1977, Frank Florence and three of his proteges, Bob Boyles, Mike Weber, and Art Troutner, bagged the first winter ascent of Borah's north face. Their marathon 26-hour climb, braving 30-35 mph winds and temperatures well below zero, was recognized in the *Idaho Statesman,* but their many other accomplishments went unreported. These four, along with Curtis Olson, placed four additional routes on Borah's north face and pioneered impressive routes on the north faces of Mount Idaho and Mount Breitenbach. While the thirty or so most dedicated climbers in the Boise valley often hung out at Sawtooth Mountaineering to share stories, they seldom discussed their current projects. Bob Boyles reminisced: "Back then, we were friends, but there was too much competition for the harder, prized routes. We never told anyone about an ongoing project until after the route was completed." Sadly, we still know too little about the accomplishments of these dedicated Idaho mountaineers.

The Selkirks—the Remake

In 1987 Randall Green published Idaho Rock, A Climbing Guide to the Selkirk Crest and Sandpoint Areas that brought northern Idaho rock climbing to the nation's attention. Green's chronicle features the accomplishments of many fine climbers from the late 1950s through the mid-1980s. Beginning with Don Bergman and J. Miller making the first ascent of Gunsight Peak's north face in 1962, Selkirk climbers spread out to other lesser known Selkirk summits like Roman Nose and Mount Harrison. Chris Kopczynski and John Roskelley both placed routes on Gunsight Peak in the late 1960s and Mount Harrison was ringed with routes in the 1980s. Randall Green and his climbing partners placed routes on the peak's south face, south buttress and west face. More importantly Green's book inspired a new generation of climbers to challenge the Selkirk's exceptional granite.

The Elephants Perch—Idaho's Big Wall

During the 1970s, the great wall on the Elephants Perch quickly became riddled with routes as the wall's reputation attracted climbers from Idaho, the Northwest, Yosemite, the South, and from the Shawangunks in the East. The major lines on the face were climbed one by one. In 1968, Gordon Webster and Steve Roper left Yosemite long enough to climb the east face, a Grade V, Class 6 route up a 500-foot dihedral;

in 1972, Jeff and Greg Lowe climbed a variation of Beckey's original line without placing bolts; Bill March and Jeff Splittgerber knocked off the northwest face in 1975; and Reid Dowdle and Don Hough climbed the line that divides the west face from the east face in 1977. Between these major lines, Reid Dowdle has placed many impressive routes up most of the remaining nonconformities in the rock. Dowdle, a modest, prolific, and highly skilled climber, has climbed the east and west faces more than ninety times since the mid-70s and is still climbing. His accomplishments on the Perch will probably never be equaled. Other climbers who have pioneered routes up the Perch's faces include Raymond Brooks, Jim Carlin, Doug Colwell, Dick Foster, Jeff Gruenburg, Jeff Hall, Jennifer Jones, Russell Oberg, Mike Paine, Steve Marts, Herb Schwabland, Gene Smith, and Kevin Swigert.

The Sawtooth Alpine Guides

Kirk Bachman, a native Idahoan, established the Sawtooth Mountain Guides in 1985. Bachman has raised Sawtooth climbing standards and he is at the forefront of efforts to preserve the Sawtooths for climbers. He began climbing in the Sawtooths in the mid-1970s while working for the Idaho State University Outdoor Program. Later in the decade, he moved to the Stanley Basin to work as a backcountry ski guide for Joe Leonard, originator of the first Sawtooth Ski Huts. Bachman also introduced yurts to the Sawtooths while working with Joe.

The Sawtooth Mountain Guides operates a climbing school, including half-day programs near Redfish Lake Lodge and full-day programs at the far end of Redfish Lake on the Super Slabs. Bachman's guides also lead climbers into the remote parts of the range to climb Mount Heyburn, the Elephants and Goats Perches, the Finger of Fate, and Warbonnet Peak. Many notable guides have been associated with the guide service over the years, including Jeff and Kellie Rhoads, Dave Bingham, Kevin Swigert, Erik Leidecker, and Bob Rosso. These guides pioneered many new and highly technical routes in the Sawtooths and trained many exceptional climbers.

Bob Boyles ascending the North Face Direct on Borah Peak in 1976 (Photo by Bob Boyles)

Rock Climbing Along the California Trail

The late 1970s and 1980s saw further refinements take place in Idaho mountaineering as the popularity of rock climbing exploded. Southern Idaho rock climbers followed the lead of Greg Lowe and many others who began to congregate in a land of beautiful granite formations tucked away in a small valley known as the "City of Rocks" at the south end of the Albion Range. No doubt many Idahoans and Idaho transplants learned to rock climb at the City; the friendly and not so friendly competition at the City advanced the abilities of many local climbers and acted as a drawing card to bring others to the state.

Spending Memorial Day weekends at the City became especially popular during the 1970s; the invasions of rock climbers, four-wheel-drive enthusiasts, campers, and sightseers often resembled a scene out of a 1960s love-in. Climbers in these gypsy groups pushed the route difficulty higher and higher. As the routes proliferated, it was inevitable that someone would write a climbing guide. In 1985, Dave Bingham fulfilled this destiny and published *City of Rocks: A Climbers Guide*. Now, at the start of a new millennium, the City of Rocks has changed forever. It is now managed as a National Preserve by the National Park Service and the Idaho Department of Parks and Recreation. Bingham's guidebook is in its fourth edition and several other authors have produced guidebooks describing the "not so silent" city.

An Ode to the Unknown Climber

Since most climbers toil in anonymity and do not write about their adventures, giving credit where credit is due is difficult. These unknown but highly committed climbers have amassed impressive peak lists, bagging hundreds of peaks over the years. There are many that I do not know. What follows is a little recognition to the few that I know.

Dana Hanson has accumulated more than three hundred Idaho summits since 1980. She was the first woman to climb all nine of Idaho's 12,000-foot peaks and her ascents, which include several firsts, stretch from Chimney Rock in the Selkirks to Quicksilver in the Owyhees to Snowdrift in the Peale Mountains to Freeman Peak in the Beaverheads, and almost every ridge in between.

Barbara Lilly, a California native, is another example. Since her first visit to Idaho in 1963 to hike and climb in the Seven Devils, she and her climbing partners have ascended more than forty Idaho peaks leaving registers atop most. Look for her registers on top of peaks stretching from Nahneke Mountain in the Sawtooths to Mount Jordan in the Salmon River Mountains to Lime Mountain in the White Knobs to Ryan Peak in the Boulders and on many peaks in between.

The peak list of Ketchum's Ben Benson includes well over a hundred Idaho summits that complement the climbs he has made all over the world. Basil Service, also of Ketchum and a contributor to this book, has lugged a fishing rod to the top of an ungodly number of Idaho summits. A fisherman at heart, he cannot resist the summits surrounding Idaho's mountain lakes.

The late Chuck Ferguson (1940–1998) was yet another stalwart mountaineer. During his life he climbed Borah Peak twenty-five times and climbed hundreds of other Idaho peaks and undoubtedly recorded several first ascents. He shared his climbs with relatives, colleagues, students, and friends and left an enduring legacy in Idaho's climbing history.

Rick Baugher of Idaho Falls, who made major contributions to this book, has spent years documenting and following in the footsteps of the government surveyors. Without his efforts, this interesting and important history would have been lost forever. Baugher has climbed nearly every Lost River, Lemhi, and Beaverhead peak, an accomplishment so difficult that it is hard for most to appreciate, and even harder to duplicate. Many of his routes are first ascents and I doubt anyone knows or will ever know the Lost River country better than Baugher.

The 1990s and Beyond

In the 1990s Idaho climbers formed a Boise chapter of the American Alpine Club. The chapter has promoted Idaho climbing and the preservation and maintenance of Idaho climbing areas in a time of rapid population growth. The chapter's members are responsible for many new routes across the state.

Idaho still offers many untried faces, isolated spires, and unexplored country far from crowds. Since climbing activity has traditionally gravitated to a few well-defined areas, most of Idaho's endless mountains remain untested. As late as 1988, a major Idaho peak (9,968-foot Cabin Creek Peak) was climbed for the first time. The peak, as picturesque and complex as any in the state, suffered from one disability—it was hidden in an out-of-the-way neighborhood where no mountaineer would have expected to find it. Despite the best efforts of climbers, it is likely that a few Idaho summits remain unclimbed and there is still an assortment of towers, faces, and pinnacles scattered around the state awaiting first ascents. Many other peaks offer high-quality route problems. Likewise, winter mountaineering has been limited to a few areas, with Mount Borah and the Lost River Range, and the Sawtooths and the Pioneers seeing the most winter activity. This book is only the second chapter of the story.

GEOLOGY

The present-day surface of Idaho is a composite of bits and pieces of literally thousands of ancient landscapes. This puzzle holds the story of Idaho's geologic history in its strata and formations.

The oldest known pieces of the Idaho jigsaw puzzle are Precambrian rocks 2.7 billion years old. These ancient rocks can be found in the Salmon River Mountains of central Idaho, the Albion Range, south of the Snake River, and other locations. The origins of these rocks are uncertain because they have been subjected repeatedly to metamorphism (restructuring due to exposure to heat and pressure) and are drastically altered from their original condition.

Idaho's most common Precambrian rock, found in northern Idaho, is a continuation of formations found in southern Alberta and western Montana. These rocks, known as the "Belt Supergroup," are from 850 million to 1.5 billion years old. They were originally sedimentary rocks, but are often lightly metamorphosed. From observation of the physical features present in these sedimentary and metamorphic rocks (such as ripple marks, fossil algae, and mud cracks), geologists have pieced together the ancient landscape and now know that the sediment that forms these rocks was deposited in an extremely shallow sea on the edge of an ancient continental plate. The sea received sediments from the many rivers that emptied into it and this sediment eventually formed into the very old rock visible in the Purcell, Cabinet, and Coeur d'Alene Mountains.

The next oldest Idaho rocks were formed much later, during the Paleozoic era, in what was then an ancient sea. Approximately 570 million to 245 million years ago, more than 30,000 feet of sedimentary deposits formed in this Paleozoic sea that was much deeper than the Precambrian sea. These Paleozoic rocks include limestone, shale, sandstone (some of which later metamorphosed into quartzite), conglomerates, and phosphorite and are found in the Lost River, Lemhi, Beaverhead, Centennial, Big Hole, Caribou, Peale, and Bear River mountains.

Four hundred million years ago, all of the earth's continental crustal plates formed one massive continent, most of which was in the southern hemisphere. This "super continent" began to break up around 300 million years ago, and the resulting pieces began to go their separate ways. Moving at roughly one inch per year, the crustal plates have traveled many miles over 3.8 billion years, constantly forming and reforming. At times, the plates have joined to form super continents; at other times, they separated to create new oceans. From Idaho's point of view, the most significant event in this sojourn began around 100 million years ago, when the North American plate began to move west, overriding the Oceanic Pacific plate.

When a continental plate overrides an oceanic plate, the denser oceanic plate is forced under the lighter continental plate. As the oceanic plate is forced down, pressure and friction liquefy the oceanic rocks, forming magma. Because magma is lighter than solid rock, it rises toward the earth's surface, where it either forms massive bodies of granite known as batholiths, or magma chambers, which fuel volcanic activity. As is plainly evident in Idaho, the collision of the plates results in the uplifting of the earth's surface and the formation of mountains. Today, the process continues as the North American plate moves imperceptibly westward over the Pacific plate, which is also moving slowly to the northwest.

During the late Mesozoic era, the North American/Pacific plate subduction zone was responsible for the intrusion of large amounts of granite into the area that is now Idaho. The Idaho Batholith is the largest and most interesting of these Mesozoic intrusions. This incredible batholith took more than 30 million years to form and covers roughly 15,000 square miles of land, stretching almost 300 miles from north to south and 100 miles east to west. Saint Maries marks the batholith's northwest corner; Missoula, Montana, the northeast corner; Challis, the southeast corner; and Boise, the southwest corner. The batholith was formed by many granitic intrusions, the oldest of which are on its western edges and are 90 million years old. The youngest intrusions are on the eastern edge of the batholith and are roughly 60 million years old.

Intrusion of the Idaho Batholith lifted central Idaho into a high tableland, which has since eroded into the present-day mountain terrain. Topographically, the lowest corner of the batholith is its northwest corner where the peaks are low, seldom exceeding 6,000 feet; the highest corner is the southeast, where Mount McGuire reaches above 10,000 feet. As the mountains fan out toward the northeast and southwest corners, elevations gradually change to roughly 8,000 feet. Much of the batholith is still covered by older sedimentary and metamorphic rocks, which have not yet eroded away.

Because of the extensive amounts of exposed sedimentary and metamorphic rock and the many different granitic intrusions that formed the batholith, there is great variety in the types and quality of rocks found on the surface in this region.

In fact, Idaho Batholith granite varies considerably in texture and form and at least a half dozen different types of granitic rock are present in the batholith. Besides the Idaho Batholith, several other batholiths formed during the Mesozoic era. These included the Kanisku Batholith (the foundation of the Selkirk Mountains) and the Owyhee Batholith (the foundation of the Owyhee Mountains).

Two hundred million years ago the Pacific coast formed a line between present-day Boise and Riggins; far out to sea, there was a remote island chain. Although seemingly unrelated, the continent and the islands were destined to unite as the subduction of the Pacific plate continued to draw the islands slowly but inexorably toward the coastline. Between 150 and 75 million years ago, the islands and the North American plate collided to form the western edge of Idaho. The process that "accreted" the chain of islands to the continent is responsible for the complex geologic terrain of the Craig, Seven Devils, West, Cuddy, and Hitt Mountains. These ranges are highlighted by a wild variety of oceanic and continental rock types including, among many others, granite, metamorphosed chert, argillite, tuff, andesite, limestone, basalt, metamorphosed basalt, dacite, and rhyolite.

While the Idaho Batholith was being intruded into central Idaho and the island arcs were being accreted to the batholith's western edge, the land east of the batholith was folded up and pushed eastward. Perhaps this was a result of the forces associated with the collision of the islands with North America, or those associated with the creation of the batholith. At any rate, this massive eastward movement of rock, known as the "overthrust belt," effectively shortened or compressed the earth's crust. In places, older rock formations moved from 30 to 40 miles over the top of younger rock formations.

The overthrust belt forms a broad arc beginning in Alberta and extending south through eastern Idaho into Utah; it is known primarily for the oil and gas deposits trapped within its rock layers. (Oil and gas tend to accumulate in areas where a porous rock layer is found below nonporous rock, such as where sandstone is covered by shale.) The Caribou and Snake River Mountains are the most likely spots in Idaho for oil discovery.

Fifty-one million years ago, a volcanic episode began in the area around present-day Challis. During the next 10 million years, this volcanic activity spread like a cancer to cover more than half the state with volcanic debris. Repeated eruptions formed accumulations of lava and ash more than 10,000 feet deep, and buried older Precambrian, Paleozoic, and Mesozoic rocks. These volcanic rocks (known as the Challis Volcanics), even after 40 million years of erosion, still cover nearly 2,000 square miles of Idaho.

Challis Volcanics form the eastern edges of the Salmon River Mountains and cover much of the area south and west of Challis, where they form the highly colored and barren slopes of the northern Lost River Range and the multicolored summits of the Boulder Mountains. Just west of Challis are many ash flows and tuffs associated with the Twin Peaks Caldera that was created when a massive volcano collapsed (the same type of event formed Crater Lake in Oregon) some 45 million years ago. Today, the caldera and its rim form the geologic backbone of the eastern edge of the Salmon River Mountains.

After 10 million years of volcanic activity, when change could be abrupt and catastrophic, Idaho settled into a period of less dramatic change. In central Idaho more granite was injected into the Idaho Batholith. Between 46 and 42 million years ago, forty plutons (smaller and younger granitic intrusions that are injected into an older granite batholith) were injected into the main Idaho Batholith. Pluton granite differs from the older granite in three ways. First, the original batholith granites are gray in color; the pluton granites possess a slightly different chemical makeup and are pink in color. Second, these plutons were implanted closer to the earth's surface and as the older rock erodes away, pluton granite is exposed at the surface. Finally, pluton granite is characterized by vertical jointing (cracking in vertical lines), which is responsible for the granite eroding into jagged edges rather than rounded domes. Hence, the pinkish granite we see forming high jagged granite mountains, such as those in the Sawtooths and the Bighorn Crags, is pluton granite, while the older batholith granite is most often found in canyon bottoms.

At approximately the same time that the plutons were implanted into the Idaho Batholith, changes were also taking place farther south. The forces that created the overthrust belt reversed and now the earth's crust was stretched apart and lengthened from east to west. As the crust was stretched apart, long linear cracks or faults developed. This faulting, known as block faulting, formed narrow bands of crust that moved vertically in relation to each other.

Block faulting is the process that formed the Great Basin, which encompasses all of Nevada and parts of Arizona, California, Oregon, Utah, and Idaho. The basin is characterized by hundreds of north-south-trending mountain ranges separated by long, narrow graben valleys, which are formed by a crustal block that is dropping in relationship to flanking mountains. The Lost River, Lemhi, Beaverhead, Albion, Black Pine, Deep Creek, Bannock, and Portneuf mountain ranges are among the most prominent Idaho mountains formed at this time. While block faulting is most evident in southern Idaho, there are many other examples of this type of faulting visible throughout the state. The most prominent of these graben valleys are the Big Wood River Valley (home of Ketchum and Sun Valley) and the Purcell Trench in northernmost Idaho, which forms a broad valley between the Selkirk and Cabinet Mountains.

Fifteen million years ago volcanic activity on a massive scale began again in Idaho. This activity created the expansive Snake River Plain and is continuing, with the last eruptions occurring only two thousand years ago. Geologists are still formulating the theoretical explanation of the forces that formed the Snake River Plain. Some hold to the theory that the plain was formed by a massive subsidence of the earth's crust; there is evidence to support this theory. More recently it has been theorized that the volcanic plain is the result of the North American plate crossing over a "hot spot" in the mantle similar to the one credited with the formation of the Hawaiian Islands. According to this theory, the hot spot is now under the Yellowstone Plateau—where evidence of volcanic activity is apparent. The age of the rocks in the Snake River Plain supports this theory; the youngest rocks are near Yellowstone, with the rocks getting progressively older to the west.

Whatever the explanation behind its formation, the Snake River Plain is a veritable museum exhibit of volcanic activity, with both volcanic cones and large fissures (where the earth simply opened and lava poured out) on display. Many lava flows are so fresh that vegetation has barely taken hold. The features found in this region include massive calderas, shield volcanoes, symmetrical cinder cones, spatter cones, lava flows, lava tubes, ice caves, and many rift systems.

The Great Rift runs from Craters of the Moon National Monument southeast and south for 50 miles and is up to 5 miles wide. An aerial view of the Great Rift reveals more about how the Snake River Plain formed than words might ever express. From the air, the rift appears as a huge crack that runs for miles. On either side of the crack, dark lava flows have poured out like blood from a cut and then hardened like crusty scabs.

While the Snake River Plain was forming, volcanic activity was occurring to the west on the Columbia Plateau. Some of this activity spilled into Idaho in the form of massive lava flows. These flows, which originated in Oregon, have built up, one over another, to a depth of more than 11,000 feet and are known as the Saint Maries, Clearwater, and Weiser Embayments. The Hitt, Cuddy, Seven Devils, and Craig Mountains are formed in part by this activity. The flows added to the

island arc terrain that had accreted to the continent millions of years earlier.

Finally, the last pieces of the present-day Idaho jigsaw puzzle were cut by glacial ice during the great Pleistocene Ice Age. Although the Pleistocene Ice Age began 2.5 million years ago, it was not until the last one hundred thousand years that the ice moved south out of British Columbia and invaded Idaho. The ice sheet that crept into northern Idaho consisted of massive lobes from the peerless continental ice fields, which formed in western Canada. This ice flowed south over northern Idaho, completely covering the Selkirks, Purcell, and Cabinet Mountains. The weight of the ice, estimated to have been 4,000 feet deep, cut and shaped the mountains, dug out the deep beds of Priest, Pend Orielle, and Coeur d'Alene Lakes, and forever altered the primeval terrain.

South of the Saint Joe River, glaciation was less catastrophic and limited to mountain glaciers that carved and sculpted the high peaks, leaving many alpine cirques. The southern alpine glaciation was most intense from twenty-five to seven thousand years ago, while a second series of glaciers were present around four thousand years ago on the highest mountain summits. A few of the larger alpine glaciers extended down into adjacent valleys, leaving lakes such as Redfish Lake in the Sawtooths, in their aftermath. Throughout central Idaho, there are many stunning examples of U-shaped valleys, moraines, and alpine lake basins. A less obvious, yet an equally significant effect of the glacial period was the increased volume of water carried by Idaho rivers when the glaciers melted. The glacial melt water dramatically increased stream flow, adding to the cutting power of rivers, which in turn allowed the rivers to rapidly cut the deep, narrow canyons found in central Idaho.

WEATHER

Because of prevailing westerly winds carrying moist maritime storms inland from the Pacific, Idaho annually receives 100 million acre feet of precipitation, with 80 percent of this total falling as winter snows. This is enough water to irrigate more than 250,000 acres of crop land, water 21.6 million acres of forest, fill the immense Snake River Aquifer and drive the Snake, Boise, Payette, Weiser, Salmon, Clearwater, Spokane, Clark Fork, and Kootenai River drainages. Idaho's precipitation varies significantly from year to year, depending largely on the position of the jet stream, which shifts with the seasons. During the summer, the jet stream runs north through Canada shunting major Pacific storms north of Idaho. The result is dry, mostly clear weather. In winter the jet stream sags southward, carrying Pacific storms across Oregon and Washington into Idaho. Some winters, for reasons not entirely clear, the jet stream shifts farther to the south than usual, carrying storms across California and Nevada. When this pattern develops, Idaho experiences its coldest weather.

Idaho's mountains play a significant role in modifying these broad weather patterns. When prevailing winds push air eastward across the state's mountains, it rises and cools, causing moisture in the air to condense and fall as precipitation on the windward (western) slopes. Once over the mountain tops, the air sinks and warms; moisture evaporates and precipitation on the leeward (eastern) slopes tapers off or ceases. The resulting areas of increased aridity are said to lie in the rain shadows of the mountain upwind.

Air temperature, like precipitation, is directly affected by latitude and elevation, decreasing as both increase. The hottest areas in Idaho are low-elevation canyons of the major rivers. Swan Falls Dam, deep in the Snake River Canyon, has the highest annual mean temperature in the state at 55 degrees F. The highest recorded temperature—118 degrees F—was recorded along the Clearwater River at Orofino. The deep river canyons form desert-like environments where, with irrigation, melons, apples, peaches, and apricots can be grown a few short miles from snow-covered mountain summits. Idaho's coldest temperatures are found at higher elevations. At 6,780 feet, Obsidian in the Stanley Valley has the lowest annual average at 35.4 degrees F. The state's record low temperature is minus 60 degrees F, recorded at Island Park in 1943.

The land north of the Columbia River receives much of its moisture from the Pacific Ocean. Because moist air can travel up the Columbia River Gorge without crossing the Cascades, northern Idaho feels the effects of the Pacific Ocean more than the central and southern parts of the state. This air is normally moister than that over southern Idaho. As a result, north of the Salmon River, mean annual precipitation levels range between 12 and 24 inches for the western valleys and 24 and 80 inches for the mountains. Because of its higher elevation and position at the head of an east/west mountain valley Wallace, Idaho, receives the heaviest annual precipitation for any city in the state, 41.69 inches. Furthermore, the proximity of northern Idaho to the Pacific serves to moderate the panhandle's winter weather, compared with equivalent areas in Montana, North Dakota, Minnesota, and Maine. This moderation comes with a price: northern Idaho receives only about 50 percent of the possible sunshine during any given year and less than 30 percent during the winter months.

The region between the Salmon River and the Snake River Plain contains the most mountainous terrain in the state and, because of its high elevations, receives massive amounts of winter snow. Precipitation in the region ranges between 12 and 80 inches, the totals generally increasing with elevation. Precipitation is rare in summer, particularly late in the season, when strong high-pressure systems often develop over this region, weakening or pushing aside incoming Pacific storms. The rain shadow of the Salmon River Mountains extends to the Challis, Big Lost, Little Lost, and Lemhi Valleys, all of which receive less than 12 inches of precipitation per year. This region receives nearly 70 percent of the annual average of available sunshine, more than 80 percent of which comes in July and August.

South of the central mountains, Idaho experiences greater climatic extremes over relatively short distances. The entire Snake River Plain, for example, receives less than 12 inches of precipitation during the average year and is classified as a high desert, while the Owyhee Mountains and the other southern mountain ranges rising out of the plain annually receive between 12 and 24 inches. A few of the higher southern peaks receive between 24 and 48 inches per year. Besides the storms that hit central Idaho, the southeast corner of the state often receives the brunt of winter storm systems that originally cross inland in southern and central California. During a winter in which the Sierra Nevada has an above-average snowfall, the Albion Range and its eastern neighbors can receive incredible snowfalls for mountains that are essentially part of a semi-desert environment.

The maritime influence of Idaho's climate is weakest in the easternmost portions of the state, where the climate exhibits greater extremes in seasonal temperatures and a shift in precipitation to a predominantly wet summer/dry winter weather pattern. Many eastern Idaho weather stations record more than 50 percent of their annual precipitation between April and September. The source of this summertime moisture is high-level, moisture-laden air that originates in the Gulfs of Mexico and California and migrates north to produce thunderstorm activity. In years when high pressure over the continent fails to weaken, and winter or spring precipitation is shunted to the north, Idaho suffers drought. At such times, large wildfires affect many areas.

USING THIS BOOK
Organization
This book divides Idaho into four sections. Section I covers northern Idaho and includes all of Idaho north of the Main Salmon River. Section II covers western Idaho and includes

an area bounded by the Snake River on the south and west, the Salmon River on the north and the Salmon and Big Wood Rivers on the east. Section III covers eastern Idaho and includes an area bounded by the Salmon and Big Wood Rivers in the west, Montana in the north, Wyoming in the east and the Snake River to the south. Section IV covers the remainder of the state and is bounded by the Snake River in the north, Oregon in the west, Nevada and Utah in the south and Wyoming in the east.

Each section includes chapters covering the mountain ranges within the section. Many Idaho ranges are so large that they have, over the years, acquired more than one name. For example, the mountains that comprise the Lost River Range are known as the Pahsimeroi Mountains in the north and the Lost Rivers in the south, and an eastern Lost River ridgeline is known as the Hawley Mountains. Since geographically this group is one distinct mountain range, it is treated as a whole; but the subranges are identified and discussed within the chapter.

Each chapter includes specific information on that range, individual peak listings, and an approach section. The peak descriptions are listed generally from north to south and west to east. Within the description, there is information on the peak's location, its mountaineering history (if any), and climbing routes. Approach information for each peak is referenced in the write-up by bracketed entries that look like this: [(A)(1)(b)]. (See next paragraph for explanation.) Finally, the peak listing includes the name of the United States Geological Survey (USGS) quadrangle(s) on which the peak is located, and a keyed reference to a designated Wilderness Area, if the peak is located within one. For example, in "USGS Chimney Peak/SBW," the SBW is the abbreviation for the Selway-Bitterroot Wilderness area.

Using the Approach Directions

The Approach section at the end of each chapter is organized as an outline. Bracketed entries (character strings) in the text refer to the information approach route for the peaks in the chapter's approach section. The capital letter designates a major approach point or highway. The next character, a number, refers to a secondary road (which can be anything from a good paved road to a primitive jeep trail) that leaves from the major approach point. (A number with a decimal point(s) denotes a road that branches off from a secondary road.) The last character, a lowercase letter, refers to a trail accessed from the road identified by the previous character. A lowercase letter with a decimal point and number indicates a trail that branches off the preceding trail. For example, (a) is

the main trail, (a.1) indicates a trail that branches off (a) and (a.1.2) indicates a trail that branches off (a.1). Additionally, roads and trails are identified by their Forest Service number and by name, for example FST-124, Parker Ridge Trail. However, keep in mind that the Forest Service numbering scheme is always subject to change and that a road or trail's number may change when the road or trail crosses a boundary between two different forests.

Abbreviations

In the interest of economy of space, this guidebook uses several abbreviations.

4WD	Four-wheel drive, high-clearance vehicle
BLM	Bureau of Land Management
CDT	Continental Divide Trail
CG	Campground
FH-#	A numbered Forest Service highway, as identified on a national forest map
FS-#	A numbered Forest Service road, as identified on a national forest map
FST-#	A numbered Forest Service trail, as identified on a national forest map
GHW	Gospel Hump Wilderness
GS	Forest Service Guard Station
HCW	Hells Canyon Wilderness
I-#	An Interstate Highway
ID-#	An Idaho State Highway
INEEL	Idaho National Engineering and Environmental Laboratory
MLPA	Mallard-Larkins Pioneer Area
ORV	Off-Road Vehicle
Quad	A USGS 7.5-minute quadrangle map
RNRW	River of No Return Wilderness
SBW	Selway-Bitterroot Wilderness
SNRA	Sawtooth National Recreation Area
US-#	A United States highway
USGS	United States Geologic Survey
WA	Washington State Highway
WCP	White Cloud Peak

Roads and Trails

Expect the unexpected. Historically, recreational use of Idaho's mountains has taken a back seat to logging, mining, and grazing. Consequently, road access in many places is poor. Recreational use has drastically increased over the last twenty years and land managers have slowly improved access routes in response. Almost all of Idaho's mountain roads (paved, gravel, or dirt) will, depending on weather conditions, require the use of four-wheel drive (4WD) or a high-clearance vehicle at one time or another. In many places, you will find that the approach to a climb can be accomplished only on foot or with 4WD. Some roads are so poor that they require not only 4WD, but also the driving skills to use the vehicle safely.

This book attempts to identify all roads that require something more rugged than a passenger sedan, stating "A 4WD is recommended" or "A 4WD is required." However, keep in mind that conditions change from season to season and year to year and roads listed in this book may have become impassable. Be prepared for the worst on every trip, because trees fall across roads, mud holes come and go, and vehicles break down. Carry extra water and a good tire jack. Make sure there is air in your spare tire. Consider taking tire chains, a shovel, and a axe if you are going to one of the state's many remote trailheads. Most of all, be prepared to take your time, drive slowly, and expect the drive to take twice as long as you planned!

This advice also applies to trail conditions. Remember that just because a trail is shown on a map it does not necessarily follow that there is a well-worn path on the ground. Many trails listed in this book are too difficult for novice hikers and some will test the route-finding skills of intermediate and expert hikers. Although trail maintenance is on the upswing, route-finding skills and common sense are essential tools for venturing into much of Idaho's backcountry. Make your goals consistent with your abilities. To paraphrase Clint Eastwood's movie character Dirty Harry, "A climber has just got to know his limitations."

Distance measurements are listed throughout the book. Over the last twenty-five years, I have checked and rechecked distances with a variety of vehicles. Each vehicle gave a slightly different reading. Please be understanding, usually the road junction or trailhead will be close to the mileage in the book, if not dead on. However, I may be off in some places and some measurements are simply estimates. This is especially true of trail distances. I have yet to hike a trail where the signed mileage seemed accurate. Finally, road access and trails are constantly changing; roads are closed, new roads are built, and trails that have not been maintained for thirty years are reopened. In summary, exacting accuracy is impossible. Enjoy the journey.

Maps

Maps form the essential foundation for almost every climb in this book. You should not consider attempting a climb without the necessary maps—and the expertise to use them.

Idaho is a big state and, in some places, getting lost is easier than you might ever imagine. If you are a novice, read up on map use (*Mountaineering: The Freedom of the Hills*, by the Mountaineers, contains an excellent discussion on how to use topographic maps) and learn the basics from an experienced wilderness navigator before you start a climb. As a final note, remember that although maps are essential equipment, no map is perfect or absolutely complete and maps near more-developed areas become outdated with surprising speed.

The climbing route descriptions include references to the landmarks and notations on the USGS 7.5-minute quadrangle map(s) that feature that peak. For example, elevation references are commonly placed on high points on USGS maps. These references are often referred to in the route descriptions (e.g., "climb toward Point 10251" or "from Lake 8756 follow the base of the cliffs to the east"). Keep in mind that occasionally you will need two, three, or even four USGS quads to complete a climb. Road and trail numbers are taken from Forest Service maps, and information on land ownership is based on Bureau of Land Management (BLM) "Land Surface Management Status" maps. Depending on where you are going, you may need to use all three map types to reach your goal.

USGS Topographic Maps
The USGS 7.5-minute quadrangle map series (with a scale of 1:24,000 or nearly 2.5 inches to a mile) is an essential tool for every Idaho mountaineer. Each map covers an area of 6 miles by 9 miles. No one is a complete mountaineer or backpacker without a good working ability to navigate using these excellent maps.

While the USGS quads are extremely accurate in displaying physical features, they can be very inaccurate as to roads, trails, and other human developments. Some maps are more than thirty years old and were published when Idaho was unpopulated and undeveloped and, as such, often do not show newer roads and other recent developments. Nor do they show land ownership, which is essential in areas where public and private lands are intertwined.

Idaho indexes to the USGS quads are available by writing the U.S. Geological Survey, Federal Center, Denver, Colorado 80225. USGS topo maps cost from $4 to $6, depending on the retailer. Most outdoor shops carry these maps, and many government land management agencies also sell them.

Forest Service Maps
Your first map acquisitions should include the national forest map for the area you intend to visit. Forest Service maps

vary greatly in quality, size, and accuracy. Use them for orientation, but not for navigation. These maps are much smaller in scale than USGS quads (generally, 0.5 inches equals a mile) and many do not show topographic lines. These maps include numbered roads and trails and display land ownership patterns. Keep in mind that, as a rule, Forest Service maps do not include all logging roads and that they often show trails that have not been maintained for years. Forest Service maps also include a handy index to the USGS quads that cover each forest. Of special note are the Forest Service maps of the Selway-Bitterroot and River of No Return Wildernesses; both maps are comprehensive, up-to-date, and include topographic lines.

BLM Land Surface Management Status Maps
BLM maps are among the newest government maps. They depict drainages, roads, trails, land ownership, and sometimes topographic lines. These are large-scale maps (1:100,000) and are very helpful for orientation purposes, for large-scale coverage, and for determining who owns the land, but they are poor for finding your way to a summit. These maps are essential for negotiating the Owyhee Mountains. They are sold at the bureau's offices throughout Idaho.

Mountain Names
Naming a mountain often is a controversial project. Since there are as many unnamed peaks as named peaks in Idaho, this book walks the wild side in its use of many unofficial names. The book does use official names (those peaks named on the USGS quads) whenever they exist. These names are simply identified as follows: Mount Heyburn. Peaks identified by unofficial names are identified by an asterisk at the end of the name: Knuckle Peak*. These unofficial names are taken from mountaineering literature, Forest Service maps, commercial publications, and local usage. The book also includes names suggested by various persons. These recommendations are identified as follows: Peak 9101 (Shoban Peak). Finally, unnamed peaks are simply identified by their elevations: Peak 11887 or Peak 10240+. The plus shows that the actual height is not known and the elevation refers simply to the last contour on the USGS quad.

Throughout history, the names for geologic features have evolved as part of the collective consciousness. Through word of mouth, a mountain became known as Diamond Peak or Sleeping Deer and then, when the first maps were published, some of this oral tradition became quasi-official and legitimized. Over the years, many names have disappeared, including some that have appeared on maps at one time or another. Many of Idaho's most striking summits are not officially named. The lack of an official name does not lessen the formidable nature of the peak or its aesthetic value, but instead is a reflection of the bureaucratic barriers confronting those who suggest names.

Today, the naming of geologic features is systematized and integrated into the government's bureaucracy. In 1947, Congress passed Public Law 242, which created a central authority for standardizing geographic names. The new law's purpose was to eliminate the duplication of names attached to geologic features in the United States. The law places the authority to name unnamed features, and to standardize the names of features with multiple names, with the Secretary of Interior acting jointly with the Board of Geographic Names. The various states have also established their own boards of geographic names that act with the federal board to approve or disapprove suggested names.

Historically, local citizens named the peaks visible from their homesteads and the climbing community has long adhered to the principal that the climbers who make the first ascent of an unnamed peak are entitled to name it. Thus, the Sawtooth peaks visible from the Stanley Valley were named by settlers and the peaks further back were mostly named by climbers. Public Law 242 short circuited this process. Citizens can still recommend names, but those who have attempted to secure official recognition for names have found the bureaucrats are jealous masters who guard their kingdom well. Theoretically, the process is simple. A recommendation is made. The USGS documents the suggestion and turns it over to the Board of Geographic Names, which in turn consults with the state board. The name is evaluated against a set of principles, which mandate that when naming geographic features the board must (1) retain local names, (2) retain suitable, euphonious Indian names, or names of a foreign origin; (3) use names suggested by peculiarities of topographic features; (4) name features only after deceased persons; (5) not use names with derogatory implications; (6) avoid the multiplication of names for different parts of the same geologic feature; (7) replace existing names only to eliminate duplicates or inappropriate names, and (8) adopt new names for geographic features in federally designated wilderness areas only when an overriding need is identified. (Some board members believe that all of these criteria must be present before a name will be adopted. Others do not.) Once the proposed name has been evaluated, the board, more often than not, rejects it. Bureaucracy triumphs!

Although a great number of suggested names are rejected each year, the board has done little to reconcile the confusion caused by the existence of multiple features bearing the same name. Thus, Idaho has many Granite Peaks and Mountains, several Deer Creeks, and at least a dozen mountains bearing some form of the word "bald" in their title: Old Baldy, Old Baldy Peak, Bald Mountain (five peaks), Bald Peak, Baldy Mountain (two peaks), Mount Baldy, and Saint Joe Baldy.

As of today, the government has not chosen to legislate the legal definition of what constitutes a true mountain summit. Climbers generally require, at a minimum, a 300-foot drop in a connecting ridgeline before two points will be considered separate mountain peaks. The government does not abide by this rule and several peaks in this book have official names but are missing the 300-foot drop. These include Reward Peak in the Sawtooths, Junction Peak in the Lemhis, and Patterson Peak in the White Clouds. Finally, the name is irrelevant if the route is challenging and enjoyable.

The Climbing Routes

The climbing routes compiled in this book have been gathered from many sources including my own climbs, climbing journals and magazines (including the *American Alpine Journal,* the *Mountaineers Journal,* the *Mazamas Journal,* the *Iowa Mountaineers Journal, Summit, Off Belay, Rock and Ice,* and *Climbing*), records left in summit registers, and, most importantly, information supplied by other climbers. I have tried to credit these climbers throughout the book.

The route descriptions vary in detail. At a minimum, I have included a rating and directions to the peak. Some routes contain a lengthy write-up. My overall intent is to inform readers of the difficulty and to allow them to make an informed judgement as to whether a climb is within their abilities. Philosophically, I believe climbing should be both an adventure and a test of our skills. Route descriptions with too much detail detract from both challenges. If you need a detailed, pitch-by-pitch description or a step-by-step guide with photos and diagrams, you should climb with a guide.

While I have attempted to assure the accuracy of every entry in this book, climbing every mountain by every route is impossible for one person. Both writing and reading route descriptions can be frustrating. Many guidebooks list detailed descriptions of every twist and turn of a complex route—yet, when you attempt to follow the route on the rock you come to believe you are on the wrong mountain. Other guidebooks tell you to "follow the easy slopes to the summit" and you find a near vertical "slope" capped by overhanging cliffs.

These discrepancies are not due to any duplicity on the author's part or lack of reading ability on the readers part, but from the inability of both the reader and the writer to translate a constantly changing natural environment into words.

To minimize these translation difficulties, the route descriptions rely heavily on USGS topographic maps. Reading the description with the map in front of you will clarify the description. For example, many route descriptions refer to the elevation references found on the USGS quads as follows: Climb toward Point 10251 or from Point 10251 turn east and follow the ridge toward the summit. Contour lines, lakes (named and unnamed), and other physical features such as rivers are also used as reference points.

The following nomenclature notes also will be helpful in understanding the route descriptions contained in this book. When I use the word **ridge**, I am referring to a distinct, narrow line that drops away steeply on two sides. Ridges run from point to point and may connect two high peaks or rise out of a valley and run directly to a summit. When I use the word **rib**, I am referring to a steep angular, ridge-like formation that buttresses a face or a ridge. Ribs are part of another feature and do not connect points. **Saddles, passes, gaps,** and **summits,** as in Pass Creek Summit, are used synonymously and refer to a low point on a ridge. A **col** is also a low point on a ridge. When I use col, I am referring to a low point that can only be reached by Class 3 or higher climbing. **Gullies, ravines,** and **couloirs** also are used synonymously to refer to a channel or hollow worn in the earth by a current of water. **Aiguille, arêtes, gendarmes, towers,** and **pinnacles** are similar formations that occupy ridges. **Cirques** are natural amphitheaters cut in the side of a mountain, usually by glaciers.

The Ratings Game

The ratings attached to climbing routes are designed to inform a person of the difficulty of the climb. While the numbers seem objective, there is a great deal of subjectivity built into them. Both the person rating the climb and the person following the route are human and what may be difficult to one may be "a piece of cake" to another.

This book uses the Yosemite Decimal System (YDS), which was introduced in the U.S. by the Sierra Club in 1937. This system rates climbing routes by the type of climbing (the class), and by the length of commitment needed to complete a climb (the grade). (For complete descriptions and a comparison chart of the various rating systems, see *Mountaineering: The Freedom of the Hills,* 8th edition, published by Mountaineers

Books.) Thus, a YDS-rated climb will have a grade and class designation. There are six classes, 1–5 and six grades, I–VI, for technical climbs.

Routes are graded based on the interplay of the route's length, average difficulty, exposure, quality of the rock, and any other factors that might affect the difficulty of a technical climb. Grade I climbs take one to two hours, Grade II climbs up to four hours, Grade III climbs may take the entire day, Grade IV climbs take at least a day with difficult technical climbing, and Grades V and VI climbs encompass big-wall climbing of increasing difficulty. While only a few of the routes in the book are graded, many of the Class 3 routes are at least Grade III.

All of the routes have been classified into one of six classes. Keep in mind that the rating is for the most difficult move on the route (the crux). Thus, a Class 3 climb might have only one short pitch of Class 3 climbing and is otherwise a walk-up. On the other hand, a Class 3 route might involve continuous climbing along the way.

CLASS 1   Hiking. There is a trail the entire way to the summit (though the trail may not be in great condition).

CLASS 2   Off-trail scrambling. These routes are off-trail but you can probably walk to the summit. You may occasionally have to use your hands for balance, but not to climb.

CLASS 3   Climbing. These routes involve actual climbing where your arms and hands are used to propel yourself up the slope. Class 3 climbing uses obvious holds and involves minimal exposure. Nevertheless, a fall will hurt.

CLASS 4   Belayed climbing. These routes involve climbing that may be no more difficult than Class 3 climbing, but does subject the climber to increased exposure where a fall will likely cause serious injury. Training and proper equipment is essential.

CLASS 5   Belayed climbing with leader placing protection. This is "technical" rock climbing, pure and simple. Training and proper equipment is a necessity.

CLASS 6   Involves artificial-aid climbing using pitons, bolts, or any other hardware placed in the rock to serve as a hold or for support.

Class 5 climbing is further broken down into degrees of difficulty under the Yosemite Decimal System. The fourth edition of *Mountaineering: The Freedom of the Hills* attempted, somewhat tongue-in-cheek, to put objective criteria to what has often been a very subjective set of numbers. Although not all climbers will agree with this breakdown, it does provide some objectivity to what has tended to be an extremely subjective set of numbers.

5.0–5.4	There are good, obvious handholds and footholds for each move. The smaller the hold, the greater the difficulty.
5.5–5.6	Handholds and footholds exist, but are not obvious to the untrained.
5.7	Either one handhold or foothold is missing.
5.8	Two holds out of four are missing.
5.9	Only one hold exists for each move.
5.10	There are no holds at all.
5.11	Such routes are impossible to climb, but someone has done it.
5.12	The rock is smooth and flawless.
5.13	The rock is both smooth and flawless and overhanging.
5.14	Use your imagination.

Class 6 climbing is also broken into six subcategories. Although this book is not directed toward this type of climbing, a few of the routes within involve aid climbing and so the following breakdown is provided. It should be noted that rock climbers are now climbing without aid what were originally aid routes.

A0	Placement is used as a hold or to allow a resting spot.
A1	Etriers (aid slings for your feet) are utilized. Placements are solid and safe.
A2	Placements are harder to find and are less secure.
A3	Placements are not likely to hold a significant fall.
A4	Placements are downright shaky and cannot be expected to hold a fall.
A5	Continuous use of A4 placements.

NORTHERN IDAHO

From the Canadian Border South to the Salmon River; From the Washington and Oregon Borders East to the Montana Border

1

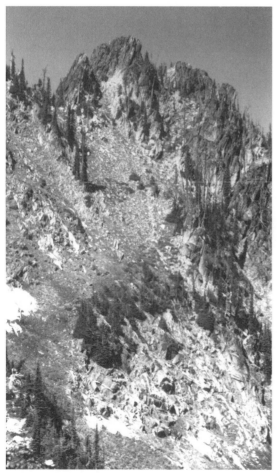

THE SELKIRK MOUNTAINS

with Randall Green

The Selkirk Mountains begin on Mica Peak west of Coeur d'Alene, Idaho, and extend north into Canada, paralleling the Idaho/Washington border for more than 100 miles. These mountains, which are up to 30 miles wide in places, surround the Priest Lake Basin. The Selkirk peaks are formed of granite from the Kaniksu Batholith and Spokane Dome and Precambrian rocks from the Belt Supergroup series. The name "Kaniksu Range" is sometimes used to identify the mountains west of the Priest Lakes; the central crest is sometimes known as the "Priest Range."

Parker Peak, at 7,670 feet, is the highest named summit in the U.S. portion of the range, while the highest point is un-named Peak 7709, which is 0.5 mile northwest of Big Fisher Lake. Selkirk valley-to-summit elevation differences are nearly 5,000 feet in places and the terrain is extremely rugged.

During the Pleistocene era, the Selkirk range was scraped clean by massive continental glaciers, which removed much of the Precambrian rock that covered the Kaniksu Batholith and carved the underlying granite into an appealing collection of alpine peaks. Besides shaping the high peaks, the glaciers also gouged out the Priest Lake Basin. As the glaciers retreated, a luxuriant forest filled the Selkirk valleys and ridges. The resulting combination of complex glaciated ridges, cirques, and a thick primeval forest created a spectacular mountain environment. Unfortunately, much of the Selkirk's terrain is no longer pristine. Logging operations have placed roads in most drainages, leaving a number of disjointed roadless areas. Recently many of these roads have been gated shut and some permanently closed. There are worthwhile hiking and climbing opportunities throughout the range.

Chimney Peak in the Selway–Bitteroot Wilderness

Land ownership in the Selkirks is a hodgepodge. The State of Idaho's Priest Lake State Forest and the Idaho Panhandle National Forest are the two largest landowners. (The state's land holdings include most of the scenic Priest Lake Basin.) The BLM manages a few small borderline areas, and several private corporations own substantial portions of the range. Nevertheless, logging is on the decline and much of the range is now managed as habitat for endangered species.

Recreational use of the range is on the upswing. In 1971 the State of Idaho and the Forest Service established the Selkirk Crest Management Area, which protects the highest Selkirk peaks and ridges. Additionally, two other areas, Long Canyon (west of Bonners Ferry) and Salmon-Priest (near the Canadian/Washington/Idaho borders), are under consideration for wilderness designation. Both are pristine and worthy of protection on scenic, recreational, and wildlife management grounds. Perhaps the strongest argument for protecting portions of the Selkirks as wilderness is the presence of highly threatened big game animals—the grizzly bear and the rare mountain caribou. There is a good chance that neither will survive in the Selkirks if the remaining roadless areas are not preserved.

Selkirk peaks offer a variety of climbing and hiking opportunities. True wilderness terrain still hides delightful and remote summits, roads lead nearly to the bottoms of imposing rock walls, and dozens of summits are excellent day-hiking destinations from valley camps. Rock climbers will find "super" granite in many spots. Randall Green, who published *Idaho Rock* (Mountaineers Books, 1987), has contributed to this chapter. His book is still an excellent guide to Selkirk and Sandpoint rock.

Snowy Top Mountain   *7,572 feet (Class 2)*

Snowy Top is a big hulking mountain and the highest point in this northernmost corner of Idaho. The summit is barren, windswept, and very enticing. To reach the top, scramble up the peak's south slopes from Snowy Top Pass (the main saddle between it and Little Snowy Top Mountain). The saddle is reached by FST-506 [(A)(1)(a) and (b)]. USGS Continental Mountain

Snowy Top Mountain (Photo by Sheldon Bluestein)

Little Snowy Top   6,829 feet (Class 1)

Although 700 feet lower than its northerly big brother, this summit, adorned by a fire lookout, is an excellent destination for northern peak baggers. The summit is an easy 1-mile hike from FST-315 via the side trail that leads to the lookout [(A)(1)(a) and (b)]. USGS Salmo Mountain

Parker Peak   7,670 feet (Class 2)

Parker Peak is found 8.5 miles south of the Canadian border, on the eastern edge of the Selkirk Range. The peak is an easy walk-up via its south ridge from FST-221 [(D)(2)(b) or (D)(3)(a)]. Although technically easy, the walk is long—7 miles—and steep—5,500 feet—when approached from the Parker Ridge trailhead (even farther if you choose to do the approach from Long Canyon). This area is especially alpine in nature in early summer, before the snow has completely disappeared from the glacially sculpted peaks. USGS Pyramid Peak

Fisher Peak   7,580 feet (Class 1)

Pyramid-shaped Fisher Peak is 2.5 miles east of Parker Peak. It features a precipitous north face, which rises almost 1,000 feet. The summit is reached via FST-27 [(D)(4)(a)] which, although in poor shape, leads to the summit. USGS Pyramid Peak

Peak 7709   7,709 feet (Class 2)

The highest point in the American Selkirk Range is unnamed and located east of the main crest and 1.5 miles southwest of Fisher Peak and 2 miles southeast of Parker Peak. The summit is a short scramble after the long hike to Big Fisher Lake [(D)(4)(c)]. From the lake, work your way up through the peak's forested western slopes to the south ridge, which leads to the summit. USGS Pyramid Peak

Peak 7445   7,445 feet (Class 2)

This unnamed peak is a continuation of the Long Mountain/Parker Peak ridge that parallels the east side of Long Canyon. The summit is 1 mile north of Long Mountain and 2 miles southwest of Parker Peak. FST-221 [(D)(3)(a) or (D)(2)(b)] nearly reaches the summit, which is a hop, skip, and a jump from the trail. USGS Pyramid Peak

Long Mountain   7,265 feet (Class 1)

Long Mountain has a distinctive 0.5-mile-long summit ridge that forms part of the Long Canyon/Parker Creek Divide. Its summit is 3 miles southwest of Parker Peak. The summit is reached by taking FST-221 [(D)(3)(a) or (D)(2)(b)] either

Peak 7445 (Photo by Chris Paulson)

south from Parker Peak or north from Trout Creek. USGS Pyramid Peak

West Fork Mountain   6,416 feet (Class 1-2)

West Fork Mountain, the big mountain that looms above West Fork Lake, is located 3 miles west of Long Mountain. The peak's northeast face is an impressive wall. The summit is a 600-foot climb from the lake, mostly along the old trail that leads to the abandoned lookout site west of the true summit. From the lookout site, follow the ridge to the summit. FST-347 [(D)(1)(a)] is a well-traveled system that leads to West Fork Lake from FS-2446 (a.k.a. FS-2464). Unfortunately, several years ago the historic West Fork Cabin near the trailhead was destroyed by arson. Consequently, the Forest Service gated the road 1 mile below the trailhead to protect a replica of the original cabin that volunteers are planning to build. USGS Smith Peak

Smith Peak   *7,653 feet (Class 3)*

Smith Peak is among the remotest of the Selkirk peaks. The peak's 800-foot north face is also one of the steepest in the Selkirks. The shortest approach is from Smith Creek [(D)(1)]. From Smith Creek, climb to the peak's northwest ridge and then follow the ridge directly to the summit. The longest approach is from Long Canyon [(D)(2)(a)]. Climbing the peak from Long Canyon involves a backpacking trip up that spectacular and very lengthy glacial valley. Hike up Long Canyon to the point where the outlet from Smith Lake empties into Long Canyon Creek and follow the drainage up to the lake. Above the lake, a steep granite wall must be bypassed by climbing to Point 7303. Once on the ridgeline, follow the ridge south and then southeast to the summit. USGS Smith Peak

Abandon Mountain   *7,022 feet (Class 2)*

Abandon Mountain is 1.5 miles south of West Fork Mountain. The peak is best climbed via Smith Creek and its northeast ridge, but may be climbed by any of its three ridges [(D)(1)]. USGS Smith Peak

Pyramid Peak   *7,355 feet (Class 2)*

Pyramid Peak is 1.25 miles south of Long Mountain. The summit is climbed directly from FST-7 [(D)(2)(b)]. Take the trail north from Trout Creek to Pyramid Pass on the peak's northeast side and climb directly to the summit from the pass. USGS Pyramid Peak

The Lions Head   *7,288 feet*

The Lions Head stands high above Abandon, Smith, and Lion Creeks and 1.5 miles south of Abandon Mountain. This delightful peak exhibits twin summits, which are known as East Lions Head and West Lions Head. In 1964, Neil McAvoy of Kellogg led first ascents of both summits and left summit registers. According to Neil, a group of Spokane Mountaineers climbed the two peaks one week later and a first-ascent controversy has existed ever since. Because the peaks are not easily accessed, little technical climbing has been noted on the peaks in recent years. The shortest approach to the peak is from the Priest Lake Basin and Lion Creek [(B)(1.4)]. Access is also possible from the northeast via Smith Creek [(D)(1)] and Lookout Mountain [(B)(1.5)(a)]. USGS Smith Peak

West Lions Head (Class 4). The lower of the two summits does not have a walk-up route. The standard route climbs

the southwest face on a series of slabs with good holds and belay spots.

East Lions Head (Class 3). The highest summit is climbed by its north ridge from the saddle just north of the peak. The climb involves a friction scamper on slanting slabs.

Lookout Mountain   *6,727 feet (Class 1)*

Lookout Mountain and its classic north face are found 2 miles west of The Lions Head. This fire lookout site can be reached from Lookout Lake to the northwest by way of a short trail hike. The lake is accessed from one of two trails and a State of Idaho timber road [(B)(1.5)(a) and (b)] that runs up Caribou Creek from the top of Priest Lake to a point near Lookout Lake. From the trailhead, hike to the lake and then on to the summit in 2 miles. USGS Caribou Creek

Kent Peak   *7,243 feet (Class 2)*

Kent Peak sits west of the main Selkirk Crest on a high ridgeline between Kent Creek and Lion Creek 1.8 miles northeast of The Wigwams. The peak is reportedly climbable from either of these creeks, both of which are roadless and difficult to traverse. Access these creeks from the Lion Creek Road [(B) (1.4)]. The best access is from the south, either from the summit of The Wigwams or from Two Mouth Lakes, which is served by FST-286 [(B)(1.3)(a.1) or (B)(1.3)(b)]. From either of these starting points, follow the connecting ridgeline to the point where it connects with Kent's south ridge and then follow this ridge north to the summit. USGS The Wigwams

Myrtle Peak   *7,121 feet (Class 1)*

This peak was once a fire lookout site and naturally offers a good view of the surrounding countryside. It is 2 miles northeast of Kent Peak on the main Selkirk Crest. The summit is a 4-mile hike from the Myrtle Creek trailhead of FST-286 [(D)(5)(a)]. Because this trail continues past the summit to Myrtle Lake, it sees substantial traffic. USGS The Wigwams

The Wigwams   *7,033 feet (Class 1)*

The Wigwams are 5.5 miles east of Squaw Bay at the north end of Priest Lake on a ridgeline that runs west from the main crest. A road/jeep trail/trail leads to the west summit of this twin-summited peak from the Two Mouth Creek drainage [(B)(1.3)(b)]. From the saddle between the two peaks, the east summit is an easy scramble. USGS The Wigwams

Harrison Peak   *7,292 feet*

Harrison Peak sits 0.5 mile north of Harrison Lake. It is a rugged mountain with spectacular south, west, and north walls and only one nontechnical route to its summit. The peak ranks with Idaho's best, a fact not lost on Idaho mountaineers. Randall Green described nine routes on the mountain, all rated 5.7 or higher. For the routes described below take FST-271 [(C)(1.3)(a)] to Harrison Lake. From the point where the Harrison Lake Trail arrives at the lake, head north along the east end of the lake to the rib that leads directly up to Point 6558 on the USGS map. Continue to the south face that is visible ahead. USGS The Wigwams

East Side (Class 3). Traverse across the lower south face to reach this route. From near the base of the south face of the peak, traverse east over the talus slope at the base of the face until you are past the east buttress that forms the boundary of the south face. From this point, it is possible to work your way up to the peak's eastern slopes. Once on these easier slopes, climb due west to the summit.

South Face/Standard (II, 5.6). The 800-foot south face sports roughly 600 feet of good technical climbing. Green's *Idaho Rock* details eight challenging routes on the wide face. This classic line on the face is found just to the right of center. Scramble up and to your right toward the line that leads directly toward a distinctive notch just below and east of the summit. This route's three pitches cross blocks, slabs, cracks, and corner systems. From the notch, scramble up the ridge to the summit.

Keystone (II, 5.8). Follow the South Face/Standard route to just above the second lie back on the third pitch. An obvious sloping ledge gives access to a direct line to the summit via a steep face. A fixed pin protects the awkward moves to a crack that leads to an alcove and another fixed pin. Move to the left and continue up a crack to a square block (keystone). Under the keystone is an alcove rest. Climb a thin crack up and to the right of the keystone to gain larger cracks and broken blocks below the summit. First ascent: R. Green, M. Kubiak, and K. Nystrom in 1984.

Southeast Buttress/Running Flakes (II, 5.8). Randall Green reports that this route is roughly 300 feet to the right (north) of the South Face/Standard route. Look for a trail that leads from the base of the standard route to the base of this route. Pitch 1: Follow a small cleft 40 feet from the base of the wall to a small ledge. Continue up a right-facing flake system for 100 feet on very clean, granular rock. The belay platform is evident at the end of a 165-foot rope. Pitch 2: Lead directly up and slightly to the left over a bulge and through a small system of dihedral and face moves, good protection. Halfway up this pitch, climb through a small overhang to the "rock cornice" that makes up Harrison's southeastern skyline. Gain the belay stance directly under the right (northeast) edge of

the cornice. Pitch 3: From a white pocket, reach up and over a blind corner to the right. A bucket gives access to easy Class 5 mantels that will take you to the summit. First ascent: M. Potucek in 1982.

West Face Flake (I, 5.7+). Approach the west face of the peak by walking around the west ridge to its base or by rappelling 150 feet off the summit. Looking at the peak's west face, there is a prominent notch near the summit. The West Face Flake route ascends a series of cracks, flakes, and blocks to a point that is just to the left of the notch. Follow a small dihedral with a crack up to a large detached flake. Mantel onto a sloping shelf, go up to and behind large flakes and blocks with a cave. Go left behind the block or face climb to the right to the summit. First ascent: R. Green and T. Green in 1981.

Twin Peaks   *7,599 and 7,374 feet (Class 2-3)*
These peaks are 2.5 miles north of Chimney Rock and are quite impressive when viewed from the summit of Chimney Rock. The Twins are the highest points on the crest between Harrison Peak in the north and Silver Dollar Peak in the south. Although both summits are climbed from the saddle that connects them, climbing the north summit first from the southernmost Beehive Lake is best, then follow the ridge south to the second summit. Access the peaks from Beehive Lakes [(C)(1)(a)]. USGS The Wigwams

Silver Dollar Peak   *7,181 feet*
This nearly symmetrical peak has four ridges and three lofty faces. It is found 1.5 miles northeast of Chimney Rock. The peak is divided into quadrants by four ridgelines. Many technical climbing opportunities exist on this peak. The east ridge, which extends down to the Pack River, is broad and gentle, and covered with stunted alpine firs. The north ridge, a continuation of the Selkirk Crest, branches off the peak halfway up the north face, dividing it into two separate cirques—northeast and northwest. The lower faces in the cirques are slabby and broken, but relatively easy to climb. The upper north face is broken and blocky, with many route possibilities in the moderate range. The west ridge is a rugged knife edge, guarded by several large blocky gendarmes. This ridge separates the northwest and southwest faces. The south ridge is the backbone of the crest. The west side of this ridge is very steep and offers many technical climbing possibilities. The east side of the south ridge is gentler, and is covered with alpine firs and strewn with boulders. The peak is most easily reached from the east and the Pack River Road [(C)(1.2)]. From the road, hike into the Chimney Rock cirque and then scramble cross-country north to the peak. USGS The Wigwams

Southwest Slopes (Class 2-3). The summit is an easy scramble from the southeast.

West Ridge (II, 5.3). Randall Green notes that the west ridge is a classic mountaineering route: aesthetic, exposed, and technical enough to be interesting. His recommendation is to "gain access to the peak's west face by descending from the notch in the south ridge. Traverse under the west face until it is possible to begin scrambling up the south side of the west ridge. Scramble up to the crest of the ridge and continue following the line of least resistance to the top (two or three pitches, rated 5.2–5.3)."

Bottleneck Peak   *6,923 feet (Class 3)*
This summit sits at the head of the Snow Creek drainage 1.5 miles north of Roman Nose [(D)(5)(c)]. Climb to the summit from Bottleneck Lake by hiking along the lake's southeast shore. Scramble up the talus toward the cliffs at the base of the summit. Climb the obvious narrow chute to the summit ridge. The northeast ridge can be climbed directly to the summit or you can drop off the ridge and follow the easier slopes to the summit. USGS Roman Nose

Roman Nose   *7,260 feet*
The Forest Service placed a fire lookout on the summit of this imposing peak in 1917. Roman Nose is found 4 miles east of Silver Dollar Peak (and the main Selkirk Crest) on a subsidiary ridge that divides the Pack River and Kootenai River valleys. The northern rock faces below Roman Nose provide many challenging climbing opportunities, but are mostly untested. C. M. Holt and M. Guthrie made the first ascent of the north face of what they identified as Little Roman Nose in 1975. This climb evidently took place on Point 6943, which is the eastern summit of Roman Nose. They rated the climb as II, 5.8 A2. USGS Roman Nose

Fire Lookout (Class 1). The summit and its lookout can be reached by FST-1 [(C)(1.4)(a)].

Upper Roman Nose Lake Route (Class 3). This route is a 1,100-foot scramble that leads from the lake's western shore up to the north ridge and then onto the summit [(C)(1.4)(a)].

Chimney Rock   *7,124 feet*
North Idaho's most imposing summit sits at the top of the Selkirk Crest just north of Mount Roothaan. The "rock" is a vertical column of granite that provides a variety of technical rock climbing opportunities. Vertical cracks and small, often blocked, chimneys make up the three faces of the wedged-shaped spire. The first ascent was in 1934 by John Carey, Mart Chamberlain, Fred Thieme, and Byron Ward. The first winter

ascent was by Spokane climbers Chris Kopczynski and W. Parks. Today, there are more than twenty-six routes and many variations on the spire's three major faces. Randall Green's book Idaho Rock includes additional routes not included in this guide. Routes on the east and north faces are uniformly rated 5.9 or higher. Chimney Rock is reached from the Priest Lake Basin via the Horton Ridge Lookout site [(B)(1.2)(a)]; or from the Pack River drainage to the east via FST-256 [(C)(1.2)]. Rappelling the northwest shoulder is the normal descent route. The rappel anchors are easy to find. A short 40-foot rappel drops from the summit to the shoulder and the top of the west face. From this point, a double-rope rappel will get you down far enough to allow easy down-climbing on the lower portion of the face. Another rappel anchor is found halfway down the face and it can be used by those with only one rope. USGS Mount Roothaan

(1) Sancho's (II, 5.9). This west face route is on the left side of the face. It starts in the grooves that lead to a small tree. From here, it works up to the northwest corner to join the West Face Standard. Pitch 1: At the tree, climb a left-sloping groove to a right-facing corner, lie back and jam to a roomy ledge (rappel station). Pitch 2: Move to the left end of the ledge and climb a curving flake, 4-inch protection is helpful here. At the flake's end, move right to another lie-back flake and continue up to the next belay on large blocks. Pitch 3: Move left to easier ground, then climb over large blocks. First ascent: J. Roskelley and C. Kopczynski in 1973.

(2) Rappel Chimney (II, 5.6). This route begins west of the West Face Standard. Although sharing a name with the descent route, it does not follow the line your ropes do on rappel. Keep moving right as difficulties increase. Follow the line of least resistance up grooves and flakes until you are in the chimney proper. Climb up toward the notch (rappel station) on the northwest shoulder. Pitch 1: Follow grooves up and right of the blank open book below the last rappel station. When level with anchors, traverse left to a belay. Pitch 2: Belay from the rappel anchors, traverse out right to grooves leading to large flakes. Halfway up this pitch, step left into a chimney that leads to the next ledge. There are fixed anchors at this point. Pitch 3: Move left around a corner from belay to easy Class 4 climbing over large blocks to the summit.

(3) West Face Standard (II, 5.3). This is the original and still most popular route. From the ridgeline just south of the face, climb out onto the face on an easy ledge system. The route leaves this ledge in the middle of the face. From this point, the route leads up for 20 feet, then veers to the left, using several fairly obvious cracks as it works its way toward the western edge of the face and a broad step about 50 feet below the summit. From its start, the route to the step involves two moderate-length pitches where the exposure is much more noticeable than the degree of difficulty. The middle belay point is a very small ledge two-thirds of the way up. (Some climbers use a double rope to avoid the intermediate belay point.) From the broad step, the route goes to the north around a bulging rock to an easy chimney. A short climb up the chimney leads to the summit.

(4) **West Face Direct (II, 5.9).** This route begins at the same point as the West Face Standard. It is Class 4 to the open book in the middle of the face. During wet years the open book is often wet from a seep. Pitch 1: Ascend the corner (off-width, 5 inches) to a spacious ledge shared by a dead tree. Halfway up the corner, watch for a small crack on the left wall. It takes nuts well. Pitch 2: From the belay, move past a tree to climb cracks and blocks to the next groove/flake system on the left, which brings you to the top. First ascent: J. Jones and G. Silver in 1972.

(5) **Cooper-Hiser East Face (III, 5.9).** This was the first route to be climbed on the east side of Chimney Rock. Cooper and Hiser used aid but the route is now rated a free climb. It ascends a line that begins in the middle of the east face and gradually works up and left. Pitch 1: Scramble to a groove that leans left and has a small dead tree clinging to it. Climb past the tree (awkward) to a large groove. At the old rappel slings, climb up and right past an old ring piton into some steep hand cracks that are part of large blocks inside a huge chimney. Finish on a sloping ledge. Pitch 2: At the belay, hand-traverse left with plenty of exposure to a flake system that is climbed by lie-back move and jamming to another ledge at the top of a large block. Go left on a ledge to a large detached block (chimney behind the block) and climb to the belay on the prow. Pitch 3: From the belay on the prow, go up an easy slab that slopes down and to the east until the wall becomes vertical. A fixed pin and bolt protect thin, tricky moves out left onto the prow. Usually a tension traverse is used from the bolt to gain easier, but overhanging,

Chimney Rock west face routes: Sancho's (1), Rappel Chimney (2), West Face Standard (3), West Face Direct (4) (Photo by Joe Benson with permission of Randall Green)

Chimney Rock east and north face routes: Cooper-Hiser (5), North Face/Graymatter (6) (Photo by Randall Green)

blocks to the summit. The moves past the bolt to the summit are at least 5.9. First ascent: E. Cooper and D. Hiser in 1962. First ascent of Cooper-Hiser Direct by C. Kopczynski and J. Roskelley in 1972.

(6) North Face/Graymatter (III, 5.11+). For the most part, the north face is steep, dark, and dirty. However, on the right side is a leaning, gray dihedral capped by a 3-foot roof that is relatively clean of lichens. This climb is well worth doing, but it does require extra cautiousness because of the large, loose block at the top of the first pitch. The first ascent of this route was by D. Burns and C. Hartshorn in 1980.

Pitch 1: Ascend a grungy crack to a bush. Awkward moves will be necessary to gain another crack that skirts a small roof. Then pass a bush and huge, loose block. Belay at the ledge and base of the gray dihedral. Pitch 2: A large, loose block must be passed to gain the crack that splits the dihedral above. Below the roof, where many No. 2 Friends are helpful, the crack is mostly sustained (crux), but past the roof easier slabs lead to an alcove on the left. Belay above the alcove. Pitch 3: The

hand crack on the left ascends directly to the summit right of the main summit roof.

Mount Roothaan   *7,326 feet (Class 2-3)*
Mount Roothaan, an impressive triangular-shaped summit, sits just south of Chimney Rock and is nearly as rugged as its more famous counterpart. It may be the most visited Selkirk summit. The summit can be easily reached by the west ridge, which is reached by the trail from the Horton Ridge parking lot [(B)(1.2)(a)]. The ridge walk to the base of the peak and the easy scramble on the ridge are as rewarding as the view of Chimney Rock to the north. The peak also can be accessed from the east side over the Pack River road to FS-2653, which leads up into the Chimney Creek area [(C) (1.2)]. USGS Mount Roothaan

Gunsight Peak   *7,352 feet*
This massive peak with its hulking 800-foot northeast and 500-foot east faces provides many technical climbing opportunities

Gunsight Peak north face routes (Photo by Joe Benson with permission of Randall Green)

and enjoyable scrambles on its ridges. The peak is located on the main crest 2 miles south of Mount Roothaan. The peak can be accessed from the Priest Lake Basin from either the Chimney Rock area [(B)(1.2)(a)] or Hunt Lake in the east [(B)(1.1)(a)]. From the east and the Pack River drainage, access the peak from Fault Lake [(C)(1.1)(a)]. The north, south, and east ridges provide Class 2 routes to the summit. USGS Mount Roothaan

Winchester East Face (III, 5.8+). R. Green and R. Gibbons pioneered this route up the east face in 1985. From the base of the face, ascend talus boulders above the tarn to the base of the headwall. To reach this route, climb from the tarn up and over the clean, light gray slabs and benches that form an apron at the base of the face. Aim for a point just right of the plumbline from the summit, where you will find a large, detached block and orange lichen growing on the wall nearby. Rope up at this point. Pitch 1: From the rope-up spot, face-climb up to a shallow corner above the large, detached block. Continue up steep rock to a small dihedral. A difficult mantel (crux) leads up and left to a series of flakes. Climb

up on good holds to another groove formed by a large block separated from the wall. Pitch 2: Continue up to the top of a large, detached flake to an ugly, dirty roof. Skirt the roof by face-climbing the wall on the right. Sharp-edged holds abound. Continue up grooves for 150 feet, past a small dead tree, to a belay ledge. Pitch 3: Climb over short cliffs and blocks on easier ground for 150 feet to the summit ridge. To descend, walk off McCormick Ridge to the northeast until descending to the tarn is possible.

Oka/Bates North Face Route (III, 5.8). Three routes have been pioneered up the face. Bergman and Miller climbed the major line that cuts the middle of the face to the summit and rated it a Class 6 climb. Roskelley and Castle climbed a line west of the Bergman/Miller line, also rated a Class 6 climb, and Oka and Bates in 1978 climbed a third chimney/dike system that splits the north face on its western side. Their route is roughly four pitches. No other details are available. Access the north face from the Horton Ridge Road [(B)(1.2)]. From the end of the road, hike up the ridge toward Mount

Gunsight Peak from Mount Roothaan

Roothaan until the north face of Gunsight Peak is in view. From this point, contour around the southwestern slopes of Mount Roothaan to a notch in the ridge between the two peaks. From the notch, it is possible to scramble into the cirque below the face.

Hunt Peak   *7,058 feet (Class 2-3)*
This is the last peak to reach above 7,000 feet at the southern end of the Selkirks. The peak, which was caught in the great Sundance Fire, is a rugged piece of real estate with two large cirques on its northern and eastern slopes that tower above Fault and McCormick Lakes respectively. The north face is the mountain's most impressive feature as it rises more than 800 feet above Fault Lake. The USGS Mount Roothaan quad shows trails leading to the summit from both Hunt Creek and the South Fork of Hunt Creek, [(B)(1.1)(a)]. East side access is best achieved via FST-059 [(C)(1.1)(a)]. The peak is a Class 2 climb via its southern slopes, and a Class 3 climb via its north and east ridges. There are no reported ascents of the north face. USGS Mount Roothaan

APPROACHES TO THE SELKIRK MOUNTAINS

Both primary highways and many forest roads (of varying condition) provide access to almost every nook and cranny within the range. However, in the northwest portion of the range many of the roads are gated and access is limited. Many roads that show up on the ground are not shown on Forest Service and USGS maps.

(A) WASHINGTON STATE ACCESS POINTS
Reaching the northern and westernmost corner of Idaho is no easy task, and involves a drive into Washington State. From I-90 (either in Spokane or from the ID-41 exit), go north to WA-20 at Newport, Washington, and then drive north on WA-20 for 46 miles to its junction with WA-31. Continue north on WA-31 for another 16.8 miles to the Sullivan Lake Road located just south of Ione, Washington.

(1) Sullivan Lake/Salmo Mountain Access. This route leads northeast from WA-31 toward Salmo Mountain. From WA-31, follow the Sullivan Creek road to Sullivan Lake and FS-22. Take FS-22 east for roughly 6 miles to FS-2220, which leads left toward Salmo Mountain. Follow this road for 13 miles to a maintained trailhead. Two trails leave from this point: the first leaves directly from the trailhead and the second begins 1 mile up the gated road that continues from the trailhead. These two

trails can be linked together for an 18-mile backpacking trip.

(a) Salmo River Cutoff/Salmo River Trails. FST-506 begins just below Salmo Mountain and descends to the Salmo River in just under 4 miles. It follows the Salmo River upstream and east to Snowy Top Pass in another 7 miles, just south of the Snowy Top Mountain, where it joins FST-535 [(A)(1)(b)].

(b) FST-535/FST-512, Shedroof Divide Trails. From the trailhead, follow the road past the locked gate for roughly 1 mile to the FST-535 trailhead. This trail leads 4 miles to FST-512 and the Idaho border. Once on the Shedroof Divide, the trail stays high and leads north to Snowy Top Pass in another 6 miles.

(B) PRIEST LAKE ACCESS POINTS
ID-57 is the primary approach route into the Priest Lake Basin and the western side of the Selkirk Crest. For much of its distance, this is a good paved road. The state highway designation ends on the west side of Priest Lake north of Nordman. Several Forest Service roads continue to the north from here. The state of Idaho owns much of the land on the east side of the basin, and has designated its roads on that side with two-digit numbers.

(1) East Shore Road. From Coolin, follow the road approximately 3.2 paved miles to a junction with Cavanaugh Bay Road. Mile markers begin at 0 from this junction. From here, the road, which is chip-sealed for approximately 17.5 miles before turning to generally well-maintained gravel, follows the east side of the two lakes and leads to a junction with FS-655, north of Upper Priest Lake.

(1.1) Hunt Creek Road System. The Hunt Creek drainage is riddled with logging roads, most of which do not show up on even the most recent maps. The Hunt Creek Road leaves the East Shore Road, 7 miles north of Coolin. Turn right off the East Shore Road just after crossing Hunt Creek. The road leads east up Hunt Creek to the area below Hunt and Gunsight Peaks. Roads in the upper drainage are rough and require high-clearance or 4WD vehicles. Good route finding skills are recommended for those venturing into this area.

(a) Hunt Lake Trail. Turn right off the East Shore Road just after crossing Hunt Creek onto Road 24. Continue on Road 24 for approximately 4 miles to the junction of Road 2/24. Continue on Road 24, cross Hunt Creek and bear to the left, still on Road 24. Continue for another mile to the junction with the Road 24 loop. Bear left and travel for 3.5 miles to the posted trailhead.

(b) Hunt Peak Trails. The 1967 USGS Mount Roothaan quad shows a trail leading from the end of the Hunt Creek Road to the summit of Hunt Peak in roughly 3.5 miles. The status of this trail is unknown.

(1.2) Horton Ridge Road. The road system accessing Horton Ridge is a well-maintained system for the first 7.5 miles, followed by a steep, rough road for 2 miles. The latter section is accessible only by high-clearance or 4WD vehicles. Turn right off East Shore Road after crossing Hunt Creek on Road 24. Proceed for 4 miles to the junction of Road 24/2. Take a left on Road 2 and follow it for 1.2 miles to the junction with Road 2/25. Take a right on Road 25, travel for 2.1 miles to the junction of Road 25/253 (a gated road). This is the end of the well-maintained road. Continue on Road 25 for 1.2 miles to a junction with Road 25/254. Bear right on Road 25, climb steep, rough roadway for 0.8 mile to the trailhead.

(a) Cross-country to Chimney Rock. From the lookout site parking area, a trail leads to the ridge below Mount Roothaan, where climbers will get their first sight of the Rock. The route from this point is cross-country and involves either dropping off the ridge into the drainage below Chimney Rock, or crossing the saddle north of Mount Roothaan and traversing the east side of the ridge to the saddle north of Chimney Rock.

(1.3) Two Mouth Creek Road. This road leaves the East Shore Road at Huckleberry Bay and ascends toward the crest. About 3 miles from the lake, a side road departs to the north and climbs toward The Wigwams and Two Mouth Lakes. The main road in the drainage (Road 32) is a well-maintained, graveled road for the first 3 miles along Two Mouth Creek, then turns into a rough road requiring high-clearance or 4WD vehicles.

(a) The Wigwams Road/Jeep Trail/Trail. Turn right off the East Shore Road after mile marker 15 onto Road 32. Continue on Road 32 for approximately 3 miles, passing several spur road junctions until the gravel ends at Camp 11 (old logging camp). The road beyond is steep and rough. Continue for 7.3 miles to the junction of Road 32/324. Bear right on Road 324 and follow it for 1.1 miles to the trailhead. The trail to the old lookout site climbs gradually on the north side of the ridge for approximately 2 miles.

(a.1) The Wigwams to Two Mouth Lake Route. This route follows the ridgeline that runs east toward the main crest in around 3 miles. The trail has not been maintained in many years.

(b) Two Mouth Lake Trail. Turn right off the East Shore Road after mile marker 15 onto Road 32. Continue on Road 32 for approximately 3 miles, passing several spur road junctions until the end of the gravel road at Camp 11 (old logging camp). An old overgrown road leaves Road 32 at the first switchback above Camp 11 (0.2 mile). Walk the old road for 1.8 miles to a trailhead. The trail to Two Mouth Lakes has not been maintained for many years and is difficult to follow, but stays on the north side of Two Mouth Creek for approximately 5 miles. A better approach to Two Mouth Lakes is from the Bonners Ferry side of the range on maintained FST-286 [(D)(5)(a)].

(1.4) Lion Creek Road. This road is accessed from the East Shore Road just south of Lionhead State Park. The road follows Lion Creek east to a point due south of the Lions Head. A sketchy trail that parallels the streambed can be followed from the road's end to Kent Lake.

(1.5) Caribou/Abandon Creek Roads. This road system has been improved with additional drainage structures and some gravel, but remains rough and requires high-clearance or 4WD vehicles. Access this road, which runs northeast up the Caribou Creek drainage, from the East Shore Road 10.5 miles north of Coolin. Look for a logging road on your right 0.2 mile past milepost 21. There are two points along the road system that provide access to Lookout Mountain's trails. The first is roughly 2 miles from the East Shore Road and the second is 9.5 rugged miles from the road. Check with Priest Lake State Forest personnel before attempting to take your car to the second trailhead. To reach the second trailhead, take the main road to a fork in about 4.2 miles and go right. After another 2.3 miles, turn right onto a poor road that will take you another 3.5 miles.

(a) South Lookout Lake Trail. From the trailhead, the route climbs to a junction just south of Lookout Lake in about 3.5 miles. From this junction it is roughly 1 mile via a good trail to the summit.

(b) North Lookout Lake Trail. Turn right off the East Shore Road onto Road 44, which is 0.5 mile past mile marker 23. Follow Road 44 for 2.5 miles to the junction of Road 44/432. Turn right onto Road 432 and climb steadily for 3.2 miles to the trailhead.

(C) PACK RIVER ACCESS POINTS

The Pack River drains a large area of the Selkirk Range between Roman Nose in the east, Harrison Peak in the north, and Chimney Rock in the west. The Pack River Road, described below, provides alternative approach routes to most southern Selkirk peaks.

(1) FS-231, Pack River Road. This road leaves US-2/US-95 at Walsh Lake and proceeds north for almost 20 miles to a point just south of Harrison Peak. The land it traverses is controlled by the Forest Service, with interspersed sections of private and state land.

(a) FST-279, Beehive Lakes Trail. This trail leaves FS-23 18 miles from US-2/US 95 beginning. The trail leaves the road, quickly crosses a footbridge across the Pack River and then climbs northwest to the southern Beehive Lakes in 4.5 miles.

(1.1) Hunt and Gunsight Peaks Access. Drive on FS-231 11.5 miles and turn east onto McCormick Creek Road. The road ends shortly.

(a) FST-059, Fault Lake Trail. This trail leads from the end of the McCormick Creek Road to Fault Lake at 5,980 feet.

(1.2) Chimney Rock East Side Access. From the junction of

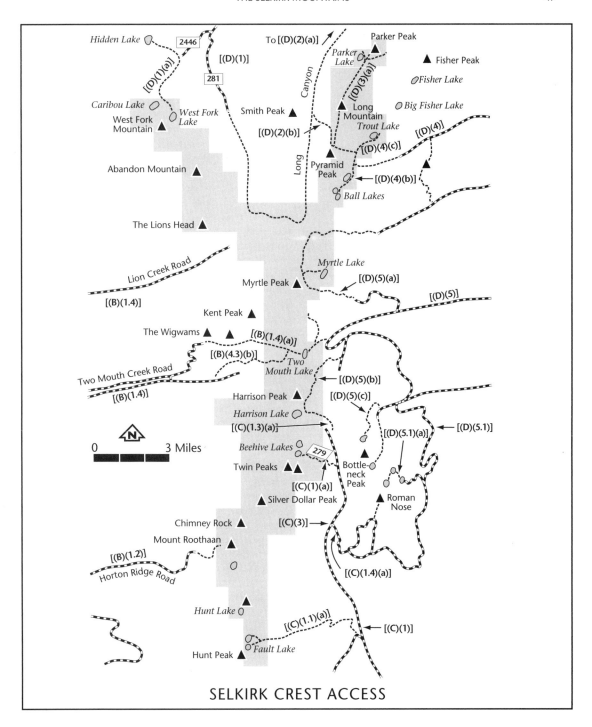

SELKIRK CREST ACCESS

US-2/US-95 and FS-231, drive north on the Pack River Road for roughly 16 miles to FS-2653. Turn west on FS-2653 and follow this road (staying on the most worn tracks) for about 2.5 miles until it becomes too difficult to traverse. A 4WD is recommended. Hike up the road for about 0.5 mile, cross Chimney Creek on a log bridge and then follow the old logging road up to the top of the ridge that divides the Chimney Creek and West Fork drainages. From this point, it is an additional 2 miles to the crest. Follow the path, which is marked with blazes on the trees and rock cairns along the ridge crest, into the cirque on a bench at the base of Mount Roothaan.

(1.3) **Harrison Peak Access.** The trailhead for Harrison Lake is 0.25 mile south of the end of FS-231 or roughly 20 miles from the beginning of the Pack River Road.

(a) **FST-271, Harrison Lake Trail.** This 2.5-mile long trail leads to the lake, FST-271, follows an old jeep road. The trail links with FST-6 [(D)(5)(b)] just before the lake.

(1.4) **Roman Nose South Access.** FS-2605 leaves FS-231 and climbs to the east, eventually reaching the ridgeline near Dodge Peak. At this point, the road becomes FS-291. This road drops off the ridge and heads north until it connects with the extensive road system leading into the range from Bonners Ferry [(D)(5)].

(a) **FST-1, Roman Nose Trail.** This trail climbs to the top of Apache Ridge and continues to the summit of Roman Nose in 4.5 miles.

(D) EAST SIDE ACCESS POINTS

Primary access to the eastern side of the Selkirk Range is from the Westside Road that can be accessed from US-2/US-95 at Porthill, Copeland, Bonners Ferry, and Naples, Idaho. The Westside Road parallels the base of the Selkirks on the west side of the Kootenai River and connects to the following access routes. The access routes listed below all leave from the Westside Road and are listed from north to south.

(1) **FS-281 and FS-2464 (a.k.a. FS-2446), Smith Creek Roads.** The Smith Creek Road provides access to the northeastern Selkirks. The shortest access is from US-1 at Porthill on the Idaho/Canada border, but the road also can be reached from Copeland farther to the south. In Porthill, follow Main Street west to a bridge that crosses the Kootenai River. Cross the bridge and follow the road west along the border and then south to the Smith Creek turn in 4 miles. To reach the FST-102/21 trailhead, follow the road into the mountains for 8 miles where the road makes a hard right turn. (The right fork goes on for another 4 miles and ends west of Smith Peak.) Follow the left fork, FS-655, for another mile to a second junction and FS-2545. Take the left fork and follow the road up Beaver Creek for roughly 3 miles to the West Fork Lake trailhead.

(a) **FST-102/FST-21/FST-347, West Fork Lake and Mountain Access.** These trails lead to the top of West Fork Lake below West Fork Mountain in roughly 6 miles. From the FS-2464 (a.k.a. FS-2446) trailhead, the trail climbs up to Hidden Lake in a short mile. From Hidden Lake the trail climbs over a pass and then drops down into the West Fork of Smith Creek, which it follows upstream to a saddle above West Fork Lake in 3.5 miles. From this point, one trail drops down to the lake while a second, unmaintained trail climbs up to the old lookout site near the summit of West Fork Mountain. The Forest Service has a gate across FS-2446 1 mile below the trailhead.

(2) **Long Canyon Access.** Take ID-1 north from its junction with US-95 for 1 mile to the Copeland turn. Drive through Copeland, cross the Kootenai River, continue to the Westside Road, and then turn north. Drive another 6.7 miles north to the trailhead.

(a) **FST-16, Canyon Creek Trail.** Long Canyon is the largest section of primeval Selkirk wilderness remaining. The trail is well-maintained (primarily thanks to volunteer efforts) as it climbs up Long Canyon to a junction with FST-7 in 13 forested miles. Beyond this junction, the trail is unmaintained and eventually reaches Long Canyon Pass after many difficult miles.

(b) **FST-7, Pyramid Pass Trail.** This trail links Long Canyon with the Parker Ridge Trail, FST-221 [(D)(3)(a)] in 4 steep miles.

(3) **Parker Ridge Trailhead.** Take ID-1 north from its junction with US-95 and follow it for 1 mile to the Copeland turn. Drive through Copeland, cross the Kootenai River, continue to the Westside Road, and then turn north. Drive another 2.75 miles north to the trailhead.

(a) **FST-221, Parker Ridge Trail.** From the trailhead, FST-221 begins with a series of easy switchbacks and then makes a rugged traverse of Parker Ridge. It provides access to the Long Mountain Parker Peak ridge leading to Pyramid Peak. The trail ends just below Pyramid Pass where it connects with FST-7, which provides access to Long Canyon [(D)(2)(a) and (b)]. FST-221 travels from Pyramid Pass into the Trout Creek Drainage where it links with FS-634, the Trout Creek Road [(D)(4)].

(4) **FS-634, Trout Creek Road.** Take ID-1 north from its junction with US-95 and follow it for 1 mile to the Copeland turn. Drive through Copeland and cross the Kootenai River and continue to the Westside Road and then turn south on the Westside Road and follow it to FS-634 in a little over 3 miles. Turn west onto FST-634. The road reaches the FST-27, Fisher Peak Trail in 5.5 miles, and the Pyramid Pass, Ball Lake, and Big Fisher Lake trailhead in 9.5 miles.

(a) **FST-27, Fisher Peak Trail.** From its Trout Creek Road trailhead, this trail climbs to the summit of Fisher Peak in about 7 miles. The trail is in reasonably good condition.

2

(b) **FST-43, Pyramid Pass and Ball Lakes Trail.** FST-43 leads to Ball Lakes just below the Selkirk Crest in 2.5 miles with a 1,300-foot elevation gain. Roughly 0.5 mile from the trailhead, the trail intersects with FST-41 leading to Trout Lake and at 1.75 miles the trail intersects with FST-221 and FST-7 [(D)(2)(b)] to Long Canyon.

(c) **FST-13/41 Big Fisher Lake Trail.** This trail leads to Big Fisher Lake after 6.5 miles of rugged walking. It crosses three drainages and passes Trout Lake. The route starts on the Pyramid Pass Trail, FST-13 [(D)(4)(b)], which it follows for 0.5 mile to the junction with FST-41. Turn right onto FST-41. Trout Lake is another 2.5 miles. From Trout Lake, the trail climbs to a pass just west of Big Fisher Lake in another 3.5 miles and 1,110 feet of elevation gain. From the pass, the trail drops steeply to Big Fisher Lake at 6,732 feet.

(5) **FS-633, 661, and 402, Myrtle Creek/Snow Creek Loop.** West of Bonners Ferry, a major Forest Service road system loops through the Snow Creek and Myrtle Creek drainages, almost reaching the Selkirk Crest at one point. Drive west from Bonners Ferry along the banks of the Kootenai River to the Westside Road (signs will direct you to the Kootenai National Wildlife Refuge). When the road ends, turn north and drive to the refuge head-quarters to reach Myrtle Creek (FS-663), or turn south to access Snow Creek (FS-402).

(a) **FST-286, Myrtle Peak Trail.** Near the top of Myrtle Creek, turn off FS-633 and onto FS-2406. Follow it to its end. FST-286 begins at this point and leads to the peak in about 4 strenuous miles. From the top of the peak, the trail drops down to Myrtle Lake, which is well worth a visit.

(b) **FST-6, Harrison Lake Trail.** To reach this trail, leave the Myrtle Creek Road just after the road crosses Myrtle Creek and loops back to the east. Turn right (south) onto FS-2409 and follow it to its end, where the trailhead is located. The trail begins at this point and runs for 4 miles to Harrison Lake.

(c) **FST-187, Bottleneck Lake Trail.** Follow the Snow Creek Road west for roughly 7 miles to a point just past FS-661, the Cooks Pass Road that runs north to Myrtle Creek. In another 0.5 mile you will come to a gate. The trail follows an old road southwest past the gate. The lake is 3.5 miles up the trail. FST-185 can be accessed from this trail and leads to Snow Lake.

(5.1) **Roman Nose Lakes Access.** This road is accessed from FS-402, which is followed roughly 7 miles to FS-1007. Drive this road south, up and over Ruby Pass, to FS-2667. Turn right and follow this road for 2 miles to the first Roman Nose Lake. A 4WD is required.

(a) **FST-160, Roman Nose Lakes Trail.** This trail leaves the first lake and climbs to the uppermost lake in 1.6 miles with a 300-foot elevation gain.

THE PURCELL MOUNTAINS

The Purcell Mountains, a Canadian range that extends south across the border into Idaho and Montana, is situated north-east of Bonners Ferry. The Purcells are bounded by US-95 and US-1 on the west and the Kootenai River and US-2 to the south. The Montana and Canadian borders form the eastern and northern boundaries, respectively. The highest point in the Idaho section of the Purcells—6,779-foot Buckhorn Mountain—sits along the Idaho/Montana border.

The range was completely blanketed by Pleistocene era glaciers, which scraped away much of the range's Precambrian rock. The Moyie River Canyon, which splits the Idaho section of the Purcell Mountains, is the most spectacular geologic feature within the range. Despite the sub-7,000-foot elevations, the Purcells are much more rugged than most would expect.

The Purcells are managed by the Idaho Panhandle National Forest and timber harvesting has been the dominant use. As a result, the range has an extensive road system, but a very small and broken trail system, though the Forest Service recently has relocated and repaired some of the original trail system and further improvements are planned. Today, only short day hikes are available for hikers and some of these are on trails open to ORVs. Roads lead to all of the mountain lakes in the Purcells and two popular summits, Deer Ridge at 4,755 feet and Hall Mountain at 5,343 feet. Consequently, climbing opportunities are limited to nontechnical Class 1 and Class 2 ascents.

Mission Mountain	*6,206 feet (Class 2)*
Harvey Mountain*	*6,402 feet (Class 2)*

These two peaks are located just south of the Idaho/Canadian border and are short climbs from either FST-156 or FST-409 [(A)(2)(a)]. USGS Hall Mountain

Bussard Mountain	*5,968 feet (Class 1)*

Bussard Mountain is located 1 mile north of Queen Mountain. Its summit can be reached from the north via FST-415 [(A)(1)(a)] or the east via FST-32 (a.k.a. FST-52) [(A)(3)(a)], which leads west from the Moyie River past Bussard Lake to the summit in 3.5 miles. Bussard Mountain also can be climbed via the Danquist Trail, FST-225, which traverses the east side of Tungsten Mountain. The trailhead for this route is found along FS-2485, roughly 3.5 miles northwest of Bussard Mountain. USGS Hall Mountain

Queen Mountain   *6,112 feet (Class 1)*
Queen Mountain is located 0.8 mile west of Queen Lake on the high ridge that divides the Moyie and Kootenai Rivers. The peak is approached from FST-152 [(A)(3)(b)], which begins on the Moyie River, or from FS-2542, which intersects FST-152 1 mile below the summit. USGS Eastport

Goat Mountain   *6,641 feet (Class 2)*
Goat Mountain stands northeast of Perkins Lake and 0.5 mile west of the Idaho/Montana border. The remnants of an old Forest Service fire lookout sit on the summit. Hike to the summit via FST-43 [(A)(4.1)(a)]. This trail climbs more than 3,400 feet. The summit also can be approached from Montana via FST-44, which more or less traverses a north/south ridgeline from Keno Mountain in Montana to Line Point and Goat Mountain in Idaho. Segments of FST-44 are difficult to find, but maintenance is expected in the future. USGS Line Point

Buckhorn Mountain*   *6,779 feet (Class 2)*
Although unnamed on the current USGS quad, this peak is known locally as Buckhorn Mountain. Its summit is the highest point in the Idaho Purcells. Located 0.5 mile south of Goat Mountain [(A)(4.1)(a)], its summit can be reached from the saddle between the two peaks. USGS Line Point

APPROACHES TO THE PURCELL MOUNTAINS

(A) PURCELL MOUNTAIN ACCESS POINTS
The primary approach is from US-2 in the south and US-95 and ID-1 along the range's western fringes. In addition, US-95 cuts across the range's northwest corner and the Moyie River Road and the Deer Creek Road (both major secondary roads) cut through the central sections of the range from north to south.

(1) US-95 from US-1 to Eastport. US-95 leaves its junction with US-1 11.7 miles north of Bonners Ferry and runs northeast to the Canadian border at Eastport in 16 miles.

(a) FST-415, Sidehill Trail/Bussard Mountain Access. This trail is accessed from US-1 and a short Forest Service road just southwest of Robinson Lake (which is on the north side of US-95). The trail leaves the trailhead and traverses mountain slopes for 5 miles to a junction with FST-32 (a.k.a. FST-52). From

this junction, ascend FST-32 for 1.8 miles to the summit of Bussard Mountain. On the summit, this trail joins FST-152 [(A)(3)(b)], which runs south to Queens Mountain, and FST-225, which runs northwest toward Tungsten Mountain.

(2) FS-272 and FS-2481, Hall Mountain and Harvey Mountain Roads. FS-272 leaves US-95 4.4 miles east of US-1 and runs north to the Canadian border. A mile from the border, FS-2481 forks off to the east and proceeds up East Fork Mission Creek before meandering to the Miller Creek drainage, where it is blocked by a gate.

(a) FST-156 and FST-409, Mission Mountain Trail. These trails combine to form a travel route between the Harvey Mountain Road and Gillion Creek. The western end of the trail can be accessed from the Harvey Mountain Road at the divide between Mission Creek and Miller Creek. It then follows the ridgeline north to Mission Mountain in a little more than 1 mile. At Mission Mountain, the trail turns due east and descends a ridgeline past Harvey Mountain to Gillion Creek. The trail's east end connects with FS-273 and Gillion Creek 1.4 miles north of US-95.

(3) FS-211, Moyie River Road. FS-211 is accessed from

Buckhorn Peak from Goat Mountain (Photo by Chris Paulson)

US-2, 10 miles from Bonners Ferry. Turn north off US-2 on the first road west of the Moyie River bridge. This road runs north along the river for 20 miles to a junction with US-95 just south of the Canadian border.

(a) **FST-32 (a.k.a. FST-52), Bussard Mountain Trail.** FST-32 leaves FS-211 just north of Bussard Lake and climbs to the summit of Bussard Mountain in 3.5 miles, where it joins with FST-225 and 152.

(b) **FST-152, Queen Mountain Trail.** This trail leaves FS-211 mile south of Twin Bridges and climbs to the summit of Queens Mountain in 3.5 miles. It then continues to the summit of Bussard Mountain in another 1.2 miles.

(4) **FS-435, Deer Creek Road.** Reach this road by following ID-72, which leaves US-2 1.4 miles east of the Moyie River bridge. Drive north on ID-72 to the FS-435 junction and turn left onto FS-435. FS-435 continues north along Deer Creek and eventually passes into Montana near Cannuck Peak.

(4.1) **FS-627, Skin Creek Road.** To reach this road, follow FS-435 north to Perkins Lake Road. Follow Perkins Lake Road east toward the lake and turn left on FS-627 1.5 miles before Perkins Lake. FS-627 is signed for Soloman Lake. At one time it continued east just before the lake, but the Forest Service has obliterated that portion of the road.

(a) **FST-43, Goat Mountain Trail.** This trail leaves the Skin Creek Road roughly 50 feet north of where the road crosses Skin Creek. The trail was reopened in 1998 and is not shown on recent maps. It climbs 3,450 feet to Goat Mountain summit in 4.5 miles.

3

THE CABINET MOUNTAINS

The Cabinet Mountains extend into Idaho from Montana. The range is situated southeast of Bonners Ferry and is bounded on the north by US-2 and the Kootenai River, on the west by US-2 and US-95, on the southeast by Lake Pend Oreille, and to the south by ID-200 and the Clark Fork River. The range stretches 40 miles from north to south and extends westerly into Idaho for 16 miles at its widest spot.

The Cabinet Mountains share many similarities with the Purcell and Selkirk Mountains. The range's foundation is Precambrian Belt Supergroup rocks carved and shaped by Pleistocene glaciation. Many peaks are high, dome-shaped mountains, while a few, such as Scotchman Peak, are sharp, sheer-edged summits reminiscent of the North Cascades. Summit elevations range between 6,000 and 7,000 feet. At 7,009 feet, Scotchman Peak is the highest Cabinet summit. East of the border, the Montana Cabinet Mountains are much higher than their Idaho counterparts.

The Idaho Cabinet Mountains are traversed by a north/south-trending ridge that wiggles its way south from the Boulder City ghost town to the Idaho/Montana border near Scotchman Peak. The Idaho Panhandle National Forest administers the range west of this divide and the Kootenai National Forest controls the east side. Although much of the range has been logged in the past, high-quality, roadless country still exists for climbers and hikers. There are many miles of inviting, well-maintained hiking trails that traverse both high, treeless ridgelines and stream bottoms. Most Cabinet peaks are rated Class 1. These are big, beautiful challenging mountains. Road access to trailheads is above average. The Forest Service is in the process of closing and removing some roads and gradually improving trails.

Clifty Mountain	*6,705 feet (Class 2)*
Katka Peak	*6,208 feet (Class 2)*

Clifty Mountain and Katka Peak are found in the northern section of the range, 6 miles southeast of Bonners Ferry. Both peaks are reached from the Black Mountain Road, FS-274 [(B) (1.1)]. Leave FS-274 at the road's last major switchback and take the Katka Peak Trail FST-182 (a.k.a. FST-46) [(B)(1.1)(a)] east toward Clifty Mountain, which is only about 1 mile from the trailhead. When the trail enters the large clearing below the summit, ascend the south slopes to Clifty's summit, a 500-foot elevation gain. From Clifty's slopes, continue northeast via the trail to reach Katka's twin summits in another 2.5 miles. The trail goes into the saddle between the summits. The eastern summit is the highest. Ascend it from the trail via its south slopes. USGS Clifty Mountain/Moyie Springs

Iron Mountain	*6,426 feet (Class 1)*

Iron Mountain sits 3.5 miles south of Clifty Mountain. The peak is climbed from FS-408 and the Iron Mountain Trail, FST-180 (a.k.a. FST-179), which is part of the Boulder Mountain trail system [(B)(1)(a)]. FST-180 leads to the summit. USGS Clifty Mountain

Boulder Mountain   *6,298 feet (Class 2)*
Boulder Mountain sits 3 miles south of Iron Mountain on the high ridgeline that runs from Iron Mountain in the north to Lunch Peak in the south. FST-176 [(B)(1)(a)] reaches to within 300 feet of the summit. From the trail, follow either the north or south ridges up to the summit. The summit also can be approached from Boulder City [(B)(2)(a)] or from the south via FST-67 [(A)(2.1)(a)]. USGS Clifty Mountain

Middle Mountain   *6,220 feet (Class 2)*
This peak is 1.5 miles southeast of Boulder Mountain and can be reached from FST-51 [(B)(2)(a)]. FST-51 originates at the Boulder City ghost town near the Kootenai River. The trail traverses the divide that is the boundary between the Idaho Panhandle and Kootenai National Forests. Along the way, it passes near the summits of Timber Mountain, 6,395 feet, Star Mountain, 6,107 feet, and Middle Mountain. Middle Mountain also can be climbed from the north via FST-179 [(B)(1)(a)] or the south via FST-67 [(A)(2.1)(a)]. USGS Clifty Mountain

Grouse Mountain   *5,982 feet (Class 2)*
Bald Eagle Mountain   *6,098 feet (Class 1)*
These two summits share a ridgeline 3 miles west of Calder Mountain. The remnants of a fire lookout can be found on Bald Eagle along with a panoramic view of the Purcell Trench and the Selkirk Mountains. These summits can be reached via FS-404 and FST-53 [(B)(3)(a)] or FS-447 [(B)(3)(b)]. These two trails and FS-404 can be combined into a loop hike. The summits also can be ascended from Boulder Meadows to the northwest. USGS Elmira/Twentymile.

Calder Mountain*   *5,699 feet (Class 2)*
Purdy Mountain   *6,062 feet (Class 2)*
Mount Willard   *6,536 feet (Class 2)*
These three summits stand on the main Cabinet ridgeline between Boulder Mountain and Mount Pend Oreille. The summits are all accessed by following FST-67 [(A)(2.1)(a)], either from Lunch Peak in the south or from Boulder Mountain or Boulder Meadows in the north. Each summit is an easy walk from the very popular FST-67 as it passes nearby. USGS Mount Pend Oreille

Mount Pend Oreille   *6,755 (Class 1)*
Mount Pend Oreille is a big dome-shaped mountain with an extraordinarily pleasant grass-covered summit featuring astonishing views in all directions. The summit is reached from either Lightning Creek and FST-52 [(A)(1)(a)] or Lunch Peak and FST-67 [(A)(2.1)(a)]. USGS Mount Pend Oreille

Smith Mountain   *6,510 feet (Class 2)*
Smith Mountain, an old fire lookout site, sits above Smith Lake. The peak is 3.5 miles east of Mount Pend Oreille. The summit is approached from either Idaho or Montana. The Montana route is Class 1 by hiking FS-4530, a gated logging road to the summit. Idaho access is from the end of the Lightning Creek Road. Hike north on FST-52 [(A)(1)(a)] to a junction just below Darling Lake. From this junction, take FST-54 to South Callahan Creek. Leave the trail at this point and ascend the peak's steep southwest slope to the ridge and walk to the summit. USGS Smith Mountain

Moose Mountain   *6,543 feet (Class 1)*
Moose Mountain is situated 1 mile southwest of Moose Lake. To reach the summit, take FST-213 from the Rattle Creek Road [(A)(1.3)(b)]. Follow the trail north toward Moose Lake to the divide above the lake. From the divide, follow the old trail up the ridgeline to the peak. The peak also can be approached from Moose and Deer Creeks. USGS Benning Mountain

Lunch Peak   *6,414 feet (Class 1)*
Lunch Peak is the southernmost peak on the main north/ south ridgeline that dominates the northern Idaho Cabinet Mountains. The mountain serves as a fire lookout site and is reached by FS-1091 [(A)(2.1)]. Lunch Peak serves as the trailhead for the popular FST-67 [(A)(2.1)(a)]. Even with the road to its summit, the peak is an excellent goal because of its tremendous view. Hike to this summit from Darling Lake or Mount Pend Oreille (to avoid the road). USGS Trestle Peak/ Mount Pend Oreille

Trestle Peak   *6,320 feet*
Round Top Mountain   *6,149 feet (Class 1)*
These two peaks are found in the southern Idaho Cabinet Mountains along a major north/south ridgeline that divides the Lightning Creek drainage from Lake Pend Oreille. FST-120 traverses this ridgeline for almost its entire distance [(A)(2)(a)]. Both peaks have striking summits with lofty views. The best route begins from FS-275 at the divide between Trestle Creek and Quartz Creek. From the saddle in the north, it is 3 miles to Trestle Peak and 6 miles to Round Top. USGS Trestle Peak

Bee Top Mountain   *6,212 feet (Class 1)*
This former fire lookout site stands above the entrance to Lightning Creek 7 miles north of Clark Fork. It provides excellent vistas in all directions. Access the summit from the Alpine Way Trail and FST-63 [(A)(3)(a.1)], which leads to the summit. USGS Clark Fork

Scotchman No. 2   *6,989 feet (Class 3)*

This beautiful and rugged summit is found 2 miles northeast of Scotchman Peak, almost directly on the Idaho/Montana border. Although the summit can probably be reached from the west via either Morris or Savage Creeks, the only route information available was from a climber who made the long, tedious traverse of the rugged ridgeline between Scotchman Peak and Scotchman No. 2. This route involves considerable climbing just to descend Scotchman Peak's north ridge. Allow plenty of time for this trip. USGS Scotchman Peak

Black Top Mountain   *6,517 feet (Class 3)*

This peak sits midway between the two Scotchman peaks. To reach the summit, climb directly from Morris Creek on the west or traverse the ridgeline north from Scotchman Peak. USGS Scotchman Peak

Scotchman Peak   *7,009 feet (Class 1)*

This summit, probably the hardest Class 1 peak in the state, is a craggy monster built of tilting metamorphic rocks that seem ready to slip down into Montana at any minute. The view of the "big" Cabinet peaks in Montana is awesome. To reach the highest point in Idaho's Cabinet Range, take FST-65 to the summit [(A)(1.2)(a)]. The trail is steep and rocky, and roughly 5 miles in length with a 3,500-foot elevation gain. USGS Scotchman Peak

Goat Mountain   *6,390 feet (Class 2)*

Goat Mountain is a minor, nondescript summit found due west of Scotchman Peak. Climb this peak from the east where

FST-65 [(A)(1.2)(a)] enters the saddle between Goat Mountain and Scotchman Peak. Leave the trail at this point and follow the easy ridgeline west to the summit. Although a minor summit, the view of Scotchman from here makes the walk worthwhile. USGS Scotchman Peak

APPROACHES TO THE CABINET MOUNTAINS

(A) SOUTHERN CABINET MOUNTAIN ACCESS POINTS

The primary southern approaches are via US-95 from Sandpoint to Bonners Ferry, which travels along the western edge of the Cabinet Mountains, and ID-200, which provides access along the south edge.

(1) FS-419, Lightning Creek Road. This is the major vehicular entrance into the southern sections of the range. The road departs from the center of the town of Clark Fork and goes north. Many trails and side roads are accessible from this road.

(a) FST-52, Lake Darling/Mount Pend Oreille Trail. The road up Lightning Creek ends roughly 18 miles from Clark Fork. At this point, FST-52 continues up the drainage to Lake Darling in 2 miles and to the top of Mount Pend Oreille in 5 miles.

(1.2) FS-1058, Mosquito Creek Road. This road is accessed from the Lightning Creek Road 0.75 mile north of ID-200. Turn east onto the road and follow it for almost 4 miles to the Scotchman Peak trailhead.

(a) FST-65, Scotchman Peak Trail. This steep (repeat, steep) trail is 5 miles long and ends at the ruins of a fire lookout on the summit of Scotchman Peak. As the trail nears the summit,

Cabinet crest looking north from Scotchman Peak toward Scotchman No. 2

The west face of Scotchman Peak

you will not believe that it traverses the final treacherous ridge-line. It does!

(1.3) FS-473, Rattle Creek Road. This road leaves FS-419 roughly 14 miles north of Clark Fork, and traverses eastward into Montana.

(a) FST-134, Lightning Peak Trail. Access this trail 4 miles from the Lightning Creek/Rattle Creek junction. The trail gives access to Lightning Peak's east slopes.

(b) FST-213, Moose Lake Trail. FST-213 leaves FST-134 3.5 miles east of Lightning Creek and runs due north to Moose Lake and Moose Creek in 4.25 miles.

(2) FS-275, Trestle Creek Road. The junction for this road is 17 miles from Clark Fork on the Lightning Creek Road. The road climbs to a pass north of Trestle Peak and then descends to ID-200 in 13 miles. This rough road has been traveled by car, but it is quite rugged on the western side of the saddle where it detours up and around a section that is constantly being washed away by Trestle Creek.

(a) FST-120, Alpine Trail. This trail is designated as a National Recreational Trail. Hopefully, this designation will insure that the route will not be violated by any more roads. The trail begins at the top of Trestle Creek (the trailhead is directly on the

saddle). From the saddle, the trail quickly climbs to the ridge top and follows the divide south for 14 miles to its end on Lightning Creek (just north of Clark Fork). In route, the trail climbs over several peaks. The route is divided into two sections by FS-489. The walk is highly recommended for those who can shuttle to the high end and walk to the low end.

(2.1)FST-1091, Lunch Peak Road. From the saddle at the top of Trestle Creek on FS-275, drive north on a good gravel road almost to the top of Lunch Peak. A lookout tower stands on the summit.

(a) FST-67, Cabinet Divide Trail. From Lunch Peak, FST-67 follows the undulating ridgeline north toward Mount Pend Oreille and beyond. It is 3.5 miles to that summit, another 1.3 miles to Purdy Mountain, another 2.1 miles to Calder Mountain, and 3 more miles to Boulder Mountain. The trail, which stays on the ridgeline for the entire distance, is a premier alpine hike. The Forest Service recently obliterated FS-427 0.5 mile north of Calder Mountain and replaced it with a trail that parallels the old road and drops down into Boulder Meadows. FST-67 connects with FST-51 [(B)(2)(a)] at Middle Mountain.

(3) State Fish Hatchery Access. Just west of Clark Fork, ID-200 crosses Lightning Creek. Turn north on the road that leads to the State Fish Hatchery and drive 2.25 miles to a junction. Turn right onto a private road (open to the public) and follow this road east to an intersection in 1.2 miles. Turn right at this intersection and then in 0.1 mile turn left where you will find the trailhead for FST-120.

(a) FST-120, Bee Top/Round Top Trail. This well-maintained trail climbs north toward the Cabinet high country. After 3.5 miles it intersects with FST-63.

(a.1) FST-63, Bee Top Mountain Trail. From its beginning at FST-120, this trail follows a scenic ridge top to the summit of Bee Top Mountain in 2 miles.

(B) NORTHERN CABINET MOUNTAIN ACCESS ROUTES.

Primary access to the north Cabinet Mountains is from US-2 and US-95.

(1) County Road 9-FS-408, Twentymile Creek Road. This road is accessed just north of Naples on US-95. The road proceeds up Twentymile Creek into the area surrounding Boulder Mountain. Follow this road east for 12 miles over a pass and onto the Boulder Creek Road. The Boulder Creek Road can be followed south toward the creek's headwaters or west toward the Kootenai River. Either choice will lead to trailheads that access the Boulder Mountain area. FS-408 continues to FS-314 near Boulder City [(B)(2)].

(a) Iron and Boulder Mountain Trails. These trails include FST-180, 176, and 179. Look for the trailhead along FS-408, about 3 miles west of Boulder City. The route starts by

4

crossing Boulder Creek and splits after climbing for about 0.25 mile. The right-hand fork, FST-180, climbs west/southwest to Iron Mountain in 3 miles. Just south of the summit, it intersects with FST-179 running south to Boulder Mountain and FST-51 at Divide Lake. The left-hand fork, FST-176, climbs up Slate Ridge, passing by Buck Mountain, and intersects with FST-179 between Iron Mountain and Boulder Mountain.

(1.1) **FS-274, Black Mountain Road.** This road leaves FS-408 at Twentymile Pass and climbs to the summit of Black Mountain.

(a) **FST-182, Katka Peak Trail.** This trail leaves the Black Mountain Road at its easternmost switchback and runs east past Clifty Mountain to Katka Pass near the summit of Katka Peak. It then continues southeast, descending to FS-408 [(B)(1)] about 1 mile west of Boulder City.

(2) **County Road 24/FS-314, Boulder City Access.** This road system parallels the south side of the Kootenai River from Bonners Ferry east to the Boulder City ghost town. This is a good road for its entire distance.

(a) **Middle Mountain Trails.** The country between Boulder Mountain and the Boulder City ghost town encompasses several roadless drainages with fine trails that follow the drainages or the accompanying, long and winding ridgelines. From the Boulder City ghost town, FST-51, the Divide Trail, climbs south to the top of the main Cabinet divide and then follows the divide south past Timber Mountain and Star Mountain to Middle Mountain in about 9 miles. FS-51 meets FST-136 at this point. FST-136 ascends the East Fork Boulder Creek from Boulder City to Middle Mountain in 7 miles. From Middle Mountain, FST-51 continues west to Divide Lake where it meets FST-176 (a.k.a. FST-179) [(B)(1)(a)]. From the lake, the route now runs along the divide southwest toward Calder Mountain where it intersects with FST-67 [(A)(2.1)(a)] at Divide Lake.

(3) **FS-404, Beaver Dam Pass Road.** This road leaves US-95 at Naples and proceeds southeast up Trail Creek to Beaver Dam Pass just north of Jay Peak. From the pass, the trail runs east to the FST-53 trailhead in about 1 mile. From this trailhead, the road continues east in roughly 1.2 miles to the trailhead for FST-447. A 4WD is recommended.

(a) **FST-53, Grouse Mountain Trail.** From its beginning along Grouse Creek, this trail quickly crosses the creek and climbs to the summit of Grouse Mountain in about 3.5 miles. From the summit, it runs northeast past Bald Eagle Mountain to Kelly Pass in another 2.5 miles. On Kelly Pass, it intersects with FST-447 [(B)(3)(b)] and FST-155.

(b) **FST-447, Kelly Pass Trail.** This trail leaves the end of FS-404 and climbs to Kelly Pass in 2 miles. On the pass, it intersects with FST-53 [(B)(3)(a)] and FST-155.

THE COEUR D'ALENE MOUNTAINS

The Coeur d'Alene mountains are a triangular group of peaks stretching from Lake Pend Oreille in the north to Lake Coeur d'Alene in the south, to Kellogg in the east and then back to Lake Pend Oreille. The range is bounded by the Bitterroot Mountains in the east, the Coeur d'Alene River in the south, and Coeur d'Alene Lake and the Purcell Trench in the west. Grizzly Mountain, at 5,950 feet, is the highest point in the range. The Chilco Mountains are a small subrange of the Coeur d'Alene Mountains on the western fringes of the main range, between Lake Pend Oreille and Lake Coeur d'Alene. The highest mountain in this subrange is Chilco Mountain, which reaches 5,685 feet.

The Coeur d'Alene Mountains are formed by twisted layers of Precambrian sedimentary and metamorphic rocks that have been extensively faulted by the Osborn Fault system. During its history, the fault has moved Coeur d'Alene rock almost 16 miles. This faulting caused massive cracks to develop within the Coeur d'Alene rockbeds; these cracks filled with superheated, mineral-laden water, which precipitated the rich ore bodies that have made this region a famous mining district. Although gold was discovered in 1881, subsequent discoveries of silver made the area famous. In the last one hundred years more than a billion ounces of silver have been pulled out of mining shafts, some as deep as 8,000 feet.

The Idaho Panhandle National Forest administers most of the area. Some private land is interspersed throughout the mountains in the form of patented mining claims. The range has an extensive road system to serve logging and mining interests. Little of the early trail system has survived the bulldozer.

Despite the overabundance of roads, there are still good hiking opportunities available in these mountains. The Coeur d'Alene River Trail and the Independence Creek area are two popular destinations for hikers. The Forest Service has set the Independence Creek Trail System aside as a roadless area with a variety of trails. The area has historic and natural significance. The main trail down Independence Creek was originally a wagon road used to supply mining camps until the early 1930s, when the mining industry suffered a general collapse.

| Chilco Mountain | 5,685 feet (Class 1) |
| South Chilco Mountain | 5,634 feet (Class 1) |

The only two named summits in the Chilco subrange of the Coeur d'Alene Mountains rise due south of Lake Pend Oreille. Both peaks are reached by FST-14, which climbs to the summit of Chilco Mountain and continues south to South Chilco in another 1.5 miles [(A)(1)(a)]. From the summit of Chilco Mountain you can see both Lake Coeur d'Alene and Lake Pend Oreille. USGS Bayview/Spades Mountain

| Grizzly Mountain | 5,950 feet (Class 1) |

To reach the highest Coeur d'Alene summit, take the Coeur d'Alene River Road [(A)(2)] north. Roughly 16 miles north of I-90, FS-260 runs up Grizzly Creek and eventually to the summit of Grizzly Mountain. It is about 8 miles up FS-260 to the summit. USGS Grizzly Mountain

| Graham Mountain | 5,727 feet (Class 1) |

Graham Mountain sits 4 miles north of Kellogg. Its summit was once a fire lookout site. The peak can be reached from the north via Coal Creek [(A)(2)(a)] or the east from Moon Saddle. From Moon Saddle, hike FST-17 [(A)(3)(a)] southwest and then northwest across the ridge top to the summit. USGS Kellogg West

| Mount Coeur d'Alene | 4,439 (Class 1) |

This peak, a popular destination for northern hikers, is found above the eastern shores of Lake Coeur d'Alene. There is both a long hike and short hike to the summit. The long route is a 5-mile hike on FST-79 Caribou Ridge Trail [(A)(4)] starting at Beauty Creek CG. The short route is by a 0.5-mile hike from the junction of the Coeur d'Alene Road and FST-79. USGS Mount Coeur d'Alene

APPROACHES TO THE COEUR D'ALENE MOUNTAINS

(A) COEUR D'ALENE MOUNTAIN ACCESS POINTS

(1) **Chilco Mountains Access.** FS-290 is the primary access route to this subrange. Take US-95 north from Hayden Lake. Turn east onto FS-290 1.5 miles south of Athol and follow this road 10.5 miles to the well-marked Chilco Mountain trailhead.

(a) **FST-14, Chilco Mountain Trail.** This trail leaves FS-290 10.5 miles from US-95 and runs to the summit of Chilco Mountain in 2 miles and South Chilco Mountain in another 1.5 miles.

(2) **Coeur d'Alene River Road.** Access this road from I-90 at the Kingston exit No. 43. The road follows the river north into the heart of the range. Dozens of Forest Service roads depart from it to penetrate every corner of the range.

(a) **FST-41, Coal Creek Trail.** This trailhead is 12.5 miles from I-90 at the Coal Creek CG. The trail climbs up Coal Creek to the summit of Graham Mountain in 5.5 miles and a hefty 3,500-foot elevation gain.

(3) **FS-930, Moon Saddle Road.** FS-930 is accessed from I-90 east of Kellogg. Take the first exit east of Kellogg, drive to the north side of the freeway and then drive west along the freeway to Moon Creek. Follow this good road north about 7.5 miles to the ridgeline above it. At this T-intersection, go left to Moon Saddle.

(a) **FST-17, Graham Mountain Trail.** FST-17 is accessed at Moon Saddle. The trail follows the ridgeline west roughly 5.5 miles to Graham Mountain. The trail is not open to trail bikes and, therefore, gets little maintenance.

(4) **Mount Coeur d'Alene Access.** FST-79, the Caribou Ridge Trail, leads to the summit of Mount Coeur d'Alene in 5 pleasant miles. To reach the trailhead, drive east out of Coeur d'Alene on I-90 to exit No. 22. From the exit, continue toward Harrison on ID-97 for 2.5 miles to FS-438. Take this road for 0.75 mile to Beauty Creek CG where you will find the trailhead. The Coeur d'Alene Mountain road is reached after 4.5 miles and the summit of Coeur d'Alene Mountain is in another 0.5 mile.

5

THE SAINT JOE MOUNTAINS

The Saint Joe Mountains form a high ridgeline that runs 45 miles east to west between the Saint Joe and the Coeur d'Alene Rivers. The range reaches its highest and most rugged heights northeast of Saint Maries, on a ridge anchored by Reeds Baldy and Latour Peak. The latter mountain is the highest Saint Joe summit at 6,408 feet. Geologically, the Saint Joe Mountains are made up of Belt Series sedimentary rocks, as are the nearby Coeur d'Alene Mountains. Much of the contorted and complicated crest line is barren of trees because of elevation and a great forest fire in 1910. The crest zigzags east and west, north and south, as it makes its way from the Bitterroots to its terminus at Lake Coeur d'Alene.

The Idaho Panhandle National Forest, the Idaho Department of Lands, and the BLM administer the public portions of this mountain group. The Coeur d'Alene Indian Reservation encompasses the western end of the range; the Forest Service land is mostly grouped at the east end of the range; and the BLM land is in the middle. While roads penetrate much of the Saint Joes, some roadless areas still exist.

The Saint Joe Mountains offer excellent opportunities for hiking, peak bagging, and cross-country skiing. The range's high open ridges are reminiscent of the Smoky Mountains of Tennessee and North Carolina. It is a shame that more hikers are not more familiar with these mountains. The best hiking is found between Latour Baldy and Reeds Baldy and in the Big Creek drainage.

The Saint Joes are a great place to find unsurpassed spring cross-country skiing. The area around Saint Joe Baldy and Reeds Baldy provides particularly good skiing in March and April (and sometimes even in May). The Phillips Draw and Rochat Divide roads, which begin at the Saint Joe River, melt out long before the snow-covered ridges above. Drive up either of these roads until you reach snow line, and then ski the roads to the high country above. In stable snow conditions, miles of open, rolling ridges can be traversed. The ridge between Reeds Baldy and Latour Peak is particularly enticing.

Climbing opportunities in the Saint Joes are limited to Class 1 and Class 2 excursions. Although the peaks are not technically difficult, trail conditions often warrant expert route-finding abilities and a lot of endurance. Saint Joe vistas, however, are as good as any in the state.

Latour Baldy   *6,232 feet (Class 2)*

Latour Baldy, which is 7.5 southwest of Pinehurst, anchors the north end of a major north/south ridgeline that stretches for more than 8 miles between the Coeur d'Alene River and the Saint Joe River. The summit is a short hike from the road that runs to the top of Frost Peak [(A)(2)]. USGS Twin Crags

Latour Peak   *6,408 feet (Class 2)*

The highest point in the Saint Joe Mountains is 2.5 miles south of Latour Baldy. Its summit is reached by the Pine Creek Road [(A)(2)]. The summit also can be reached by hiking north cross-country from Reeds Baldy. This route follows the wide, open ridge between Latour Peak and Reeds Baldy. Total distance is 6 miles one way. USGS Twin Crags

Iron Mast Mountain*   *6,160 feet (Class 2)*

Iron Mast is unnamed on the USGS quad, but named on the Forest Service map. The summit sits 1.5 miles south of Latour Peak on the ridge that connects Latour and Reeds Baldy. To reach the top of this peak, follow the rolling, grass-covered ridge from either of the named peaks to the summit. USGS Twin Crags

Reeds Baldy   *6,153 feet (Class 1)*

Reeds Baldy is a big dirigible-shaped peak located 2.8 miles south of Iron Mast Mountain and 2 miles northeast of Saint Joe Baldy. From the roadway north of Saint Joe Baldy [(B)

Saint Joe Baldy to Latour Peak; this crest is anchored by Latour Peak in the north (right) and Saint Joe Baldy in the south.

(2)(a)], follow the unmaintained ridge trail to the summit. This trail used to be maintained all the way to Latour Peak. USGS Rochat Peak

Saint Joe Baldy   *5,825 feet (Class 1)*
This beautiful, cone-shaped peak is visible from Saint Maries as well as other more distant locations. Although a road reaches the summit, the peak offers an excellent winter or early spring ski ascent. Follow either the Phillips Draw Road [(B)(1)] or the Rochat Divide Road [(B)(2)] to the saddle north of the peak, and then ski up the northeast ridge. An Idaho Department of Lands fire lookout is on top. USGS Saint Joe Baldy

Wardner Peak   *6,198 feet*
Kellogg Peak   *6,397 feet (Class 1)*
These two peaks are located just south of Kellogg and the Silver Mountain downhill ski resort. To reach the summits, drive 4 miles east of Kellogg on I-90. Take the Big Creek Road, FS-264 south into the mountains. Follow FS-264 south to the FST-111 trailhead. Hike FST-111 south along Big Creek, then turn west and follow the trail to the divide and FST-16, which leads northwest over Silver Hill to Wardner Peak. To reach Kellogg Peak, take a side trail from FST-16 to the summit. USGS Masonia

Lemonade Peak   *5,651 feet (Class 1)*
This summit is on the divide between Big Creek and Trout Creek. The peak offers a fine destination with a 360-degree view. A classically designed, fire lookout crowns the summit, but, unfortunately, vandals trashed the building, and it is no longer fit for human habitation. From the end of the Big Creek Road, take Pierce Ridge FST-563, which begins with a very wet crossing of Big Creek [(B)(3)(a)]. At last report, portions of the Big Creek Trail were brushy and difficult to follow, so allow extra time for a trip into this area. USGS Masonia

Placer Peak   *5,240 feet*
Bad Tom Peak   *5,587 feet*
Striped Peak   *6,316 feet (Class 1)*
These three minor summits are located due south of Wallace. All three are Class 1 and are accessed via FST-16 from Slate Creek Saddle [(A)(3)(a)]. Although not as impressive as many other Saint Joe peaks, the ridge walk to these summits is enjoyable. USGS Wallace

Elsie Peak   *5,257 feet (Class 2)*
Elsie Peak is the high point on the ridgeline that divides the West Fork of Big Creek from the Middle Fork. The trail is

climbed from FST-568 [(B)(3)(a)], which climbs the ridge to a point within 80 vertical feet of the summit before descending to Kellogg saddle. Scramble to the top from the trail. USGS Polaris Peak

APPROACHES TO THE SAINT JOE MOUNTAINS

(A) NORTH SIDE APPROACHES
I-90, which runs along the north side of the Saint Joe Mountains between Coeur d'Alene and the Montana border, is the primary approach in the north.

(1) Cataldo Exit. From the Cataldo exit on I-90, the Latour Creek/Rochat Divide Road runs south along Latour Creek and crosses the Saint Joe Mountains near Rochat Peak. The road is often passable for passenger autos, but is very rough.

(2) Pine Creek Road. This unnumbered road follows Pine Creek south from I-90 at Pinehurst. From this road, two feeder roads lead to the tops of two Saint Joe peaks, Frost and Latour.

(3) FS-456/FS-225, Slate Creek Saddle Road. From the Wallace area, this road crosses the Saint Joe range and leads to Hoyt Flats on the Saint Joe River. To access this road, drive south from Wallace on the Placer Creek Road, which eventually climbs to Slate Creek Saddle high above Wallace, and then descends to Hoyt Flats via Slate Creek.

(a) FST-16, Striped Peak Trail. This trail leaves Slate Creek Saddle and runs west to Striped Peak in 6 miles, crossing Placer Peak and Bad Tom Mountain on the way.

(b) South Fork Coeur d'Alene River Trails. The Forest Service maintains several trails along the Saint Joe divide. The trails traverse the higher Saint Joe ridges between the Silver Mountain Ski Area and Placer Peak south of the towns of Kellogg, Osborne, and Wallace. This true high-country trail is called the Saint Joe Divide Trail. The system is closed to motorcycles.

(B) SOUTH SIDE APPROACHES
The Saint Joe River Road is the primary approach route in the south. The road leaves ID-97 on the west edge of Saint Maries.

(1) Phillips Draw Road. Turn onto this road 10 miles east of Saint Maries. The road climbs the divide and joins with the Rochat Divide Road. The summit of Saint Joe Baldy is accessed via a feeder road.

(2) Rochat Divide Road. This is the major approach road in the west end of the Saint Joes. The road is found 14 miles east of Saint Maries. It connects with the I-90 Cataldo exit in the north.

(a) Crystal Lake Trail. The trailhead is on the saddle north of Saint Joe Baldy. This busy little trail is 2 miles in length and leads to a small but picturesque lake below Reeds Baldy.

(3) Calder Area Roads. Turn north from the Saint Joe River Road and drive into the village of Calder. From Calder, turn east and follow the gravel road that parallels the north shore of the Saint Joe River for 5 miles to join with the Big Creek Road, FS-537. FS-537 leads to several scenic trails deep in the heart of the range.

(a) Big Creek Drainage Trails. The Big Creek drainage covers a lot of ground. At one time it contained stately stands of white pine and small mining operations. Today, it is mostly un-forested as a result of the great 1910 forest fire. The present trail system is surprisingly good considering the low emphasis on recreation in this ranger district. These trails intersect with the trails above Wallace to provide miles of exceptionally good hiking.

6

THE CLEARWATER MOUNTAINS

The Clearwater Mountains are the largest of the Idaho Batholith mountain ranges and are located in north central Idaho. The Clearwaters stretch 125 miles north to south and from 40 to 75 miles east to west. The Saint Joe River forms the northern boundary, the main fork of the Salmon River forms the southern boundary, and the Bitterroot Mountains form the eastern boundary. There is no logical or clear dividing point between the Clearwater and Bitterroot Mountains. In fact, they are physically the same set of mountains. Likewise, the western boundary is not a definite geographic line, but roughly extends between Saint Maries, Moscow, Orofino, Grangeville, and Riggins.

The Clearwaters are formed mostly of Idaho Batholith granite, covered in places by scattered deposits of older sedimentary and metamorphic rocks that have yet to erode away. During the Pleistocene Ice Age alpine glaciers carved cirques and lake basins into the sides of higher Clearwater peaks. The effects of the glaciers are most readily visible in the Mallard-Larkins and Selway Crags areas of the range. Although the Clearwater terrain is somewhat uniform in its overall appearance, several distinct ridges within the range have been singled out by topographers as subranges. These include the Selway Crags, the Moose Mountains, the Sheep Mountain Range, and the Little Goat Mountains.

Clearwater peaks are seldom more than 6,500 feet high in the north, but gradually gain elevation as one moves to the south. The highest peaks are found just north of the Salmon River, where Buffalo Hump, Gospel Peak, and Stripe Mountain, the highest Clearwater peak at 9,001 feet, rise abruptly from the Salmon's deep canyon.

The Forest Service administers the vast majority of the range, although it takes several national forests to accomplish this task. In the north, the Idaho Panhandle National Forest is in charge, followed by the Clearwater, Bitterroot, and Nez Perce, respectively, from north to south. Much of the land in the northwest Clearwater Mountains is owned by large private timber companies. This land, once owned by all Americans, fell into private ownership in the last century when Congress gave private corporations huge tracts of land as an incentive to build transcontinental railroad lines.

The congressional scheme to stimulate development of the west entitled the railroads to receive, free of charge, their right-of-ways and alternating square-mile sections of land next to the right-of-ways. This created the checkerboard pattern of alternating sections of federal land and private land that is readily visible on the Clearwater National Forest map. More than 90 million acres of valuable public lands were given to the railroads under various pieces of legislation. In a few cases, rail lines were constructed just to secure the land.

Although Congress intended that the railroads raise investment capital by selling the "gift lands" to settlers, the railroads simply used it as collateral and exploited the timber reserves. In the end, the railroads were built, but the U.S. Treasury saw little return on this incredible investment. The only good news is that for the most part, these lands are still open to the public without a permit. However, the land is private and its access may be restricted anytime.

Opportunities for hiking and climbing in the Clearwater Mountains are as unlimited as the mountains themselves. The variety of hikes is impressive, ranging from short forested hikes to long alpine adventures. Although climbing routes primarily fall in the Class 1 to Class 3 categories, many technical routes exist. Clearwater peaks come in an infinite variety and any hiker or peak bagger who ventures into the range will experience wonderful hiking and—above all—solitude.

Three great designated wilderness areas, the Selway-Bitterroot, the Gospel Hump, and the northern edge of the River of No Return, protect much of the Clearwater country. In addition, many other roadless areas worthy of wilderness designation might someday be protected. These de facto wilderness areas include, but are not limited to, the Mallard-Larkins, Kelly Creek, Great Burn, and Pot Mountain areas.

HOODOO MOUNTAINS

This group of Clearwater summits is separated from the Clearwater Mountains to the east by the Saint Maries River. The Hoodoos are oval-shaped and run from the river west to the Washington/Idaho border, north to Lake Coeur d'Alene, and south to Potlatch. Summits are low and rounded and, for the most part, forested. The highest point is Bald Mountain at 5,334 feet. Logging has taken place throughout the Hoodoos. Some summits have been clear-cut and the expanding road system has left most trails abbreviated or broken and nearly useless. Roads have replaced trails at a staggering rate and hiking and climbing are minimal. There are two bright notes. First, at the Giant White Pine CG along ID-6, the Forest Service has tried to establish and preserve a series of short loop trails recommended for day hiking. Second, the Idaho Department of Parks and Recreation has set up a park and ski area on North South Pass along ID-6 [(C)(2)]. Cross-country skiers can make ascents of 4,626-foot East Dennis Peak via the roads that lead west from the pass.

Bald Mountain   *5,334 feet (Class 1)*
Bald Mountain is the highest peak in the Hoodoos. Its summit is reached by dirt road from ID-6 [(C)(2)] or via a trail from Giant White Pines CG on ID-6 [(C)(1)(a)]. Although the trail's corridor is violated several times by roadways, the hike to the summit from the campground is a good early season conditioning hike for the diehard hiker. It is 9 miles one way. The dirt road to the summit from North South Pass is closed in winter and offers a good long ski trip to the top. USGS Emida

Three Tree Butte   *3,330 feet (Class 1)*
This is the lowest summit listed in this guidebook. The summit is reached by trail from ID-6 and Giant White Pine CG [(C)(1)]. The view from the top is limited, but the walk through the woods is quite pleasant. USGS Deary

PALOUSE RANGE

This small subrange is the westernmost extension of the Clearwater Mountains. It rises north of Moscow to form a divide 18 miles long and 10 miles wide, with a rolling forested crest containing a few granite outcroppings. At 4,983 feet, Moscow Mountain is the tallest peak in the range. Its summit is on private land, as is most of the Palouse Range.

The Forest Service and the University of Idaho control a small portion of the range. The University of Idaho land is open to the public, but much of the private land is posted with NO TRESPASSING signs. East Moscow Mountain is the only summit on public land and it is reached by a road. See [(D)(1) and(2)].

NORTHERN DIVIDE PEAKS

The Clearwater Mountains begin south of the Saint Joe River, rising up as a series of moderate forested ridges. While there are many named peaks in this area, most are nothing more than tree-covered hills and only a few are of interest. The following peaks are bordered by the Saint Joe River in the north and the North Fork Clearwater River and the Mallard-Larkins Pioneer Area in the south. This stretch of mountains is dissected by roads and access is generally good. The following peaks are listed from west to east.

Grandfather Mountain   *6,306 feet (Class 1)*
Grandmother Mountain   *6,369 feet (Class 1)*
Grandfather Mountain and Grandmother Mountain are located in the Clearwaters' northwest corner on BLM land, 9 miles northeast of Clarkia. From FS-301 [(B)(2)(a)] at Freezeout Saddle, follow the signed and well-maintained trail to Grandmother's summit, which is 2 miles from the road. Grandfather is another 2 miles along FST-275 to the northwest and a total of 4 miles from Freezeout Saddle. Although these peaks are not much more than large humps, the hike offers an excellent introduction to the Clearwater Mountains and the views are vast all along the grassy ridge top. USGS Grandmother Mountain

Lookout Mountain   *6,789 feet (Class 1)*
Widow Mountain   *6,828 feet (Class 1)*
Lookout and Widow Mountains are located east of the Grandfather/Grandmother Mountains on a parallel north/south ridge. It is 1.5 miles via FST-52 [(B)(2)(b)] to Widow's summit and another 2 miles north to Lookout Mountain by the same trail. USGS Widow Mountain

Snow Peak   *6,760 feet (Class 1)*
Snow Peak is 14 miles west of Red Ives GS on the Saint Joe River and 4 miles north of the Mallard-Larkins Pioneer Area. The upper reaches of Snow Peak are pyramid-shaped and quite picturesque. The summit, which contains a fire lookout, can be reached by trail. Reportedly, mountain goats are sometimes visible on the peak's rocky east ridge and there is a large elk herd that populates the roadless area surrounding the peak.

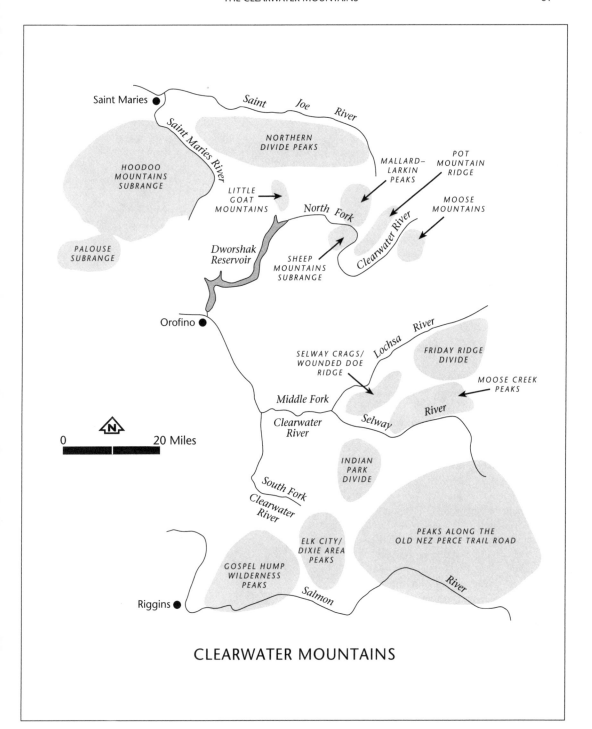

Saint Maries

Saint Joe River

Saint Maries River

NORTHERN DIVIDE PEAKS

MALLARD–LARKIN PEAKS

POT MOUNTAIN RIDGE

HOODOO MOUNTAINS SUBRANGE

LITTLE GOAT MOUNTAINS

North Fork

MOOSE MOUNTAINS

Clearwater River

PALOUSE SUBRANGE

Dworshak Reservoir

SHEEP MOUNTAINS SUBRANGE

Orofino

Lochsa River

FRIDAY RIDGE DIVIDE

SELWAY CRAGS/ WOUNDED DOE RIDGE

MOOSE CREEK PEAKS

Middle Fork Clearwater River

Selway River

0   20 Miles

INDIAN PARK DIVIDE

South Fork Clearwater River

PEAKS ALONG THE OLD NEZ PERCE TRAIL ROAD

ELK CITY/ DIXIE AREA PEAKS

GOSPEL HUMP WILDERNESS PEAKS

River

Riggins

Salmon

CLEARWATER MOUNTAINS

The peak is reached by taking FST-55 for 5 miles from its start at FS-201 [(A)(1.3)(a)]. Camping is available in the meadows below the summit, where there is a small spring that flows year round. USGS Montana Peak

LITTLE GOAT MOUNTAINS

The Little Goat Mountains are a petite subrange of the Clearwater Mountains. The range is located north of Dworshak Reservoir and is roughly 7 miles by 4 miles in size. These granite-based peaks have a northwest-to-southeast orientation and reach their highest point at Blackdome Peak, 6,412 feet. The range has one mountain lake located on the east side of the crest.

Blackdome Peak   *6,412 feet (Class 2)*
Blackdome Peak is located north of the Little North Fork Clearwater River, just a short distance north of FS-457 [(B)(2.1)]. The summit is a short walk from the road. USGS Little Goat Mountains

MALLARD-LARKINS PEAKS

The Mallard-Larkins Pioneer Area is the largest and most threatened of the Clearwater's de facto wilderness areas. According to the Forest Service, "pioneer" status "recognizes Mallard-Larkins' unique natural beauty and recreation values and gives special consideration to wildlife and fisheries." It is likely that this area eventually will receive wilderness designation because it is extremely important habitat for big game animals that bring the state "hunter dollars" each fall. The Mallard-Larkins country is semi-alpine in nature, with several mountain lakes and glacial cirques. Elevation changes are quite extreme, ranging from 2,600 feet to more than 7,000 feet at Black Mountain. This precipitous terrain is responsible for the area's diverse flora. The high alpine areas are characterized by grasses and wildflowers. Along the lower slopes, the hiker can still find incredible stands of cedar. This area is administered jointly by the Idaho Panhandle and Clearwater National Forests and encompasses 30,500 acres; another 150,000 acres adjoining it are roadless and still worthy of wilderness designation. Unfortunately, pressure from logging interests constantly threatens this superb area.

Larkins Peak   *6,661 feet (Class 1)*
Larkins Peak is located 7 miles due south of Snow Peak and is the westernmost of the Mallard-Larkins Pioneer Area peaks.

The summit sits south of Larkins Lake on the main east/west ridgeline that divides the Little North Fork and North Fork Clearwater drainages. To reach the summit, hike either FST-240 [(E)(1.1.2)(a)] which leads directly to the summit or hike up Isabella Creek to FST-96 [(E)(1.1.2.1)(b)], which follows Elmer Creek via FST-96 to meet FST-240 south of the peak. USGS Mallard Peak/MLPA

Crag Peak   *6,879 feet*
Heart Peak   *6,870 feet (Class 2)*
Both tree-covered peaks stand above the southwest edge of Heart Lake, a little more than 1 mile east of Larkins Peak. FST-65 crosses a saddle between these two peaks [(E)(1.1.2)(b)]. Climb both peaks from the saddle. USGS Mallard Peak/MLPA

Mallard Peak   *6,870 feet (Class 1)*
This old lookout site, the easternmost peak on the Mallard-Larkins divide, is located 3 miles east of Heart Peak. The summit can

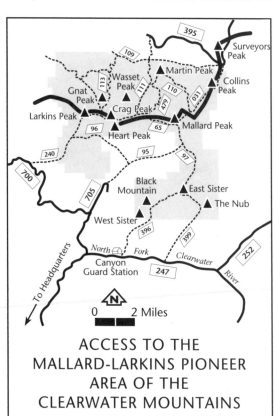

ACCESS TO THE MALLARD-LARKINS PIONEER AREA OF THE CLEARWATER MOUNTAINS

be gained by a ridge trail from the south. From FS-705, hike up Isabella Creek (FST-95) until the ridge trail (FS-91) is gained in about 5 miles [(E)(1.1.2.1)(a)]. USGS Mallard Peak/MLPA

Black Mountain   *7,077 feet (Class 1)*
Black Mountain is located south of the main Mallard-Larkins divide and east of Isabella Creek. The peak has a precipitous north face; its summit (an old lookout site) is reached by the trail that runs from Black Lake to the peak's south slopes [(E)(1.3)(a)]. USGS Mallard Peak/MLPA

SHEEP MOUNTAIN RANGE

The Sheep Mountain Range is located northeast of the town of Headquarters and is situated inside a major bend in the North Fork Clearwater River. This Clearwater subrange is 8 miles long and 4 miles wide. Eagle Point, at 5,709 feet, is the highest point in this heavily roaded and logged area.

Sheep Mountain   *5,708 feet (Class 1)*
Eagle Point   *5,709 feet (Class 1)*
Sheep Mountain is located south of the Mallard-Larkins Pioneer Area near the Sousie Creek CG. To reach its summit, hike FST-93, which is a ridge trail, west from FS-682 [(E)(1.1.1)(a)] for less than 1 mile to Eagle Point and for roughly 2 miles to Sheep Mountain. USGS Sheep Mountain.

POT MOUNTAIN RIDGE

Pot Mountain Ridge rises inside a great loop in the North Fork Clearwater River southeast of the Mallard-Larkins area. This ridgeline trends from southwest to northeast for more than 20 miles. Pot Mountain is at the ridge's southern end and Chamberlain Mountain is at the northern end.

Pot Mountain   *7,139 feet (Class 1)*
Pot Mountain, the highest Clearwater peak in the region, is situated near the southwest end of the Pot Mountain Ridge. It is the center of an unofficial wilderness area complete with a surprising number of mountain lakes and scenic vistas. To ascend Pot Mountain follow FST-144 [(E)(2.1)(a)] south for 3 miles to the west side of the summit at roughly 5,800 feet. Climb the peak's western slopes. USGS Pot Mountain

Cold Springs Peak   *6,731 feet (Class 1)*
Cold Springs Peak is surrounded by mountain lakes and is located 5 miles northwest of the Kelly Forks GS and 6 miles northeast of Pot Mountain. The Class 1 summit is adorned by an abandoned fire lookout and reached from the GS via FST-176 and FST-169 [(E)(2)(a)]. The summit also can be reached from FST-445, which runs between Cold Springs Peak and Elizabeth Mountain [(E)(2)(b)]. USGS Pot Mountain

Elizabeth Mountain   *6,464 feet (Class 1)*
This picturesque summit is located 2.5 miles due east of Cold Springs Peak. The shortest route to the summit is FST-445, which climbs steeply from FS-250 to the summit in 2.5 miles [(E)(2)(b)]. USGS Elizabeth Lake

Flat Mountain   *6,606 feet (Class 1)*
Flat Mountain, located 2 miles northwest of Kelly Forks GS, is the southernmost summit on the ridge that divides Cold Springs Creek from Kelly Creek. The summit is reached by FST-176 [(E)(2)(a)]. USGS Elizabeth Lake

MOOSE MOUNTAINS

The Moose Mountains were named after the mining town of Moose, which sat on the subrange's eastern slopes. These mountains are located just east of the Pot Mountain Ridge and roughly 30 miles east of Pierce in the Y formed by the North Fork Clearwater River and Kelly Creek. This subrange is approximately 10 miles in length from east to west and 4 miles wide. Moose Creek Butte is the highest point at 6,937 feet. Although the Forest Service recommended the Moose Mountains for wilderness protection in the late 1970s, Congress has yet to act.

Sheldon Bluestein, in his book *North Idaho Hiking Trails,* states that "the Moose Creek Buttes rank among Idaho's most rugged mountains." He goes on to say, "They have an inspirational value that makes them worthy of preservation...the Buttes' north sides dazzle you with a three-tiered display of blue sky, tan rock, and green meadows." While the scenery is spectacular, use of the area is low. The Moose Mountains offer a large, roadless area that is seldom visited, because it is located a long way from anywhere.

Moose Mountain   *6,603 feet (Class 1)*
Moose Mountain sits at the head of Moose Creek. Its western slopes descend steeply in 2 miles to Black Canyon on the North Fork Clearwater River. The summit is accessed by trail from both the east and the north [(E)(2.2)(a) and (b)]. USGS Moose Mountain

The Moose Creek Buttes (Photo by Sheldon Bluestein)

Moose Creek Buttes   *6,937 (Class 2)*

Although no trail leads to the Buttes, scramblers can follow the ridgeline from Moose Mountain to its summits. The Buttes are rugged—a good knowledge of cross-country travel is essential [(E)(2.2)(a) and (b)]. USGS Scurvy Mountain

CLEARWATER PEAKS BETWEEN THE LOCHSA AND SELWAY RIVERS

The entire area between the Lochsa and Selway Rivers and west of the Bitterroot Mountains is located in the Selway-Bitterroot Wilderness Area. The 1.2 million-acre wilderness area also encompasses land south of the Selway and large stretches of the Bitterroot mountains. Lowell, Idaho, Missoula, Montana, and Darby, Montana, roughly form the corners of the Selway-Bitterroot Wilderness, the first of Idaho's great wilderness areas to be designated by Congress.

The natural history of this great wilderness is affected by three factors. First, glacial action gouged out immense quantities of overburden in this area, which has exposed a monumental amount of batholith granite, especially on the eastern fringes. Second, the many rivers that drain the Selway-Bitterroot country cut deep canyons when the glaciers melted. Third, the great fires of 1910 cauterized many slopes to such an extent that trees have yet to repopulate the sterile soil. Thus, though the maximum elevations range only from 7,000 to 9,000 feet, much of the wilderness is open, treeless, and alpine in nature. This area is divided into three areas: Selway Crags/Wounded Doe Ridge, the Friday Ridge Divide, and the Moose Creek Peaks.

Selway Crags/Wounded Doe Ridge

The Selway Crags are found at the western edge of the Selway-Bitterroot Wilderness Area where the Selway and Lochsa rivers join at Lowell at the terminus of a prominent ridgeline known as Wounded Doe Ridge. This ridge system parallels the Lochsa River for more than 40 miles. The Selway Crags, the most extensively glaciated peaks in the central Clearwaters, are located at the end of the ridge. This country is steep with several sharp, vertical summits and high mountain lakes. The trails are poorly maintained and difficult. Elevations range from 2,000 feet along the Lochsa and Selway Rivers to more than 8,000 feet near Fenn Mountain.

Ghost Mountain   *6,861 feet (Class 1)*
Ghost Mountain is the westernmost Selway Crags peak listed in this guidebook. It is located 12 miles east of Lowell. FST-3 leads to the summit [(E)(3.1.1)(a)]. USGS Chimney Peak/SBW

Cantaloupe Peak   *6,133 feet (Class 1)*
Huckleberry Butte   *6,710 feet (Class 1)*
These peaks are reached after a strenuous climb from Wilderness Gateway trailhead via FST-220 [(E)(3)(c)]. Start early and carry plenty of water. Cantaloupe Peak is really just a high point on the ridgeline that leads to Huckleberry Butte. USGS Huckleberry Butte/SBW

Chimney Peak   *7,840 feet*
Chimney Peak, an extremely rugged mountain for this part of the Idaho Batholith, resembles a soot-stained chimney. The peak is located at the heads of Chimney and Old Man Creeks a little more than 1 mile west of Old Man Lake. Although Chimney Peak's east and west faces present more interesting terrain, the peak apparently has only been climbed from the pass to its southeast via the south ridge. FST-3 provides access to the peak with the shortest route beginning from Big Fog Saddle Road [(E)(3.1.2)(a)]. USGS Chimney Peak/SBW

South Ridge (Class 3). From FST-3, at the saddle southeast of the summit, a long slanting gully is visible slicing up through the dark rock of the south ridge. This gully leads to the east side of Chimney's lower south peak. To reach the gully, leave the trail and drop off the saddle near the base of the south ridge by down-climbing a steep, rocky step through a thick stand of small firs. Once down the step, traverse west into a small boulder field and drop down through the boulders to a grassy bench on the east side of the south ridge. Traverse north along the narrow bench to the bottom of a slanting gully. Climb the gully to its top and then traverse around the south summit to the ridgeline between the south and main summits and continue north to the base of the main summit. At this point, the route drops west off the ridge top through thick timber to a gully filled with "whitish" rock. Climb this Class 2 to Class 3 gully until it ends at the base of a large block. Traverse around this block on the west and climb the next large summit block to the ridge top. From this point, the route follows the knife-edged ridgeline north to the true summit across 100 feet of slanting blocks.

Gedney Mountain   *7,360+ feet (Class 2)*
Gedney Mountain is a fin-shaped summit located just west of Cove Lakes. The summit is a short scramble from FST-708 [(E) (3.1)(a) or [(E)(3.1.2)(c)]. USGS Chimney Peak/SBW

Fenn Mountain   *8,021 feet*
Fenn Mountain is named after Major Frank Fenn, who served three terms in the Idaho Territorial Legislature and was the first supervisor of the Sawtooth National Forest. The mountain selected to honor Fenn is the culmination of a large, craggy, northeast-trending ridge with multiple summits, which reaches its highest point at its northern end. It is the highest point in the Selway Crags and offers a lot of route possibilities, but is seldom climbed. USGS Fenn Mountain/SBW

Chimney Peak is the most vertical summit in the Selway Crags. This view is from the ridge top just southeast of the summit.

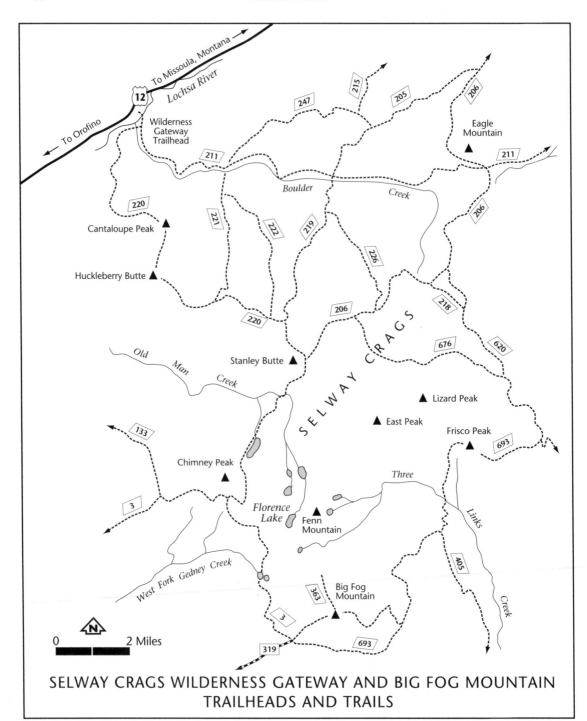

SELWAY CRAGS WILDERNESS GATEWAY AND BIG FOG MOUNTAIN TRAILHEADS AND TRAILS

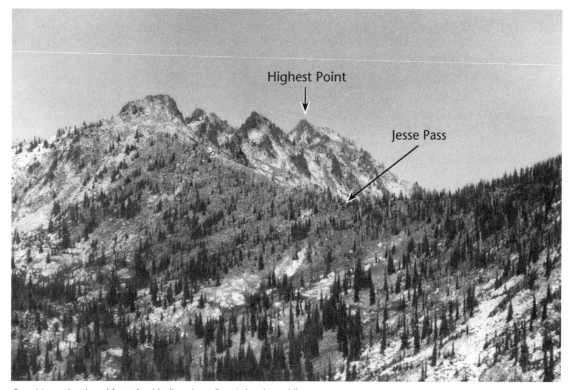

Fenn Mountain, viewed from the ridgeline above Cove Lake; the saddle

Jesse Pass Route (Class 3). Three major summits are distinguishable from Jesse Pass [(E)(3.1.2)(b)]. Picking out the summit of Fenn Mountain is difficult because the foreground melds into the background. Follow the trail east off the pass to a boulder field in roughly 0.3 mile. Climb up the boulder field to a grass-filled gully on the east side of the third summit. At the top of the gully, head north, crossing another boulder field, to the ridge top and then continue toward a rock fin that sits squarely on the ridgeline. From this point to the true summit's southern slopes, route-finding is difficult. As a rule, when faced with an option to go up or go down—go down and around. Bypass the first fin on the west side and then cross back to the east side of the ridge to bypass the next fin. Cross again to the west side of the ridge to bypass the last fin. Once past the last fin, cross back to the east side of the ridge and climb out onto the south slopes of the true summit. Climb up and north, past a window in the peak's south ridge, to the summit.

Lower Three Links Lake Route (Class 2-3). This route climbs the large gully that runs from the lower Three Links Lake directly to the summit. The gully is filled with almost 2,000 feet of loose talus, but presents no real difficulties.

Big Fog Mountain   *7,122 feet (Class 1)*
Big Fog Mountain contains a massive summit field that was burned off in the 1910 fires. The view of the peaks to the north is one of the finest views in Idaho. FST-343 leads to the summit from the Big Fog Mountain Road [(E)(3.1.2)(d)]. USGS Fenn Mountain/SBW

East Peak   *7,852 feet (Class 2)*
East Peak is located 3 miles northeast of Fenn Mountain and towers over the largest of the Lizard Lakes, climbing more than 1,500 feet in 0.25 mile. Climb this peak from the saddle just south of Stanley Butte and FST-206 [(E)(3)(d)]. Follow the ridge south to the summit. USGS Fenn Mountain/SBW

Eagle Mountain   *7,427 feet (Class 2)*
Eagle Mountain is an attractive summit located 8.5 miles northeast of East Peak. Sponge Mountain 0.5 mile to the

south is its lower summit. To reach the peak, take FST-206 [(E)(3)(d)] from Boulder Pass to its south ridge. Leave the trail, which continues along the peak's west slopes, and climb up the south ridge to the summit. USGS Fish Lake/SBW

Greystone Butte   *6,545 feet (Class 1)*
Flytrap Butte   *6,338 feet (Class 1)*
Greystone Butte and Flytrap Butte are notable because they sit on a high ridge between the Lochsa River to the north and Sponge Creek to the south. Greystone Lake is to the east. FST-206 [(E)(3)(d)] leads to the saddle between the two peaks and then turns southwest to cross the summit of Greystone Butte in 0.4 mile. FST-208 leaves from the saddle and runs to the northwest to Flytrap Butte in 1.6 miles. This hike involves a hefty elevation gain. USGS Greystone Butte/SBW

Freezeout Mountain   *5,986 feet (Class 2)*
Freezeout Mountain is located 3.5 miles east of Flytrap Butte. The summit is accessed via FST-209 [(E)(3)(e)], which crosses over the peak's northern slopes. (The trail is accessed from the Mocus Point trailhead along US-12.) Be prepared for a couple of excessive elevation gains with a steep descent in-between. USGS Bear Mountain/SBW

Bear Mountain   *7,184 feet (Class 1)*
Bear Mountain is located north of Wounded Doe Ridge, at the head of Kinnikinic, Mountain, Colgate, and Queen Creeks, and 3 miles south of the Lochsa River. Take FST-209 to FST-21, which leads to this lookout site [(E)(3)(e)], or [(E)(3)(f)]. The quickest approach is via the Warm Springs Pack Bridge trailhead along US-12. Beware, it is a long climb. USGS Bear Mountain/SBW

McConnel Mountain   *7,424 feet (Class 1)*
McConnel Mountain, the last named peak along the Wounded Doe Ridge system, is a remote summit that divides four drainages—Pedro, Wag, Chain, and Moose Creeks. FST-213 leads to the summit [(E)(3)(b)]. USGS McConnel Mountain/SBW

The Friday Ridge Divide

This ridge, located east of Wounded Doe Ridge and south of the Lochsa River, trends from north to south and is a major watershed. Although the arcing ridgeline is only 10 miles in length, eighteen different streams drain its slopes. Primary access is from US-12. Tom Beal Peak is on its northern end and Graves Peak is on its southern end.

Tom Beal Peak   *7,568 feet (Class 2)*
This peak is located 5.5 miles southeast of the Powell GS. Climb to the peak's upper slopes via either FST-37 [(E)(3)(g)] or FST-44 [(E)(3)(f)]. FST-44 provides the shortest approach, while FST-37 offers an excellent ridge walk to the summit. USGS Tom Beal Peak/SBW

Grave Peak   *8,282 feet (Class 1)*
Grave Peak is surrounded by lakes in possibly the most attractive setting of any Clearwater peak. It sits 4 miles south of Tom Beal Peak. The summit is reached via an old, unmaintained trail up the south ridge from Friday Pass, which is reached via FST-45 [(E)(3.2)(a)]. From FS-358, it is 4.5 miles to the summit. USGS Grave Peak/SBW

Moose Creek Peaks

Moose Creek flows into the Selway at the Moose Creek GS midway between Lowell and the Idaho/Montana border. From where it flows into the Selway River, the Moose Creek drainage runs north for several miles and then forks. Its north fork cuts to the northwest and its east fork works generally to the east. The five very remote and worthwhile summits listed below are found in the wild country on either side of this creek and its tributaries.

Diablo Mountain   *7,461 feet (Class 1)*
This peak is located 2.5 miles southwest of Hoodoo Lake. A fire lookout adorns its summit. Reach the top via FST-18 [(E)(3.2)(c)]. USGS Jeanette Mountain/SWB

Bailey Mountain   *7,386 feet (Class 1)*
Remote, desolate, and isolated, Bailey Mountain really is in the middle of nowhere. Look for it between the north and east forks of Moose Creek and just west of May Lake. This lookout site is reached by two trails, one from the north and one from the south. The shortest route from a road is to approach the peak from the Selway River Road via the Moose Creek GS by taking FST-619 to the summit [(E)(3.1)(c.1)]. Remember that "shortest route" is a relative term. USGS Hungry Rock/SBW

Goat Heaven Peaks   *7,254 feet (Class 2-3)*
These peaks embrace the Goat Lakes many miles due south of Powell and US-12. While there are no trails to the lakes, FST-491 [(E)(3.1)(b)] (see also [(E)(3.2)(c)]) leads across their south slopes within a short distance of the summits. Goat Lakes also can be accessed from FST-42 along the East Fork

Moose Creek by hiking cross-country up the outlet stream. To climb the Goat Heaven Peaks from the lakes, gain the ridge and follow it to the various summits. USGS Cedar Ridge/SBW

Freeman Peak   *7,294 feet (Class 1)*

Freeman Peak, an island in the sky, is located 7 miles east of the Moose Creek GS between Moose Creek and the Selway River. It is the highest point in the vast expanse of wilderness between Moose Creek and the Bitterroot Crest many miles to the east. The shortest route to the summit from the GS is via FST-430 [(E)(3.1)(d)]. USGS Freeman Peak/SBW

Wahoo Peak   *7,682 feet (Class 1)*

Wahoo Peak is located 7.5 miles east of Freeman Peak and 6 miles south of Goat Heaven Peaks. Its forested summit is reached by five different trails. The shortest approach is from Montana via FST-430 and FST-432. See the Bitterroot Mountains chapter [(D)(4)(a)]. The most enjoyable approach is probably from Freeman Peak via FST-430, which begins at the Moose Creek GS many miles to the west [(E)(3.1)(d)]. USGS Wahoo Peak/SBW

GOSPEL HUMP WILDERNESS PEAKS

The Gospel Hump Wilderness Area encompasses 206,000 acres in the southern Clearwater Mountains. This area is home to beautiful forest, open meadows, mountain lakes, and several notable summits. Many of its trails follow ridge tops and cross mountain tops with spectacular views. At 8,924 feet, Buffalo Hump is the preeminent peak in the wilderness area and one of the highest points in the Clearwaters.

Because of the abundance of moose and elk, the Gospel Hump area was a favorite hunting ground of the Nez Perce tribe, which occupied this area as early as 6000 B.C. Gold was discovered in Florence Basin in 1861, and by 1889 five thousand miners poured into the area, forcing the Nez Perce out and temporarily ending the wilderness quality of the environment. In the early 1900s, the mining boom subsided and this high plateau returned to a wild, remote hinterland.

Round Top   *7,842 feet*
Little Round Top   *7,495 feet (Class 2)*

These twin peaks, the westernmost peaks in the wilderness, are located across Slate Creek, 2 miles southwest of Gospel Peak. The peaks can be climbed from FST-313 [(F)(1.2)(c)]. From either its western or eastern trailheads, hike until you reach the small drainage that descends to Slate Creek from the saddle between the two summits. Follow this drainage to the saddle and climb the peaks from this point. USGS Hanover Mountain/GHW

Gospel Peak   *8,345 feet (Class 2)*

The peak gained its name because of a man named Billie Knox, a district court clerk in Grangeville in the 1890s, who

Gospel Peak (Photo by Bruce Dreher)

preached Sunday sermons as a hobby. One Sunday, while on a horseback trip through the country south of Grangeville, he came upon a road gang and gave them one of his favorite sermons. Evidently moved by the sermon and Knox's spiritual blessings, the road gang named the nearest mountain Gospel Peak. Gospel Peak is located on the western edge of the Gospel Hump Wilderness hundreds of feet above Gospel Lakes. Its long, arcing summit has five high points. The easternmost is known as Tower Knob. The summit is a short, easy walk from FS-444 [(F)(2.1)]. USGS Hanover Mountain/GHW

Tower Knob*   *8,010 feet (Class 3)*
This impressive eastern summit of Gospel Mountain is located just south of Tower Knob Lake. From the lake, the peak's north wall is a series of impressive faces. No technical climbing has been reported. Climb the peak from FS-444 [(F)(2.1)] by hiking north to the 7,800-foot saddle on Gospel Peak's east ridge. From this saddle, climb the high point due east and then descend its east ridge until traversing it into the next saddle to the north is possible. Once in the saddle, ascend Tower Knob's south ridge to the summit. USGS Hanover Mountain

Pyramid Peak   *8,369 feet (Class 2)*
Pyramid Peak is located 1 mile north of Gospel Peak and east of Gospel Lakes. The summit is easily reached from Gospel Lakes, reached in turn by a short cross-country hike from FS-444 [(F)(2.1)]. USGS Sawyer Ridge/GHW

Hanover Mountain   *7,966 feet (Class 1)*
Hanover Mountain is located 5 miles due south of Gospel Peak. Take FST-125 south from FS-444 to this summit [(F)(2.1)(b)]. USGS Hanover Mountain/GHW

Baking Powder Mountain   *7,593 feet (Class 2)*
Baking Powder Mountain is located along the northern boundary of the Gospel Hump Wilderness, southeast of Sourdough Fire Lookout. This peak is an easy cross-country walk from FST-300 [(F)(1.1)(b)], which leaves the Sourdough road just below the summit of Sourdough Peak. USGS Sourdough Peak/GHW

North Pole   *8,818 feet (Class 1)*
North Pole anchors a north/south ridgeline that connects with Buffalo Hump to the south. The ridge forms the eastern border of the Gospel Hump Wilderness. The region east and south of the ridge is not included in the wilderness because of the extensive mining activity that took place in the area during the late 1800s and early 1900s. Take FST-299 [(F)(1.2)

(b)] west from Wildhorse CG to the summit area less than 2 miles away. From this trail, a side trail just north of the summit climbs the peak's north ridge in 0.25 mile. USGS North Pole/GHW

Buffalo Hump   *8,938 feet (Class 2)*
This peak , the highest in the Gospel Hump Wilderness Area, is located 2 miles south of North Pole and is surrounded by four mountain lakes. The summit is (you guessed it) a hump-shaped ridge that reaches its high point at dead center. Take either FST-299 [(F)(1.2)(b)] from Wildhorse CG over North Pole and on to Crystal Lake and Hump Lake, or FST-313 to Hump Lake [(F)(1.2)(c)]. From Hump Lake, the remnants of an old jeep road may be found running due west from the lake and over the ridgeline just south of the Buffalo Hump summit. Follow this route from the lake and then climb the ridge due north to the summit. USGS Buffalo Hump/GHW

Oregon Butte   *8,464 feet (Class 2)*
Quartzite Butte   *8,371 feet (Class 2)*
These two peaks are located south of Buffalo Hump in the southeastern section of the Gospel Hump Wilderness. Both peaks are reached by trail and both are a long way from any road. There are three potential starting points. The first two begin at Orogrande Summit where FST-313 [(F)(1.2)(c)] and FST-204 [(F)(1.2)(a)] lead south. Follow either trail south to FST-230 and then follow FST-230 until it forks past the Del Río mine. FST-202 and 225 lead to Oregon Butte. FST-221 and 226 lead to Quartzite Butte. The third way into the area around Oregon and Quartzite Buttes is from Dixie via FST-215 [(F)(1.3.2)(a)]. USGS Buffalo Hump/GHW

Nipple Mountain   *7,098 feet (Class 1)*
Nipple Mountain is located on the northeast boundary of the Gospel Hump Wilderness. From Orogrande CG, take FST-801 for 3.6 miles until it joins FST-800, which leads to the summit [(F)(1.2)(d)]. USGS Orogrande/GHW

INDIAN PARK DIVIDE
This divide located south of the Lochsa River midway between Selway Falls GS and Moose Creek GS runs south from Mink Peak to Grave Meadow Peak where it divides into two prongs. Its western prong runs southwest to Vermillion Peak. Its eastern prong runs south to Elk Mountain, the northern half of the ridge is in the Selway-Bitteroot Wilderness (SBW) and the southern half should be. Primary access to the ridge is from the Selway River Road in the north and ID-14 in the south.

Mink Peak   *7,054 feet (Class 1)*
Mink Peak is located south of the Selway River, roughly 12.5 miles east of the Selway Falls GS. Approachable by trail from all four compass points, the summit is crossed by FST-438 [(E) (3.1)(b.2)]. The shortest approach from the Selway Falls GS is via FST-4 and FST-438. Mink Peak is a very long way from anywhere. USGS Mink Peak/SBW

Grave Meadow Peak   *7,373 feet (Class 2)*
Grave Meadow Peak is located 5.5 miles south of Mink Peak. The summit is a relatively easy scramble from FST-602, which passes over the saddle just west of the peak [(E)(3.1)(b.2)]. USGS Running Lake/SBW

Indian Peak   *7,728 feet (Class 2)*
Indian Peak is 2 miles southwest of Grave Meadow Peak and sits directly on the boundary of the Selway-Bitterroot Wilderness. To climb the peak, hike on FST-602 to the saddle west of Grave Meadow Peak and follow the snaking ridge southwest to the summit [(E)(3.1)(b.2)]. USGS Running Lake/SBW

Rocky Peak   *7,640 feet (Class 3)*
Rocky Peak is located 1 mile due south of Indian Peak. This peak can be climbed by traversing the ridgeline between it and Indian Peak. USGS Running Lake

Vermilion Butte   *7,575 feet (Class 2)*
Disgrace Butte   *6,589 feet (Class 1)*
From Fenn Ranger GS drive up the Selway River Road, FS-223, to Slim's CG. Take FST-726 to FST-609, located 0.5 mile east of the Meadow Creek GS [(E)(3.1.3)(b)]. FST-609 climbs a ridge, crosses Disgrace Butte and then comes within a short distance of the Vermilion Butte summit. It is 19 miles from the CG to the summit. USGS Vermilion Peak

Elk Mountain   *7,826 feet (Class 2)*
Bilk Mountain   *7,610 feet (Class 2)*
Take FST-517 [(G)(1.1)(a)] to the north side of the peak and scramble to the top. Return to the trail to continue to Bilk Mountain. The total distance to Bilk is 7 miles. USGS Running Lake

Vermilion Peak (Photo by Sheldon Bluestein)

Wylies Peak   *7,799 feet (Class 1)*
This summit located 4.5 miles northeast of Bilk Mountain
was named for an old prospector who originally blazed some
of the trails in this section of the SBW. FST-526 leads to the
summit. It can be accessed from FST-602 [(E)(3.1)(b.2)] or
from FST-4 [(G)(1.4)(d) and (d.3)]. USGS Wylies Peak/SBW

Box Car Mountain   *7,589 feet (Class 2)*
Box Car Mountain is located 4 miles south of Wylies Peak.
FST-529 crosses the peak's south slopes. Leave the trail and
scramble to the top along the peak's south ridge [(G)(1.4)(d.2)].
USGS Wylies Peak/SBW

Archer Mountain   *7,492 feet (Class 2)*
This peak is named for George Archer, a trapper who died
after skiing off a cliff on this peak in 1909. The peak is located
2 miles east of Box Car Mountain. FST-529 crosses Archer
Saddle west of the summit and then traverses the peak's north
side to a point near the summit. Leave the trail at this point
and hike to the peak's highest point [(G)(1.4)(d.2)]. USGS
Wylies Peak/SBW

ELK CITY/DIXIE AREA PEAKS

Elk City, a former mining camp, is located along the South
Fork Clearwater River due east of Grangeville. Dixie is another
former mining camp found along the southern margin of the
Clearwater Mountains due south of Elk City. These outposts
are between the Gospel Hump Wilderness to the west and
the Selway-Bitterroot and River of No Return Wildernesses
to the east. Although this area is not protected by wilderness
designation, there are many good hiking peaks. Primary access is via ID-14.

Blue Ribbon Mountain   *6,055 feet (Class 1)*
Blue Ribbon Mountain is located 4 miles due east of downtown Elk City. From Elk City, drive FS-1818 south to FS-1807.
Turn east onto FS-1807 and follow it to the trailhead 2.3 miles
from town [(F)(1.4)(a)]. From the trailhead, follow FST-833,
an old jeep road, to the summit in about 2 miles. USGS Black
Hawk Mountain

Black Hawk Mountain   *6,091 feet (Class 1)*
Black Hawk Mountain sits 4.5 miles east of Blue Ribbon
Mountain. Take FS-423 north from the Red River Road to
where the road is closed within a mile of the summit. From
this point, follow the road to the top and a terrific view [(F)

(1.3.1.1)]. For those with plenty of time, the area north of
Black Hawk's summit is a de facto wilderness area encompassing the Meadow Creek drainages that stretch north to the
Selway River. The hiking is reported to be excellent in this
area. USGS Black Hawk Mountain

Moose Butte   *7,121 feet (Class 1)*
Moose Butte, located south of Elk City, is the highest point
on a major north/south ridgeline that divides Big Creek from
the South Fork of the Red River. The summit is accessed via
FST-207 from either the north or south [(F)(1.3)(a.1)]. USGS
Moose Butte

Porters Mountain*   *6,421 feet (Class 1)*
Porters Mountain is located 4 miles north of Moose Butte on
the same ridgeline. FST-508 [(F)(1.3)(a)] leads to the summit
in 8 miles. USGS Moose Butte

Burpee Mountain   *6,848 feet (Class 1)*
Burpee Mountain is located southwest of Dixie Summit on
the same ridgeline with Moose Butte. FST-209 and then FST-
207 [(F)(1.3)(a.1)] lead 3 miles to the summit from FS-222.
USGS Moose Butte

Churchill Mountain   *6,687 feet (Class 1)*
Churchill Mountain is located 3.25 miles west of Dixie and
is the highest point on Blue Ridge. The trailhead for FST-210
is found in Dixie at the south end of town [(F)(1.3)(c)]. It is
4.3 miles to the summit. USGS Dixie

Blowout Mountain   *6,629 feet (Class 1)*
Blowout Mountain is situated east of the Dixie GS. The Class
1 summit is a 3.5-mile walk from the GS via FST-211 and
FST-212 [(F)(1.2)(d)]. The summit also can be reached from
the northeast by turning off FS-222 onto FS-222D just south
of Dixie and following FS-222D for 2.5 miles to the FST-233
trailhead. The condition of this route is unknown, but it is only
2 miles to the summit from the end of the road. USGS Dixie

PEAKS ALONG
THE OLD NEZ PERCE TRAIL ROAD

The Old Nez Perce Trail Road runs between Red River GS and
Nez Perce Pass on the Idaho/Montana border. Several good
hiking peaks are accessed from this slow, winding road. The
following peaks are located both north and south of the road.
They are listed from west to east.

Boston Mountain   *7,648 feet (Class 1)*
Boston Mountain is located south of the Old Nez Perce Trail Road on a north/south ridgeline that divides Mallard Creek from Bargain Creek. Its summit is located on the edge of the River of No Return Wilderness (RNRW) and there is a large tree on its grassy summit. The old ladder attached to the tree was used in the 1930s by a fire lookout who climbed the tree for an even better view. Although trails reach the summit from all compass directions, the best route is from the Nez Perce Road by way of FST-580 [(G)(1)(a)]. USGS Boston Mountain

Green Mountain   *7,227 feet (Class 1)*
Little Green Mountain   *6,980 feet (Class 1)*
These two summits sit 5 miles east of Red River Hot Springs. A Forest Service road leads to the summit of Green Mountain and its lookout site. FST-541 gives quick access to the smaller peak in 1.2 miles [(G)(1.1.1)(a)]. USGS Green Mountain

Center Mountain   *8,260 feet (Class 2)*
Center Mountain is located north of the Salmon River in the RNRW, 8 miles south of Burnt Knob Lookout and the Old Nez Perce Trail Road. The summit, boasting three mountain lakes on its eastern flanks, is reached via a moderate scramble up the peak's east ridge from where FST-578 crosses the ridge [(G)(1)(b)]. USGS Sheep Hill/RNRW

Granite Peak   *7,232 feet (Class 1)*
Granite Peak is located 7 miles northeast of Red River Hot Springs and 3.5 miles south of Bilk Mountain on a high ridgeline that divides Three Prong Creek and the East Fork Meadow Creek. FST-647 leads to the summit from the Windy Saddle Road [(G)(1.1)(c)]. The trailhead area has seen considerable mining activity in the past, and the trail begins by following a mining road to the ridge top. It is 6 miles to the summit, with many good vistas along the way. USGS Green Mountain

White Top Mountain   *7,886 feet (Class 2)*
White Top Mountain is 2 miles northwest of Burnt Knob Lookout. To climb the peak from Burnt Knob Lookout, follow FST-539 north for 1.5 miles and then take the intersecting ridgeline due east for 0.5 mile [(G)(1.2)(a)]. USGS Sabe Mountain/SBW

Sabe Mountain   *8,245 feet (Class 1)*
This peak is located southeast of Burnt Knob Lookout and just north of the Old Nez Perce Trail Road. It is accessed by FST-61, which leads from the road to the summit in less than 1 mile [(G)(1)(c)]. USGS Sabe Mountain/SBW

Three Prong Mountain   *8,182 feet (Class 2)*
Three Prong Mountain is located in a rugged area on the western boundary of the Selway-Bitterroot Wilderness. Take FST-539 [(G)(1.2)(a)] north from Burnt Knob Lookout; it follows a ridgeline to a saddle on the south slopes of the peak in 5 miles. Scramble to the top from the saddle. USGS Three Prong Mountain

Magruder Mountain   *7,421 feet (Class 1)*
Lloyd MaGruder was a packer who operated pack trains between Lewiston and Virginia City, Montana. In 1863, while returning to Lewiston after selling goods to miners in Montana, MaGruder and several of his employees were murdered for the $25,000 he was carrying. The murderers were eventually caught in San Francisco and hanged in Lewiston. FST-7 and FST-13 provide an easy approach to Magruder's summit. From the Old Nez Perce Trail Road, it is 3 miles to the top [(G)(1)(f)]. USGS Magruder Mountain/SBW

Harrington Mountain   *8,186 feet (Class 1)*
Harrington Mountain is 6 miles southeast of Center Mountain and 6 miles north of the Salmon River. FST-28 and FST-9 lead to the summit from the Old Nez Perce Trail Road after 15 very long miles [(G)(1)(d)]. USGS Dennis Mountain

Salmon Mountain   *8,943 feet (Class 1)*
Salmon Mountain is located just south of the Old Nez Perce Trail Road and is reached by a short trail leading from the road. The summit has a fire lookout tower and an exceptional view [(G)(1.3)]. Goat Mountain is the minor peak to the southeast. USGS Stripe Mountain

Waugh Mountain   *8,887 feet (Class 1)*
This peak is located 8 miles south of Salmon Mountain. The summit is reached by trails from the north, south, and east. The recommended approach is from the Old Nez Perce Trail Road to the north via FST-019 [(G)(1)(e)]. USGS Waugh Mountain/RNRW

Stripe Mountain   *9,001 feet (Class 2)*
This peak, the tallest Clearwater Mountain summit, sits atop a west/east trending ridgeline that forms the headwaters of the Selway River near the boundary between the Clearwater Mountains and the Bitterroot Range. It is located 1.8 miles

northeast of Waugh Mountain. The peak is climbed via its east ridge from FST-069. The route, [(G)(1)(e) or (G)(1)(g.1)], presents no difficulties. USGS Stripe Mountain/RNRW

Thirteen Mountain   *8,973 feet (Class 2)*
Thirteen Mountain is located directly north of Stripe Mountain. The peak has a horseshoe-shaped summit surrounding a beautiful lake. The peak should be climbed in conjunction with a climb of Stripe Mountain by simply crossing the connecting ridge between the two peaks. USGS Stripe Mountain/RNRW

Parker Mountain   *8,503 feet (Class 1)*
The final Clearwater Mountain summit listed in this guidebook can be reached from the south after an enjoyable backpack. Its grassy summit provides great views to the south over the Salmon River canyon and on to the Bighorn Crags. Approach from the west on good trails [(H)(1)(a)]. USGS Square Top

APPROACHES TO
THE CLEARWATER MOUNTAINS

The Clearwater Mountains are nearly as big as some states and, consequently, the combination of federal, state, county, and Forest Service roads that crisscross the range is as complex as any state highway system. For clarity's sake, this section describes the Clearwater road system as it exists in relation to the following locations: (A) Saint Maries, (B) Clarkia, (C) Potlatch, (D) Moscow, (E) Orofino, (F) Grangeville, (G) the Nez Perce Trail, and (H) Salmon. Most Clearwater journeys will begin from one of these locations. Expect it to take a lot of time to drive anywhere in this country.

(A) SAINT MARIES APPROACHES
Saint Maries, a town of 3,000, is located on the northeast corner of the Clearwater range and offers all essential services.
(1) FH-50/FS-218, Saint Joe River Road. This road leaves ID-3 on the west edge of Saint Maries and stretches east and then south for 74 miles to Red Ives GS. This road also can be accessed from Saint Regous, Montana, via I-90. Leave the freeway 1 mile west of Saint Regous and drive south from the exit on the Little Joe River Road, cross the Idaho/Montana border at Roland Summit, and drive down the North Fork Saint Joe River to the Saint Joe River Road at Avery.
(1.1) FS-321, Marble Creek Road. This road leaves the Saint Joe River Road 34.5 miles east of Saint Maries. The well-signed road makes a 31-mile journey over 4,500-foot Hobo Pass on its

way to Clarkia. This road is open to passenger autos, but can have a rough surface.
(1.2) FS-301, Fishhook Creek Road/Freezeout Saddle Road. This road leaves the Saint Joe River Road just east of Avery, 43 miles east of Saint Maries. It leads south and then west to Clarkia, crossing some of the more remote northern Clearwaters on the way. The road requires a high-clearance vehicle for much of its distance. Also see [(B)(2)], below.
(1.3) FS-201, Sisters Creek Road. This road begins 9.75 miles south of Avery at FS-301 and runs east for nearly 40 miles to the summit of Granite Peak and a junction with FS-395, which leads south to the Mallard-Larkins Area. The route traverses checkerboard patterns of public and private land where a great deal of road construction and logging has taken place; consequently, route-finding requires a map, but most major junctions are signed.
(a) FST-55, Snow Peak Trail. FST-55 leaves FS-201 26.6 miles east of its junction with FS-301. The trailhead is signed and has room for several vehicles. The trail traverses an undulating ridge for 5 miles to the base of Snow Peak, where there is some camping in a meadow and a small spring for water. The trail forks after the meadow. The right fork continues west toward Spotted Louie Point and the left fork climbs to the top of Snow Peak.
(1.3.1) FS-395, Surveyors Ridge Road. This road leaves FS-201 and proceeds to Sawtooth Saddle in roughly 10 miles. This is a rough road and passenger cars are not recommended.
(a) FST-111, Northbound Creek Trail. This trail provides the longest and most difficult approach route into the Mallard-Larkins Pioneer Area. The trail begins at the end of FS-395 at Sawtooth Saddle and then steeply descends to Sawtooth Creek, where it climbs up Northbound Creek to join FST-65 on the Mallard-Larkins Crest. See [(E)(1.1.2)(b) and (c)], below.
(1.4) FS-303, Beaver Creek Road. This road is a connector between the Saint Joe River Road and FS-201. The road is accessed 1.7 miles north of Red Ives and is a better alternative for those going to the north end of the Mallard-Larkins Pioneer Area.
(B) CLARKIA AREA ACCESS POINTS
Clarkia is a wide spot in ID-3, 32 miles south of Saint Maries and 51 miles east of Moscow. Although this village is a heavily used gateway into the northern Clearwaters, it provides few traveler services. Gas and food are available during regular business hours.
(1) FS-321, Hobo Pass/Marble Creek Road. This road heads due east out of Clarkia and proceeds east and then north to the Saint Joe River in 31 miles [(A)(1.1)]. One mile from Clarkia, this road intersects with FS-301.
(2) FS-301, Freezeout Saddle Road/Fishhook Creek Road.

Take FS-312 east from Clarkia for 1 mile and turn right onto this road which leads to Gold Center CG in 4.5 miles. Turn left at Gold Center and follow the road for about 12 bumpy, twisty miles to Freezeout Saddle and FST-275. The Widow Mountain trailhead is another 5 miles down FS-301. This is a good gravel road, though a bit narrow, and is open to autos when the weather is mild. Note that during the winter FS-301 is often plowed to within a few miles of Freezeout Saddle to allow loggers to remove logs. This allows cross-country skiers to use the road on weekends to reach relatively high terrain and good snow. Also note that while FS-301 can be utilized to reach Snow Peak, the better route to this mountain leaves the Saint Joe River Road [(A)(1.3)(a)].

(a) **FST-275, Grandmother Mountain Trail.** This popular trail leaves Freezeout Saddle and leads to Grandmother Mountain in 2 miles and Grandfather Mountain in 4 miles; it is well maintained.

(b) **FST-52, Widow Mountain Trail.** This trail leaves FS-301 21 miles east of Clarkia and traverses a ridge east for 6 miles to Widow Mountain. The trail is on BLM land and is seldom, if ever, maintained.

(2.1) **FS-457, Little Goat Mountain Road.** From Clarkia, take FS-301 past Freezeout Saddle to the FS-457 junction, which climbs up to the Little Goat divide and Goat Mountain. This road eventually traverses along the crest of this minor Clearwater subrange and provides access to all of its peaks. A 4WD is recommended.

(C) POTLATCH AREA ACCESS POINTS

Potlatch provides all major services. From Potlatch, working clockwise, the Hoodoo Mountains are circled by US-95, ID-5, ID-3, ID-9, and ID-6. ID-6 traverses the range from Harvard to Sanders, through the remnants of a great western white pine forest.

(1) **Giant White Pine Campground Trail System.** This campground is located 16 miles northeast of Potlatch along ID-6. The Forest Service has constructed a series of short loop trails in the area. All provide beautiful forest hikes.

(a) **FST-228, Bald Mountain Trail.** The old Bald Mountain Trail "ain't what it used to be." Although it is well signed, has a good tread, and traverses exciting scenery, the Bald Mountain Trail crosses two major roads (which do not show up on the map board in the CG) as it climbs 9.5 miles to the summit of Bald Mountain. Nevertheless, the trail provides a good, long hike and melts out early in the hiking season.

(2) **North South Pass Access Points.** ID-3 crosses this pass 19 miles from Potlatch. From the pass, gravel roads lead both east and west along the Hoodoo Mountain divide. The east road

ends on Bald Mountain and the west road eventually leads to US-95. During the winter, these roads are closed and regularly groomed, serving as a state-run park and ski area.

(D) MOSCOW ACCESS POINTS

Moscow is a college town of 16,000 with all essential services, plus outdoor equipment suppliers. The town is the primary approach point for the Palouse Range, which is surrounded by federal and state highways. US-95 forms the west boundary of the range, ID-8 the south, ID-9 the east, and ID-6 the north.

(1) **Old Tamarack Ski Area Road.** To reach this road, take Sixth Street east from the Moscow business district until the road ends; turn right and drive 0.25 mile, then turn left and follow the good paved road 4 miles to the Robinson Lake Park. (Note: there is no longer a lake at the park.) Turn right and cross the old dam and follow the gravel road for another 5 miles to Tamarack Road. Turn left onto this road leading to the old ski area (closed) in 4 miles, and the Palouse Crest Road in 5.5 miles.

(2) **Palouse Crest Road.** This road follows the crest of the Palouse Range, traversing state, federal, and private land along the way. It is often passable to autos, weather permitting. The road is a favorite cross-country ski route of University of Idaho students during the winter.

(E) OROFINO ACCESS POINTS

Orofino is a town of 4,000 located along the Clearwater River on US-12, 42 miles east of Lewiston. The town provides all essential services.

(1) **ID-11, Orofino to Headquarters.** From Orofino, drive east on US-12 for 7 miles and turn left onto ID-11, which leads east to Weippe, then northeast to Pierce and, finally, north to Headquarters in 42.4 miles. This good paved road climbs out of the Clearwater canyon and crosses the Weippe Prairie before eventually returning to the mountains and arriving at Headquarters, population 300. Headquarters is owned by the Potlatch Corporation.

(1.1) **FS-247, Beaver Creek Road.** This paved road continues the route from Headquarters to the North Fork Clearwater River over Beaver Creek Divide in 24 miles.

(1.1.1) **FS-248, Sheep Mountains Access.** This road leaves FS-247 about 3 miles south of the North Fork Clearwater River and leads east into the Sheep Mountain Range. FS-248 almost completely circles this group. The areas it does not reach can be accessed by FS-682, which crosses the range from north to south. Eagle Point is reached by a side road (FS-6050) off FS-248, or by trail from FS-682.

(a) **FST-93, Sheep Mountain Trail.** This route leaves FS-682 at its high point and proceeds west to the summit of Sheep Mountain in 2 short miles from the trailhead.

(b) FST-93 to Eagle Point. Eagle point is a short 1-mile walk to the east from the trailhead and FS-682.

(1.1.2) FS-700, Smith Ridge Road. From Headquarters, take the Beaver Creek Road (FS-247) north for 24 miles to the North Fork Clearwater River. At this junction, go left on FS-700, which follows the North Fork Clearwater River for 0.6 mile before turning up Isabella Creek. Follow this road for roughly 3 miles up Isabella Creek to a junction. At this point, FS-705 continues up the Isabella drainage to a trailhead, while FS-700 runs east to Smith Ridge and the main Mallard-Larkins trailhead in about 10 miles.

(a) FST-240, Goat Ridge Trail. FST-240 leaves the trailhead on FS-700 and connects with FST-65 in 8 miles, following the ridge top over Goat Ridge Peak.

(b) FST-65, Mallard Divide Trail. This trail follows the Mallard-Larkins Divide, staying near the crest of the ridge, and provides access to a number of peaks. Access to this trail is available from many different points including [(E)(1.1.1)(a)] and [(A)(1.3.1)(a)].

(c) FST-111, Northbound Trail. This trail leaves FST-65 1 mile east of Heart Peak, descends to the north to Northbound Lake, and then continues on to Martin Creek and Sawtooth Creek. At Sawtooth Creek, the trail immediately climbs up steep north slopes to Sawtooth Saddle where it joins FS-395/FS-102, which connects with FS-201 near Snow Peak. See [(A)(1.3.1) (a)], above. The total distance from FST-65 to Sawtooth Saddle is roughly 5 miles.

(d) FST-475, Martin Creek Trail. This trail leaves FST-65 0.5 mile east of its junction with FST-111 and descends along Martin Creek to Sawtooth Creek in 1.5 miles. See [(A)(1.3.1) (a)], above.

(e) FST-97, Upper Northwest Trail. This trail leads south from FST-65 and Mallard Peak to a trail junction east of East Sister, where it joins FST-685 and FST-399 in 4 miles. Midway, it intersects with FST-95, which descends to Isabella Creek. This road climbs 3,300 feet and is only in fair condition.

(1.1.2.1) FS-705, Isabella Creek Road. This road leaves FS-700 1.4 miles up Isabella Creek and then crosses the creek. The trailhead for FST-95 is shortly after the crossing.

(a) FST-95, Isabella Creek Trail. FST-95 leaves FS-705 and runs northeast to join FST-97 in 5 miles. It is a well-maintained route that gains 3,600 feet in elevation. FST-96 forks off of this trail 1.9 miles from the trailhead.

(b) FST-96, Elmer Creek Trail. This trail begins where FST-97 passes Elmer Creek, and then climbs up the drainage to the northwest for 4 miles to a junction with FST-65 on Goat Ridge. This trail is in bad condition and requires expert skills.

(1.2) FS-249, North Fork Clearwater River Road. This road begins where FS-247 ends and follows the meandering river east to Orogrande Creek, where it joins FS-250 running south to Pierce and northeast to Kelly Forks GS. The road is passable for autos.

(a) FST-396, Black Mountain Trail. Access this trail at the Canyon GS, 1.5 miles east of the FS-247/FS-249 junction. The steep trail begins at 1,800 feet and leads to Black Mountain Lookout at 7,400 feet in 7 long, steep miles.

(b) FST-399, The Nub Trail. FST-399 follows Upper Twin Creek past the steep walls of the North Fork canyon to the vicinity of the Nub and a junction with FS-97. This trail, a difficult, rocky, and brushy route, is accessed east of the Canyon GS.

(2) FS-250, Pierce, Idaho, to Montana Road. This road is accessed from ID-11 just south of Pierce. FS-250, known as the French Mountain Road, climbs over French Saddle, follows French Creek and then descends along Orogrande Creek to the North Fork Clearwater River and FS-249 [(E)(1.3)]. Once the road meets the North Fork, it proceeds east to Kelly Forks GS and then north to Hoodoo Pass on the Idaho/Montana border.

(a) FST-176/FST-169, Cold Springs Mountain Trail. This trail leaves FS-250 at the Kelly Forks GS and climbs north up a ridge that divides the Cold Springs drainage from the North Fork Clearwater drainage. Fiat Mountain is 3 switchback-filled miles from the road, and Cold Springs Mountain is 6 miles from the road. Beyond Cold Springs Mountain, the trail designation becomes FST-169 and the trail continues north along a ridgeline for many miles to Fly Hill and FS-715. Alternative access is via FS-711 to FS-5295 to FS-5297 and FS-5297A. A 4WD is required.

(b) FST-445, Elizabeth Mountain Trail. FST-445 leaves FS-250 4 twisting miles north of Kelly Forks GS and climbs out of the North Fork canyon toward Elizabeth Mountain, which is reached in 2.5 miles. From this summit, the trail turns due west to meet FST-176 in another 3 miles just south of Cold Springs Mountain. Alternative access is via FS-711 to FS-5295 to FS-5297, and FS-5297A and FST-176 to avoid a hefty elevation gain. A 4WD is required.

(2.1) FS-253/FS-711, Pot Mountain Cutoff Road. These two roads form a shortcut across a large bend in the North Fork Clearwater River between the outlet of Quartz Creek and the Cold Springs GS. FS-253, the western entrance to the cutoff, can be accessed from FS-249 7 miles east of the Canyon GS. FS-711, at the Cold Springs GS, is the eastern entrance to the cutoff. Mush Saddle, the high point along the cutoff, is located 8.5 miles from the GS and 12 miles from the outlet of Quartz Creek.

(a) FST-144, Pot Mountain Ridge Trails. Access for FST-144 is gained just west of Mush Saddle. Turn south onto

FST-5259, an old logging road that wiggles on for 1.5 miles to where the road becomes too rough for all but 4WDs. The road eventually turns into a trail at roughly 2,400 feet, runs south past the summit of Pot Mountain in 3 miles, and descends to the North Fork Clearwater River in another 11 miles. All of the trails in the area south of Pot Mountain can be accessed from FST-144.

(b) **FST-169, Pot Mountain Trail.** This trail leaves Mush Saddle at 2,400 feet and follows a ridge northeast to Cold Springs Mountain in 4 miles with moderately steep sections.

(2.2) **FS-255, Kelly Creek Road.** This road leaves the North Fork Clearwater River at the Kelly Fork GS and follows Kelly Creek north until it eventually turns off at Ruby Creek and continues north to Moose City. Several trailheads are available from this road.

(a) **FST-690, Moose Mountain Trail.** From FS-255 2 miles north of Ruby Creek CG, drive on FS-5440 up Moose Creek for 2 miles. Pick up the trail and follow it 3 miles to the summit of Moose Mountain. A 4WD is recommended.

(b) **FST-427, Moose Mountain Trail.** From FS-255 and Deception Saddle take FS-730 to its end and the FST-427 trailhead at 5,600 feet. The trail runs south to Moose Mountain in about 3.5 miles where it intersects with FST-690 [(E)(2.2)(a)].

(3) **US-12 Access Points.** US-12 runs between Lewiston, Idaho, and Lolo, Montana, by first following the Clearwater River and then the Lochsa River to Lolo Pass. A number of trailheads which furnish access to the Selway-Bitterroot Wilderness Area are located along US-12. US-12 is a long, narrow, twisting two-lane road that requires a lot of patience to drive, so leave extra time in your schedule to get to the trailhead.

(a) **FST-133, Split Creek Trail.** This trailhead is 10 miles east of Wilderness Gateway. After crossing the river on a suspension bridge, the trail goes east along the river to Split Creek and then almost immediately climbs up Split Creek Ridge. Chimney Peak is reached after a massive climb in roughly 12, very steep, miles. A spring at 3 miles is the only water.

(b) **FST-211/FST-213, Boulder Creek Trail and Beyond.** This trail leaves from the Wilderness Gateway trailhead and CG located 26 miles east of Lowell. The Boulder Creek Trail provides direct access to the north end of the Selway Crags and the entire SBW. It is roughly 15 miles to Boulder Pass from the trailhead. East of the pass, the trail continues on to Fish Lake and its GS and then down Fish Creek, where it intersects with FST-213 and FST-60. FST-213 runs north and south and provides access to McConnel Mountain to the south and Bear Mountain to the north. FST-60 crosses two drainages and then follows a ridgeline east before joining the Warm Springs Creek Trail.

(c) **FST-220, Lochsa Peak Trail.** This trail leaves the Wilderness Gateway trailhead, climbs up and crosses Cantaloupe

Peak, Huckleberry Butte, and Stanley Butte before reaching Old Man Lake and the Chimney Peak area after 20 miles.

(d) **FST-206, Eagle Mountain Trail.** This trail is the main east/west approach route in the Selway Crags. It begins along US-12, 15 miles east of Wilderness Gateway at the Eagle Mountain Pack Bridge, climbs up to the Selway Crags divide north of Greystone Butte and then proceeds southwest, roughly following the divide (on the ridge/off the ridge) to Chimney Peak. From where the trail reaches the divide, it is 1 mile to Greystone Butte, 8 miles to Boulder Pass and FST-211, 19 miles to Shasta Lake, and 26 miles to Chimney Peak.

(e) **FST-469, Mocus Point Pack Bridge.** This trailhead is located 25 miles east of Wilderness Gateway along US-12. FST-469 leads to FST-209, which is a principal wilderness trail. From this trail, FST-21 provides quick access to the summit of Bear Mountain.

(f) **FST-49 and FST-44, Warm Springs Pack Bridge Trails.** These trails are located 36 miles east of Wilderness Gateway along US-12 (52 miles east of Lowell). FST-49 and FST-44 lead into the wilderness by making the long climb from the river to the ridge top. Jerry Johnson Hot Springs is located 2 miles up FST-49, so the first part of this trail system sees considerable use from day hikers.

(3.1) **FS-223, Selway River Road.** This road leaves US-12 at Lowell, 26 miles east of Kooskia, and follows the Selway River for 19 miles to Selway Falls. Although paved for much of its distance, it is exceedingly narrow in places and should be driven slowly.

(a) **FST-708, Pete King Ridge.** The trailhead is located 17 miles up the Selway River from Lowell on US-12. Take FST-708, first up Gedney Creek and then up Gedney Mountain's long south ridge to the summit in 10.5 miles and 5,100 feet of elevation gain. The trail is not maintained regularly and is brushy and hard to find in places.

(b) **FST-4, Selway River Trail.** The westernmost section of the Selway River Trail begins at the end of FS-223. This trail follows the Selway River upstream through the entire SBW to the Paradise GS [(G)(1.4)].

(b.1) **FST-606, Sixtytwo Ridge Trail.** FST-606 leaves FST-4 and proceeds north for 9 miles to a junction with FST-693, which leads west to Big Fog Saddle [(E)(3.1.2)(e)] and east to Shissler Peak and the Moose Creek GS. Big Rock Mountain is located 1 mile north of the junction.

(b.2) **FST-438/FST-602, Mink Peak/Bilk Mountain Trail.** This trail leaves FST-4 opposite the Sixtytwo Ridge Trail and runs south to Mink Peak in 6 miles and Bilk Mountain in 16 miles. From Bilk Mountain, FST-602 can be followed north-east toward Wylies Peak; FST-517 leads south to FS-285 [(G)(1.1) (a)]. This very rugged trail requires near-expert abilities and good conditioning.

(c) **FST-421, Moose Creek Trail.** This trail is the major east/west travel route in the Selway-Bitterroot Wilderness. The trail runs for approximately 42 miles between Moose Creek GS and Twin Lakes, which are on the Montana side of the Bitterroot divide.

(c.1) **FST-619, Bailey Mountain Trail.** FST-619 leaves FS-421 5 miles north of the Selway River and climbs to Bailey Mountain in 9.5 steep miles.

(d) **FST-430, Freeman Peak/Wahoo Pass Trail.** This trail gives hikers another way to hike between the Moose Creek GS and Montana. Although shorter than FST-421, it involves considerable up-and-down travel. The trail leaves the GS and climbs to Freeman Peak in 10 miles, continues on to the southern slopes of Wahoo Peak in another 10 miles and to Wahoo Pass on the Idaho/Montana border in another 9 miles. FST-631 and FST-432 both lead to the summit of Wahoo Peak from this trail.

(3.1.1) **FS-317, Coolwater Ridge Road.** FS-317 leaves the Selway River Road less than 1 mile south of Lowell and climbs to the summit of Round Top Mountain. A 4WD is recommended, but not required.

(a) **FST-3, Chimney Peak Trail.** Leaves FS-317 roughly 1 mile short of the summit of Round Top Mountain and heads northeast toward Ghost Mountain and then continues along a ridge over Louse Point and on to the Chimney Peak area in a total of 10 miles.

(3.1.2) **FS-319, Big Fog Saddle Road.** This road is the prime southern approach point into the Selway Crags. The Fog Mountain Road is steep and usually graded, but contains literally hundreds of deep water bars that force one to drive very slowly. Although a passenger auto can use this road, it is not recommended for cars with automatic transmissions because their brakes are destined to overheat on the descent. The trailhead is 12 miles from the river. Three trails leave the road at its end.

(a) **FST-3, Cove Lake Trail.** This trail leaves Big Fog Saddle and drops down into the Canteen Creek drainage, climbs up to a saddle west of Cove Lakes and east of Gedney Mountain, descends to the lakes and then continues on to Chimney Peak for a total of 10 miles. Even though the trail begins right on Big Fog Saddle, it is hard to find its starting point because an old road leading to the north is distracting. The trail begins in the trees just north of where the road drops off the saddle. Although this trail has a well-worn tread (to the extent of being seriously eroded), it is very brushy in places and completely overgrown in other spots. Expert route-finding abilities are required beyond Cove Lake.

(b) **Jesse Pass Trail.** This trail is not an official Forest Service route and does not show up on their maps. However, the trail, which is accurately shown on the Fenn Mountain USGS quad, actually exists and is in no worse condition than the Cove Lake Trail. The junction for this trail is located 0.7 mile north of Cove Lake, exactly as shown on the USGS quad. Look for the junction in a clump of trees, where a somewhat obvious tread leaves the main trail and climbs uphill. It is 0.8 mile from the junction to Jesse Pass. A spring below the pass is the last water before the pass. From the pass, the trail descends into the Three Links drainage and eventually connects with FST-693.

(c) **FST-708, Pete King Ridge Trail.** This trail leaves FST-3 just west and above Cove Lakes, climbs over Gedney Mountain and then descends down to the Selway River [(E)(3.1.1)(a)]. The trail is not regularly maintained but can be followed easily to the top of Gedney Mountain.

(d) **FST-343 and 363, Big Fog Mountain and Big Fog Lake Trails.** Although these trails are no longer maintained by the Forest Service, they are still passable. From Big Fog Saddle, the unsigned FST-343 is hard to find. From the obvious trailhead complete with a large sign for FST-693, walk north along the edge of the trees until you see the trail heading uphill. Once on the trail, it is easy to follow it to the top of Big Fog Mountain. From Big Fog's summit, the tread of FST-363 is no longer visible, but the ridgeline to the north is visible and easy to follow. Keep on the ridgeline and, as it narrows, the trail will show up. Although a fairly good tread leads down to the lake from the ridge top, cross-country expertise is essential. For those wishing for quick access to the Fenn Mountain area, the ridgeline can be followed north to Three Links Lake and Jesse Pass with a minimum of Class 3 climbing.

(e) **FST-693, Big Fog Saddle to Moose Creek GS Trail.** This trail leaves Big Fog Saddle and it runs east for many miles along the higher ridges before descending to the Moose Creek GS, which provides access to many Selway-Bitterroot trails.

(3.1.3) **Meadow Creek Road.** This road leaves the Selway River Road 18.75 miles from Lowell. Cross the Selway Falls Bridge and drive up Meadow Creek to the trailhead, which is at the Slims CG.

(a) **FST-726, Meadow Creek Trail.** FST-726 leaves the trailhead and follows Meadow Creek south and then east to FS-285 near Windy Saddle. Meadow Creek is centered in an extremely beautiful roadless area just west of the SBW.

(b) **FST-609, Vermilion Creek Trail.** This trail leaves FST-726 at the Meadow Creek GS and proceeds northeast to FST-438. On the way, the trail crosses Disgrace Butte and Vermilion Peak.

(3.2) **FS-111, Elk Summit Road.** This road provides one of the highest approach points in the SBW. It is roughly 18 miles from Powell to Hoodoo Lake. The road also provides access to a number of trails that lead east into the Bitterroot Range.

(a) **FST-45 , Kooskooskia to Grave Peak.** To reach this trail, drive up FS-111 to its junction with FS-358. Follow this road east to its end where the trail begins. It is 3 miles to Friday Pass, 4 miles to Wind Lakes, and 4.5 miles to the peak via an unmaintained side trail. This is steep, rocky country.

(b) **FST-486 to the Moose Creek Drainage.** This trail leaves the end of FS-111 and proceeds south to the upper reaches of East Fork Moose Creek in 6 miles, where it joins FST-421. FST-421 follows East Fork Moose Creek between the Moose Creek GS (to the west) [(E)(3.1)(c)] and Twin Lakes (in Montana).

(c) **FST-004/018, Diablo Mountain Access.** This route begins by following FST-004 east and then FST-018 to the summit in about 5.6 miles. The trail is in good shape.

(F) GRANGEVILLE ACCESS

Grangeville, a town of 4,000, offers all necessary services and is the headquarters of the Nez Perce National Forest.

(1) **ID-14, The Elk City Road.** This good paved road is reached from Grangeville by following ID-13 east out of town for 10 miles to its junction with ID-14. This road follows the South Fork Clearwater River to Elk City in 49.6 miles.

(1.1) **FS-492, Sourdough Peak Road.** Thirty miles east of the ID-13/ID-14 junction, turn south off ID-14 onto this recently rebuilt road, which ends on the summit of Sourdough Peak.

(a) **FST-415, Tenmile Creek Trail.** This trail begins 12 miles south of ID-14 and leads directly into the northeast corner of the Gospel Hump Wilderness, where it connects with numerous other wilderness trails.

(b) **FST-300, Baking Powder Mountain Trail.** FST-300 leaves FS-492 just short of the road's end and provides access to the entire northern section of the Gospel Hump. The south flanks of Baking Powder Mountain are 3 miles from the trailhead.

(1.2) **FS-233, Crooked River/Orogrande Road.** This road leaves ID-14 8 miles west of Elk City and runs for 21 miles through Orogrande and on to Orogrande Summit, where the road splits. The right fork leads to Wildhorse CG in 3 miles; the left fork goes to a trailhead on Lake Creek in 2.5 miles. The Lake Creek extension is generally too rough for passenger cars.

(a) **FST-204, Fish Lake/Jumbo Canyon Trail.** This trail leaves the Lake Creek trailhead and extends 13 miles across the southeast corner of the Gospel Hump Wilderness to the Halfway House CG, just south of Dixie. See [(F)(1.3.2)(a)], above.

(b) **FST-299, North Pole Trail.** FST-299 leaves from Wildhorse CG, heads west and then south over North Pole, and then onto the east slopes of Buffalo Hump.

(c) **FST-313, Orogrande Trail.** From Orogrande Summit, a road descends south into the basin below. The road is exceedingly rough (4WD only); it is advisable to park on the summit and walk 2 miles to the road's end, where FST-313 begins. The trail runs across private land (public access on the trail only) to Hump Lake in 2.5 miles, where it joins FST-299. This area south of Orogrande is crisscrossed by trails that provide excellent hiking.

(d) **FST-801/FST-800, Wilderness Boundary Trail.** This trail is accessed from the Orogrande CG on FS-233. From the trailhead, it is 3 miles on FST-801 to FST-800, which can be followed south to Wildhorse CG or north to Nipple Mountain.

(1.3) **FS-222, Red River/Dixie Road.** This paved road leaves ID-14, 2.7 miles west of Elk City. It is 14 miles to the Red River GS and 30 miles to Dixie. South of Dixie, the road turns to gravel and eventually leads to MacKay Bar on the main Salmon River.

(a) **FST-508, Porters Mountain Trail.** Drive 21 mile south of Elk City on FS-222 to the Porter Mountain trailhead. Follow FST-508 up the West Fork Red River for 4.5 miles to FST-207, which leads to the summit in 1 mile.

(a.1) **FST-207, Moose Butte Trail.** This trail stretches between FST-508 on the West Fork Red River and Burpee Mountain, a distance of 7 miles. The trail also can be accessed on its south end from FS-222 on Dixie Summit via FST-209, which is described in the next entry.

(b) **FST-209, Dixie Summit Trail.** This trail leaves Dixie summit and runs west along a ridgeline for 1.8 miles to a junction with FST-207 north of Burpee Mountain.

(c) **FST-210, Churchill Mountain Trail.** FST-210 is accessed from Dixie. The trail runs due east over Churchill Mountain and on to the Salmon River.

(d) **FST-211/FST-212, Blowout Mountain Trail.** This trail leaves FS-222 at the Dixie GS and runs east and then south to the top of Blowout Mountain. From the top of the mountain, the trail can be followed southeast to the Salmon River.

(1.3.1) **FS-234, Red River Hot Springs Road.** This road leaves FS-222 at the Red River GS and reaches the resort after 11 miles.

(a) **FST-541, Green Mountain Trail.** The trail leaves the Red River Hot Springs area and proceeds east to Green Mountain and FS-285 in 8 miles.

(1.3.2) **FS-2221, Halfway House CG Road.** Access this road at the Dixie GS at the south end of the runway. Follow it to the CG, where the Halfway House trailhead is located.

(a) **FST-215/FST-204/FST-215, Southeast Gospel Hump Trails.** The entire southeast corner of the Gospel Hump Wilderness is accessed from the Halfway House trailhead. Follow FST-215 west for 3 miles to where it joins the other trails. FST-204 leads north to Orogrande Summit. FST-215 leads south to the

Salmon River and FST-203, which leads west to Oregon Butte.

(b) **FST-204, Lake Creek Trail.** See [(F)(1.2)(a)], below.

(1.4) **FS-1818/FS-1807.** This road leaves downtown Elk City and proceeds southeast to Wigwam Creek, which is full of dredge tailings, in about 3 miles. When the road reaches Wigwam Creek, it forks. The right fork connects with FS-222 in less than 0.5 mile; take the left fork 0.5 mile to the trailhead for Blue Ribbon Mountain.

(1.3.1.1) **FS-423, Black Hawk Mountain Road.** This road leaves FS-234 roughly 6 miles from the Red River GS and proceeds north toward Black Hawk Mountain. The road is closed 1 mile from the summit. A number of trails are accessible from the summit, including FST-833 [(F)(1.4)(a)], which leads to Blue Ribbon Mountain. A 4WD is required.

(a) **FST-833, Blue Ribbon Mountain Trail.** FST-833 was formerly a mining road that left FS-1807 and led to the top of Blue Ribbon Mountain. Today, it is a footpath that travels eastward from Blue Ribbon Mountain along a ridge to Black Hawk Mountain. This route receives a lot of motorcycle use.

(2) **FS-221, Grangeville/Salmon Road.** This road leaves Grangeville from the east edge of town and proceeds south toward the Fish Creek Recreation Area.

(2.1) **FS-444, Moores Station Road.** This road leaves FS-221 30 miles south of Grangeville and runs east into the Gospel Peak Wilderness and Moores GS. The last 12 miles are rugged and require a 4WD, especially when the road is wet. This ridge road has remained open as a compromise between the Forest Service and the people claiming mining rights in the area.

(a) **FST-313, Slate Creek Trail.** This trail, which leaves FS-444 just east of its starting point, climbs up Slate Creek for 5 miles to Slate Lakes. At this point, a side road leads east back to FS-444.

(b) **FST-125, Hanover Mountain Trail.** FST-125 begins at Slate Lakes and runs due south to the Salmon River in 11 miles.

(c) **FST-312, Marble Butte Trail.** This trail begins at the Moores GS and traverses the Gospel Hump central sections, running south along ridges for more than 12 miles. Marble Butte is 9 miles from the trailhead.

(G) NEZ PERCE TRAIL ACCESS POINTS

The Nez Perce Trail runs between Red River GS in the west and Darby, Montana, in the east. It is a well graded but primitive road that provides access to miles of wilderness trails as it splits the Selway-Bitterroot and River of No Return Wildernesses.

(1) **FS-468, Old Nez Perce Trail Road.** This road stretches 113 miles between Red River GS and Darby, Montana. This twisty dirt road, the only "nonwilderness" break between the massive Selway-Bitterroot and Frank Church–River of No Return Wilderness areas, offers a wonderful combination of scenery, history, and washboard road that makes for a slow crossing of the once-impenetrable Clearwater Mountains. There are no services along the road, and it takes hours and hours to drive it—even when it's dry and graded. The road has numerous trailheads of interest to those who are wilderness bound. To reach the road from the Montana side, turn west off US-93 4 miles south of Darby and follow paved road till it splits at the West Fork GS. Take the right fork to Nez Perce Pass.

(a) **FST-580, Boston Mountain Trail.** FST-580 leaves FS-468 10.25 miles east of Red River CG and reaches Boston Mountain in 4 miles. From the peak, trails leave in all directions, while FS-580 proceeds southeast to Barganin Creek.

(b) **FST-575/FST-578, Center Mountain Trail.** This trail leaves FS-468 at Dry Saddle, 26 miles east of Red River. The Center Mountain Trail follows a high ridge with numerous lakes on its flanks, heading south toward Sheep Hill Lookout and Center Mountain. Five miles from the trailhead, the trail forks. The right fork, FST-576, goes to Sheep Hill Lookout; the left fork goes toward Center Mountain. After roughly 2 miles, the left fork trail passes Center Mountain's western slopes. Once the trail passes by the summit and is on the peak's south side, FST-578 forks off and proceeds east out onto Center Mountain's east ridge, where it eventually ends. South of the FST-578 junction, the Center Mountain Trail connects with FST-577, which descends to the Salmon River.

(c) **FST-61, Sabe Mountain Trail.** The Sabe Mountain trailhead is located 2 miles south of Sabe Saddle. From the road, the trail quickly climbs to the summit of Sabe Mountain in less than 1 mile.

(d) **FST-28/FST-29, Harrington Mountain Trail.** This trail leaves FS-468 at the Horse Heaven Saddle trailhead and heads south toward Harrington Mountain, which is reached after approximately 15 long up-and-down miles.

(e) **FST-019, Waugh Mountain Trail.** FST-019 is another long ridge trail that eventually leads from the Old Nez Perce Trail Road to the Salmon River. Waugh Mountain is located 14 miles south of the trailhead.

(f) **FST-7/FST-13, Magruder Mountain Trail.** This trail leaves FS-468 10.5 mile south of the Selway River and leads to Magruder Mountain in 2 miles.

(g) **FST-004, Selway River Trail.** This portion of the Selway River Trail follows the river south from the Magruder GS to the river's headwaters below Stripe Mountain, a distance of nearly 20 miles. Numerous side trails are accessed from the main travel route, the most important being FST-069 leading to Waugh Mountain.

(g.1) FST-069, Stripe Mountain Trail. FST-069 leaves FST-004 at Stripe Creek and proceeds southwest to FST-019 in 6 miles.

(1.1) FS-285, Windy Saddle Road. This road leaves Old Nez Perce Trail Road 20 miles east of Red River and proceeds north along a ridge to the south slopes of Elk Mountain in 15 miles. This road can be quite rough and a 4WD might come in handy if it rains.

(a) FST-517, Elk Mountain/Bilk Mountain Trail. FST-517 leaves FS-285 at the road's end, climbs to the top of Elk Mountain in less than 1 mile, and then continues on to Bilk Mountain on the SBW boundary. North of Bilk Mountain, the trail joins FST-602 [(E)(3.1)(b.2)], which leads north toward the Selway River.

(b) FST-529, Windy Saddle/Archer Mountain Trail. This trail leaves FS-285 at Windy Saddle (2 miles from the road's end) and runs northeast to Archer Mountain and then to the Selway River, which it meets north of the Paradise GS.

(c) FST-647, Granite Mountain Trail. This trail leaves FS-285 9.5 miles from its beginning, and follows the ridge to the summit in 4 miles.

(1.1.1) Green Mountain Road. This road is accessed 3 miles from the beginning of FS-285. The summit of Green Mountain is less than 1 mile from the main road.

(a) FST-541, Green Mountain Trail. This trail leaves from the top of Green Mountain and proceeds west to Red River Hot Springs [(F)(1.3.1)(a)].

(1.2) Burnt Knob Lookout Road. This road leaves the Old Nez Perce Trail Road just north of Dry Saddle and climbs up to the lookout site in 1 mile.

(a) FST-539, Three Prong Mountain Trail. This trail traverses the ridge between Burnt Knob Lookout and Three Prong Mountain in 6 miles.

(b) FST-3, Spot Mountain Trail. FST-3 leaves FST-539 just south of Three Prong Mountain and follows a ridge east to Spot Mountain in 4 miles. From Spot Mountain, the trail descends to the Selway River.

(1.3) FS-765, Salmon Mountain Lookout Road. This road is now closed and maintained as a trail. It begins along FS-468 at a signed trailhead 14 miles from the Selway River.

(1.4) FS-6223, Paradise Road. This road is the most important southern approach point into the SBW. From Magruder GS on FS-468, FS-6223 runs 12 miles up a nonwilderness corridor into the heart of the SBW to the Paradise GS. Five major trails leave from the road's end, and three major trails leave the road between the two guard stations.

(a) FS-3 to Spot Mountain. The trailhead is 1 mile north of Raven Creek CG. The trail climbs a ridge to Spot Mountain

in 4.5 miles. FS-40 follows a ridge north over Mount Aura and then drops down to the Selway River just above Paradise GS. See [(G)(1.4)(b)].

(b) FS-13/East and West. This trail is one of Idaho's premier ridge trails. The trailhead is located on FS-6223 just south of Raven Creek CG. The west fork goes up Magruder Ridge to Magruder Mountain [(G)(1)(f)]; the east fork of the trail climbs a ridge that leads to Nick Wynn Mountain, Beaver Jack Mountain, Cayuse Mountain, and Nez Perce Peak. The trail eventually ends at Nez Perce Pass.

(c) FST-10, Indian Ridge Trail. The trailhead is at Indian Creek CG. The trail switchbacks up to the ridgeline, which it follows to Green Mountain and Burnt Strip Mountain.

(d) FS-4, Selway River Trail. This trail traverses the unroaded sections of the Selway River, eventually ending at the Selway River Road [(E)(3.1)(b)]. Although this area is more attractive to river runners and kayakers than to hikers, it offers the quickest approach available to many Selway-Bitterroot peaks and lake basins.

(d.1) FST-517, Gardiner Peak Trail. This trail leaves FS-4 opposite the Running Creek Ranch and climbs up Gardiner Creek to Gardiner Peak in 6 miles.

(d.2) FST-529, Archer Mountain Trail. FST-529 leaves FS-4 2 miles south of the Shearer GS and climbs southeast to Archer Mountain in 7 miles. From the peak, the trail continues on to Windy Saddle and FS-285.

(d.3) FST-526, Wylies Peak Trail. This trail leaves FST-4 at the Shearer GS and follows Goat Ridge west to Wylies Peak. West of Wylies Peak, the trail intersects with FST-602 [(E)(3.1)(b.2)], FST-436, and FST-562.

(H) SALMON ACCESS POINTS

Salmon is located southeast of the Clearwater Mountains. All services are available as long as you do not need them too late in the evening.

(1) Spring Creek Road. Drive north from Salmon to North Fork. Turn west on FS-030, the Salmon River Road, and drive 16.7 miles to the Spring Creek Road, FS-038. Drive north on this road, which becomes FS-044, for 19.1 miles to Horse Creek Pass on the Idaho/Montana border. Turn west at the pass and continue on FS-044 for another 12.9 miles to the Reynolds Lake trailhead. A 4WD is required.

(a) FST-158/FST-018, Parker Mountain Trail. From the trailhead, this trail follows a ridge top to the southwest and leads past Reynolds Lake in 1.5 miles to a junction in 3.2 miles. Take FST-018 from this junction, still following the ridge. After 9.8 miles you will reach a junction just north of Parker Mountain and south of Hidden Lake.

7

THE BITTERROOT MOUNTAINS

The Bitterroot Mountains are a group of mountains primarily created by map makers and not by fault blocking or granitic intrusions. The map makers' creation arbitrarily combines parts of the Coeur d'Alene and Clearwater Mountains. The crest line designated as the Bitterroot Mountains begins in the north along the eastern shores of Lake Pend Oreille and runs south to Lost Trail Pass, north of Salmon. For 150 miles of this distance, the Bitterroot Crest also forms the Idaho/Montana border. In the north, the peaks designated as the Bitterroot Mountains are simply a high divide, undistinguishable from the surrounding Coeur d'Alene Mountains. In the south, the Bitterroot peaks are the eastern edge of the Idaho Batholith and are physically indistinguishable from the Clearwater peaks to the west. Nevertheless, this range is legendary.

Nevin M. Fenneman, in his book *Physiography of The Western United States,* described the southern Bitterroot Mountains as follows: "These mountains, while not remarkable for great height, are among the most characteristically alpine of the United States. Everywhere the effects of glaciation are prominent." As a range tied together only by a geographical location rather than a consistent geological makeup, the Bitterroots offer a varied and exciting mountain environment for climbers.

As with most Idaho ranges, the Bitterroot gains elevation from north to south, with 10,131-foot Trapper Peak (which is completely in Montana) its highest point. The highest point in the Idaho portion of the range, 9,439-foot Bare Peak, is found along the main divide forming the state boundary.

The range is administered in the north by the Idaho Panhandle National Forest and Montana's Lolo National Forest. Further south, the Bitterroot and Clearwater National Forests assume management responsibilities. In the Lolo Pass Area, many sections of land are held by private landowners.

Hiking and climbing opportunities are abundant throughout the Bitterroots. Although the most technically challenging summits are wholly within Montana and are not covered in this book, many Idaho peaks are worthwhile goals for both hikers and climbers. Between Lolo Pass and Nez Perce Pass, the vast majority of the range is within the Selway-Bitterroot

Wilderness. Between Lolo Pass and Hoodoo Pass, most of the divide is roadless and offers excellent wilderness terrain to those willing to explore remote country. North of Hoodoo Pass, several Bitterroot peaks sit at the centers of tiny pockets of wilderness and are excellent destinations for overnight and day trips. Foremost among these areas are Packsaddle Mountain and Binocular Peak.

CLARK FORK RIVER TO LOOKOUT PASS

The northernmost stretch of the Bitterroot Crest begins on the eastern shores of Lake Pend Oreille and then makes a gentle arc to the southeast to meet the Idaho/Montana border near Heron, Montana. From this point on, the range's crest forms the Idaho/Montana border until the range ends at Lost Trail Pass north of Salmon. From Packsaddle Mountain to Lookout Pass, which is crossed by I-90, the crest is forested and many roadways penetrate clear to the crest.

Packsaddle Mountain   *6,402 feet (Class 1)*
Packsaddle Mountain anchors the northern end of the Bitterroot Mountains in a grand fashion. The peak towers over surrounding peaks by nearly 1,000 feet. Standing 4,400 feet above Lake Pend Oreille, Packsaddle provides an enormous view of Idaho and Montana. The peak can be reached from the west by hiking up the Fall Creek, Minerva Ridge [(A)(1)(a)], or Granite Creek trails. However, the recommended route begins on the peak's east side, where a steep, 2-mile trail leads to the summit from the saddle at the head of Granite Creek [(A)(2)(a)]. Because of the many logging roads in the area, a recent Idaho Panhandle National Forest map is essential for finding the trailheads. USGS Packsaddle Mountain

Divide Peak   *5,205 feet (Class 2)*
Divide Peak is the northernmost Bitterroot Peak directly on the Idaho/Montana border. The summit is a short walk from FS-430 [(A)(3)], which traverses the Bitterroot divide to within a short distance of the summit. USGS Jordan Creek

Ulm Peak   *6,444 feet (Class 2)*
Ulm Peak is found 5 miles southeast of Divide Peak. Like Divide Peak, its summit is easily reached from FS-430, which continues to traverse the divide. This road provides quick access to the summit [(A)(3)]. USGS Gem Peak

Black Peak   *6,548 feet (Class I)*
Black Peak is the prominent summit that sits at the heads of East Fork Eagle Creek (on the Idaho side of the border) and

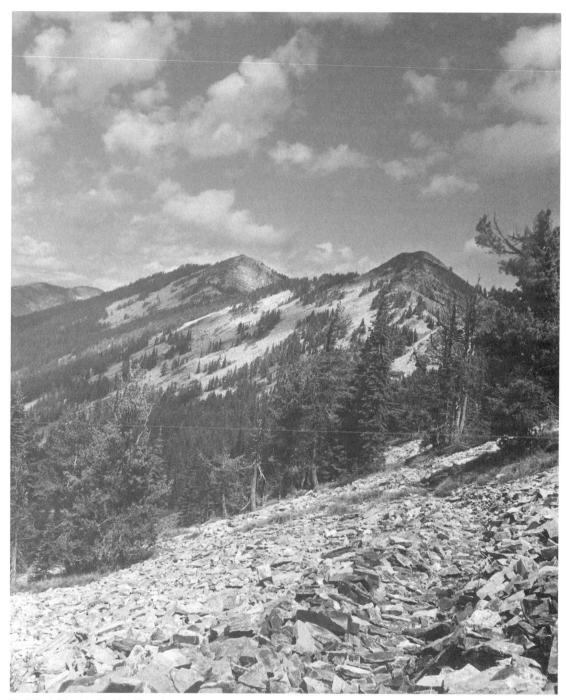

Black Peak (Photo by Sheldon Bluestein)

White Pine Creek (on the Montana side). The peak's Class 1 summit is easily accessed from both states as FST-7 traverses the border in this region. To reach the peak from the Idaho side, drive up FS-152 and then hike up FST-148 to FST-7 [(A) (4.1)(a) and (b)]. USGS Black Peak

Granite Peak   *6,815 feet (Class 1)*
Granite Peak sits east of the Idaho/Montana border above Revert Lake, 7 miles north of Mullan. The summit is reached via FST-137 from Sunset Mountain, which is a Coeur d'Alene Mountains peak. From Sunset Peak, follow FST-137 [(A)(5) (a)] east along a connecting ridgeline to the Granite Peak summit. USGS Burke

SHOSHONE RANGE

The Shoshone Range is a small subrange tucked into the west side of the Bitterroot Mountains northeast of Kellogg. This small, north-to-south trending range is roughly 12 miles long and 5 miles in width. It is separated from the Coeur d'Alene Mountains on the west by the Coeur d'Alene River and from the Bitterroot by Big Creek and Shoshone Creek. This tree-covered range reaches its highest point at Bennett Peak, 6,209 feet. Other peaks include Sentinel Peak and Little Sentinel Peak.

Bennett Peak   *6,209 feet (Class 1)*
Bennett Peak is found 10 miles due south of Divide Peak. Its Class 1 summit can be reached via FST-81 from both the north and the south. The north approach is via Shoshone Creek Road [(A)(4.2)] and the Hemlock Creek Road [(A)(4.2.1)]. The southern approach is from the Shoshone Crest Road [(A)(4.3) (a)]. FST-81 traverses the ridge between these two roads and provides easy access to the highest Shoshone Range summit. USGS Taylor Peak

LOOKOUT PASS TO LOLO PASS

South of Lookout Pass, the Bitterroot Crest begins to climb and take on a more alpine motif. While this section of the range is penetrated by many roads, there are still pockets of wild, roadless country suitable for wilderness designation.

Stevens Peak   *6,838 feet (Class 2-3)*
Stevens Peak, a rugged alpine summit, sits west of the main Bitterroot divide and 2.5 miles south of Mullan and I-90. The Spokane Mountaineers used this peak for their snow-climbing school for years. According to Neil McAvoy, "the likes of John

Roskelley, Chris Kopszynski, and hundreds more learned to use ice axes and crampons on this pleasant little hill." The Forest Service has designated the area around the summit as the Stevens Peak Alpine Lakes Area. The peak can be reached from most directions. The two most popular routes are from I-90 via either the Willow Creek Road [(B)(2)(a)] and one of the trails that lead up to Stevens Lakes and Long Lake, or from the Lookout Pass Ski Resort [(B)(1)]. A third approach route from Mullan leads up Boulder Creek on FST-128 to the peak's west shoulder [(B)(3)(a)].

The precipitous summit has been climbed from almost every direction and in every season. The most direct route to the summit is from Mullan via FST-128. Hike the trail south to the divide and then follow the divide due east to the western slopes of the peak. Leave the trail and hike the moderate slopes to the summit. The total distance is about 4.5 miles, with a 3,600-foot elevation gain. Another popular route climbs to the summit from Stevens Lake via the north ridge or the northwest slopes. USGS Mullan

Bald Mountain   *6,033 feet (Class 2)*
Dominion Peak   *6,032 feet (Class 2)*
Crittenden Peak   *6,416 feet (Class 2)*
Following the Bitterroot Crest south from Stevens Peak, one encounters these three summits over a 5-mile stretch of the divide. They are easily scaled from FS-391 [(B)(6)], which passes near their summits. The best approach begins in Montana. Take the Saltese, Montana, exit from I-90 and then follow the road that parallels the freeway west to Rainy Creek and FS-506. This road leads up to the Bitterroot divide and FS-391. Because the road passes by these summits, these peaks are suited to mountain bike approaches. USGS Saltese/Adair

Quarles Peak   *6,560+ feet (Class 1)*
Quarles Peak is found 2.5 miles south of Crittenden Peak. An old jeep road leads to the summit of this long narrow peak from FS-391 [(B)(6)]. There is a lookout site on the Idaho side of the border. Consider making this ascent on a mountain bike. USGS Adair

Ward Peak   *7,312 feet (Class 2)*
Ward Peak is the northernmost Bitterroot peak, more than 7,000 feet in height. It is a former fire lookout site and was named for George Ward, who mined in the area in the late 1800s. The summit is easily reached from FS-391, which crosses the peak's southern slopes. From FS-391, FST-250 leaves the road south of the peak [(B)(6)(a)]. Hike the trail

northwest to the border and then climb the west slope from the trail. If you prefer a longer hike, approach the peak from Montana and climb to the summit from Hub Lake. USGS McGee Peak

Eagle Cliff   7,543 feet (Class 2)

Eagle Cliff sits high above Cliff Lake, 11 miles southwest of Saint Regis, Montana. FST-738 follows the border in this area and passes along the peak's western slopes [(B)(7)(a)]. The summit is a short scramble from the trail at almost any point along the western slopes. USGS Torino Peak

Binocular Peak   7,266 feet (Class 2)

Binocular Peak is the large, impressive peak with a treeless summit that is 2.5 miles south of Eagle Cliff. Binocular's north face drops almost 900 feet to Heart Lake in less than 0.25 mile. The peak is accessed from FST-738 [(B)(7)(a)]. This trail traverses around the peak by swinging south around its southern slopes. Climb the peak from the point where the trail crosses the 6,800-foot contour line on the USGS map. USGS Sherlock Peak

Illinois Peak   7,690 feet (Class 1)
Graves Peak   7,200 feet (Class 2)

The Saint Joe River begins in a scenic alpine cirque nestled in the western slopes of these peaks. Both peaks are climbed from Saint Joe Lake via FST-49 [(B)(8)(a)]. The trail leaves the north side of the lake and climbs to the divide above, where it meets FST-738 [(B)(7)(a)], which follows the border from north to south. From this point, the trail crosses over the top of Illinois Peak, and then drops down the peak's east ridge into Montana. To climb Graves Peak, follow FST-738 south from its junction with FST-49 to the peak's west ridge and then climb the ridge to the summit. USGS Illinois Peak

Admiral Peak   7,323 feet (Class 2)

Admiral Peak is at the head of South Fork Kelly Creek, 2 miles east of Fish Lake. Fish Lake can be reached via Lake Creek

Binocular Peak (Photo by Sheldon Bluestein)

and FST-419/FST-478 [(C)(1.1)(b)] or FST-478 [(C)(2)(a)] or via the State Divide Trail, FST-738 [(C)(1)(a)]. The summit is climbed from FST-738 [(B)(7)(a)] by following the trail east from Fish Lake to its highest point on the peak's southeast ridge. Leave the trail at this point and follow the ridge to the summit. USGS Schley Mountain

Shale Mountain   *7,612 feet (Class 3)*
This is one of the more rugged peaks in the area. Climb it from the point where FST-508 [(C)(3)(a)] crosses the Bitterroot divide at Cache Saddle and leads into Montana. The saddle can be accessed from FS-581 via FST-508 or from Granite Pass via FST-46 [(C)(5)(a)]. Leave the trail at the divide and follow the ridgeline north to the summit in 1 mile. USGS Rhodes Peak

Rhodes Peak   *7,930 feet (Class 2)*
Rhodes Peak sits 3 miles south of Shale Mountain. The peak sits on a subsidiary ridge south of the Idaho/Montana border. Climb the peak from FST-508, which passes along its western slopes [(C)(3)(a)]. (See the directions for Williams Peak below.) USGS Rhodes Peak

Granite Peak   *7,551 feet (Class 2)*
Although this is the second Bitterroot peak to bear this name, there is little danger of confusing the two peaks since they are separated by many miles. This Granite Peak sits 3.5 miles directly east of Shale Mountain. The summit is reached by climbing either the peak's western or northern ridge from FST-46 [(C)(5)(a)]. USGS Granite Pass

WILLIAMS RANGE

The Williams Range, located south of Rhodes Peak and west of Lolo Pass, is a subrange of the Bitterroot Range. This range is composed of a major subsidiary ridge that runs south from the main Bitterroot Crest for 9 miles and has a width of 4 miles. Williams Peak, 7,501 feet, is the highest peak in the range.

Williams Peak   *7,705 feet (Class 1-2)*
The highest point in the Williams subrange is found high above Williams and Goat Lakes. To reach the summit of this peak, follow FST-248 [(C)(3)(a)] up Silver Creek to where it joins FST-508, which leads to Goat Lake. From the lake, follow the trail eastward toward the summit. Although the top is only a short scramble from the trail, the trail is difficult to follow in places and physically demanding. USGS Cayuse Junction

LOLO PASS TO NEZ PERCE PASS

Between Lolo Pass and Nez Perce Pass is the highest, wildest, and most rugged stretch of the Bitterroots. While the highest peaks sit east of the main crest, the peaks on the border are also impressive and admirable goals for climbers. Most of this section sits within the SBW. Primary access to this portion of the crest is via US-12, US-93, and FS-468, the Old Nez Perce Trail Road.

Old Stormy   *8,203 feet (Class 2)*
Old Stormy is located south of US-12 and Lolo Pass and just west of Stormy Pass in the Selway-Bitterroot Wilderness Area. The peak is easily climbed from FST-307 [(D)(1)(a)] at Stormy Pass via its east ridge. USGS Ranger Peak/SBW

Ranger Peak   *8,817 feet (Class 3)*
Ranger Peak sits 1 mile due west of Old Stormy. Although the peak can be climbed from the Idaho side of the border, approach considerations dictate that the easiest route to the summit is from the Big Creek Lakes on the Montana side of the border. Follow FST-11 [(D)(1)(a)] around the largest Big Creek Lake to its west side and the first inlet stream. Follow this stream up to the high basin on the peak's southeast slopes. From the basin, climb to Ranger Peak's south ridgeline and then follow the ridge to the summit. USGS Ranger Peak/SBW

Sky Pilot Peak   *8,792 feet (Class 3)*
Sky Pilot Peak is located 4.5 miles south of Old Stormy, at the head of the North Fork Bear Creek. The peak is best reached from the Montana side of the border by hiking up FST-5 [(D)(2)(a)] to Bear Creek Pass. (Note: this trail is designated FST-43 on the Idaho side of the border.) From the pass, follow the ridgeline east to the summit. USGS Cash Point/SBW

Hidden Peak   *7,826 feet (Class 1)*
Hidden Peak is a pyramid-shaped summit 6 miles southwest of Sky Pilot Peak and just west of the Bitterroot Crest. Its summit is home to a fire lookout and offers great views of this rugged and remote area. Take FST-10 [(D)(6)(c)] to the summit.

Frog Peak   *8,078 feet (Class 2)*
Frog Peak sits west of the main Bitterroot Crest on a subsidiary ridge that runs south from Hidden Peak, which is 1.9 miles to the north. Climb to the summit from FST-906 [(D)(6)(b)]. From Frog Lake, the trail climbs up the peak's south ridge and then cuts across the west face to the north ridge. Hike either ridge to the summit. The peak also can be climbed from Hidden Peak via FST-10 [(D)(6)(c)], although this route

is not maintained between the peaks and is in poor condition. USGS Blodgett Mountain/SBW

Shattuck Mountain   *8,459 feet (Class 3)*
Shattuck Mountain sits 0.9 mile north of Blodgett Mountain and the border near Blodgett Pass. Direct access to the summit from Blodgett Pass is blocked by cliffs. Descend Blodgett's west ridge until it is possible to cross Blodgett's west face to the base of Shattuck Mountain. Climb to the summit via its southwest slopes. Although the only reported route began on the summit of Blodgett Mountain, there are undoubtedly other ways to approach this seldom-climbed summit. USGS Blodgett Mountain/SBW

Blodgett Mountain   *8,647 feet (Class 3)*
Blodgett Mountain was named after Joseph Blodgett, who was an early packer in the Bitterroot valley. The peak is located 15 miles due west of Hamilton, Montana, and sits directly on the Idaho/Montana border. Climb the east ridge

from Blodgett Pass [(D)(3)(a)] until it is blocked by steeper terrain. Move onto the south side of the ridge at roughly 7,800 feet and traverse over to the peak's south ridge. Follow the west side of the south ridge to the summit. USGS Blodgett Mountain/SBW

Saddle Mountain   *8,258 feet (Class 2)*
Twin-summited Saddle Mountain is located west of the main divide, near Twin Lakes. To reach the summit, follow FST-430 [(D)(4)(a)] west from the Twin Lakes trailhead to the divide at Wahoo Pass in about 1 mile. Leave the trail and climb due north to the ridge top west of Lost Horse Pass. At this point, the ridge forks. Take the western fork and follow the ridge for 2.25 miles to Saddle Mountain's summit. USGS Saddle Mountain/SBW

Hunter Peak   *8,472 feet (Class 2-3)*
Hunter Peak is a triangular summit located 1 mile west of the crest near Bell Lake. To reach this isolated summit, start

The Bitterroot peaks above Big Flat Creek (Photo by Sheldon Bluestein)

in Montana at Lake Como and hike west on FST-580 [(D)(5)(a)] to the border. From the border, descend FST-522, past Bell Lake to the first stream crossing. Turn south and follow this stream to the ridge top above. Once on the ridge, turn west and follow the ridge to the summit. USGS Hunter Peak/SBW

Mount Paloma   *8,371 feet (Class 2)*
Mount Paloma is located west of the Idaho/Montana border on a major subsidiary ridge that runs from the border to the Selway River at Elevator Mountain in 17 long miles. Paloma is the highest point along this ridge. To reach the summit, take FST-24 [(E)(1.4)(a)] up White Cap Creek from Paradise GS to FST-717 [(E)(1.4)(b)], which leads to Cedar Saddle, Mount George, and Mount Paloma. This is a long, mostly dry hike along ridgelines. The trail deteriorates after Cedar Saddle. Keep on the ridgeline. Please note that the quadrangle does not display the present-day trail system. The cirques below the peak offer good overnight destinations. USGS Mount Paloma/SBW

Mount George   *7,714 feet (Class 1)*
Named after Ben George, a trapper and Forest Service employee, this peak is located 3.5 miles south of Mount Paloma. Follow the route described for Mount Paloma above. USGS Mount George/SBW

Nipple Knob   *8,505 feet (Class 3)*
Peak 8479   *8,479 feet (Class 3)*
Peak 8524   *8,524 feet (Class 3)*
These peaks are northeast of Mount Paloma and are part of the same rugged subsidiary ridge. They are among Idaho's least known and most remote summits. Climbing these three wilderness peaks is an accomplishment that few have even attempted. There are no maintained trails within a reasonable

The Bitterroot Crest at the head of White Cap Creek (Photo by Sheldon Bluestein)

distance of these peaks and you must approach via a climb of Mount Paloma. Nipple Knob's north face drops almost 900 vertical feet from the summit and Peak 8479's west face drops 400 vertical feet. Conical-shaped Peak 8524 has a vertical 200-foot north face. From Mount Paloma, follow the ridgeline northeast to Point 8340 and then follow the connecting ridge east to Peak 8524's summit.

To continue to Nipple Knob and Peak 8479, descend Point 8340's north ridge until it is possible to drop off the ridge to the east and descend to Brushy Fork Lake. (While I have heard rumors that horse packers have made a trail up Brushy Fork Creek, no one has verified this fact.) From the lake, climb to the saddle between Nipple Knob and Peak 8479 and climb via the connecting ridge. USGS Mount Paloma/SBW

Vance Mountain   *8,793 feet (Class 2)*
Vance Mountain is a high vantage point named for James Vance, a Forest Service ranger. The peak is located west of the border near White Cap Lakes. Climb this peak via its northwest ridge, which is reachable from either FST-45 or FST-46 [(E)(1.4)(c)]. USGS Tin Cup Lake/SBW

Bare Peak   *9,439 feet (Class 2-3)*
Bare Peak, the highest point in the Idaho section of the Bitterroot Mountains, sits directly on the border. Its northwest to southeast-trending summit ridge extends into Montana. The USGS has attached the name to the peak's lower eastern summit that sits completely in Montana. Bare has a picturesque north face that rises above Canyon Lake, 0.6 mile to the northwest. The summit can be climbed from the southwest via Soda Springs Creek, which is traversed by FST-250 [(E)(1.2)(a)]. The peak also can be approached from Boulder Lake to the north via FST-617 [(E)(1.1)(a)]. Although a route up the peak's northern slopes looks feasible, no one has reported climbing the peak from this direction. USGS Mount Jerusalem

Watchtower Peak   *8,790 feet (Class 3)*
Watchtower Peak is located 8 miles north of Nez Perce Pass and is the last major summit within the SBW along the Bitterroot divide. The peak is climbed via its southeast ridge, which is reached from FST-699 [(E)(1.3)(a)]. USGS Watchtower Peak/SBW

Nez Perce Peak   *7,531 feet (Class 1)*
Nez Perce Peak is located 2.5 miles east of the Idaho/Montana border and Nez Perce Pass. The summit is crossed by FST-13. To climb to the summit start on Nez Perce Pass and either

follow FST-16 to FST-13 [(E)(1)(a)] or take FST-14 from the Old Nez Perce Trail to FST-13 [(E)(1)(b)]. USGS Nez Perce Peak

NEZ PERCE PASS TO LOST TRAIL PASS

This stretch of the divide runs south from Nez Perce Pass, turns to the southeast, then climbs northeast and eventually ends at Lost Trail Pass and US-93. This seldom-visited stretch of the Bitterroot Crest is paralleled by road and trails and is highly recommended. From Lost Trail Pass the State Divide Trail runs south and west for more than 30 miles to the Spring Creek Road. The next 16 miles of crest are traversed by Forest Service roads that lead to the eastern edge of the RNRW. From the end of the road, it is possible to continue again by trail north toward Nez Perce Pass.

Steep Hill   *7,977 (Class 2)*
This is the first named summit south of Nez Perce Pass. The State Divide Trail [(E)(1)(a)] leads south to the west side of the peak in about 4 miles. Follow the crest from the trail south to the summit. USGS Blue Joint

Blue Joint   *8,597 (Class 2)*
Blue Joint sits just west of the Bitterroot Crest at the point where the boundary begins its northern run to Nez Perce Pass and eastern run to Lost Trail Pass. Follow the State Divide Trail [(F)(4.1)(b)] west to its junction with the Blue Joint Trail. Take the Blue Joint Trail west to Blue Joint. USGS Blue Joint

Allen Mountain   *9,154 feet (Class 3)*
Allen Mountain is located 8.5 miles southwest of Lost Trail Pass and just east of the main crest. While the recommended route starts at Twin Creek CG [(F)(2)(a)] along US-93, there are many alternatives. See [(F)(1)(a) and (F)(3)(a)]. USGS Allen Mountain

Rocky Mountain   *8,690 (Class 3)*
This peak sits 1.5 miles southeast of Allen Mountain. Climb Rocky Mountain in conjunction with an ascent of Allen Mountain. USGS Allen Mountain

APPROACHES TO THE BITTERROOT MOUNTAINS

As expected for a mountain range that runs almost 175 miles from north to south, there are many approach points to the range's many valleys. The vast majority of Bitterroot vehicular access points begin on the Montana side of the border, because much of the Idaho side is contained within the Selway-Bitterroot Wilderness. The approaches are divided into four sections and are listed from north to south.

(A) ID-200 SOUTH TO LOOKOUT PASS/I-90

The northernmost stretch of the Bitterroots is served by two major east/west highways: ID-200, which runs between Sandpoint, Idaho, and Noxon, Montana, in the north; and I-90, which stretches between Wallace, Idaho, and Missoula, Montana, in the south.

(1) FS-278, Pend Oreille Shore Road. Access this road at Clark Fork, Idaho, which is 26 miles east of the junction of ID-200 and US-2/US-95. From ID-200, turn south at the National Forest access sign, cross the Clark Fork bridge and follow the river west several miles before it swings south and climbs up into the mountains. This road parallels the entire east shore of Lake Pend Oreille before connecting with FS-209, far to the south.

(a) FST-610, Minerva Ridge Trail. This trail is accessed from FS-278. To reach the trailhead, turn off FS-278 onto the Fall Creek Road and drive up Fall Creek Road for 0.1 mile, and then turn left (northeast) onto a rough road. The trailhead is 0.25 mile ahead. The trail quickly climbs to the top of Minerva Ridge and follows the ridgeline up to the base of Packsaddle Mountain in 7 miles.

(2) FS-332, Pend Oreille Divide Road. This road is reached from FS-278 [(A)(1)] by taking FS-1060 across Monarch Ridge. This road, like FS-278, parallels the east shore of Lake Pend Oreille, but, unlike FS-278, its route is near the top of the mountains. From its junction with FS-1060, the road runs east and then southeast to the Idaho/Montana border. Although this road is narrow and steep in places, in good weather it is generally passable to autos. However, the eastern end of the road is primitive and a 4WD could be required.

(a) FS-611, Packsaddle Mountain Trail. This trail begins in the saddle southeast of the summit of Packsaddle Mountain and climbs to that peak's summit in 2 miles, gaining 1,900 feet in elevation.

(3) FS-430, State Divide Road. This road begins where FS-332 ends at the Idaho/Montana border and follows the border south. It runs on or near the crest for many miles, providing access to many summits. Check with the Forest Service for current driving conditions before using this road.

(4) Coeur d'Alene River Road. This road is accessed from the Kingston exit on I-90. The road follows the meandering river east and north.

(4.1) FS-152, East Fork Eagle Creek Road. This road is accessed from the Coeur d'Alene River Road at Prichard. From Prichard, drive east for 2.6 miles to Eagle Creek, turn north up Eagle Creek, and then, after 1.3 miles, turn east.

(a) FST-148, Casper Creek Trail. FST-148 leaves FS-152 at a signed trailhead and climbs up Casper Creek in just over 2 steep miles, where it joins FST-7.

(b) FST-7, State Divide Trail. At one time, this trail followed the Bitterroot Crest along the Idaho/Montana border for much of its distance. Currently, much of the trail has been replaced by roads (such as FS-430). The trail between Bloom Peak and Black Peak remains long and unbroken, however, and can be accessed from FST-148.

(4.2) FS-151/FS-412, Shoshone Creek Road. This road leaves the Coeur d'Alene River Road at the Shoshone Creek GS and follows Shoshone Creek north for roughly 17 miles to Hemlock Creek and FS-992. From Hemlock Creek, the road makes a half circle to the west, where it again joins the Coeur d'Alene River Road. Many logging roads of varying quality climb up into the Bitterroot and Shoshone Ranges from this road.

(4.2.1) Hemlock Creek Road. This road leaves FS-412 and climbs up Hemlock Creek to the Shoshone Range divide. Once on the divide, the road runs south along the crest to Pond Peak and FST-81. This is a rough road and a 4WD is recommended.

(a) FST-81, Shoshone Crest Trail. See [(A)(4.3)(a)], below.

(4.3) FS-502, Shoshone Crest Road. This road leaves the Coeur d'Alene River Road near the Shoshone Creek GS and climbs 10 miles up a ridge (passing several side roads along the way) to a point on the crest of the Shoshone Range below Downey Peak. From this point, the road continues to Little Guard Peak; this section is closed to motorized vehicles.

(a) FST-81, Shoshone Crest Trail. This trail leaves FS-502 and runs north along the Shoshone Range Crest to Pond Peak and FS-992 in just over 3 miles, crossing over Bennett, Little Sentinel, and Sentinel Peaks along the way.

(5) FST-456 and FS-261.1, Sunset Peak Road. These two roads lead from Wallace to the summit of Sunset Peak. It is roughly 8 miles to the summit.

(a) FST-137, Granite Peak Trail. This trail follows the ridgeline eastward for 3.5 miles from Sunset Peak to Granite Peak.

(B) LOOKOUT PASS SOUTH TO HOODOO PASS

Primary access to this section of the Bitterroots is provided by I-90 and many secondary and Forest Service roads. Most of the Bitterroot divide between Lookout and Hoodoo Passes is roaded.

(1) Lookout Ski Area Road. Access this road from the Lookout Pass exit on I-90. The road runs a short distance to the south to the Lookout Pass Ski Area.

(2) Willow Creek Road. This road leaves I-90 at the east end of Mullan and follows Willow Creek south for 1.3 miles. This is the primary approach road for the Stevens Peak Alpine Lakes Area.

(a) **FST-165, Stevens Lake Trail.** FST-165 leaves the Willow Creek Road and runs 1.1 miles to Stevens Lake at the base of Stevens Peak.

(3) **Boulder Creek Road.** This road is accessed from Mullan by following Boulder Creek south from town for less than 1 mile to the national forest boundary.

(a) **FST-128, Boulder Creek Trail.** FST-128 begins at the end of the Boulder Creek Road. The poorly maintained trail climbs 2.75 miles up Boulder Creek to the ridgeline above, where it joins the ridge trail that leads due east to the Stevens Peak area and FS-278.

(4) **Saint Joe River Road.** This road leaves ID-3 on the west edge of Saint Maries and stretches east and then south for 74 miles to Red Ives. It also can be accessed from Montana and I-90 as described in [(B)(5)], below. The road is paved from Saint Maries to Marble Creek, just west of Avery.

(5) **FS-456/FS-388, Rolland Summit Road.** This road connects I-90 with the Saint Joe River Road. It is accessed from I-90 1 mile west of Saint Regis, Montana. From the I-90 exit, drive south up the North Fork Little Joe Creek to Rolland Summit in 12.8 miles, then descend to the Saint Joe River Road. The road is gravel for much of its distance and is suitable for passenger autos during good weather.

(6) **FS-391, State Divide Road.** FS-391 begins on Rolland Summit and follows the Bitterroot Crest and the Idaho/Montana border south for more than 40 miles to a point south of Little Joe Mountain. This primitive road can be accessed from many points on both sides of the border.

(a) **FST-250, Eagle Peak Trail.** This trail leaves FS-391 directly south of Ward Peak and runs due north across the border and into Montana in 0.5 mile. From the border, the trail traverses Eagle Peak and Gold Peak before joining FS-3816 near Up Up Mountain.

(7) **FS-389, East Fork Gold Creek Road.** This road leaves FS-388 1.75 miles east of the Saint Joe River Road and climbs to the Bitterroot divide in 14.6 miles.

(a) **FST-738, State Divide Trail.** This section of the State Divide Trail is one of Idaho's least known and most outstanding trails. It begins south of Little Joe Mountain and follows the Bitterroot Crest south for more than 20 miles to Hoodoo Pass.

(8) **FS-320, Red Ives Creek Road.** This road leaves the Saint Joe River Road just south of Red Ives GS, and then climbs up to Simmons Ridge and a junction with FS-346. From this point, the road drops down to the upper reaches of the Saint Joe River. A 4WD is recommended.

(a) **FST-49, Saint Joe Lake Trail.** This trail follows the Saint Joe River 5 miles to Saint Joe Lake. From the lake, the trail climbs up and joins FST-738 [(B)(7)(a)] just below Illinois Peak.

Access the trail from FS-320 16 miles east of the Red Ives GS.

(9) **FS-346, Simmons Ridge Road.** This road leaves FS-320 9.3 miles from the Red Ives GS and follows the ridgeline to the north. A 4WD is recommended.

(a) **FST-74, Heller Ridge Trail.** FST-74 leaves FS-346 0.5 mile north of its junction with FS-320 [(B)(8)(a)] and runs to FST-738, the State Divide Trail, between Eagle Cliff and Binocular Peak.

(b) **FST-78, Simmons Ridge Trail.** FST-78 leaves FS-346 and proceeds northwest past Simmons Peak to Midget Peak before eventually descending to the Saint Joe River.

(10) **FS-715/FS-720, Saint Joe/North Fork Road.** This road connects the Saint Joe River drainage with the North Fork Clearwater drainage. It is accessed from FS-320 [(B)(8)] roughly 3.25 miles south of Heller Creek CG and runs south to join FS-250 [(C)(1)] in 24 miles. Although this is a good gravel road, it is about the longest and slowest 24 miles you will ever drive.

(C) HOODOO PASS SOUTH TO LOLO PASS

The primary approach to this section is provided by FS-250, which crosses the Bitterroot divide at Hoodoo Pass as it runs between Pierce, Idaho, and Superior, Montana.

(1) **FS-250, North Fork Clearwater River Road.** This road begins at Pierce, Idaho, and then runs east along French Creek and Orogrande Creek until it eventually meets the North Fork Clearwater River. Once it meets the river, the road follows the river east to the confluence of the North Fork and Kelly Creek. (The right-hand fork, FS-255 [(C)(2)], is discussed below.) From this junction, FS-250 continues up the North Fork Clearwater River through Black Canyon to Hoodoo Pass. Many people prefer to take the longer FS-255, because it is a better road. From Hoodoo Pass, the road continues to Superior, Montana.

(a) **FST-738/FST-46, State Divide Trail.** From Hoodoo Pass, this most pristine section of the State Divide Trail runs south for more than 40 miles to Kelly Creek Saddle (above the Middle Fork Kelly Creek), following the Bitterroot divide as it forms the Idaho/Montana border. Further south at Cache Saddle, the State Divide Trail continues as FST-46 and proceeds along the crest to Granite Pass. (See [(C)(5)(a)], below.) Many feeder trails provide access to this trail from both the Montana and Idaho sides of the border.

(1.1) **FS-295, Lake Creek Road.** This road leaves FS-250 roughly 10 miles south of Hoodoo Pass and follows Lake Creek east until it forks in about 4 miles. The road forks with the left fork, designated FS-5440, leading up Goose Creek for 1 mile to where it is gated shut. The right fork continues along Lake Creek for another mile to where it, too, is gated shut.

(a) **FST-414, Goose Lake Trail.** From the gate on the Goose Creek Road at 4,200 feet, follow the road for almost 0.5 mile to the trailhead. It is 4 miles and 1,500 feet up Goose Creek to Goose Lake and the State Divide Trail [(C)(1)(a)].

(b) FST-419/FST-478, Fish Lake Trail. From the gate on FS-295 at 4,400 feet, continue along Lake Creek on the closed road, which soon turns into a trail. It is roughly 5 miles and 1,600 feet to Fish Lake and the State Divide Trail [(C)(1)(a)]. This trail is open to ORV use.

(2) FS-255, Kelly Creek/Moose Road. This road leaves FS-250 and the North Fork Clearwater River and follows Kelly Creek north to the Kelly Creek GS, where Moose Creek flows into Kelly Creek. At this point, the road turns up Moose Creek toward Moose and eventually rejoins FS-250 north of Deception Saddle.

(a) FST-478, Pollock Hill Trail. This trail leaves FS-255 roughly 2 miles north of the Kelly Creek GS at 3,400 feet. The trail quickly forks twice—keep to the right at both junctions. After the trail leaves Swamp Creek, it climbs steeply up to the top of Pollock Hill and follows the ridge for 8 long miles to the northern slopes of Wapito Peak. After climbing 2,600 feet, the trail bypasses the peak and drops down to Fish Lake in another 2 miles where it connects with FST-478 [(C)(1.1)(b)] and the State Divide Trail [(C)(1)(a)].

(b) FST-567, Kelly Creek Trail. This trail is accessed just east of the Kelly Creek GS, where FS-581 crosses Kelly Creek. Kelly Creek, a large drainage, is still in a wilderness condition and could be included in the proposed Big Burn Wilderness. This well-maintained trail follows Kelly Creek for 10 miles with a 600-foot elevation gain to a point past Hanson Meadows, where it quickly divides into three trails, two of which are listed below.

(b.1) FST-493, North Fork Kelly Creek Trail. This trail continues for another 9 miles up Kelly Creek and then the North Fork Kelly Creek, gaining 600 feet, to join with the State Divide Trail [(C)(1)(a)] between Fish Lake and Admiral Peak.

(b.2) FST-503, Middle Fork Kelly Creek Trail. This well-maintained trail leaves FST-493 and quickly climbs up the Middle Fork Kelly Creek to the State Divide Trail [(C)(1)(a)] in 5 miles, gaining 2,000 feet along the way.

(3) FS-581, Toboggan Ridge Road. This road leaves FS-255 just east of the Kelly Creek GS, crosses Kelly Creek, climbs the ridge to the south, and drops into the Cayuse Creek valley. The road crosses Cayuse Creek, then wiggles and worms its way east for many miles to FS-500, the Lewis and Clark Road. (See [(C)(4)], below.)

(a) FST-248/FST-508, Silver Creek/Williams Peak/Cache Saddle Trail. This route begins by leaving FS-581 1.5 miles north of Cayuse Junction, where FS-581 and FS-500 meet. The trail climbs up Silver Creek, which is open, on a poor but passable tread. After roughly 3.5 miles, the route intersects with FST-508. FST-508 quickly reaches Goat Lake, then swings around the

south side of Williams Peak and continues to Rhodes Peak. From Rhodes Peak to Cache Saddle, the trail disappears, but this 2.5-mile stretch crosses a high alpine landscape that is conducive to cross-country travel. At Cache Saddle, the route intersects with the State Divide Trail, FST-46 [(C)(5)(a)].

(4) FS-500, Lewis and Clark Road. FS-500 is designated as the route followed by Lewis and Clark. It parallels US-12, running from north to south, and can be accessed from most points that connect with US-12. The quickest way to use FS-500 for Bitterroot access is via FS-569, the Parachute Hill Road, located 72 miles east of Lowell on US-12. Turn north off US-12 and follow FS-569 2.5 miles to FS-500. Turn left and follow this good gravel road to Cayuse Junction and FS-581, which drops off the ridge and crosses Cayuse Creek.

(5) FS-595, Granite Pass Road. This road leaves US-12 at Lolo Pass and follows the divide north through Granite Pass. Two miles north of the pass, the road ends and FST-738/FST-46, the State Divide Trail, begins.

(a) FST-46, State Divide Trail. The southernmost portion of the State Divide Trail is accessed from Granite Pass by taking the gravel road that leads from the pass north along the border. Follow the road for about 1 mile until it drops off the ridge to the east. At this point, the trail continues along the ridgeline toward Rocky Peak and Cache Saddle, where it intersects with FST-508 [(C)(3)(a)].

(D) LOLO PASS SOUTH TO NEZ PERCE PASS

Primary access to this section of the Bitterroots is via US-12 and US-93. US-12 crosses Lolo Pass as it runs between Lewiston, Idaho, and Lolo, Montana. US-93 runs along the eastern front of the Bitterroots between Lolo and Darby, Montana.

(1) FS-1321, Big Creek Road. Turn off US-93 1.5 miles north of Victor and follow the road to the Big Creek CG and trailhead.

(a) FST-11, Big Creek Trail. From FS-1321, it is roughly 9 miles to Big Creek Lake. From the lake, FST-11 continues along the western shore of the lake and south over Packbox Pass and into Idaho. FST-307/FST-99 also leaves the lake and travels due north to nearby Stormy Pass and then drops down into the south fork of Storm Creek on the Idaho side of the border. The Idaho portion of the trail is in poor condition.

(2) FS-737, Bear Creek Road. Take the paved road that leaves Victor heading west and follow the signs to Bear Creek CG and trailhead.

(a) FST-5, Bear Creek Pass Trail. From the trailhead, follow FST-5 for 10 miles northwest to Bear Creek Pass and the Idaho border. Once at the pass, the trail designation changes to FST-43 on the Idaho side. FST-43 descends to Garmet Creek then joins FST-50, which follows White Sandy Creek north and south. FST-50 can be followed south to reach the Frog Peak Trail, FST-906 [(D)(6)(b)] or north over Packbox Pass to Big Creek Lake and FST-11 [(D)(1)(a)].

(3) **Blodgett Creek Road.** This road leaves US-93 at Hamilton and proceeds west to Blodgett Canyon CG and the Blodgett Pass Trail.

(a) **FST-19, Blodgett Pass Trail.** This trail leads over Blodgett Pass and into Idaho in 14 miles. At the divide, the trail climbs steeply to the pass on a series of switchbacks and then drops north into Idaho and Big Sand Creek, where it is designated FST-4. FST-4 then leads to FS-111, the Big Elk Road, in Idaho. (See [(D)(6)(a)], below.)

(4) **FS-429, Lost Horse Creek Road.** This road system penetrates the Bitterroot divide clear to its crest. Drive 3.6 miles north of Darby, turn west onto FS-429, and follow it to where it splits. FS-5605 ends at Twin Lakes and FS-429 ends on the divide at Bear Creek Pass. Several peaks and high mountain lakes are accessible from the three trails that leave this road's trailheads.

(a) **FST-430, Wahoo Pass/Freeman Peak Trail.** This trail leaves Lost Horse Pass, crosses Wahoo Pass, and runs due west to the Moose GS on the Selway River. (See [(E)(3.1)(d)] in the Clearwater access section.)

(5) **FS-550, Lake Como Road.** Access this road from US-93 at a signed junction 6 miles north of Darby, Montana. The signed road quickly leads to Lake Como, which has trailheads on both sides of its dam.

(a) **FST-580/FST-522, Elk Lake Trail.** This trail leaves from the south side of the Lake Como dam and runs directly west up Rock Creek to Elk Lake, crosses the Idaho/Montana border, and descends into Idaho to reach Bell Lake in about 16.5 miles. West of Bell Lake, the trail is poorly maintained and difficult to follow in places.

(6) **FS-111, Elk Summit Road.** This is one of the few western vehicular approach points on the Idaho side of the Bitterroots in the SBW Area. Access the road at Powell on US-12 and follow it north to the Elk Summit GS trailhead for FST-4.

(a) **FST-4, Big Sand Lake Area Trails.** This trail system begins at the Elk Summit GS and covers the area east of the GS. FST-4 proceeds due east to Big Sand Creek in 4 miles and then continues to Big Sand Lake in another 4 miles. One mile from the trailhead, FST-18 forks off and climbs to Diablo Mountain. FST-18 was reconstructed in 1995 and is in good shape. From Big Sand Lake, FST-4 continues to the east and arrives at Blodgett Pass in 3 more miles. FST-906 is accessed at Big Sand Lake.

(b) **FST-906, Frog Peak Trail.** This trail leaves FST-4 at Big Sand Lake and proceeds up a ridgeline to the northeast. Once up the ridge, the trail drops into the Frog Lake Basin and then

climbs again, this time to Frog Lake, which is just 1 mile north of Big Sand Lake. This trail is brushy, rutted, rocky, and steep. It crosses a divide just south of Frog Lake and then descends steeply to the lake. Beyond the lake, the trail deteriorates as it leads to Frog Peak and then Hidden Peak.

(c) **FST-10, Hidden Lake Trail.** Access this trail from FST-4 [(D)(6)(a)] where it meets Big Sand Creek. Ford Big Sand Creek (difficult in high water) and follow FST-1 south to a junction with FST-10 in 0.75 mile. Go right on FST-10, which climbs to a ridge top and Hidden Peak lookout. This trail is in fair condition. Although the map shows the route continuing to Frog Lake, the Forest Service does not maintain the section beyond the lookout.

(E) NEZ PERCE PASS AREA ACCESS

Primary access to this section of the Bitterroots is provided by FS-468, the Old Nez Perce Trail Road, and US-93.

(1) **FS-468, Old Nez Perce Trail Road.** This road leaves US-93 7 miles south of Darby, Montana, and crosses Nez Perce Pass at 6,587 feet. The road eventually traverses the entire state of Idaho, cutting between the Selway-Bitterroot and River of No Return Wilderness Areas. (See the approach section for the Clearwater Mountains for additional information on trails accessible from this road.)

(a) **FST-16, Indian Hill Trail.** This trail leaves FS-468 at Nez Perce Pass and follows the Bitterroot divide both north and south. The northern section of the trail ends at a pass on the western slopes of Indian Hill 9 miles from Nez Perce Pass. Several trails fork off from here, including FST-35, which follows a ridgeline west to Cayuse and Beaver Jack Mountains (both are Clearwater peaks), and FST-14, discussed below.

(a.1) **FST-14, Nez Perce Peak Trail.** This trail runs north between FS-468 and FST-16 over Nez Perce Peak for a distance of approximately 6.5 miles. From FST-16, access this trail 3 miles northwest of Nez Perce Pass; from FS-468, access the trail just west of Schumaker Creek.

(b) **FST-16, State Divide Trail South.** This trail runs south along the Bitterroot Crest from Nez Perce Pass. The trail is in good condition.

(1.1) **Boulder Creek.** Turn off FS-468 just east of the West Fork GS and drive 1 mile to Boulder Creek Campground and trailhead.

(a) **FST-617, Boulder Creek Trail.** This trail leads from the end of the Boulder Creek Road into a remote section of Idaho near Vance Mountain. It reaches the Idaho/Montana border in 10.5 miles. The trail is deeply rutted in places, but also well-marked and easy to follow. From a small pond just east of the border, FST-249 leads south to Boulder Lake in about 1 mile.

(1.2) FST-5635, Soda Springs Creek Road. FST-5635 leaves FS-468 5 miles west of the West Fork GS. Follow FS-5635 north to the trailhead in a little more than 1 mile.

(a) FST-250, Soda Springs Creek Trail. This trail leaves the FS-5635 trailhead and follows the creek up its drainage for 7 miles to a small unnamed lake at the base of Bare Peak.

(1.3) Watchtower Creek Trailhead. The trailhead for FST-699 is accessed from FS-468 1.5 miles east of Fales Flat CG by turning north onto a short access road and driving a short distance to the road's end.

(a) FST-699, Watchtower Creek Trail. This trail runs up Watchtower Creek for 7.5 miles to a point on the border of the Bitterroot divide southwest of Watchtower Peak.

(1.4) FS-6223, Paradise Road. This road is the most important southern access point into the SBW Area. From Magruder GS on FS-468, FS-6223 runs 12 miles up a non-Wilderness peninsula to the Paradise GS in the heart of the Wilderness. Five major trails leave from the road's end, and three major trails leave the road between the two guard stations.

(a) FST-24, White Cap Creek Trail. FST-24 leaves the Paradise GS and follows White Cap Creek eastward to the Bitterroot divide in 26 miles.

(b) FST-717, Mount Paloma Trail. This trail is accessed from FST-24 3.75 miles east of the Paradise GS. The trail leaves White Cap Creek and immediately climbs a ridgeline that leads north to Cedar Saddle in 2.5 miles. From the saddle, the trail turns east, climbs almost to the summit of Mount George in another 1 mile and then again turns north and leads to Mount Paloma in 4 more miles. (Note that FST-711 also runs between White Cap Creek and Mount George. This trail leaves White Cap Creek 6 miles east of the Paradise GS and follows Barefoot Creek to Mount George in roughly 3 miles. The Forest Service no longer maintains this trail on a regular basis, and following it will be difficult in places.)

(c) FST-45/FST-46, Vance Mountain Trail. This loop trail leads from White Cap Creek to the cirque below the western slopes of Vance Mountain, then returns to White Cap Creek. Access FST-46 at Cooper Flat 7 miles east of the Paradise GS by crossing the bridge and heading southeast along Canyon Creek for a short distance to where the trail forks. Take the right-hand fork and follow the trail up the ridgeline that divides White Cap Creek and Canyon Creek. The trail runs east for about 7 miles to the base of Vance Mountain, where it joins FST-45. FST-45

descends along Fall Creek to White Cap Creek in 3 miles.

(F) NEZ PERCE PASS TO LOST TRAIL PASS ACCESS

The southernmost stretches of the Bitterroot Range are accessed from US-93 and the Salmon River Road.

(1) Lost Trail Pass/State Divide Trail Trailhead. From Lost Trail Pass CG follow FS-0181 west for a short distance to the trailhead.

(a) FST-106, State Divide Trail. From the trailhead, this follows the divide southwest for 30 miles to FS-038 [(F)(4.1)]. It is a premier route.

(2) Twin Creek CG Trailhead. Twin Creek CG is located roughly 6 miles north of Gibbonsville on US-93.

(a) FST-108, Twin Creek Trail. This trail leaves the CG and climbs to the State Divide Trail in 5.5 miles

(3) FS-091, Hughes Creek Roads. This road leads northwest from US-93 a little over 5 miles north of North Fork. From the highway the road leads up Hughes Creek and provides access to several other roads including FS-089 that leads to the top of Granite Mountain. To reach FST-113, stay on FS-091 when the road forks at Allen Creek. Continue on FS-091 until the road switchbacks and climbs out of Allen Creek. FST-113/FST-107 starts at this point.

(a) FST-113/FST-107, Ax Park Way/Allen Lake Access. These trails provide access to the State Divide Trail and Allen Lake on the slopes of Allen Mountain.

(4) Salmon River River Road. Salmon is located southeast of the Clearwater Mountains. Access the Salmon River Road from US-93 north of Salmon at North Fork.

(4.1) FS-038, Spring Creek Road. From North Fork, turn west off US-93 onto FS-030, the Salmon River Road, and drive 16.7 miles to the Spring Creek Road, FS-038. Drive north on this road for 19.1 miles to Horse Creek Pass on the Idaho/Montana border. FST-106 is accessible from here. The road is now designated as FS-044. Follow this road west from the pass for another 12.9 miles to the Reynolds Lake trailhead that is used to access FST-016. A 4WD is required.

(a) FST-106, State Divide Trail—East to Lost Trail Pass. From the trailhead, this trail follows the divide northeast to Lost Trail Pass in about 30 miles [(F)(1)].

(b) FST-16, State Divide Trail—North to Nez Perce Pass. From the end of FS-044, this trail leads west for about 2 miles along the divide to a junction with FST-016, which leads north to Nez Perce Pass.

WESTERN IDAHO

From the Salmon River South to the Snake River;

From the Oregon Border East to Idaho-75 and

US-93

1

THE WESTERN BORDER: THE CRAIG, SEVEN DEVILS, CUDDY, AND HITT MOUNTAINS

Idaho's western border between Ontario, Oregon, and Lewiston, Idaho, is formed by the Snake River. The eastern shore of the river quickly rises to lofty mountain ridges. These ridges have been identified by four geographic names from north to south: the Craig, Seven Devils, Cuddy, and Hitt Mountains. These ranges are geologically similar.

THE CRAIG MOUNTAINS

This small range is the northernmost of the border ranges. It is located west of Grangeville and separated from the Seven Devils Mountains by the Salmon River. The range extends north from the point where the Salmon and Snake Rivers join. The range is named after Colonel William Craig. This country is more akin to a high plateau than a mountain range and contains only five named peaks, the highest of which is Craig Mountain at 5,341 feet. Much of the range is in private ownership, with the public lands administered by the BLM. See [(A)(1)]. USGS Frye Point

THE SEVEN DEVILS MOUNTAINS

The Seven Devils Mountains extend along the Idaho/Oregon border for roughly 40 miles between the Idaho towns of Whitebird and Council and are bounded by the Snake River on the west and the Salmon and Little Salmon Rivers

The Elephant Perch: the Sawtooth batholith's boldest statement

95

on the east. The range, which ranks high among Idaho's mountain chains in terms of ruggedness and scenic quality, is the state's most precipitous range. Elevations vary from just above 1,000 feet along the Snake River to 9,393 feet on the summit of He Devil.

The range was formed by block faulting of the region's very complicated rock layers, which contain a little of everything, from oceanic sedimentary rocks to intrusive igneous rock and limestone, all within a short walking distance of each other. In the past, mining activity exploited the contact zones between the igneous and sedimentary rock; old digs can still be found, mostly at the lower elevations. While the Seven Devils block was uplifting, the Salmon River cut an immense trench on its eastern side, and the Snake River cut an even deeper canyon along the western side. Between the two river canyons, a high bench forms the Seven Devils high country. This crest runs north to south and is most pronounced on its east side, where all of the major peaks are found. The western slope of the range, while at first more moderate than the eastern side, descends rapidly into Hells Canyon of the Snake River. The effects of Pleistocene era glaciers are evident everywhere in the upper regions of the range, where there are dozens of prominent cirques and some thirty mountain lakes. From the central portion of the range, the Seven Devils crest loses elevation as it runs north and south.

In 1975, Congress established the Hells Canyon National Recreation Area, which includes territory in both Idaho and Washington. This pseudo national park encompasses most of the Seven Devils Mountains; 190,000 acres (including the entire high-peak area of the central range) are designated as the Hells Canyon Wilderness (HCW). The southern section of the range is managed by the Payette National Forest, and the eastern foothills are managed by the Nez Perce National Forest.

The range is readily accessible, with the most popular route beginning in Riggins, Idaho, allowing autos to drive above 8,000 feet at Windy Gap. While the southern and northern approach routes are more primitive, they offer quick access to the most important summits. Hiking and climbing opportunities are above average. Because of the large elevation differentials, the Seven Devils have the longest hiking season of any Idaho mountain range, with hiking along the Snake River beginning in early March. While the best-known trails are within the HCW, many excellent trails are found in the southern Seven Devils west of Council.

Because the peaks are conglomerations of hard and de-teriorated rock strata, shattered towers, massive talus slopes, and slanted rock bedding, climbing opportunities run the gamut from Class 1 hikes to Class 5 climbs. Seven Devils peaks have a deceptive quality that often puts route-finding abilities to the test. Ledges appear and end in the most unlikely places, and chimneys that look very prominent are often traps for the unwary. Climbing is a combination of slushing in talus, boulder-hopping, and climbing short, broken ledges. Technical climbing opportunities are limited by the loose rock that clutters every ledge, shelf, or ridge top. Using a rope for protection would, in most instances, invite rock fall that would more than likely destroy the rope or injure the climber.

THE CUDDY AND HITT MOUNTAINS

These two small mountain ranges are found north and west of US-93 as it runs between the Idaho towns of Weiser and Council. These ranges, which are physically connected, are a geological continuation of the Seven Devils Mountains terrain and share that range's complex geologic history. The Cuddy Mountains, the northernmost group, reach their highest point on 7,867-foot Cuddy Mountain. The Hitt Mountains, located just to the south, reach their highest point on 7,589-foot Sturgill Peak.

Both ranges are managed by the Payette National Forest through its Council Ranger District. The state of Idaho owns large sections of land within the national forest boundaries. Hiking and climbing opportunities are available, but seldom used. Climbing opportunities are limited to Class 1 and Class 2 walks.

SEVEN DEVILS PEAKS

Devils Tooth *7,760+ feet*
This imposing andesite spire is located north of Sheep Lake in the Sheep Creek drainage. Actually, there are two teeth (summits) separated by a narrow gap, the northernmost being the most formidable. Devils Tooth rises more than 200 vertical feet on three sides, with the south face measuring about 1,130 feet. The southernmost summit is easily reached from the south via a short pitch of Class 3 climbing. The northern and highest summit is a technical climb. The peak is reached from the Seven Devils Loop Trail [(A)(3)(a)] or from Sheep Lake, which can be accessed via [(A)(3)(a.1.2)] or cross-country from Windy Gap [(A)(3)(b)]. USGS He Devil/HCW

North Face Route (Class 5). The Devils Tooth is almost

The Devils Tooth as seen from the east

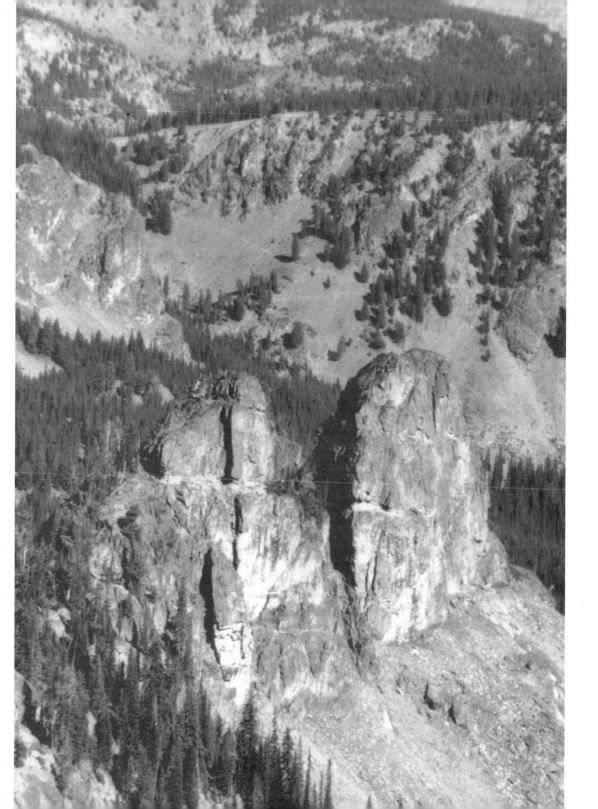

2,000 feet shorter than the neighboring peaks. However, what it lacks in altitude it makes up by the perpendicular nature of its walls. The first ascent was made in 1963 by D. Eastman and J. Angell. After circling the tower and exploring several alternatives, they attacked the north face, which they believed to be the "easy way" up. They eventually encountered smooth, hard andesite ranging from 65 degrees to overhanging, and reached the summit after five pitches and four terraces.

Tower of Babel   *9,269 feet*

This formidable peak is located 0.5 mile east of Sheep Lake. It is visible from Windy Gap, from which point it resembles the witch's castle in the *Wizard of Oz*. The first ascent was in June 1939 by A. H. Marshall. According to Marshall, the route followed ledges that "made a complete spiral to reach the top." This spiral ramp reminded him of a picture of the Tower of Babel he had seen as a child; hence the name. Marshall called the climb the "most interesting climb I had ever made, bar none." Access the peak from Sheep Lake [(A)(3)(a.1.2) or (A)(3)(b)]. USGS He Devil/HCW

The Marshall Ledges Route (Class 3). This route is not obvious. According to Marshall, the route begins at the southwest base of the peak, circles the peak (becoming steeper as it crosses the east face), and then climbs across a ledge to the north face, where it narrows, eventually reaching a rubble slope that leads to the summit. The Mazamas climbed the route in 1963 and described it as a broad 30-degree slope covered with loose rock on the lower sections and more solid rock above. According to the Mazamas, the route begins on the west face then curves onto the south face, crosses the south ridge, and moves onto the northeast face. From here, climb up on solid rock to a boulder field and continue to the top.

South Ridge (Class 3). This climb, a top-ten scramble, begins in the col between Mount Baal and She Devil. The col can be reached from Sheep Lake [(A)(3)(a.1.2) or (A)(3)(b)] or from Windy Saddle via the east side of the Seven Devils Loop Trail [(A)(3)(a)]. Between Mount Baal and the Tower of Babel, you will encounter four towers as you approach the summit. Pass the first two towers on the east and then drop down about 100 feet on the west side of the third and fourth towers. Cross

Tower of Babel from She Devil

the talus to what appears to be a dead-end corner. From this point, good ledges lead up a steep wall to the knife-edged notch above. Climb the boulder leaning against the north wall of the notch to reach the slanting slabs above. Follow the slabs up to and then under a large overhanging roof to the talus slopes above. Climb loose rock from here to the summit.

Mount Baal*   9,040+ feet (Class 2)
This peak, unnamed on the He Devil USGS quad, is located midway between She Devil and the Tower of Babel on the intervening ridge. A register in an old metal film container dates from 1960. The date of the first ascent is unknown. The peak strikes an imposing west face above Sheep Lake. The east and south slopes are easy scrambles and are accessed from Sheep Lake [(A)(3)(a.1.2) or (A)(3)(b)]. From Sheep Lake, climb the 1,200-foot scree gully that leads to the ridge between Mount Baal and She Devil, and then scramble up the south ridge to the summit. The west face is probably unclimbed. USGS He Devil/HCW

She Devil   9,280+ feet
She Devil is 0.6 mile southwest of the Tower of Babel. It was first climbed by A. H. Marshall in June 1940. Marshall named the peak Lucifer—he had already attached the name She Devil to a peak farther to the south, which the USGS later renamed Devils Throne. Many routes have been tried on this peak; the two most popular are described here. Access the peak from Sheep Lake [(A)(3)(a.1.2) or (A)(3)(b)]. USGS He Devil/HCW

Northeast Ridge Route (Class 2). This is the original route followed by Marshall. Climb from Sheep Lake to the saddle northeast of the peak and then follow the northeast ridge to the summit. Stay high up on the northwest side of the ridge. This is a long, but easy walk.

West Ridge (Class 3). This route climbs up from the She Devil/He Devil col. From the col, move up the south side of the west ridge to a large, talus-filled gully leading up to a point near the ridge crest where a number of rock walls of varying difficulty are encountered. Choose a route best suited to your ability around or over the walls and climb to the summit ridge, which you can follow to the top.

He Devil   9,393 feet
He Devil, the highest Seven Devils summit, sits due west of She Devil and southwest of Sheep Lake. A. H. Marshall reached the summit in June 1938. At the top, he found a piece of wood with the following names carved on it: B. Savage, C. Brown, H. Barton, and J. W. Ratcliff. There was no date. He Devil is an impressive dark tower with steep walls on all sides of its three summits. The north summit is the highest. Access the peak from FST-123 [(A)(3)(a.1.2)] or from Sheep Lake [(A)(3)(b)]. USGS He Devil/HCW

Northwest Ridge Route (Class 3). This ridge can be accessed from either He Devil Lake or Gem Lake, or from the saddle above Sheep Lake. From either the saddle or the lakes, follow the relatively gentle slopes up to the ridge top; from there, hike to the summit along the ridge, which splits the north and west faces of the peak. Although this route looks difficult from below, it is nothing more than a simple scramble.

East Ridge Route (Class 3). A more difficult route than the northwest ridge, this route leads up from the col between

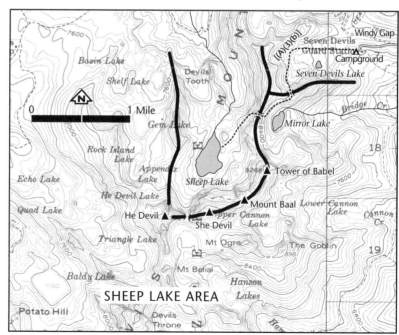

Sheep Lake area and cross-country route [(A)(3)(b)]

He Devil, viewed from Sheep Lake

peak three years later by its west ridge, he found no record of who made the first ascent and named the peak Mount Appollyon (a name that was not adopted by the USGS). The peak presents a massive 1,200-foot northeast face to tiny Upper Canyon Lake. The peak is accessed from the Boise Trail section of the Seven Devils Loop Trail [(A)(3)(a.3)] by hiking south from Windy Gap to either Cannon Creek (2 miles) or Hanson Creek (almost 4 miles) and then following one of these drainages to the base of the peak. USGS He Devil/HCW

West Ridge (Class 2). This ridge is accessed from the low saddle between Mount Ogre and She Devil. It is easily followed to the summit.

East Ridge (Class 3). From the saddle between the Ogre and the Goblin, the peak appears to be a series of unclimbable towers. The route from the saddle traverses out onto the center of the peak's south face into a small amphitheater filled with gullies and ledges. Take the southernmost (left) gully to the east ridge above. Follow the ridge back to the west over several small blocks.

North Face (Class 4). The first ascent was by the Mazamas. The route climbs the large central couloir and chimney system. The chimney is roofed by a chockstone. The route begins by climbing a series of steps to reach the west wall of the couloir. Then a Class 4 crack is climbed to a sloping ledge that runs under an overhanging wall. From here, the route leads to a triangular snowfield in the couloir one third of the way up the face. Look for a smooth V-shaped crack with a tree at the top. The Mazamas climbed toward the tree until the leader could escape the crack, moving out onto the face where he found a "sheltered cleft." From this point, several options lead to the top.

He Devil and She Devil. From the col, the route works across the ledges on the south side of the ridge to the base of the mountain. The route from here is somewhat obscure, but follows two connecting gullies to the summit. Take care on the very rotten talus that fills these gullies.

Southeast Face (Class 4). The first ascent was made by the Mazamas in 1963. Climb the lower scree slopes to the lowest point on the face. Climb the face to the summit. The Mazamas used pitons for protection.

Mount Ogre   9,200+ feet

Mount Ogre stands 0.5 mile southeast of She Devil, east of the main Seven Devils crest. When Marshall reached the summit of She Devil in 1940, he spotted a large cairn on the top of the then-unnamed Mount Ogre. When he finally climbed the

The Goblin   *8,981 feet (Class 2-3)*

The Ogre's companion is located due east of the Ogre on the same ridgeline. The Goblin was first climbed from the Boise Trail section of the Seven Devils Loop Trail via its eastern slopes by A. H. Marshall and Ed Hughes in August 1935. Marshall gave the peak its name, attempting to stay with the original devilish theme given to the range by local Native Americans. Views of the main crest to the west are spectacular. Although the peak may be approached from several directions, the recommended route to the summit is from Hanson Lake [(A)(3)(a.3)]. From the lake, climb southeast directly to the summit. USGS He Devil/HCW

Mount Belial   *8,880 feet (Class 2)*

Mount Belial is located midway between He Devil and the Devils Throne on the main Seven Devils crest. The first ascent

She Devil (left) and Mount Ogre, viewed from summit of He Devil

of this tri-summited peak probably belongs to A. H. Marshall, who in 1943 tentatively named the peak after Belial, a fallen rebel angel in Milton's *Paradise Lost*. The peak, while not imposing from a distance, possesses three very rugged summits and offers a multitude of mostly untested route possibilities. It is unknown whether the middle and north summits have been climbed.

Access the peak from either Hanson Creek in the east or via Triangle Lake in the west. Both approaches are accessed from the Seven Devils Loop Trail [(A)(3)(a)]. The south summit is the highest point, and is climbed via its southwest ridge (from the saddle between it and the Devils Throne), or via its east ridge. USGS He Devil/HCW

Painted Peak*   8,160+ feet (Class 3)

Painted Peak, unnamed on the He Devil USGS quad, is the crumbling summit on a subsidiary ridge 1 mile west of Mount Belial and directly south and above Triangle Lake. The first reported ascent was by the Mazamas, who climbed it in 1963. Access the peak from the Seven Devils Loop Trail and Baldy Lake [(A)(3)(a.2)]. USGS He Devil/HCW

Devils Throne   9,280+ feet

Relying on the advice of an old miner, A. H. Marshall climbed this peak in June 1938, believing it to be She Devil—which it may have been called in 1938 before the USGS published the "official" maps. The peak is located 1 mile due south of He Devil on the main crest and has an impressive summit buttressed by three ridges. Marshall climbed the west ridge and left a register on the summit. The current register was left by the Mazamas in 1963. The view down into Hells Canyon is excellent as are the views to the north and south. Access is from the Seven Devils Loop Trail and Baldy Lake in the west [(A)(3)(a.2)] or via the cirque on the peak's northeast side [(A)(3)(a.3)]. USGS He Devil/HCW

West Ridge (Class 3-4). The details of Marshall's original route are unknown. The ridge is a ragged conglomeration of towers and blocks, which will present some route-finding difficulties. It looks to be difficult Class 3 to 4 terrain.

Northeast Face (Class 4). This route follows a steep gully on the right side of the face. This gully runs 500 feet to the top of the north ridge. The Mazamas climbed the gully for 300 feet to where they discovered a second gully heading up to the left. The Mazamas took this gully to the summit. The first ascent was led by D. Eastman in 1963.

East Cirque/South Ridge Route (Class 3). This route begins in the cirque on the peak's east side. The cirque can be reached from FST-517 [(A)(3)(a)] or from Cannon Lake [(A)(3)(a.3.1)]. From the trail, hike directly west into the cirque over moderately difficult terrain. From Hanson Lakes, hike west into the upper cirque and then cross the saddle to the south on mostly Class 2 terrain. From the cirque, this route

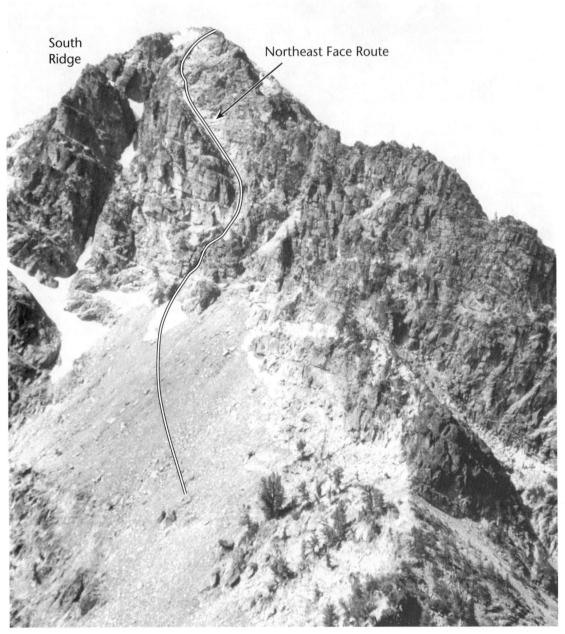

South
Ridge

Northeast Face Route

The Devils Throne, viewed from summit of Mount Belial

climbs due south to the top of the subsidiary ridge that runs east from the crest. Once on top of this ridge the broad ridge top leads east and then north to the summit.

Southwest Boulder Field/South Ridge (Class 3). This is the easiest route to the summit. From Baldy Lake [(A)(3)(a.2)], hike into the cirque on the peak's southwest side and climb southeast until the slope becomes noticeably steeper. From this point, turn northeast and climb to the top of the south ridge just south of the summit and follow the broad ridge to the summit.

Twin Imps   *9,240+ feet*
This twin-summited peak is located 0.7 mile south of the Devils Throne. The first ascent of the higher, north summit was by a Mazama group in 1963. The first ascent of the southern summit was by (who else?) A. H. Marshall on June 20, 1938, the same day he made the first ascent of Devils Throne. The peak's base can be reached from the west [(A)(3)(a.2)] and probably from Dog Lake on the range's east side. To reach Dog Lake, follow the Boise section of the Seven Devils Loop Trail [(A)(3)(a.3)] south from Windy Gap for 5.2 miles to where it crosses Dog Creek. Leave the trail and hike up the drainage for 1 mile to the lake. USGS He Devil/HCW

South Peak (Class 3). Climb from the saddle between the two summits. Approach from the east via an obvious ledge system.

North Peak (Class 5). The Mazamas climbed this summit via its northeastern arête. Approach from the northeast across a mostly talus slope through scattered trees to the wall above. Follow a ledge that leads onto the north face. At the beginning of the ledge, take a crack system that leads 100 feet up to a second ledge on the crest of the arête. At this point, the crest is blocked by a large tower and it is necessary to descend 30 feet down a gully on the south side of the arête. Move out onto the arête's south face and slide around a "bulging rock." A V-shaped gully should now be visible—climb this gully to the crest above the tower. The route from here follows the crest, switching from side to side.

Jackley Mountain   *8,747 feet (Class 2)*
Jackley Mountain is located 3 miles southeast of Horse Heaven Lookout and is a former lookout site. The summit is reached by an easy scramble up the peak's south ridge from Holbrook Saddle crossed by FST-191 [(A)(4)(b)]. USGS Purgatory Saddle

Monument Peak   *8,957 feet (Class 2)*
Monument Peak sits 2 miles southwest of Jackley Peak and directly north of Crystal Lake. The peak is the most formidable summit in the southern Seven Devils and route-finding on its slopes can be tricky. Reach this peak from FST-214 that passes by its western side [(A)(4)(a)]. Leave the trail 1 mile north of Emerald Lake and climb into the gully that leads to the saddle south of the summit. Once in the gully, you will eventually arrive at a headwall. Turn due north at this point and climb up, aiming for a point just west of and 100 feet below the summit. Look for a chute that leads to the summit. USGS Purgatory Saddle

Smith Mountain   *8,005 feet (Class 1)*
Smith Mountain is located 3.5 miles south of Black Lake and just east of FS-112, which passes within 300 vertical feet of the summit. This mountain was named after an early prospector, Crazyhorse Smith. The summit is reached by a short trail from the road [(A)(4)]. USGS Purgatory Saddle

THE CUDDY AND HITT MOUNTAIN PEAKS

Cuddy Mountain   *7,867 feet (Class 2)*
The highest point in the Cuddy Mountains is located 18 miles west of Council. Take ID-71 west from Cambridge to the Brownlee GS. From the GS, follow FS-044 until it splits. Continue up the creek bottom until the road ends, then follow the old trail for 3.5 miles to the summit [(A)(5.1)(a)]. USGS Sturgill Peak

Sturgill Peak   *7,589 feet*
The highest point in the Hitt Mountains is a fire lookout site with a road to the summit. The lookout and road were built in 1933 by the Civilian Conservation Corps. A 4WD is needed to reach the summit via the road. The road, which sees little use, makes a good hiking route to the summit [(A)(6.1)]. USGS Sturgill Peak

Hitt Peak   *7,410 feet (Class 2)*
Hitt Peak is located 2 miles southeast of Sturgill Peak. The summit can be climbed from FST-276 [(A)(6.1)(a)], which crosses the saddle east of the peak. From the saddle, follow the ridgeline north from the saddle to the summit.

APPROACHES TO THE WESTERN BORDER RANGES

(A) US-95 ACCESS POINTS

US-95 provides primary access to much of the Seven Devils as it runs between the Idaho towns of Council, New Meadows,

Riggins, and Cottonwood. These towns can provide gas, food, and lodging. The following access points are from north to south.

(1) Craig Mountains Access. Access is via back roads from either Cottonwood or Lewiston. A secondary road connects these two towns with Soldier Meadow Reservoir, which is located roughly midway along the route. In the north, leave Lewiston on County Road P2 and drive east to the Waha Road, which runs south through Waha to Cottonwood. From US-95 at Cottonwood, drive west from town toward Waha. From the Waha Road, several feeder roads provide access to the heart of the Craig Mountains. Check with the BLM's Cottonwood office regarding road conditions before making a trip into this area. There are no designated trails in the Craig Mountains.

(2) FST-493, Pittsburgh Landing Road. This approach point is used by those wishing to approach the range from the west. It is the longest and most difficult access route in the Seven Devils country. From the White Bird junction on US-95, drive south for 1.5 miles and then turn west on the road (signed Hammer Creek Recreation Area) that follows the Salmon River downstream. At 1.5 miles, a bridge crosses the river. Cross the bridge and turn left on Deer Creek Road. From this point, there are many minor feeder roads, but the main road is well marked. This road climbs over a high saddle, but is often passable throughout the winter with 4WD.

(a) FST-102, Snake River Trail. This trail leaves Pittsburgh Landing and follows the Snake River south for 29 miles to the Hells Canyon Dam. The trail provides important early season access to the western slopes of the Seven Devils. FST-57 and FST-112 lead from the river to the Seven Devils high country.

(3) FST-517, Windy Gap and Heavens Gate Lookout Road. Take US-95 1 mile south of Riggins and turn west onto Squaw Creek Road. This steep gravel road climbs and winds for 17 miles to Windy Gap; Heavens Gate is another 2 miles farther along the road.

(a) FST-112/FST-56/FST-101, Seven Devils Loop Trail. A loop trail leaves from the saddle and circles the major peaks in 27 miles. Side and feeder trails lead to many of the high mountain lakes and provide access to the base of most of the peaks. The trail is broken into three main sections, which are listed below under (a.1), (a.2) and (a.3).

(a.1) FST-112, Windy Gap to Snake River Trail. This trail forms part of the northern section of the Seven Devils Loop Trail as it traverses around the high peaks area 7.2 miles from Windy Gap to Hibbs Cow Camp. From Hibbs Cow Camp, the trail descends 13.5 miles along Little Granite Creek to the Snake River and FST-102 [(A)(2)(a)].

(a.1.1) FST-57, Dry Diggins Trail. This trail leads west from FST-112 to Dry Diggins Lookout, which is 8.2 miles from Windy Gap.

(a.1.2) FST-123, Sheep Lake Trail. Sheep Lake is a primary destination for mountaineers. This is the only trail to the lake, but there is also a cross-country route [(A)(3)(b)]. Leave Seven Devils Loop Trail at Windy Gap and head west to Dry Diggins Ridge. Turn south on the ridge and hike about 0.5 mile to the FST-123 junction. From Windy Gap, it is more than 9 long miles to Sheep Lake. Note that this trail is shown on the Nez Perce National Forest map, but not on the He Devil USGS quad. The route can be shortened by leaving the main trail where the trail crosses Sheep Creek 3.5 miles from Windy Gap and hiking cross-country up the west side of the Devils Tooth to Sheep Lake. This is a strenuous route that most will find difficult.

(a.2) FST-56, West Side Trail. This trail begins along the Snake River, climbs steeply to Dry Diggins Lookout, and then turns south to a junction with FST-112. From this junction, the trail becomes part of the Seven Devils Loop Trail as it runs from Dry Diggins 6.5 miles south to Horse Heaven Lookout.

(a.3) FST-101, Boise Trail. This is the final 12.2-mile link in the Seven Devils Loop Trail, connecting Horse Heaven Lookout to Windy Gap. This trail provides access to all of the major east-facing drainages along the Seven Devils high country, from the Tower of Babel south to the Twin Imps. Fishermen's trails lead to both Hanson and Dog Lakes. To reach Hanson Lake from the Boise Trail, leave the trail where it crosses Hanson Creek and then stay on the creek's north side. Watch your footing and look for a poorly defined trail. The trail to Dog Lake leaves the Boise Trail on the south side of Dog Creek, but soon crosses back to the north side. This trail is sketchy in places, but passable.

(a.3.1) Lower Cannon Lake Trail. This trail is not shown on the Nez Perce National Forest map, but is well marked where it leaves the Boise Trail at Cannon Creek. The trail quickly climbs to the lake at the base of the Goblin, a distance of 4 miles from Windy Gap.

(b) Goat Pass Cross-Country Route. Goat Pass is the second way into Sheep Lake from Windy Gap. This route is not marked on the USGS He Devil quad. In just 2 short miles you will traverse from Windy Gap to Sheep Lake across two high saddles and a spectacular ledge. Goat Pass is unnamed on the He Devil USGS quad, but apparently it and this route were identified on older Forest Service maps. The trail has been subject to occasional trail maintenance efforts in the past, but today the management policy apparently is to leave the route for the adventurous only.

From the trailhead parking lot, follow the gravel road south to the lower campground. Keep right where the road forks in the campground and follow this fork to the first campsite after the second set of restrooms. The cross-country route starts from here. A short way into the trees, there is a bulletin board marking the beginning of the trail. The trail is in good condition and generally easy to follow. The trail climbs out of the trees and up to the saddle on the ridge separating the Seven Devils Lake and Mirror Lake Basins. Two spots along this section of the route are steep and somewhat exposed, and will cause some people to pause and think about the wisdom of continuing on. After crossing the first saddle, the route traverses to Goat Pass (0.25 mile west of Mirror Lake) along fairly stable slopes. From Goat Pass, the route drops to the west side of the ridge, where it traverses down to Sheep Lake, passing several spectacular views of the Devils Tooth. The last section of the trail descends along an exciting ledge that clings to a vertical cliff. The route, while generally easy to follow, is a cross-country route—it can be dangerous and should be used only by the experienced.

(4) Southern Seven Devils Access. The south end of the range is heavily roaded. Access begins at Council via FS-002, the Hornet Creek Road. Turn west at the city park in Council (where US-93 makes a 90-degree turn) and follow the signs to the village of Bear. (Bear junction is 31 miles from Council.) The road forks at Bear. FS-002, the left fork, leads west toward Hells Canyon. Continue on the right fork, FS-105, through Bear for 4.9 miles, and turn right onto the Black Lake Road that leads to Black Lake. A Forest Service map is essential in reaching this destination; also, be advised that this road usually is not clear of snow until the middle of July. A 4WD is recommended.

(a) FST-214, Horse Heaven Trail. FST-214 is the most important of the trails accessed from the Black Lake area. It can be followed north past Emerald Lake to Horse Heaven Lookout where it joins the Seven Devils Loop Trail in 8 miles. See [(A)(3) (a)], above.

(a.1) FST-218/FST-216, Oxbow Saddle Trail. These two trails form a loop on the west side of FST-214. FST-218 leaves FST-214 in Horse Pasture Basin and runs west to Six Lakes Basin in 5 miles. The trail continues west, past the lakes, and joins FST-216 and FST-217. FST-217 descends to Deep Creek and the Snake River. FST-216 runs northeast to Oxbow Saddle and then continues west to rejoin FST-214.

(b) FST-191, Holbrook Saddle Trail. FST-191 leaves FS-002 just east of Black Lake and follows an indirect course north to Holbrook Saddle in about 4 miles. From the saddle, the trail drops into the West Fork of the Rapid River, where it intersects with FST-113. FST-113 descends along Rapid River and meets FST-192 and FST-194, both of which connect with FST-214 [(A) (4)(a)] to the west.

(b.1) FST-189, Ruth Lake Trail. This trail runs between FST-191 and FST-214 in 4 miles. Midway along the trail, a short feeder trail provides access to Ruth Lake.

(5) ID-71. This state highway leaves US-95 at Cambridge and crosses a pass between the Cuddy and Hitt Mountains as it runs northwest to the Snake River and Oregon.

(5.1) FS-044, Brownlee Creek Road. This road leaves ID-71 where it crosses East Brownlee Creek and runs east to Brownlee CG. Just past the CG, the road forks. Follow the left-hand fork until it ends.

(a) East Fork Brownlee Creek Trail. This trail leaves from the end of FS-044 and follows the drainage north to the ridgeline north of Cuddy Mountain. Once on the ridge, the trail turns southeast and leads to the top of Cuddy Mountain.

(6) FS-009, Mann Creek Road. Access this road just north of Weiser. It leads north to the Mann Creek GS and eventually to the top of Sturgill Peak. Beyond Lower Spring Creek CG, the road requires a 4WD.

(6.1) FST-573, Hitt Creek Road. This road leaves FS-009 north of the Mann Creek GS and follows Hitt Creek north for 4 miles to FST-276.

(a) FST-276, Hitt Peak Trail. FST-276 leaves the end of the Hitt Creek Road and climbs to the eastern slopes of Hitt Peak in 3.25 miles. Beyond Hitt Peak, the road continues north to Sturgill Peak in another 2 miles.

2

THE WEST MOUNTAINS

The West Mountains are separated from the Salmon River Mountains by the Little Salmon River and the North Fork Payette River. The range forms a long upland that runs from New Meadows in the north 75 miles to a southern terminus near Horseshoe Bend. The range, a complicated series of ridges and drainages, varies in width from 10 to 15 miles. The towns of New Meadows, McCall, Cascade, and Banks are found along the range's eastern edge; Council is found in the west.

Geologically, the West Mountains form a meeting ground between the Idaho Batholith and the Island Arc geology of the Cuddy and Hitt Mountains to the west. Fault blocking has lifted the range to 8,322 feet on Snowbank Mountain and has formed a crest that consistently stays above 7,000 feet. While the range is heavily forested along its lower slopes, the highest peaks are above timberline and large meadows dot the crest.

The range is managed by the Payette National Forest in the north and the Boise National Forest in the south. The state of Idaho owns sections of land throughout the range and there are a few major private holdings within the national forest boundaries. The Federal Aviation Administration (FAA) operates a radar facility on Snowbank Mountain.

Though not well known, the exceptionally good Snowbank Mountain Road (which leads to the FAA facility) provides quick access to the beautiful high country in the center of the range. Farther north, Council Mountain sits at the center of a small but scenic roadless area. Along the crest, several West Mountains peaks and several high-altitude lakes provide interesting destinations for hikers. Climbing is limited primarily to Class 1 and Class 2 walks, with Council and Tripod Peaks the most popular destinations. Additionally, several small granite faces are available for rock climbers between Tripod and Snowbank Mountain.

Council Mountain   *8,126 feet (Class 2-3)*
Although its elevation is only 8,126 feet, it is a big, domineering mountain that rises high above all of the surrounding peaks. Its summit sits well above tree line in the middle of a mini wilderness. Council Mountain is 8 miles east of Council, Idaho, at the north end of the range. The summit area can be reached by several trails of varying lengths and conditions. Two routes are recommended. The first is via FST-201 [(A)(2.1)(a)] and the second is via FST-210 [(A)(2)(b)]. The two trails meet northeast of the summit and soon intersect with FST-198 on the north side of a saddle between the East Fork Weiser River and Granite Creek. From this junction, follow FST-198 until it crosses Council Mountain's north ridge. Follow the short but steep ridge to the top across about 10 feet of Class 3 terrain. The west ridge also can be climbed from FST-198. Note: The USGS quads and the Payette National Forest map do not accurately reflect the roads and trails in this area. USGS Council Mountain

Lookout Peak   *7,813 feet (Class 2)*
Lookout Peak sits along the main West Mountains crest directly east of Cascade, Idaho, and roughly 6 miles north of Snowbank Mountain. The peak is reached by trail via FST-133, which is reached from either the Snowbank Mountain Road in the south [(A)(4)(e)] or the Big Flat Road in the north [(A)(3)(a)]. The trail across the crest is listed as a jeep trail on the USGS quad but is now closed to vehicles. Follow the trail to its highest point on the peak's western slopes and then scramble to the top. USGS Cold Springs Ridge/Cascade

Wilson Peak   *7,865 feet (Class 2)*
Wilson Peak is a minor summit 1.5 miles northwest of Snowbank Mountain and west of the main West Mountains divide. Hike to the peak from the Snowbank Mountain Road via trail FST-135 [(A)(4)(d)], which crosses over the peak's southern shoulder. Once on the peak, climb up its gentle south slopes. USGS Tripod Peak

Snowbank Mountain   *8,322 feet*
The summit of this, the highest peak in the West Mountains, is occupied by a FAA radar dome that is clearly visible from ID-55 south of Cascade. The summit of Snowbank forms a large flat plateau with east and west high points. The western summit is crowned by the radar dome; the eastern summit (also reached by road) has a small radio transmission facility. The summit is reached by FS-446 [(A)(4)]. It is roughly 8 miles to the summit from ID-55. USGS Tripod Peak

Gabes Peak   *7,655 feet (Class 2)*
Gabes Peak is located 2 miles south of Wilson Peak and almost due west of Granite Peak. The summit is clearly visible from the Snowbank Mountain Road, since it sits to the west of the road across a large meadow. A small lake known as Gabe's Bathtub sits northwest of the summit. Climb Gabes Peak from the Snowbank Mountain Road via trail FST-136, which leads nearly to the summit [(A)(4)(b)]. USGS Tripod Peak

Granite Peak   *8,273 feet (Class 2)*
Granite Peak sits on the West Mountains crest 1 mile due south of Snowbank Mountain. This summit is a 5-minute walk from FS-446 [(A)(4)], the Snowbank Mountain Road. Park on the pass just south of the summit and walk up the south ridge to the summit. USGS Tripod Peak

Tripod Peak   *8,086 feet (Class 2)*
This is the premier summit in the southern West Mountains. The view from the lookout tower is expansive and the walk to the summit threads through a beautiful mix of forest and meadow. The summit is reached by FST-131 from the Snowbank Mountain Road [(A)(4)(c)]. The hike to the

Tripod Peak dominates the southern end of the West Mountains

summit takes in about 5 miles of the West Mountains crest. USGS Tripod Peak

APPROACHES TO THE WEST MOUNTAINS

(A) EAST SIDE ACCESS

The primary approach to the east side of the West Mountains is via ID-55, which runs between Boise and New Meadows.

(1) FS-422, Cascade Reservoir Road. This road follows the west shore of Cascade Reservoir from north to south. Access the road from ID-55 at either Donnelly or Cascade. From Cascade, drive west at a signed junction at the north end of town to the reservoir, and then follow the road around the south end of the reservoir to FS-422. From Donnelly, drive due west for 1.6 miles, turn south and drive 1 mile, then turn west and drive to FS-422 in about 1.5 miles.

(2) FS-186/185, Middle Fork Weiser River Road. This road leaves FS-422 from the north end of Cascade Reservoir, runs north climbing steeply, then heads west crossing No Business Saddle, then south and finally west to US-93 5 miles south of Council.

(a) **FST-206, Crest Trail.** FST-206 leaves FS-186 at No Business Saddle and follows the West Mountains crest south to FS-435.

(b) **FST-210, Granite Creek Trail.** This trail is accessed from FS-186 just south of its junction with FS-245. The trail leads due east toward the north ridge of Council Mountain, reaching FST-201 in 3.75 miles. This trail has been reworked. On its way up the mountain, it traverses several logging roads and clearcuts that are not shown on the maps. Despite these blights, it is a good way to approach Council Mountain.

(c) **FST-205, Crystal Creek Trail.** FST-205 follows the Crystal Creek drainage east to the southern slopes of Council Mountain, where it joins FST-198. FST-198 continues to the northwest, where it joins FST-201 and FST-203. To reach the trailhead, follow FS-186 south from No Business Saddle for about 5.25 miles.

(2.1) FS-245/FS-172, East Fork Weiser River Road. This road is accessed from FS-186 west of No Business Saddle, where No Business Creek meets the Middle Fork Weiser River. Turn north on FS-245 and follow it for 5 miles to a junction; turn left onto FS-185, which cuts west to the East Fork and FS-172. (This cutoff is not advised in wet weather.)

(a) **FST-201, Deseret Cabin Trail.** This moderately difficult trail is reached from FS-172. Leave FS-172 where it switches back out of the East Fork drainage by turning on the old logging road that follows the river south. Take this road south until it becomes too rough for your vehicle (or ends—whichever comes first).

(3) FST-435/FST-835/FST-206, Big Flat Road. This road leaves FS-422 on the west side of Cascade Reservoir just north of the turn to Cambell Creek CG. The road climbs up to the West Mountains crest in 6 miles and then drops down to the west into Anderson Creek. The road follows Anderson Creek south to the Little Weiser River, then follows the Little Weiser west to US-93.

(a) **FST-206, Crest Trail South.** This trail leaves the Big Flat Road at the top of the West Mountains crest. This trail runs both north and south from FS-206. Park at the pass. The trail runs north along the crest for 15 miles to FS-186 [(A)(2)] at No Business Saddle and south to the Snowbank Mountain Road [(A)(4)] in 11 miles.

(4) **FS-446, Snowbank Mountain Road.** This road provides quick access to the crest of the West Mountains and the summit of Snowbank Mountain. Leave ID-55 at the Clerk Creek Store 8 miles south of Cascade and drive west toward Cabarton. Follow the paved road west until it abuts the base of the mountains. The paved road turns north, crosses a bridge, and FS-435 begins shortly afterward. This exceptional gravel road is steep, but passable to passenger autos.

(a) **FST-119, Blue Lake Trail.** This 1-mile trail leaves FS-446 just before that road crosses the crest and runs to Blue Lake. It is possible to hike cross-country from the lake to FST-131 by traversing around to the south side of the lake and climbing to the saddle 0.5 mile south of the lake. This route is rated at Class 2 and requires the use of a topo map.

(b) **FST-136, Gabes Peak Trail.** This trail leaves FS-446 after it crosses the West Mountains crest and turns north. The trail begins as an old road and runs due west across a large meadow toward Gabes Peak, which is less than 2 miles from the road. From the peak, the trail continues to the south, where it joins FS-653 north of Sage Hen Reservoir.

(c) **FST-131, West Mountain Trail.** This trail is accessed from the Gabes Creek Trail a short distance west of FS-446. It runs north and south between Squaw Creek and Little Sage Hell Basin (east of Sage Hen Reservoir). (See [(A)(5)(a)], below for more details.) Approximately 3 miles south of its junction with FST-136, a short side trail leaves FST-131 and climbs to the top of Tripod Peak in 0.25 mile. This side trail is faint in places, washed out in others, but still relatively easy to follow. When in doubt, just go up!

(d) **FST-135, Wilson Peak Trail.** This trail forks off FST-131 about 1 mile north of that trail's junction with FST-136. From where it leaves FST-131, the trail proceeds due north toward Wilson Peak and then descends to the southwest to Squaw Creek.

(e) **FST-133, Crest Trail.** This trail leaves FS-446 at Snowbank Mountain and proceeds north along the crest to FS-206 in 11 miles. The trail leaves FS-446 on an old roadway, which is only signed to say that it is closed to motor vehicles.

(5) **FS-644/FS-645/FS-626, Sage Hen Reservoir Road.** Sage Hen Reservoir is accessed from ID-55 at Smiths Ferry. Leave ID-55, turning west, following FS-644 west and then north for roughly 3.5 miles to its junction with FS-626. Turn west on FS-626 and follow it to the reservoir. From the reservoir, several road options continue to the north, west, and south and provide alternative access routes into the southern West Mountains.

(a) **FST-131, Snowbank Mountain Trail.** This trail leaves the Sage Hen Reservoir road west of Tripod Creek and runs north toward Tripod Peak. See [(A)(4)(c)], above for additional details.

(B) WEST SIDE ACCESS

Primary access is from US-95 between Cambridge and New Meadows.

(1) **FS-165/172, East Fork Weiser River Road.** This route begins as FS-165, which leaves US-95 10 miles north of Council and follows the river into the mountains. Follow FS-165 to Shingle Flat and the FS-183 junction. Turn onto FS-183 and follow it 1.5 miles to the FS-172 junction. Turn on FS-172 and follow it to Squaw Flat in another 8 miles. See [(A)(2.1)], above for additional road and trail information.

(2) **FS-186, Middle Fork Weiser River Road.** This road leaves US-93 about 5 miles south of Council just before the highway crosses the Middle Fork Weiser River. See [(A)(2)], above for road and trail information.

3

THE SALMON RIVER MOUNTAINS

The Salmon River Mountains are the second largest of the Idaho Batholith mountain groups. When the name was approved by the U.S. Board of Geographic Names in 1921, these mountains were described as "a great mountain mass covering more than 7,300 square miles, broken only by narrow valleys...." This massive range encompasses an immense area in south-central Idaho that includes 2 million acres of officially designated wilderness, hundreds of rugged summits, and scores of deep river canyons. These mountains are named for the Salmon River, which encircles nearly the entire range, forming its boundary from Riggins in the northwest, to Salmon in the northeast, to Challis in the southeast, and finally to Stanley, halfway across the range's south boundary. From Stanley, the southern boundary is formed by the Sawtooth Mountains and then by the South Fork Payette River. The western margins are formed by the North Fork Payette and the Little Salmon Rivers.

Salmon River terrain is primarily associated with its drainages rather than its mountains, as erosion has formed a great natural maze in the Idaho Batholith. Elevations range from 1,400 feet at Riggins to more than 10,400 feet on White Mountain. Abrupt 5,000-foot elevation changes are common throughout the range. Although the geology of this range is primarily the geology of the Idaho Batholith, the predominance of the batholith granite is spiced by many overlying sedimentary and metamorphic strata and volcanic rocks. The oldest rocks in the area are found along Big Creek near Edwardsburg where the quartzites, slates, and schists are of Precambrian age. The area west of Challis is composed of extensive deposits from the Challis Volcanics, which form the youngest Salmon River terrain. Five major ridge networks within the Salmon River Mountains have been singled out as subranges. They are the Bighorn Crags, the Yellowjacket Mountains, the Lick Creek Range, the North Fork Range, and the Grass Mountains.

The Boise, Payette, and Salmon-Challis National Forests administer sections of the Salmon River Mountains. The state of Idaho owns part of the southwest corner of these mountains, and a number of scattered sections in other locations. Nearly 2 million acres of these mountains are included in the Frank Church–River of No Return Wilderness (RNRW), but many more acres of the Salmon River country are worthy of wilderness designation.

Though having Congress declare an area a wilderness is never easy, the creation of the River of No Return Wilderness is a casebook study of what can be accomplished when the right political ducks are lined up. The political history of the area began in 1930, when a group of prominent Idaho citizens led by former governor H. C. Baldridge encouraged the Forest Service to set the area aside and protect its natural, roadless condition. Remarkably, in April of 1931, the Idaho Primitive Area was established to protect 1.2 million acres of public land. More remarkably, this "primitive area" status was maintained for many years—without strong environmental lobbying—against ever-growing pressures to open the area to logging, mining, and road building.

In the late 1970s, as mining and logging interests turned up the rhetoric, Congress (acting against all odds) established the present RNRW, not only protecting the original 1.2 million-

acre "primitive area," but also tossing in another 1 million acres of surrounding mountains. This final victory required a Democratic Congress, a senior Democratic U.S. Senator (Frank Church, who was a devout conservationist), a Secretary of the Interior (Cecil Andrus, who was a former governor of Idaho and a staunch conservationist), and a Democratic president who had taken a presidential float trip down the Middle Fork two years earlier. Beyond the luster of the big names, thousands of people worked to insure the establishment of a wilderness area that is almost too big to comprehend.

Hiking and climbing opportunities are almost unlimited in the Salmon River Mountains. In addition to an extensive road system, the Salmon River Mountains possess a number of public airstrips that allow quick access to many points within the RNRW. Though the RNRW is known throughout the nation, it is seldom crowded because the vastness of the wilderness can swallow up thousands of hikers. (Margaret Fuller's *Trails of the Frank Church–River of No Return Wilderness* is the definitive hiker's guide). Recreation opportunities beyond the RNRW are also virtually unlimited. While the region around McCall sees the most use from hikers and climbers, everywhere you go in the Salmon River Mountains you will find trails to hike and peaks to climb.

To ease locating peaks, the 7,300 square miles of the Salmon River Mountains have been broken down into eleven smaller, more comprehensible areas. While the boundaries of several of these areas are somewhat indefinite, most are bounded by rivers. Please refer to the overview map to orient yourself.

NORTHWEST CORNER PEAKS

The northwest corner of the Salmon River Mountains sits between Riggins and McCall. It is bounded on the west by the Little Salmon River and on the east by the North Fork Payette River and its tributaries.

Patrick Butte   *8,841 feet (Class 2)*
Patrick Butte is located 8.5 miles southeast of Riggins, Idaho. Its summit is the highest peak in the northwest corner of the Salmon River Mountains and commands a stunning vista of the surrounding country. The summit is reached after a moderate scramble up the peak's southern slopes from FST-153 [(B)(1)(c.3)]. USGS Patrick Butte

Hard Butte   *8,695 feet (Class 1)*
Hard Butte is almost 4 miles south of Patrick Butte and stands above Rainbow Lake. It is a rugged granite mountain

SALMON RIVER MOUNTAINS

with many cliffs that abruptly rises above the surrounding rolling terrain. The peak's rocky summit, which still holds the crumbling ruins of an abandoned fire lookout, is a Class 1 hike on a poorly maintained trail [(B)(1)(c.2)]. The view of the Seven Devils and the surrounding peaks is stunning. USGS Patrick Butte

Hershey Point   8,232 feet (Class 1)
This peak is found 4 miles due east of Patrick Butte, where it forms a high promontory above the Salmon River and serves

as a lookout site for the Forest Service. The stunning view from the summit is reached after a Class 1 hike via FST-149 [(B)(1.1)(a)]. USGS Hershey Point

Sams Throne   8,283 feet (Class 3)
Sams Throne is located 4 miles southeast of Patrick Butte on the east side of Partridge Creek. The peak offers exceptional views of this remote area. Climb the peak's south ridge from the point where FST-152 crosses the saddle between the ridge [(B)(1.1)(b)]. When the ridge is blocked by a wall, pass it on its

east side and then scramble up over large granite boulders to the ragged summit area. There are two summits. It is difficult to discern which is the highest. USGS Hershey Point/Patrick Butte

Lava Butte   *8,328 feet (Class 3)*
Lava Butte, located 0.9 mile due south of Sams Throne on the same north/south ridgeline, is a tri-summited mountain with impressive north and east faces. Leave FST-152 [(B)(1.1)(b)] in the meadow on the north side of the peak and climb the north slopes or hike the south slopes from Butte Lake. USGS Hershey Point

Bear Pete Mountain   *8,751 feet (Class 1)*
This former lookout site is located 3 miles west of Burgdorf. Its summit is reached via FST-142 [(B)(2.3)(a)] which can be reached from either the north or the south or via FST-143 or FST-144, which begin near Burgdorf. USGS Burgdorf

Bruin Mountain   *8,767 feet (Class 3)*
Bruin Peak*   *8,607 feet (Class 2)*
These two mountains are found east of Upper Hazard Lake on a connecting ridgeline. Both summits were given the same name for some unknown reason. Since both have the same name on the USGS maps, I will call the highest summit Bruin Mountain and the lower Bruin Peak. Both summits are worthy destinations.

Bruin Mountain is a sharp fin-shaped summit with impressive north and east faces. Climb to the summit from Hazard Lake [(B)(1)(d)] by climbing the west face or the south ridge. Bruin Peak is a more complex peak with steep cliffs on its east and north sides. From the saddle to the north, hike toward the peak, staying on the west side of the ridge. Enter and ascend the wide chute that divides the north and northwest ridges. The northwest ridge is also an enjoyable scramble. Take the trail south from Hard Creek Lake to the pass above and then follow the ridgeline east and then southeast to the summit. USGS Black Tip

Black Tip   *8,292 feet (Class 2)*
Black Tip sits at the head of eight drainages, northwest of Upper Payette Lake and 1.5 miles east of Fisher Creek Saddle. The peak is best reached from either French Creek via FST-308 [(B)(2.1)(a)] or Fisher Creek Saddle, which is reached by FS-281 [(B)(1.2)]. From Fisher Creek Saddle, the route traverses the ridgeline east to the summit in roughly 1.5 miles. Though FST-308 leads to the summit, it is not well maintained—the ridge traverse from Fisher Creek Saddle is recommended because it is much shorter. USGS Black Tip

Slab Butte   *8,225 feet (Class 3)*
Slab Butte is located 4 miles south of Bruin Peak and due west of Granite Peak. Climb the peak from the meadow where the Granite Mountain Trail [(B)(1)(a)] leaves the Hazard Lake Road. Hike to the southeast through meadows and forest to the north ridge. Follow the north ridge to the summit. USGS Brundage Mountain

THE GRASS MOUNTAINS

The Grass Mountains are located northeast of New Meadows and east of US-93. The Goose Creek/Hazard Lake Road parallels the east side of this subrange. This convoluted divide trends from north to south for roughly 16 miles and encompasses several mountain lakes and bald ridgelines that offer scenic vistas and good hiking. Granite Mountain is the highest peak at 8,478 feet.

Grass Mountain*   *8,138 feet (Class 2)*
This rolling mountain has four nearly equal summits spread over its 3.3-mile-long summit ridge. The Hard triangulation station is on the second summit from the north. Climb the peak via FST-163 [(B)(1)(b)] by taking the trail past Grass Mountain Lakes and over the top of the summit ridge, then following the ridge south to the highest point. USGS Hazard Lake

Granite Peak   *8,478 feet (Class 1)*
Granite Peak, the highest point in the Grass Mountains, is an impressive dome-shaped summit with two cirques cut into its northern slopes and a 30-foot high fire lookout on its southern summit. It is located high above Twin Lakes and 2 miles west of Goose Lake. The summit is reached by FST-165 from the east or the west [(B)(1)(a)]. USGS Brundage Mountain

THE LICK CREEK RANGE

The name Lick Creek Range has not been adopted by the USGS. Nevertheless, many people use it to identify the divide that sits between the North Fork Payette River and the South Fork Salmon River. As such, it comprises the largest of the Salmon River Mountains subranges. The Lick Creek Range forms an impressive divide about 40 miles long from north to south and more than 20 miles wide at its widest point. The highest Lick Creek peaks are clustered at the range's northern end; at 9,322 feet, North Loon Peak takes the honors as the highest of the bunch.

While this area is better known for its hiking than its

climbing opportunities, the climbing is also highly rated. Granite walls and outcrops are found throughout the range and many peaks have untested, nearly vertical north faces. The Needles, a group of granite spires in the Gold Fork River drainage are well known to rock climbers. Nick Peak and Jughandle Mountain are perhaps the best-known peaks in the range, but another dozen peaks offer good goals for peak baggers.

Much of the Lick Creek Range is roadless and is recommended for wilderness designation. The southern section of the range is administered by the Boise National Forest. In the north, the Payette National Forest runs the show. Access is plentiful, but often requires high-clearance or 4WD vehicles.

Victor Peak   8,718 feet (Class 2)

Victor Peak is located 9 miles south of Burgdorf and is the northernmost Lick Creek Range summit in this book. Storm Peak is 2 miles to the southwest along a very rugged connecting ridgeline. No one has reported traversing the ridge between the two summits, but it should be possible, given enough time. Climb to the summit from Loon Lake [(B)(2)(b) or (B)(4)(c)] by leaving the trail at the center of the lake's western shore and climbing due west to the small, poorly defined ridgeline above. Once on the ridge, turn south and climb to Point 6773. From this point, the route turns due west and climbs up a steep, timbered slope to the summit, which is another 1.5 miles away and 2,000 feet above. USGS Victor Peak

Storm Peak   9,080+ feet (Class 2-3)

Storm Peak is 4.5 miles east of Upper Payette Lake and 6 miles north of Lick Creek Summit. Although tree-covered, the peak has a lot of exposed granite and several cliffs can block your way. The summit views are terrific, especially North and South Loon peaks and the north face of Storm Dome. The shortest approach is via FST-085/FST-315, which leads east to the Twentymile Lake Basin [(B)(2)(a)]. Hike east on FST-315 to North Twentymile Lake. From the lake, climb northeast to the ridgeline just east of the peak and then follow the ridge northwest to the summit. USGS Victor Peak

Storm Dome   8,758 feet (Class 2)

This formation is 0.6 mile southeast of Storm Peak. From the south side it is nothing more than a bump on a ridge but from the north it is one of Idaho's most attractive granite walls. This face rises 600 feet vertically out of Storm Peak Lake. To date, no one has climbed this face formed by downward trending slabs. Climb to the summit from the west and Twentymile Lakes [(B)(2)(a)]. USGS Victor Peak/Box Lake

Peak 8808   8,808 feet (Class 3)

This tri-summited peak forms the southern backdrop of Twentymile Lakes. The high point is 0.9 mile south of Storm Peak. Climb the peak from Long Lake to the north. From the lake, climb to the summit ridge between the middle and western summits. Follow the summit ridge east to the top. USGS Victor Peak

North Loon Mountain   9,322 feet (Class 2)

This Loon Mountain summit is situated 3 miles southeast of Storm Peak and northwest of Enos Lake. The summit is most easily reached via the mountain's east ridge. Enos Lake is remote and not reachable by trail, making the hike to the lake the most difficult part of the journey. To reach the lake, hike south from Loon Lake on FST-081 [(B)(2)(b)] or north from FH-21 on FST-081 [(B)(3)(d)] to the point where the trail crosses Enos Creek, and then follow the drainage southwest to the lake. From Enos Lake, at Point 7800, climb directly north to the top of the ridge and then follow the ridge west to the summit. USGS Enos Lake

South Loon Mountain   9,287 feet (Class 2)

South Loon Mountain is directly south of North Loon Mountain and is by far the most impressive of the two peaks. While this peak can, like North Loon Mountain, be climbed from Enos Lake, the shortest approach is from FH-21 via FST-083 and FST-082 [(B)(3)(c.1)]. Hike from the road to Hum Lake. Just west of the lake, FST-083 switches its way back north to the ridgeline above and then traverses northeast to Point 8056 on the southwest ridge of South Loon Mountain. Leave the trail at this point and climb the ridgeline directly to the summit. USGS Box Lake

Tail Holt Peak*   7,769 feet (Class 1)

The USGS used this peak as a triangulation station identified as Tail Holt. Tail Holt, 9 miles due east of South Loon Peak, sits on the long north/south ridgeline that divides the Secesh and South Fork Salmon River drainages. The summit is reached by a trail that begins near Ponderosa CG on FH-48, the Lick Creek Road [(B)(3)(f)]. It is roughly a 5-mile walk to the summit. USGS Williams Peak

Peak 9027   9,027 feet (Class 2)

This unnamed summit, one of the highest peaks in the Lick Creek Range, is located 4.8 miles south of South Loon Mountain. Climb to its summit from the North Fork Fitsum Creek Trail, FST-086 [(B)(3)(e)]. Follow the trail east until roughly the 6,000-foot contour on the map. Leave the trail and hike north toward Point 8662. Once on the summit ridge, continue due north to the summit. USGS Enos Lake

Rain Peak*   8,755 feet (Class 3)

This attractive summit's north face rises more than 1,100 feet above a beautiful, unnamed lake 2.9 miles north of Beaverdam Peak. Climb the peak from Duck Lake [(B)(3)(c)]. From the lake, hike to Lake 7523, then hike north to the base of the peak's west ridge and proceed northwest to the southeast face. Climb the face over boulders, talus, and short steps to the south ridge 100 feet below the summit. Climb to the summit over large blocks. USGS Box Lake

Beaverdam Peak   8,653 feet (Class 2-3)

This pyramid-shaped peak northeast of Box Lake has a sharp north face and is composed of light-colored granite. Climb the peak from the north end of Box Lake [(B)(3)(b)] via its western slopes. Scramble up to the peak's summit ridge just southwest of the summit and then follow the ridge to the top. USGS Box Lake

Sawtooth Peak   8,875 feet

Sawtooth Peak is located 1.2 miles north of Snowslide Lake. Despite Sawtooth Peak's somewhat innocuous-looking south side, its north face is among the most impressive granite walls in Idaho, rising vertically for 600 feet. There are no reports of climbing attempts on the north face. USGS Fitsum Summit

South Ridge (Class 3). The ridge begins at Snowslide Pass and rises 900 feet in 1 mile to the summit. Take FST-104 from Snowslide Lake to reach the pass above and the base of the ridge [(B)(3)(b)]. The ridge is easy to follow at first, but eventually narrows and is blocked in several spots by rock walls and pinnacles. Generally, follow the west side of the ridge to bypass the first obstacles and the east side of the ridge to avoid later obstacles. At times, it is necessary to drop well below the ridgeline to get by.

Snowslide Peak   8,522 feet

Snowslide Peak is 1.2 miles due south of Sawtooth Peak. Its vertical north face, which rises abruptly above Snowslide Lake and climbs more than 1,400 feet in less than 0.5 mile, is clearly visible from FH-48 as one descends from Lick Creek Summit toward McCall. Although the last 700 feet of face are nearly vertical, no one has recorded its first ascent. Like Sawtooth Peak, it is a great scrambler's peak. USGS Fitsum Summit

Northwest Ridge (Class 3). Traverse around the east end of Snowslide Lake and climb up to the small pond above.

(This involves traveling through very brushy terrain.) From the pond, go due south to the base of a prominent gully that cuts slightly to the southwest. Climb the gully until it ends at the base of several short, broken, tree-covered cliffs. Look for a steep shelf that cuts to the left (east) and use this to bypass the cliffs. Work around the cliffs to a small gully and then climb directly up to the ridgeline above. Once on the ridge, it is possible to follow it northeast to the summit without too much difficulty. Obviously, route-finding is the most difficult part of this climb. In all likelihood, several options besides the one described above exist. Whatever you do, keep off the cliffs directly below the summit unless you are experienced with and equipped for high-angle rock climbing. Snowslide Lake is reached by following FST-104 east from FH-48 for 2 miles [(B)(3)(b)].

Northeast Ridge (Class 3). From Snowslide Lake, hike FST-104 [(B)(3)(b)] to the pass above. From the pass, follow the southeast side of the ridgeline southwest to the summit. The route is straightforward for the first two thirds of its distance. The final third of the route involves a little more difficult route-finding and steeper climbing. Stay on the ridgeline if your skill level allows it. Otherwise, traverse out onto the southeast slopes until you find a gully (several options exist) that appeals to you. Follow the gully to the ridge top and then continue up the ridge to the summit.

Fitsum Peak   8,737 feet (Class 3)

This peak has three summits spread over a 1.2-mile summit ridge. The USGS placed the name on the middle summit (on the Fitsum Peak quad) and not on the highest western summit (on the Fitsum Summit quad). Climb the peak from North Fitsum Summit [(B)(3)(b) or (e)] via the north ridge. USGS Fitsum Summit/Fitsum Peak

Nick Peak   9,064 feet (Class 3)

Nick Peak is 2.8 miles south of Fitsum Peak (and 11 miles east of McCall). Though Nick Peak has attracted some interest from peak baggers because its summit is visible from downtown McCall, the peak is not easily approached from any direction. The shortest approach to the summit is from Lake Fork CG on the peak's west side via FST-104 [(B)(3)(b)]. Follow this trail north until it crosses Idler Creek directly below Fitsum Summit (Pass). Leave the trail and climb the steep slope up to the pass. A second approach is via the peak's northwest side via FST-087 [(C)(1.1)(a)] which follows Fitsum Creek to Fitsum Summit. This route provides the easiest route to Fitsum Summit, but it too involves a very long hike. Once on Fitsum Summit, it is a relatively easy task to follow the ridge to the summit, 1 mile to the south and 800 feet higher. USGS Fitsum Peak.

Boulder Mountain   *8,377 feet (Class 1-2)*

Boulder Peak is located 7 miles due east of the McCall Airport. At one time, the Forest Service maintained a short trail to the summit of this peak from FST-103, which crosses Boulder Pass just east of the peak. Although the summit trail is no longer an official trail, its remnants can be easily followed from Boulder Summit [(B)(4)(b)]. USGS Fitsum Summit

Jughandle Mountain   *8,340 feet*

Jughandle is the big peak with a long north/south summit ridge that sits south of Boulder Lake. The peak's north face, like many Lick Creek Range mountains, is nearly vertical as it plunges down into Louie Lake. USGS Paddy Flat

   Louie Lake (Class 2). A jeep trail leads to Louie Lake from FS-403 [(B)(4)(a)]. Follow this trail to the lake, go around the

west shoreline to the peak's northwest ridge and follow the ridge to the summit.

   Northeast Ridge (Class 2). Approach this ridge from either Louie Lake or Boulder Lake [(B)(4)(a) or (c)]. The ridge provides a straightforward route to the summit.

Buckhorn Mountain   *8,457 feet (Class 2)*

Buckhorn Mountain is 1.7 miles due east of Boulder Lake. The pyramid-shaped peak is flanked by small lakes on its north, east, and south sides. The peak is easily climbed from Buckhorn Summit and FST-096 [(B)(4)(b)] via its southeast ridge. From Buckhorn Summit (Pass), climb the tree-covered slopes to the north until the top of the ridge is reached. From this point, work along the mostly treeless ridge to the summit 0.5 mile to the northwest. USGS Paddy Flat

Rapid Peak   *8,264 feet (Class 2)*

Rapid Peak is 0.5 mile south of Buckhorn Mountain. Its summit sits just south and a little more than 400 feet above

The west face of Buckhorn Mountain, as seen from Boulder Lake

Buckhorn Pass [(B)(4)(b)]. Leave the trail at the summit and climb the peak's north ridge to the top. USGS Paddy Flat

Blackmare Peak   *8,724 feet (Class 1)*
This lookout site is found 4 miles north of Square Top Mountain. FST-303 leads to the summit from the Cougar Creek Summit (Pass), which is reached via FST-099 [(B)(5)(a)]. USGS Blackmare Peak

Square Top Mountain   *8,681 feet (Class 2)*
Square Top Mountain is the distinctive summit 2.25 miles northeast of the Needles. Access the peak from Kennally Creek CG and FST-101 [(B)(5)(b)], which leads to Needles Summit (Pass) just north of the Needles. From the pass, follow seldom-maintained FST-303 north along the ridge to the second saddle above Blackmare Lake. From this point, climb over the high point just south of Square Top to reach the saddle due south of the peak. It is an easy walk from this saddle to the mountain's prominent top. This route is 7 miles from trailhead to summit. The peak also can be reached via a long scramble from Blackmare Lake. USGS Blackmare Peak

Needles Peak*   *8,302 feet*
Needles Peak is located 2.25 miles south of Square Top Mountain and just south of Needles Summit (Pass) along the main Lick Creek crest. The peak is identified as "The Needles" on the USGS quad. This mountain would be just another hump-shaped mountain except that its summit is crowned by three impressive granite formations. The northernmost formation is a teepee-shaped spire that is the peak's highest point, while the southern and middle formations are fin-shaped and slightly lower in elevation. Additionally, several other granite formations are found on the peak's lower slopes. The most impressive of these is found 0.25 mile west of the summit. The granite, for the most part, is solid and clean and possesses many good faces and cracks that promise high quality one-or two-pitch climbing opportunities. A lot of activity has taken place on these towers over the past ten years, but the climbers who placed the routes are unwilling to talk about their accomplishments. Besides the route described below, the main tower has a two-and-half-pitch Grade II, 5.9 route on its southwest face. The southernmost summit tower has two, two-pitch Grade II, 5.10 routes, and the middle tower has at least a dozen one- to two-pitch Grade II, 5.8 to 5.11 routes. Many anchors and bolts are present on these routes.

Access to the summit area is from either the north via Kennally Creek or the south from the Gold Fork trailhead. From the north, take FST-101 [(B)(5)(b)] to Needles Summit

and then follow the western side of the Lick Creek divide to the south until the ridge crest can be reached. Follow the ridge to the summit area. From the south, near the Gold Fork trailhead [(B)(6)(a)], climb directly to the summit area via the peak's south ridge. USGS Gold Fork Rock

North Summit (Class 4). The north teepee-shaped spire rises 100 to 150 feet above the surrounding terrain and is climbed on its north side. Hike around the spire's east face to the small saddle on the northeast corner. This saddle is between the summit spire and a small granite formation 100 feet to the northeast. From this point, one can view the entire route as it follows a prominent crack system to the small notch on the summit's north side. From the base of the spire, scramble up the northeast corner until a wall blocks your way. Climb this wall on its left side, where it forms a 10-foot step with good holds. Once above the step, climb up a steep diagonal shelf to the northwest (to your right) to the base of a second wall (8 or 10 feet high), which is capped by a small pine tree. (Because this tree blocks the route, the move

The highest point on Needles Peak is climbed via an east Class 4 route. (Photo by Dana Hansen)

over this wall is more difficult than it might be.) Climb this wall directly up through the tree to the shelf above. From this point, follow the shelf back to the east for 10 feet and then climb over a boulder and into the diagonal gully that leads to the summit notch. Follow the gully up to the notch on deteriorating rock. From the notch, climb around to the west side of the peak and stem up for 10 feet between the northernmost and middle summit blocks.

THE NORTH FORK RANGE

This Salmon River Mountains subrange is found in the extreme southwest corner of the Salmon River Mountains, above the confluence of the North Fork Payette River and the Payette River. ID-55 and the North Fork Payette River form the range's western boundary, while the Middle Fork Payette River and South Fork Salmon River forms the range's rather indefinite eastern boundary. The North Fork Range reaches 40 miles from north to south between Banks and Warm Lake and has a maximum width of 8 miles. East Mountain, 7,752 feet is the highest point. With only a few named summits in the range, it is best known for Cougar Rock, a spectacular granite dome visible from Warm Lake.

Cougar Rock   (I, 5.8)

Cougar Rock is the impressive granite dome that is 1 mile north of Stolle Peak. The rock is accessed from the South Fork Salmon River near Stolle Meadows [(C)(1.1)(f)]. While little is known of the formation's climbing history, it is certain that the rock has been climbed several times. Although there are many possible climbing lines, all known ascents were on the west face.

The two-pitch route, which leads up the west face, begins at the notch between Cougar Rock and a smaller formation on its west side. From the Cougar Rock Trail, climb a 10-foot pitch into the notch and set your belay. (You may also circle the base of the smaller formation and approach the notch from the south.) From the notch, the route climbs the vertical west wall, following an obvious line up a thin flake and alongside a left-facing open book that overhangs slightly at its top. From the top of the flake, the route moves south (or to your right) into a narrow crack in the overhanging open book's wall. Jam up the crack and climb up onto the ledge above. Stand up on the narrow ledge and move left to its most exposed point. From this point, you must take one giant airy step to your left across the lower portion of the route to a good, bucket-sized ledge, 6 to 8 feet away. Once on this ledge, traverse out and around toward the north face for 10 to 15

feet to a small pine tree. (Note: Do not drop down onto the more prominent ledge that is just below you.) Go by the tree to the base of a wide crack that leads directly up to a shelf in about 25 feet. The first pitch ends on this shelf.

The second pitch is shorter and less exposed. From the shelf, the route climbs due east with good holds for 25 feet up and over the wall that faces the shelf. Above this wall, the technical climbing ends at a medium-sized pine tree (a good rappel anchor for the descent). The final summit block is an easy scramble. The rappel from the tree to the notch will require two 165-foot ropes and a large sling for an anchor. USGS Rice Peak

Stolle Peak*   7,563 feet (Class 1-2)

Stolle Peak is located just south of Cougar Rock and directly east of Stolle Meadows. This peak is identified on the USGS quad as the Cougar triangulation station. The summit is formed by a granite outcropping adorned with the remains of an ancient fire lookout that once used the peak's commanding

The unclimbed east face of Cougar Rock

viewpoint to good advantage. The summit is nominally reached by a very poor trail, FST-109, which according to the Forest Service map begins at the Stolle Meadows GS. Do not be fooled by the map—see [(C)(1.1)(f)], below. USGS Rice Peak

East Mountain *7,752 feet (Class 1)*
Located southeast of Cascade, the highest peak in the North Fork Range is reached by both road and trail. The recommended route to the top (for truly addicted peak baggers) is via FST-033/FST-100 [(D)(1.1)(a)], which begins at Boiling Springs GS and eventually reaches the summit after 10 long miles. USGS Bull Creek Hot Springs

LOG MOUNTAIN/DEADWOOD DIVIDE

Moving to the east from the North Fork Range, the Log Mountain/Deadwood Divide forms the next major watershed. This impressive ridge system runs unbroken for more than 60 miles between the East Fork and South Fork Salmon River in the north and the South Fork Payette River in the south. The western boundary is formed by the South Fork Salmon River and Middle Fork Payette River; the eastern boundary is formed by Johnson Creek, the Deadwood River, and Clear Creek. The peaks in this section are listed from north to south.

Log Mountain *9,179 feet (Class 1-2)*
Log Mountain, which sits midway between Yellow Pine and Warm Lake, is the highest point on the divide. Its summit was once a fire lookout site and its tiny summit block still contains wood planks and rusty nails, remnants of the primitive hut that once served as the lookout tower. Log Mountain is reached via a trail after hiking nearly 10 miles and gaining 5,000 feet in elevation from where Fourmile Creek dumps into the South Fork. The last portion of the trail is seldom maintained and requires Class 2 skills [(C)(1.1)(c.1)]. USGS Log Mountain

Shell Rock Peak *8,574 feet (Class 2)*
Shell Rock peak sits 1.2 miles east of Log Mountain. Climb the peak via its northern slopes from FST-094 [(C)(1.3.1)(a)]. USGS Log Mountain

Thunderbolt Mountain *8,652 feet (Class 1)*
Thunderbolt Mountain, a large granite dome with an active fire lookout on its summit, sits 6 miles south of Log Mountain. This may be the best viewpoint in the entire Salmon River Mountains. From the summit you can view all of the surrounding summits, the West Mountains, the Sawtooths,

and even the White Clouds, including Castle Peak. The summit can be reached by trail from either Johnson Creek (the longer route) [(C)(1.3)(a)], or Cabin Creek [(C)(1.2)(a)]. The Johnson Creek route is recommended because it crosses more interesting terrain. For something different, try the east face, a Class 3 scramble with minimal route-finding problems. USGS Warm Lake

Rice Mountain *8,696 feet (Class 1)*
The long north/south summit of Rice Mountain was once a fire lookout site. The peak sits on at the southern end of Log Mountain/Deadwood Divide, 12 miles north of Deadwood Reservoir. The summit, which offers a good view of this region, is easily reached by three different trails. The preferred route uses the Switchback Trail, FST-009/FST-102, to reach the summit from the Deadwood Reservoir Road [(C)(1)(a)]. USGS Rice Peak

JOHNSON CREEK/MIDDLE FORK DIVIDE

A third north/south trending divide is found west of the Log Mountain/Deadwood Divide. This divide is situated between Johnson Creek, the Deadwood River, and Clear Creek in the west and ID-21 and the Middle Fork Salmon River in the east. In the north, the divide begins at Murphy Peak on Red Ridge (see Big Creek to Red Ridge Peaks below) near Monumental Summit and then snakes south for roughly 60 miles to end near Lowman. Much of the northern portion of this convoluted divide is within the RNRW, and a large portion in the south around Red Mountain is roadless and suitable for wilderness designation. Roads and trails follow the crest of this divide for most of its distance. Peaks along this divide are listed from north to south.

Pistol Rock *9,178 feet (Class 3)*
Pistol Rock is located 9 miles southwest of Murphy Peak. Climb to the summit via the rock's south ridge from FST-088 [(C)(1.4)(a)] to the south. Trapper Mountain is a lower southern summit of this mountain. USGS Chilcoot Peak

Big Baldy Peak *9,705 feet (Class 1)*
This massive summit, which should be on every hiker's to-do list, is an island in the sky. It anchors the east end of Big Baldy Ridge, which runs east from Pistol Rock. It is the highest Salmon River summit west of the Middle Fork and dominates a huge section of country. The Forest Service maintains a fire lookout on its summit for most of the summer. From the east, trails lead out of the Middle Fork and Little Pistol Creek drainages to the summit, climbing nearly 5,000 feet in

the process. From the west, FST-227 is accessed from FST-088 [(C)(1.4)(a) or (1.3.2)(a)] and follows Big Baldy Ridge east to the summit, passing beautiful Buck Lake along the way. All three approaches are long and require a serious commitment. USGS Big Baldy

Chilcoot Peak   *8,988 feet (Class 1)*
Chilcoot Peak, located 2 miles southwest of Pistol Rock, has an attractive north face that towers over Chilcoot Lake. Its summit is reached by a side trail that climbs up its south ridge from FST-088 [(C)(1.4)(a) or (1.3.2)(a)] and Chilcoot Peak. USGS Chilcoot Peak

Lake Mountain   *8,928 feet (Class)*
Lake Mountain, which is 3 miles south of Chilcoot Peak, is one of the most rugged summits in the western Salmon Rivers. Its four summits are arranged on a west to east summit ridge. Climb the peak from the point where FST-088 [(C)(1.4) (a) or (1.3.2)(a)] crosses either its southern or northern ridges. USGS Pistol Lake

Chinook Mountain   *9,113 feet (Class 3)*
Chinook Mountain is 2.5 miles due east of Lake Mountain. FST-216 leaves FST-088 [(C)(1.4)(a) or (1.3.2)(a)] south of Lake Mountain and follows a ridgeline southeast and then northeast before descending into Forty-four Creek. Leave the trail where it leaves the ridge top to descend into the drainage and follow the ridge northeast to the summit. USGS Chinook Mountain

Morehead Mountain   *8,506 feet (Class 1)*
Morehead Mountain is 11 miles south of Chinook Mountain and just west of the Middle Fork Salmon River. This peak, a fire lookout site overlooking the Middle Fork, offers rewarding views into the awesome Middle Fork Canyon. The summit is reached by trails from three different directions. The recommended route uses FST-068 and FST-082 [(C)(1.5)(a)]. USGS Big Soldier Mountain/RNRW

Blue Bunch Mountain   *9,710 feet (Class 1)*
Blue Bunch Mountain is 7 miles south of Morehead Mountain and towers above the Middle Fork Salmon River, which flows on its north and east sides. FST-013 [(C)(1)(b)] leads to the summit in 4.5 miles. USGS Blue Bunch Mountain

Cape Horn Mountain   *9,526 feet (Class 2)*
This peak's long narrow summit, located 5.5 miles south/ southeast of Blue Bunch Mountain, also sits high above the

headwaters of the Middle Fork Salmon River. The summit provides excellent views of the entire region—so good, in fact, that the mountain was used as a triangulation station for the initial USGS mapping of the area in 1922. The summit is reached after a beautiful ridge walk from the south. Approach the summit by hiking FST-024 from Cape Horn Summit on the Landmark-Lowman Road [(C)(1)(c)]. The trail climbs more than 2,500 feet in 3.5 miles to the ridgeline, and then follows the ridge north for 1 mile to a point above the Lolo Creek drainage. The trail is faint on the ridge top and, although the map shows it making a descent into the Lolo Creek drainage, the route is not readily apparent. From the ridge above Lolo Lake, follow the ridgeline cross-country to the summit. USGS Cape Horn Lakes/RNRW

Red Mountain   *8,733 feet (Class 1)*
Red Mountain is a somewhat isolated peak 13 miles southwest of Cape Horn Peak and 15 miles northeast of Lowman and ID-21. The former lookout site is a popular destination for day hikers. Take FST-145 (which eventually leads to the many small lakes east of the summit) to its junction with FST-083, which climbs to the mountain's summit [(E)(1.1)(a)]. The summit also can be reached via a Class 3 scramble from the lakes east of the peak. USGS Cache Creek

CHAMBERLAIN BASIN PEAKS

The north-central section of the Salmon River Mountains is bordered by the Salmon River on the north, Panther Creek on the east, Big Creek on the south and the tributaries of the South Fork Salmon River in the west. It is a vast area of high rolling country with miles of forest and interspersed peaks. All but the western fringes of this section are within the RNRW. The peaks in this section are listed from west to east.

Chicken Peak   *8,600 feet (Class 1)*
Chicken Peak, which is 12 miles north of Edwardsburg, is the culmination of three long ridges (Mosquito Ridge, Horse Ridge, and Sheepeater Ridge). Its summit provides a fine view of the wilderness country to the northeast. Several trails converge on the summit. The shortest approach is from the Werdenhoff Mine trailhead via FST-003 [(B)(3.2.1)(b)]. It is roughly 6 miles to the summit from the trailhead. USGS Chicken Peak/RNRW

Mosquito Peak   *8,774 feet (Class 2)*
Mosquito Peak is a seldom-visited summit located 2 miles southeast of Chicken Peak and above Mosquito Lake. The

peak can be reached from FST-003 [(B)(3.2.1)(b)]. Leave the trail where it crosses the peak's southwest ridge and follow the ridgeline to the summit, which is about 1 mile to the northeast. USGS Mosquito Peak/RNRW

Sheepeater Mountain   *8,486 feet (Class 1)*
Sheepeater Mountain is found 3 miles northeast of Chicken Peak and 7 miles west of Chamberlain Meadows in the northern section of the RNRW. This large peak, which sits above and west of Sheepeater Lake, is one of the most isolated mountains in the entire state. Reaching its summit will take most people several days of hiking. The peak is reached from FST-003 [(B)(3.2.1)(b)], which crosses its summit. USGS Sheepeater/RNRW

Bismark Mountain   *8,128 feet (Class 2-3)*
This peak is situated 12 miles south of Chamberlain GS and 2.2 miles north of Big Creek. The mountain is accessed after a long hike from FST-009 [(B)(3.2.1)(a),(c), and (d)], which crosses its southeast and northeast ridgelines. The information is sketchy, but the best route to the top apparently utilizes the northeast ridge and may or may not involve Class 3 climbing. USGS Bismark Mountain/RNRW

Cold Mountain   *8,084 feet (Class 1)*
This peak with a lookout is 10 miles east/northeast of Bismark Mountain and directly south of Cold Meadows GS. The Class 1 summit is reached by FST-043 [(B)(3.2.1)(a.2.2)]. USGS Vinegar Hill/RNRW

Camel Peak   *9,225 feet (Class 2)*
Camel Peak is located in the northeast corner of the RNRW and 5.5 miles southwest of Corn Creek CG on the main Salmon River. It is the first high summit along FST-168, the Black Butte Trail [(H)(3)(b)] and sits high over Basin Creek to the north. The summit is a short walk from the trail. USGS Cottonwood Butte/RNRW

Cottonwood Butte   *9,349 feet (Class 2)*
The peak is situated 1.75 miles southwest of Camel Peak and east of Cold Meadows GS. FST-168 [(H)(3)(b)] provides direct access to the mountain's summit. USGS Cottonwood Butte

Farrow Mountain   *8,992 feet (Class 2)*
Farrow is located 2.25 miles southwest of Cottonwood Butte along the route of FST-168 [(H)(3)(b)], which crosses its eastern slopes. Because the trail stays relatively high along the mountain's slopes, the summit is easily reached. USGS Cottonwood Butte/RNRW

Black Butte   *8,711 feet (Class 1-2)*
Black Butte is 5.5 miles south of Farrow Mountain and 5 miles north of Big Creek. Once, a maintained trail led from near the junction of FST-168 and FST-044 [(H)(3)(b)] to the top of this isolated mountain. Reportedly, the old trail can still be followed, but hikers should be prepared to follow the ridgeline without the aid of a trail. USGS Papoose Peak/RNRW

Horse Mountain   *8,184 feet (Class 1)*
Horse Mountain is located 4.75 miles southwest of Black Butte. Its summit, which served as a fire lookout site at one time, rises steeply above Big Creek (gaining more than 4,000 feet in less than 1.5 miles). The summit is accessible by FST-044 [(B)(3.2.1)(a.3)]. Like many peaks in the RNRW, its summit is a very long walk from anywhere. USGS Vinegar Hill/RNRW

BIG CREEK TO RED RIDGE PEAKS

This section covers another massive stretch of north-central Salmon River Mountains. The northern border is formed by Big Creek and the eastern border is the Middle Fork Salmon River. The southern border is framed by the Red Ridge on its east end and the East Fork South Fork Salmon River on the west end. Finally, the western boundary of this section follows the South Fork Salmon River. All but the westernmost summits listed in this section are within the RNRW. Peaks are listed from west to east.

Williams Peak   *6,826 (Class 1)*
The summit of Williams Peak sits east of the confluence of the South Fork Salmon River and the East Fork South Fork Salmon River. Though the summit is low, its position commands an exceptional view, making it a perfect location for its Forest Service fire lookout. The summit is reached by trails from the north, east, and south. The recommended route follows FST-073 from FH-48 [(B)(3)(g)] for 3 steep miles. USGS Williams Peak

Parks Peak   *8,833 feet (Class 1)*
This beautiful summit anchors the western end of the Hidden Divide and forms the culmination of Rainbow Ridge. The summit is a jumble of broken rock and the old fire lookout is in ruins, but the view is exceptional. The summit is reached by trail from the East Fork South Fork Salmon River. For an outstanding hike, take FST-069, the Parks Peak Trail, to the summit [(B)(3)(i)]. USGS Parks Peak/Caton Lake

Wolf Fang Peak, viewed from the south

Wolf Fang Peak   *9,007 feet (Class 2)*

Wolf Fang Peak is a rugged, triangle-shaped mountain located 2 miles north of Elk Summit (Pass) on FS-340 [(B)(3.2)]. On its east side, the rocky summit juts out from a group of pinnacles and crags called the Wolfs Fangs. Although the name conjures up thoughts of steep, pointed spires, the Fangs are less impressive than you might imagine and only one metamorphic fang might be of some interest to rock climbers.

Climb the peak from Elk Summit. From the highest point on the pass, a road leaves FS-340 and leads to the top of the 9,000-foot, unnamed peak just north of the pass. Follow this road until it forks on the north side of the unnamed peak. Take the left fork and park on the ridge top 100 yards ahead. From this point, follow the undulating ridge north for 1.5 miles to the summit. The ridge is broad and offers a decent tread for most of its distance. Once on the peak's south ridge, pick your route around a few small obstacles and keep to the center of the slope as much as possible.

Mount Eldridge   *9,207 feet (Class 2)*

This is the prominent peak that sits directly southeast of Elk Summit (Pass) and FS-340 [(B)(3.2). Mount Eldridge is 3 miles due south of Wolf Fang Peak and 1 mile southeast of Elk Summit. Climb the peak from the pass via the connecting ridge. A good, but hard to find game trail leads from Elk Summit directly to the low spot in the ridge due south of Elk Summit. If you cannot find this trail in the timber, climb to the high point southwest of the ridge over loose talus and then follow the connecting ridge to the summit. USGS Wolf Fang Peak

Dixie Mountain   *9,070 feet (Class 2)*

The next summit south of Eldridge is Dixie Mountain, about 1.4 miles away. The easiest route to the top follows the connecting ridgeline south from Mount Eldridge. USGS Profile Gap

Greeley Mountain   *9,233 feet (Class 2)*

Continuing south from Dixie Mountain for another 1.8 miles will bring enterprising ridge walkers to Greeley Mountain, the highest summit in the immediate area. USGS Profile Gap

Profile Peak   *8,965 feet*

Profile Peak is a sharp, steep-walled peak at the top of the Logan Creek drainage east of Profile Gap. The peak, as well as Profile Gap and Wilson Peak, are named after Profile Sam Wilson, who prospected in the area during the early 1900s. Profile Peak is not easily approached from any direction—climbing the peak involves long, strenuous cross-country travel. USGS Profile Gap

Profile Gap (Class 2). Profile Peak may be climbed from Profile Gap in conjunction with ascents of Crater Peak, Wilson Peak, and Big Creek Point. This route involves a long (4 miles one-way) ridge walk with considerable ups and downs. Park on Profile Gap [(B)(3.2)] and climb to Point 8325 on the ridgeline due west of the road. From this point, follow the ridge south to the summit of Crater Peak, then turn west and follow the ridge over Point 8856. From the top of this unnamed peak, the ridgeline swings northwest and leads over the summits of Wilson Peak, Big Creek Point, and finally to the top of Profile Peak. Leave early and carry plenty of water.

Profile Lake (Class 2-3). Profile Lake sits 0.5 mile north of the summit of Profile Peak. FST-284 leads up the South Fork Elk Creek to within 1 mile of the lake [(B)(3.2)(d)]. The last portions of the drainage are steep and not easily crossed. If you reach the lake, climb the slopes directly to the south toward the ridgeline just west of the cliffs that form the final summit block. Once on the ridge, stay on the south side and hike to the top.

Big Creek Point   *8,893 feet (Class 2)*
This big rectangular summit sits west of Profile Gap between Profile Peak and Wilson Peak. The peak is climbed from Profile Gap. See the Profile Gap route, listed under Profile Peak, for directions. The summit is 3 miles from Profile Gap. USGS Profile Gap

Wilson Peak   *8,955 feet (Class 2)*
Wilson Peak is located southeast of Profile Peak on the same ridgeline. To reach the summit, which is a 2-mile ridge walk from Profile Gap, see the Profile Gap route, listed under Profile Peak. USGS Profile Gap

Crater Peak   *8,800+ feet (Class 2)*
Crater Peak is a pointed, tree-covered summit just west of Profile Gap and directly north of Crater Lake. The summit is 1 mile from Profile Gap. See the Profile Gap route, listed under Profile Peak. USGS Coin Mountain Profile Gap

Coin Mountain   *8,994 feet (Class 2)*
Coin Mountain forms the eastern wall of Profile Gap. The summit is 1.5 miles southeast of Profile Gap and is reached via the tree-covered connecting ridge [(B)(3.2)]. USGS Profile Gap

Pinnacles Peak*   *9,273 feet (Class 3)*
Pinnacles Peak is found northeast of Yellow Pine at the highest point of the Missouri Ridge above Profile Creek. This peak is identified as the "The Pinnacles" on the Edwardsburg

USGS quad. Although the mountain is less precipitous than its name implies, it is still the most rugged Salmon River mountain in the entire area. The peak, which towers over the upper portion of the Missouri Creek drainage, consists of three rock towers. The middle tower is the highest and the northernmost is the most rugged. The peak can be climbed from either the unofficial Missouri Ridge Trail or the small lake at the top of the Missouri Creek drainage. Both routes are long and at times steep. USGS Edwardsburg/RNRW

Missouri Ridge (Class 3). Take the Missouri Ridge Trail [(B)(3.2)(a)] to the top of the Missouri Ridge and follow the ridgeline north to the summit, passing all obstacles on the east side of the ridge. At the final summit block, cross over onto the west side of the ridge to bypass the small tower that blocks the ridge, and climb to the notch between the tower and the summit. Cross through the notch and traverse out onto the east face for 25 feet on the obvious ledge, and then climb straight up on good rock to the summit.

Missouri Creek (Class 3). Follow the Missouri Ridge Trail [(B)(3.2)(a)] until you reach a cabin where the trail crosses the creek. Leave the trail and, staying on the west side of the drainage, follow the creek up to the small lake below the west face of the peak. The forested terrain is difficult to pass through at first, but quickly opens up to allow fast progress to the upper basin. From the small lake, climb the gully that runs directly up to the notch on the south side of the summit. From this point, follow the directions for the final portion of the Missouri Ridge route.

Marble Mountain   *9,128 feet (Class 2)*
Marble Mountain is the big, bulky mountain that sits east of the Big Creek GS. The summit is reached by a long, but easy climb from the Cougar Basin Trail [(B)(3.2)(c)]. USGS Edwardsburg/RNRW

Cougar Peak   *9,120 feet (Class 2)*
Cougar Peak is 5 miles east of Coin Mountain and sits up above pristine Cougar Basin in the RNRW Area. The peak is an easy scramble from the basin, which is reached from FS-340 [(B)(3.2)(c)]. USGS Edwardsburg/RNRW

Center Mountain   *9,323 feet (Class 2)*
Snowslide Peak   *9,104 feet (Class 2)*
Both summits are located northeast of Cougar Peak on the same ridgeline. Both peaks are accessed from Cougar Basin and FST-065 [(B)(3.2)(c) and (c.1)], which is not signed and no longer receives regular maintenance. Follow the trail north from FST-004 where it crosses the pass northeast of

Cougar Peak. The trail stays high above the Snowslide and Little Marble Creek drainages as it climbs nearly to the top of Snowslide Peak in 3.3 miles and then continues to the summit of Center Mountain in another 2.2 miles. USGS Center Mountain/RNRW

Rainbow Peak   *9,325 feet (Class 2-3)*
Rainbow Peak is 13 miles due east of Yellow Pine, Idaho. According to the miners who first visited this country in the 1800s, the peak's slopes are composed of many strata of rock that sparkle like a rainbow when the sun strikes them—hence the name. Climb Rainbow Peak from the Monumental Creek Road, FS-375. Follow Rainbow Creek to its upper reaches and climb the steep, southeast slopes to the summit [(B)(3.1)]. USGS Rainbow Peak/RNRW

Murphy Peak   *9,238 feet (Class 2)*
Murphy Peak sits on the west end of Red Ridge 13 miles east/southeast of Yellow Pine and south of Monumental Summit. It is also the northern anchor for the Johnson Creek/Middle Fork Divide. The Thunder Mountain Road [(C)(1.3.2)] comes within a short distance of this summit. Climb the peak via its western slopes from the road. USGS Rainbow Peak/Stibnite/RNRW

Red Peak   *9,571 (Class 2)*
Red Peak   *9,468 (Class 2)*
No, it is not a typo! The USGS named two peaks on one quad Red Peak. The westernmost summit was the Red Peak triangulation station and the easternmost summit gets the official name. Both summits are worth climbing. Start from the Thunder Mountain Road [(C)(1.3.2)] on the western slopes of Murphy Peak, hike over Murphy Mountain, and then follow the ridgeline southeast to these summits. It is a strenuous 9-mile round trip with great views for the entire distance. USGS Big Baldy/RNRW

Lookout Mountain   *8,680 feet (Class 1)*
Lookout Mountain is found 14 miles east of Pinnacles Peak and sits high above Monumental Creek. The mountain is the highest point on Lookout Mountain Ridge, which begins at the end of the Monumental Creek Road and runs north for many miles. Access to the top is via an 8-mile hike along FST-061 [(B)(3.1)(b)] from the nearest trailhead to the southeast. Although trails approach the summit from every direction, only FST-061 provides a moderately short approach to the summit. USGS Monument/RNRW

Shellrock Peak   *9,435 feet (Class 2)*
Shellrock Peak anchors the southwest end of a long divide that runs northeast to Dave Lewis Peak in 8 miles. This ridge includes Two Point Mountain and Mormon Mountain. Shellrock served as a fire lookout for many years beginning in the 1930s; its summit still holds the ruins of the old lookout. When the lookout was in use, a trail was maintained to the top via the ridgeline that runs north to Two Point Mountain. Since the lookout was abandoned, the trail has deteriorated, but the ridgeline is passable and provides easy access to the summit [(B)(3.1)(b)]. USGS Shellrock Peak/RNRW

Two Point Mountain   *9,426 feet (Class 2)*
Two Point Mountain is the rocky twin-summited peak on the ridge that connects Shellrock Peak to Mormon Mountain. The peak served as a fire lookout site in the early 1920s, but in the 1930s it was replaced by a superior site on Shellrock Peak. Its summit is an easy scramble from the point where FST-061 crosses Bush Creek Summit [(B)(3.1)(b)]. USGS Shellrock Peak/RNRW

Mormon Mountain   *9,545 feet (Class 1)*
This domineering peak is 2 miles north/northeast of Two Point Mountain. It overlooks the Middle Fork Salmon River and forms one of the highest and most remote uplands in the entire RNRW Area. The summit is reached via FST-061 [(B)(3.1)(b)], a seldom-maintained trail that climbs out of Brush Creek to Two Point Mountain before turning north to cross Mormon Mountain. From Mormon Mountain, the trail follows the ridgeline north to the saddle west of Dave Lewis Peak. USGS Mormon Mountain/RNRW

Dave Lewis Peak   *9,252 feet (Class 2)*
Dave Lewis Peak is 3.25 miles northeast of Mormon Mountain and 7 miles northwest of the Bernard Creek GS on the Middle Fork Salmon River. This peak anchors the northeast end of the long divide that runs southwest to Shellrock Peak in a little more than 8 miles and includes Mormon Mountain, Two Point Peak, and Shellrock Peak. The summit is reached by making an easy scramble from the saddle to the southwest, which is reached by FST-061 [(B)(3.1)(b)]. USGS Dave Lewis Peak/RNRW

THE BIGHORN CRAGS

The Bighorn Crags form a distinctive, high-granite divide more than 20 miles in length. This divide, which stands on the east side of the Middle Fork Salmon River, towers nearly 1,000 feet above the surrounding mountains. Although these peaks are part of the Salmon River Mountains, they are unique in their physical shape and geologic makeup because Crags granite was formed by a younger granitic intrusion called a pluton that was interjected into the older Idaho Batholith granite roughly 40 million years ago. This chemically different, younger granite is characterized by vertical jointing, which has eroded it into spires and sharp walls.

The Bighorn Crags offer many excellent challenges to mountaineers and a surprising amount of good rock to challenge rock climbers. The quality of the Crags granite is much like Sawtooth granite: hard and clean in some places, soft and deteriorated in others. Many of the best walls and rock are found down in the canyons rather than on the peaks, which in some cases are still covered by metamorphic overburden. Climbers who come to the Crags should expect to find little in the way of company or conveniences such as established bolts for rappelling.

There are two major rock-climbing areas within the Crags. The first is the "Cathedral's Cemetery," which begins 2 miles from Crags CG and occupies an area along the main trail for almost 2 miles to the base of Cathedral Rock. (The domes and spires resemble giant tombstones; Cathedral Rock, of course, resembles a cathedral.) The Cemetery includes 14 spires and domes, which vary considerably in size and shape and offer simple bouldering problems as well as more complicated one- and two-pitch route rock-climbing projects. The second area of interest to rock climbers is a tangled collection of spires, faces, and cliffs at the west end of Ship Island Lake called the Litner Group. Because it is more than 10 miles from the nearest trailhead, little climbing activity has taken place in the Litner Group, but, rest assured, the area has high potential for serious rock climbers.

Beehive *9,610 feet (Class 2)*
This rugged peak stands at the north end of the Crags, 1.5 miles southwest of Dome Mountain. The summit is most easily approached via the southwest ridge where it is crossed by the Crags Trail [(H)(4.1.1)(a)]. The first recorded ascent was by T. M. Bannon in 1912. USGS Mount McGuire/RNRW

Goat Mountain *9,607 feet (Class 2)*
This peak, which is 3 miles north of Mount McGuire, is the most remote Bighorn Crag peak. It can be reached only after a long cross-country march from either Ship Island Lake or Goat Lake. If you really want to go "where no one has gone

before," this is the place. The summit is an easy scramble from either its east or south ridges [(H)(4.1.1.1)(a.2) and (a.2.1)]. USGS Mount McGuire/RNRW

Litner Peak* *8,837 feet (Class 5)*
Litner Peak is the highest point in the Litner Group; it is found at the west end of Ship Island Lake [(H)(4.1.1.1)(a.2) and (a.2.1)]. Little is known about the route of first ascent by L. Hales and P. Schoening in 1955. The peak's numerous formations and faces offer many potential technical lines. USGS Aggipah Mountain/RNRW

The Chisel* *8,920+ feet (Class 4)*
This descriptively named formation is located west of Ship Island Lake [(H)(4.1.1.1)(a.2) and (a.2.1)]. The peak is the highest point on the northwest ridge of Aggipah Mountain. It was first climbed by Hales and Schoening in 1955. USGS Aggipah Mountain/RNRW

Mount McGuire *10,082 feet (Class 2)*
The highest peak in the Bighorn Crags rises directly north of Airplane Lake and is composed of a huge pile of broken metamorphic overburden on a granite base. The pyramid-shaped peak has a steep, but rotten north face and offers no technical climbing. The peak was named after Dan McGuire, a mining engineer. T. M. Bannon made the first ascent in 1912. The Forest Service placed a benchmark on the summit in 1924.

The most economical route to the summit is from the south via the stream that runs into Airplane Lake from the north. From the trail to Ship Island Lake [(H)(4.1.1.1)(a.2) and (a.2.1)], follow the stream until you reach its source, a small pond at 9,150 feet. From the pond, continue up to the saddle over increasingly broken ground for another 250 feet, then turn west and climb directly up the southeast ridge, skirting a couple of granite towers on their south side. The summit is a double, with the east summit being the highest. USGS Mount McGuire/RNRW

Aggipah Mountain *9,920 feet (Class 3)*
This large peak rises just to the southwest of Ship Island Lake to form a massive, flat-topped mountain that presents a bold face to the lake. Aggipah, which means salmon in the Chinook Indian dialect, is on the west end of a subsidiary ridge that connects with the main Bighorn Crag crest at Knuckle Peak. The peak is (probably) most easily climbed from Ship Island Lake. This route begins at the unnamed lake just south of Ship Island Lake [(H)(4.1.1.1)(a), (a.2) and

Mount McGuire, the highest point in the Bighorn Crags, viewed from the summit of Knuckle Peak

(a.2.1)]. Start by climbing a scree slope to a col on Aggipah's southeast ridge, then follow the steep ridge to the summit. Although many other route possibilities exist, these would involve much longer and more difficult approaches. USGS Aggipah Mountain/RNRW

Sheepeater Mountain*   *9,920 feet (Class 2-3)*
This is the large peak that rises due north of Terrace Lakes. The view of Ship Island Lake from the summit is beautiful. Climb from the southeast ridge (Class 3) or the south ridge (Class 2) [(H)(4.1.1.1)(a) and (a.2)]. USGS Mount McGuire/ RNRW

Fishfin Ridge
The USGS Mount McGuire quad lists the most complex feature in the Bighorn Crags as simply Fishfin Ridge. Climbers, on the other hand, have recognized the complexity of this exceptional ridge comprised of four major formations, all of which are unofficially named. The highest and westernmost point is known as Knuckle Peak; to the east, in order of appearance, are the Rusty Nail, Pinnacle 3, and Pinnacle 4.

Knuckle Peak*   *9,700 feet*
Knuckle Peak, the most impressive feature of the Bighorn Crags, is the highest point on the Fishfin Ridge. It was named by Lincoln Hales and Pete Schoening, who made the first

ascent in 1955. The three-sided mountain has no simple route to its top, which is a jumble of small jagged spires and blocks. Although the peak's granite is generally hard, climbers should be aware that its quality can vary a great deal in a short distance.

The peak has three faces. On its west side, the peak presents an 800-foot face to Wilson Lake. This face is a conglomeration of smooth slabs without any major cracks. A variety of overhanging obstacles block many possible routes, sometimes repeatedly. The north face rises impressively above Birdbill Lake and is 300 feet higher than the west face. On this side, the face can be reached from the upper portion of the Beaver Tail Trail [(H)(4.1.1.1)(a.2)], where the trail hits the crest above the Birdbill Lake. The east face is the least impressive of the three—but is still imposing. It rises above the Crags Trail, which provides easy access to its lower slopes. The route of the first ascent, described by Hales in the *Mountaineers Journal*, is unclear. USGS Mount McGuire/RNRW

East Face/South Ridge (I, 5.2). From the Crags Trail [(H) (4.1.1.1) (a)], climb the easy ledges up to the base of the face. From the top of the easy ledges, find a narrow ramp that cuts diagonally to the south. Follow this ramp until it ends. From this point, a series of moderately difficult steps lead almost directly up to the south ridge with one small section of 5.2 climbing (and moderate exposure). Once on the ridge, ascend it to the summit, over Class 3 to Class 4 terrain. The south ridge also has been climbed directly from the notch between Knuckle Peak and the Rusty Nail; the move out of the notch has been rated 5.7.

The Rusty Nail*   *(Class 5)*

This spire is next to Knuckle Peak, near its southeast corner. Lincoln Hales, who named this spire, was unable to reach its summit. In the late 1950s and early 1960s several members of the Idaho Alpine Club attempted the formation, but without success. Someone eventually did climb the spire, but there is no information on who did it or what route they took [(H)(4.1.1)(a)]. USGS Mount McGuire/RNRW

Pinnacle 3*   *(Class 3)*

This stubby, obelisk-shaped spire is the second peak from the south end of Fishfin Ridge. The route climbs the numerous ledges that form the formation's west side [(H)(4.1.1.1)(a)]. First ascent: Bob Hammer and a group of Idaho Alpine Club members in 1963. USGS Mount McGuire/RNRW

Pinnacle 4*   *(Class 4)*

The easternmost of the Fishfin Ridge formations is climbed by way of a thin crack system on the spire's north side [(H)(4.1.1.1)(a)]. First ascent: Bob Hammer and a group of Idaho Alpine Club members in 1963. USGS Mount McGuire/RNRW

Bighorn Peak*   *9,821 feet (Class 2)*

This peak, located west of and above Harbor Lake, has a broad summit ridge and a rough broken face that is half metamorphic rock and half loose debris. From Harbor Lake, the peak can be climbed by either its north or south ridges. Class 3 climbing could be encountered climbing to the north ridge, depending on the route chosen. From Harbor Lake, climb the scree slopes to one of the ridge tops and then follow the chosen ridge to the summit [(H)(4.1.1.1)(a) and (a.2)]. USGS Mount McGuire/RNRW

Ramskull Peak*   *9,460 feet (Class 4)*

This peak was named by Pete Schoening and Lincoln Hales in 1955, after they made the first ascent. It dominates its surroundings, presenting an almost unbroken 1,000-foot face to Wilson Creek. From Wilson Lake, it resembles a two-pronged granite spire. The summit can only be reached by climbing on very poor quality granite. The route begins at Harbor Lake [(H)(4.1.1.1)(a) and (a.2)]. From the lake, scramble up to the ridgeline west of the peak and then follow the ridge to the base of the summit block. From this point, drop down the south side of the ridge for roughly 40 feet, keeping to the base of the summit block, until you are at the base of a large gully that leads up to the summit in one Class 4 pitch. The crux of the climb is the descent, because the summit is composed of

Knuckle Peak and the Rusty Nail from Ramshorn Peak, Bighorn Crags

The Rust Nail, as seen from Wilson Lake

deteriorated granite and placing an adequate rappel anchor is impossible. USGS Mount McGuire/RNRW

Heart Peak*   9,573 feet (Class 2)

This is a pointed peak that rises to the south of Heart Lake. Its lofty summit can be reached via its gentle east ridge. Technical climbing opportunities exist on this peak, including a major snow gully on the northeast face [(H)(4.1.1.1)(a.1)]. USGS Mount McGuire/RNRW

Cathedral Rock   9,400+ feet

This impressive peak is 2 miles east of Fishfin Ridge and directly above its namesake, Cathedral Lake. From the lake,

it is an impressive collection of granite cliffs and slabs that quickly rise 800 feet. Cathedral Rock is composed of three major summits. The north summit had been climbed by 1924, the year a Forest Service benchmark was cemented to its summit. The more difficult (and highest) south summit was first climbed by Hales and Schoening in 1955. The middle summit evidently has not been climbed; nor has the Rock's imposing east face [(H)(4.1.1.1)(a)]. USGS Mount McGuire/RNRW

North Summit (Class 3). From the trail, work your way through the tree-covered slopes to the highest point on the west face, next to the northernmost summit. Climb the small north summit block from the west side via a 25-foot scramble from a boulder field that reaches nearly to the summit.

South Summit (I, 5.4). The middle and south summits are separated by a steep gully on their western side. Climb the gully (on bombproof holds) in one short pitch, and then traverse south to the summit.

Puddin Mountain   9,684 feet (Class 2)

This peak is 1.5 miles south of Harbor Peak. It is named after Puddin River Wilson, who was the saloon keeper at Yellowjacket during that mining town's heyday. Climb via the southeast ridge from Turquoise Lake by keeping on the south side of the ridge near its crest [(H)(4.1.1.1)(a.1.1)]. The first recorded ascent was by T. M. Bannon in 1912. USGS Puddin Mountain/RNRW

Wilson Mountain   9,520 feet (Class 3)

Wilson is the other Bighorn Crags peak named for Puddin River Wilson. It is located 1.5 miles south of Puddin Mountain. Climb the peak from either Ramshorn or Paragon Lakes to the east via the east ridge [(H)(4.1.1.1)(a.1.1)]. Bannon also made the first recorded ascent of this peak in 1912. USGS Hoodoo Meadows/RNRW

YELLOWJACKET MOUNTAINS

This subrange of the Salmon River Mountains was named by miners after the now-abandoned town of Yellowjacket. The range runs 24 miles from southwest to northeast and is situated due east of the Bighorn Crags. These mountains are almost indistinguishable from the surrounding Salmon River peaks. The highest point is in the south on Middle Fork Peak at 9,127 feet. This book includes four Yellowjacket summits: Gant Mountain, Sugar Loaf, Mount McEleny, and Middle Fork Peak.

The east face of Ramskull Peak, viewed from Boulder Lake

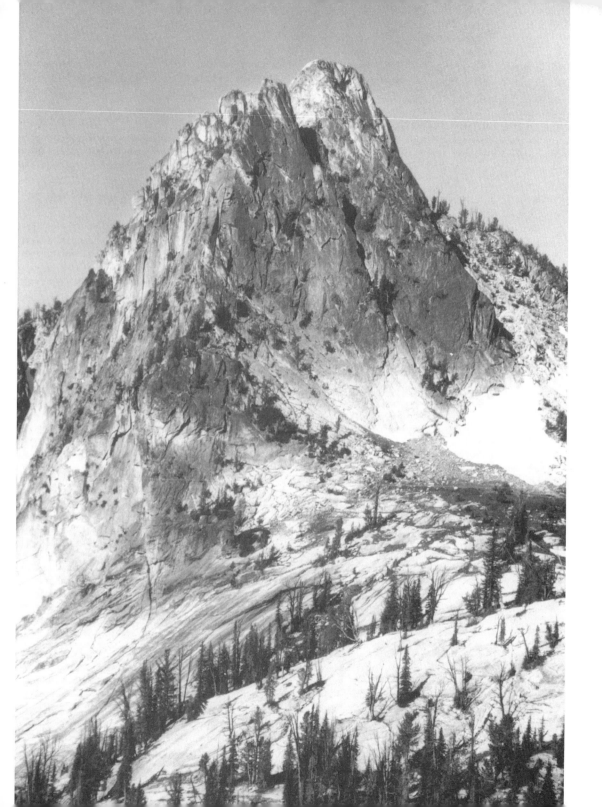

Gant Mountain   *8,276 feet (Class 1)*
Gant Mountain anchors the north end of the Yellowjacket Mountains. It is part of massive Gant Ridge 6 miles north of the point where Panther Creek flows into the main Salmon River. One of the earliest fire lookouts in the Salmon National Forest was placed on its summit in 1933 or 1934. The lookout was used for several years and then abandoned. To reach the summit from the Panther Creek Road, take the Birch Trail, FST-023, to the summit [(H)(4)(a)]. The trail gains more than 4,500 feet and teaches an excellent lesson on how vertical the Salmon River country can be. USGS Gant Mountain/RNRW

Sugar Loaf   *9,045 feet (Class 2)*
Sugar Loaf, rising directly west of Yellowjacket Lake [(H)(4.1.1)], is a half-dome-shaped peak that has an 800-foot vertical east wall. Rock climbers who have approached the granite wall with great anticipation have been disappointed by its deteriorated condition. I do not know of any attempt to climb it. The Sugar

Sugar Loaf in the Yellowjacket Mountains, viewed from the Crags Trail in the Bighorn Crags

Loaf summit can be reached by a short cross-country walk from the Yellowjacket Lake CG via either its south or north sides. USGS Hoodoo Meadows

McEleny Mountain   *8,938 feet (Class 1)*
McEleny Mountain is 3 miles southeast of Sugar Loaf. This peak is reached via a 3-mile walk up FST-039 from Hoodoo Meadows and the end of FS-113 [(H)(4.1.1)(a)]. The trail leads almost the entire distance to the summit, passing along the peak's west side. From the trail, it is a short stroll to the top. USGS Hoodoo Meadows

Middle Fork Peak   *9,127 feet*
Middle Fork Peak, the highest Yellowjacket mountain peak, is historically significant. The peak is reached by both a road and a trail. The trail (FST-112) climbs up Warm Springs Creek from the Middle Fork Salmon River, gaining more than 5,000 feet in the process [(H)(4.1)]. USGS Aparejo Point
Rick Baugher notes that

> *"Despite the road, a visit to the summit is worthwhile. It is still 60 miles to the nearest pavement. At your feet is a 5,000-foot crack in the earth's crust, through which the Middle Fork flows. The historic Thunder Mountain Trail passed this way in the 1890s. T.M. Bannon visited the summit in 1913 and the Forest Service placed the first lookout on top in 1929."*

SOUTHEAST CORNER PEAKS

The southeast corner of the Salmon River Mountains is bordered on its southwest and northeast side by the Middle Fork Salmon River and Panther Creek and along its southern and eastern boundaries by the main Salmon River. While much of this area is outside the RNRW, it is still excellent country for hiking and scrambling and the access is much better. The peaks below are listed beginning in the southwest corner and moving to the east and then north.

Big Soldier Mountain   *8,984 feet (Class 1)*
This fire lookout site is located southwest of Greyhound Mountain and directly east of the Middle Fork Salmon River. The peak is approached by four different trails. The best approach is from the Josephus Lake CG [(F)(1)(d)] via FST-019, passing by Soldier and Cutthroat Lakes and then on to the summit. USGS Chinook Mountain/RNRW

Greyhound Mountain   *8,995 feet (Class 1)*
Greyhound Mountain's bald summit is 4.5 miles northwest of the Seafoam GS, which in turn is northwest of Stanley.

Approach the peak from the south on FS-011 [(F)(1)(e)], which leads to the Greyhound Mine. Drive or walk to the end of the road and then take FST-006 north to the summit. USGS Greyhound Mountain/RNRW

Little Soldier Mountain   *8,813 feet (Class 1)*
Another fire lookout site, this peak sits 7.4 miles north of Greyhound Mountain in a big bend in the Middle Fork Salmon River that surrounds it on three sides and is more than 4,000 feet below. Although the peak is reached from several directions by trail, the recommended route follows FST-006 [(F)(1)(e.1)] north from Greyhound Peak. USGS Little Soldier Mountain

Mount Mills   *9,185 feet (Class 2)*
Mount Mills is located southeast of Big Soldier Mountain and just south of Lost Lake. The summit is an easy scramble from FST-014. From the Josephus Lake CG, take FST-019 and then FST-014 to the peak's northwest ridge [(F)(1)(d) and (a)]. Climb the easy ridge to the summit. The peak also can be reached from the Langer Peak area. USGS Greyhound Ridge/RNRW

Langer Peak   *9,315 feet (Class 2)*
Langer Peak is a minor summit located 3 miles southeast of Mount Mills, above Rocky Lake. Its summit is a simple scramble from the lake. Take FST-014 [(F)(1)(a)] to Langer Lake and then hike cross-country to Rocky Lake. From this lake, climb to the saddle due north of the summit and follow the ridge south to the summit. USGS Langer Peak/RNRW

Roughneck Peak   *9,419 feet (Class 1)*
Roughneck Peak, an active fire lookout site, sits 2 miles southwest of Langer Peak. The peak is nearly surrounded by mountain lakes and is a popular destination during the summer via a well-maintained trail from Island Lake. This trail is an easy, but long Class 1 ascent [(F)(1)(a)]. USGS Langer Peak

Mount Loening   *10,012 feet (Class 3)*
This peak sits at the north end of a north/south ridgeline 10.5 miles northwest of Bonanza GS. The ridge is sometimes called the Tango Peaks. The peak's name is official but has not yet appeared on the Knapp Lake quad, which identifies the summit as the Knapp triangulation station. Loening, a prodigious jumble of shattered rock towers, is named for a bush pilot who spent many years flying the Salmon River backcountry. The peak can be climbed via its south ridge and face by using a system of gullies and ribs that carve up the broken face. Approach the face from Crimson Lake [(F)(3.1)(a)] by climbing to the main ridge north of Cabin Creek

Roughneck Peak, 9,419 feet, from Langer Lake

Peak and then follow this ridge to the north over Last Tango Peak to the base of the south face. Although the ridgeline is narrow in places, it is easily followed.

At the base of the peak, the route is blocked by a tower. Drop down on the west side of the ridge to a ledge and traverse to the northwest until you reach the base of a steep, rotten couloir. Follow this couloir until it dead ends, cross over to the east to enter the next couloir, and follow it up to the summit blocks. The final summit blocks are climbed on the west side. USGS Knapp Lakes

Last Tango Peak*   9,647 feet (Class 2)

Last Tango is a minor summit on the main ridge between Cabin Creek Peak and Mount Loening. It is easily bagged as part of an ascent of Mount Loening. See [(F)(3.1)(a)]. USGS Knapp Lakes

Cabin Creek Peak   9,968 feet

This remote tower is one of the most rugged peaks in the entire state. Its first ascent was apparently not made until 1988. The knife-edged summit, formed by fine-grained gran-ite, stands nearly 400 feet high on its east face and almost 1,200 feet high on its west face. The summit is broken into two major sections by a deep, narrow notch. The highest point is on the south side of the notch. North of the notch, the summit ridge is razor thin. USGS Knapp Lakes

East Face (I, 5.3). To reach the east face from Crimson Lake [(F)(3.1)(a)], climb to the saddle due south of the lake (between the twin dark towers that are visible from the lake). Descend the saddle below the north tower and then climb to the saddle on its west side. To reach the face from the south, take the Basin Butte Road [(F)(2)] for 18 miles to the locked gate, and then hike the road to the point where it crosses the creek that drains the east side of the peak. Follow the creek up to the east face.

The east face is cut by three gullies. The northernmost gully is vertical, the middle meanders back and forth across the face, and the southernmost (and widest) is highlighted by a cave at its base. The route begins just to the right of the southernmost gully and follows the small buttress up and to the left for two and one-half pitches. The fine-grained granite that forms the summit block is highly fractured, so

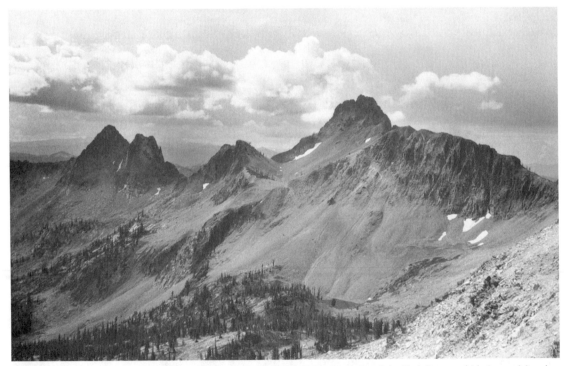

The southern end of the Tango Peaks is anchored by Cabin Creek Peak (right of center) and the Black Towers, which rise precipitously above Crimson Lake.

wear a helmet. First ascent: led by P. Bellamy with D. Lopez and T. Lopez in 1988.

Red Mountain 9,387 feet (Class 2)
This Red Mountain is 2 miles east of Cabin Creek Peak. The eastern and northern talus slopes of this mountain display a bright red tint as they rise steeply above the surrounding drainages. The summit can be climbed from almost any direction, but the most direct approach is from the West Fork Yankee Fork [(F)(3.1)(a)]. Those with a 4WD may approach by taking the Basin Butte Road to the point where it is closed by a locked gate, then following the mining road to the peak's west ridge [(F)(2)]. T. M. Bannon climbed the peak in 1915. USGS Mount Jordan

Peak 10006 10,006 feet (Class 2)
This unnamed 10,000-footer is found 1.1 miles southwest of The General and 5 miles northeast of Red Mountain. Climb due west from the unnamed lake on the peak's east slopes to the summit ridge. Follow the ridge north to the summit. Access the peak from the Lightning Creek Trail, FST-156 [(F)(3.2.1)(a)]. USGS Mount Jordan

The General* 10,329 feet (Class 2)
The General is an attractive summit that rises sharply above Mystery Lake just 1.5 miles northwest of Mount Jordan. The peak was named after the nearby General Custer Gold Mine. The mountain's two summits both reach above 10,000 feet. The south summit is the highest point. It is recommended that the peak be climbed by traversing the ridgeline from Mount Jordan, although the peak is approachable from most directions [(F)(3.2.1)]. T. M. Bannon climbed the peak in 1915, but it is likely that prospectors made it to the summit before him. USGS Mount Jordan

Mount Jordan 10,063 feet (Class 2)
Mount Jordan is named after Sylvester Jordan, who discovered gold in this area in the 1870s. The peak is located north of the town of Bonanza and due west of Loon Creek Summit. It is climbed via its south ridge from the jeep trail that runs up Jordan Creek from just below Loon Creek Summit [(F)(3.2.1)]. Follow the old roadway to the south ridge and then scamper up the ridge. T. M. Bannon ascended the peak in 1915. USGS Mount Jordan

Mayfield Peak 9,846 feet (Class 2)
Mayfield Peak is the big isolated summit that sits 3.75 miles north/northeast of Mount Jordan. Its pyramid-shaped summit is surrounded by the Mayfield Creek drainage, which has cut deep trenches around the peak. Climb to the summit from FS-172 [(F)(3.2)] via the unnamed drainage that crosses the road due south of the summit. From the ridge top, turn northwest and follow the peak's southwest ridge to the summit. USGS Sherman Peak

Sherman Peak 9,892 feet (Class 2)
Sherman Peak, another big, isolated summit is 5 miles due east of Mayfield Peak. The USGS quad shows a trail passing within 600 feet of this peak's summit. This trail is not shown on the Forest Service maps. Climb the peak from FST-114 [(F)(3)(b)], which crosses the peak's south ridge 2 miles south of the summit. USGS Sherman Peak

Estes Mountain 9,643 feet (Class 3)
Estes Mountain is located 4 miles southeast of Mount Jordan and 4.5 miles north of Bonanza. Access the peak from FS-172 [(F)(3.2)] via the mining road that traverses its southern slopes. This road eventually crosses a saddle on the peak's east ridge and a side road leads from this point to more than 9,400 feet. Follow the road to its high point and then scramble to the top. USGS Custer

Mount Greylock 9,857 (Class 2)
Greylock, which Rick Baugher notes is yet another peak ascended by T. M. Bannon in 1915, is the attractive, pyramid-shaped summit 1.9 miles south of Estes Mountain. A lookout was placed on the summit in 1934. Although it was abandoned in 1942, it is still habitable today. Early Tertiary fossils are found below the summit. According to Baugher, the most direct ascent follows the ridgeline south from Estes Mountain/Mount Greylock saddle. USGS Custer

Custer Peak 9,753 feet (Class 1)
Custer Peak is located 5 miles east of the Bonanza GS and the Yankee Fork Salmon River. The summit is identified on the Challis National Forest map as the Custer fire lookout. The defunct lookout is available for public use on a first-come, first-served basis. Custer Peak, the culmination of several rugged ridges, stands in the heart of a small slice of de facto wilderness that is seldom visited. From the top, the expansive view includes Mount Borah and Mount McCaleb in the Lost River Range, Cabin Creek Peak and Twin Peaks in the Salmon River Mountains, and the Sawtooths. Trails lead to the summit from north, east, south, and west. The 6-mile north route, which uses FST-161 [(F)(3)(a)], is recommended because of its scenic qualities. T. M. Bannon climbed Custer in

Custer Peak's north face

1915. Baugher reports that the east face provides an excellent ski descent. USGS Custer

Ramshorn Mountain — 9,895 feet (Class 2-3)

Rocky Ramshorn Mountain is located west of Challis and north of Bayhorse Creek. The peak's lower slopes were extensively mined in the past and are strewn with debris from this activity, including the ruins of a tramway that used to lead up to the mine shafts on the upper slopes. The peak is climbed from lower Bayhorse Lake [(G)(1)]. From the lake, a faint trail leads off toward the summit. Although the route is not physically difficult, finding the correct course can be a problem. Bannon called this peak Bay Horse. Mining digs on the summit suggest that prospectors preceded his 1915 ascent. USGS Bayhorse

Bald Mountain — 10,313 feet (Class 2)

This peak is not only the third-highest point in the Salmon River Mountains, it also rises more than 5,000 feet in just 3.2 miles, making it one of the steepest peaks in Idaho. The best route up the peak is from the north. Drive up the Bayhorse Creek Road, FS-051 [(G)(1)(a)], to the forest boundary. Take the jeep trail that leads to the south until it ends, then follow the unnamed drainage to the summit. Bannon climbed this peak in 1915 and named it Ram. USGS Bald Mountain

Falconberry Peak — 9,465 feet (Class 2)

This remote summit is well worth the effort. Falconberry is located north of the Falconberry GS on Loon Creek and 3.6 miles west/southwest of Sleeping Deer Mountain. The peak's 700-foot north face plunges into Falconberry Lake, which is also one of Idaho's most remote mountain lakes at 8,700 feet. Since climbing the peak from Loon Creek (the nearest trail) would involve a climb of more than 4,000 feet, the recommended route it to approach the peak from Sleeping Deer Mountain via the strenuous connecting ridge. USGS Falconberry Peak/Ramey Hill/Sleeping Deer/Rock Creek

Sleeping Deer Mountain — 9,881 feet (Class 1)

This large mountain located 28 miles northwest of Challis shows signs of past alpine glaciation in its many cirques, several of which contain beautiful lakes. The fire lookout on the summit was built in 1933. In 1879, Captain Reuben F. Bernard and his U.S. Army troops pursued a band of Sheepeater Indians over the summit, causing a forced first ascent by the Native Americans. The trail to the summit is reached from FS-086 [(G)(2)(a)] and a trailhead at 9,100 feet elevation on the peak's east side. From the trailhead, it is a short walk to the summit. USGS Sleeping Deer Mountain/RNRW

Martin Mountain — 9,406 feet (Class 1)

Martin Mountain is located west of Challis and north of Sleeping Deer Mountain. From Sleeping Deer, follow FST-103 [(G)(2)(b)] north for 5 miles to the summit. USGS Sleeping Deer Mountain/RNRW

The Twin Peaks:
South Twin Peak	10,340 feet
North Twin Peak	10,196 feet

The area just west of Challis, the center of the Challis Volcanics, features the tallest real estate in the Salmon River Mountains. The Twin Peaks rise more than 5,000 feet above the Salmon River, just 5 miles away. The Twins and many surrounding peaks sit on the south rim of a huge caldera left when a massive volcano (much like Mount Rainier) collapsed millions of years ago. South Twin Peak, the second highest mountain in the Salmon River Mountains, contains a fire lookout reached by road. USGS Twin Peaks

North Twin Peak (Class 2). Climb this peak via its southern ridge from the saddle between it and South Twin Peak. It is 1 mile and 1,000 feet of elevation gain to the summit over moderate slopes. Leave FS-086 [(G)(2)] and walk due north up through the forest and barren upper slopes to the ridge top. From this point, stay on the ridge as it curves northeast to the summit.

South Twin Peak (Class 1). FS-090 [(G)(2.2)] leads directly to the summit, and is taken by 99 percent of those who visit the summit. The road requires a 4WD and thus—for those interested in walking to the top—does not see much traffic. Bannon climbed the peak in 1913. The peak's steep north ridge has been skied.

White Mountain   *10,400+ feet*

The highest summit in the Salmon River Mountains is located 1.5 miles southwest of Twin Peaks. The name is derived from the peak's western ridge, which is composed of a brilliant white rock visible from all the major summits to the west. Nevertheless, there is some confusion about this peak because the USGS originally attached the name "White Mountain"

to a lower subsidiary point on the peak's shoulder rather than to the actual highest point, which is 0.5 mile to the west. There is nothing "white" about this subsidiary point, however. USGS Twin Peaks

North Ridge (Class 3). Access the north ridge from South Twin Peak and FS-090 [(G)(2.2)]. Turn onto FS-090 and follow it to the second switchback at 1.5 miles. There is a large turnout and a sign that proclaims TWIN CREEK LAKES TRAIL at this point. This trail, which is not on the maps, leads down South Twin Peak's south ridge to the saddle just below White Mountain. Leave the trail at this point and follow the ridge up on mostly stable rock (the last 400 vertical feet cross extremely broken and loose rock) to the base of the summit. Pass the first fin on the ridge by staying low and traversing its west side. From this point, stay mostly on the top or the east side of the ridge for the remaining distance. Some may find it easier to detour down onto the lower eastern slopes of this ridge to avoid a tricky notch about midway along the ridge.

Southwest Ridge (Class 3). This route begins at Challis Creek [(G)(2.1)]. To reach the lakes, take the Challis Creek road out of Challis and follow it to its end at Mosquito Flat Reservoir. From the reservoir, follow the jeep trail west and then north up Challis Creek to the lakes. The ascent to the summit presents no objective difficulties until the base of the summit pyramid, where some Class 3 climbing is encountered.

The north face of White Mountain, the highest summit in the vast Salmon River Mountains. The right skyline is the north ridge

White Goat Mountain   *9,421 (Class 1)*

This former fire lookout site offers an excellent viewpoint on the eastern edge of the RNRW. Its summit is located 9.5 miles north of the Twin Peaks. It is best accessed from the West Fork Morgan Creek via FST-143 [(G)(3.1)(a)]. USGS Black Mountain

Van Horn Peak   *9,616 (Class 2)*

This cone-shape summit, located 7 miles northeast of White Goat Mountain, dominates the view as one drives up the Morgan Creek Road. Climb from Van Horn Creek [(G)(3.3)(a)]. Take the trail west to its junction with FST-221. From the junction, climb south to Point 9236 and then continue east to the summit. USGS Black Mountain

Woods Peak   *9,730 (Class 2)*

This large summit sits squarely on the divide that runs southwest from Taylor Mountain to Twin Peaks. It is 7 miles southwest of Taylor Mountain and 1.5 miles north of Van Horn Peak. The peak is accessible from almost any direction. The shortest route begins in Alder Creek [(G)(3.4)(a)]. Leave the road at its westernmost turn and follow the peak's northwest ridge to the summit. USGS Black Mountain

Black Mountain   *9,510 feet*

Black Mountain's remote summit is located 3 miles northwest of Woods Peak. The best approach is to follow the Alder Creek Road [(G)(3.4)(a)] to its end and then take FST-135 to FST-221. This trail leads to the unnamed lake on the peak's southern slopes. From the lake it is 0.4 mile and a 600-foot elevation gain to the summit. USGS Black Mountain

Taylor Mountain   *9,960 feet (Class 2)*

This big peak is located 26 miles north of Challis and north of the Morgan Creek Summit in a small, roadless area accessible from either the north or the south. Eleven mountain lakes are visible from the summit of Taylor Mountain. Taylor was first used as a fire lookout site in the 1920s. By the late 1930s, Taylor Mountain was relegated to an emergency lookout. While it has long since been abandoned, remnants of the access trail and the lookout are still visible on the summit. R. Baugher reports that a Native American hunting blind is also located near the summit, suggesting someone preceded Bannon's 1915 climb.

The recommended approach is from Morgan Creek Summit [(G)(3.5)(b)]. Take the trail to the lake basin southeast of the peak. The summit is reached after a scramble on moderate slopes from the lake basin to the saddle south of the summit.

From this point, take the old lookout trail to the top. USGS Taylor Mountain

APPROACHES TO THE SALMON RIVER MOUNTAINS

Second in size only to the Clearwater Mountains, the Salmon River Mountains include a massive and diverse chunk of Idaho within their circumference. Literally hundreds of roads and trails crisscross the land, creating a complex and varied approach system. This section describes approaches beginning at the nearest "gateway towns," which are (A) Riggins, (B) McCall, (C) Cascade, (D) Banks, (E) Lowman, (F) Stanley, (G) Challis, and (H) Salmon.

(A) RIGGINS APPROACHES

Riggins, a village of 527 people, is located on US-95 at the extreme northwest corner of the Salmon River Mountains. The town provides all essential services.

(1) FS-1614, Salmon River Road. This road leaves US-95 at the south end of Riggins and runs up the main fork of the Salmon River for 27.2 miles. It provides an alternative access to the northwest corner of these mountains.

(1.1) FS-246, French Creek Burgdorf Road. This road leaves FS-1614 and the Salmon River 20 miles east of Riggins, climbs to Burgdorf in 23 miles, and connects with FH-21, the Warren Wagon Road, in 2 more miles. See [(B)(2)], below.

(B) MCCALL APPROACHES

McCall is a major resort town on the shores of Payette Lake. Primary access to the town is via ID-55. Food, gas, lodging, and even some outdoor equipment is available from the town's merchants.

(1) FS-257, Goose Creek/Hazard Lake Road. This road is reached from McCall by driving northwest on ID-55 for 6 miles to the Brundage Mountain Ski Area turnoff. From the highway, this road leads north for more than 25 miles, ending north of Hazard Lake. The road is paved to the junction for the ski area, which is 3.9 miles from ID-55. Beyond this point, it is usually passable to autos. Nevertheless, a 4WD is recommended.

(a) FST-165, Granite Mountain Trail. To reach this trail, follow FS-257 north for 13.4 miles to the FST-165 trailhead. The trail climbs west to the summit of Granite Mountain in just under 3 miles. Once over the summit, the trail descends to FS-294, which connects with US-95 near New Meadows. To reach the trail from New Meadows, drive north on US-95 for 4 miles and turn right onto FS-294, which parallels the edge of the mountains for many miles before reaching the trailhead along Browns Creek.

(b) FST-163, Grass Mountains Divide Trail. This trail leaves FS-257 just south of the Hard Creek GS, which is 18.7 miles north of ID-55. FST-163 leads into the heart of the Grass Mountains and provides access to several mountain lakes along its course.

(c) FST-347, Hard Butte Trail System. FST-347 leaves from the end of FS-257 26.1 miles north of ID-55 or 7 miles north of the Hard Creek GS. It leads northwest to Warm Springs Saddle, where the extensive Hard Butte trail system begins. This trail system crisscrosses this roadless area. Trail conditions vary from trail to trail and generally require at least intermediate skills.

(c.1) FST-344. This trail leaves FST-347 at Warm Springs Saddle and makes a half-circle around the eastern, southern, and northern ends of Hard Butte in roughly 6 miles.

(c.2) FST-508, Hard Butte Trail. This trail is not shown on the Patrick Butte quad. The beginning of the trail in Warm Springs Saddle is signed and the trail is easy to follow for the first third of the distance. There is a junction about halfway between the saddle and Upper Twin Lake. Follow the fork that runs south to Hard Butte's east ridge. The second third is marked by stone cairns, and the last third has a good tread as it ascends the east ridge.

(c.3) FST-152/FST-151/FST-153/FST-371, Paradise Lake Loop. This route leaves Warm Springs Saddle and loops north between Hard Butte and Patrick Butte, providing access to Paradise Lake. From the loop, FST-152 runs east down Partridge Creek and then climbs west to join FST-149 near Sams Throne and Lava Butte [(B)(1.1)(a) and (b)].

(d) FST-169, Upper Hazard Lake Trail. The trail can be found just south of the Hard Creek GS or at Hazard Lake CG. It loops into the country south of FS-257. After leaving the road, the trail quickly crosses a divide and drops into Hard Creek. The trail soon forks. The south fork leads to Hidden Lake, the right fork to Hard Creek and Upper Hazard Lakes. These trails are well maintained.

(1.1) FS-308, Lava Butte Road. This road leaves FS-257 25.5 miles from ID-55 or 5.5 miles north of the Hard Creek GS and continues many tortuous miles north to provide access to the area east of Lava Butte.

(a) FST-149, Lava Butte Trail. This trail follows the major north/south divide that makes up the Lava Butte area. The trail begins where FS-308 crosses Big Dave Creek. FST-149 also can be reached from several feeder trails, including FST-347, which is the shortest route into the Lava Butte area.

(b) FST-152, Partridge Creek Trail. FST-152 leaves FST-149 southeast of Sams Throne and climbs westward over a saddle before descending into Partridge Creek. The trail is not well maintained and in places is only marked by sporadic blazes on trees. See [(B)(1)(c.3)].

(1.2) FS-281, Fisher Creek Road. This road leaves FS-257 6.9 miles from ID-55 and just below Brundage Reservoir. It crosses into the Fisher Creek drainage and ends on Fisher Creek Saddle after 10.5 miles. The road can be quite rough in its upper reaches. A 4WD is recommended.

(2) FH-21, Warren Wagon Road. This is one of the major roads in the Salmon River Mountains. It begins in McCall on the west side of Payette Lake and runs up the North Fork Payette River to Secesh Summit. It then crosses eastward to the Warren GS, where it ends. It is paved for the 31.5 miles to the Burgdorf junction, and is then gravel for 14.2 miles to Warren.

(a) FST-085/FST-315, Twentymile Lakes Trail. This trail leaves FH-21 at the north end of Upper Payette Lake and leads 6 miles east to north Twentymile Lake.

(b) FST-080/FST-084/FST-081, Loon Lake Trails. These trails are accessed from the Chinook CG just south of FH-21 and lead to Loon Lake at the north end of the Lick Creek Range. To reach the trailhead, take FH-21 north from McCall for 35.1 miles and turn into the CG that is 1.2 miles from the main road. FST-080 follows the Secesh River to Loon Creek, where it becomes FST-084 and climbs up Loon Creek to Loon Lake in a total of 5.5 miles. FST-081 leads directly from the CG to the lake by following the slopes above the river. From Loon Lake, FST-084 continues south for 12 miles to Duck Lake, Foolhen Meadows, and FH-48 [(B)(4)(b)].

(2.1) FS-260, Squaw Meadows Road. This road forks off FH-21 just north of Upper Payette Lake and follows the North Fork Payette River north for nearly 4 miles.

(a) FST-504/FST-308, Black Tip Northern Approach Route. From the end of FS-260, FST-504 proceeds west and then northwest to French Creek in 4 miles. At French Creek, FST-504 intersects with FST-308, which follows French Creek both north and south. To reach Black Tip, turn left (south) onto FST-308 and hike 6 miles to the summit. This trail sees little use and is difficult to follow in many places.

(2.2) FS-340, Warren to Big Creek. This gravel road leads from Warren to the South Fork Salmon River and the South Fork GS. It crosses the river on a new bridge and continues onto Big Creek [(B)(6)].

(2.3) FS-246, Burgdorf/French Creek Road. This road leaves FH-21 and leads north to the Salmon River east of Riggins [(A)(1.1)].

(a) FST-143/FST-142, Bear Pete Mountain Access. This trailhead is located north of Burgdorf where Pete Creek flows into Lake Creek. The trail climbs to a ridgeline north of Bear Pete

Mountain in 4.1 miles, where it meets FST-142. Follow FST-142 south for 2 miles until it intersects with the trail that leads north to the Bear Petes summit.

(3) FH-48, Yellow Pine Road. Access to this road is in downtown McCall at ID-55, just south of Payette Lake. Turn east off of ID-55 on Thompson Street. Follow Thompson east to Davis Avenue. Turn left and drive north on Davis to Lick Creek Road. This road proceeds along the east shore of Payette Lake to Little Payette Lake, Lick Creek Summit, and the town of Yellow Pine.

(a) Black Lee Creek Trail. This trail leaves FH-48 11 miles north of McCall and climbs to Box Lake in 3.5 miles. This is a steep route; the first mile climbs more than 800 feet and the second mile is not much better. The trail crosses a saddle just east of the lake and then drops 300 feet to the lake.

(b) FST-104, East Fork Lake Fork/Snowslide Lake Loop Trail. This trail has two trailheads along FH-48. The first is at Lake Fork CG 10 miles northeast of McCall. The second is located 6 miles north of the Lake Fork CG. **Lake Fork CG Trailhead.** From the CG, the trail follows the Lake Fork Creek east to a trail junction in roughly 1 mile. At this junction, FST-103 [(B)(4)(b)] runs south to Boulder Summit (Pass); FST-104 continues east a short distance and then turns north to follow the East Fork Lake Fork drainage north for 5 miles to a second junction. At this second junction, FST-104 meets FST-086 [(B)(3)(e)] and then turns west, crosses the Lick Creek Range crest between Snowslide and Sawtooth Peaks and then descends to rejoin FH-48 in another 4 miles. **Snowslide Lake Trailhead.** The northern trailhead is identified by a sign on FH-48 11 miles north of McCall. There is parking for only two or three vehicles at this trailhead. From this trailhead, the trail immediately crosses the North Fork Lake Fork (a difficult crossing in high water) and almost immediately begins to climb to Snowslide Lake in 2 very steep miles. From the lake, the trail takes an even steeper 1-mile route to the saddle between Snowslide and Sawtooth Peaks.

(b.1) FST-086, North Fork Fitsum Summit Trail. This trail leaves FST-104 6 miles north of Lake Fork CG and provides access to the North Fork Fitsum Creek. See [(B)(3)(e)].

(c) FST-084, Duck Lake/Loon Lake Trail. This trail is accessed roughly 1.5 miles north of Lick Creek Summit at a large, new trailhead. From FH-48, the trail runs north to Duck Lake in about 1 mile and then continues northeast over a divide and into the upper section of the Loon Creek drainage, eventually reaching Loon Lake after 12 miles [(B)(2)(b)].

(c.1) FST-083/FST-082, Hum Lake/North Fork Lick Creek Trail. This trail forks off FST-084 at Duck Lake and runs northeast to Hum Lake. At Hum Lake the route divides. FST-083 descends Hum Creek to meet FH-48, while FST-082 climbs up to the top of the divide north of the lake and then traverses northeast to

the southern slopes of South Loon Mountain in 2 miles. From the high point on South Loon Mountain, FST-082 descends along the North Fork Lick Creek to a junction with FST-081 in 5 miles.

(d) FST-081, Loon Lake Trail. This trail is accessed from FH-48 where the North Fork Lick Creek crosses the road just west of Ponderosa CG and the Secesh River. The trail runs north from FH-48 to Loon Lake in 10 miles. Also see [(B)(2)(b)], above.

(e) FST-086, North Fork Fitsum Creek Trail. This trail leaves FH-48 near Ponderosa CG, climbs Cow Creek in a southern direction, crosses a divide and drops into the North Fork Fitsum Creek. Once the route reaches the bottom of the drainage it follows the creek west to North Fitsum Summit, crosses the pass and descends to join FST-104 [(B)(3)(b)] east of Snowslide Peak.

(f) FST-079, Tail Holt Peak Trail. The lower portion of this trail is not shown on the Payette National Forest map; nevertheless, FST-079 leaves FH-48 at a signed trailhead west of the point where the Secesh flows into the South Fork Salmon River. The trail climbs steeply to Tail Holt Peak in roughly 6 miles and then follows a ridgeline north to Bear Lake in another 7 miles.

(g) FST-073, Williams Peak Lookout Trail. This trail leaves FH-48 where that road crosses Williams Creek. It makes a short, but steep, 3-mile ascent of Williams Peak.

(h) FST-070, Rainbow Ridge Trail. FST-070 begins at a signed junction just past the Williams Peak summit and runs east (as the crow flies) to a point below Parks Peak, where it joins FST-069. This rugged and poorly maintained trail is roughly 12 miles long.

(i) FST-069, Parks Peak Trail. This trail leaves FH-48 and the East Fork South Fork Salmon River 0.4 mile east of where the road crosses Park Creek (or roughly 2 miles east of Yellow Pine). The trail begins as a closed road. The last time I visited, the trailhead was not signed but the road and trail are exactly where they are shown on the USGS quads. Park and follow the road up to a little saddle where the trail can be found. The route is steep, climbing 4,200 feet in 6.5 miles. There is plenty of water along the trail, which has a good tread for most of its distance. It is a little sketchy along the last mile. Look for rock cairns.

(3.1) FS-412/FS-375, Yellow Pine to Monumental Creek. From Yellow Pine, FS-412 continues east. In 5 miles, it intersects with FS-340 [(B)(3.2)], which leads to Big Creek. From this junction, the road continues east over Monumental Summit to Monumental Creek. After 25 miles, the road reaches the Upper Monumental Creek trailhead. From this trailhead, FS-375 leaves Monumental Creek and climbs up Coon Creek to the Lookout Mountain Ridge trailhead and FST-061. Leave plenty of time in your schedule to reach these trailheads. Also, be warned that these roads receive heavy traffic from mining-related vehicles. Watch out!

(a) FST-005, Monumental Creek Trail. This trail leaves FS-375 at Coon Creek and follows Monumental Creek north to Big Creek in the RNRW, a distance of more than 20 miles [(B) (3.2.1)(a)].

(b) FST-061, Lookout Mountain Ridge Trail. This trail leaves the end of FS-375 and crosses Lookout Mountain Ridge to Lookout Mountain in 8 miles.

(3.2) FS-340, Yellow Pine to Big Creek to Warren. This road leaves FS-412 5 miles east of Yellow Pine and runs north, climbing over 7,605-foot Profile Gap in 14 miles and then descending to the Big Creek Work Center at mile 24. Just south of the work center, the road turns west and heads over 8,670-foot Elk Summit in another 9.3 miles. From Elk Summit, the road descends to the South Fork Salmon River and eventually continues to Warren (and FS-21) in a total of 75.3 miles. See [(B)(2.2)] for further details.

(a) Missouri Ridge Trail. This trail leaves FS-340 4.4 miles north of its junction with FS-412. The trail is an old mining road that leads up Missouri Creek for 3 miles. Park at the beginning of the roadway—it is impassable to all vehicles a short distance from FS-340. The trail follows the stream bottom for 2 miles to a cabin, crosses the creek, and then begins to switchback up Missouri Ridge. After many switchbacks, the roadway narrows and becomes a trail for the last 1 mile to the top of Missouri Ridge, where it ends. Although the trail is moderately easy to follow at this time, it is not a maintained Forest Service route and could become impassable in the future.

(b) FST-066, Missouri Ridge Lookout Trail. FST-066 forks off the Missouri Ridge Trail 0.5 mile east of FS-340 and ends at a viewpoint on the western end of the ridge.

(c) FST-004, Cougar Basin Trail. This trail leaves FS-340 22 miles north of its junction with FS-412, 1.5 miles south of the Edwardsburg/Big Creek junction. The trail runs southeast over Cougar Saddle into Cougar Basin, and then meets FST-005 and continues to Monumental Creek [(B)(3.1)(a)]. The total distance is about 17 miles.

(c.1) FST-065, Center Mountain Trail. This is a primitive trail that leaves FST-004 north of Cougar Basin and climbs over Snowslide Peak and Center Mountain in 5.5 miles and then descends to Big Creek in 12.5 miles.

(d) FST-120/FST-284, South Fork Elk Creek Trail. This trail leaves FS-340 roughly 8 miles west of Elk Summit and climbs the South Fork Elk Creek toward Profile Lake at the base of Profile Peak. The 6-mile trail is maintained to within 1 mile of the lake.

(3.2.1) FS-371/FS-373, Smith Creek Road/Werdenhoff Mine Road. FS-371 begins at the Edwardsburg/Big Creek junction on FS-340 [(B)(3.2)] and follows Big Creek north, past the

Big Creek Work Center to its junction with Smith Creek and the Big Creek trailhead in 3 miles. The road then turns northwest and follows Smith Creek for 5 miles to a signed junction. From this junction, FS-371 continues up Smith Creek and is either impassable or nearly impassable. (A sign states MINING ACCESS ROAD/ NOT RECOMMENDED FOR PUBLIC USE. The sign is accurate.) FS-373, the Werdenhoff Mine Road, is also rough and a 4WD is required to reach these trailheads. From the junction, FS-373 leads to the Mosquito Ridge trailhead in 2.3 miles and the Pueblo Summit trailhead in 4 miles.

(a) FST-196, Big Creek Trail. This is one of the major east/west routes through the RNRW. The trail covers more than 40 miles as it follows Big Creek east to the Middle Fork Salmon River.

(a.1) FST-001, Beaver Creek/Chamberlain GS Trail. This trail leaves Big Creek and FST-196 4.5 miles east of FS-371 and runs north through Chamberlain Basin to the main Salmon in 39 miles.

(a.2) FST-002, Crooked Creek/Cold Meadows GS/Chamberlain Basin GS Trail. This is a primary north/south route through the northern portion of the RNRW known as the Chamberlain Basin. It leaves Big Creek and FST-196 at Crooked Creek and proceeds northeast to Cold Meadows GS in 16 miles, then turns northwest and follows a ridgeline to Chamberlain Basin in another 20 miles.

(a.2.1) FST-009, Bismark Mountain Trail. This trail leaves FST-002 2.8 miles above Big Creek and climbs up to Bismark Saddle in 4 miles.

(a.2.2) FST-043, Cold Mountain Trail. FST-043 leaves FST-002 0.5 mile south of Cold Springs GS and climbs up to the summit of Cold Mountain in 2.5 miles.

(a.3) FST-044, Horse Mountain/Black Butte Trail. This trail leaves Big Creek at Cabin Creek and then climbs up to the summit of Horse Mountain in 6 miles. From this point, it continues northeast to Black Butte and a junction with FST-168 [(H) (3)(b)] in another 5.5 miles.

(b) FST-003, Mosquito Ridge Trail. FST-003 leaves FS-371/FST-373 7.3 miles above Big Creek and climbs steeply up to the top of Mosquito Ridge. The trail then follows the ridge north to Mosquito Peak in 12 miles and Sheepeater Mountain in another 9 miles. From Sheepeater Mountain, the trail turns east and continues to Chamberlain Basin GS in another 11 miles. Chicken Springs and Mosquito Springs provide adequate water even in the driest years.

(4) FS-403, Boulder Creek Road. Turn east off ID-55 just south of the McCall Airport at highway milepost 142. (A Mormon church is located just east of ID-55 at this turn.) Follow this paved road east as it makes several 90-degree turns and eventually intersects with FS-403 at a signed intersection. Turn onto FS-403, which is paved, and follow it east. The pavement ends in 1 mile and crosses a cattleguard at 1.8 miles. Just after the cattleguard there is a major junction—continue straight ahead here and at all other minor junctions. FS-403 dead-ends after 4.8 miles at the base of the Boulder Meadows Reservoir dam. There are two trailheads at the end of the road.

(a) **Louie Lake Trail.** This trail begins at a signed trailhead 100 yards west of the Boulder Meadows Reservoir dam and runs for 2 miles to Louie Lake at the base of Jughandle Mountain's picturesque north face. The last 1 mile of the trail is along a jeep trail that also can be accessed from the west.

(b) **FST-105/FST-103/FST-096, Boulder Creek Trail System.** From the end of FS-403 at the north end of the Boulder Meadows Reservoir, this trail system leads to Boulder Lake and beyond and gives access to many of the Lick Creek Range's most interesting peaks. FST-105 runs due east from the trailhead for 3 miles past Boulder Lake to a trail junction. From this junction, FST-103 runs north and south. Taking FST-103 north will lead to Boulder Summit (Pass) in just over 1 mile and to Lake Fork CG on FH-48 [(B)(4)(a)] in another 4 miles. Traveling south on FST-103 leads to the Paddy Flat GS in 7 miles. Also from this junction, FST-096 runs due east over Buckhorn Summit and eventually to the South Fork Salmon River at Poverty Flat [(C)(1.1)(d)].

(c) **Boulder Lake to Louie Lake Trail.** The Paddy Flat USGS quad shows a trail leaving FST-105 just east of Boulder Lake and proceeding south to the pass between Jughandle Mountain and Twin Peaks, where it descends to Louie Lake. Though this trail is not shown on the newest Payette National Forest maps, it does exist as shown on the USGS map. An old, vandalized sign on a tree (visible only to those walking west on FST-105) marks the beginning of the trail. Although the tread is difficult to follow at first (and disappears occasionally), this very scenic trail is well worth the effort. The USGS map will prove invaluable for following this route.

(5) **FS-388, Kennally Creek Road.** This road leaves ID-55 3 miles north of Donnelly. Turn east onto a county road that becomes FS-388. This road leads to Kennally Creek CG. From the road's end, FST-099, FST-101, and FST-102 lead deep into the range's roadless country and provide access to many peaks. The road is passable to passenger cars. Access to the Jughandle Mountain area is also possible from FS-388, but you will need a 4WD.

(a) **FST-099/FST-306, East Fork to Blackmare Lookout Trail.** This trail leaves the Kennally Creek trailhead and proceeds up Kennally Creek to Cougar Creek Summit in 5.5 miles, where it intersects with several other trails, including FST-306, which leads to the top of Blackmare Peak in another 0.8 mile.

(b) **FST-101, Needles Trail.** FST-101 leaves FST-099 just

east of the Kennally Creek trailhead and climbs steeply to Needles Summit (Pass) in 4 steep miles. At the summit, the trail enters the Boise National Forest and intersects with FST-115, which runs south into the Gold Fork drainage and FST-303 [(C)(1.1)(e)]. FST-303 supposedly follows a ridge top east toward White Rock Peak and then northeast to the South Fork Salmon River, but the tread can be difficult to locate east of Needles Summit.

(6) **FS-498/FS-402, Gold Fork Access.** From the Cascade Post Office, drive north on ID-55 for 12.9 miles to a point just south of where the highway crosses the Gold Fork River. Turn east and drive 0.2 mile, turn right again and drive south for 0.3 mile and then turn left onto FS-498. Follow FS-498 east for 9.3 miles to the first FS-498/FS-402 junction. (Note that FS-402 loops east and then rejoins FS-498 farther north.) Continue straight ahead for another 2.7 miles and turn left at the second FS-402 junction. Turn right and follow FS-402 for 7.2 miles to the Gold Fork trailhead. From this trailhead, FST-114 and then FST-115 give access to the southern Lick Creek Divide. (Note: FS-498 continues north from its junction with FS-402 and eventually leads to Kennally Creek CG [(B)(5)].) A 4WD is recommended.

(a) **Needles Peak Access.** This approach point is located 100 yards west of the Gold Fork trailhead where an old skid road numbered FS-402D (and not shown on the Forest Service map) runs off to the northeast. The old skid road requires a 4WD—it may be best to park on FS-402 and walk it as it cuts around a hillside to a clear-cut. Once in the clear-cut, leave the road, climb west up to the ridge top and then hike the ridge north cross-country up to the top of Needles Peak. The first part of the ridge is very brushy.

(C) **CASCADE APPROACHES**

Cascade is a small resort/logging town on ID-55. The town of 1,000 provides food, gas, and lodging.

(1) **FS-22/FS-579, Warm Lake Highway/Landmark/ Stanley Road.** This road leaves Cascade and ID-55 at the north edge of town and goes 26 miles to Warm Lake, another 11 miles to Landmark and to 10/21 and Stanley after 108 miles. The road is paved to Landmark and is plowed in the winter to Warm Lake. After the pavement ends, the road continues as a high-quality gravel road. Using this road, ID-21, and the Warm Lake Road, it is 108 miles between Cascade and Stanley.

(a) **FST-009/FST-102, Rice Peak Trail.** The route to Rice Peak begins 3 miles south of Deadwood Summit and climbs up to a ridge top in 4 miles. From the top of the ridge, FST-102 runs north and south. Rice Peak is 2 miles south of the junction. This trail receives little use or maintenance.

(b) **FST-013, Blue Bunch Mountain Trail.** This trail leaves the Landmark/Stanley Road 5 miles northwest of Cape

Horn Summit at Fir Creek CG. It climbs to the top of Blue Bunch Mountain in a long 4.5 miles.

(c) FST-024, Lolo Lakes Trail. FST-024 begins at Cape Horn Summit on the Stanley/Landmark Road and climbs up to the base of Cape Horn Mountain before dropping down into Lolo Creek. The trail along the top of the ridge and down the ridge into Lolo Creek is sketchy in places. However, the open nature of the terrain allows for easy cross-country travel.

(1.1) FS-474/FS-674, South Fork Salmon River Road. This road follows the South Fork Salmon River from near its headwaters (south of Stolle Meadows) to its confluence with the East Fork South Fork Salmon River (east of Yellow Pine), a distance of 45 miles. The section of the road between the Warm Lake Road and FH-21 is paved and often plowed in the winter to provide access to Yellow Pine. This is a narrow road with many blind corners. Drive slowly.

(a) FST-087, Fitsum Creek Trail. This trail leaves the South Fork Salmon River Road just south of its junction with FH-21, the Lick Creek Summit/Yellow Pine Road. The trail runs southwest up Fitsum Creek for 12 miles to Fitsum Summit northwest of Nick Peak. Though brushy, the trail has a good tread. Stream crossing is difficult early in the season.

(b) FST-090, Indian Ridge Trail. FST-090 leaves the South Fork Salmon River Road at the Krassel Work Center. It follows Indian Ridge southeast to Indian Peak in 8 miles and on to Eagle Rock in an additional 3 miles. Near Eagle Rock, the trail intersects with several other trails, including FST-091 to Caton Lake, FST-092, which leads south to Log Mountain, and FST-093, which is discussed below.

(c) FST-093, Fourmile Creek Trail. This trail leaves the South Fork Salmon River Road 17.4 miles south of the Warm Lake Road and climbs up to Fourmile Summit (just south of Eagle Rock) in 7 miles. From here, it joins with the Indian Ridge trail system.

(c.1) FST-092, Log Mountain Trail. FST-092 leaves FST-093 just south of Fourmile Summit and follows a ridgeline south to Log Mountain in 5 miles. The tread varies from good to nonexistent. For the most part, the trail is easy to follow when it is in the trees, and hard to find when it goes through meadows. Keep your eyes open.

(d) FST-100, Blackmare Creek Trail. This trail leaves FS-674 and the South Fork Salmon River at the Poverty Flat trailhead, which is 14.4 miles north of the Warm Lake/Landmark Road. There is camping available at the trailhead and a good steel bridge across the river. FST-100 reaches Blackmare Summit after 8 miles. From Blackmare Summit, FST-306 runs northeast to Blackmare Peak, FST-098 leads north to Cougar Creek and FST-099 leads west to the Boulder Lake area. See [(B)(4)(b)], above.

(e) FST-303, White Rock Peak Trail. This trail leaves the South Fork Salmon River Road at the same point as FST-100 described above and climbs southwest to White Rock Peak in 5 miles and Needles Summit in about 9, sometimes obscure, miles [(B)(5)(b)].

(f) FST-109, Cougar Rock Trail. This trail leaves FS-674 south of the Warm Lake/Landmark Road. On the latest edition of the Payette National Forest map and on the USGS Warm Lake quad, this trail is clearly shown leaving the South Fork Salmon River Road at the Stolle Meadows GS. Both maps are out of date and inaccurate. Ignore the route shown on the maps. Instead, take FS-474 south from FS-22 for 4.7 miles and then turn west onto FS-483, which is signed LOGGING ROAD. FS-483 is partially shown on the Payette National Forest map, but is not shown on the Warm Lake quad. Drive across the river on a good bridge, turn left when the road forks, and follow it up to a saddle at 5,640 feet 1 mile southeast of Cougar Rock. At this saddle, the road turns sharply and drops steeply downhill. Park on the saddle. Look carefully for a trail running uphill. The route is vague in places, but sharp eyes can find blazes on trees for the entire distance. Cougar Rock is reached in 1 mile; Stolle Peak is 2 miles from the start of the trail. A 4WD is required to drive FS-483 and expert skills are required to hike the trail.

(1.2) FS-467, Cabin Creek Road. This road leaves the Warm Lake Road north of Warm Lake and follows Cabin Creek north for 5 miles. A 4WD is recommended.

(a) FST-086, Thunderbolt Mountain Trail. FST-086 leaves FS-467 at its end and proceeds to the top of Thunderbolt Mountain in 1.2 miles.

(1.3) FS-413, Johnson Creek Road. This road begins at Landmark and follows Johnson Creek north for 23 miles to Yellow Pine Road [(B)(3)]. This road is graded and suitable for autos.

(a) FST-091, Trout Creek Trail. Access this road by turning west off the Johnson Creek Road 7.2 miles north of Landmark. Follow the dirt road to its end, where the trail begins. It is roughly 3 miles to the top of Thunderbolt Mountain.

(1.3.1) FS-410, Shell Rock Road. This road leaves the Johnson Creek Road at Coffee Creek and then wiggles its way northwest to a trailhead east of Shell Rock Peak.

(a) FST-094/FST-093/FST-096, Caton Lake Trail. The Caton Lake Trail leaves the Shell Rock Road trailhead and proceeds north to Caton Lake in 6 miles and then joins up with the FST-090 on Indian Ridge in 9 miles. See [(C)(1.1)(b)], above.

(1.3.2) FS-440, Thunder Mountain Road. This road leaves Johnson Creek midway between Landmark and Yellow Pine. It is a 4WD road from the start. It leads northeast to Monumental Summit [(B)(3.1)] by first following Trapper Creek, then traversing the Riordan Creek drainage, and then climbing to the top of the Johnson Creek/Middle Fork Divide. Near Monumental Summit, the road crosses the western slopes of Murphy Peak.

(a) FST-088, Summit Trail. The summit trail leaves the Thunder Mountain Road on a ridge top east of Riordan Creek and runs south past Chilcoot Peak and Lake Mountain to the Artillery Dome Road many miles to the south. See [(C)(1.4)(a)].

(1.4) FS-447, Big Baldy/Chinook Mountain Access. Leave Landmark on FS-447, Burnt Log Road. In 2 miles this route turns left (north). Go straight at a junction in another 2 miles. There are many side roads along this route. Generally, the best road is FS-447. At roughly 6 miles the road crosses Burnt Log Creek and at 12 miles FS-448 leads off to the right. Continue on FS-447 to a trailhead in another 5.9 miles or 17.9 miles from Landmark.

(a) FST-090/FST-088, Summit Trail. FST-090 leads due west for 0.5 mile to FST-088, the Summit Trail. FST-088 runs north for many miles to FS-440, the Thunder Mountain Road [(C)(1.3.2)], and south to FS-447E, Artillery Dome Road. Lake Mountain is 3 miles to the south and Chilcoot Peak is 1 mile to the north. South of Chilcoot Mountain, FST-227, Big Baldy Ridge Trail, runs east toward Big Baldy Peak in about 8 miles.

(1.5) FS-568, Dagger Falls Road. This road leaves the Landmark/Stanley Road in Bruce Meadows and runs north to the Middle Fork Salmon River in 11 miles.

(a) FST-068/FST-082, Morehead Mountain Trail. These two trails provide the best access to the summit of Morehead Mountain. FST-068 is the main trail down the Middle Fork Salmon. Follow it for 3 miles and then, just past the Morgan Airstrip, turn west and follow FST-082 up Prospect Creek to the summit.

(D) BANKS APPROACHES

Banks is located 36 miles north of Boise on ID-55, at the point where the north and main forks of the Payette River converge. Banks is the proverbial "wide spot in the road" and offers only gas and food as services.

(1) Payette River Road. This paved road leaves ID-55 at Banks and follows the South Fork Payette River east through Garden Valley to Lowman and ID-21 in 33 miles.

(1.1) FS-698, Middle Fork Payette River Road. This road leaves the Payette River Road at Crouch (8.1 miles east of ID-55) and runs north to Boiling Springs GS.

(a) FST-033/FST-100, East Mountain Trail. This trail leaves the Boiling Springs GS and follows Middle Fork Payette River north for many miles to Clear Creek Summit. At mile 6, FST-100 runs up Fool Creek Ridge to reach East Mountain in another 5 miles.

(1.2) FS-555, Deadwood Reservoir Road. This road leaves the Payette River Road 23.1 miles east of ID-55 (and 9 miles west of Lowman) at Big Pine Creek and runs north to Deadwood

Reservoir and FS-579, the Landmark/Stanley Road [(C)(1)]. It is 26 long, narrow miles to Deadwood Reservoir and a total of 36 miles to the Landmark/Stanley Road.

(E) LOWMAN APPROACHES

Lowman is a small village situated on the South Fork Payette River. Primary access is via ID-21. Lowman is 72 miles northeast of Boise and 57 miles southwest of Stanley. The village is connected with Banks by the Payette River Road [(D)(1)]. Lowman has a few year-round residents and offers gas and food.

(1) FS-582, Clear Creek Road. This road leaves ID-21 at Lowman and proceeds north to FST-579, the Landmark/Stanley Road, in 21 miles [(C)(1)].

(1.1) FS-515, Red Mountain Road. This road leaves FS-582 12 miles north of Lowman and runs northeast for 5 miles to the Red Mountain trailhead.

(a) FST-143/FST-145, Red Mountain Area Trails. These trails leads to Red Mountain and Mountain and Cat Creek Lakes. For Red Mountain, take FS-145 toward the lakes. Roughly 1 mile from the trailhead, look for an unsigned junction in a meadow-covered side hill. Take this trail, FS-143, to the summit in another 1.5 miles. From the junction, FST-145 continues to the lakes that are 3.5 to 4.5 miles away from the trailhead.

(F) STANLEY APPROACHES

Stanley was once just a small ranching town at the base of the Sawtooth Range, Salmon River, and White Cloud Mountains. With the creation of the Sawtooth National Recreation Area, Stanley's economy is changing from herding cattle to herding people. ID-21 reaches Stanley from Boise after 129 miles; ID-75 reaches Stanley from both Ketchum and Challis. Gas, food, lodging, and outfitters are available.

(1) FS-008, Seafoam Road. This road leaves ID-21 19 miles west of Stanley at a well-signed junction. The road forks immediately after it leaves ID-21. Take the right fork and then, in 0.5 mile, take the left-hand fork toward Seafoam GS. This road runs north and then west for 21 miles to the Josephus Lake CG.

(a) FST-014, Langer Lake Trail. This trail leaves FS-008 6.8 miles north of ID-21. The trail runs west to Langer Lake in 2.6 miles and connects with the trail to Roughneck Peak fire lookout in 3.75 miles. From here, FST-014 turns north and leads to FST-013 and Helldiver Lake in 6 miles.

(b) FST-007, Rapid River Trail. To reach this trail, follow FS-008 1.2 miles north from the Seafoam GS and then turn onto a dirt road that runs north up Rapid River for a short distance to the trailhead. This trail connects with FST-207 [(F)(1)(c)] in 10 miles and reaches the Middle Fork Salmon River in 14 miles.

(c) FST-207, Cabin Creek Trail. This trail leaves FST-007 10 miles north of its trailhead, then follows Cabin Creek north to the base of Little Soldier Mountain and a junction with the short trail that leads to its summit in 4 miles. From the summit, the trail descends to the Middle Fork Salmon River near the Pistol Creek Ranch landing strip in another 4 miles.

(d) **FST-013, Big Shoulder Mountain Trail.** This trail begins at the end of FS-008 at Josephus Lake and runs to the Middle Fork Salmon River. Big Soldier Mountain is 10 miles from the trailhead along a route that passes many lakes and crosses a long, scenic ridge.

(e) **FS-011/FST-008, Greyhound Mountain Trail.** This route leaves FS-008 roughly 2 miles before the Josephus CG. The road was originally built to service the Greyhound Mine. A 4WD is recommended.

(e.1) **FST-006, Access to Little Soldier Mountain.** This route leads north from Greyhound Mountain along a ridge for several miles before descending into and crossing the Rapid River. Once across the river, the route follows Cabin Creek north for 4 miles to the east side of Little Soldier Mountain, where a side trail leads to the summit. This is a long, tiring route.

(2) **FS-032, Basin Butte Road.** This road leaves ID-21 5 miles west of Stanley and climbs up to Basin Butte Lookout in 9 miles. From a junction just south of the lookout, the road continues to Hindman Lake and then to a locked gate at 18 miles. The last 9 miles to the gate require a 4WD. Beyond the gate, the mining access road continues almost to the summit of Red Mountain.

(3) **FS-013/FS-070, Yankee Fork to Challis Road.** To reach this road, drive east on ID-75 toward Challis for 14 miles to Sunbeam (42 miles west of Challis). At this wide spot in the highway, turn north on the Yankee Fork Road, FS-013, and go 9 miles to Bonanza. At Bonanza, the road forks. FS-070 leads northeast and east to Challis. A 4WD is recommended for this route past Bonanza (which is the slow way to drive to Challis).

(a) **FST-161/FST-163, Custer Peak Trail.** This route is accessed where FS-013 crosses Five Mile Creek, 4.5 miles northeast of Bonanza. The trail runs to the top of Custer Peak in 6 long miles. The route is easy to follow and well maintained. The only confusing spot is around a large meadow 3 miles in. At this point, an obvious trail leads uphill; take the less obvious trail (actually the main trail) around the meadow.

(b) **FST-114, Yankee Fork/Mayfield Creek Trail.** This trail leaves FS-070 at the point where the road leaves the Yankee Fork and proceeds southeast up McKay Creek. This trail follows the Yankee Fork north for 3 miles and then west to the river's headwaters south of Sherman Peak. The trail crosses a divide, drops into Trapper Creek, climbs out of Trapper Creek and crosses a second divide south of Sherman Peak and then descends into Mayfield Creek. This route is regularly maintained.

(3.1) **FS-074, West Fork Road.** This road leaves Bonanza at the GS and runs west for roughly 1 mile to a gate. This is a rough

road, but autos can probably make it to the gate.

(a) **FST-155, West Fork Trail.** FST-155 leaves from the end of FS-074 and works its way up the West Fork Yankee Fork for 5.5 miles to the confluence of Cabin Creek. From this point, follow FST-113 up Cabin Creek until the turn for Crimson Lake is reached. The Crimson Lake Trail is not shown on Forest Service or USGS maps, but it is signed and in passable condition.

(3.2) **FS-172, Loon Creek Summit Road.** This road begins 0.75 mile north of Bonanza (just past the old Yankee Fork dredge sitting by the road). The road climbs to Loon Creek Summit in 10 miles, and then descends to Loon Creek GS deep inside the RNRW in another 13 miles. From the GS, roads lead north, west, and south to provide access to most hiking trails that penetrate the southern portion of the RNRW. A 4WD is recommended.

(3.2.1) **FS-356, Jordan Creek Road.** This 4WD road leaves FS-172, the Loon Creek Summit Road, 6.1 miles north of its beginning. Turn west off FS-172 onto this road, which ends in 2.5 miles at roughly 9,300 feet in elevation. Beyond the road's end, a sketchy trail continues west, crosses the slopes of Mount Jordan and then drops into the Lightning Creek drainage.

(a) **FST-156, Lighting Creek Trail.** This trail leaves the end of FS-356 and quickly drops into Lighting Creek to the west. This trail can be followed south to the West Fork Yankee Fork [(F) (3.1)(a)]. The tread is a little hard to find in places.

(G) CHALLIS APPROACHES

Challis is a boom-or-bust town, dependent on the price of cattle and molybdenite, which is mined locally. Gas, food, and lodging are available. US-93 and ID-75 run north and west, respectively, from Challis and provide primary access to the eastern end of the range.

(1) **FS-051, Bayhorse Creek Road.** This road leaves ID-75 10 miles west of its junction with US-93 and climbs steeply up to Bayhorse Lake CG in 10 miles. Along the way, the road passes the mining town of Bayhorse. A 4WD is recommended.

(a) **FST-206, Juliette Creek Trail.** FST-206 leaves FS-051 1.3 miles above the ghost town of Bayhorse and runs due south to Kinnikinic Creek. A saddle on the west flanks of Bald Mountain is crossed 5 miles from Bayhorse Creek. This saddle is the best access point to the peak.

(2) **FS-086, Challis Creek/Sleeping Deer Mountain Road.** This road leaves downtown Challis and proceeds west for 43.1 miles to the base of Sleeping Deer Mountain. To reach this road, turn west off US-93 onto the Challis main street and then, in 0.5 mile, turn right onto the signed Challis Creek Road and follow it north and then west. The road is paved at first, then gravel. It eventually becomes very narrow and quite steep. FS-080 [(G) (2.1)] is reached in 10.5 mile, FS-090 (which leads to the South Twin Peak lookout [(G)(2.2)]) in 18.5 miles, and the saddle

between Twin Peaks in 19 miles. From the saddle, the road follows winding ridgelines west for another 23.9 miles to its end high above Rock Lakes. A 4WD is recommended.

(a) **FST-112, Sleeping Deer Mountain Trail.** This trail leaves from the end of FS-086 and climbs to the top of the mountain in 2 miles. It is an easy-to-follow trail that gains 760 feet along the way.

(b) **FST-103, Woodtick Summit Trail.** This superb ridge walk leaves FST-112 about 1 mile below the summit of Sleeping Deer Mountain. The trail reaches Woodtick Summit in 4 miles, and the base of Martin Mountain in another 2.5 miles.

(2.1) **FS-080/FST-091, Challis Creek Lakes Road.** This road leaves FS-086 10.5 mile west of Challis and runs to Mosquito Reservoir and Challis Creek Lakes in 18 miles. Beyond the reservoir, a 4WD is recommended.

(2.2) **FS-090, South Twin Peak Road.** This road leaves FS-086 18.5 miles west of Challis (0.5 mile east of the Twin Peaks saddle). The road climbs to South Twin Peak's 10,340-foot summit in just over 1 mile. A 4WD is recommended.

(3) **FS-055, Morgan Creek Road.** This road leaves ID-93 10 miles north of Challis. It climbs to Morgan Creek Summit in 19 miles, and then descends to Panther Creek, where it becomes the Panther Creek Road [(H)(4)], which eventually reaches the Main Fork Salmon east of US-93.

(3.1) **FS-057, West Fork Road.** The West Fork Road leaves FS-055 1 mile north of the BLM's Morgan Creek CG and 6.2 miles from US-93. This rough road runs northwest for 7 miles toward the Blow Fly CG. The trailhead is a short distance beyond the campground.

(a) **FS-143/138, White Goat Mountain Trail.** FST-143 and FST-138 provide the best access to White Goat Mountain. FST-143 follows West Fork Morgan Creek toward West Fork Lakes. Follow FST-143 3.5 miles from the road to a signed junction for the lakes. Go left at this junction and follow FST-143 southwest to the ridgeline southeast of White Goat Mountain where there is a large flat meadow. FST-138 passes obliquely through this meadow from left to right. Look for signs that mark the points where the trail leaves the meadow. Follow FST-138 generally northwest to the summit in slighty more than 1 mile.

(3.2) **FS-058, Lick Creek Road.** This road leaves the Morgan Creek Road 9 miles north of US-93 and follows Lick Creek northwest for roughly 3 miles. A 4WD is recommended.

(a) **FST-142, Lick Creek Trail.** This short trail runs northwest to join FST-138/139 near the divide that runs between Morgan Creek Summit and Twin Peaks where it connects with FST-139 [(G)(3.3)(a)].

(3.3) **FS-061, Van Horn Creek Road.** Access this road from

the Morgan Creek Road 12.4 miles from US-93. The road climbs for a little more than 2 miles. A 4WD is recommended.

(a) **FST-139, Van Horn Creek/Furnace Creek Trail.** This trail runs northwest to the Morgan Creek Summit/Twin Peaks Divide, then turns southwest and descends Furnace Creek to join the Lick Creek Trail (G)(3.2)(a).

(3.4) **FS-341, Alder Creek Road.** This road leaves the Morgan Creek Road at the north end of a large pasture roughly 14.8 miles from US-93, then works its way up toward the west slopes of Woods Mountain. A 4WD is required.

(a) **FST-135, Alder Creek Trail.** This trail climbs up to the Morgan Creek Summit/Twin Peaks Divide where it joins FST-138 northeast of Woods Peak.

(3.5) **FS-129, Upper Corral Creek Road.** This road leaves the Morgan Creek Road at Morgan Creek Summit, 19.4 miles from US-93 and winds 2.4 miles east to the upper portion of Corral Creek and the FST-251 trailhead. This bumpy road passes several side roads as it winds through a clear-cut, but the main road is easy to follow.

(a) **FST-251/FST-093, Hat Creek Lakes Trail.** From its trailhead, this trail takes a roundabout route to the Hat Creek Lakes, which it reaches in 4 up-and-down miles. From the lakes, it continues north to Iron Lake and the Salmon River Mountain Road, FS-020. A side trail not shown on the maps leaves the main trail just north of Lake 8805 and climbs to the highest lake where there is good camping and access to Taylor Mountain.

(b) **Taylor Mountain Trail.** This old trail once led to the summit of Taylor Mountain from FST-251. Above tree line, it is in surprisingly good shape, but is difficult to find when it moves into the forest.

(H) SALMON APPROACHES

Salmon, a town of 3,400 population, is reached via US-93 from Missoula and Challis, and via ID-28 from eastern Idaho. Food, gas, lodging, and some outdoor equipment shops can be found in town.

(1) **FS-021, Williams Creek Road.** This road is accessed from US-93 5.1 miles south of Salmon. Turn west off the highway and cross the Salmon River. Follow the road west for 0.5 mile and then follow it south along the Salmon River to Williams Creek. It is roughly 16.2 miles from this point to Williams Creek Summit, and another 10 miles to Panther Creek and FS-055.

(2) **FS-020, Salmon River Mountain Road.** This road runs along the eastern crest of the Salmon River Mountains for 42 miles between Iron Lake CG in the south and Napoleon Hill in the north. The road is accessed by many roads, including FS-021 as discussed above. A 4WD is advisable for much of the road.

(a) **FST-093, Hat Creek Lakes Trail.** FST-093 leaves

FS-020 at its southern terminus at Iron Lake CG and runs due south 2.5 miles to Hat Creek Lakes. It meets FS-055 [(G)(3)] 6 miles beyond the lakes.

(3) FS-030, Salmon River Road. This road leaves US-93 at North Fork 21 miles north of Salmon and follows the Salmon River west for 26 miles to Corn Creek CG. The road is paved at first, then gravel, and provides access to FS-055, the Panther Creek Road [(H)(4)], and the Middle Fork Canyon.

(a) FST-162, Salmon River Trail. From the end of FS-030, this trail follows the Salmon's main fork west and provides access to many trails that make the long climb out of the canyon and up to Chamberlain Basin. The trail eventually connects with FS-1614 [(A)(1)], which leads to Riggins and US-95.

(b) FST-202/FST-168, Black Butte Trail. This trail leaves FS-30 at Corn Creek CG and climbs steeply to Butts Creek Point. From the point, the trail soon joins FST-168, which leads south to Black Butte in 16 miles. Southeast of the butte, the trail joins FST-169, discussed below. Also see [(B)(3.2.1)(a.3)].

(c) FST-169, Stoddard Trail. This trail leaves the end of FS-030, crosses a bridge, and almost immediately climbs toward Chamberlain Basin. It is the most direct approach into the basin from the east—direct, but also long and difficult.

(d) FST-172, Dome Mountain Trail. This trail leaves FS-030 just west of Panther Creek and then climbs to Dome Mountain in 11 steep miles. At Dome Mountain, the trail joins FST-021 [(H)(4.1.1.1)(a)], then turns northeast, crosses Horse Heaven Peak, and makes a steep descent to the Salmon River, which can be crossed with the aid of a cable cart.

(4) FS-055, Panther Creek Road. This road leaves FS-030 and the main Salmon River Road 26 miles west of North Fork. It runs north to Morgan Creek Summit, where it becomes the Morgan Creek Road [(G)(3)] and leads south to US-93 at a point 10 miles north of Challis. This well-maintained gravel road is a major avenue in the eastern Salmon River Mountains.

(a) FST-023, Birch Trail. This trail leaves FS-055 roughly 7 miles south of the main Salmon River and climbs to Gant Peak and FST-026 in 6 long miles.

(4.1) FS-112, Yellowjacket Road. This road leaves the Panther Creek Road at Porphyry Creek. In 6 miles, the road crosses a saddle where FS-113 [(H)(4.1.1.1)] forks off to the north. FS-112 continues to the summit of Middle Fork Peak. Yellowjacket CG is located along the way at Yellowjacket Lake, which is at the base of Sugar Loaf peak.

(4.1.1) FS-113, Yellowjacket Lake Road. Turn off FS-112 onto FS-113, which leads to a junction with FS-114 in roughly 10 miles. Continuing straight ahead leads to Yellowjacket Lake in 4 miles, and the road's end in 5 miles.

(a) FST-039, McEleny Mountain Trail. This trail begins at the end of FS-113 and climbs to the top of McEleny Mountain in 3 miles, then descends to FS-112 at the old Yellowjacket town site.

(4.1.1.1) FS-114, Bighorn Crags Road. This road leaves FS-113 and proceeds north to Crags CG in 1.8 miles. The road is usually washboard-rough, but passable to autos.

(a) FST-021, Crags Trail. This is the longest of the Bighorn Crags trails. It starts at Crags CG and ends at Panther Creek, 31 miles later. Wilson Lake is about 7 miles from the CG and Dome Mountain is 15 miles farther in. For most of its distance, the trail follows a major ridge system and passes the following landmarks in this order: trail junction for Frog Meadows, view of Golden Trout Lake, the "tombstone" area (of the Cemetery, below), trail junction for Gant Ridge Trail, trail junction for the Waterfall and Clear Creek Trails, the Cemetery, Cathedral Rock,

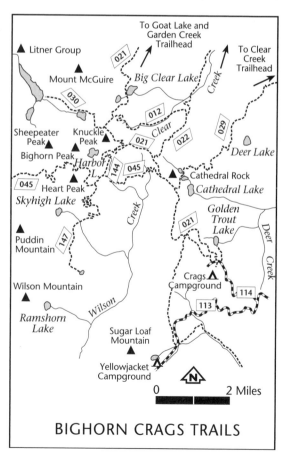

BIGHORN CRAGS TRAILS

Fishfin Ridge, Wilson Lake, Dome Mountain, and Sagebrush Lookout. FST-029 leads to Cathedral Lake.

(a.1) **FST-045, Waterfall Trail.** Starting at the Crags Trail just west of Cathedral Rock, this trail goes for 16 miles across the Crags and down to the Middle Fork Salmon.

(a.1.1) **FST-147, South End Trail.** It is 6.1 miles from Welcome Lake to Buck Lake. The trail provides access to several lakes and many named and unnamed peaks.

(a.2) **FST-144, Beaver Tail Trail.** This trail connects Welcome and Birdbill Lakes. At its midpoint, just east of Wilson Lake, it connects with the Crags Trail. The short north section of the trail runs from this junction to Birdbill Lake in 1.7 miles. (This trail is often covered by snow until late in the summer.) The equally short (also 1.7 miles) south section connects with the Waterfall Trail and the South End Trail.

(a.2.1) **FST-030, Ship Island Lake Trail.** This trail leads from Birdbill Lake to Airplane Lake, crosses a saddle, and then descends to Ship Island Lake in 3.9 miles. Aggipah Mountain and the Litner Group can be easily reached from the lake. It is 12 miles from Crags CG to the lake.

4

THE BOISE MOUNTAINS

The Boise Mountains occupy the southernmost portion of the Idaho Batholith. The range is bounded by the South Fork Payette River in the north, the Sawtooth, Smoky, and Soldier Mountains in the east, and the Snake River Plain in the south. The range's western boundary is roughly formed by ID-55, which runs between Boise, Horseshoe Bend, and Banks.

The Boise Mountains topography holds more than 20 mountain lakes and 35 named summits. Its terrain runs the gamut from gentle and rolling, to rocky and vertical. Two Point Mountain, which reaches 10,124 feet, is the highest point. The Boise Mountains are hotter and drier than the northern Idaho Batholith mountains. The Boise River's south, middle, and north forks drain most of the range.

The Boise Mountains are the main component of the

Boise National Forest, which manages the vast majority of the range. The Sawtooth National Forest manages the eastern edge of the range, the state of Idaho manages a large track of land near Danskin Peak and the BLM manages some of the range's southern foothills.

Though mining and logging activities have long dominated the region's economy, several large tracks of roadless mountains still offer good opportunities for hiking and exploring. The largest roadless areas are the Trinity Mountain region and the upper reaches of the South Fork Boise River drainage. Besides these spots, hikers will find many other seldom-used trails worthy of their consideration. Several Boise peaks are worthwhile goals in the Class 1, Class 2, and Class 3 categories. Rock climbers will turn up many challenging rock walls and formations. Most of the summits listed below provide great panoramic views, at a minimum.

Road access to the Boise Mountains is good. In the north, a high-quality road follows the South Fork Payette River along the range's northern boundary. ID-21 cuts diagonally across the range's northeastern corner between Boise and Lowman. A good (but exhausting) gravel road follows the Middle Fork Boise River between Lucky Peak Reservoir and Atlanta. Finally, a paved road penetrates from the south into the heart of the range at Featherville. Many gravel and dirt roads lead from these primary routes into every nook and cranny of the range.

PEAKS NORTH OF ID-21

Mores Peak   *7,237 feet (Class 1)*
Mores Peak is located along the extreme western edge of the Boise Mountains 12 miles north of Boise. The summit is reached from the Shaffer Butte picnic area, which is in a saddle between Mores Peak and Shaffer Butte via a 2-mile nature trail. Follow the trail around the peak until you are on its western side. Leave the trail at this point and walk the short distance to the broad granite-crowned summit. The picnic area is 20 road miles from Boise via the Bogus Basin Road [(A)(1)]. On a clear day, the views of the Sawtooths from the summit are striking. USGS Shaffer Butte

Shaw Mountain/Lucky Peak   *5,908 feet (Class 1)*
This small, but attractive peak forms the backdrop for east Boise. The summit is 5 miles due east of Boise and 5 miles north of the Lucky Peak Reservoir Dam. Because of its proximity to town, it is a popular destination. This summit is reached by roads from several directions. None of the roads see much traffic and, thus, provide good hiking and mountain biking experiences. The first route leaves the Rocky Canyon Road

just below the south side of Aldape Summit and climbs to the summit in about 2.5 miles [(A)(2)]. The second route leaves Warm Springs Road just east of Eckardt Road at the Golden Dawn Trailer Park. Follow the road on the west side of the trailer park to the base of the mountains where it is closed by a gate, and park. Behind the gate, the first part of the road crosses private property, open to the public thanks to the landowners and the Idaho Department of Fish and Game. Continue up the canyon on the obvious road, which eventually crosses into the next drainage to the east. After a steep climb, the road intersects with another road, keep left. The road will continue to climb steeply through a couple of switchbacks and then passes along the south ridgeline descending from Lucky Peak. From this point you can continue on the road to the saddle west of the summit where the summit road leads east to the top of Lucky Peak, or you can make a Class 2 hike up the ridge. The third route begins along ID-21 [(B)], 2.4 miles north of the Lucky Peak dam. Turn west off the highway and follow the Highland Valley Road uphill for a short distance to a cattleguard. Park here. (Note: This road is closed to vehicles in the spring.) Hike the road west, keeping right at the first two junctions and left at the third. The road passes just below the summit on its northeastern side. Leave the trail and scramble to the top. All three routes

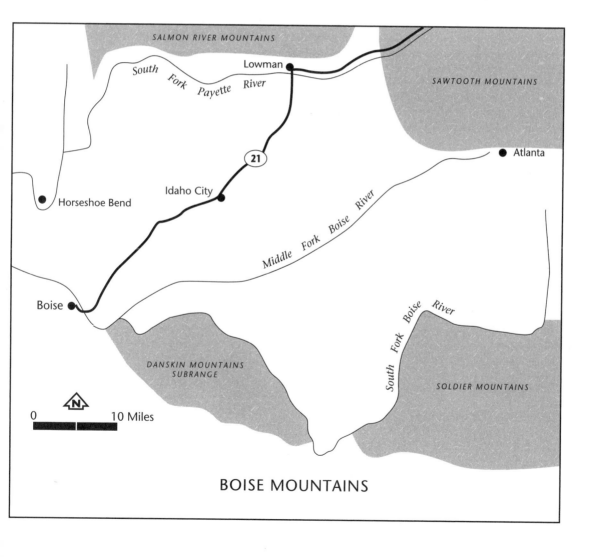

BOISE MOUNTAINS

are good spring conditioning hikes. The first is usually open in mid-April, the last two routes often can be hiked as early as March. USGS Lucky Peak

Wilson Peak   *7,837 feet (Class 1-2)*
Wilson Peak is located 11 miles northeast of Idaho City and 3.5 miles west of Pilot Peak. From the road between Pilot and Free-man Peaks, an old Forest Service trail leads to the summit. The trail was included on the 1977 version of the Boise National Forest map, but is missing on later versions. It is unknown if the trail will be maintained in the future, but because it follows a ridgeline for its entire distance, the route can be followed with a map [(B)(1)(a)]. USGS Sunset Mountain

Freeman Peak*   *8,096 feet (Class 2)*
This peak is just 1.25 miles southwest of Pilot Peak and is named on the Boise National Forest map, but not on the USGS quad. Drive or ski to the saddle between the two peaks and then hike or ski up the peak's eastern slopes to the summit [(B)(1)]. USGS Sunset Mountain

Pilot Peak   *8,128 feet (Class 1)*
Pilot Peak sits 2 miles north of ID-21, where it crosses Mores Creek Summit. This former lookout site, the present site of a radio communications station, is reached by FS-380 [(B)(1)]. I recommend mountain biking to the summit in the summer and skiing to the top in the winter. On winter weekends, doz-ens of cross-country skiers and many snowmobiles ascend the peak via the snowbound road. There is potential avalanche danger at various points along the road and the ridge. USGS Sunset Mountain

PEAKS BETWEEN ID-21 AND THE MIDDLE FORK BOISE RIVER

Peak Cervidae   *4,987 feet (Class 2)*
This summit, which provides an excellent introduction to mountain climbing, is 4 miles east of Shaw Mountain and 1.5 miles west of Spring Shores State Park. This peak is often without snow as early as February. There are two excellent routes to the top. The first climbs up from the east and the second from the west. For the eastern route, drive just past the northern boundary of Spring Shores State Park and park. Climb due west up the very steep hillside aiming for the ridge top above and to your right. Follow this first ridge until it merges with a second ridge that leads to the summit ridge in about 1.5 miles. Once on the summit ridge, turn north, descend into the intervening saddle and then climb to the summit.

The west side route begins in a turnout on the left (west) side of ID-21 [(B)] 1.1 miles north of the bridge that crosses the spectacular Mores Creek Canyon (the turn for Spring Shores State Park is on the north side of the bridge). The route climbs the peak's southwest ridge. From the turnout, cross the road to the point where a big road cut ends and a cement barrier begins. Start up the gully on a side hill by traversing up to a game trail about 50 feet above. Follow the game trail up the gully for about 0.1 mile until the gully divides. Cross the gully and hike directly up the ridge that separates the gully's two forks. As you climb, the route crosses two old road cuts. The route is very steep in places, but it narrows and the pitch moderates as you progress toward the summit ridge. The southwest ridge tops out 0.1 mile south of the summit. Follow the ridge north to the top. USGS Arrowrock Dam

Sunset Mountain   *7,869 feet (Class 1)*
Sunset sits 11 miles east/northeast of Idaho City and 5 miles south of Pilot Peak. It is an active fire lookout site during the summer, and is reached by FS-380 [(B)(1)], which leaves ID-21 at the top of Mores Creek Summit. Because of the road, the peak is an excellent mountain biking destination in the summer months; in the winter a parking area is plowed on Mores Creek Summit and the road is a popular ski touring and snowmobiling route. It is 5 miles to the summit from Mores Creek Summit and ID-21. USGS Sunset Mountain

Wolf Mountain   *8,876 feet (Class 2)*
Wolf Mountain is one of the more noteworthy Boise Moun-tain summits. It is composed of many cliffs and faces, which culminate in an impressive granite summit block. The peak is located 12 miles southeast of Lowman, where it sits at the headwaters of the Crooked and Bear Rivers. The peak is climbed from FS-312 [(B)(2.1)] by driving to Shonip Creek, which is roughly 3 miles east of the road's junction with the Jackson Peak Road. A side road leads south from the main road just past the SHONIP CREEK sign. Turn onto this road and park after 100 yards. From this point, the route involves dif-ficult cross-country travel.

Start the ascent by crossing the Crooked River (difficult in high water), then continue by slogging through a swamp of beaver ponds and mud. Once past the swamp, the route climbs up and to the south, paralleling Shonip Creek through thick timber for 1 mile. The timber eventually begins to thin out, and a view of the summit opens up to the south. Con-tinue to the large meadow at 8,000 feet.

From this point, reaching both the peak's north and west ridges is possible. Either route will encounter little difficulty,

The west face of remote Wolf Mountain

with the west ridge the easier one. To climb to the north ridge, follow the spur ridge just north of the meadow over easy but steep ground to the ridgeline above. Avoid several obstacles by staying on the east side of the north ridge as it climbs to the summit. To climb the west ridge, hike due south from the meadow through a short stretch of timber to the peak's open north slopes. Set a course that will bring you to the top of the ridgeline at roughly the 8,500-foot level. Once on the west ridge, the route is open to the summit block. To avoid technical climbing, climb the summit block from the south. USGS Jackson Peak

Tyee Mountain   *8,753 feet (Class 2)*

Tyee Mountain is situated 4.25 miles due east of Wolf Mountain and just a little more than 1 mile east of FS-312 [(B)(2.1)]. Climb to the summit from FS-312 via the connecting ridge that leads from the road east to the peak's summit. USGS Tyee Mountain

Shepard Peak   *8,833 feet (Class 2)*
Silver Mountain   *8,573 feet (Class 2-3)*

These two peaks are 3.5 and 4 miles south of Tyee Mountain; both are climbed from FS-312 [(B)(2.1)]. Park where the road crosses the saddle northwest of the peaks at the head of Big Silver Creek. From that saddle, contour southeast to another saddle, which is northeast and directly below Shepard Peak's northwest ridge. From here, climb the ridge to the summit in 1.5 miles of Class 2 climbing.

Silver Peak sits 0.75 mile southeast of Shepard Peak and is the southern summit of Shepard Peak. Though it is 250 feet lower than its neighbor, it is a much more impressive looking peak. Silver's north face is a 400+-foot vertical wall that has never been tested by climbers. Climb this peak via the Shepard Peak connecting ridge. The route is straightforward until the last 200 vertical feet, which are climbed on the southwest side of the ridge. USGS Swanholm

Peak 8970 (North Goat)   *8,970 feet (Class 3)*
Goat Mountain   *8,915 feet (Class 3)*

These two peaks form the high points on a 3-mile ridge system located 3.5 miles south/southeast of Wolf Mountain. Shepard Peak is 1.75 miles to the east. The ridge is a very rugged north/south trending structure that climbs 3,500 feet from the North Fork Boise River in just over 2 miles. Many ponds and lakes are found along the ridgeline. On the Swanholm Peak USGS quad, the name Goat Mountain is attached to the wrong point. The true summit is 0.4 mile due south of the named point. Two routes lead to the summit of Goat Mountain. The most direct and steepest route to the summit begins from FS-248 [(C)(1.3)] where it crosses Hunter Creek. Park at the crossing and follow the drainage east to the saddle just north of the peak and then climb the north ridge to the summit.

The second route leaves FS-312 [(B)(2.1)] at the saddle at the head of Big Silver Creek and allows you to climb Peak 8970 en route. From the saddle, climb southwest to the top of the ridgeline that leads to Point 8625. Follow the ridge south to Point 8625, then turn west and descend to the Peak 8970 (North Goat)/Point 8625 saddle. The remainder of this ridge is blocked by rugged towers, so drop down to the small lake to the south. Walk southwest from the lake to the rib that buttresses the south ridge of Peak 8970 just south of the summit. Climb the steep rib to the summit ridge. Following the ridge south to Goat Mountain or north to Peak 8970 is now possible. To follow the Class 3 ridge south, stay on its top where possible and when the route is blocked, drop off the ridge on its east side.

Climbing Goat Mountain from the Point 8625/Shephard Peak saddle is also possibe. From the saddle, contour to the 8,700-foot lake north of the summit. From this lake, climb to the Point 8835/Point 8816 saddle. From the saddle, contour to the Point 8835/Goat Mountain saddle. (Note: Each of these routes require stamina and expert route-finding abilities.) USGS Swanholm Peak

Swanholm Peak   *8,727 feet (Class 1)*
Swanholm Peak, located 5.5 miles south of Goat Mountain and 2 miles north of the North Fork Boise River, is a big mountain with a fire lookout on its summit. While the map shows several trails leading to this lookout site, the quality of these trails varies. In 1997, FST-050 had disappeared. The recommended route follows FST-051 and a system of confusing logging roads to reach the summit from the west. This peak also can be reached from Black Warrior Creek to the east after a very long hike. Begin on FS-327 [(B)(3)] and drive to the saddle between the middle and north forks of the Boise River. From this saddle, take the logging road that leads to the east. Park at this point and hike the closed road east to the point where it intersects with FST-051. You will need the Bear River and Grand Mountain USGS quads to make this approach. FST-051 is a 4WD road that climbs steeply to the summit in another 3 miles. The fire lookout was placed on this summit because of the massive view. Don't miss it! USGS Swanholm Peak

Warrior Peak   *8,930 feet (Class 2)*
West Warrior sits 1.5 miles southeast of Swanholm Peak and directly above Warrior Lakes, which occupy a broad cirque on the peak's northeast side. The summit is a Class 2 climb along the peak's north ridge from the point where it is crossed by FST-051 [(B)(3)(b)]. USGS Swanholm Peak

Grand Mountain   *7,264 feet (Class 1-2)*
Granite Mountain   *7,084 feet (Class 1-2)*
These peaks are 5 miles southwest of Swanholm Peak on a high divide that separates the Middle Fork and North Fork

Goat Mountain forms the highest point on a long north/south ridgeline that harbors a number of seldom visited lakes.

Boise River. Both peaks can be climbed by either FST-049 [(B)(3)(a)] or FST-048 [(C)(b)]. These trails are poorly marked and seldom used—make sure you take a USGS quad map. The recommended route uses FST-049. Using this trail, it is roughly 2 miles to Granite Mountain and 3 miles to Grand Mountain. USGS Grand Mountain

PEAKS BETWEEN THE MIDDLE FORK AND SOUTH FORK BOISE RIVER

Rattlesnake Mountain   *8,177 feet (Class 2)*
This attractive summit is situated 6.5 miles southwest of Sheep Mountain and is approached by trails from several different directions. The shortest walk is from Tipton Flat CG via FST-128 [(C)(1.1)(a)], which crosses the peak's southern slopes. Follow the trail from the CG to a small saddle between the peak and Point 6310. From this saddle, climb directly north toward Point 7977. When the route reaches tree line, it is a quick scramble to the summit ridge that leads northeast to the summit. Other approach routes to consider are FST-128 [(C)(a)], which reaches the peak from Sheep Creek in the north, and FST-125/FST-126 [(E)(2.2)(a) and (b)], which reaches the peak from the Trinity Mountain area to the east. USGS Prairie

Lava Mountain*   *8,703 feet (Class 2)*
The name Lava Mountain is attached to the midpoint of a long ridgeline that begins at North Star Lake and runs southwest for 7 miles. The high point is found 0.7 mile north of North Star Lake and 2.5 miles due east of Rattlesnake Mountain. The shortest route to the summit is from the west. Drive FS-222B to FST-124 [(C)(1.2)(a)], which quickly climbs to the ridgeline. Once on the ridge, follow the trail northeast to a junction just past Point 7862. From this junction leave the trail and follow the ridge northeast and then north to the summit. A second alternative begins to the southwest in Lava Creek. The USGS quad (but not the national forest map) shows a trail that leaves the end of FS-222B and climbs up the Lava Mountain ridge. It is in fair condition. As a longer alternative, the peak can be approached from the Trinity Mountain region. See [(E)(2.2)(a)], below. USGS Prairie

Sheep Mountain   *8,148 feet (Class 2)*
Sheep Mountain sits 12 miles south of Grand Mountain and 10 southwest of Steele Mountain. FST-124 traverses the north/south ridgeline that contains Sheep Mountain. From the south, approach this trail from the Roaring River Road and FST-124 [(C)(1.2)(a)], or in the east from the same road

and FST-045 [(C)(1.2)(b)]. The longest approach route begins where Sheep Creek empties into the Middle Fork Boise River and follows Sheep Creek east to a junction with FST-124 [(C)(a)]. Once on FST-124, take it to the peak's eastern side and then scramble to the summit. USGS Little Trinity Lake

Trinity Mountain   *9,451 feet (Class 1)*
Trinity Mountain is the very rugged culmination of the Trinity Mountains, a long, high north/south ridgeline that runs from Dog Mountain (just above Anderson Ranch Reservoir) to Sheep Mountain (just north of the Middle Fork Boise River) was known to prospectors as the Trinity Mountains. However, the USGS failed to adopt this name on its most recent maps and the name is disappearing from the collective consciousness. Much of what was once known as the Trinity Mountains reaches above the tree line and contains scattered mountain lakes in glacially carved cirques. The biggest of these cirques, on the northeast side of Trinity Mountain, contains eight lakes. Its steep northeast facade harbors impressive cliffs that tower over several lakes. The peak, which is 8.5 miles west of Featherville, has a fire lookout on its summit. A service road, which is closed to private motor vehicles, provides a good route for a walk to the summit [(E)(2.2)(c)]. USGS Trinity Mountain

Peak 9037   *9,037 feet (Class 2)*
This unnamed summit sits 1.25 miles northeast of Trinity Mountain. From FS-129 [(E)(2.2)], ascend the peak's west ridge to the summit, a vertical distance of a little more than 500 feet. The view of Trinity Mountain from the top is as good a reason as any to climb this peak. USGS Trinity Mountain

Steele Mountain   *9,730 feet*
Steele Mountain is an island in the sky that dominates the surrounding country. It has two granite summits that rise quickly out of the surrounding drainages. The northern summit is formed by a series of rugged cliffs, faces, and towers. Several technical routes on the northern summit were pioneered by Greg Parker. Steele Mountain is 10 miles north of Featherville. The Forest Service has placed a radio transmission facility on the summit. USGS Rocky Bar

Elk Creek Route (Class 3). To reach this route, start in Featherville. Leave town on FS-156 and drive to Rocky Bar. At Rocky Bar, turn right onto FS-126, the James Creek Road [(F)(1.1)], which runs northeast to Atlanta. In 4 miles, this road crosses Elk Creek where an unmarked trail leads up Elk Creek. Follow the trail up the drainage until it ends, and then continue up the eastern slopes of Steele Mountain's north peak.

Steel Mountain from the southeast

Pass the north peak on its southeastern side and climb the higher southern summit via the notch between the two peaks.

West Slope Route (Class 2). The summit can be reached from the west via the short but steep west side. From Rocky Bar, take FS-156 [(F)(1)] to the saddle just west of the peak. Park on the saddle and head up the broad slopes through thick timber. The ridge eventually narrows, the timber thins, and the route becomes more obvious. A couple of granite towers block the ridge top, but they are easily bypassed.

North Ridge (Class 3-4). The north ridge is approached via a logging road from the Pheifer Creek Road, FS-156 [(F)(1)]. Leave the Pheifer Creek Road roughly 3 miles south of the Middle Fork Boise River and follow the unnumbered logging road east to Hot Creek. According to Greg Parker, the climb starts at the end of the logging road. Begin by scrambling over and around the cliff faces to the north ridge (Class 3 or 4 depending on how ambitious a line you choose) and then continue up the ridge to the summit.

North Summit Routes. Steele Mountain's north summit reaches above 9,680 feet and sits slightly northeast of the main summit. The north summit is more rugged and enticing than Steele's true summit. It is possible to make a Class 3 scramble up the north summit from the saddle between the two peaks.

Quasi-Moat-O (II, 5.5). Greg Parker describes this route as beginning in Steele Mountain's north bowl and climbing the obvious wide crack on the right side of the bowl's face. The two-pitch route crosses steep ramps and overhanging chockstones on its way to the top of the northwest summit ridge. From this point, follow the ridge to the summit. The rock is very solid granite. First ascent: G. Parker and M. Riffie in 1997.

North Face (II, 5.9). This three-pitch route, also described by Greg Parker, begins in Steele Mountain's north bowl. Look for the route to the right of Quasi-Moat-O where a diagonal crack and ledge system begins just to the right of the bowl's center. Start the climb by heading north on a small diagonal ledge system. Traverse up and to the left almost to the center of the face. Turn back and climb to the right utilizing one of the numerous face or ledge systems that lead to the summit ridge. A short rappel and Class 3 down-climb gains the northwest ridgeline. Continue to the summit. First ascent: G. Parker and K. McFarley in 1997.

Parallel Universe (snow climb). Yet another Greg Parker route offers a good early season snow climb. Approach this route by the west ridge. Approximately one-half to one-third of the way up the ridge, there is an interesting split-rock formation with almost parallel sides. Early in the year, climb the split on steep snow—a pitch of 45 to 50 degrees—and ice. If climbed in the summer, this will be a brush and scree scramble. First ascent: G. Parker in March 1995.

Bald Mountain   9,389 feet (Class 3)

This often overlooked summit, located 4 miles due east of Steele Mountain, offers a great view toward the Sawtooths and the Atlanta area. Take FS-126 [(F)(1.1)] to the saddle northwest of the summit and park. From the saddle, hike the ridgeline southeast to the summit. The ridge is not well defined in its lower reaches and crosses through thick forest. USGS Cayuse Point

Gunsight Peak   9,527 feet (Class 2)

Gunsight Peak is in the Willow Creek drainage, 3.25 miles southwest of Ross Peak. Its summit does look like a gunsight. The peak is climbed from FST-019 [(F)(2)(a)], which traverses Willow Creek. One person reported that while deer hunting, he left the trail at Fern Gulch, climbed up the gulch, crossed over the summit, and then descended Gunsight Creek to the trail. Though the account of this journey was sketchy, it probably is a reasonable route. USGS Ross Peak

Jumbo Mountain   8,216 feet (Class 2)

Jumbo, located 6 miles south of Gunsight Peak and 2 miles north of the South Fork Boise River, is a small mountain with a massive view. From the top, the following 360-degree view will reward you: starting to the north and moving clockwise, Two Point Mountain, Newman Peak, the Smokey Mountain crest, Buttercup Mountain, Smoky Dome, Iron Mountain, South Fork Boise River, Trinity Mountain, Steele Mountain, and Gunsight Mountain. Follow FST-027 [(F)(2)(b)] to the saddle above Little Water Gulch where there is a junction with FST-020. (Note: The trail on the Sawtooth National Forest map that continues up Jumbo Creek is not maintained.) From the saddle, FST-020 leads east to a second saddle on a steep but good tread. Leave the trail in this saddle and hike north through forest to the bald, jumbo summit. USGS Ross Peak

Ross Peak   9,773 feet (Class 2-3)

Ross Peak is 2 miles southwest of Two Top Mountain. The only reported route is from the saddle on the peak's northwest side. From this saddle, the summit is about 0.5 mile away. To reach this saddle, two approach routes are suggested: (1) From the south, drive up FS-227, then hike FST-019 [(F)(2)(a)], which follows Willow Creek north for 10 miles to the saddle, or (2) approach from the east via Bear Creek and FS-080 [(F)(2.1.1)].

This second approach is recommended since it is much shorter. From the end of the road, find FST-197 [(F)(2.1.1)(b)] and follow it west across the nearby divide and then down into Willow Creek to FST-019. Follow FST-019 north to the saddle. Though this peak can undoubtedly be climbed from its east side, no one has reported an ascent. USGS Ross Peak

Newman Peak   9,603 feet (Class 2)

Newman Peak's summit is formed by a pyramid of broken granite with a steep north face. On three sides, its lower slopes rise abruptly out of the deep canyons formed by Bear Creek and the South Fork Boise River. Take FS-012 from Big Smoky GS into the upper section of the South Fork drainage to the Boise Corrals (1.25 miles after FS-012 crosses the South Fork). From this point, poorly maintained FST-069 [(F)(2.1)(a)] departs and climbs up High Creek, crossing the southeastern slopes of the peak to the south ridge in 3.5 miles. It is possible to leave this trail at several points and scramble to the summit. The shortest off-trail route climbs the south ridge but involves more on-trail time. Both the northeast and east ridges are also passable. USGS Newman Peak

Two Point Mountain   10,124 feet

Two Point Mountain, a twin-summited peak, is the highest point in the Boise Mountains. It is located 28 miles northwest of Fairfield along the extreme eastern edge of the range, in a spectacular and little-visited area above the upper reaches of the South Fork Boise River. Both summits, which are 0.5 mile apart, reach above 10,000 feet—the only two points in the Boise Mountains above that elevation. The higher south summit stands only 64 feet above the north summit, which is 10,060 feet tall. USGS Newman Peak

West Ridge (Class 3). From the South Fork and FS-012 follow FS-080 [(F)(2.1.1)(a)] up Bear Creek 4 miles to Goat Creek. A mining road leads up Goat Creek to an old mine. Park here and hike up this road until you reach the 8,400-foot contour line on the USGS quad. From here, gain the ridge top, which leads up and around the cirque on the peak's west side. The ridge eventually reaches the lower (but very rugged) north summit without much difficulty. From this summit, follow the ridge to the main summit, staying mostly on the west side. Pass the difficult middle tower by winding around a rubble-filled ledge on its eastern side.

South Ridge (Class 2). Use the same approach directions as those provided for the West Ridge, but leave the road at the first stream crossing and follow a broad tree-covered ridge north for 1.5 steep miles to the summit.

Two Point Mountain, the highest point in the Boise Mountains, is a ragged collection of shattered towers and steep faces when viewed from the mountain's lower northern summit.

THE DANSKIN MOUNTAINS

This small Boise Mountain subrange is 15 miles long, 3 to 5 miles in width, and encompasses all of the Boise Mountains south of the South Fork Boise River. The highest summit in the range is Danskin Peak at 6,694 feet. Because of their low elevation and proximity to the Snake River Plain, the Danskins thaw out earlier than most Idaho mountains and are sometimes accessible as early as March. Although the range does not reach 7,000 feet in elevation, it rises more than 2,500 feet from the South Fork to the summit of Danskin Peak in just 3 miles. The terrain is mostly open, with a few small stands of pine and fir on the wetter slopes. Many primitive roads penetrate the range. The Danskins' ridges and unnamed summits provide excellent trailless hiking destinations. Additionally, motorcycles have pioneered several unofficial trails along ridgelines.

Kepros Mountain   5,428 feet (Class 1-2)

Kepros offers a good early season hike. Its summit is located west of Lucky Peak Reservoir and 3.5 miles north of Three Point Mountain. Access the peak from FS-189 [(G)(1)(a)] and Three Point Mountain. From Black Creek Summit, climb to the ridgeline 0.25 mile to the west and just south of Three Point Mountain. From this point, a well-worn path leads north following the undulating ridge over Points 5272 and 5283 in about 1.5 miles. After Point 5283, the ridgeline turns northwest to connect with another ridge at a point just north of a small but distinctive granite outcropping. A closed road is met at this point. Follow it north. After 0.75 mile there is a junction. Continue north on the road for another 1.5 miles to the Kepros summit. USGS Arrowrock Dam

Three Point Mountain   5,300+ feet (Class 1-2)

This is the obvious, tri-summited mountain visible from I-84 at the Black Creek Road exit. Because of its low elevation and proximity to the Snake River Plain, this summit is probably the first summit to melt out in Idaho. To reach the summit from Blacks Creek Pass, which is crossed by FS-189 [(G)(1)(a)], hike west up the jeep trail that leads to the ridgeline just north of the north summit, and then follow the ridgeline south over the middle summit to the southernmost summit, which is the highest. A USGS survey marker is found on the summit, along with a terrific view of the Snake River Plain. USGS Arrowrock Dam

Danskin Peak   *6,694 feet (Class 1)*

Danskin Peak is a worthy goal, not only because it is the highest point in the Danskin Mountains, but also because it is a beautiful, isolated summit with a terrific 360-degree view. The peak is located due north of Mountain Home and 7 miles southwest of Prairie. Most years, snowdrifts will keep the summit access road closed until July, allowing hikers to visit the summit without being bothered by motor vehicles. Throughout the spring, the shortest route to the summit follows FS-167 [(D)(1)] from where it crosses the Danskin Mountain crest east to the summit. The peak also can be approached from the southeast via FS-143, but this would involve a long hike over trailless terrain. USGS Danskin Peak

APPROACHES TO THE BOISE MOUNTAINS

(A) BOISE ACCESS APPROACHES

(1) **FS-297, Bogus Basin Road.** This road begins as part of Harrison Boulevard in Boise. From the corner of Main and 15th in downtown Boise, drive north on 15th (one-way to West Hays). Turn left (west) on Hays and drive one block to the beginning of Harrison Boulevard. Turn right (north) on Harrison and follow it north into the Boise Mountains. It is 19 miles to the Shaffer Butte CG, which is between Shaffer Butte and Mores Mountain. The road is paved almost to the Bogus Basin Ski Resort.

(a) **Mores Mountain Trail.** This trail is made up of two short loop trails. The shortest is a nature trail. The second loop circles the summit of Mores Mountain in roughly 2 miles. This second trail follows the nature trail to a junction in about 0.25 mile. Take the less worn path to the left. The trail now crosses the south face of Mores Mountain and then continues to circle the summit. After circling the summit, it drops to the peak's eastern slopes to join the nature trail again.

(2) **Shaw Mountain Road/Rocky Canyon Road.** From downtown Boise, find the Fort Boise softball fields. The fields are at the east end of State Street and the north end of Broadway by St. Lukes Regional Medical Center. Reserve Street is on the east side of the park. Follow Reserve north. Reserve becomes Shaw Mountain Road and curves its way up through the Foothills East subdivision. At the top of the subdivision, the road forks. Table Rock Road is the right fork and Rocky Canyon is the left fork.

Go left. It is 8 miles to the top of Aldape Summit and another 6 miles from the summit to ID-21.

(B) ID-21 APPROACHES

ID-21 is accessed from I-84. Take the Gowen Road exit and drive north. From Boise, ID-21 cuts through the heart of the Boise Mountains as it passes through Idaho City and Lowman. From Lowman to Grandjean, the highway follows the South Fork Payette River, which divides the Boise and Salmon River Mountains. This highway is narrow and twisty, and often congested on summer weekends. Leave extra time in your travel schedule for those busy days.

(1) **FS-380, Sunset Peak/Pilot Peak Road.** This road leaves ID-21 at Mores Creek Summit and runs both north and south from the highway. South of the highway, the road runs to the fire lookout on top of Sunset Peak in 5 miles. North of the highway, the road runs to a saddle north of Pilot Peak and then continues to Pioneerville. From the saddle, a rough gravel road leads to the top of Pilot Peak. A 4WD is recommended.

(a) **Wilson Peak Trail.** This trail is no longer maintained by the Forest Service. The route, which is identified on the USGS quads and older Boise Forest maps, begins as an old road between Freeman and Pilot Peaks, and then continues northwest along a ridgeline for 1.5 miles before turning due west along another ridgeline and running to Wilson Peak in another 1.5 miles. This trail has not been maintained or signed in some time.

(2) **FS-384, Willow Creek Road.** This road leaves ID-21 just east of Mores Creek Summit. It leads south to FS-327 and the North Fork Boise River, and is the best approach available to the upper drainages of the North and Middle Forks Boise. The road opens late in the summer and is often congested with logging trucks.

(2.1) **FS-312, Graham GS Road.** This road is accessed from ID-21 via FS-384. It usually requires a 4WD and the ability to drive it safely. Turn off ID-21 and follow FS-384 for 4 miles, then turn east onto FS-312, which eventually leads to the Graham GS on the edge of the Sawtooths. It begins by following Banner Creek and then quickly turns onto Pikes Fork Creek, which it follows northeast to a high ridgeline just south of Jackson Peak. East of the junction for Jackson Peak, the road drops into the Crooked River drainage, which it follows east, eventually climbing out of the drainage between Tyee Mountain and Wolf Mountain. For the next few miles, the road runs south along a ridgeline and then drops into Big Silver Creek, which leads to the North Fork Boise River.

(3) **FS-327, Granite Creek/North Fork Boise River Road.** This road leaves ID-21 just east of Idaho City, climbs up Granite Creek, crosses over to Rabbit Creek and then descends to the North Fork Boise River, which it follows east to the Deer Park GS.

From the GS, the road runs south over a divide to meet FS-269 along the Middle Fork Boise River.

(a) **FST-049, Grand Mountain Trail.** FST-049 follows the high ridgeline that divides the North and Middle Forks Boise River. The trail leaves FS-327 near the Barber Flat GS and runs northeast for 12 miles to Swanholm Creek Summit, where it again joins FS-327. Along the way, the trail intersects with FST-048 [(C)(b)] just east of Grand Mountain.

(b) **FST-050/FST-051/FST-052, Horse Heaven Creek/Swanholm Peak Trails.** These trails are accessed from FS-327 1.8 miles south of Deer Park. Follow the old logging road up the Horse Heaven Creek drainage until it crosses the creek for the second time. At this point, the trail leaves the road and climbs up the drainage to the northeast to eventually cross Blue Jay and Lodgepole Creeks. FST-052 runs up Lodgepole Creek and connects with FST-051 on the ridge at the top of the drainage. FST-051 runs from Swanholm Peak east into Warrior Lakes Basin and then continues east to a junction with FST-053 along the banks of Black Warrior Creek.

(C) MIDDLE FORK BOISE RIVER ROAD APPROACHES

FS-269 leaves ID-21 6.1 miles north of Lucky Peak Dam and follows the Middle Fork Boise east to Atlanta in 72 miles. It begins by tracing the edges of Lucky Peak and Arrowrock reservoirs for many dangerous miles before following the river east to Atlanta. Drive slowly and keep on your side of the road. Utilize FS-327 [(B)(3)] to avoid the dangerous sections along the reservoir.

(a) **FST-122, Sheep Creek Trails.** FST-122 begins 30.1 miles east of ID-21. The Sheep Creek drainage runs to the base of Trinity Mountain and encompasses several trails that follow the drainage's tributaries and ridges. Two of these side trails are of particular interest. FST-128 leaves FST-122 4.5 miles east of the trailhead and leads south to Rattlesnake Mountain in another 6 miles of "now you see it, now you don't" trail. FST-124 leads to Sheep Mountain. Take FST-122 east for 11 miles, then follow FST-124 northwest for 1 mile to Sheep Mountain.

(b) **FST-048, Browns Creek Trail.** This trail leaves FS-269 east of the Ninemyer CG and runs north to FST-049 in 7.5 miles. The trail is hard to follow in its upper end and its many stream crossings are difficult in periods of high water.

(1) **FS-113, Slide Gulch/Long Gulch GS Road.** This road connects FS-269 (near the Middle Fork Boise River) with FS-189 (near the South Fork Boise River). The road is accessed from FS-269 just east of Willow Creek CG or from FS-189, 3 miles east of Prairie. Long Gulch GS is midway between the road's two ends.

(1.1) **FS-217, Tipton Flat Road.** This road leaves FS-113 where the road crosses Rattlesnake Creek. The road follows the creek east to Tipton Flat CG in about 4.5 miles.

(a) **FST-128, Rattlesnake Mountain Trail.** FST-128 begins at the Tipton Flat CG and proceeds north along the south side of Rattlesnake Mountain in 3 miles and then descends along Devils Creek to meet Sheep Creek and FST-122 [(C)(a)]. North of Rattlesnake Mountain, the trail intersects with FST-127, which also provides access to Sheep Creek.

(1.1.2) **FS-222, Lava Mountain Access Road.** This road leaves FS-113 where it crosses Spring Creek, then runs northeast toward Lava Mountain. In about 1 mile, the junction with FS-222B is reached. Follow this road, which is rough and sometimes impassable, to its end in 3.5 miles.

(a) **FST-125, Smith Creek Lake Trail.** FST-125 begins near the end of FS-222B, just west of the summit of Lava Mountain. From its start, it leads to the summit area before running northeast to Smith Creek Lake and eventually to the Trinity Mountain area [(E)(2.2)(a)].

(1.2) **FS-255, Roaring River Road.** This route begins several miles west of the Dutch Creek GS, runs south up Roaring River and then east to FS-129 [(E)(2.2)] in roughly 15 miles.

(a) **FST-124, Sheep Mountain Trail.** FST-124 leaves FS-255 3 miles south of that road's beginning at the Middle Fork Boise River. This trail climbs due west to the ridgeline that includes Sheep Mountain, and then runs due south to Sheep Mountain in about 5 miles. South of the mountain, it joins with FST-122 [(C)(a)].

(b) **FST-045, Roaring River Trail.** This trail leaves FS-225 at its southernmost crossing of the Roaring River and begins the long climb out of the drainage to run due south to the Trinity Mountain area. It intersects with FST-122 [(C)(a)] 2 miles from where it begins.

(1.3) **FS-248, Bear River Road.** This road begins at the Deer Park GS and runs north past Steamboat Creek, the Bear River, and then into the Crooked River drainage before intersecting with FS-384 [(B)(2)] near the Willow Creek CG. This road was constructed to provide access to logging operations. A 4WD is recommended.

(D) MOUNTAIN HOME APPROACHES

Mountain Home is 45 miles east of Boise and 89 miles west of Twin Falls along I-84. The town of more than 8,000 inhabitants offers all services.

(1) **FS-167, Canyon Creek/Danskin Peak Road.** This road is accessed from Mountain Home. From I-84, take exit 90 and follow the old highway east toward town for 3.1 miles. Turn north on Canyon Creek Road and follow it through town and into the desert. In 8.2 miles, the pavement ends and a well-graded gravel road begins. The road forks at this point—keep left. Follow the gravel road to the northwest across a drainage for another 5.9 miles to a point where the main gravel road veers sharply to the

west. FS-167 begins here and climbs directly uphill to the north. From this point on the road is dirt—steep, rutted, and almost impassable when wet—and a 4WD is highly recommended. Many side roads lead off the main road and will cause some confusion for those following the road without a map. Keep on the most-used road at each junction until a small reservoir is reached after 8.8 miles. Drive just past the reservoir and turn north up Case Creek. In another 4.5 miles, the road reaches the crest of the Danskin Mountains, west of Danskin Peak. From this point, a road descends to the South Fork Boise River, where it ends at a closed gate on a private property boundary. FS-167 continues to the summit of Danskin Peak in 3 steep miles.

(E) ID-20 APPROACHES

This state highway leaves I-84 at exit 95 in Mountain Home and runs north and east to Fairfield. A major approach route, it is one of the best-constructed highways in Idaho. Expect a lot of recreational vehicle traffic on weekends.

(1) FS-131, Pony Creek Road. This road leaves ID-20 15.5 miles north of Mountain Home (3.7 miles past the Tollgate Cafe). Turn north on a distinct gravel road that runs north to the South Fork Boise River, where it connects with FS-113.

(2) FS-134, Anderson Ranch Dam Road. This road leaves ID-20 20.8 miles north of Mountain Home and runs north to the dam, where it connects with FS-113. The road is paved to within 1 mile of the dam.

(2.1) FS-113, South Fork Boise River Road. This road begins at the Anderson Ranch Dam and follows the South Fork Boise River west to the site of the old Danskin GS. From this point, the road climbs north out of the canyon and goes to the village of Prairie and FS-189 [(G)(1)] in 8.2 miles.

(2.2) FS-123/FS-129 Trinity Mountain Road. This road leaves Anderson Ranch Reservoir 8.8 miles east of the dam at Fall Creek. The road follows Fall Creek north to the top of the Trinity Mountain divide in 16.5 miles. From the high point, the road follows a ridgeline north and joins up with FS-156 [(F)(1)] just west of Steele Mountain. Though a major thoroughfare, this route is narrow, steep, and rough in places.

(a) FST-125, Smith Creek Lake Trail. This trail leaves FS-129, runs west to Smith Creek Lake in 1.5 miles, and then continues to Lava Mountain in another 5.5 miles.

(b) FST-126, Bear Gulch Cutoff Trail. FST-126 leaves FST-125 3 miles west of Smith Creek Lake and runs north to join with the Sheep Creek Trail system east of Rattlesnake Mountain. See [(C)(a)], above.

(c) FS-129A, Trinity Mountain Road. This road leaves FS-129 and runs east. It is open for about 0.5 mile and then gated shut. From the gate, it is 1.5 miles to the summit of Trinity Mountain.

(F) FEATHERVILLE APPROACHES

FH-61 leaves ID-20 31.9 miles northeast of I-84 at exit 95 and runs north to Featherville. The road is paved to Featherville.

(1) FS-156, South Fork/Middle Fork Road. This road begins in Featherville and runs northwest to Rocky Bar in 8 miles, to FS-129 in about 6 more miles, and then eventually to the Middle Fork Boise River and FS-269 [(C)]. Just north of its junction with FS-129, the road crosses a saddle on the western flanks of Steele Mountain.

(1.1) FS-126, James Creek Road. This road is an alternative route to Atlanta. It begins at the Rocky Bar ghost town and runs north to Atlanta. A 4WD is recommended, but is not required.

(2) FS-227, South Fork Road. This excellent gravel road begins in Featherville and proceeds east along the South Fork Boise River to Big Smoky GS. Note that this road also can be reached from both Fairfield and Ketchum via Forest Service roads. See [(A)(7)] in the Smoky Mountains approaches and [(A)(1)] under the Soldier Mountains approaches.

(a) FST-019, Willow Creek Trail. This trail leaves FS-227 at the Willow Creek CG and follows Willow Creek northeast for nearly 10 miles to a pass northeast of Ross Peak, where it joins FST-227 [(F)(2.1)(b)].

(b) FST-027, Jumbo Creek Trail. This trail leaves FS-227 just east of the Baumgartner CG and follows Jumbo Creek northeast to a ridgeline north of Jumbo Mountain.

(2.1) FS-012/FS-079, Upper South Fork Road. This road is accessed from FS-227 at the Big Smoky CS. It runs northwest from the Big Smoky area, crosses a small divide and drops into the upper reaches of the South Fork drainage. The road follows the river north, nearly to the Sawtooth Wilderness boundary. Be advised that the upper stretches of this road require a 4WD.

(a) FST-069, Newman Peak Trail. This route begins at the South Boise Corral. From FS-012, the trail climbs along High Creek for almost 2 miles, then runs south and west to the upper reaches of the Bridge Creek drainage. At this point, the trail is situated on the high slopes of Newman Peak. It continues west across the southern slopes of that peak, then continues farther to the west, where it joins an extensive trail system not covered by this book.

(b) FST-227, South Fork Trail. This trail begins at the end of FS-012 and proceeds south to Ross Pass, northwest of Ross Peak. At the pass, the trail joins FST-019, which traverses Willow Creek [(F)(2)(a)].

(2.1.1) FS-080, Bear Creek Road. This road leaves FS-012 near the South Fork CG. It is a rough, rutted primitive road that requires a 4WD. It begins with a stream crossing, then continues due west from the South Fork to the old Red Horse Mine in about 6 miles.

(a) **FST-061, Goat Creek Trail.** FST-061 leaves FS-080 where Goat Creek flows into Bear Creek, then climbs north to the Tip Top Mine and Goat Lake. Although not shown on the Forest Service map, the trail continues over the divide to the north and drops down into Bass Creek, where it is designated FST-061. This trail is actually a 4WD road for most of its distance.

(b) **FST-197, Bear Divide Trail.** This trail begins at the end of FS-080, runs west, climbs almost immediately over a divide and then drops down into Willow Creek, where it joins FST-019 [(F)(2)(a)].

(G) I-84 APPROACHES.

This Interstate Highway is the major east/west connector in Idaho.

(1) **FS-189, Upper Blacks Creek Road.** This road leaves I-84 at exit 64, 10 miles east of Boise. The good gravel road extends north from the exit to Blacks Creek Pass in 9 miles. Keep left at the only major fork. From the pass, the road descends to the South Fork Boise River, which is located in a spectacular gorge cut out of lava rock. The road crosses the river and works its way east for 24 miles to Prairie.

(a) **Arrowrock Ridge Tracks.** At the top of Blacks Creek Pass, there is a mining operation on private property. On the north side of the cattleguard on the pass, a jeep track traverses Forest Service land and heads west up the ridgeline to a point just north of Three Point Mountain. Once the ridgeline is surmounted, the jeep tracks can be followed along the ridgeline north to Kepros Mountain and beyond. These tracks provide excellent early-season hiking.

(1.1) **FS-113, Long Gulch/Slide Gulch Road.** See [(C)(1)].

5

THE SAWTOOTH RANGE

with contributions by Lyman Dye, Reid Dowdle, and Kirk Bachman

The Sawtooth Range is located completely within the Sawtooth National Recreation Area (SNRA), just southwest of Stanley. This oval-shaped group of mountains is bounded by ID-75 in the east and by ID-21 in the north and west.

The Boise and Smoky Mountains form the less well-defined southern boundary of the Sawtooth Range, which ends on the slopes of Greylock Mountain north of Atlanta. The Queens, Boise, Payette, and Salmon Rivers all begin in the Sawtooths.

The Sawtooth Range is the home of Idaho mountaineering and is the best-known of Idaho's many mountain ranges. The range is an extremely rugged collection of granite peaks and alpine lakes with an eastern escarpment that is perhaps Idaho's most impressive mountain wall. Scattered throughout the range are 33 peaks that exceed 10,000 feet, and many spires and towers crowd the high Sawtooth ridges. The main Sawtooth crest stretches more than 32 miles from north to south. From east to west, the range measures 20 miles across at its widest point and includes several impressive divides. Thompson Peak is the highest Sawtooth summit at 10,751 feet.

In the north, the main crest begins on McGown Peak. It snakes south for 35 miles past Alturas Lake and then merges with the Smoky Mountains crest near Galena Summit. Along this route, several impressive subsidiary ridges spread out from the crest and include some of the range's most challenging summits. These subsidiary ridges include the Verita Ridge, the Cony/Reward Divide, and the Grand Mogul/Cramer Divide. Additionally, west of the main crest, two impressive north-south divides rise above the Boise and Queens Rivers country. The Mount Everly/Greylock Peak Divide separates the Boise River from the Queens River and the Mount Pinchot/Nahneke Peak Divide separates the Queens River from the Little Queens River. This latter divide is home of the Rakers, Idaho's most imposing and remote granite spires.

Geologically, granite and glaciation are the main characters in the Sawtooth story. The Sawtooth pluton was injected into the larger Idaho Batholith 40 million years ago at a depth of only 3 to 4 miles. Its granite is pinker than most Idaho Batholith granite, because it contains more feldspar. Sawtooth granite is also extensively fractured by vertical jointing, which has caused the range to erode into jagged edges and towers rather than the hump-shaped appearance characteristic of most Idaho Batholith mountains. Sawtooth glaciation was both merciless and artistic as it cut away millions of tons of rock and created the state's largest alpine lake basins—and a technical climbing environment second to none.

The Sawtooth granite offers climbers the largest number and variety of climbing opportunities in Idaho. Although good climbing rock is found throughout the range, the best rock is found in a triangular-shaped area bounded by Redfish Lake in the north, Hell Roaring Lake in the south, and Grandjean in the west. This Sawtooth triangle is dominated by the solid pink granite of the Sawtooth pluton and was also the most glaciated portion of the range. These two factors are responsible for the triangle's classic collection of alpine icons.

The Elephants Perch, found in the triangle's northeastern corner, harbors Idaho's most impressive mountain wall and has more than twenty-five highly technical routes on its faces. While most of these routes are rarely repeated aid climbs, several are often repeated classic big wall routes with national reputations. Among these, the Mountaineers Route, Beckey Direct, Astro Elephant, and Sunrise Book are the most popular.

Other popular destinations near Redfish Lake include Mount Heyburn, which offers a variety of challenging routes including the classic Stur Chimney and the Chipmunk, Goats, and Eagles Perches. Lesser known but equally challenging formations in this area include the Aiguilles and Le Bec d'Aigle. In addition, Sawtooth Mountain Guides, Idaho's only full time mountaineering guide service, uses a group of solid granite slabs known as the Super Slabs in Redfish Lake Creek Canyon throughout the summer to teach introductory climbing classes.

At the southern end of the triangle, the Finger of Fate in the Hell Roaring drainage is one of the most striking towers in the Sawtooths. A half-dozen or so established routes lead to its airy summit. The most popular is the Open Book, a moderate route on the north face. West of the Finger of Fate, on the main Sawtooth crest, Red Bluff, the Arrowhead, and Mount Sevy offer challenging routes on good rock.

To the west, the Verita Ridge forms much of the triangle's northern hypotenuse as it runs from the main crest, near Alpine Lake to Grandjean. Although remote, hard to reach and seldom visited, its solid granite provides many exceptional climbing opportunities. The ridge's northwest end is anchored by five-summited Grandjean Peak. Moving southeast from Grandjean Peak to the main crest, the next peak is little-known Tohobit Peak, followed by incisor-shaped Warbonnet Peak, the multiple spires of Cirque Lake Peak, and, finally, Monte Verita, a veritable "witches castle" of spires, faces, and arêtes. More than fifty years of climbing history on Verita Ridge demonstrate that Warbonnet Peak is the most sought after destination on the ridge, but the other summits and towers have their adherents. Just to the south of Verita Ridge, Packrat Peak's classic summit block and the many facets of the Mayan Temple are also tremendous granite sentinels that should not be overlooked.

North and south of the triangle, the character of the Sawtooth rock changes. The climber-friendly Sawtooth pluton granite gives way to a mixture of Idaho Batholith granite and metamorphic rock. Nevertheless, mountaineers have explored and placed many challenging routes on these other Sawtooth peaks, which including Thompson Peak and Mount Cramer, the two highest Sawtooth summits, and photogenic beauties like Mount Regan, El Capitán, and Mount McGown. Because the rock is broken, climbers most often tackle snowfields, couloirs, and broken ridges to reach these summits. Yet, many technical rock routes are found on many of these peaks.

The Forest Service manages the Sawtooth Range through the SNRA. From almost the beginning of the twentieth century, there have been many unsuccessful proposals to include the Sawtooths in the national park system. Finally, in 1972, with the aid of a favorable political climate, Congress created the SNRA as a compromise between environmentalists and resource developers. In effect, the SNRA is a de facto national park that has given the Sawtooths protection without creating a Yosemite-like atmosphere. The concept, which emphasizes recreation, protects 200,000 acres of wilderness, and preserves the traditional ranching economy, is working well and has gained wide acceptance within the state.

The SNRA offers limited services by national park standards, but more than adequate services by Idaho standards. There are many developed campgrounds, and camping is generally allowed along most roads. Stanley, a truly unique town, forms the hub around which Sawtooth life revolves. Food, lodging, gasoline, and guide services are all available—so long as you do not need them too late at night.

Overall, the Sawtooths are the most accessible of all of Idaho's mountains. The Forest Service is slowly upgrading the roads, trailheads, and trails within the SNRA. Some roads are still unforgiving destroyers of automobiles, but most are surprisingly pleasant. The trail system is almost too good—most trails have been rebuilt over the last twenty years and are in near-perfect condition. No permits are required to enter the backcountry unless you have an unusually big group or are using horses. Strenuous cross-country travel is possible in many trailless drainages. Although hikers cluster around the major Stanley area destinations, the entire Sawtooth backcountry is worthy of consideration.

THE MAIN CREST: MCGOWN PEAK TO ALPEN PEAK

McGown Peak   *9,860 Feet*

This spectacular summit is the Idaho summit most likely to appear on a calendar. Its pointed summit splits the sky 2 miles south of Stanley Lake. Except for Mount Regan, it is the most photogenic of the Sawtooth peaks. First ascent:

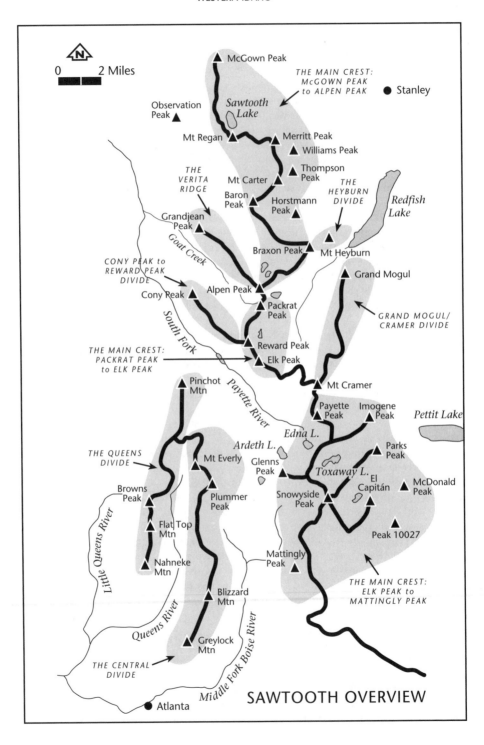

N

0   2 Miles

McGown Peak

THE MAIN CREST:
McGOWN PEAK
to ALPEN PEAK

● Stanley

Observation
Peak ▲

*Sawtooth
Lake*

Mt Regan ▲

Merritt Peak ▲

▲ Williams Peak

THE
VERITA
RIDGE

▲ Thompson
Peak

Mt Carter ▲

THE
HEYBURN
DIVIDE

*Redfish
Lake*

Baron
Peak ▲

▲ Horstmann
Peak

Grandjean
Peak ▲

Goat Creek

Braxon Peak ▲

▲ Mt Heyburn

▲ Grand Mogul

CONY PEAK to
REWARD PEAK
DIVIDE

GRAND MOGUL/
CRAMER DIVIDE

Cony Peak ▲

Alpen Peak ▲

▲ Packrat
Peak

South Fork

THE MAIN CREST:
PACKRAT PEAK
to ELK PEAK

▲ Reward Peak

▲ Elk Peak

Payette River

▲ Mt Cramer

Pinchot
Mtn ▲

Payette
Peak ▲

Imogene
Peak ▲

Pettit Lake

Edna L.

THE QUEENS
DIVIDE

Ardeth L.

Mt Everly ▲

Glenns
Peak ▲

▲ Parks
Peak

Browns
Peak ▲

Plummer
Peak ▲

Toxaway L.

El
Capitán ▲

▲ McDonald
Peak

Snowyside
Peak ▲

Little Queens River

Flat Top
Mtn ▲

▲ Peak 10027

Nahneke
Mtn ▲

Mattingly
Peak ▲

THE MAIN CREST:
ELK PEAK to
MATTINGLY PEAK

Blizzard
Mtn ▲

Queens River

Middle Fork Boise River

Greylock
Mtn ▲

THE CENTRAL
DIVIDE

SAWTOOTH OVERVIEW

● Atlanta

R. Underhill, M. Underhill, and D. Williams in 1934. USGS Stanley Lake/SW

East Face (Class 3). This route begins in the cirque on the east side of the peak [(B)(2)(b.1)] and climbs the ill-defined rib that ascends the south side of the peak's east face. The rib bypasses the massive granite wall that forms the lower two-thirds of the face. Start at the base of the rib, which ends between the two small lakes in the cirque. Climbing the lower sections of the rib involves route-finding around two short walls. Above the walls, the upper section of the rib steepens and crosses loose talus and sand and leads to the base of the summit block. From this point, the route climbs up to the right over several broken walls to the north ridge just below the summit. Follow the ridge to the summit.

Northeast Diagonal Route (II, Class 4). From Stanley Lake, take the Stanley Lake Creek Trail [(B)(2)(a)] and then the Alpine Way Trail [(B)(2)(b)] until the trail crosses a stream due north of the large diagonal couloir that cuts the face from southwest to northeast. Leave the trail at this point and climb the moraine just north of the stream. When the stream forks, continue by following the westernmost fork into the couloir. The path from the trail to the base of the route involves difficult cross-country travel through thick underbrush and downed timber. Climb the couloir to the peak's north ridge near Point 9248. Gain the ridge and climb to the south, staying on the ridge's west side until reaching a saddle with a long, high, smooth cliff on the right. The summit is not the broad peak directly to the north. To reach the true summit, cross the entire base of the smooth cliff on snow patches and ledges, then double back and climb to the southeast up to the northeast rim. From this point, the 300-foot summit block is visible. The route continues up the pinnacle and makes a nearly-complete spiral to the summit.

Peak 9820   *9,820 feet (Class 2)*
This unnamed summit, which is just 0.8 mile southeast of McGown Peak, is that peak's fraternal twin. Both peaks rise precipitously above the intervening cirque. The view from this summit is superb and includes views of Stanley and Sawtooth Lakes as well as all of the northern Sawtooth summits. The route to the summit begins in the cirque that is just north of the peak [(B)(2)(b.1)]. The route begins at a small pond found along the creek and just below the 8,600-foot contour. From this point, angle up to the southeast until a broad shelf is reached at 9,000 feet. From this flat area a steep, debris-filled gully is visible cutting up to the northeast. Follow this gully to the summit ridge. From the top of the gully, it is 5 minutes to the summit. USGS Stanley Lake/SW

Peak 9709   *9,709 feet (Class 2)*
This unnamed summit is the third peak bounding the Mc-Gown cirque. It sits 1 mile due south of McGown Peak. Its isolated summit is best reached from the cirque that separates it from McGown [(B)(2)(b.1)]. Climb to the summit via the peak's north ridge. USGS Stanley Lake/SW

Observation Peak   *9,151 feet (Class 1)*
Observation peak sits off the main crest 3 miles south of McGown Peak. The peak's summit is reached by a good trail that can be accessed from the north, south, and east. The most direct route uses FST-640 [(B)(2)(a)], which it follows south up Stanley Creek for 6 miles to a well-marked junction with FST-024 [(B)(2)(a.1)]. FST-024 leads to the summit. USGS Stanley Lake

Alpine Peak   *9,861 feet (Class 2)*
This peak rises directly east of Sawtooth Lake and provides excellent vistas of the lake and Mount Regan. From FST-478 [(B)(1)(c)], at the south end of Sawtooth Lake, climb any one of the gullies that ascend to the easy slopes above. Gain the summit ridge east of the summit and follow it to the top. Other than loose scree, the route is straightforward. USGS Stanley Lake/SW

Mount Regan   *10,190 feet*
Mount Regan's northwest face has graced dozens of calendars and book covers. The peak is at the south end of Sawtooth Lake and 1 mile southwest of Alpine Peak. The first recorded ascent was by R. Underhill, M. Underhill, and D. Williams in 1934. To approach the peak for all of the routes listed below, first hike to Sawtooth Lake [(B)(1)(b)]. USGS Stanley Lake/SW

Southeast Ridge (Class 3-4). This classic scramble was the route of the first ascent. From the south end of Sawtooth Lake, take the trail south across the broad saddle and drop down to Lake 8271. From the lake, contour around the base of the southeast ridge and enter a large (and rotten) gully. Follow the west side of the gully until it is nearly vertical, and then exit to the west onto a steep, tree-covered slope that leads to the top of the ridge. Follow the ridge until it dead-ends at the base of the summit dome. From this point, the route follows an exposed ledge out onto the east face for 50 feet to an exposed, concave pocket. There are two exposed lines up the pocket's walls to the ridge above. Climb up to the summit ridge, then weave in and out of the large blocks to reach the summit.

Lower East Face (II, 5.5). From the high point on FST-478 [(B)(1)(c)] between Lake 8489 and Sawtooth Lake, climb up steep talus in a southerly direction toward the jagged couloir that cuts the face on its south side. The couloir ends on the southeast ridge roughly 400 feet below the summit. The lower half of the couloir is climbed in two and a half pitches with the crux midway up the first pitch. The upper half of the couloir is a grungy scramble on narrow ledges and loose blocks. The couloir is usually filled with good snow early in the summer. From the top of the ridge follow the Southeast Ridge route to the summit.

North Ridge (II, 5.3). Climb the steep slabs at the south end of Sawtooth Lake. Follow the ridge toward the summit to the highest point directly above the prominent notch that separates the ridge from the mountain. Rappel down into the notch until it narrows enough so that you can safely anchor yourself on the opposite wall. Climb up the notch wall to the ridge and follow it to the summit. First ascent: L. Dye.

Merritt Peak*   *10,312 feet*

Merritt is a complex, tri-summited mountain capped by metamorphic rock. The middle summit is the highest point. The peak is located 1.9 miles east of Mount Regan and 0.5 mile south of Goat Lake. The peak's name is taken from a contemporary copy of the Sawtooth National Forest map. The summit is barred by near-vertical walls on almost every side. Access the peak from Goat Lake [(B)(1)(a.1)]. USGS Stanley Lake/SW

Southeast Face/South Ridge (Class 3-4). From the unnamed lake just east of Point 9088, climb due west up an intermittent stream that flows out of the snow bowl just below the south and middle summits at roughly 9,480 feet. From the snow bowl, climb northeast up the bowl's headwall toward the saddle that separates the south summit from the middle summit. A grayish dike cuts across the face and leads directly to the saddle. Follow this dike until directly below the saddle where several lines will lead up to the saddle and the beginning of the south ridge. Stay on the ridge top until it is blocked by a tower. To bypass this tower, drop down onto the west face and then traverse north on very broken terrain to a gully that climbs up to the middle summit, which is crowned by a summit block. Climb the block's west face. The highest point of this block is found on its north end and it is reached via an easy, but exposed Class 4 traverse. The north summit also can be climbed from the base of the summit block via an easy scramble. It offers a great view of Goat Lake and the upper stretch of the Snowfield Route.

South Face (Class 4). Follow the Southeast Face/South Ridge route to the snow bowl. From the snow bowl, the route climbs directly up the south face without any route-finding

difficulties. This line is best done as a snow climb in June. First ascent: K. Bachman and H. McComish in 1985.

Snowfield Route (II, Snow Climb, Class 4). Climb via the snowfield system that begins above Goat Lake and leads up the peak's northeast side (this system is shown on the Stanley Lake USGS quad). The route is straightforward when good snow conditions exist, and ends in a notch on the west side of the north summit.

Point 10084   *10,084 feet*

This high point, located 0.6 mile north of Williams Peak, is part of Williams Peak. Although it is not a separate summit, it is an enjoyable alpine goal for mountaineers. USGS Stanley Lake/SW

Southeast Slopes (Class 3). Approach the peak's southeast slopes from FST-528 [(A)(6)(d)]. The route from the trail leads to the base of the southeast slopes and then climbs directly to the summit. These slopes offer a spectacular scramble in the summer and a challenging winter/spring ski descent.

Northeast Cirque/Northeast Face (Class 4). Approach the cirque from FST-528 [(A)(6)(d)]. Hike from the trail to the snowfield (shown on the USGS quad) in the northeast cirque. This walk involves some interesting route-finding problems. Ascend the snowfield, which requires ice axes and crampons over moderately difficult and exposed terrain. From the top of the snowfield, climb directly up the face. First ascent: K. Bachman.

Williams Peak   *10,635 feet (Class 3)*

This peak is named after Dave Williams, the Stanley Valley rancher who teamed up with the Underhills to make the first ascent in 1934. Williams Peak is a large fin-shaped summit located 5.5 miles southwest of Stanley. USGS Stanley Peak/SW

Southwest Couloir (Class 3). When viewed from the upper lakes in the Goat Creek drainage, this couloir is located to the southeast and is identified by a small but dense grove of fir trees at its base. The couloir, which can be reached from either the Williams/Thompson Peak saddle or Lake 8865 to the northwest. Access the saddle from FST-528 [(A)(6)(d)] or from the Iron Creek trailhead via Goat Lake to the west [(B)(1)(a.1)].

The bottom of the couloir is blocked by vertical gray cliffs. From the lake just southeast of Point 9088, climb up the small drainage that splits the cliffs to the talus slopes above and then traverse to the base of the gully. If you are approaching from the Williams/Thompson Peak saddle, contour across the face along the 9,800-foot contour. If the snow has melted away, you will discover that the southwest couloir is full of loose talus. It is best to stay on the south side of the couloir where the footing is somewhat better.

At the top of the couloir, turn north and follow the ridge-line to the first tower. Cross behind this tower, drop down 5 feet, and climb to your right onto a goat-traveled ledge. This ledge leads up and down across the base of the next set of towers. The ledge turns a corner and three more towers come into view. Climb over the first tower. Pass the second tower on the east by climbing around a gray rock rib on an airy step. The third tower is the peak's whitish-rock summit block. Traverse out onto its west face to a block that leans on the summit block and then climb directly up to the summit.

Northeast Face, June Couloir (III, Alpine Ice, 5.7). This couloir is the prominent steep couloir that cuts up the northeast face to the notch just east of the main summit. Access the couloir from the Alpine Way Trail [(A)(6)(d)]. The route, which involves 60-degree gully ice where crampons and tools are necessary, is best climbed early in the season. In dry years, expect rotten volcanic rock to be exposed. Be aware that the route is overhung by a large cornice in winter. First ascent: K. Bachman and B. Franklin in 1986.

Southeast Slopes (Class 3). Access these slopes from the Alpine Way Trail [(A)(6)(d)]. The southeast slopes are climbed via an easy scramble. During stable snow conditions, these slopes offer an exciting winter climb and ski descent.

Thompson Peak   *10,751 feet*

This peak, the highest summit in the Sawtooth Range, is clearly visible from both ID-21 and ID-75. The peak, which is 0.8 mile south of Williams Peak, is composed of metasedimentary rocks believed to be Precambrian in age. Although the peak is visible from the valley, it is remote by Sawtooth standards, with no easy access points. The first known ascent was by R. Underhill, M. Underhill, and D. Williams in 1934. The most advantageous approach route is from the Alpine Way Trail [(A)(6)(d)]. Leave the trail at its highest point on the east ridge of Williams Peak. Turn south and traverse into the basin that holds a large, unnamed lake at roughly 9,000 feet. From a point just below the north face of Thompson Peak, scramble up the terraces to the Thompson/Williams saddle. This saddle also can be approached from Goat Lake to the west [(B)(1)(a.1)]. USGS Stanley Peak/SW

South Couloir (Class 3). From the Williams/Thompson saddle, hike around Thompson's west face to the Thompson Peak/Mickeys Spire saddle. From this vantage point, Thompson's south face is split by is a broad couloir. The couloir, which contains a lot of loose rock, rises directly up to the notch between the peak's east and west summits. Climb to

Thompson Peak, the northeast face (Photo by Lyman Dye)

the notch, and then scramble to the west over solid rock to the summit.

Southwest Couloir (II, 5.4). The route begins on the Thompson Peak/Mickeys Spire saddle. From the saddle, traverse across the west face toward the southwest couloir. The couloir is fairly open and lies west of the South Couloir route described above. The couloir is entered about 150 feet below the saddle and is relatively free of loose rock. Two alternatives lead to the summit. The first leaves the couloir where it narrows below the notch in the west rib, and climbs out onto the southwest face following easy Class 5 ledges to the summit. The second alternative climbs the couloir directly to the notch in the west ridge. (This point is roughly 60 feet west of the summit block.) From the ridge crest, climb a short 30-foot section of 5.2 rock and then scramble to the summit.

Northeast Face (II, 5.8). According to Lyman Dye, this route climbs to the large couloir that splits the face and eventually summits on the north ridge. He describes the climb as

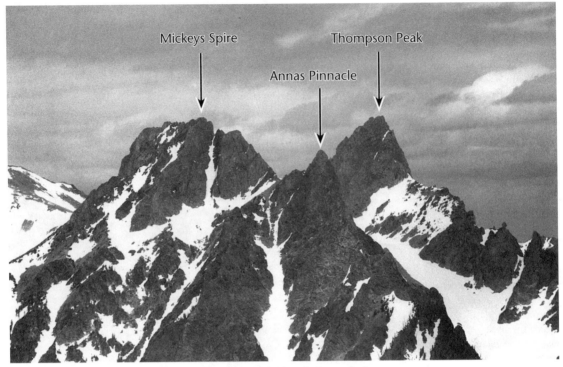

Left to right: Mickeys Spire, Annas Pinnacle, and Thompson Peak (Photo by Lyman Dye)

following the right side of the couloir for several leads, then entering a chimney, which is partially climbed to an "alcove." From the alcove, the route turns right and follows a crack system to the north ridge. First ascent: T. Gathe and J. Kahn in 1968. They rated the climb as moderate-to-difficult Class 5.

West Crack (II, 5.2). This is a complicated, multi-pitch route. From the Williams/Thompson saddle, the west face is cut by a prominent couloir that leads to a notch in the north ridge. In early summer, this couloir is entirely filled with snow at approximately a 50-degree angle. In late summer, the upper portions of the couloir are filled with hazardous loose rock. The route climbs the couloir to the notch roughly 200 feet above the saddle. From the notch, climb up the northwest face for about 100 feet to a large crack that cuts directly up the northwest face.

The first pitch up the crack leads to an overhang and a pile of loose rock. The second pitch requires a touchy move up and over the overhang. Above the overhang, scramble out across the west wall to the southwest on an easy ledge. The third pitch takes you back to the crack directly above a notch that overlooks the north face. (This point is directly west of

the first tower on the west ridge.) The fourth pitch traverses across an easy ledge on the north face to the notch between the first and second tower. The fifth pitch climbs directly out of the notch and onto the north face for about 60 feet, then climbs up to the ridge again. From this point, climb to the summit of the second tower and then descend into the notch between the second tower and the summit pinnacle. From this point, the route joins the Southwest Couloir route. Climb a short 30-foot step out of the notch and then scramble up the ridge to the summit. First ascent: L. Dye.

Mickeys Spire*   *10,680+ feet*
This peak is directly south of Thompson Peak. Its present (unofficial) name was given to it by the Iowa Mountaineers in 1948. The summit is not a spire, but rather a long line of broken towers. The easternmost tower appears to be the highest point. First ascent: R. Underhill in 1934. USGS Stanley Lake/SW

North Ridge (Class 3). This climb begins in the Thompson Peak/Mickeys Spire saddle. The easiest access to this saddle is from Goat Lake [(B)(1)(a.1)] to the north. (See the

South Thompson Peak Cirque route below for an approach to the saddle from the east.) The ridge is straightforward Class 3. From the top of the ridge, follow the Summit Ridge Traverse route described below to reach the peak's high point.

West Ridge (Class 3). This route begins on the Mickeys Spire/Mount Carter saddle that is reached from Goat Lake in the north [(B)(1)(a.1)] or Fishhook Creek [(A)(6)(d.1)] in the south. The ridge is straightforward Class 3 with a few obstacles that you can either climb over or bypass on their north side. To reach the west ridge from Fishhook Creek take the left fork of the upper Fishhook Creek drainage and ascend into the upper basin past Lake 9425. To reach the upper basin, you must climb the lower headwall below the lake on the north side of the stream. Once in the upper basin, turn north and hike to the saddle between Mount Carter and Mickeys Spire. From the top of the ridge follow the Summit Ridge Traverse route described below to reach the peak's high point.

Summit Ridge Traverse (Class 3). If you climb the peak by either its north or west ridges you must climb across the peak's complicated summit ridge to reach the highest point. The route across the ridge follows its south side. From the summit ridge's west end, scramble to the notch between the first and second towers. From the notch, down-climb a rotten gully to a ledge. This narrow, airy, and broken ledge leads across the base of the second tower to easier slopes that lead to the ridge crest just below and west of the summit.

South Thompson Peak Cirque (II, Class 4). This route provides technical climbing on Thompson Peak's lower slopes to reach the Thompson Peak/Mickeys Spire saddle. Take the Fishhook Creek Trail [(A)(6)(d.1)] to its end and continue cross-country on the north side of the drainage until the creek forks. Heavy brush makes this a tiring endeavor. As you hike up the canyon, look for a cliff formation with a visible dark concave rock structure dividing the canyon. Take the right fork of the drainage. As you ascend the drainage, the route climbs to the headwall between Thompson Peak and Mickeys Spire. Climb the headwall on your right side to the saddle. The route from the saddle follows the North Ridge route described above.

East Ridge (II, 5.5). The approach to this route follows Fishhook Creek [(A)(6)(d.1)] as described in the West Ridge route above. The east ridge forms the north wall of the canyon leading to Lake 9425. The spire near the east end of the ridge is known as Annas Pinnacle. The route begins in a large meadow just above the tree line. From this spot, locate the large couloir that leads from the lower end of the meadow to a large notch. Climb to the notch.

From the notch, there are three alternatives. The first

continues through the notch and crosses out onto the north face. From this point, follow the steep ledges (often covered with snow) west to the summit. The second alternative attacks the east ridge directly. This route involves either climbing or bypassing the many small gendarmes on the way to the summit. The third alternative leaves the notch and climbs the southeast face toward the south ridge spur. The route then climbs up this spur to the east ridge. First ascent: L. Dye, A. Barnes, and W. Boyer in 1972.

South Ridge Headwall (II, 5.4). Approach this route via Fishhook Creek [(A)(6)(d.1)]. From the upper basin near Lake 9425, climb toward the prominent diagonal crack that ascends the headwall to the north. This crack begins about halfway up the headwall. It is somewhat broken and contains some loose rock. Climbing within the crack moderates the exposure. Near the top of the crack, the route reaches a small saddle. Cross to the saddle and then continue to the spur on the peak's southwest face. The spur is climbed with two 60-foot pitches separated by a short traverse. At the top of the second pitch, scramble back west to the summit ridge. First ascent: L. Dye and the Iowa Mountaineers in 1972.

Mount Carter*   **10,590 feet (Class 2)**

This peak, a big pile of talus and sand, offers great 360-degree Sawtooth views, including a great view of Sawtooth Lake. It is 0.25 mile due east of Mickeys Spire. The first reported ascent was by the Iowa Mountaineers in 1948. They named the peak after James E. Carter, who was president of the University of Iowa. Climb to the saddle just east of the peak from either the Goat Creek [(B)(1)(a.1)] or Fishhook drainages [(A)(6)(d.1)] and climb to the summit. USGS Stanley Lake/SW

Mount Limbert*   **10,385 feet (Class 3)**

This peak, which is located 0.5 mile south of Mount Carter, was first climbed by the Iowa Mountaineers. Though the Iowa Mountaineers named it after Ede Ebert, who was the wife of their leader, Mount Limbert seems a more appropriate name. Climb the peak from Lake 9425 in the upper Fishhook drainage [(A)(6)(d.1)] via the easy eastern slopes. USGS Stanley Lake/SW

THE IOWA MOUNTAINEERS PINNACLES

The ragged, 1.5-mile ridgeline that extends east from Mount Limbert was a favorite haunt of the Iowa Mountaineers. After World War II, the Iowa climbers placed routes on each of the ridge's four main formations and tagged each with a name. The ridge rises north of Fishhook Creek and directly north of Horstmann Peak. The formations from west to east are Schwartz Pinnacle, Harriets Pinnacle, Mount Bruce, and Mount Bush.

Schwartz Pinnacle*   10,000+ feet

This formation is the westernmost of the Iowa Mountaineers Pinnacles. Schwartz was originally called Pattys Pinnacle by the Iowa Mountaineers, but has more recently been known as Schwartz Pinnacle in honor of Hans Schwartz, a professional mountain guide from Canada who guided the Iowa Mountaineers in the Sawtooths in the late 1940s. First ascent: Iowa Mountaineers in 1948. USGS Stanley Lake/SW

East Ridge (I, Class 4). Access this route from the Fishhook drainage and Lake 9425 [(A)(6)(d.1)]. Climb to the prominent notch in the east ridge and follow the ridge to the summit. The ridge route occasionally moves out onto the pinnacle's broken south slopes. The route is obvious until about 100 feet below the summit, where a low-angle slab forms the crux. Good holds lead up a short crack, which quickly places you on the summit. First ascent: Iowa Mountaineers.

Southwest Crack (II, 5.4). From the west side of Lake 9425 [(A)(6)(d.1)], climb the obvious couloir to the notch between Mount Limbert and Schwartz Pinnacle. Snow remains in the lower sections of the couloir through most of the summer. From the notch, traverse around the west shoulder of the pinnacle, bypassing a minor crack, to the first large crack that opens to the south. The route now follows the crack up for 140 feet to a cove in the face. Climb above the cove for 30 feet to a thin ledge, which allows a tricky traverse across the face and onto the ridge. Follow the ridge to the summit. The traverse is the crux of the climb. First ascent: L. Dye, Springer, Howard, Taylor, and Bravence in 1973.

South Couloir (II, Class 4). Follow the East Ridge route from Lake 9425 [(A)(6)(a.1)] to the notch on the east ridge. From the notch, traverse out onto the south face until this major couloir is reached. Follow the couloir across very loose rock to the ridge spur and then follow the spur to the summit on sound, but broken rock. First ascent: L. Dye in 1973.

Harriets Pinnacle*   (II, 5.4)

This pinnacle sits due east of Schwartz Pinnacle. It is a scramble from the east, south, or west [(A)(6)(d.1)]. A short technical climb leads up the west face, but little is known about this route. USGS Stanley Lake/SW

Mount Bruce*   9,800+ feet (II, 5.2)

This formation is located 0.25 mile due west of Mount Bush. From the Fishhook drainage [(A)(6)(d.1)], climb to the saddle

west of the peak and then follow the west ridge to the summit. The route alternates between the ridge and the ridge's north face. USGS Stanley Lake/SW

Mount Bush*   9,600+ feet

Mount Bush is located 0.9 mile directly north of Horstmann Peak and 1 mile east of Mount Limbert on the Limbert-to-Bush ridge. It is the highest point on the ridge, east of Schwartz Pinnacle, and directly east of the first major notch as it rises out of Fishhook Creek. While Mount Bush is much lower than the surrounding peaks, it attracted the attention of the Iowa Mountaineers because of its impressively thin, pointy shape. Access the peak from the Fishhook drainage [(A)(6)(d.1)]. First ascent: Iowa Mountaineers in 1948. USGS Stanley Lake/SW

East Ridge (II, Class 4). Lyman Dye believes this is probably the route used by the Iowa Mountaineers in 1948. Approach via the Fishhook Creek Trail and the bench west of the creek until you are well beyond the eastern end of the east ridge. Directly north of the prominent snow couloir on Horstmann Peak's north face, a couloir ascends the south side of Mount Bush's east ridge. This couloir leads to the first notch west of the ridge's eastern end. Climb the couloir three-quarters of the way to the notch. At this point, turn west and climb up ledges and a crack system to the summit.

North Face (II, 5.6). This climb starts at the base of a crack that descends to the valley floor from the notch west of the summit. To reach the crack, you must first cross some low-angle slabs that lead to the base of crack. Climb up the crack, keeping mostly on its east side, to an overhang. To avoid the overhang, traverse out onto the east wall, toward a small ledge with a twisted tree. (There are ample holds along the way.) This tree serves as an excellent rappel anchor for the descent. From the tree, follow a ledge back to the crack. Climb the crack directly to the notch. From the notch, take a small ledge system to the east. The ledges end against the peak's northwest face. A small break in the face is climbed back to the west toward a step located about 40 feet above the notch. Continue up the face for 80 feet using small, but beautiful holds. Descent is by two rappels down the north face. First ascent: L. Dye and K. Morrison in 1972.

Southwest Face (II, 5.4). This route follows the North Face route to the notch west of the summit. From the notch, climb up the west ridge for about 40 feet to a step. From the step, the route moves out onto the west face, ascending a ledge system to a bowl halfway across the face. The most difficult pitch leads out of a pocket located below the bowl. From the bowl, the summit is a short scramble. First ascent: L. Dye in 1972.

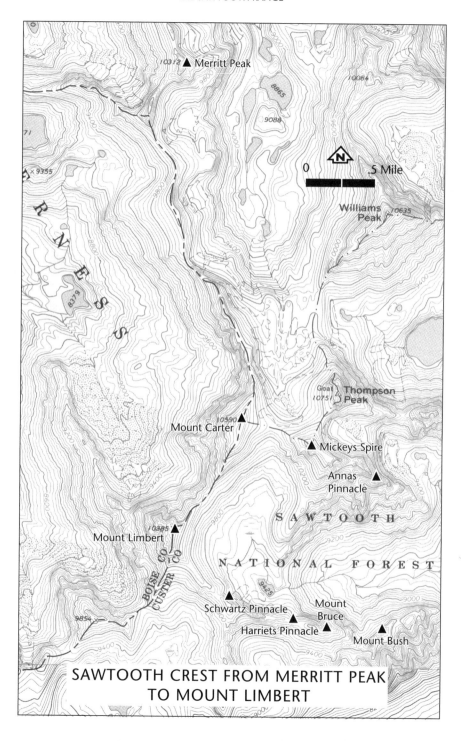

SAWTOOTH CREST FROM MERRITT PEAK TO MOUNT LIMBERT

Peak 10330   *10,330 feet (Class 3)*

This peak, which is north of the main Sawtooth crest on a spur ridge and directly north of Baron Peak, may be the least visited Sawtooth summit even though it has an impressive north face and Matterhorn-like lines. Climb the peak from the vicinity of the Peak 10330/Baron Peak saddle. Approach the saddle either from Baron Peak or from the Baron Creek Trail [(B)(3)(c)] and Moolack Creek to the west. Since the beginning of the south ridge is blocked by vertical granite walls, the route begins on the west side of the saddle roughly 150 feet below the saddle.

From this point, follow the steep talus slopes directly to the south ridge just above the cliffs. Follow the ridge on its west side until the route is blocked by broken walls and ledges. Pick your way through these obstacles staying as close as possible to the top of the ridge. Just below the peak's west summit block, a ledge leads to a small saddle between the peak's two summits. Follow it into the saddle and then climb directly west to the higher, western summit. USGS Stanley Lake/SW

Baron Peak   *10,297 feet*

Baron Peak is a well-hidden, impressive summit that sits at the top the Fishhook, Baron, and North Fork Baron drainages. The peak is protected on the north by an 800-foot vertical face. Nevertheless, its towering summit is not as difficult as it first appears. First ascent: R. Underhill, M. Underhill, and D. Williams in 1934. USGS Warbonnet Peak/SW

South Ridge (Class 2). The south ridge, which is most easily reached from the Stephens Lakes in Fishhook Creek [(A)(6)(c.4)], is an enjoyable walk. From the lake southeast of the peak, hike northwest until roughly 9,200 feet in elevation. Turn due west and climb to the ridge top. Follow the ridge to the summit.

West Ridge/West Face (Class 3). Access this route from the Baron Creek Trail [(B)(3)(c)] where Moolack Creek crosses the trail. Climb the long west ridge directly over Point 8962 and continue to the base of the face. The face is climbed via a steep, rotten gully. This strenuous route gains almost 4,000 feet from where it leaves the trail.

Northwest Ridge (Class 3). This route begins on the Baron Peak/Peak 10330 saddle and follows the north ridge to the summit. The saddle can be reached by following Moolack Creek from the Baron Creek Trail [(B)(3)(c)].

Mount Ebert*   *9,880+ feet*

This ragged peak is found on the ridge that runs between Baron and Braxon Peaks 1.5 miles southeast of Baron. The peak was named for John Ebert, president of the Iowa Mountaineers. First ascent: Iowa Mountaineers in 1957. USGS Warbonnet Peak/SW

West Ridge (II, 5.6). This is the route of the first ascent. The ridge that connects Ebert with Baron Peak to the north is considered Ebert's west ridge. The route begins in the

Ed-Da-How Spire and Mount Ebert from the southeast

Fishhook drainage [(A)(6)(c.4) or (A)(6)(d.1)] at the base of the main couloir on the north side of the peak. The couloir leads to a notch in the west ridge. The climb up the couloir crosses plush meadows and easy slabs to a landing formed by a shallow cliff band. Just above this landing, climb up the east side of the wall to a scree delta at the base of the couloir. The climb up the couloir to the notch is straightforward. From the notch, the route continues up the west ridge (with an occasional traverse onto the southwest face) to the summit. First ascent: Iowa Mountaineers.

East Face Dike (II, 5.4). Access this route from the Stephens Lakes in the upper sections of the Fishhook drainage [(A)(6)(c.4) or (A)(6)(d.1)]. The route climbs the east face's prominent black dike, and then traverses the face. This dike ends to the right of a large notch south of the summit. The climb up the dike to the notch is straightforward. From the notch, traverse north to the top of an easy ledge that leads to a crack system that leads to the next notch up the face. Climb this crack, using a small ledge on the face, to a solid belay point. Continue to the second notch. From this notch, descend the east face for 40 feet to a ledge system that runs across the face toward the north. Take this ledge system across the face and up to the spur ridge, which is located near the third notch. Two pitches up, this spur brings you to a fourth notch. Climb out of this notch to the summit in another 80 feet. To descend, follow the spur directly down from the summit until you are above the main cliffs. Cross the face to the black dike and follow it back down. First ascent: L. Dye, Springer, Howard, Taylor, and Bravence in 1973.

Ed-Da-How Spire*   9,333 feet (II, 5.2)

This pinnacle resembles a big thumb. It is found on Mount Ebert's southeast ridge. The pinnacle is separated from Ebert by a large notch. The first ascent was by L. Dye, Springer, Howard, Taylor, and Bravence in 1973 via the north ridge. To climb the north ridge, descend from the notch above the black dike on Mount Ebert's east face (see the description under Mount Ebert) to the saddle slab. The north side of the pinnacle is attacked directly from the saddle. The ridge becomes more difficult as it climbs toward the summit. USGS Warbonnet Peak/SW

Stephens Spire*   9,440+ feet (I, 5.1)

This picturesque pinnacle is southeast of Ed-Da-How Spire and directly west of Rothorn Spire. It rises about 100 feet above the ridge crest. Climb the spire from Stephens Lakes [(A)(6)(c.4)] via its north couloir. Scramble up the loose scree and talus occupying the lower slopes. From the ridge crest,

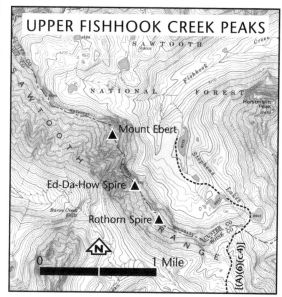

the spire can be climbed from east, west, or south with about the same degree of difficulty. Lyman Dye notes that the actual technical climbing is only about 60 feet. USGS Warbonnet Peak/SW

Rothorn Spire*   9,440+ feet (II, 5.7)

This formation is located southeast of Ed-Da-How. It was first climbed by Dye and Brodie in 1973. This spire is the largest pinnacle in the area. Its rock is reddish in color and sound in consistency. The only known ascent route climbs up the north face. Dye and Brodie's route starts from the saddle north of the spire, and descends out across the north face to a large crack near the northwest corner of the spire. This crack has a large chockstone wedged in about 60 feet up the wall. Climb the crack to the chockstone. There is a second chockstone above the first. Bypass both on the left. Above the second chockstone, the route moves out onto the wall on thin holds and climbs up to a slightly overhanging slab. A 30-foot layback up another crack system takes you to a point above this slab. From here, the route moves to the west and reaches an open shelf about 100 feet below the summit block. Climb from here to the summit. USGS Warbonnet Peak/SW

Horstmann Peak   10,470 feet

This peak was originally called Mount Hancher by the Iowa Mountaineers, but was later officially named after an early Stanley Basin homesteader and friend of Dave Williams.

The peak is located 1.4 miles due east of Mount Ebert and is a spectacular conglomeration of ridges, couloirs, and gendarmes with several rewarding routes. The first ascent was by R. Underhill, M. Underhill, and D. Williams in 1934. Access for all routes listed below begins at various locations in the Fishhook drainage [(A)(6)(c.4) or (A)(6)(d.1)]. USGS Warbonnet Peak/SW

South Ridge (Class 3). From the highest of the Stephens Lakes, Lake 8945, hike up and due north to the lowest point on Horstmann's south ridge (between Horstmann and Fishhook Spire). From this point, ascend the ridge for a short distance until you can look across Horstmann's southeast face. Look for a goat path that crosses the talus from the ridge toward the base of the face. This path meanders up and down, losing about 75 feet in the process. Follow it to the gully that climbs diagonally toward the high point. Two major notches are visible at the top of the gully. While the summit may be ascended from either notch, the notch farthest to the right is the most direct route. Beware that the gully, though passable, is cluttered with loose rock. From the notch, climb up diagonally for 50 feet to the west face and then straight up the face to the summit ridge. Cross back over to the summit ridge to its east side and follow it to a point where the summit block can be climbed.

Sickle Couloir (II, Snow and Ice Climb). This popular route climbs the sickle-shaped couloir that climbs up the east side of the north face. Approach via Fishhook Creek [(A)(6)(d.1)]. At a point opposite the face, look for the hanging cirque on the face above. Cross the creek and climb into the cirque. The curving couloir leads out of the cirque and onto the summit. (K. Bachman)

North Face (II, 5.2). The complicated north face was first climbed by the Iowa Mountaineers in 1957, but the exact line of the ascent is unknown. A variety of options are available on the face and the difficulty of the options can vary greatly. Access is from the Fishhook [(A)(6)(d.1)].

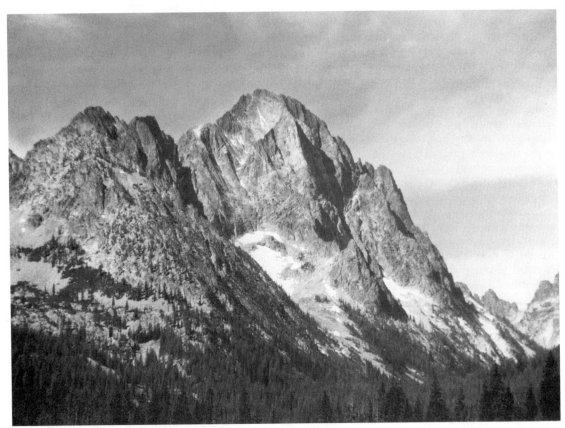

Horstmann Peak, 10,470 feet, dominates the Fishhook Creek drainage.

Northwest Buttress (IV, 5.9). The Northwest Buttress is the peak's prominent right-side, skyline ridge viewed from the Stanley Basin. This is a long route on rock of variable quality. From roughly 8,000 feet along Fishhook Creek [(A)(6)(d.1)], hike south to the base of a massive buttress that rises out of the upper drainage toward the northwest ridge. Ascend this buttress to the upper northwest ridge which is formed by a series of gendarmes and towers. Follow this ridge to the summit. The lower buttress requires above-average route-finding skills as there is no dominant crack system to follow. First ascent: K. Bachman and R. Young in 1979.

Northeast Ridge (II, 5.7). Access this route by hiking cross-country up Fishhook Creek [(A)(6)(d.1)], staying north of the creek, until you are directly north of the northeast ridge. Cross the creek and go up through the timber to the ridge's east side. Continue along the base of the ridge, climbing across terraced platforms, to the point where the ridge swings to the west. From this point, climb a couloir that leads to the ridge crest southeast of Point 9738. Follow the ridge, occasionally moving out onto the north face, to the summit. The last 50 feet is climbed on the north face. First ascent: L. Dye, A. Barnes, and W. Boyer in 1965.

North Ridge Spur (II, 5.6). Access this route from Fishhook Creek [(A)(6)(d.1)]. Stay north of the creek until you are directly north of the large snowfield at the base of the north couloir. Cross the creek and look for a small pinnacle near this snowfield—just beyond it is a subsidiary ridge that descends from the main north ridge. This is the north ridge spur. It is composed of shattered, down-sloping granitic rock. The entire climb is on this unsettling rock. First ascent: M. Howard and D. Walters in 1971.

East Face (II, Class 4). This was probably the route used by the Underhills and Dave Williams in 1934. The route, which moves directly up the face with no route-finding difficulties, begins in Fishhook Creek's south fork [(A)(6)(d.1)]. Leave the creek and climb to the bowl below the face. From the bowl, several routes, including the line described in the South Ridge route, climb the ledge network to the summit. This is a good spring route when snow conditions are right.

Fishhook Spire*

This impressive formation is located between Horstmann Peak and Mount Iowa. Its history provides a good example of how confusing names can become. The "original" Fishhook Spire was in the Baron Creek drainage. That formation, now called El Pima, was called Fishhook Spire by Beckey and others because it looks like a fishhook. However, to the northeast, in the Fishhook Creek drainage, other spires could be mistaken

for the "original" Fishhook Spire. Thus, to avoid confusion, the name of the Baron Creek spire was changed to El Pima (it also looks like a cat claw). The Iowa Mountaineers then dubbed the Fishhook Creek formation "Fishhook Spire," not so much for its appearance, but because it is at the top of the Fishhook drainage. Access is from either Fishhook Creek [(A)(6)(d.1)] or Stephens Lakes [(A)(6)(c.4)]. USGS Warbonnet Peak/SW

Southwest Couloir (II, 5.5). The route follows this prominent couloir on the formation's southwest side up over very broken rock. First ascent: R. Maynard and F. Chappel.

Mount Iowa*   *10,327 feet*

This peak is named in honor of the Iowa Mountaineers. This summit is located on a connecting ridge midway between Braxon Peak and Horstmann Peak and just south of Fishhook Spire. First ascent: attributed to P. Petzoldt, B. Adams, B. Merrian, J. Speck, C. Wilcox, and C. Fisher in 1947. USGS Mount Cramer/SW

West Face (Class 3). Access the west face from the highest Stephens Lake [(A)(6)(c.4)]. From the lake, hike north toward Horstmann Peak until you are directly below Fishhook Spire. Climb up to the base of the spire and hike southeast into the Fishhook Spire/Mount Iowa saddle. From the saddle, contour up and across the face to a notch just below the summit. This route avoids several obstacles on the peak's northwest ridge.

Northwest Ridge (Class 4). This route also begins in the Fishhook Spire/Mount Iowa saddle, which is accessed from Stephens Lakes [(A)(6)(c.4)]. The route climbs the ridge either on its top or on its east side. First ascent: Iowa Mountaineers in 1947.

Rotten Monolith*

This formation, which is visible from Stanley Basin, is located on the north side of Braxon Peak, near its summit. The east side of the tower is 500 feet high and the west side is 150 feet high. USGS Mount Cramer/SW

West Face (Class 6). This formation was first climbed by F. Beckey and L. Stur in 1961. Stur reports that the rock was "unbelievably rotten." Twelve pitons and one bolt were used on the ascent. In several spots, the pitons were hammered directly into the granite wall (sans cracks).

Braxon Peak   *10,353 feet*

This summit, with the best 360-degree view in Idaho, is 1.1 miles southwest of Mount Heyburn. The peak's summit, a strenuous scramble, is a ragged, decomposed granite block.

The ascent is best done in early spring when the snow covers the talus. Details of the first ascent are unknown. USGS Mount Cramer/SW

East Ridge (Class 3). Leave the Redfish Lake Inlet boat dock and hike up Redfish Lake Creek Trail [(A)(6)(b)] until the trail crosses a small stream roughly 2 miles from Redfish Lake. This point is due northwest of the Elephants Perch's west face at roughly 7,200 feet. Climb up the stream, working around small cliffs and through heavy brush and downfall for roughly 400 feet of elevation gain. This section, because of the brush and downfall, is the unappealing crux of the climb. The terrain opens into a mixed pine and fir forest with an occasional cliff to block your way. Just below 9,000 feet the route reaches two small ponds. From the ponds, turn due north and climb to the saddle above. Aim for a point west of the saddle's lowest point to avoid the two towers that sit in the saddle. From the saddle, climb the ridge to the summit that is roughly 700 feet above. The only Class 3 climbing is just below the summit.

West Side (II, Class 4). From the vicinity of the saddle (between Braxon Lake and Stephens Lakes) [(A)(6)(c.4)], climb to the west up the snowfields and steep scree and talus to the summit. Pass the horn-shaped formation on its north side. Once above the tower, scramble up the loose scree to the base of the east wall. From this point, the route follows the base of the wall to a notch that separates the horns south of the summit from the summit itself.

Quartzite Peak*   *9,682 feet*
Quartzite Peak, located 0.7 mile due south of Braxon Peak on a subsidiary ridge that runs east from the main crest, is a cylindrical-shaped summit. The first and only known ascent was by H. Gmosser, W. Joura, and the Iowa Mountaineers. The line and details of this ascent are unknown. To reach the peak, use the Braxon Peak East Ridge route. USGS Mount Cramer/SW

Red Sentinel*   *9,980 (II, 5.4 A1)*
This formation is also known as Flatrock Needle. It is a sheer, orange-colored wall located 1.1 miles south/southwest of Braxon Peak. It is visible from the Redfish Lake Creek Trail

Quartzite Peak (left) and Braxon Peak from the cross-country route to Saddleback Lakes

near Flatrock Junction [(A)(6)(b) and (c)]. The formation can be climbed from the junction by ascending to the narrow south couloir that eventually leads to the ridge top west of the formation. Climb the couloir until it is blocked by a boulder about one quarter of the way up. Bypass the boulder via a chimney and a delicate ledge system on the left-hand wall. Climb this system until moving back into the upper couloir is possible, then continue in the couloir to the ridge top. Once on the needle proper, the route traverses its south side to the corner. The route moves onto the east face; direct aid is needed to reach a platform just below the summit. The final move to the summit is short and exposed. First ascent: H. Gmosser, B. Echo, D. Milisap, and C. Brown. USGS Mount Cramer/SW

The Chessman* (III, 5.10). This is the dark, freestanding tower just west of the Red Sentinel summit. The route is approached and visible from Braxon Lake. The climb follows a crack that runs up the entire length of the north face, some of which is off-width. Five pitches lead to the summit. Descend off the backside with a single rappel. First ascent: K. Bachman and R. Young in 1982.

Le Bec D'Aigle*   *9,727 feet*
This peak is situated directly north of Airplane Lake and northeast of Baron Pass. Its pointed summit is composed of extremely smooth rock on the west side and broken ledges and cracks on the east side. The first ascent was up the east face, but the peak has many solid untried cracks and walls. Access the peak from FST-101 [(A)(6)(c)]. USGS Warbonnet Peak/SW

East Face (I, 5.3). The route begins at the small lakes north of Alpine Lake [(A)(6)(c.4)]. Scramble up the hardpan scree and talus slope northeast of the uppermost lake. South of the summit buttress there is a level spot in the south ridge. Cross the ridge at this point and move onto the peak's east side. There is an obvious ledge leading out onto the face that becomes broken near a tree halfway across. From the tree, a friction step-up leads to a broken terrace. Follow this terrace to a fragmented crack at its far northeast end. Climb this crack to the platform above. From the platform, a long diagonal crack ascends to the base of the summit block to a step about 15 feet below the actual summit. Climb the crack to the step. Above the step, follow a horizontal flake (which moves when you touch it) to the summit. First ascent: H. Adams Carter and G. Constan in 1957.

North Buttress (I, 5.2). From Alpine Lake, hike to the Alpine/Braxon Lakes saddle [(A)(6)(c.4)]. Just below the pass, leave the trail and contour northeast to the saddle just west of the summit. From this saddle, scramble up to the base of the buttress. (Note: From this point, you can reach the East Face route by traversing south across the west face to the south ridge and crossing the ridge via one of its many chimneys.) At the base of the North Buttress, there is a large crack that leads up and over a hump to the top of the buttress. The buttress provides a fine, 120-foot lead to the summit. The final 30 feet cross exposed rotten rock. First ascent: L. Dye, M. Howard, and the Mazamas.

Peak 9769   *9,769 feet (Class 3)*
This peak, which is located on the main Sawtooth crest 0.6 mile west of Alpine Lake, is the southern anchor of the Verita Ridge that is covered in detail below. It has been called Monte Verita in the climbing literature. However, the USGS placed that name on a peak further west. The peak is a strenuous, but enjoyable scramble from the saddle to the west [(A)(6)(c)]. USGS Warbonnet Peak/SW

Mount Alpen*   *9,680+ feet (Class 3)*
This twin-summited peak is located 1 mile southwest of Alpine Lake. It is plainly visible from the lake. It is erroneously identified as Packrat Peak by the USGS. From Alpine Lake, follow the stream to the west and then turn south and climb the gully to the saddle west of the peak. There is a permanent snowfield in the upper stretches of the gully. From the saddle, it is a short scramble to the summit. USGS Warbonnet Peak/SW

THE HEYBURN DIVIDE
The Heyburn Divide runs east from the main Sawtooth crest at Braxon Peak and encompasses some of the most challenging Sawtooth formations. The divide was the first to catch the interest of the mountaineers following in the footsteps of the Underhills. Mount Heyburn's three summits crown the eastern end of the ridge. On the southern slopes of the divide, northwest of Redfish Lake Creek, are five extraordinary granite formations that were first described by Robert Underhill: the Grand Aiguille, Small Aiguille, Black Aiguille, Split Tooth, and Splinter Towers.

Mount Heyburn   *10,200+ feet*
This complex peak is situated east of Braxon Peak and the main crest, and just west of Redfish Lake. It is the best-known Sawtooth peak and possibly Idaho's most majestic mountain. As seen from the highway near Stanley, the peak has three major summits. The two highest summits are separated by a

deep snow couloir known as the Silver Saddle. The western-most of these two summits is the highest by 1 or 2 feet. It was first climbed by Robert and Miriam Underhill in 1935. The east peak was probably first climbed by Robert Limbert in 1927. Since the first ascent, the peak has been a focal point for Sawtooth climbers. A third summit, the West Pinnacle, is located southwest of Heyburn's two main summits. USGS Mount Cramer/SW

West Summit Routes. Unfortunately much of the west summit is composed of deteriorated granite, which eliminates several fine climbing lines from consideration. Fortunately, there also is some good granite and several fine routes lead up the peak, including the classic Stur Chimney on the West Summit's west face.

Stur Chimney (II, 5.2). Access the west face from the up-permost Bench Lake by crossing the saddle at the top of the

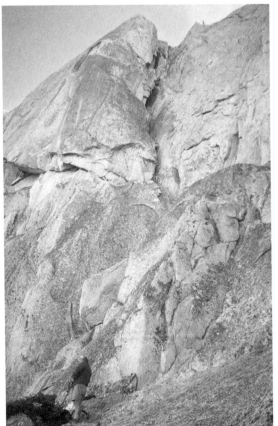

The Stur Chimney splits the west face of Mount Heyburn's west summit.

drainage [(A)(6)(a)]. (Note that the saddle also can be reached from the Redfish Lake Creek Trail [(A)(6)(b)] by following a small drainage up toward the northwest. In the upper sections of the drainage, a steep, talus-filled couloir leads to the saddle.) Once across the saddle, traverse across scree slopes below the west face toward the West Summit/West Pinnacle saddle. From the saddle, look back across the face to the north and you will see the Stur Chimney, an almost-vertical chimney splitting the solid granite in the face. Descend off the saddle, toward the crack, to the base of a large crack on the south or right-hand side of the west face. Climb this Class 4 crack or the slab next to it up toward a notch on the southwest ridge until you reach the broad ledge that crosses the face to the base of the chimney. Cross to the chimney.

The first pitch climbs 40 feet up the chimney, crosses a chockstone, and then continues to a large room in the chimney that serves as a good belay station. The second pitch leaves the room by climbing out onto the west face, over the roof and into a small pocket above. From this point, there are two alternatives: climb out of the chimney on the right on good cracks to the open pocket 30 feet below the summit; or continue to climb the chimney directly. The second alternative requires a move out and over the second, larger chockstone. This move involves maintaining one hand jam under the chockstone while the other hand searches for a hold above the stone. The last pitch from the pocket is an easy lead on a fracture line that cuts to the south. First ascent: L. Stur, J. Fuller, and J. Ball in 1958. First winter ascent: W. Cove and L. Adkins on February 25, 1975—or by L. Stur and F. Beckey on April 3, 1961, depending on your definition of winter.

Southwest Ridge (II, 5.6). The route, first climbed by the Underhills and Dave Williams, begins on the saddle between the west summit and the West Pinnacle [(A)(6)(a)]. From the saddle, the southwest ridge is blocked by a pinnacle. Bypass this pinnacle by following the lower portion of the Stur Chimney route to the broad ledge that crosses the west face. Instead of traversing across the west face, continue up the crack to the notch. The move into this notch is the crux of the entire route. From the notch, continue climbing the ridge to the summit. The upper ridge is moderate in difficulty but, according to Underhill, is a "crumbling mess."

An alternate route to the southwest ridge, which avoids the rotten move out of the notch, begins on the opposite side of the southwest ridge in the couloir separating the east and west summits. From this couloir, a series of rotten slabs can be followed to the notch on the southwest ridge. The exposure is minimal, but the rock is something else. Yet another variation on this route was climbed by the Iowa Mountaineers in 1947. This route is rated 5.2 and was first climbed by K. Jones, B. Adams, J. Ebert, G. Goodrich, and J. Speck. About halfway up the crack leading to the notch (followed by the Underhills), the Iowa Mountaineers followed a smaller crack that also leads to the notch. This crack bypasses the difficult move below the notch.

East Face/Snow Couloir (II, 5.3 A1 or 5.9). From the upper Bench Lake [(A)(6)(a)] area, a prominent but rotten couloir leads to the Silver Saddle that separates the two summits. Follow this steep couloir up past the north-face cliffs to the saddle. From the saddle, the west summit's short east face is a vertical wall. A 40-foot section on this wall is the only technical difficulty encountered on this route. Paul Petzoldt first climbed the wall with a group of Iowa Mountaineers (E. Carter, C. Fisher, B. Merriam, and C. Wilcox) in 1947, using a double-rope, tension technique. Above this pitch, the summit is easily reached. The normal descent route makes two rappels down the wall to the saddle. The final rappel is set up just above the tension pitch in a crack located on the south cliff wall.

Northwest Ridge (II, 5.6). Climb across the scree slopes directly above and west of the highest Bench Lake [(A)(6)(a)] to the west corner of Heyburn and then enter a steep, goat-traveled couloir. Climb halfway up the couloir and then traverse sharply to the left onto the west wall. Follow the ridge in three pitches to the summit. First ascent: Iowa Mountaineers in 1948.

Other Routes. Two other routes are reported in the *American Alpine Journal*. F. Beckey and J. Fuller climbed the Northwest Ridge/North Face **(II, 5.6)** in 1961. This multi-pitch route climbs the northwest ridge and north face. Then, later in the summer, L. Stur and J. Ball completed the Beckey and Fuller route on the northwest ridge without detouring onto the north face. They rated the Northwest Ridge Direct at **II, 5.6**. It is unlikely that either of these routes has ever been repeated.

East Summit Routes. Once the west summit of Heyburn was unofficially declared the peak's highest point (by two Iowa Mountaineers with a spirit level), much of the appeal of the equally beautiful East Summit was lost. The East Summit offers good climbing, a good view, and what difference does a couple of feet make anyway? The East Summit's highest granite block is formed by a shaft of rock rising 30 feet from a ledge. When the Underhills and Dave Williams reached the East Summit in 1934, they found evidence of a previous ascent.

South Rib (II, 5.2). This route climbs to the Silver Saddle via the main south couloir from the Redfish Lake Creek Trail

[(A)(6)(b)] or from the Bench Lake area [(A)(6)(a)]. Both approaches are steep and require care. The northern approach is usually icy, even into the fall. From the saddle, climb to the east onto the peak's west wall until you reach a crack that leads up the west face of the summit pinnacle. The crack angles up to the south and finally exits on the south wall. From this point, follow the ledge to the east and to the south rib. Climb directly up the exposed rib.

Northeast Ridge (II, Class 4). This pinnacle-studded ridge rises out of the lateral moraine that divides the Redfish drainage from the Bench Lake drainage. The ridge can be reached from the Bench Lake Trail [(A)(6)(a)] or by climbing the prominent couloir that appears directly above the Redfish Inlet Campground. Gain the ridge above the trees and climb onto the ledge system. A pinnacle that looks like a person wearing a robe (Saint Peters Pinnacle) is visible up the ridge. Follow the ridge, meandering from east to west to avoid various assorted towers, to the summit block. The summit block can be climbed from the north or east sides. Route-finding around the many pinnacles on the ridge is time consuming.

West Pinnacle/Tunnel Route (III, Class 6). The West Pinnacle, Heyburn's third summit, has failed to attract climbers despite its imposing shape and good rock. Only one route, climbed more than fifty years ago, has been recorded. It begins on the West Summit/West Pinnacle saddle [(A)(6)(a)]. From the saddle, hike to the base of the pinnacle and look on the north side of the tower for a long, narrow tunnel behind an enormous flake. The tunnel leads to a large platform. From the platform, scramble down the pinnacle's northern side to its base. This wall above contains two piton-sized cracks, which eventually join. The first ascent climbed this wall by using a double-rope tension technique. There is a small rock projection on the wall. Pass a sling over it and use two anchors to overcome the first 10 feet. The next 20 feet are overhanging. Use four anchors for direct aid to get over this obstacle to the ledge above. The moves involved in getting to the ledge are awkward and difficult. Six feet above the ledge is a large rock projection. Place another sling over it to provide direct aid. Climb up the next high-angle flake and past a 20-foot slab to reach the summit. First ascent: R. Widrig, J. Hieb, W. Grande, and G. Matthews in 1948.

The Aiguilles, Split Tooth, and Splinter Towers

These five formations sit on the Heyburn Divide between the West Pinnacle and Braxon Peak. To approach these formations, leave Redfish Lake Creek Trail [(A)(6)(b)] where it crosses

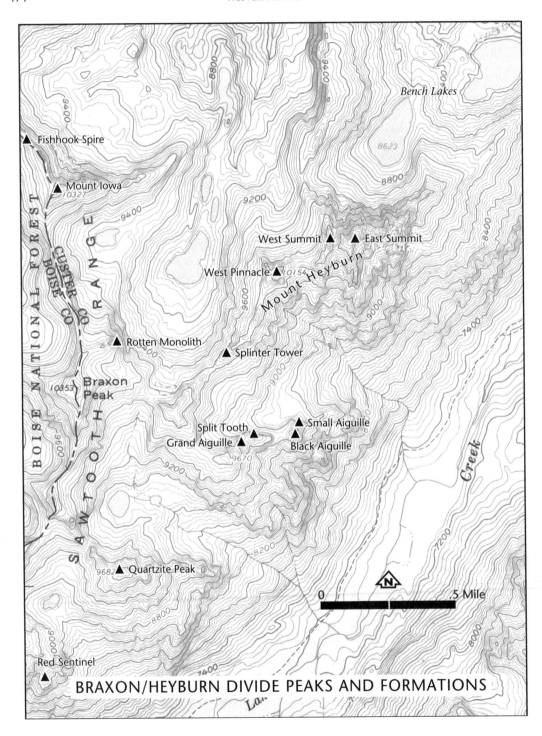

BRAXON/HEYBURN DIVIDE PEAKS AND FORMATIONS

the 7,200-foot contour line on the USGS quad and climb the large slide area on Mount Heyburn until it narrows to a slot. Then turn to the southwest, climb into the cirque above, and then continue to the ridgeline.

Grand Aiguille*

This formation, visible from the south end of Redfish Lake, appears as a shallow fishtail summit with an overhanging north face. First ascent: J. Hieb, W. Grande, R. Widrig, and W. V. Graham Mathews in 1946. USGS Mount Cramer/SW

Northwest Side (II, 5.4). This was the line of the first ascent. The climb begins from the notch on the west side of the formation, where it joins with the Split Tooth. The route to the notch is relatively easy, though climbing the snow-filled couloir early in the season may present some problems. The route above the notch consists of four or five pitches of moderate, but exposed climbing. The first pitch leads up the northwest face past several trees and ends behind a large flake. The second pitch runs from the flake to a second notch found on the southeast face by crossing a deep pit and squeezing up a 40-foot chimney. From the notch, the third pitch leads (using a layback) to some large granite flakes out on the face. (These flakes are shaky when pulled outward, but are secure when downward pressure is placed directly on them.) From the flakes, the final lead traverses back to the southeast on the crest of the summit block.

South Face (II, Class 5). This route was first climbed by F. Beckey and J. Fuller in 1962. The route climbs up a rotten southwest gully to more solid rock above. From the top of the gully, Beckey made a pendulum traverse around a blind corner to a platform. From this spot, he followed a crack up for 250 feet to a tree. The route follows the original crack above the tree until a more prominent crack system can be entered. The new crack is followed for two and one-half pitches to where it joins the original crack, which is then followed to the summit.

Small Aiguille*

Located east of the Grande Aiguille and next to the Black Aiguille, this formation is much less impressive than its neighbors and contains spots of rotten rock. First ascent: H. King and A. Holben in 1948. USGS Mount Cramer/SW

North Face (II, 5.3). This route begins on the col to the west. The first pitch climbs to the left up a roughly horizontal dike on the north face. From the dike, a tricky diagonal traverse on unsound rock leads to a chimney. The next pitch climbs this chimney to a large block, moves out onto the face to climb a short, vertical pitch, then moves back into

the chimney, which leads to the summit. Two long rappels can be used to return to the col. First ascent: H. King and A. Holben in 1948.

South Face (II, 5.4). From the Redfish Lake Creek Trail [(A)(6)(b)], several chimneys are visible in the Small Aiguille's east wall. All of the chimneys offer alternative routes to the knife-edged summit ridge. Climb up and across a boulder field just east of the tower to the base of the south face. Scramble west from this point to the base of a smooth wall. Climb the chimney southwest of this wall to its top, where a second chimney, above and to the right of the first chimney, is accessed. The second chimney is broken by a ledge and several trees as it leads straight up to the east end of the summit ridge. A shoulder stand was used to reach the final few feet to the summit. The summit ridge is exposed and composed of extremely poor rock. First ascent: L. Stur and J. Fuller in 1960.

Black Aiguille*

This spire, named by the Iowa Mountaineers, is south of the Small Aiguille. The summit block is rounded and has a definite black color. It is free of cracks and composed of friable granitic rock that is so rotten the first ascent party easily carved a saddle horn-like fixture into the rock to use as a rappel anchor. First ascent: H. Gmosser and R. Harris. USGS Mount Cramer/SW

East Couloir (II, 5.2). This route starts by scrambling up the main couloir on the east face. This couloir contains two very sharp spires. Relatively easy ledges and chimneys lead out of the couloir and up the east face to the summit.

South Side (rating and route unknown.). First ascent: the Iowa Mountaineers lead by Idaho Falls–native Bill Echo in 1960.

Split Tooth*

This spectacular tower is immediately west of the Grand Aiguille. The tower is split by a massive crack dividing the formation into two summits. The lower summit is the easier of the two. First ascent: B. Echo and a group from the Idaho Falls Alpine Club in 1960. USGS Mount Cramer/SW

Northeast Tower (I, Class 6). This route climbs the lower summit from the notch on the formation's west side and then uses a Tyrolean traverse to reach the summit. The route, about 110 feet in length, is on exposed, rotten rock.

Northeast Crack (I, 5.7). This route begins in the notch between Split Tooth and the Grand Aiguille and climbs the obvious crack in the northeast face as far as possible by stemming. The route then moves onto the northeast side of the south pinnacle. Follow this face to the top. An old piton is visible, marking F. Beckey's 1963 first-ascent route.

Southwest Ridge (II, 5.6 A1). Climb into the cirque to the southwest of the formation and approach the cirque's southeast wall. Take the first major crack in this wall to the ridge above. From this point, you are above and to the west of the formation. Descend the ridge to the northeast and climb to the summit of the lower spire. Make a Tyrolean traverse to the higher spire.

Splinter Towers*

These towers are found on the ridge between Mount Heyburn's West Pinnacle and Braxon Peak. The spires are named Splinter, Steeple, and Thimble. All three were first climbed in 1948. Splinter was climbed in 1948 by A. Holben and H. Schwabland via eight Class 4 pitches up the south face. Steeple was first climbed by H. King and F. Beckey via the west ridge. Thimble was first climbed by King and Beckey, who used direct aid on the summit block. USGS Mount Cramer/SW

Grand Mogul (Photo by Lyman Dye)

THE GRAND MOGUL TO MOUNT CRAMER DIVIDE

This divide is east of the main crest and runs from the Grand Mogul just south of Redfish Lake to Cramer Peak. This long, high ridgeline contains the Elephants Perch's east face, numerous 10,000-foot peaks and many impressive spires offering good clean alpine climbing. The primary access routes for this divide are Redfish and Hell Roaring Lakes.

Grand Mogul   9, 733 feet

This enticing peak is located at the southwest end of Redfish Lake, where it and Mount Heyburn form ramparts on either side of Redfish Lake Creek. The peak is composed of sections

Splinter Tower (Photo by Lyman Dye)

of both hard and deteriorated granite that has formed alternating walls and talus slopes. Little technical climbing has taken place on its slopes. USGS Mount Cramer/SW

Northeast Ridge (Class 3). From the Inlet Transfer Camp at the south end of Redfish Lake, take FST-092 [(A)(6)(b.1)] around the southwest end of the lake. Follow the trail to the base of the prominent avalanche chute that cuts the lower portion of the ridge and follows the chute up toward the ridge top. The chute eventually turns right. Follow the turn and continue climbing up through the trees toward the ridge top. At tree line, look for a small protrusion that resembles a serpent's head. There is a notch directly west of this formation. Scramble up to this notch. From the notch, the route generally follows the gendarme-studded ridge, with occasional visits to the east face to avoid the more difficult terrain.

North Face Snow Couloir (II, Class 5). The north face of the Grand Mogul is split by a large couloir that gives the peak its distinctive look. (The couloir is usually filled with snow until late summer.) From the Redfish Lake Inlet trailhead take FST-092 [(A)(6)(b.1)] a short distance until you cross the small stream that descends out of the couloir. Follow this drainage up into the couloir. Once in the couloir, the route rises quickly to a notch directly west of the summit. First ascent: Iowa Mountaineers in 1957.

Saddleback Peak/Elephants Perch*   9,870 feet

West and south of the Grand Mogul, the Sawtooth granite has been carved and cut into a complex system of faces, ridges, and high points. Nine of these high points reach above 9,600 feet and two, Peaks 9870 and 9847, exceed the Grand Mogul in height. Early settlers in the Stanley Valley dubbed this big mountain Saddleback Peak because of the swayback ridge between two of its high points. Others called it Sawtooth Dome. Mountaineers know it as the Elephants Perch, a name bestowed on it by the Iowa Mountaineers in 1960. Today, it is a favorite haunt for big wall climbers because its east and west faces are unquestionably Idaho's foremost granite walls.

The Elephants Perch's two main walls face Saddleback Lakes. As of 1998, twenty-five routes climbed these two faces. The face has been climbed in the winter and has been soloed. Reid Dowdle and his climbing partners pioneered fourteen of the twenty-five routes and he has ascended the face ninety times. The two arêtes just south of the southeast face are known as EP Arête and the Tusk. Both have been climbed. The Perch's northern prow also has two faces of interest to climbers: Black Buttress and Outside Chance. USGS Mount Cramer/SW

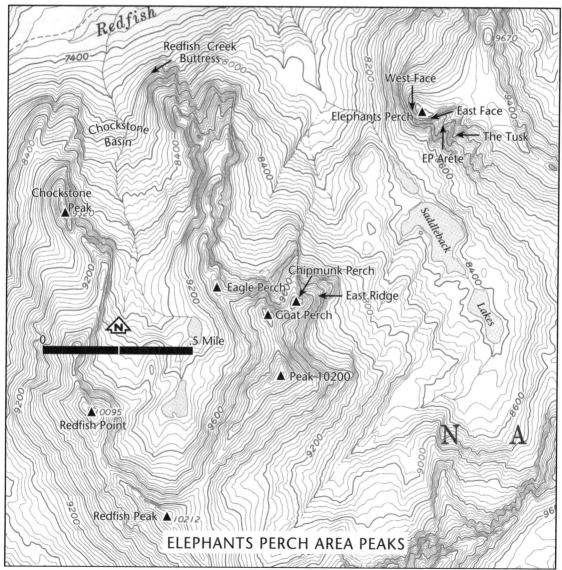

ELEPHANTS PERCH AREA PEAKS

The Face Routes

Route information for the following complicated routes was provided by Reid Dowdle.

(1) **Northwest Face (II, Class 4).** This route climbs the complicated, but rather nondescript northwest face. This terrain is more a collection of ledges, ramps, and talus than a face. Cross Redfish Lake Creek about 2.5 miles above the Inlet Campground [(A)(6)(b.2)]. After crossing, look for several prominent granite slabs near the northwest face. Using the slabs as a landmark, climb toward the northwest shoulder. From the base of the shoulder, turn northeast and use a zigzag route to climb the many steps and ledges that lead to the saddle between the two summits of Elephants Perch. The first two steps are the most difficult. Once the route reaches the upper broken ledges, the climbing moderates.

(2) **Northwest Shoulder (II, 5.3).** This is the original ascent route used by the Iowa Mountaineers in 1960. The shoulder is the north edge of the west face. This route is found west of the Northwest Face route and north of the Mountaineers Route. Follow the cross-country course [(A)(6)(b.2)] toward Saddleback Lakes to the base of the northwest shoulder and locate a sound chimney and crack system that leads up the shoulder. Stay on the northeast side of the shoulder.

(3) **Mountaineers Route (III, 5.9).** This is probably the most popular route on the Perch. Most of the route's six to seven pitches cross 5.7 to 5.8 terrain with significant exposure. Depending on how you climb some pitches, the rating can be as high as 5.9. The route climbs over, around, and near several large, loose blocks. Two people were killed on this route in the mid-1980s when their anchors pulled off a large block. The route starts up a large gully system on the left edge of the main west face (see photo). Route-finding is tricky near the bottom where the route leaves the gully to head off to the left.

The first pitch climbs a 5.5, left-leaning gully to the point where it cuts back to the right. The second pitch continues up the gully for 20 to 30 feet. Exit the gully at this point and move left to the base of a crack that leads past a small tree. This section involves a 5.8 mantel move to reach the crack and then climbs the crack past the tree. The third pitch begins by climbing a 5.8 crack to the left and then moves horizontally to the left and continues up to a point below a three-tiered roof system. The fourth pitch avoids the roof by climbing the 5.7 rock to the left. Above the roof, the pitch moves back to the right to the base of the large, blank diamond that dominates this portion of the face. The fifth pitch crosses 5.8 slabs to the left of the diamond and then climbs to the left to its northernmost edge. The sixth pitch

climbs left of the major line that ascends across 5.7 terrain directly from the edge of the diamond. The seventh pitch moves to the right into the line and crosses several jammed blocks to a wide crack. Climb the crack to the ledge above. The remainder of the route crosses Class 3 terrain. This route does not get sun until late and is best climbed on a warm day.

(4) **The Beckey Routes (the Original Beckey V, 5.11; the Beckey Direct V, 5.11+).** The first ascent of the west face occurred in 1963 and was made by F. Beckey, S. Marts, and H. Schwabland. Beckey picked the most obvious line up the middle part of the west face. The route follows beautiful cracks and flakes the entire way. Beckey and his crew used 110 pitons and several bolts. The original rating was V, 5.8 A2. J. Lowe and G. Lowe climbed a variation of the original route in 1972 and did not use bolts. Over the years, aid climbing was whittled down to just the first and third pitches. The Beckey Direct bypasses these two harder pitches taking a more direct line. It joins the Original Beckey after the fourth pitch.

The Original Beckey follows the original aid line and is much harder, 5.11+ or 5.12 depending on how the first pitch is done. Most of the climbing is in finger to hand-size cracks. Protection is good and belay ledges are found on almost every pitch. A prominent feature on these routes is a large pine at the top of the ninth pitch. Both routes are normally done in eleven to thirteen pitches and take from 7 to 9 hours. It is possible to exit the route from the pine tree by climbing left to a notch via an easy Class 5 line.

(5) **Astro Elephant (IV, 5.10).** This east-face route receives sunlight early making it one of the most popular routes on the Perch. Start this climb by ascending route 7, the Descent Gully, along the base of the east face across moderate Class 5 terrain to the huge chockstone that blocks the gully. Climb above the chockstone for about 100 feet to a right leaning and facing dihedral near two small trees. The route leaves the descent gully at this point.

The first two pitches up the dihedral are 5.10. Early in the summer or after a wet winter the first pitch is often through running water. The third pitch angles to the right to a ledge and is 5.7. The fourth pitch is to the right and follows a crack to a big traverse ledge. For the fifth pitch, follow the ledge to the right to exit the face or to the left to continue the climb in a 5.8 crack that some will have difficulty finding. The sixth pitch climbs a crack just to the left of an arête. Climb the 5.9 crack until it is possible to step around the arête and move up and left to the base of a disjointed vertical crack. The 5.8 eighth pitch climbs straight up this crack and then moves along the flakes above to the right. The 5.7 ninth pitch climbs a crack and then a small gully. The final pitch follows either of

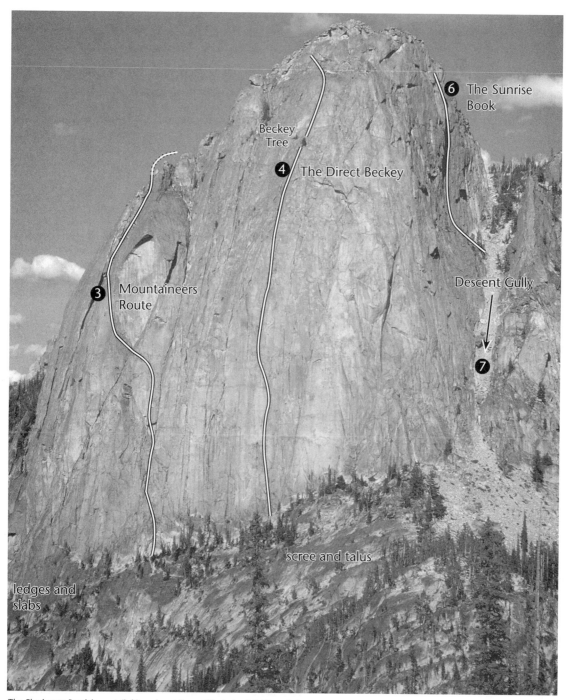

The Elephants Perch's west (left) and east faces (Photo by Reid Dowdle)

two short 5.9 cracks and the slabs above. A variation, which avoids the first two 5.10 pitches, starts 15 to 20 feet to the right of the dihedral. The variation was first climbed in 1985 by R. Dowdle and D. Hough. See also AAJ 1979.

(6) **The Sunrise Book (III, 5.10, A1 or 5.12).** This east-face route was pioneered by G. Webster and S. Roper in 1969 as a classic nail-up. It ascends a striking, 500-foot dihedral that catches the first morning light. R. Dowdle and J. Niwa climbed all but three of the moves free in 1981 and J. Mileski and J. Gruenberg climbed the entire route free in 1983. To reach the start of the route, ascend route 7, the Descent Gully, past the start of Astro Elephant. This route features short pitches, good cracks, and a spectacular horizontal chimney at the top. From the gully, climb left to the base of dihedral. Climb the 5.9+ face to the right of the crack and continue up the first belay ledge. The second pitch crosses the moves usually done with direct aid. The third pitch is 5.9+ and the fourth 5.10. The fifth pitch follows the horizontal chimney about midway and is 5.9+.

(7) **Descent Gully (Class 5).** The standard descent route follows the gully spliting the east face and the EP Arête. This gully is obvious from Saddleback Lakes, because it is blocked by a giant chockstone. There are several good rappel anchors along the way.

(8) **South Gully (Class 3).** Those wishing to scramble to the top of the Perch are limited to one route. Start this climb between the first and second Saddleback Lakes [(A)(6)(b.2)]. From this point, climb up to the east until you reach the base of a steep, but well-used gully that is to the right of the Tusk. This is the first gully not blocked by a chockstone or granite wall. This gully is full of loose rock and sand, but presents little trouble. Once on the summit plateau at the top of the gully, three high points are visible. The one to the north is the highest. It is climbed by crossing a boulder field at its base and then climbing up the short wall to the left. The western summit at the top of the east face is also an easy walk.

Other Perch Routes. If you are interested in the other routes on the Perch's great walls, stop by the Elephants Perch outdoor shop in Ketchum or contact Sawtooth Mountain Guides in Stanley. EP Arête's southwest face is III, 5.11 A0. There are three routes on the Tusk. The Prow is rated III, 5.11 A1.

Peak 9870   (Class 3)
Saddleback Mountain's unnamed high point is located 1 mile due south of the Grand Mogul and 0.8 mile west of the Elephants Perch face. It is seldom climbed. The summit is a scramble from the uppermost Saddleback Lake [(A)(6)(b.2)].

From the lake, climb northeast aiming for the 9,480-foot saddle at the base of the summit. From the saddle, follow the short ridge the last 390 feet to the top.

Peak 9847   9,847 feet (Class 4)
On the 1963 version of the Mount Cramer quad, this peak was incorrectly identified as Decker Peak. On the 1972 version of the map, that name had been shifted to another peak. This peak is occasionally, incorrectly, called the Chipmunks Perch. This peak can be climbed from the Saddleback Lakes via the west face [(A)(6)(b.2)]. USGS Mount Cramer/SW

Peak 10200   10,200+ feet (Class 3)
The Goat, Eagle, and Chipmunk Perches
This unnamed peak southeast of the Elephants Perch is a favorite destination for mountaineers, thanks to its series of towers, faces, and ridges. The peak is best known for the three spires that form the north wall. From west to east, these three high points are called the Eagle Perch, the Goat Perch, and the Chipmunk Perch. All three points have challenging routes up their north ridges. The actual high point of this peak is located to the south of the perches and can be reached via its Class 3 southwest ridge from the Saddleback Lakes Basin [(A)(6)(b.2)]. USGS Mount Cramer/SW

Eagle Perch*   9,560+ feet (Class 5)
This point, the westernmost of the perches, is located due north of the two unnamed lakes in the Chockstone Basin [(A)(6)(b.2)]. The first ascent was by the Iowa Mountaineers, led by H. Adams Carter, in 1972 via the northwest buttress. The route ascends the northwest buttress on an obvious line to the summit ridge. Follow the summit ridge to the top. The north ridge direct route was climbed by R. Dowdle and J. Niwa and is rated II, 5.8. USGS Mount Cramer/SW

Goat Perch*   10,080+ feet
This, the middle perch, is just north of Peak 10200's true summit. The first ascent was made via the north ridge by the Iowa Mountaineers, led by Hans Gmosser, in 1960. USGS Mount Cramer/SW

North Ridge (III, 5.7-5.9). This exposed route starts on the east face and then climbs up to the right to the north ridge. The ridgeline is then followed to the summit with an occasional brief foray out onto the face. Access the route from the second Saddleback Lake by contouring around the north base of the Chipmunk Perch. H. Gmosser, who led the climb, compared it with a famous climb in the Alps on the Piz Badille [(A)(6)(b.2)].

Goat Perch to Redfish Point (Photo by Lyman Dye)

Southwest Ridge (II, Class 5). To reach this route, follow the Redfish Lake Creek Trail [(A)(6)(b)] until directly north of Chockstone Basin [(A)(6)(b.3)]. Chockstone Basin is the next drainage west of the Saddleback Lakes drainage. Cross the creek (dangerous during high water) and hike due south cross-country into the basin. The route begins by climbing a snow couloir on the west face to the notch on the southwest ridge between Peak 10200 and the Goat Perch (climbing difficulty is Class 4 to this point). From the notch, climb directly to the summit block. An exposed rib on the block leads to the summit.

Chipmunk Perch   *9,840+ feet*
This tower is the easternmost of the three perches on Peak 10200.

North Ridge (IV, 5.9+). The north ridge offers steep, challenging climbing almost from your camp at the first Saddleback Lake. First ascent: R. Dowdle and J. Niwa in 1980.

The Four Horsemen/East Ridge (IV, 5.9). The east ridge rises from a point between the first and second Saddleback Lakes and is comprised of four towers. From the first lake, hike to the base of the upper ridge and start up on the left-hand side of the north face of the first tower. From this point, there are many variations. The entire route takes 14 to 15 pitches. First ascent: R. Dowdle.

Chockstone Peak*   *9,320 feet*
This formation is found 2.1 miles southwest of the Grand Mogul on the south side of Redfish Lake Creek. The summit is derived from the large boulder wedged in the col that divides the peak's two summits. First ascent: Iowa Mountaineers in 1954. USGS Mount Cramer/SW

Iowa Couloir (II, Class 4). Cross Redfish Lake Creek [(A)(6)(b)], which can be difficult in high water, and hike cross-country into Chockstone Basin [(A)(6)(b.3)] up to the peak's east face. Climb the central couloir to just below the chockstone and then skirt around the lower summit block to a large chimney that separates the east face from the col between the two summits. Climb this chimney to a point where it divides roughly after two thirds of its distance. At this point, the route toward the south summit eventually leads out onto the face. To reach the north summit, continue up the chimney to the chockstone and then go to the summit. First ascent: Iowa Mountaineers in 1954.

The Chipmunk Perch: the Four Horsemen route follows the left ridge and the Chipmunk Arête follows the right ridgeline (Photo by Reid Dowdle)

East Face (II, 5.3). From Chockstone Basin [(A)(6)(b.3)], a Class 3 scramble leads several hundred feet up the Iowa Couloir (described above) to a point that provides good access to the east face. Twelve pitches of Class 4 and Class 5 climbing leads to the notch just east of the true summit. Two more pitches with small holds lead across the exposed east face to the summit. First ascent: L. Dye.

West Face (II, 5.6). This route follows the Iowa Couloir (described above) to the chockstone [(A)(6)(b.3)]. Climb out from underneath the chockstone to the west summit on easy, but rotten rock. From here, move to the west face of the higher eastern summit. The climb up the face begins on two ledges (both about 3 inches wide) and continues around the corner to the west face. At this point, the upper of the two ledges narrows to 1 inch and the lower ledge disappears. Two almost imperceptible, down-sloping holds allow you to make a long step to a 20-foot vertical flake. Climb to the top of this flake and then contour upward to either an open book or a narrow exposed crack. At the top of this pitch, the route finishes on a short friction pitch to the summit.

Redfish Point*   *10,095 feet*

Point 10095, known as Redfish Point, is the next high point to the south of Chockstone Peak. Although not a separate peak, this high point has attracted considerable interest from mountaineers. The peak's southeast slopes, which can be accessed from the Redfish Lake Creek Trail [(A)(6)(b)], are a Class 3 scramble. Although the Iowa Mountaineers probably made the first ascent in 1948, it is unclear what route they followed. USGS Mount Cramer/SW

West Face (I, Class 4). This route begins on the ledges southwest of Chockstone Peak and climbs into a diminutive upper bowl. Once in the bowl, the route follows a series of ledge and crack systems to the summit. Approach this route from the Redfish Lake Creek Trail [(A)(6)(b)] by leaving the trail south of Flatrock Junction. First ascent: L. Dye.

East Face (II, 5.2). This route begins in Chockstone Basin [(A)(6)(b.3)] between the two lakes east of the summit. Climb the Class 3 to Class 4 ridge that begins at the outlet of the upper lake to the face. The final 200 feet on the face are Class 5. First ascent: L. Dye and A. Barnes in 1965.

Redfish Peak*   *10,212 feet (Class 3)*
This peak is the next high point up the ridge from Redfish
Point. It is located 1.75 miles southwest of the Elephants Perch
at the junction of two ridges. The first ridge leads south to
Chockstone Peak and the second northeast to the Goat Perch.
The summit is reached via a straightforward scramble up the
east face or via the peak's northeast or southeast ridges. All
three routes can be accessed from the Saddleback Lakes Basin
[(A)(6)(b.2)]. First ascent: probably R. Underhill, D. Underhill,
and D. Williams in 1934. USGS Mount Cramer/SW

Decker Peak   *10,704 feet*
Although Decker, the third-highest Sawtooth summit, has
an impressive north face, it has received little attention from
climbers. It is located 2.5 miles almost due south of the Grand
Mogul. USGS Mount Cramer/SW

    South Ridge (Class 3). The main saddle on the south
ridge can be accessed from either Decker Creek [(A)(5)(b)] on
the east or Redfish Lake Creek Trail at Cramer Lakes on the
west [(A)(6)(b)]. From the Redfish Lake Creek Trail, hike up
through the thick forest from either Upper or Middle Cramer
Lake to the base of the saddle. The last 300 feet are over steep,
loose talus and quite trying. From Decker Creek, hike to the
headwall below the saddle. Climb the headwall via the short
Class 3 walls on its north side. The south ridge itself involves
mostly boulder hopping.

    North Ridge (Class 4). The north ridge is usually accessed
from Saddleback Lakes [(A)(6)(b.2)], but also can be accessed
from the Redfish Lake Creek Trail [(A)(6)(b)] near Cramer
Lakes. Both routes are steep with poor footing. From either
side, aim for the narrow saddle at the northern end of the
peak's long north ridge. From the saddle, climb out onto the
ridge's steep south face and edge up until it is possible to
return to the ridge top just east of Point 10300. Follow the
ridge south, eventually crossing a broad plateau between
10,200 and 10,400 feet. At the end of the plateau, the route is
blocked by several Class 4 towers. It may be possible to bypass
the tower by down-climbing around the base of the towers
and then climbing a gully back up to the summit.

Finger of Fate   *9, 760+ feet*
This striking tower sits east of the Grand Mogul/Cramer
Divide directly above Hell Roaring Lake. Its soaring granite
walls are visible in the distance from ID-75. Although the
formation's clean granite and majestic lines quickly attracted
climbers, the first ascent, by L. Stur and J. Fuller, did not oc-
cur until 1958. As of 1998, there were at least nine routes
on the Finger of Fate's two main faces east and north. All

routes are reached from Hell Roaring Lake [(A)(5)(a.1)]. The
east face is the big wall visible from ID-75 and Hell Roaring
Lake. The east face is composed of a Lower East Buttress and
an upper face. The Lower East Buttress has four routes that
can be done as three-pitch climbs, which tend to funnel into
the same upper pitches. The East Face route (6) described
below is the main line up the Lower East Buttress. Above the
buttress, the East Face route continues to the summit in a
total of nine pitches. R. Dowdle and D. Hough climbed the
two obvious lines to left of the East Face route in 1978. The
Finger's summit block has two obvious 5.8 lines that will lead
to the top. USGS Mount Cramer/SW

    (1) The Book (II, 5.8). This is probably the most popular
route up the Finger of Fate. The route's first four pitches follow
an obvious open book. Climbing is Class 3 to the notch at the
base of the main pinnacle. The route then climbs through a
tunnel underneath the 5.8 summit block.

    (2) Tiptoe (II, 5.10). This route starts by climbing Class 3
ledges to the base of a wide (30 to 40 feet) open book system

The Finger of Fate's north face (Photo by Reid Dowdle)

to the right of route 1. Routes 3, 4, and 5 all follow the initial line, which requires careful route-finding. For this route, keep as far to the left as possible without getting on the arête on the right side of route 1. The first pitch is a thin crack in a dihedral. The second pitch uses finger and hand holds to reach the notch on route 1. From the notch, continue to the summit as described above.

(3) Feel Free (II, 5.8). Follow route 2 to the open book. This route begins on the high angle slabs to the right of route 2 and climbs an obvious crack system for two pitches to a large overhang. The third pitch leads to the notch. From the notch, continue to the summit, as described above.

(4) Bino's Book (II, 5.9). This route ascends the first book to the right of route 3. The first pitch is the crux. It starts up an awkward lie-back in a groove and finishes in a finger crack. The second and third pitches are 5.7 and top out near the tunnel described in route 1.

(5) Drizzlepuss (II, 5.7). This route ascends an open book to the right of Bino's Book and is located on the northwest corner of the formation. The first ascent was by B. Gorton and S. Collins. Access the route as described in route 2. Climb the open book for two pitches. At the top of the second pitch the route moves off the corner and onto the west face. Continue up toward the west ridge until roughly 30 feet below the top of the ridge. Climb a jam crack that diagonals to the right.

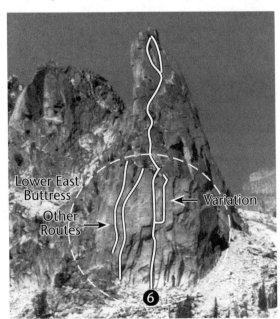

The Finger of Fate's east face (Photo by Reid Dowdle)

At the top of this crack, work into a horizontal chimney that leads right and exits on the east face.

(6) East Face (III, 5.11). This route begins in the right-facing open book leading up the Lower East Buttress. Climb up the book on cracks and then up the face to an overhang. Bypass the overhang on the right to a small belay ledge. From here, climb up the book for two more leads to a broad flat area. The next lead uses a chimney that leads up the right side of a large blocky area to a jam crack, which is followed up and to the right to a ledge. From this ledge, climb up into a prominent chimney just above. Climb this chimney to a shelf. Above the shelf, climb up and right to where another short chimney can be entered. This chimney ends near the summit block. Finish the climb on the Southeast Face route. The total climb is nearly 1,000 feet in length. It is believed that the first ascent was by J. Beaupre and G. Webster in 1967. However, they reported the climb at only 5.8 and, thus, they may have climbed another line.

Red Bluff*   *10,272 feet*
This impressive formation composed of reddish rock sits on the Sawtooth crest just north of Mount Sevy. (The small pinnacle due north of the Red Bluff is known as the Sentry; the large block north of the Sentry is called the Coffin.) This formation can be accessed with difficulty from Upper Cramer Lake in the west [(A)(6)(b)] or via Hell Roaring Lake in the east [(A)(5)(a.1)]. First ascent: G. Vendor and E. Vendor in 1960. USGS Mount Cramer/SW

East Face (II, 5.4). This was the route of the first ascent. The route climbs a conspicuous crack in the east face.

Northeast Ridge (II, 5.3). Begin this route by climbing north across the east face to the northeast ridge. The route up the ridge to the summit block varies from scrambling to easy Class 5. The summit block is impressive from this approach. It is split by an 80-foot-high crack that narrows as it ascends. The first 30 feet of the crack are the most difficult. Despite the exposure, there are plenty of good holds. First ascent: M. Howard and V. Howard in 1972.

West Couloir (II, 5.4). This route begins on the western side of the divide at the Upper Cramer Lake. Scramble up the scree and talus to the base of the north branch of the main west couloir, and then up the couloir to the notch separating the west tower from the face. (This is the junction point of the north and south branches of the couloir, about two-thirds of the distance up the face.) The rock is loose, but not treacherous. Climb from this notch to the main notch in the northeast ridge. From the main notch, follow ledges out onto the northeast ridge. The summit block is clearly visible to the south.

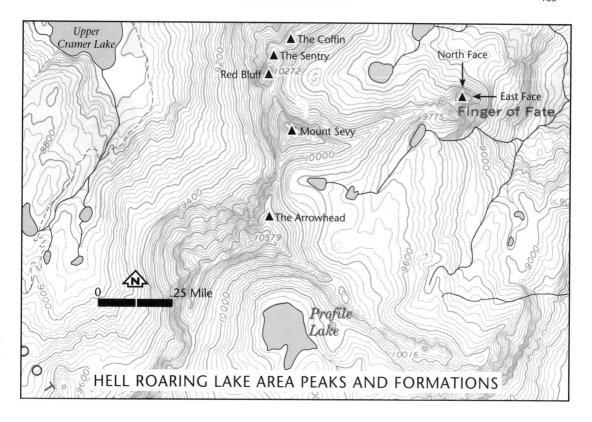

HELL ROARING LAKE AREA PEAKS AND FORMATIONS

Climb up and over two small cliffs, following the obvious route. From here, the summit block can be surmounted with some difficulty. First ascent: L. Dye and M. Ranger in 1972.

Mount Sevy* 10,480+ feet (5.2)
Mount Sevy is on the main Sawtooth crest 0.6 mile west of the Finger of Fate and is misidentified as the Arrowhead on the 1963 USGS quad. This fang-shaped summit is climbed via its eastern ridge and south face. Sevy's summit block is a typical Sawtooth upright block surrounded by smaller, broken blocks. Though this peak offers several challenging lines, few have tried its granite; there is only one reported route to its summit.

Lyman Dye's route on the peak follows: From the west end of Hell Roaring Lake [(A)(5)(a.1)] climb directly toward the Finger of Fate and the unnamed lake at its eastern base. Pass under the Finger close to its base, then continue to the small ponds at the base of Mount Sevy's southern slopes. From the uppermost pond, climb directly north to Sevy's east ridge and then follow the ridge to a notch about 80 feet below the sum-

mit. (This section of the route involves about 400 feet of easy Class 4 climbing.) From this notch, the route moves out onto the south face, and then up the face for another 40 to 50 feet of moderately difficult Class 4 climbing to a small notch at the base of the upright summit block. The final moves up the summit block are on thin, airy holds. USGS Mount Cramer/SW

The Arrowhead (II, 5.9)
This formation is located on the Sawtooth crest on the north slopes of Peak 10579. The rock looks exactly like a giant arrowhead. (Note: On the 1963 version of the Mount Cramer quad, the Arrowhead was erroneously located on the summit of Mount Sevy.) Climb the west face from the ridge crest. This one-pitch climb first leads up to a small ledge. From the ledge, traverse about 15 feet to the left, to a small right-facing open book (the 5.9 crux). Ascend the short open book via a jam crack to a flake. From the flake, moderate Class 5 climbing leads to the summit. First ascent: G. Webster and J. Beaupre (date unknown). USGS Mount Cramer/SW

THE VERITA RIDGE: FROM THE MAIN CREST WEST TO GRANDJEAN PEAK

From the main Sawtooth crest near Alpine Lake an impressive ridge runs 5 miles northwest to Grandjean Peak. The section of the ridge between the main crest and Warbonnet Peak is cluttered with a complex collection of summits, spires, and towers composed of solid granite. These formations have received more attention by mountaineers than any other single place in Idaho. When you first see this area, you will know why. The ridge's southern exposure, toward Goat Creek, is a steep mass of scree, talus, and granite walls. The northern side of the ridge, which rises above Baron Creek, is generally composed of lovely, solid, high-angle slabs. Access the north side of the ridge from FST-101, which begins at either Redfish Lake [(A)(6)(c)] or Grandjean [(B)(3)(c)], and the south side of the ridge from Alpine Lake via the various cross-country routes [(A)(6)(c.1) and (c.3)]. The Warbonnet Peak USGS quad covers all the formations. The summits and formations are described below from southeast to northwest starting with the Monte Verita Group.

The Monte Verita Group

The first mountain west of the main crest is Monte Verita, an extremely complex group of granite spires with a climbing history stretching back more than fifty years. Unfortunately, the climbing literature is unclear regarding the location of several of the formations.

Dessert Tower*   9,500+ feet (Class 4)

This is the first formation northwest of the main Sawtooth crest that is of interest to mountaineers. It is the first of the four "meal" towers: Dessert, Breakfast, Lunch, and Dinner. It is located directly above the saddle that is directly west of Peak 9769. The first ascent was by D. Davis in 1961. Davis followed a crack system on the southeast face. The rock is crumbly and the cracks are rounded on their corners. USGS Warbonnet Peak/SW

Breakfast Tower*   9,700+ feet (Class 6)

This is the next tower in the line viewed from southeast to northwest. The first ascent was by E. Bjornstad and D. Davis in 1961. They climbed up the south rib. The first pitch leads to the top of the rib and is easy Class 5 climbing. The second pitch follows a poor crack system—it required five pitons, which were used for direct aid. USGS Warbonnet Peak/SW

Lunch Tower*   9,900+ feet (Class 4)

This tower is next to and west of Breakfast Tower. It sits just southwest and slightly below the ridge crest. The route follows a chimney on the tower's northwest side. The major difficulty is the traverse into the chimney at the start. First ascent: E. Bjornstad and D. Davis in 1961. USGS Warbonnet Peak/SW

Dinner Tower*   9,900+ feet (Class 5)

This is the westernmost "meal" tower. The route climbs the southeast face, up an easy Class 5 crack system. First ascent: F. Beckey, E. Bjornstad, D. Davis, and S. Marts in 1961. USGS Warbonnet Peak/SW

Damocles*   9,800+ feet (Class 5)

Written accounts that mention this formation are in conflict as to its exact location. It is reportedly found on the south side of the Verita Ridge below the ridge crest and to the south of the Leaning Tower of Pisa. The first ascent was made by F. Beckey and S. Marts in 1961. Their route, called the Merry-Go-Round, begins at the northeast base of the pinnacle. From there, the route goes diagonally to the right on a ledge system that circles about two-thirds of the tower to a belay spot. From the belay spot, turn back to the left on a finger traverse to a roomy ledge. From this ledge, a short chimney leads to the summit. USGS Warbonnet Peak/SW

Monte Verita   10,080+ feet (Class 4)

Monte Verita is the highest point in the Monte Verita Group. It is a twin-summited peak. The southernmost summit is the high point; the northernmost summit, which is only slightly lower in elevation, is known as the Perforated Pinnacle. A complex peak, Monte Verita appears as a collection of spires from the Alpine/Baron Lakes divide. The ridge's east face is loose talus and scree. The ridge's west face steepens and becomes a beautiful sheer wall above Baron Lake. It is surprising that most climbers ignore it.

The route to the summit begins at Upper Baron Lake and climbs up the northeast ridge. The northeast ridge descends to the western shore of the lake. It is composed of low-angle polished ledges. These ledges are severely broken on the ridge's crest. Follow the ridge up to the summit blocks. From the north, the summit blocks are climbed by a short, obvious pitch. USGS Warbonnet Peak/SW

Perforated Pinnacle*   10,080+ feet (Class 4)

This is Monte Verita's lower, northern summit. The granite summit block is broken—or perforated—and flat on top. Once

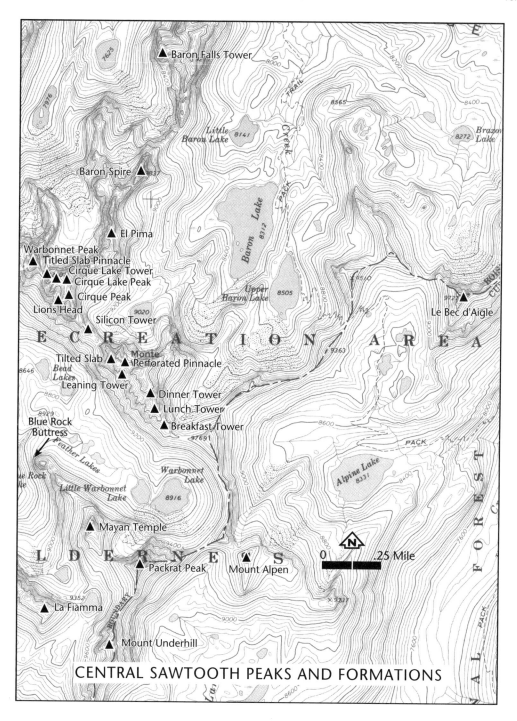

Baron Falls Tower

Little
Baron Lake

Baron Spire

El Pima

Warbonnet Peak
Titled Slab Pinnacle
Cirque Lake Tower
Cirque Lake Peak
Cirque Peak
Lions Head
Silicon Tower

Baron Lake

Upper
Baron Lake

Le Bec d'Aigle

R E C R E A T I O N   A R E A

Tilted Slab
Monte
Perforated Pinnacle
Bead
Lakes
Leaning Tower

Dinner Tower
Lunch Tower

Blue Rock
Buttress
Breakfast Tower

Feather Lakes

Warbonnet
Lake

Little Warbonnet
Lake

Alpine Lake

Mayan Temple

W I L D E R N E S S

Packrat Peak   Mount Alpen

N
0   .25 Mile

La Fiamma

F O R E S T

Mount Underhill

CENTRAL SAWTOOTH PEAKS AND FORMATIONS

Monte Verita (Photo by Reid Dowdle)

you are at its base, the summit block is an easy climb from any side and involves only one lead. (See the Monte Verita description for more details.) USGS Warbonnet Peak/SW

Leaning Tower of Pisa*   *10,040+ feet (II, Class 6, A1)*
This is the massive granite tower on the ridge crest just west of Monte Verita. The first ascent was done via the northwest side. The climb involved continuous direct aid. It was made by F. Beckey, D. Davis, and S. Marts in 1961. USGS Warbonnet Peak/SW

Tilted Slab Pinnacle*   *10,000+ feet (5.3)*
This pinnacle is located on the west side of the Verita Ridge just east of the major saddle that separates the Warbonnet Group from the Monte Verita Group. The pinnacle is capped by a tilted slab that looks as if it is balanced on the formation's shaft. From Bead Lakes, climb to the saddle just northwest of the formation. Descend from the saddle for 20 feet to a fragile ledge on the southwest slope. Traverse east over several spur ridges until you are on the east side of the formation. A large crack leads to a talus pocket at the base of the pinnacle above. There is a chockstone about halfway up this crack. Climb behind the stone and scramble out behind it. From this point, scramble out of the crack to the west over several ledges to the base of the north face of the pinnacle.

The summit slab is tilted to the north at 50 degrees. Use a mantel move to get onto the shelf at the base of the block and then friction climb to the summit. First ascent: L. Dye in 1971. USGS Warbonnet Peak/SW

The Cirque Lake Peak Group

This complicated group of spires and towers is located directly southeast of Warbonnet Peak above the uppermost Baron Lake. It also has a long climbing history. There is some controversy over the names of some of the spires. This book attaches the name Cirque Lake Peak to the true summit, which cannot be seen from Bead and Feather Lakes on the peak's southwestern side. However, four distinctive, high granite towers are visible from this side. Each has been named by mountaineers, although not everyone agrees on the following names. From northwest to southeast the formations are: Cirque Lake Tower, Cirque Peak, the Lions Head (a.k.a. Japhys Ear), and Silicon Tower (see photo).

Cirque Lake Peak*   *10,210 feet*
Despite some rotten and broken rock, the views of the surrounding peaks make this summit well worth the climb. The first ascent was originally credited to H. Adams Carter and G. Constan in 1954. However, a register left by the Seattle

Mountaineers in 1949 was found on the summit during a 1973 ascent. The older register incorrectly identified the summit as Warbonnet Peak. Access is via FST-101 that begins at either Redfish Lake [(A)(4)(c)] or Grandjean [(B)(3)(c)]. USGS Warbonnet Peak/SW

East Face (II, 5.1). Scramble up the moraine debris south of Baron Lake until you reach Lake 9020 above. From this lake, climb the gentle friction slabs on the west side of the lake to the upper debris-filled ledges. From here, a crack is visible in the east face. Follow the crack up good rock through the cliff bands to the upper, decomposed face. First ascent: L. Dye.

West Slope (I, Class 4). This route begins on the Warbonnet/Cirque Lake Peak saddle. From the saddle, scramble east up the talus-covered slopes toward the Lions Head and past Cirque Lake Tower and Cirque Peak. The only obstacle involves crossing several large slabs near the base of Cirque Lake Tower. From above these slabs, the route is nothing more than a scramble over relatively stable large blocks and slabs.

North Ridge (II, 5.2). The north ridge can be accessed from Baron Lake [(A)(4)(c)], and then Lake 9020. First ascent: H. Adams Carter and G. Constan in 1954.

Cirque Lake Tower*　　　　　　*9,600+ feet (I, 5.4)*
This pinnacle is the northwesternmost point on Cirque Lake Peak. The top of the formation is reached by a 40-foot lead up the south face. First ascent: L. Dye.

Cirque Peak (a.k.a. Cirque Lake Peak)　　*(II, 5.9, A1)*
This formation is located between Cirque Lake and the Lions Head. The first ascent—by Helmeke, Schmidt, and Errington in 1972—ascended the formation's southwest spur. The route begins at Bead Lakes [(A)(6)(c.3)]. Climb toward the Warbonnet/Cirque Lake Peak saddle. About 300 feet below the saddle, the route crosses diagonally right to a headwall between Cirque Lake Tower and Cirque Peak. From this point, the route continues diagonally right to a platform, and then diagonally left to a dihedral and large flake. The first ascent party climbed the flake until it reached the ridge top north of Cirque Peak. From the ridge top, it was one pitch to the

The Verita Ridge (Photo by Lyman Dye)

west ridge and two pitches along the west ridge to the summit tower. A chimney on the tower's south face was then followed to the summit.

The Lions Head/Japhys Ear   (II, 5.9)

This is the obvious reddish wall visible from Bead and Feather Lakes. Climb the tower via its east face. K. Bachman and J. Hokom climbed this formation in 1976. The route begins several hundred feet down the face from the Lions Head/Silicon Tower notch. Ascend a shallow corner system to the distinctive south/southwest rib. First ascent: either R. Dowdle or Bachman and Hokom.

Silicon Tower*   9,680+ feet (III, 5.9)

This pinnacle is the southeasternmost formation on Cirque Lake Peak and the smallest of the four towers. The route climbs the northeast corner via a chimney system. The first climb—by H. Adams Carter in 1961—used direct aid. R. Dowdle and R. Jonas climbed the route in 1996 and gave it the current rating. USGS Warbonnet Peak/SW

Warbonnet Peak   10,200+ feet

Warbonnet, which is located just northwest of Cirque Lake Peak, is the crowning glory of the Verita Ridge. The peak has been called the "Grand Teton of Idaho." No matter what you call it, Warbonnet is an impressive peak from any direction. All routes to the top involve Class 5 climbing. In the article "Sawtooth Mountaineering" from the February 1975 issue of Off Belay magazine, Louis Stur said of the peak:

> The sheer walls on both sides of the 'rooftop' overhang menacingly into nothingness down below; holds are a bare minimum and piton cracks zero…the view from the top…is exceptionally breathtaking. Quite understandably so since a stone dropped from this point will fall for 9 seconds before disintegrating on the boulder fields below. The peak is distinctive because of the massive fin-shaped summit block that caps it. The fin is split by a large fissure that splits the block into two massive blocks. At the south end of the summit block is a prominent notch, which is the focus of most routes on the mountain.

The original reconnaissance and first ascent was led by Bob Merriam and Paul Petzoldt as part of the Iowa Mountaineers' 1947 Sawtooth outing. Louis Stur made the first ascents of the peak's south, west, and east faces in the late 1950s. More recently, Jeff Lowe and Kevin Swigert brought their rock-climbing expertise to Warbonnet and established the Black Crystal Route up the north face. This route, which involves the most difficult climbing on the peak to date,

included 5.10 and 5.11 pitches. All routes described below, except Black Crystal, begin at Bead Lakes [(A)(6)(c.3)] USGS Warbonnet Peak/SW

West Face (II, 5.7). This route begins at Bead Lakes. From the lakes, climb up to the saddle directly west of the summit. From this point, traverse first to the southeast and then back toward the west, gaining elevation on moderate terrain. Climb to a spot just below the sheer west wall and two-thirds of the way across the face. The route now climbs up a difficult crack that eventually dies out. At this point, a tension swing is necessary to cross over to an adjoining crack in a large debris-filled pocket. Follow a crack and chimney system out of the pocket to a platform 40 feet below the summit. From the platform, a solid fissure leads to the notch in the summit block. (The view of the summit from the notch is breathtaking.) From the notch, step across the fissure onto a narrow ledge and start up the summit block. The holds are moderately large at first, but become progressively smaller near the top. There is a bolt just over the lip of the fin that provides protection for the move up to the broken ledge near the apex. The first 40 feet of the summit block offers little opportunity for placing protection other than bolts. Bolts were placed on the upper stretches of the block in 1971. First ascent: Iowa Mountaineers in 1947; the party included B. Merriam, J. Speck, C. Wilcox, B. Adams, C. Fisher, and P. Petzoldt.

South Face (II, 5.7). This route also begins at Bead Lakes southwest of the summit. From the lakes, climb to the Warbonnet/Cirque Lake Peak saddle southeast side of the peak. From the saddle, the route follows a series of connecting chimneys. Begin by climbing up the face for 40 or 50 feet to a ledge system that runs diagonally left to the peak's southeast corner. The access to this ledge system is somewhat flaky, but sound. The ledge system ends behind a large detached slab. Climb over or below this slab to the west side of the ridge. From this point, there are three alternative chimney routes, all of which lead to a shelf below the "staircase"—a talus-filled crack that leads up to the "friction highway." The far left chimney, which is rated at 5.4, involves considerable exposure. The center chimney, also rated at 5.4, contains a chockstone and is shaped like an hourglass (one climber—despite having only a 31-inch waist—became wedged into the narrow section of the chimney). The far right chimney, the most difficult of the three, is rated at 5.6. This chimney is directly above the detached slab and contains a chockstone that should be avoided. Exiting this chimney requires stemming up under the crack's roof and then doing a twisting pull-up (mantel) on a thin handhold. From the top of the chimney, climb up the "staircase" to the "friction highway" leading west on a ledge that connects with the notch at the base of the summit block. Follow the West Face route to the top from this point. First ascent: L. Stur, B. Ring, N. Bennet, and S. Franke in 1957.

Southwest Ridge (II, 5.4). This route climbs a large ravine that parallels the west side of the southwest ridge. To reach the route, contour from Bead Lakes to the couloir. L. Stur described the route as "tremendously wide and extremely steep." The route crosses four rock walls separated by talus and grass slopes and eventually joins the West Face route near the summit block. The climbing gets more difficult as each wall is climbed. The platform at the top of the fourth wall is the 40-foot fissure in the summit block. Climb the fissure to the notch at the top and follow the West Face route to the summit. First ascent: L. Stur and J. Fuller in 1958.

Southwest Rib (IV, 5.9). This route climbs to the right of the Southwest Ridge route and crosses 5.8 to 5.9 terrain. The route starts in a large ravine on the lowest point of Warbonnet's south side. It immediately climbs out of the ravine using cracks on the right face for four pitches. At this point, there is a large, left-facing corner/chimney system. Climb this system for four pitches to the point where it joins the South Face route. First ascent: R. Dowdle and Bob Jonals in 1995.

Northeast Face (II, Class 6, A1). To reach this route, climb southeast from Bead Lakes, traverse out onto the ledges that cross the north face, and follow the ledges until they end. At this point, climb a chimney with a chockstone by bypassing the steep lower section to the right on a steep slab. This pitch leads to a ledge. Follow this ledge back into the chimney above the slab. The chimney ends on the ridge crest at a vertical headwall. (The first-ascent team overcame the vertical wall with the aid of seven bolts.) From the top of the wall, a steep slab leads to the summit. First ascent: D. Davis, S. Marts, and F. Beckey in 1962.

Black Crystal Route (II, 5.11+). This route begins on the snowfield at the base of the north face. Access this snowfield from FST-101 [(B)(3)(c)]. Leave the trail directly north of the summit, drop down, cross the creek, and hike up the cirque. The route climbs 1,200 feet to the summit. It covers 5.10

The east face of Warbonnet Peak (Photo by Lyman Dye)

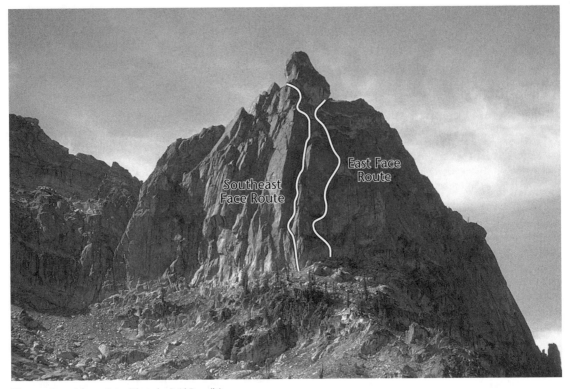

The east face of Baron Spire (Photo by Reid Dowdle)

terrain on its lower sections and then joins the northeast face route for the final pitch. First ascent: K. Swigert and J. Lowe in 1981. They climbed the final pitch without resorting to the Beckey bolt ladder and rated it 5.11+.

East Face (II, 5.5). This route begins at the base of the main vertical chimney on the east face. This chimney is usually filled with ice and dripping water. The route moves up on solid slabs and ledges on the left side of the crack to a notch about 60 feet below the summit fin. Follow the West Face route from the notch to the summit. First ascent: L. Stur and J. Fuller in 1960.

El Pima*   9,837 feet

El Pima is located midway between Cirque Lake Peak and Baron Spire, just west of Baron Lake. Beckey and his partners originally dubbed this formation Fishhook Spire, a name now attached to a spire in the Fishhook drainage. El Pima signifies that the summit block resembles a great cat claw. Access is via FST-101, which begins at either Redfish Lake [(A)(6)(c)] or Grandjean [(B)(3)(c)]. First ascent: F. Beckey, P. Schoening, and

J. Schwabland in 1949. USGS Warbonnet Peak/SW

East Face (II, Class 6, A1). The route begins on the east face and climbs a dirt-filled chimney to a shelf below the overhanging summit block. From here, Beckey and his crew climbed toward a "monster chockstone" wedged against the summit block. From the chockstone, the party used pitons for direct aid to reach the sloping ledge that leads to the summit.

West Face (II, Class 6, A1). The first ascent was made via a rather confusing route that began on the west face. The climbers used twenty bolts and three days to overcome the many obstacles. The account is chronicled in the 1950 *American Alpine Journal* in an article by Jack Schwabland.

Baron Spire (a.k.a. Old Smoothie)*   9,211 feet

This splendid granite spire, which is topped by a summit block overhanging on all sides, is located in the Baron Creek area northwest of Little Baron Lake and 1.2 miles north/ northeast of Warbonnet Peak. The first ascent was made via the south ridge and the west face by F. Beckey, J. Schwabland, and P. Schoening in 1949. There are two routes on the spire's east face; both are currently rated **III, 5.9, A1** (see photo). Both routes are on the Baron Lake side, are five-pitch climbs, and end by ascending the Beckey bolt ladder up the west face of the summit block. Access is via FST-101, which begins at either Redfish Lake [(A)(6)(c)] or Grandjean [(B)(3)(c)]. USGS Warbonnet Peak/SW

Beckey/Schoening/Schwabland Route (III, Class 6, A1). This route begins at Little Baron Lake and works its way up to the spire's south ridge. Begin on the spur ridge that comes directly off the south ridge from an obvious hump on the south ridge. Near the top, a wide dirt ramp leads north toward the notch separating the "hump" from the main tower. This ramp ends at a ledge and crack system below the notch. Climb up this crack system to a narrow, V-shaped gully leading up to the notch. From the notch, the route moves out onto the west face and climbs a series of steps and chimneys to the base of a smooth, vertical chimney. Climb the chimney to an overhang, which is bypassed on the left using, according to Jack Schwabland, a "tricky finger traverse." The crack above the overhang runs up to the south ridge just below the overhanging summit block. The route then traverses, via a narrow ledge, onto the west face and easier terrain. When the ledge ends, climb up a steep, broken wall on good holds to a boulder field at the base of the summit block.

From the base of the overhanging summit block, the route moves up a narrowing ledge and over a corner to the north shoulder of the spire. The first ascent team began placing bolts from this point. They used fourteen bolts to get above the overhang and into a small bowl. Above the bowl, the corner steepens to nearly vertical and the first-ascent route required four more bolts before the climbers could make the summit.

Southeast Face (III, 5.9, A1 above A0). Reid Dowdle reports that this route begins directly below the summit block to the right of a prominent corner (see photo). Climb up into the gully right of the corner and follow this line until it is possible to exit to the left and climb toward the notch on the right side of the summit block. Go around the block to the Beckey bolt ladder on the west face.

East Face (III, 5.9, A1 above A0). This route, also described by Reid Dowdle, climbs a line to the right of the Southeast Face route (see photo). The route follows a series of cracks that wiggle up the face and end below the summit block. Avoid the block by climbing to the north ridge. Continue around the corner to the Beckey bolt ladder.

North Ridge (V, 5.11). The north ridge is the longest technical climb in the Sawtooths. R. Dowdle notes that it is "comparable to the Beckey-Chouinard route on the Howser Towers in the Bugaboos in length and setting, but substan-tially harder." Two-thirds of the route's eighteen pitches are 5.9 or 5.10. The 5.11 crux is encountered on the second pitch. First ascent: R. Dowdle, K. Anderson, S. Poklemba, and J. Craig in 1996.

Baron Falls Tower   *8,960+ feet (IV, 5.10)*
This tower is located north of Baron Spire and directly east of Lake 7625 on the west side of Point 9211. The tower is prominent to those hiking up Baron Creek [(B)(3)(c)]. Access the tower from Baron Creek by leaving the trail at 6,800 feet and hiking up to Lake 7625 or from Baron Lake via the Baron Spire/Point 9211 saddle. The seven-pitch route climbs the west face and starts on the only feasible spot on the face next to a large flake that leans against the wall. The first two pitches climb a chimney and the route heads off to the right. First ascent: R. Dowdle and D. Colwell in 1995. USGS Warbonnet Peak/SW

Tohobit Peak   *10,046 feet*
This peak, located 1.1 miles northwest of Warbonnet Peak, is a bewildering conglomeration of faces, slabs, and cliffs. (Tohobit means "black" in the dialect of a West Coast Indian tribe). For years it was ignored by climbers more interested in nearby icons like Warbonnet Peak and Baron Spire. But, recently, Greg Parker focused on the peak and placed a line up the peak's north face. And it has many other inviting, but untested lines. There may be easier Class 4 routes on the south side, but the approach from either Baron Lakes down Goat Creek or up Goat Creek from the South Fork Payette River requires a very long, cross-country hike. USGS Warbonnet Peak/SW

North Face/Northwest Ridge (Class 3-4). This route begins in the lower reaches of Baron Creek. Approach the peak from Grandjean via the Baron Creek Trail [(B)(3)(c)]. Cross Baron Creek. Leave the trail at Moolack Creek, which is due north of the large drainage that runs steeply up Tohobit's north face. Climb high into this drainage and directly to the snowfields (shown on the USGS quad) below the summit. At the base of the first snowfield, turn due west and contour to the rib that descends from Point 9389. Once at this point, climb the rib to Point 9389 and then follow the northwest ridge southeast to the summit, staying on the southern side of the ridge as much as possible.

North Face (II, 5.5, and 50- to 60-degree snow and ice). This very exposed direct route climbs the north (or northwest) face of Tohobit. The first ascent was a solo climb by Greg Parker in May 1997. Parker's route follows the approach for the North Face/Northwest Ridge route above and leads to the snowfields at the base of the North Face. Climb the snowfields around large rock islands to the base. Cross a small bergschrund (up to 30 feet deep) to access a steep snow ramp in the center of the North Face. The first pitch is up a snow/ice ramp that angles to the right. The second pitch exits the ramp and crosses an exposed snow face (may be rock in late summer). The next pitch exits the snow face. Above this point, the slope moderates somewhat. Continue to a very flat snow col on the ridge in another two to three pitches. Follow the Class 3 ridge to the summit. This climb will probably change to a rock route by July. The return route may be either a down-climb to the snow col and a three-pitch rappel to the bergschrund, or a five-pitch rappel from the summit.

Grandjean Peak   9,160+ feet

This complex peak with five summits was named after Emil Grandjean, who was a Danish-trained forester and the first supervisor of the Sawtooth and Payette National Forests back in 1905. Grandjean came to the United States from Denmark in 1883 and mined, trapped, and explored in central Idaho before beginning his forestry career. The peak is located at the far northwestern end of the Verita Ridge. Its summits form a ragged, sawtooth line that is seldom approached by climbers. Crossing Baron Creek in the spring can pose a very serious risk. The original summit register was placed in 1973 by Bob and Sheila Dargatz, but was damaged by water and most of the names in the register have been lost—there were 13 listed between 1973 and 1996. USGS Warbonnet Peak/SW

Peak 9105 Routes. The westernmost summit of Grandjean Peak is the point named Grandjean Peak by the USGS. This is not the peak's highest summit, but it is the point where a register was found.

Southwest Ridge (Class 3). Approach this ridge from the South Fork Payette River Trail [(B)(3)(b)]. Hike up the trail until it crosses Goat Creek, then hike up Goat Creek about 1 mile. Leave the creek and ascend to the col between Peak 9105 and the next Grandjean summit to the southeast. It is steep hiking to the ridgeline; after that the character changes to Class 3 scrambling, becoming more exposed as you reach the summit. The rock is generally rotten on this side of the mountain.

North Slope/West Ridge (Class 3). This route is easiest in the spring when snow still covers the small trees and brush on the lower slopes. Approach the route via the Baron Creek Trail [(B)(3)(c)] until you reach the obvious avalanche path through the trees. Ascend the chute to the saddle between Point 7888 and Peak 9106. From the saddle, follow the ridge to the summit.

Peak 9144 Routes. Grandjean's highest summit is its easternmost summit. Greg Parker points out that several enticing lines remain untested on this remote summit.

Summit Ridge Traverse (II, Class 4). Greg Parker's Summit Ridge route traverses Grandjean's summit ridge from Peak 9105 to Peak 9144. After climbing 9105, down-climb or rappel a short pitch to gain a ridge heading to the east. Scramble through very exposed rotten rock to the summit. First ascent: G. Parker.

Grandjean Peak from Baron Peak

Northeast Face (II, 5.9). This route is under construction by G. Parker and M. Riffie. Approach by Baron Creek Trail [(B)(3)(c)] and begin climbing steep slabs on the south side of the creek just before the trail crosses a log at North Fork Baron Creek. Follow good friction face climbing (5.6) on slabs to the ridgeline, about three pitches. Then scramble to the upper face (Class 3), where the climbing changes to steep face climbing (5.9) on generally solid granite with few protection cracks. You can avoid the harder pitches with Class 4 and easy Class 5 climbing, but there is not a really easy way to the summit. The rock deteriorates near the summit.

Point 7255   *7,255 feet (II, 5.5)*
This point is located 1.2 miles west of Point 9105. Access the spire from the Baron Creek Trail [(B)(3)(c)]. From the trail, scramble through trees and rock bands across Class 3 and 4 terrain toward the summit. The final pitch has 30 to 50 feet of 5.5 climbing. Above this pitch, scramble the remaining distance to the small summit. The rock is generally very sound granite. First ascent: G. Parker. USGS Edaho Mountain

THE MAIN CREST:
PACKRAT PEAK TO ELK PEAK
The main crest from the Verita Ridge south to Elk Peak is entirely trailless and all cross-country approaches are strenuous. The best access routes begin at Alpine Lake and lead to Upper Redfish Lakes [(A)(6)(c.1)] and Warbonnet Lake [(A)(6)

(c.2) or (c.3)]. Despite the access difficulties, this spectacular country is worth the effort.

Packrat Peak   *10,240+ feet*
The USGS has misnamed Packrat Peak on the Warbonnet quad. The peak that mountaineers know as Packrat is 0.5 mile southwest of the summit identified on the quad. The true Packrat Peak is a notable mountain distinguished by two towers on its northern side that resemble the ears of a giant rat when viewed from a distance. The actual summit of this peak is formed by an impressive leaning granite fin. The peak offers several hundred feet of technical climbing from all directions. First ascent: R. Underhill, M. Underhill, and D. Williams in 1934. USGS Warbonnet Peak/SW

Northeast Ridge (II, 5.1). This route begins on the Alpen Peak/Packrat saddle [(A)(6)(c.1.1)]. From the saddle, follow the ridge toward Packrat's summit. Stay on the ridge crest to the main notch below the buttress. From the notch, climb to the base of the north tower. From this point, two alternatives are available. The first leads to the north for 25 feet across an angled slab, turns a corner, and continues up the north face by climbing between the north towers to the upper saddle. The second alternative follows a thin horizontal crack out to the south below the tower's cliffs and across the face. From this crack, the upper saddle (which is south of the north tower) can be reached by making a delicate, 5.6 move up and over the lip of the saddle. The summit block is visible from the upper saddle. Climb the summit block via a 30-foot lie-back.

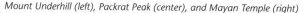

Mount Underhill (left), Packrat Peak (center), and Mayan Temple (right)

First ascent: L. Dye, M. Howard, and the Mazamas in 1971.

North Face (II, 5.4). Access the base of the North Face from the Warbonnet Lake cirque [(A)(6)(c.1)(c.3)]. The route starts at the base of the face near its center. Ledges lead at an angle from here to a large slab. Avoid the slab by climbing a chimney on its left side. From the top of the chimney, the route follows diagonal ledges to the right. This ledge system eventually intersects a left-trending ledge. Follow this for 200 feet to a grassy ledge that intersects with a second ledge. From the second ledge, a gully leads up to a point near the summit. Much of this route is Class 3 with occasional Class 4 and 5 moves. In the 1963 *American Alpine Journal,* Dan Davis wrote that the major problem is route-finding. First ascent: D. Davis, S. Marts, and F. Beckey in 1962.

East Face (II, 5.1). This route begins at Upper Redfish Lakes [(A)(6)(c.1)]. Hike to the base of the face and start up the ledges. These ledges become more difficult as you approach the main buttress. Finding a route up through the lower ledges may be difficult. Once the upper ledges are reached, the best route to the summit block is just to the left of the peak's center point. Follow an angled crack that tilts to the south, and then turn back to the north on the ledge that forms the summit base. Climb the tilted summit block up the exposed south rib. First ascent: R. Underhill, M. Underhill, and D. Williams in 1934.

South Couloir (II, 5.3). This route begins on the Packrat Peak/Mount Underhill saddle, which is accessed from Lake 9352 to the west via an easy scramble. From the saddle, the route enters the south couloir and then follows easy ledges to the base of a buttress. Turn the corner on the buttress and climb to a broken ledge. Follow this ledge to the north and onto the face. From here, an angled crack, which is tilted to the south at its upper end, leads to a higher ledge. Move to the north end of this ledge and climb one of the many cracks that infest this spot. The cracks lead to the saddle north of the summit. Walk south on the saddle ledge to the summit block.

Mayan Temple*   *10,080 feet*
This peak is located directly west of Packrat Peak on the subsidiary ridge that runs west from the main divide. It is also called Japan Peak. The shortest approach to the following routes is from Warbonnet Lake [(A)(6)(c.3)]. USGS Warbonnet Peak/SW

East Ridge (Class 4). The climb begins in Packrat Peak/Mayan Temple saddle. To reach the saddle, skirt the Temple's north face (normally accomplished on snow). The east ridge is easy terrain to the summit block, which is Class 4.

Northwest Ridge (III, 5.8+). This route ascends the strik-ing right-hand skyline as seen from upper Bead Lake. Two easy, Class 5 pitches lead to the ridge crest. Four pitches follow the ridge crest weaving through blocks, cracks, and chimneys. Descent involves several rappels down the west side. First ascent: K. Bachman, J. Splitgerber, and A. Dzmura in 1978.

Northeast Couloir (Class 5). This route begins at Feather Lakes [(A)(6)(c.3)]. From the lakes, there are two couloirs visible on the ridge's north wall. The route climbs the narrower one to the east. Except in low snow years, the route in the couloir is a moderate-angle snow climb. Climb the couloir to the notch just west of the first tower on the ridge crest and continue to the summit from this point. The couloir contains a buttress about two thirds of the way up that can be bypassed on the west wall.

Other Routes. Kirk Bachman climbed the Northeast Ridge (II, 5.9), and Jeff and Kelly Rhoads climbed the West Face, (II, 5.10). Both routes are challenging multiple-pitch climbs.

Blue Rock Dome   *9,240+ feet*
This formation is the northwesternmost point on Mayan Temple. Though it does not look like much from Bead or Feather Lakes [(A)(6)(c.3)], it is very impressive from Blue Rock Lake. R. Dowdle has placed four routes on the west face. The West Prow (III, 5.11) is recommended. The route starts at the low point of rock on the prow, next to a huge whitebark pine and then follows cracks up the prow with many 5.10 moves. K. Bachman and J. Splitgerber climbed the West Face (III, 5.10) in 1978 via six pitches on steep slabs, connecting various cracks and dihedrals. The cracks start thin and become wider near the summit.

Rainy Day Pinnacle*   *9,280+ (I, 5.10)*
This formation is an orange tower between Mayan Temple and Blue Rock Dome. The only reported ascent was by K. Bachman and B. Franklin in 1987 via the South Face Crack. This one-pitch route climbs a crack system on the south side of the formation. The approach to the crack is Class 4.

La Fiamma*   *9,900+ feet*
This formation is located near the end of and 0.5 mile south of Mayan Temple and west of the main crest. The shortest approach is from Warbonnet Lake [(A)(6)(c.3)]. From Warbonnet Lake, climb over the Packrat Peak/Mayan Temple saddle and descend into the cirque below. USGS Warbonnet Peak/SW

East Face (II, 5.6). The route starts at the notch where the tower meets the main ridge and then angles up the broken face toward the north side to a second notch. From this point, traverse across to the west face and a chimney that splits the lower tower. Climb the chimney. At the top of the chimney, the route leads out onto the upper west face. The first ascent was made using direct aid, but later climbers have done the route without aid. First ascent: F. Beckey, S. Marts, and D. Davis in 1962.

Mount Underhill*   10,160+ feet

This stunning and complex peak , which is unnamed on the USGS quad, is located 0.5 mile south of Packrat Peak on the main crest. In the past, climbers have incorrectly identified this peak in journals and magazine articles as Reward Peak. But Reward Peak, a less interesting summit, is the next one to the south. The peak is named after Sawtooth pioneers Robert and Merriam Underhill, who, along with Dave Williams, first climbed it in 1935. The west side of the peak can be accessed from the South Fork Payette River and FST-452 [(B)(3)(b)] via a long, cross-country walk up Goat Creek to Warbonnet Lake. The east side of the peak is accessed from Upper Redfish Lakes [(A)(6)(c.1)]. USGS Warbonnet Peak/SW

Southwest Couloir (II, Class 4). Access this route from Lake 9352 on the peak's west side. The first half of the couloir is a scramble. The second half is dominated by harder and steeper rock composed of multiple ledges. The crux is in the last 40 feet—but even here, the holds are good and the exposure is minimal. First ascent: R. Underhill, M. Underhill, and D. Williams in 1935.

Northwest Ridge (II, Class 4). The route starts at the Packrat Peak/Mount Underhill saddle and follows the northwest ridge to the summit. The saddle is accessed from Lake 9352 to the west. The northwest ridge rises sharply and is blocked by a tower. The climb starts at a prominent ledge that cuts diagonally across the north face of this tower and leads to a notch directly west of the tower. From this notch, the climb continues above the notch on the ridge crest (occasionally moving onto the north or southwest faces to avoid obstacles). First ascent: L. Dye, M. Howard, and the Mazamas in 1971.

Mazama Couloir (II, 5.2). This couloir offers a classic line to the summit. The couloir, which is reached from the northernmost Upper Redfish Lake [(A)(6)(c.1)], is a large vertical chimney that rises the full length of the peak's north face. It ends at a notch just east of the summit. The couloir is a 55-degree snow climb in early spring. Once the snow has melted, the climb up the couloir encounters only one obstacle: a band of cliffs two thirds of the way up. The holds through this section are good. Above the cliffs, the couloir begins to open, eventually forming a bowl in the north face. Climb up

The west face of Blue Rock Buttress (Photo by Reid Dowdle)

the broken ledges in the bowl to the northwest ridge, which is reached about 75 feet below the summit. Take a helmet. First ascent: L. Dye, M. Howard, and a Mazama Club group in 1971.

Northwest Couloir (II, 5.6). Access this route from Upper Redfish Lakes [(A)(6)(c.1)]. This couloir is smaller than the Mazama Couloir and located farther to the west on the north face. It ends at the notch east of the peak's main west tower. The entrance to the crack is easy and usually snow-covered. The first third of the route crosses a horizontal band of cliffs, which is the crux. The couloir is plagued with chockstones, and its upper portion is filled with loose and broken rock. Occasionally, the route moves out onto the face to avoid chockstones. The climbing becomes easier as the route moves between the first and second set of cliffs. The crack dies out near the second set of cliffs, and then opens again some 250 feet below the notch. From this point, the route joins the northwest ridge route. Rockfall is a constant danger on this route. First ascent: the Colorado Mountain Club in 1972.

Reward Peak   *10,074 feet (Class 2)*
This peak is located 1.25 miles due south of Mount Underhill and 0.9 mile north of Elk Peak. It was named in 1927 by Arval Anderson, who was surveying for the USGS. Anderson found a note, originally left on the summit in 1925, which offered the finder a $25 reward for returning the note. The peak is an easy scramble from the middle Upper Redfish Lake [(A)(6)(c.1)]. From the lake, hike west past the end of the peak's northeast ridge and then turn south to follow the drainage directly to the summit. USGS Warbonnet Peak/SW

Elk Peak   *10,582 feet*
Elk Peak is one of the largest Sawtooth peaks. Its distinctive twin summits are visible from almost every other Sawtooth summit. It is located 0.75 mile south of Reward Peak, on the main Sawtooth crest. The first ascent, which followed the east ridge, was by R. Underhill and D. Williams in 1934. USGS Warbonnet Peak/SW

   East Ridge (Class 3). Access the east ridge from Upper Redfish Lakes and Lake Kathryn (the southernmost of the three Upper Redfish Lakes [(A)(6)(c.1)]. The East Ridge route is gained by hiking and boulder hopping due south for 1 mile to a steep chute at the base of the ridge. Climb up the chute to the 9,800-foot col on the east ridge. Ascending the col will require an ice axe during the early part of the season. After the snow melts, the route is cluttered by steep, loose talus. The East Ridge route is easy Class 3 from the col to 10,200 feet where a Class 3 or 4 tower blocks the way. Either climb over the tower or climb out onto the south face and contour around it. If the latter option is chosen, regain the east ridge by climbing the first gully west of the tower. Above the tower, the remaining distance on the ridge involves boulder hopping over large blocks to reach the east summit. The west summit is higher. Descend into the saddle between the summits by down-climbing the intervening granite blocks. From the saddle the route to the west summit climbs directly up the obvious steep gully. There are a lot of good holds.

   West Side (Class 3). This is a long, steep climb that ends in the saddle between the peak's two summits. To approach from the west, leave FST-452 [(B)(3)(b)] roughly 2 miles above Elk Lake and climb northeast to tree line and the peak's south ridge at roughly 10,000 feet. Cross the ridge and follow the

south slopes to the saddle. Follow the route in the East Ridge description from this point to the summit.

THE CONY PEAK/REWARD PEAK DIVIDE
This divide runs between Cony and Reward Peaks and divides the trailless Goat Creek drainage from the South Fork Payette River. The divide is topped by four summits, Cony, Peak 9765, Peak 9627, and Peak 9760+, and its north side hosts seven spectacular lakes. The divide is accessed from FST-452 [(B)(3)(b)] or Warbonnet Lake [(A)(6)(c.3)]. Access to this remote divide is both strenuous and time consuming.

Cony Peak   *9,606 feet (Class 2)*
Cony Peak is situated 2.25 miles due west of Mount Underhill and 2 miles southwest of Warbonnet Peak. From the South Fork Payette River and FST-452 [(B)(3)(b)], follow Garden Creek to its upper reaches (a steep, direct slog) and then climb through the trees to the southeast ridge and follow this ridge to the summit. USGS Warbonnet Peak/SW

Peak 9765   *9,765 feet (Class 3)*
This is peak is located 2.3 miles northwest of Reward and directly south of Cony Peak. Scramble to the peak's south ridge from Meadow Lake and then follow the ridge to the summit. USGS Warbonnet Peak/SW

Peak 9627   *9,627 feet (Class 3)*
This peak is located just southwest of Three Lake. Its summit has an arrowhead-shaped footprint that points north. Scramble to the summit via the east face. First ascent: K. Bachman and J. Hokum in 1976. USGS Warbonnet Peak/SW

Peak 9760   *9,760+ feet (II, 5.8)*
This peak, an impressive pyramid with a vertical northwest face, is located south of Three and Limber Lakes and 1.5 miles northwest of Reward Peak. The only reported route climbs the northwest face. Approach the base of the face from Three Lake to the base of a prominent left-facing dihedral. This dihedral leads to the summit in four pitches. First ascent: K. Bachman and J. Hokum in 1976. USGS Warbonnet Peak/SW

Peak 9730   *9,730 feet*
This twin-summited peak sits southeast of Limber Lake. The west summit is the more difficult of the two. Scramblers can reach the summits from the north via the Packrat/Limber Lakes saddle.

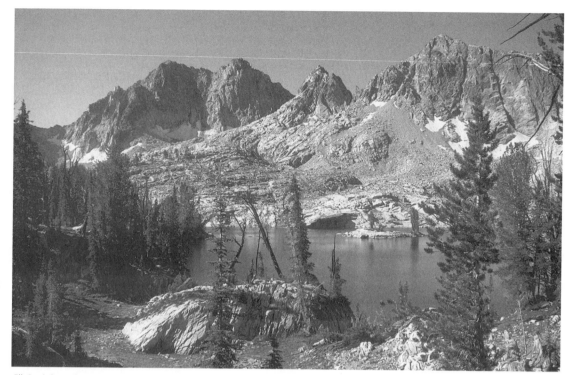

Elk Peak from the Upper Redfish Lakes

North Face/West Summit (II, 5.8). Approach this route from Limber Lake. Ascend to the snowfield at the base of the face. From the top of the snowfield, climb the dihedral that leads directly to the west summit in four pitches. First ascent: K. Bachman and J. Hokum in 1976.

THE MAIN CREST:
ELK PEAK TO MATTINGLY PEAK

From Elk Peak, the main Sawtooth crest swings east to Mount Cramer, and then runs south over Snowyside Peak, and then onto Mattingly Peak many miles to the south. Primary eastern access to this stretch of crest is from the Hell Roaring, Pettit Lake, Alturus Lake, and Smiley Creek trailheads. Accessing the western side of the crest involves a long backpacking trip.

Mount Cramer   *10,716 feet*

Mount Cramer, the second-highest peak in the Sawtooth Range, is the dominant Sawtooth peak along this stretch of the crest. Cramer sits at the top of three drainages. The main crest runs north and south from its summit and a subsidiary divide runs east to Glenns Peak. Its north face is one of the most impressive in the range and rises almost vertically for 1,000 feet. USGS Mount Cramer/SW

East Face (Class 3). This route follows the wide, prominent east ridge up to the east face, where it crosses a large boulder field just below the summit. To access the route from the Hell Roaring Lake area, follow the Imogene Lake Trail [(A) (4)(b)] to within 1 mile of Imogene Lake. Leave the trail and hike cross-country over relatively easy ground to the highest unnamed lake just south of the east ridge.

West Face (II, 5.3). This route climbs the main couloir on the face. (This vertical couloir is the first break north of the center of the west face.) The route, which begins at the bottom of the face, is straightforward [(A)(4)(b)]. Exit the crack about 150 feet below the summit and climb into a pocket on the face. (The pocket will hold snow into early summer.) Climb one of the snow gullies out of the pocket to a point southeast of the summit. The rock is fairly solid. First ascent: L. Dye, M. Ranger, and M. Herman.

Payette Peak   *10,211 feet (Class 2)*
Payette Peak is located on the main Sawtooth crest 1.5 miles
east of Imogene Lake. The eastern approach to the summit
begins at Imogene Lake. From the lake [(A)(5)(a)], hike cross-
country along the string of lakes up to the basin below the
peak. Scramble up to the saddle north of the summit and
follow the ridge to the top. From the west, begin your climb
at Hidden Lake [(A)(6)(b) or (B)(3)(b)]. The route climbs the
peak's north ridge and southwest slopes. From Hidden Lake,
hike due west to the small pond at 9,200 feet. Access the ridge
that descends from the summit to the pond and climb it to
a point below the summit where the route is blocked. Climb
out onto the southwest slopes until the route is passable to
the summit. USGS Snowyside Peak/SW

Imogene Peak*   *10,125 feet (Class 2-3)*
Imogene Peak is located east of the main crest on a divide that
separates the Imogene and Toxaway basins. It is 2.6 miles due
east of Payette Peak. The peak is identified as the Imogene
triangulation station on the USGS quad. The summit can be
reached from Farley Lake [(A)(4)(a)]. Climb from the west end
of the lake directly to the summit ridge and then follow the
ridge east to the summit. USGS Snowyside Peak/SW

Peak 10052   *10,052 feet (Class 2-3)*
This unnamed 10,000 footer is found 1 mile northeast of
Snowyside Peak and 1.8 miles southwest of Parks Peak on
the Toxaway/Alice Lakes divide. The summit is an easy
scramble from the pass to the west, which is crossed by the
trail between Alice and Toxaway Lakes [(A)(4)(a)]. USGS
Snowyside Peak/SW

Glenns Peak   *10,053 feet (Class 2)*
Cone-shaped Glenns Peak sits 2.25 miles west of Snowyside
Peak and directly south of Ardeth Lake. While it can be easily
climbed from several directions, the best route begins at the
pass west of the summit. Follow the west ridge from FST-463
[(B)(4)(a)] where that trail crosses the pass between Spangle
and Ardeth Lakes. The ridge is broad at the pass and well
defined near the summit. USGS Mount Everly/SW

Parks Peak   *10,208 feet (Class 3)*
Parks Peak is located 2 miles due south of Imogene Peak on
the Toxaway/Alice Lakes divide. To climb this mountain, take
the Alice Lake Trail, FST-095 [(A)(4)(a)], toward Alice Lake.
Leave the trail at the 8,400-foot contour and hike due north
to the base of an obtrusive buttress that trends southeast from
the summit. Climb up the west side of the buttress to just

above a granite point that overlooks the valley below. Cross
over to the east side of the buttress at this point. Climb along
the east side of the buttress toward the south face wall. Climb
the low-angle wall on broken ledges to the summit. There is
a register on the summit (left by D. Miller, T. Robertson, and
H. Wendling in 1960). This peak has also been climbed from
Farley Lake via the prominent and rotten north couloir—but
the route is not recommended because of the broken rock.
USGS Snowyside Peak/SW

Snowyside Peak   *10,651 feet*
Because of its striking appearance and its proximity to the
popular Alice/Toxaway Lakes hiking loop, this may be the
most climbed summit in the Sawtooths. The peak was a
popular destination for Idahoans long before the Underhills
climbed it in 1935. In 1926, Bob "Two Gun" Limbert wrote
an article for the *Idaho Statesman* on the east and north ridges.
Both ridges are approached from FST-095 [(A)(4)(a)] where it
crosses the pass above Twin Lakes. There is no record of who
made the first ascent. USGS Snowyside Peak/SW

   East Ridge (Class 3). Leave FST-095 at Toxaway/Alice
Lakes pass and follow the east ridge to the summit, staying on
the south side of the ridge until it turns north. Then stay near
the ridge top and climb directly over short intervening walls.
   North Ridge (I, Class 4). Start up the East Ridge route for
0.25 mile and then traverse north to the rugged shoulder of
the north ridge. From the top of the shoulder, the route makes
an airy crossing of the ridge to a wall just below the summit.

Perfect Peak*   *10,269 feet (Class 3-4)*
This interesting peak with a chiseled summit block is located
1.7 miles southeast of Snowyside Peak on the main crest. It
is unnamed on the USGS quad. The name is adopted from
Sheldon Bluestein's Hiking Trails of Southern Idaho. The
peak is climbed via the saddle on its northeast ridge. From
the saddle, climb the peak's east face to a point just south of
the lower, south summit. Cross between the summits to the
peak's west side through a small notch. Descend the west side
via a gully between the two summits to the base of a Class
3 wall. Climb this wall to the top of the north summit. The
saddle on the northeast ridge can be accessed from either
Alpine Creek and FST-094 [(A)(3)(a)] or from Alice Lake to
the north [(A)(4)(a)]. USGS Snowyside Peak/SW

El Capitán   *9,901 feet*
This peak sits just east of Alice Lake, 1.7 miles south of Parks
Peak on a divide that runs east from Perfect Peak. Its summit
block forms a small dome with a large west-facing wall remi-

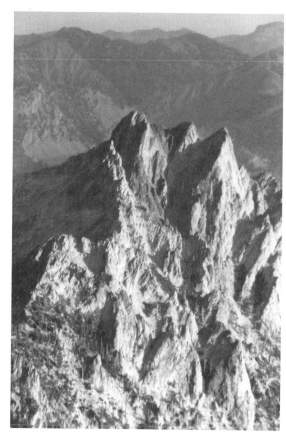

The north side of Perfect Peak, viewed from Snowyside Peak

Upper North Face (II, 5.2). This route begins at the base of the south headwall near the east face of the peak's north tower. Follow the chimney situated just east of where the base of the upper terrace joins the north tower. Climb from the top of the chimney to the notch that separates the tower from the main peak, then continue through the notch and out onto the north face on a ledge system. Ascend the ledges to the summit. First ascent: L. Dye and B. Hansen in 1972.

McDonald Peak   *10,068 feet (Class 3)*

McDonald Peak is located 2 miles south of the west end of Pettit Lake on a north/south divide that runs south from the west end of Pettit Lake to Peak 10027. From FST-095 [(A)(4)(a)] at the upper end of Pettit Lake, cross the wet, downfall-clogged flats to the base of the peak's north slopes. Climb these slopes directly through steep, forested terrain toward Point 9068. These slopes eventually turn into the peak's northern ridge, which in turn becomes the summit ridge. The route along the summit ridge is blocked by a granite fin that requires some Class 3 climbing. To traverse the ridge, stay on its top when

The west face of El Capitán is composed of broken metamorphic rock.

niscent of the real El Cap in Yosemite. Access is from Pettit Lake [(A)(4)(a)]. USGS Snowyside Peak/SW

East Side (Class 3). From the two small lakes below Alice Lake, climb into the cirque northeast of the peak. From the cirque, work your way to the east ridge, which leads to the summit. First ascent: R. Underhill, M. Underhill, and D. Williams in 1935.

Northeast Ridge (II, 5.2). This route begins on the bench north of Alice Lake [(A)(4)(a)]. Leave the trail and climb up to the first terrace. A small headwall, which forms the terrace's south side, extends clear to the east wall of the cirque. Several easy chimneys lead through this wall to a second terrace. From the second terrace, the climb continues above the south headwall in a westerly direction to the notch between the summit and the north tower. From the notch, climb up the ridge to the south and follow the crest to the summit. First ascent: L. Dye and B. Hansen in 1972.

possible; otherwise, bypass obstructions on their west side. The last tower is bypassed by climbing through a U-shaped notch and back to the east side. This peak also can be climbed from Vat Creek and the Valley View Summer Home area over easy Class 2 slopes. USGS Snowyside Peak/SW

Peak 10027   *10,027 feet (Class 2)*
This rewarding summit is one of the least known Sawtooth summits. It offers excellent views in all directions and is frequented by mountain goats. It is a southern extension of the ridgeline that forms McDonald Peak to the north. Climb the peak via its south ridge from the middle Cabin Lakes. The lake is accessed by FST-191 [(A)(3)(b)], which is not shown on the USGS quad. The official trail ends at the lake, but a fishermen's trail follows the east side of the lake and then climbs up a ridge to Lake 9078. From this lake, climb due north to the south ridge and then follow it to the summit. An alternative route climbs the peak from the trailless lake basin due east of the peak. From the point where FST-191 crosses the creek that drains this basin, follow the creek up to the lakes at the base of the peak's east face. This is a difficult but rewarding cross-country hike. To climb the face, aim for the saddle south of the summit, keeping to the left of the face to avoid a cliff band. USGS Snowyside Peak/SW

Peak 10129   *10,129 feet (Class 2)*
This unnamed summit is located between Beaver Creek and Alturas Creek. Climb the peak directly from the end of Beaver Creek Road [(A)(2)]. The route is steep, but straightforward. USGS Frenchman Creek

Abes Armchair*   *9,956 feet (Class 2)*
From ID-75, this peak, which rises 2.7 miles south of the Smiley Creek Lodge, looks like an armchair. Its summit is an excellent scramble from Smiley Creek. Leave ID-75 at the Smiley Creek Lodge and follow the Smiley Creek Road, FS-077[(A)(1)], for 3 miles to a point just before the road crosses the creek that descends out of Sawmill Canyon. If you look carefully, you can find a good trail—not shown on any maps—that climbs up Sawmill Canyon [(A)(1)(a)]. Hike up the canyon for 0.5 mile to a point due south of Point 8522. Leave the canyon bottom and hike north to the top of the peak's east ridge. Once on the ridge, turn west and follow it to the summit. USGS Frenchman Creek

Vienna Peak*   *10,224 feet (Class 2-3)*
Vienna, a large twin-summited peak, rises 1.5 miles southwest of Abes Armchair. While not spectacular or well known, its

remoteness makes it worth the effort. The peak can be accessed by traversing the connecting ridge from Abes Armchair—a Class 2 climb—or by its east face—a Class 3 climb. Hike up Sawmill Canyon [(A)(1)(a)] to the small pond at 8,700 feet. From the pond, work your way east to the base of the east face. Climb directly toward the summit until it steepens around 9,500 feet. Turn south and climb to the east ridge over Class 3 slopes and then follow the ridge to the summit. USGS Frenchman Creek

Peak 9367   *9,367 feet (Class 3)*
Surprisingly, this rugged peak is ignored by climbers. Its jagged summit divides Frenchman Creek and Smiley Creek. Access the peak from Smiley Creek [(A)(1)]. Park 4 miles from ID-75. Cross Smiley Creek and hike up to the peak's south ridge at 8,600 feet. Follow the ridge north to the peak's twisted summit. USGS Frenchman Creek

Mattingly Peak   *9,921 feet (Class 3)*
Mattingly's three summits are seldom visited. Its highest summit is 4 miles south of Snowyside Peak and 0.7 mile west of the main crest. The summit is accessed from the unnamed lake to the southeast that is in turn accessed from Mattingly Creek [(A)(3)(c) or (B)(4)(a)]. Leave the trail where it crosses the outlet stream for the lakes and climb to the lakes, staying west of the creek. From the lakes, climb into the saddle between the middle summit and the northeast summit. Ascend due west to the summit. USGS Mount Everly/SW

THE CENTRAL DIVIDE

This 8-mile divide rises between the main crest to the east and the Queens Divide to the west. The Middle Fork Boise River is on its east side and the Queens River on the west. Primary access is from the Queens River and Atlanta trailheads to the south. The Central Divide is less well defined than any other Sawtooth divide, yet it contains several excellent summits and dozens of beautiful alpine lakes. At its widest spot it is more than 4 miles across.

Mount Everly   *9,852 feet*
Mount Everly is a gorgeous, block-shaped summit that rises steeply on all sides. It is located 1.6 miles southeast of Blacknose Mountain and just west of Everly Lake. Mount Everly features several formidable walls with high potential for interesting scrambles; it is well worth the long walk into its base. USGS Mount Everly/SW

East Face (Class 3). This route is accessed from Everly

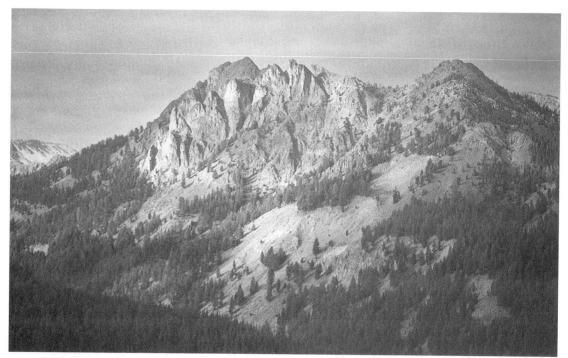

Peak 9367 from Abes Armchair

Lake [(B)(5)(a)]. The east face is steep, but broken by many short steps. The route begins at the south end of the lake where a rib descends the face. Start up the rib, keeping on its north side until above the trees. From this point, climb to the top of the rib toward the cliff above. Bypass the cliff on its south side via a steep, debris-filled gully. At the top of the gully, the route climbs the steps into the center of the face and then works toward the east ridge. In 1991 there were cairns leading up the face. Aim for a point just below the east end of the summit ridge. The summit is an easy 100-yard walk to the west.

Southeast Slopes (Class 2). This route is less rewarding than the east face, but allows for a long easy slosh up talus slopes to the summit. Access the route from Everly Lake [(B)(5)(a)]. Hike south around the east rib and follow the timber line past the cliffs that guard the base of the southeast slopes. Beware of the cliffs if you chose to use this route for your descent. Do not try to down-climb them.

Peak 9798   *9,798 feet (Class 3)*
This picturesque summit is located 0.4 mile east of Everly Lake and directly north of Plummer Peak. Climb from Plummer Lake [(B)(5)(a)] via zigzagging slopes that work around cliffs on the lower half of the route and eventually lead to the center of the peak's west slopes. From this point follow the west slopes directly to the summit. USGS Mount Everly/SW

Plummer Peak   *9,978 feet (Class 3)*
Plummer Peak is located 1.25 miles southeast of Mount Everly. Climb the peak via its northwest rib. Begin at the south end of the small, unnamed lake 0.15 miles southwest of Plummer Lake [(B)(5)(a)]. The route climbs up the south side of the rib for the first 300 feet and then follows the top of the rib through fir trees for several hundred feet. After breaking out of the trees, the route climbs broken rock to the summit, where there is a view of ten mountain lakes. USGS Mount Everly/SW

Peak 9737   *9,737 feet (Class 3)*
This remote, seldom climbed peak is the highest point on the divide that separates Timpa Creek from the Middle Fork Boise River. It is located 2.5 miles southeast of Plummer Peak. The peak can be climbed from Timpa or Confusion Lakes via its west or northeast ridges. USGS Mount Everly/SW

Greylock Mountain   *9,363 feet (Class 2-3)*
The name Greylock Mountain reportedly originated with the Chinese, who prospected in the Atlanta area in the 1800s. As the story goes, the Chinese called the mountain "Grey Rock" because of its gray color, but their accented pronunciation was taken literally and the mountain became Greylock instead. Occasionally climbed by campers from the Atlanta area campgrounds, Greylock can be a treacherous peak. In 1987, a group of amateur climbers got lost and hung up on a cliff while descending. One fell and was killed. Despite a number of easy routes to the summit, do not disregard the lesson of 1987. Access the peak from Atlanta [(B)(4)(a)]. USGS Atlanta East/SW

THE QUEENS DIVIDE

This impressive divide encompasses exceptional remote mountain terrain, including the famous Rakers and several alpine lakes. It is the westernmost Sawtooth divide. In the north, Pinchot Creek is on its western side and the South Fork Payette River is on its eastern side. Farther south, the divide splits the Little Queens and Queens Rivers. The southern stretches of the divide are accessed from the Queens River trailhead. Northern access begins at the Grandjean trailhead, but also requires difficult cross-country travel and fording the South Fork Payette River.

Pinchot Mountain   *9,502 feet (Class 2)*
Pinchot Mountain, named after Gifford Pinchot, the father of American forestry, is located at the north end of the Queens Divide, 3 miles due west of Elk Peak. Climb from the Fern Falls area along the South Fork Payette River [(B)(3)(b)] via the north ridge. Be aware that crossing the Payette River to reach the bottom of the ridge is dangerous even in low water. Look for a safe crossing. USGS Warbonnet Peak/SW

The Rakers

The Rakers are among the most imposing and remote peaks in the Sawtooths. They are found west of the South Fork Payette River above Fall and Pinchot Creeks. As delineated by the USGS on the Mount Everly quad, North Raker (which was once called Red Finger) has two summits. The northern summit is 9,970 feet; the south is more than 9,880 feet. Climbers have always called these two peaks North and South Raker. However, the USGS identified a smaller peak 1 mile to the south as South Raker. Although it is a little confusing, for the purpose of this guide, I will stick with the original designa-

tions. Because the Rakers are so remote, they have seen little climbing activity. In fact, as of 1986 only four parties had reached the summit of the very difficult North Raker.

The Rakers are visible for miles and are very enticing when viewed from almost any other Sawtooth peak. Thus, it is not surprising that the first attempt on the Rakers was made by the Underhills and Williams in 1934. Though they succeeded on the South Raker, the North Raker was not conquered until 1949 when Fred Beckey and Pete Schoening used their "hard-rock engineering techniques" to overcome the peak's last pitch. The register is located in a cigar box on the saddle between the north and south peaks. Access to the peaks requires a difficult cross-country hike from the South Fork Payette River [(B)(3)(b)]. USGS Mount Everly/SW

North Raker   *9,970 feet (III, Class 6)*
The only known route on North Raker makes an exposed traverse out to the north corner of the peak from the saddle. From this corner, traverse 15 feet on a flake to the underside of an overhang. Using direct aid, climb the overhang up a crack that splits the rotten, decomposed granite. Above this, the face becomes smooth. F. Beckey and P. Schoening used a shoulder stand from the notch above the smooth section to reach a 12-foot jam crack, which gave them access to the summit. USGS Mount Everly/SW

South Raker   *9,880+ feet (Class 3-4)*
Climb the South Raker from the North Raker/South Raker saddle. The route is an easy scramble from the saddle until the summit block. The summit block is rated at either Class 3 or 4, depending upon who you ask. USGS Mount Everly/SW

Blacknose Mountain   *9,802 feet (Class 2-3)*
There is no better spot on earth to view the Rakers than from the summit of Blacknose Mountain. The peak's summit, which is located 1.5 miles south of North Raker, is a short climb from the nearest trail, but more than 25 miles from the nearest trailhead. Climb from FST-494 [(B)(6)(a.1)] and Queens Pass above Pats Lake. From the saddle, you can climb to the summit by either following the ridgeline or by traversing out onto the south face and climbing a gully to the summit rocks. USGS Mount Everly/SW

Peak 9704   *9,704 feet (Class 3)*
Although unnamed, this summit, which is located due south of Blacknose Mountain and Arrowhead Lake, is a worthy objective. It offers a scenic north face and a well-defined northeast ridge. From Queens Pass, climb the northeast ridge,

The Rakers, North Raker on the right, viewed from Blacknose Mountain

staying on its top for the first 300 yards. From this point, climb the ridge's southeast side (staying near the top) to the summit that is a 0.5 mile from the pass. There is only a short section of Class 3 climbing. USGS Mount Everly/SW

Browns Peak   *9,705 feet (Class 2-3)*
Browns Peak is the next summit south of Peak 9704. It is located just east of Browns Lake and south of Glacier Lake. Climb this pup-tent-shaped peak from Browns Lake via its western slopes. The lake is located 1 mile east of FST-454 [(B)(5)(b)] and is reached by a short side trail, FST-480. From the lake, climb directly west to the summit. USGS Nahneke Mountain/SW

Flat Top Mountain   *9,665 feet (Class 3)*
Flat Top Mountain is located 1.2 miles south of Browns Peak. Climb the peak from Flat Top Lake (Lake 8850 on the USGS quad), which is reached by FST-456 [(B)(5)(b.1)]. From the lake, hike south to an unnamed lake 0.25 mile away. Once at this lake, turn east and climb toward the peak's south ridge. Follow the ridge directly to the summit. USGS Nahneke Mountain/SW

Nahneke Mountain   *9,582 feet (Class 3-4)*
Nahneke Mountain sits 1.6 miles due south of Flat Top Mountain. Climb the peak from the Scenic Lake drainage

[(B)(5)(b.1)]. This peak has two summits of almost equal height. The easternmost summit, the highest and the most impressive of the two, is buttressed by four attractive ridges. Although all four ridges are probably climbable, information is available only for the north ridge. To reach this ridge, bypass Scenic Lake on its east side, staying roughly 100 feet above the lake. Climb into the upper basin to a small pond. Climb to the ridge top from this point. Stay on the west side of the ridge at first and then cross over to the east side near the top to avoid obstacles. USGS Nahneke Mountain/SW

APPROACHES TO THE SAWTOOTH RANGE

(A) ID-75 APPROACHES
This highway runs along the entire eastern side of the range from the headwaters of the Salmon River to Stanley.

(1) FS-077, Smiley Creek Road. This road begins along ID-75 at the Smiley Creek Lodge. It is a good gravel road for the first few miles but then deteriorates as it approaches the Vienna mining town site.

(a) Sawmill Canyon Trail. Sometimes trails that do not exist show up on maps and sometimes trails that exist do not show up on maps. This trail falls into the latter category. No one knows who built it or why. The trail's beginning is unmarked. Look for it 3 miles south of ID-75 just before the spot where the road crosses the creek that descends out of Sawmill Canyon. The trail, which has a good tread, stays on the east side of the creek as it climbs Sawmill Canyon.

(2) FS-204, Beaver Creek Road. Access this road from ID-75 roughly 1.8 miles north of the Smiley Creek Lodge. Its junction is signed for Sawtooth City. From the highway, the road traverses up Beaver Creek for 7 miles to old mining digs.

(3) FST-205, Alturas Lake Road. This road leads from ID-75, past Alturas Lake, for 7 miles (5 miles paved and 2 miles gravel), and then continues as a rough jeep road.

(a) FST-094, Alpine Creek Trail. FST-094 leaves FS-205 1.5 miles west of Alturas Lake (or roughly 7 miles from ID-75) just before the road fords Alpine Creek. It then follows Alpine Creek northwest for 3.5 miles to Alpine Lake. The trailless portion of the upper Alpine Creek drainage, which contains more than 50 lakes and ponds, is seldom visited.

(b) FST-191, Cabin Lakes Trail. To access this trail from Alturas Lake, turn north at the east end of the lake onto FS-207. Follow this road north for 0.5 mile to the well-marked trailhead. This trail leads to Cabin Lakes in 3 miles.

(c) FST-034, Alturas/Mattingly Creek Trail. This trail leaves the end of FS-205 and proceeds southeast to a junction with FST-034. From the junction, the trail climbs northwest over the Sawtooth crest and then descends into Mattingly Creek. The trail eventually leads to FST-460 [(B)(4)(a)] just north of Atlanta.

(4) FS-208, Pettit Lake Road. This road begins 19 miles south of Stanley and runs west from ID-75 to Pettit Lake and the Tin Cup Transfer Camp trailhead in about 2.5 miles of good gravel road.

(a) FST-095, FST-092, and FST-096, Alice Lake/Toxaway Lake Loop Trail. This is one of the most popular and crowded trails in Idaho. The 19-mile loop trail leaves Pettit Lake by following Pettit Creek to Alice Lake at 6 miles. From Alice Lake, it continues to Twin Lakes at 7 miles and then crosses Snowyside Pass and drops into the Toxaway Lake Basin at 11 miles. From Toxaway Lake, the trail descends the drainage past Farley Lake. South of Farley Lake, at a junction, the trail climbs south over the intervening ridge to return to Pettit Lake.

(a.1) Toxaway Lake and Beyond. From Toxaway Lake, a trail leads up to the top of the high ridge north of the lake to a junction. From this point, two trails lead deeper into the Sawtooth backcountry. The first, FST-452, goes to Edna Lake and then to Grandjean via the South Fork Payette River Trail [(B)(3)(b)]. This trail connects with all of the main Sawtooth trails and is well marked and maintained. The second, FST-092, leads north to Imogene Lake and then out to Hell Roaring Creek [(A)(5)(b)].

(5) FS-315, Hell Roaring Creek Road. Take ID-75 south from Stanley for 12 miles, turn west, cross the Salmon River and then drive 5 miles on a rugged dirt road best suited for a 4WD to the trailhead. A 4WD is recommended.

(a) FST-092, Hell Roaring Lake/Toxaway Lake Trail. From the end of the road, this short trail reaches Hell Roaring Lake, which is located directly below the Finger of Fate, in 1.8 miles. The trail begins by fording the creek, which—as you can guess from the name—carries a lot of water early in the summer. From Hell Roaring Lake, it is another 3 miles to Imogene Lake and 6.5 miles to Toxaway Lake [(A)(4)(a)]. This trail sees much use.

(a.1) Cross-Country Route to the Upper Basin. From the western end of Hell Roaring Lake, a fishing/climbing route of fair quality leads up into the high basin to the north of the Arrowhead and the Finger of Fate. Although this trail is not maintained, it is passable and relatively easy to follow. Leave the main trail and hike around Hell Roaring Lake to the second inlet stream and look for the trail in this area.

(b) FST-092, Hell Roaring Lake to Redfish Lake Trail. This trail leaves the Hell Roaring Lake Trail roughly 0.6 mile below the lake and runs due north across a saddle and onto Redfish Lake [(A)(6)(b)]. It provides good access to Decker Creek and the west side of Decker Peak.

(6) FS-214, Redfish Lake Road. Turn west off ID-75 5 miles south of Stanley and drive 2 miles on a paved road to Redfish Lake. A large backpackers' parking lot is located just before the lake on the north side of the road.

(a) FST-155, Bench Lake Trail. This trail leaves the backpackers' parking lot and leads to the first two Bench Lakes at the base of Mount Heyburn in 4.5 miles and 1,300 feet of elevation gain. From the first lake, it is a 1.5-mile walk on a sketchy fishing trail to get to the uppermost Bench Lake and the starting point for several climbing routes on Heyburn. From the uppermost lake, it is possible to hike cross-country over the saddle north of Heyburn to approach the peak's west face and its west pinnacle.

(b) FST-101, FST-154, Redfish Lake Creek Trail. This trail begins at the top of Redfish Lake, 5 miles from the trailhead parking lot. There are two ways to reach the top of the lake: Take the boat operated by the lodge during the tourist season or hike the first 2 miles of the Bench Lake Trail and then descend a cutoff trail for 3 miles to the west end of Redfish Lake. Take the boat when it is available. The trail, which runs from the inlet on the west end of Redfish Lake to Cramer Lake, is the main approach route to the northeastern portion of the Sawtooths. The Saddleback Lakes cross-country route begins 2 miles from the Inlet [(A)(6)(b.2)]. At 3.5 miles, the trail reaches Flatrock Junction. At this junction, FST-101 [(A)(6)(c)] leaves Redfish Lake Creek and runs to Alpine Lake, Baron Pass, Baron Creek Lakes, and eventually to

Grandjean [(B)(3)(c)]. The main trail (now designated FST-154) fords Redfish Lake Creek and continues to Cramer Lake, which is 11 miles from Redfish Lake (16 miles from the parking area). From Cramer Lake, the trail continues west over the Cramer Divide, drops down to Payette Lake, and joins FST-452 [(B)(3)(b) and (A)(4)(a.1)].

(b.1) FST-092, Redfish Lake to Hell Roaring Lake Trail. Access this route at the west end of Redfish Lake. From the boat dock, hike through the CG to a signed junction for the trail. The trail runs south and eventually works its way along the lake shore. In roughly 0.5 mile, the trail begins a long climb up the lateral moraine on the south side of the lake. At the top of the moraine, it intersects with FST-045 which leads back to the northeast end of the lake and FS-092, which continues south to Hell Roaring Lake. [(A)(5)(b)].

(b.2) Saddleback Lakes Cross-Country Route. This route leads into a rugged cirque surrounded by the four perches: Elephants, Eagle, Goat, and Chipmunk. The route is not signed and will take a little time to find. Two miles above Redfish Lake, the trail crosses a stream coming down off the flanks of Mount Heyburn. Several hundred feet past this point, follow a path that drops down to Redfish Lake Creek. Find a safe place to cross, and then look for a path often marked by small rock cairns that leads uphill toward the cirque.

(b.3) Chockstone Basin Cross-Country Route. Chockstone Basin is located on the south side of Redfish Lake Creek due south of Braxon Peak. It is not named on the maps, but is the next drainage west of the drainage that holds Saddleback Lakes. Leave the trail roughly 0.5 mile east of Flatrock Junction. Cross the creek—difficult in high water—and hike up into the basin to access climbing routes on Chockstone Peak and the Goat Perch.

(c) FST-101, Alpine Lake/Baron Lakes Trail. This wide, switch-backing trail leaves the Redfish Lake Creek Trail at Flatrock Junction 3.5 miles above Redfish Lake and climbs 1,000 feet in roughly 2 miles to Alpine Lake. From Alpine Lake, the trail climbs over the Baron Divide and then drops to the Baron Lakes in 2.5 miles [(B)(3)(c)]. Alpine Lake may be the most crowded location in the Sawtooths. Try to avoid camping along its shores.

(c.1) Upper Redfish Lakes Cross-Country Route. This strenuous cross-country route leaves FST-101 at Alpine Lake. From the lake's eastern end, hike south toward the ridgeline dividing the Alpine and Upper Redfish Lakes Basins. Climb to the ridge's crest and follow it up to roughly 8,800 feet. At this point, traverse down the west side of the ridge into the gully below. Follow this gully up to the ridge top just west of Point 9337. From this point, descend directly down to the first lake without much difficulty. Once you are in the basin, travel is easy.

(c.1.1) Upper Redfish Lakes to Warbonnet Lake Cross-Country Route. This route involves a short pitch of Class 3 climbing on its east side and is difficult with heavy packs. From the northernmost of the Upper Redfish Lakes, hike west to the pond just below Packrat Peak. Turn north and hike to the very small pond at 9,200 feet and then climbs to the Alpen/Packrat col above by staying to the right side of the headwall. The descent to Warbonnet Lake involves very tedious boulder hopping.

(c.2) Alpine Lake to Warbonnet Lake Cross-Country Route: Alternative No. 1. This alternative also uses the Alpen Peak/Packrat Peak col and makes a Class 2 crossing between these two lake basins. Leave the Alpine Lake/Baron Lake Trail at the first switchback above Alpine Lakes. Hike due west from the trail until it is possible to turn south into the talus and then snow-filled gully that climbs to the saddle just east of Alpen Peak. From this saddle, traverse west to the Alpen/Packrat saddle. On the west side, ascend to Warbonnet Lake. This route involves extensive boulder hopping.

(c.3) Alpine Lake to Warbonnet Peak Cross-Country Route: Alternative No. 2. Follow FST-101 toward Baron Lakes until approximately 8,600 feet. Leave the trail and head due west toward the saddle at 9,400 feet (just northeast of Peak 9769). From the saddle, hike up the ridge until you are roughly at the same elevation as the saddle that is just west of Peak 9769. Traverse over to the saddle. There are several paths in this area to aid you. Unfortunately, none of them connect. From the saddle, hike down into the Warbonnet Basin by keeping to your left. A steep but passable trail can be followed for part of the distance. Once in the upper Warbonnet Basin, cross-country travel is not difficult.

(c.4) Alpine Lake to Baron Lake and Stephens Lakes Cross-Country Route. This cross-country route leaves FST-101 on the west side of the unnamed lake just below the east side of Baron Pass. Follow the lake's western shore north to the Alpine Lake/Braxon Lake pass at 9,080 feet. The south side of the pass is a gentle walk-up, but the north side is much steeper. Descend toward Braxon Lake and look for a game trail to your left in the sand 35 feet below the pass. This game trail allows an acceptable descent down the steepest part of the slope. Leave Braxon Lake on its east side and hike north toward Lake 8945. The terrain on the south side of the Braxon/Stephens Lakes pass is uneven and tree-covered. From the east side of Lake 8945 descend grass-covered slopes to Lake 8557 taking care to avoid the cliffs that dot the slope.

(d) FST-528, Alpine Way Trail. This is a long trail that contours along the northeast and northern fronts of the Sawtooths between Redfish Lake, the Iron Creek trailhead, and Stanley Lake. The trail varies in quality along its route; it is not regularly maintained between Iron Creek trailhead and Stanley

Lake. Access the trail from the backpackers' parking lot at Redfish Lake. Take the signed route out of the parking lot and follow it 0.75 mile past the Bench Lake Trail junction to a second junction. At this junction, the left fork trail proceeds up Fishhook Creek [(A)(6)(d.1)]. Continue on the right fork, which is the Alpine Way Trail. Follow this trail for 4 miles to reach Marshall Lake, which is a good jumping-off point for climbing Williams and Thompson Peaks. From this lake, the trail continues to the junction for the Iron Creek trailhead [(B)(1)(a)].

(d.1) FST-186, Fishhook Creek Trail. Follow the directions above for FST-528 to reach this trail. From the junction with the Alpine Way Trail, this route runs up a spectacular valley for 2 miles toward Horstmann Peak, eventually ending near some beaver ponds. The upper reaches of the Fishhook drainage are accessible via strenuous cross-country travel. Stay on the north side slopes to avoid swampy thickets along the creek bottom.

(B) ID-21 APPROACHES

ID-21 leads northwest from Stanley following the northern margins of the Sawtooths, then swings sharply south following the western edges of the Sawtooths. The highway eventually turns to the southwest and crosses through the heart of the Boise Mountains on its way to Boise.

(1) FS-619, Iron Creek Road. Drive 2 miles northwest from Stanley on ID-21. Turn onto this signed road and drive 4 miles to its end, where there is a campground and a large backpackers' parking lot. The trail leaves the trailhead just past the large information sign, gradually ascends a tree-covered alluvial fan and intersects with the Alpine Way Trail in 1 mile.

(a) FST-528, Alpine Way Trail. From the trailhead, it is 1 mile to the Alpine Way Trail. The trail runs northwest to Stanley Lake Creek [(B)(2)(b)] and southeast to Redfish Lake Creek [(A)(6)(d)].

(a.1) Goat Lake Trail. This trail is not shown on the maps. Nevertheless, you can access Goat Lake from the Alpine Way Trail [(A)(6)(d)] by hiking 1 mile southwest from the Iron Creek trailhead to the Alpine Way junction and then following the Alpine Way Trail southeast for another 1.75 miles. At this point, the trail looks over Goat Creek. The Alpine Way Trail continues to the left and descends to Goat Creek. Turn right on the Goat Lake Trail and follow it uphill for another 0.75 mile. While not maintained, this route is not difficult to follow. It ends at Goat Lake. To reach the upper basin from Goat Lake, climb up the ridgeline on the east side of the lake to the small pond at 9,120 feet (and northwest of Point 10084). Cross over the saddle just west of the lake and descend to Lake 8865.

(b) FST-640, Sawtooth Lake/McGown Lake Trail. Sawtooth Lake is a 5.5-mile hike from the Iron Creek trailhead along a well-signed, maintained trail. From this junction, follow

the trail's right fork for 0.75 mile and then turn left at the next junction. From the last junction, it's 2.25 miles to the Alpine Lake turnoff and 3.25 miles to Sawtooth Lake. Sawtooth Lake is usually crowded and camping there is not recommended. From the north end of the lake, trails lead south and west. The trail to the south leads into the North Fork Baron Creek drainage and out to the Grandjean entrance [(B)(3)]. The trail west leads 1 mile to McGown Lakes. From McGown Lakes, the trail continues to Stanley Lake Creek [(B)(3)(a)].

(c) FST-478, North Fork Baron Creek Trail. FST-478 begins at the north end of Sawtooth Lake, proceeds south along the lake, and then drops into the upper reaches of the North Fork Baron Creek. The trail joins the Baron Creek Trail in about 5 miles.

(2) FS-455, Stanley Lake Road. This road leaves ID-21 5 miles west of Stanley at a well-signed junction. The trailhead is 3.8 miles from ID-21 at Inlet CG.

(a) FST-640, Stanley Lake Creek Trail. FST-640 leaves the Stanley Lake trailhead and follows the creek south for 7.25 miles to a saddle at its headwaters. From this saddle, FST-640 continues east to McGown and Sawtooth Lakes and eventually the Iron Creek trailhead [(B)(1)(b)]. FST-453 [(B)(3)(a)] continues into Baron Creek and eventually to the Grandjean trailhead. From the saddle, FST-024 [(B)(2)(a.1)] leads to Observation Peak.

(a.1) FST-024, Observation Peak Trail. This trail leaves FST-640 from the saddle at the top of Stanley Lake Creek and climbs west to the top of Observation Peak in 1.5 steep miles.

(b) FST-528, Alpine Way Trail. FST-528 leaves FST-640 1 mile from Stanley Lake and traverses along the northern and eastern sides of McGown Peak, crossing through some of the most remote parts of the Sawtooths before ultimately reaching the Iron Creek trailhead [(B)(1)(a)]. This portion of the Alpine Way Trail is not maintained regularly.

(b.1) Cross-Country Route to McGown Cirque. This route leaves FST-528, the Alpine Way Trail, at a tree-covered saddle roughly 2.5 miles from the trail's northern end and FST-640, the Stanley Lake Creek Trail. The saddle is cluttered by downed timber. Leave the saddle at its southern end (where the trail begins to descend) and hike west uphill through the trees along the rounded ridge that climbs from the saddle toward Peak 9820. If you look hard, a good game trail can be found about 50 yards from the saddle. This game trail stays roughly 100 feet below the ridge's crest, paralleling the ridge on its southeastern side. It eventually leads to a saddle on the ridge top. From the saddle, stay on the ridge top until the ridge merges into the side of Peak 9820 at approximately 8,200 feet. From this point, follow the stream into the upper cirque.

(3) FS-524, Grandjean Entrance Road. This entrance is located 38 miles west of Stanley on ID-21. A good gravel road leads east from the signed turnoff for 7 miles to the trailhead, which is at an elevation of 5,200 feet.

(a) **FST-453, Trail Creek Trail.** This trail provides a steep and relatively long approach into the Observation Peak and Sawtooth Lake areas [(B)(2)(a)].

(b) **FST-452, South Fork Payette River Trail.** FST-452 starts from the end of FS-524 and follows the South Fork Payette south for many miles, providing access to the middle of the Sawtooth backcountry. The trail reaches Elk Lake in 11 miles, before crossing over the Sawtooth crest and linking up with the Alice Lake/Toxaway Lake Loop Trail [(A)(4)(a.1)].

(b.1) **Garden Creek/Cony Lake Cross-Country Route.** This seldom-used route leaves the South Fork Payette River Trail where Garden Creek crosses the trail at roughly 5,800 feet. Follow the creek up the steep slopes until you are directly southwest of Cony Lake at an elevation of 8,600 feet. From this point, climb over the intervening ridge to Cony Lake. From Cony Lake you can reach all the main lakes on the Cony Peak/Reward Peak Divide. This route is extremely taxing and not for the weak spirited.

(c) **FST-101, Baron Creek Trail.** This trail forks off the South Fork Payette River Trail 1.5 miles from the Grandjean trailhead. From the trailhead to Baron Lakes, it is roughly 10 miles and an elevation gain of 3,100 feet. The trail begins at the Grandjean trailhead, crosses Trail Creek, and then forks. Take the right fork and go 1.5 miles to another fork at Baron Creek. Stay left and follow Baron Creek to the lakes. From the lakes, the trail crosses the Baron divide and drops into Alpine Lake [(A)(6)(c)].

(4) **Atlanta Area Access.** Atlanta is one of the most remote towns in Idaho. It can be reached from several different directions on fair-to-primitive roads. These routes are slow and winding. Patience is required. Drive slowly. Leave ID-21 at a signed junction next to the Edna Creek CG, just east of Mores Creek Summit. From the highway, it is 47 miles to Atlanta on a good gravel road. Be sure to take the Boise and Sawtooth National Forest maps with you to assure finding Atlanta (there are many junctions and side roads to confuse you).

Atlanta also can be gained via the Middle Fork Boise River Road. This is the most direct route to Atlanta for those driving from the Boise area. However, it is also the slowest route. Drive 17 miles north from Boise on ID-21 to the top of Lucky Peak Reservoir. Turn east on FS-168 and follow this gravel road 72 miles to Atlanta.

Access is also possible from I-84 at Mountain Home. Take exit 95 at Mountain Home and drive north on ID-20 for 31.9 miles to the Featherville turn. Turn right and follow the road north to Featherville. From the north end of this small village, turn left (west) onto FS-156. At Rocky Bar, turn right (north) onto FS-126 which leads to the Middle Fork Boise River and Atlanta. FS-126

is a primitive road not suited for passenger cars. It usually does not open until late June. Once FS-156 reaches the Middle Fork Boise River Road (FS-268), turn east onto this road and follow it to Atlanta.

(a) **FST-460, Middle Fork Trail.** The Powerhouse CG and trailhead are 1.5 miles north of Atlanta. The Middle Fork Trail leads generally north into the heart of the Sawtooths, where it links with the Sawtooths' many other trails. It is roughly 15 miles from the trailhead to Spangle Lake, where the route intersects with FST-462/FST-463.

(b) **FST-462/FST-463, Spangle Lake Trail.** This trail loops from the South Fork Payette River and FST-452 [(B)(3)(b)] south up Benedict Creek to intersect with FST-458 [(B)(5)(a)], then turns southwest and traverses past Robert Jackson Lake and Lake Ingeborg to Spangle Lake. At this lake, the trail intersects with FST-460 [(B)(4)(a)]. From this point, the trail turns north and runs to Ardeth Lake. It then descends along Tenlake Creek to rejoin the South Fork Payette and FS-452 [(B)(2)(a)].

(5) **FS-206, Queens River Road.** The Queens River transfer camp is located northeast of Atlanta. From Atlanta, drive 4.5 miles west on FS-168 to the Queens River CG. Turn north on FS-206 and follow it to the trailhead. The trailhead is located at the point where the Little Queens River flows into the Queens River. Trails lead up both drainages.

(a) **FST-458, Queens River Trail.** FST-458 follows the Queens River north for 9 miles to its headwaters near Mount Everly. Eight miles from the trailhead, it intersects with FST-494 [(B)(6)(a.1)], which leads west over a divide past Arrowhead and Pats Lakes to a junction with FST-459 [(B)(6)(a) and (B)(5)(b)]. FST-459 accesses the Little Queens River and Johnson Creek drainages, respectively. From this junction, FST-458 crosses a divide on the north slopes of Mount Everly and connects with FST-462 [(B)(4)(b)] in the Benedict Creek drainage. The trail then climbs south to cross a high pass and leads to the headwaters of the Little Queens River [(B)(5)(a)].

(b) **FST-454, Little Queens River Trail.** This trail follows the Little Queens River for 9 miles to a junction with FST-459 [(B)(6)(a)], which leads west to Graham. It also intersects with FST-494 [(B)(6)(a.1)], which leads east to the Queens River drainage.

(b.1) **FST-456, Scenic Creek Trail.** FST-456 is a side trail that leads into the country around Scenic and Flat Top Lakes. Access the trail 6 miles north of the Queens River Transfer Camp. Once on this trail, follow one fork 3.5 miles to Scenic Lakes; the other goes about 3 miles to Flat Top Lakes.

(6) **Graham GS Road.** Turn off ID-21 at Edna Creek CG and follow FS-384 for 4 miles to FS-312. Turn north on FS-312 and drive 23 miles on a rugged road to the Graham GS area. This trip requires a 4WD and some driving skill.

(a) FST-156/FST-459, Bayhorse Creek/Johnson Creek Trails. Access these trails from FS-312 just before it reaches the North Fork Boise River (north of the Graham GS). From this point, the trail crosses Cow Creek and then parallels Bayhorse Creek to the southeast for 3.5 miles until it intersects with FST-459 and Johnson Creek at the boundary of the SBW. From this junction, it is 5 miles to a second junction where FST-459 turns south and crosses into the Little Queens River drainage and FST-494 [(B)(6)(a.1)]. FST-494 then runs east toward Pats Lake and Mount Everly.

(a.1) FST-494, Pats Lake Trail. This trail leaves FST-459 and runs east to join FST-458 in the Upper Queens River drainage. It is 2.6 miles to Pats Lake and 6.9 miles to the Queens River from the junction.

6

THE SMOKY MOUNTAINS

The Smoky Mountains are located on the west side of the Big Wood River Valley, the home of Ketchum and Sun Valley. The range extends south from the Sawtooth Range 40 miles to the flats of the Camas Prairie. The Big Wood River and ID-75 form the range's eastern boundary, while the South Fork Boise River and the Soldier Mountains flank its western side.

Geologists believe that the Smoky Mountains were originally forced up when the nearby Idaho Batholith was implanted 90 to 60 million years ago. The peaks are composed of deteriorated metamorphic and granite-like rocks that reach a high point of 10,441 feet on Saviers Peak. More recently, block faulting has occurred, causing the Big Wood River Valley to sink in relation to the Smoky and Boulder Mountains. Consequently, the Smoky Mountains have developed a steep eastern facade that contrasts sharply with the range's western slopes, which merge almost invisibly into the Boise and Soldier Mountains.

Besides the nine summits that exceed 10,000 feet, the range includes equally rewarding sub-9,000 peaks, exquisite mountain lakes, and a large herd of mountain goats. The Smoky Mountains are administered by the Sawtooth National Forest in the south and the Sawtooth National Recreation Area (SNRA) in the north. Logging and grazing are the primary consumptive uses.

The quality of vehicle access points within this range is above average because of the economic power of the Ketchum/Sun Valley resort centers. The Forest Service is regularly improving access points and, for the most part, Smoky Mountain trails are in tip-top shape. The major Smoky peaks of interest to climbers are located north of Ketchum between Baker Peak and Galena Summit. All are reached by Class 2 or Class 3 routes. The southern end of the range contains a maze of canyons and peaks with excellent opportunities for solitude.

Titus Peak*   *10,110 feet (Class 2)*
Titus Peak, which features a rugged north/south summit ridge, is the northernmost major summit on the Smoky Mountain skyline. It is 2.5 miles south of Galena Summit and 0.6 mile east of Bromaghin Peak. William Titus was a member of T. M. Bannon's 1915 USGS survey party. The summit can be climbed from either Titus Lake or Galena Summit. The recommended route begins at Galena Summit and follows the connecting ridgeline without much difficulty. An unmaintained trail follows the first 1.5 miles of the ridgeline from Galena Summit [(A)(1)(b)]. The trail ends at Point 10005, where there is a good view of Titus Peak to the south. The remaining ridge sections to the top of Titus Peak are well defined and present no objective problems to those experienced with cross-country travel. It is 2.6 miles from Galena Summit to the top of the peak. USGS Galena

Bromaghin Peak   *10,225 feet (Class 3)*
This peak is named after Captain Ralph Bromaghin, a former Sun Valley ski instructor and member of the 10th Mountain Division, who lost his life in World War II. It is 0.6 mile southwest of Titus Peak. The peak can be climbed from Owl Creek or by traversing the ridge from Titus Peak. Following the ridge from Titus is Class 2 until the final short section up the east face, which is Class 3. The route stays on the south side of the broken face and then follows the obvious gully to the top. From Owl Creek [(A)(2)], follow the drainage up to the saddle between Titus and Bromaghin and climb the face to the summit as described above. USGS Galena

Saviers Peak*   *10,441 feet (Class 3)*
Many local people call this peak Silver Peak. However, because there is an officially named Silver Peak due east across the

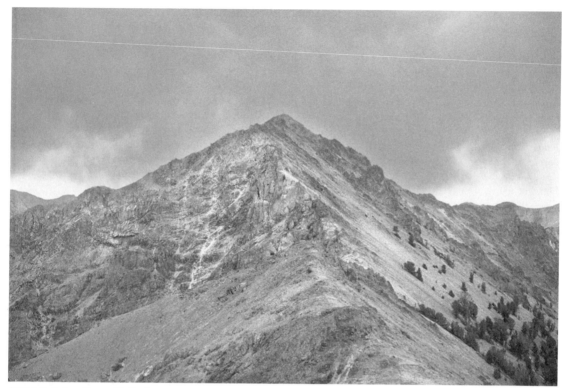

Saviers Peak from Bromaghin Peak

valley in the Boulder Mountains, it may be more appropriate to name the peak after Mr. and Mrs. George Saviers. They climbed the peak on their honeymoon in 1947 and left a register on the summit in a Band-Aid can. The peak is located 0.5 mile south of Bromaghin Peak on the main Smoky Mountain crest. Both the north ridge from Bromaghin Peak and the east ridge from Owl Creek have been climbed.

From the summit of Bromaghin Peak (see route description above) follow the ridgeline south to the summit. Pass the rocky ribs that bar the top of the ridgeline on the west and scramble up the final summit blocks on the west side. To climb the peak from Owl Creek [(A)(2)], most scramblers ascend the east ridge to reach a point just south of the summit. However, since the east side terrain is open in nature, several suitable lines can be followed to the summit. USGS Galena

Norton Peak 10,336 feet (Class 2)
Norton Peak stands east of the main Smoky Mountain crest, forming a rugged island surrounded by forest. The summit is

9 miles southeast of Saviers Peak, and directly east of Miner Lake. The rocky upper slopes, one of the best places in the state for viewing mountain goats, provide a super view of the Boulder Mountain crest across the valley. This summit is easily reached from the saddle between Miner Lake and upper Norton Lake and FST-135 [(A)(4)(b)]. From either of these lakes, follow the seldom-maintained trail that links the lakes with the saddle above. From the saddle, climb east up through a stand of pines to the rocky slopes above and then to the ridge top. From the top of the ridge, the route is obvious, running north along the summit ridge. Stay as close as possible to the ridge crest as you make the traverse. USGS Galena

Prairie Creek Peak* 10,138 feet (Class 2)
Prairie Creek Peak is located 1.5 miles southwest of Norton Peak on the Smoky Mountains crest. When viewed from Prairie Lakes, it forms the large pyramid directly to the south. To reach its summit, hike to the saddle south of upper Prairie Lake on FST-134 [(A)(3)(a)]. From the saddle, gradually work your way to the east up the peak's west ridge,

skirting a couple of small rock towers on the ridge's south side. USGS Baker Peak

Peak 10099   *10,099 feet (Class 2-3)*
This peak, which provides the stunning backdrop for Baker Lake, is found 1.4 miles north of Baker Peak. Its north, south, and east ridges are easy scrambles. The most direct route is from Baker Lake [(A)(4)(a)]. USGS Baker Peak

Baker Peak   *10,174 feet (Class 2)*
Baker is one of the most elusive Smoky Mountain peaks, hidden from ID-75 because it sits far back (more than 10 miles from the highway) and views are obstructed by intervening ridges. It is 6.5 miles southwest of Norton Peak on the range's main crest. Approach the peak by hiking to Baker Lake [(A)(4)(a)] and then hiking on FST-211 [(A)(4)(a.1)] to the saddle just north of Baker Peak. Leave the trail and follow the ridge to the summit. USGS Baker Peak

Peak 10137   *10,137 feet (Class 2)*
The southernmost 10,000-foot summit in the Smoky Mountains is 0.8 mile southeast of Baker Peak, on the main crest. Although this mountain's relatively gentle slopes can be climbed from almost any direction, access considerations make a ridge traverse from Baker Peak the best choice. USGS Baker Peak

Big Peak   *10,047 feet (Class 2)*
Big Peak, located 2.6 miles west of Baker Peak, is one of the more isolated 10,000-foot peaks in the state. The shortest route to the summit is to leave FST-211 [(A)(4)(a.1)] at the saddle north of Baker Peak and then follow the ridge north to Point 9956. From this point, take a subsidiary ridge due west for 2 miles to where it turns south and climb to the peak's summit. USGS Baker Peak

Bear Peak   *9,525 feet (Class 2)*
Bear Peak sits 10 miles due west of Ketchum and 4.5 miles east of Baker Peak. From the Warm Springs Creek Road, take FST-168 [(A)(7)(a)] up Bart Gulch to a point near the summit on the peak's southwest slopes. From this point, scramble to the top. It is roughly 3 miles one way. USGS Boyle Mountain

Griffin Butte   *8,411 feet (Class 2)*
Griffin Butte is just north of Ketchum above Adams Gulch. Hiking this peak is a totally scenic experience with super vistas of Bald Mountain and the entire Ketchum area. The ascent begins at the Adams Gulch trailhead [(A)(6)(a)]. From

the trailhead, take FST-142 north and then northwest for roughly 1 mile to the Butte's south slope, where you can leave the trail and hike cross-country to the summit. USGS Griffin Butte

Bald Mountain   *9,151 feet (Class 1)*
Home of the Sun Valley Ski Resort's main downhill ski runs, this is the most famous of Idaho's many "Bald" mountains. To reach the summit in the summer, hike the summit trail that begins at the River Run Lodge on the east side of the mountain. Although not a wilderness experience, the strenuous hike leads to unsurpassed views of this impressive area. USGS Griffin Butte

Dollarhide Mountain   *9,301 feet (Class 2)*
Dollarhide Mountain is situated 4 miles due south of Baker Peak. It is the first summit north of Dollarhide Summit on the Warm Springs Creek Road [(A)(7)]. From Ketchum, drive to the summit, park, and then hike 1.25 miles on the ridgeline north to the summit. USGS Dollarhide Mountain

Shaw Mountain   *9,650 feet (Class 2)*
Shaw mountain is located 1.5 miles east of Dollarhide Mountain. The two mountains are connected by an arcing ridgeline that is easily traversed from Dollarhide Mountain. USGS Dollarhide Mountain

Peak 9175   *9,175 feet (Class 2)*
This unnamed peak with a 3-mile summit ridge is located 6 miles southeast of Shaw Mountain near the head of Wilson Creek. Climb the peak by taking FST-223 [(B)(1)(a)] to the ridgeline north of the summit and then follow the ridge and an old trail to the summit. USGS Buttercup Mountain

Buttercup Mountain   *9,075 feet (Class 2)*
Buttercup, an attractive summit when viewed from the mouth of Wilson Creek, is 2 miles south of Peak 9175. Its summit is protected by steep slopes on all sides and is capped by a small dome. The peak can be reached from two directions. The first is from the Deer Creek drainage. From the end of the Deer Creek Road [(A)(9)(a)], take FST-158 for 1 mile and then FST-160 for 3 miles up Curran Gulch to the peak's south ridge. Leave the trail at this point and follow the ridge north to the summit. The second route approaches from the south and Wilson Creek [(B)(1)]. From the Buttercup Mine, just above the highest ruins (7,200 feet), hike due east and straight up the slope to the ridge top above. Follow the ridge northeast to 8,000 feet. Cross into the draw to the southeast

and follow the draw up to the ridge top—just south of Point 8854. Once on this ridge top, the summit is an easy 0.5 mile to the southeast. USGS Buttercup Mountain

Kelly Mountain   *8,827 feet*
Kelly is the southernmost Smoky Mountain terrain to rise above 8,000 feet. It is located 6 miles east/southeast of Buttercup Mountain. It is an excellent objective with superb views of the mountains to the north and the Camas Prairie to the south. Access is from the Croy Creek Road [(A)(10) or (B)(1)]. USGS Richardson Summit

East Ridge. Leave the Croy Creek Road at Red Elephant Gulch. Drive up the gulch to Red Elephant Mine and park. Hike the old road west up the gulch to its end. Turn south and climb to the top of the east ridge at 7,800 feet. Follow the ridge to the summit.

South Ridge. Leave the Croy Creek Road at Kelly Gulch. Follow the road north for roughly 1 mile to a fork in the road. Follow the old mining road uphill and due north to the digs about 200 feet above. Continue up the ridge until it flattens out at 7,500 feet. Turn and follow the south ridge north to the summit. This is a long, but enjoyable walk.

APPROACHES TO THE SMOKY MOUNTAINS

(A) ID-75 ACCESS POINTS

This well-maintained state highway is the major north/south corridor between Shoshone and Challis. It provides access along the entire eastern slope of the Smoky Mountains. ID-75 access points are described from north to south.

(1) Galena Summit Area. ID-75 crosses this pass north of Ketchum and then descends into the Stanley Basin. (The pass is the point where the Smoky and Boulder Mountains meet).

(a) FST-190, Titus Lake Trail. The south trail begins on the south side of Galena Summit, just before ID-75 reaches the top, on the last sharp switchback. Park across the road in the large turnout. The trail follows a jeep road a short distance and then contours around the ridges to 8,900-foot-elevation Titus Lake in just 2 miles.

(b) Galena Ridge/Titus Peak Route. From the Titus Lake trailhead, continue following the old road (the beginning of FST-190) past the sign for that trail. This road contours around the draw and ends up at the ridge top directly above the point where ID-75 passes over Galena Summit. From this point, a good, but unofficial trail goes directly up the ridge. There are excellent views along the ridge of both the Big Wood River Valley and the

Stanley Basin. The trail ends in about 1.5 miles on Point 10005.

(2) FS-181, Owl Creek Jeep Trail. Turn off ID-75 roughly 20 miles north of Ketchum. FS-181 immediately fords the Big Wood River and then runs up this drainage for 3 miles to the base of both Saviers and Bromaghin Peaks. It is best to park at ID-75 and walk this road, which otherwise requires a 4WD.

(3) FS-179, Prairie Creek Road. This road leaves ID-75 approximately 18 miles north of Ketchum and runs west 2.5 miles into the Smokys to the Prairie Creek trailhead. This dirt road is often rutted and can cause problems for passenger cars.

(a) FST-134, Prairie Lakes. From the end of the Prairie Creek Road, a well-maintained trail leads to Prairie Lakes and then continues, climbing over a pass just north of Prairie Creek Peak. The trail is roughly 5 miles long.

(b) FST-135, Miner Lake Trail. FST-135 leaves Prairie Creek Road 2.5 miles from ID-75 and climbs to Miner Lake in 4 miles [(A)(4)(b)]. From the lake, the trail climbs over a subsidiary crest of the Smoky Mountains to Norton Lakes.

(4) FS-162, Baker Creek Road. This good gravel road leaves ID-75 15.8 miles north of the traffic light in Ketchum and leads 9.5 miles into the heart of the Smoky Mountains, to near the base of Baker Mountain.

(a) FST-138, Baker Lake Trail. FST-138 begins at the end of the Baker Creek Road. A steep, 2-mile hike brings you to Baker Lake at the base of an unnamed peak. From Baker Lake, the trail runs due north and joins with FST-134 [(A)(4)(c)] at Norton Creek.

(a.1) FST-211, Baker Creek/West Fork Cutoff Trail. This trail runs between Baker Lake and West Fork Creek by crossing the Smoky Mountain divide just north of Baker Peak.

(b) FST-135, Norton Lake Trail. To reach the trailhead, drive 6 miles up the Baker Creek Road and then turn right on a signed road, which is rough but generally passable to autos. Follow this road 1.2 miles to the trailhead. The trail to Norton Lakes is well maintained and reaches the first lake in 3.5 miles and the second lake in another 0.5 mile. From the second lake, the trail climbs up to a saddle just north of Norton Peak and then drops down to Miner Lake and the Prairie Creek drainage [(A)(3)(b)].

(5) Lake Creek Trailhead. This trailhead is found on ID-75, roughly 2.5 miles north of Ketchum. It has a large parking lot complemented by a good bridge across the Wood River. Several different trails are accessible from this point. This is a popular area for day hikers, mountain bikers, and runners in the summer and cross-country skiers in the winter.

(6) FS-141, Adams Gulch Trailhead. This road leaves ID-75 1.6 miles north of Ketchum. Turn west onto the signed road, which serves as a trailhead for two important trails.

(a) FST-142, Adams Gulch High Trail. FST-142 leaves FS-141 just past the forest boundary. This is one of the best—and least known—high routes in Idaho. The trail climbs north toward Griffin Butte and then turns west to rejoin the Adams Gulch Trail in 6 miles. From this point, the trail runs east along a high ridgeline for another 7 miles to Lost Shirt Gulch, where it intersects with FST-212. FST-212 drops north down a gulch to Baker Creek and FS-162 [(A)(4)]. FST-145, FST-144, and FST-168 are all feeder trails that connect the High Trail with the Warm Springs Creek Road [(A)(7)].

(b) FST-177, Adams Gulch Trail. FST-177 leaves the end of FS-141 and runs up Adams Gulch for 4 miles, where it connects with FST-142.

(7) FS-227, Warm Springs Creek Road. This road leaves ID-75 in Ketchum just north of downtown. Look for the road that forks off to the west just past the restaurant in a railcar. The road twists and turns for 19 miles to the Dollarhide Summit. From the summit, the road continues for another 16 miles to the Big Smoky Fire Camp on the South Fork Boise River.

(a) FST-168, Bear Gulch Trail. FST-168 leaves FS-227 as a two-track road 4 miles west of Warfield Hot Springs. The road soon ends and the trail continues up Bear Gulch and eventually past the west slopes of Bear Peak to join with FST-142 [(A)(6)(a)] in 4.5 miles.

(8) FS-117, Greenhorn Gulch Road Area. This road, which is a little more than 4 miles long, leaves ID-75 5 miles south of Ketchum. FST-156 is at the road's end; a good loop hike with many side trails.

(9) FS-097, Deer Creek Road Area. This road begins at ID-75 8 miles south of Ketchum. The Deer Creek Road is part of an extensive road and trail system that sees little use by hikers despite the enjoyable nature of the terrain.

(a) FST-158/FST-160, Curran Gulch Trails. From the end of FS-097, these trails combine to climb up to the ridgeline just south of Buttercup Mountain in 3 miles. FST-160 then runs south along the Smoky Mountain crest to Wolftone Creek.

(10) Croy Creek Road. Access this road from either Hailey or US-20 east of Fairfield. The road departs west from Hailey at the center of town and crosses BLM and private land. Red Elephant Gulch, reached in roughly 6 miles, is signed. Kelly Gulch is another mile further west. If dry, a 4WD is not required, but one is recommended for the side roads.

(B) US-20 ACCESS POINTS

US-20 runs between Mountain Home and Carey.

(1) FS-017, Willow Creek Road/Buttercup Mountain Access. This road is accessed from US-20 11 miles east of Fairfield. Turn north and follow the road toward the mountains. In 10.3 mile you will reach FS-248. The main road continues up Willow Creek for a couple of miles. To reach Buttercup Mountain, turn right and follow FS-248 east. In 2 miles the road reaches an old bridge that is probably unsafe to cross. The road is washed out in 0.5 mile, but does continue past the Buttercup mine shaft, which is up to the left.

(a) FST-223, Willow Creek Trail. This trail leaves the end of the Willow Creek Road and climbs up to the Smoky Mountain crest in 3.2 miles. Along the crest, there are junctions with several designated trails. One runs south to Peak 9157, another runs north toward Dollarhide Summit, and a third drops into the twisted country to the east.

7

THE SOLDIER MOUNTAINS

The Soldier Mountains are located north of Fairfield at the southern edge of the central Idaho mountains. They cover a roughly triangular piece of real estate 30 miles wide and 15 miles long from north to south. The range is bordered by the Camas Prairie in the south, the South Fork Boise River in the north and west, and the Smoky Mountains in the east.

Physically, the range is nearly indistinguishable from the Smoky Mountains. Soldier Mountain topography is characterized by long, winding drainages and high, grass-covered ridges. While there are only two dominant summits—10,095-foot Smoky Dome and 9,694-foot Iron Mountain—both are exceptional scrambling goals. The Soldiers are dry mountains with a few stands of really dense timber that cluster on the north and eastern slopes and along the stream bottoms. The upper slopes of the highest ridges are alpine in nature. A few small lakes dot the slopes around Smoky Dome and Iron Mountain.

The Sawtooth National Forest manages almost the entire range through its Fairfield Ranger District. The BLM and the state control a few sections of land in the southern foothills. Recreational use of the Soldiers is increasing and consumptive uses are decreasing. The Soldiers are a prime wildlife habitat populated by large deer herds.

Although the Soldier Mountains are outside the hiking mainstream, the range is an exceptional recreational destination. Climbers will want to include Smoky Dome and Iron Mountain on their lists of "must do" peaks. Hikers venturing into these mountains will find that the hiking is as good as it gets. The views, the many miles of seldom-used trails, and the terrain, which is conducive to cross-country travel, contribute to an enticing mountain environment.

Road access to the Soldier Mountains begins from ID-20, which runs east to west past the range's southern flanks. The Forest Service maintains a good system of roads along the perimeter of the range and from Fairfield into the heart of the range. Some roads are well signed and maintained while others are hard to find. But, on the whole, access is acceptable. Trails pierce almost every corner of the range. Trail maintenance varies in quality, but has improved significantly over the last ten years.

Smoky Dome   10,095 feet
Smoky Dome dominates the east end of the Soldier Mountains and forms an attractive backdrop behind Fairfield. The big, crown-shaped mountain not only rises 5,000 feet above the Camas Prairie, but also stands from 1,000 to 1,200 feet above every peak in the range except Iron Mountain. Views from the summit of Smoky Dome take in a huge chunk of Idaho from the Sawtooths in the north to the Camas Prairie and Mount Bennet Hills in the south. Trinity and Steele Mountains are visible in the distance to the west, and the main crest of the Pioneer Mountains dominates the view to the east. The peak is a massive mountain with a half-dozen points above 9,000 feet on subsidiary ridges. The north summit reaches 9,937 feet and sports massive, unstable rock cliffs. USGS Fairfield

The Grand Tour (Class 2). In terms of nearby roads and trails, the highest peak in the Soldier Mountains is quite remote. Climbing Smoky Dome by this route involves a long, difficult approach hike. The route begins at the end of FS-093 [(A)(1.1)(a)]. From the road's end, follow the closed road up the South Fork Soldier Creek for 2 miles until it ends just after crossing the creek. After crossing the creek where the road runs downhill and dies out, there is a small clearing where FST-087 vaguely runs off through the trees and proceeds up the creek to the west. From this point, leave the road/trail and climb up to the ridge top to the south. Once on the ridge, the route follows the ridgeline west for several miles. Most of the ridge is traversed by a sheepherder's trail and though it is brushy in places, following it is not difficult. The ridge eventually joins the eastern slopes of Smoky Dome

below the north peak. From this point, traverse south across the meadows and talus to the saddle between the main and north peaks. It is a steep but easy scramble to both summits from this saddle. The north summit is an easy Class 2 ascent via its south ridge or east face. This route is roughly 5.5 miles in length and gains more than 4,000 feet of elevation. The Sydney and Boardman Peak USGS quads will be helpful in following this route.

Other Routes. The open nature of the Soldier Mountains makes it possible to approach the peak from almost any direction. Southern approaches would be shorter, but private land increases access problems.

Iron Mountain   9,694 feet (Class 1)
Rising to 9,694 feet, Iron Mountain is the big mountain 7 miles northwest of Smoky Dome. Its summit is a long way from anywhere, which is one of its main attractions. A fire lookout sits on the summit of this impressive rock pile. Heart Lake, the largest of the Soldier Mountain lakes, can be found just northeast of the summit. You can approach the summit, which is reached by trail, from almost any direction. The shortest approach to the summit is from the north via FST-052. This route begins along the South Fork Boise River 4,000 feet below the summit. Follow FST-052, FST-053, and FST-050 to the top [(B)(1)(a)]. The second approach begins in the west and follows FST-048 and FST-050 [(B)(2)(a)] to the summit. The hike to the summit is more than 11 miles making the round trip more than 22 miles. The highlight of this route is the long hike along a ridge known as Blue Ridge that parallels the main Soldier Mountain crest. The trail along this ridge "flows" for miles above tree line reminding hikers of the movie *The Sound of Music.* USGS Jumbo Mountain

Couch Peak   8,551 feet (Class 2)
Couch Peak served the USGS as a triangulation station and you will know why when you visit its summit. The view is all encompassing. Couch Peak sits on the eastern edge of the Soldier Mountains between Couch summit and Wells Summit on a high ridgeline. Hike to the summit from FS-095 [(A)(1.2)]. Park on Wells Summit and follow the arching ridgeline northwest to the summit, which is less than 3 up-and-down miles away. USGS Sydney Butte

Cannonball Mountain   8,330 feet (Class 2)
Liberal Mountain   8,265 feet (Class 2)
These two peaks form the high ground on Soldier Mountain's eastern end between Wells Summit and Willow Creek. The terrain is mixed trees and open slopes and the summits can be

Iron Mountain, viewed from Smoky Dome

reached from almost any direction. The recommended route is from Wells Summit and FS-095 [(A)(1.2)], because it allows for a high start. From the pass, it is 3 miles to Cannonball and another 3 to Liberal Mountain. The views of the Camas Prairie to the south from Cannonball are spectacular. USGS Cannonball Mountain

APPROACHES TO
THE SOLDIER MOUNTAINS

(A) FAIRFIELD ACCESS POINTS

Access through Fairfield leads into the central portion of the range and also to the southern portions of the Smoky Mountains. Turn north off US-20 and drive through downtown Fairfield, following the signs for the Soldier Mountain Ski Area. In 2 miles, the road enters the village of Soldier, where it jogs to the east for a short distance and then quickly turns back to the north to become FS-094.

(1) FS-094, Couch Summit Road. This good gravel road is a continuation of the Soldier Mountain Road. It leads north and intersects with FS-093 in 5 miles. FS-094 continues north from this junction to Couch summit and then drops down Little Smoky Creek to the South Fork Boise River.

(1.1) FS-093, Soldier Creek Road. This road forks off FS-094 and, shortly after passing by the Soldier Mountain Ski Area, crosses a cattleguard and ends just past the mouth of the South Fork Soldier Creek. There are several campsites here and plenty of parking. The road up the South Fork is closed.

(a) Soldier Creek Trail System. From the end of FS-094, there is access to an extensive trail system that penetrates most of the higher elevations of the Soldier Mountains. An old road (not shown on the newest Forest Service map) runs up the South Fork Soldier Creek. The road, which is closed to vehicles, connects with FST-087 and FST-185. Also, from the end of FS-093, FST-005 runs up North Fork Soldier Creek and eventually connects with FST-087.

(1.2) FS-095, Wells Summit Road. This road leaves FS-094 4.1 miles north of Soldier at a signed junction. It ascends Wardrop Creek to 7,040-foot Wells Summit and then descends Basalt Creek to Smoky Creek and FS-015.

(B) ANDERSON RANCH RESERVOIR ACCESS POINTS.

This reservoir on the South Fork Boise River divides the Soldier Mountains from the Boise Mountains. Begin in Mountain Home. Leave I-84 at exit 95 and turn onto US-20. The Anderson Ranch/Featherville turnoff is 31.9 miles ahead. Turn north off the highway and follow a good paved road to Pine and Featherville. Featherville is a central hub for access into this entire area; services are available from early summer through hunting season.

(1) FS-227, South Fork Boise River Road. From Featherville, FS-227 winds along the South Fork Boise River to Little Smoky Creek, where it connects with FS-094 [(A)(1)], which goes south to Fairfield. Many trails lead into the Soldier Mountains from this road.

(a) FST-052, FST-053, and FST-050, Iron Mountain Trail. This trailhead is roughly 11 miles east of Featherville. The trail, a main thoroughfare into the western part of the Soldier Mountains, intersects with every trail in the area. From the Boise River, it is 9.5 miles to the summit of Iron Mountain. To reach the trailhead, turn south off FS-227 at the sign for Baumgartner CG. After the road crosses the river, it forks. Take the right fork, which parallels the south fork of the river and runs west. Follow this road to its end at Kelly Creek in a little more than 1 mile.

(2) Iron Mountain Access via Blue Ridge. To reach Iron Mountain from the west, leave the Featherville Road on FS-166, the Grouse Creek Road. This road system winds through the western end of the Soldier Mountains and many unmapped side roads fork off of it. Besides the Boise National Forest map, the USGS quads will help you find the FST-048 trailhead. Follow FS-166 east up Grouse Creek. At 5.3 miles, there is a major intersection. Go right. The next junction is at 6.9 miles. Go right again. At 8.9 miles and the next intersection, turn left. At 10.8 miles, the road reaches another intersection. Turn left on a road designated FS-166N. FS-166N is less used than FS-166, which drops down into the North Fork Lime Creek. At mile 11.1, go left, and at mile 11.6, go right. At mile 12, turn right onto a unmaintained track which ends at 12.1 miles on a broad ridge top. Look for the trail that drops into the saddle to the north.

(a) FST-048. From the undeveloped trailhead, follow FST-048 north along the west side of the ridge across a saddle and then along the east side of Grouse Butte. North of Grouse Butte, the trail crosses and then joins FST-044. The two trails then drop down into the North Fork Lime Creek. After 0.25 mile, you will reach a junction. FST-044 continues down the drainage and FST-048 climbs steeply out of the drainage and into a saddle. The trail switches back out of this saddle and heads east along a broad grass and sagebrush-covered ridge. The trail wanders from side to side and up and down along this ridge until it reaches a junction with FST-055. Go left onto FST-055 and descend onto the flats to the north that are below Iron Mountain. The next junction is with FST-053 [(B)(1)(a)], which climbs up from the South Fork Boise River. Go right at this junction continue toward the peak. Just below the face, there is another junction with a trail that leads off to the east. Continue up Iron Mountain on the old road.

EASTERN IDAHO

From Idaho-75 and US-93 East to the Wyoming Border; From Montana South to the Snake River

1

THE WHITE CLOUD MOUNTAINS

The White Cloud Mountains are located southeast of Stanley and lie totally within the boundaries of the Sawtooth National Recreation Area (SNRA). The range is oval-shaped and about 22 miles long and 20 miles wide. It was uplifted by forces associated with the placement of the Idaho and Sawtooth Batholiths. Over the eons, the range has eroded into its present maze of divides and drainages. The highest peaks are clustered together in the center of the range and guarded by an extensive system of foothills. The Salmon River flanks the range's western and northern boundaries, while the East Fork Salmon River flanks its eastern and southeastern sides. In the southwest, the White Clouds and the Boulder Mountains merge with no definite division between them.

The geologic history of the range is highlighted by the Pleistocene Ice Age. Glaciers extensively carved the White Cloud rock into gracious peaks, sweeping canyons, and beautiful lake basins containing more than one hundred lakes. The White Clouds take their name from the extensive deposits of white limestone in the northwestern portion of the range, which looked like white cumulus clouds to the early settlers who named the range in the late 1800s. The highest elevation is 11,815 feet at the summit of Castle Peak. A group of fourteen peaks, all over 10,000 feet, is specifically known as the White Cloud Peaks. Many of the range's most rugged summits are unnamed.

The entire range is managed by the SNRA except for several private holdings that evolved primarily from mining claims. The presence of gold and silver brought mining activity to these mountains as early as the 1880s. The remains of this activity can be found in the Fourth of July, Three Cabins, and Washington Basin drainages. It is possible that mining

Mount Church: A classic eastern Idaho peak

activity will resume within the range. Pressure from mining interests continues to prevent Congress from declaring the range a designated wilderness. Despite the mining issue, the Forest Service manages the range primarily for recreational pursuits—a perfect use for what is probably Idaho's most varied mountain range. The upper reaches of the White Clouds are generally a barren, treeless world of alpine meadow and rock, which contrasts sharply with the dense stands of Douglas fir and lodgepole pine that blanket the intermediate slopes and the sagebrush and grasses that cover the foothills. During the short summer season, the combination of wildflowers, water, and jagged rock are unbeatable.

Vehicle access points to the range's trailheads are plentiful, although many roads are too rough for passenger cars. The SNRA is slowly upgrading roadways. The range contains many miles of trails, most in good to excellent shape. The Boulder Lake and Little Boulder Chain of Lakes areas, the busiest spots in the range, are the only areas that can be considered crowded. Climbing opportunities range from Class 1 through Class 3. Although a number of faces are appealing, technical climbing is generally out of the question because of the shattered nature of the rock.

Lookout Mountain   *9,954 feet (Class 1)*
Lookout Mountain is located in the northeast corner of the White Cloud Mountains, 9 miles east of Stanley. It is separated from the main group of White Cloud Peaks, which are 4 miles to the southeast, by the massive Warm Springs Creek drainage. This peak, an old fire lookout site, offers an exceptional view of the Sawtooths to the west as well as the surrounding mountains. It is reached by taking the Rough Creek Trail [(A)(4)(a)] or the Casino Lake Trail [(A)(3)(a)] to the point where they join FST-647, and then following FST-647 to the summit. The shortest approach (5.5 miles) is via Rough Creek. The lookout is no longer in use, but the Forest Service leaves it open for public use—please help keep it clean. USGS Casino Lakes

Potaman Peak   *9,376 feet (Class 1-2)*
Potaman Peak is situated in the northeastern corner of the range. It is an impressive hunk of volcanic rock that once had a fire lookout on its summit. The remains of the old lookout tower are still visible. The peak is located 3 miles directly south of Clayton. Its craggy summit dominates the surrounding country. In addition to the great views of the high White Cloud Peaks, from its summit you can view the Lost River Range's crest from Challis south to Mount McCaleb, the northern Lemhi Range, the northern Boulder Mountains,

and the Salmon River Mountains from Twin Peaks to Cabin Creek Peak. The best approach to the summit is from Jimmy Smith Lake via Forest Service trails 177, 617, and 247. The final 1.25 miles to the summit is more akin to cross-country travel since the trail has not been maintained in years [(B)(1)(a) and (a.1)]. USGS Potaman Peak

WCP-1*   *10,353 feet (Class 2)*
WCP-1 is the northernmost peak of the group designated as the White Cloud Peaks by the USGS. Located 5.5 miles southeast of Lookout Mountain, its summit is just 0.75 mile west of Hoodoo Lake. Access to this peak is via FS-666 and the Hoodoo Lake Trail [(A)(5)(b)], which leads to Hoodoo Lake. From Hoodoo Lake, hike into the cirque southwest of the lake until the slope grows steeper, then turn due north and hike directly toward the summit. USGS Robinson Bar

WCP-2*   *10,271 feet (Class 2)*
WCP-2 is located 1.2 miles southwest of WCP-1, just north of Swimm Lake. The peak can be climbed from Swimm Lake—the catch is that there is no trail to Swimm Lake. To reach the lake, hike cross-country up Swimm Creek from FST-671 [(A)(2)(a.1.1)] or begin in Iron Basin [(A)(2)(a.1.1.1) or (5)(c)] and climb into the Swimm Lake basin from the south over the saddle between WCP-4 and WCP-5 (a steep, grungy crossing). If you manage to get to the lake, climb from Swimm Lake to the saddle east of the summit and then follow the ridge to the summit. USGS Robinson Bar

WCP-3*   *10,588 feet (Class 2)*
This pyramid-shaped summit is located 0.75 mile south of WCP-1, just north of Swimm Lake. (See WCP-2 for approach information.) Climb from Swimm Lake via either the west or south ridges. Gaining either ridge involves crossing a considerable amount of loose scree, reportedly the hardest part of the climb. USGS Robinson Bar

WCP-4*   *10,450 feet (Class 3)*
WCP-4 is found 0.6 mile north of Watson Peak and 1.5 miles southwest of WCP-3. The peak is accessed from Iron Basin [(A)(2)(a.1.1.1) or (5)(c)]. From the general area where the trail crosses the 9,200-foot contour line on the USGS quad, climb northwest to the peak's east ridge, which leads to the summit. USGS Robinson Bar

WCP-5*   *10,597 feet (Class 3)*
WCP-5 is a three-sided column that rises precipitously for its last 600 feet. It is situated 1 mile east of WCP-4, just north of

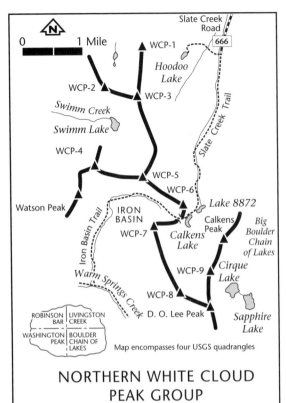

NORTHERN WHITE CLOUD PEAK GROUP

(A)(5)(c)] where it crosses Ocalkens Pass just south of the peak. Leave the trail at the pass and climb the south ridge, which rises 650 feet to the summit. USGS Robinson Bar

WCP-7*   *10,777 feet (Class 3)*
WCP-7 presents a bold, pyramid-shaped east face to Ocalkens Lake. It sits 0.7 mile due south of WCP-6 and Iron Basin. Access the peak's north ridge from the Iron Basin Trail [(A)(2)(a.1.1.1) or (A)(5)(c)]. The route climbs the north ridge and east face. The peak's north ridge is rugged and steep at first, but still Class 2. After it abuts the east face, the route becomes Class 3, with a little exposure in two places. Stay on the ridge top when possible. (Climbing the peak from other directions is possible, but this route provides the shortest access.) USGS Washington Peak/Robinson Bar

Caulkens Peak*   *11,500+ feet (Class 3)*
This peak is located 1.6 miles due east of WCP-7, just west of Tin Cup Lake. It is identified on the USGS quad as the Caulkens triangulation station. The elevation on the USGS

WCP-5 is the most interesting of the northern White Cloud Peaks. Its split summit and rotten vertical slopes are challenging for scramblers.

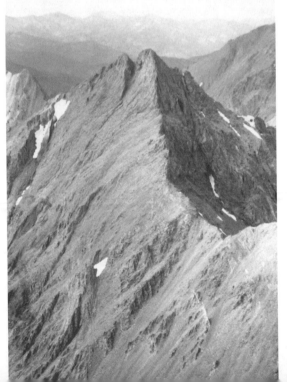

Ocalkens Lake. The west ridge has been climbed from Iron Basin [(A)(2)(a.1.1.1) or (A)(5)(c)], but no details are available. USGS Robinson Bar

Watson Peak   *10,453 feet (Class 2)*
Watson Peak sits west of the main White Cloud divide and just south of WCP-4. Climb via the south ridge, which can be reached from the Iron Basin Trail [(A)(2)(a.1.1.1) or (A)(5)(c)]. Hike north toward Iron Basin from Warm Springs Creek until the trail crosses the area represented by the 8,800-foot contour on the USGS quad. At this point, it is possible to climb up a large east-facing gully, which ends just below the east ridge. At the top of the gully, traverse southwest to the ridge top and then follow the ridge to the summit. USGS Robinson Bar

WCP-6*   *10,256 feet (Class 2)*
The summit of WCP-6 is located 0.6 mile southeast of WCP-5. Access to the peak is via the Iron Basin Trail [(A)(2)(a.1.1.1) or

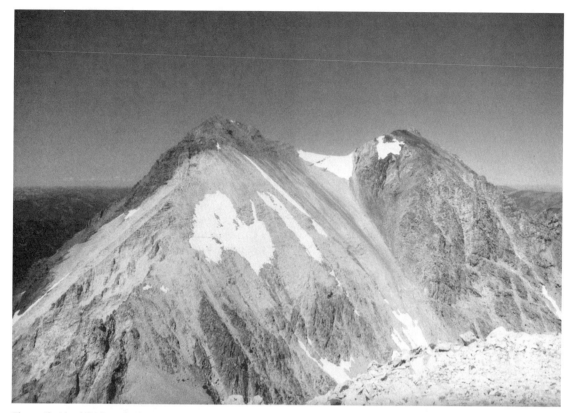

The south side of Caulkens Peak

quad is not for the true summit, which is the westernmost high point. Access the peak from the Big Boulder Chain of Lakes Trail [(B)(2)(a.1)] by crossing the 10,400-foot saddle on WCP-9's east ridge and traversing to the WCP-9/Caulkens saddle. The rocks leading to the headwall below the saddle are granite. Several Class 3 routes lead up the headwall. From the saddle, the route climbs the steep south ridge. Follow the ridge to the summit. USGS Boulder Chain of Lakes

WCP-10*   *11,102 feet (Class 3)*
WCP-10 is the high point on the ridgeline extending east from Caulkens Peak. It is 0.5 mile due east of that peak. It is the steepest of all the White Cloud Peaks. The only reported route traversed the connecting ridge between the two peaks and then returned via the same ridge. An unverified report suggests that a climb from Tin Cup Lake to the north is possible. Access the peak from the Big Boulder Creek Trail [(B) (2)(a.1)]. USGS Boulder Chain of Lakes

WCP-9*   *11,263 feet*
WCP-9 is between Caulkens Peak and D. O. Lee Peak on the intervening ridgeline. It is usually climbed in conjunction with ascents of these neighbors. The peak has a gentle south ridge, a tower-infested north ridge and a west face cut by a spectacular gully. USGS Washington Peak

Cirque Lake/South Ridge (Class 2). From Cirque Lake [(B)(2)(a.1)], hike southeast into the saddle south of the peak. At roughly 10,300 feet, turn northwest and climb directly to the peak's south ridge. Follow the ridge north to the summit.

West Buttress (Class 3). Access this buttress from Ocalkens Lake [(A)(5)(c)]. From the lake, hike south into the upper basin to the base of the buttress at elevation 9,800 feet. This prominent formation is covered by mountain goat tracks and loose talus. The route generally stays on the north side of the buttress and has only two short sections of Class 3 climbing. From the top of the buttress, follow the south ridge to the summit.

East Ridge (Class 2). Access this ridge from Cove Lake

[(B)(2)(a.1)] by following the easy slopes to the 10,400-foot saddle due north of Cirque Lake. From this point, the ridge is a walk-up with good footing.

North Ridge (Class 3). This route starts on the saddle between Caulkens Peak and WCP-9. This saddle is best accessed from its east side by traversing from the 10,400-foot saddle on WCP-9's east ridge. (See East Ridge route above.) The lower part of the north ridge is also formed by granite outcroppings. The route primarily stays on the ridge's east side with one exception, a granite tower. Bypass the tower on its west side. There is some exposure, but the holds are good. The upper portion of the ridge is composed of broken and loose limestone and is Class 2.

D. O. Lee Peak   *11,342 feet*

D. O. Lee is identified on newer Forest Service maps, but has yet to appear on the USGS quad. Dave Lee was a wilderness ranger for the SNRA and a relative of Dave Williams, Sawtooth climbing partner of Robert and Merriam Underhill. The peak the Forest Service chose to honor Lee has two summits and an impressive east face. This peak is located at the west end of the Boulder Chain of Lakes Basin at the southern terminus of the peaks known as the White Cloud Peaks. As you trek up its summits, you will pass igneous rocks near the Boulder Chain of Lakes, then metamorphic rocks, and finally, on the summit, brilliant white sedimentary limestone. USGS Washington Peak

South Ridge (Class 3). The route begins on the peak's east side at Cove Lake. From Cove Lake [(B)(2)(a.1)], hike to the small lake to the southeast and gain the saddle just southeast of that lake. Reaching the saddle is the most difficult part of the climb. In most years, a snowfield exists below the saddle late into the summer. Once on the ridge, follow it north to the summit. Climbing this peak via its south ridge from Warm Springs Creek is also possible, but the approach is much longer.

North Ridge (Class 3). From the saddle between D. O. Lee and WCP-9, the north ridge rises nearly 600 feet in 0.25 mile. The route stays on the west side of the ridge and gets

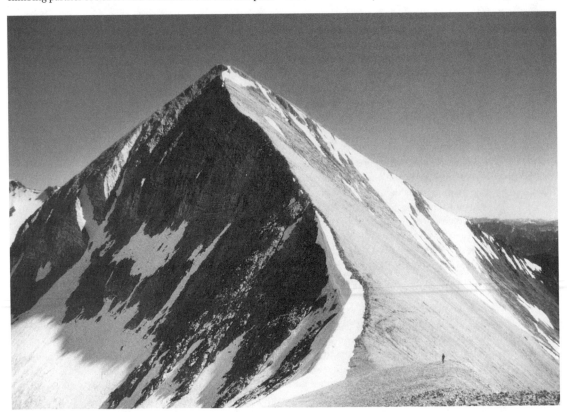

The north ridge of D.O. Lee Peak

progressively steeper as you climb. The crux is just below the summit, where a steep indentation in the ridge holds snow and ice into late summer. An ice axe is invaluable here, at least until the ice is gone. To reach this route, use the Cirque Lake/South Ridge or West Buttress route on WCP-9.

WCP-8*   10,557 feet (Class 3)

WCP-8 is situated 1.4 miles south of WCP-7 and 0.9 mile east of D. O. Lee Peak. Access is from the Warm Springs Creek Trail [(A)(2)(a.1.1)]. Leave the trail at the point where the creek that drains the peak's southern slopes crosses the trail. Follow this creek upstream until you are at approximately the 9,000-foot level. At this point, turn west and climb to the south ridge, then follow this ridge to the summit. USGS Washington Peak

Peak 11272   11,272 feet (Class 3)

This impressive, but unnamed summit, sits directly east of D. O. Lee Peak and 0.6 steep miles south of Cove Lake. It is a pyramid-shaped granite mountain that culminates in a pointed summit block that barely accommodates two climb-ers. Since it is centrally located it is an ideal place to orient yourself to the surrounding peaks and the nearby Sawtooth, Lost River, and Pioneer ranges. The peak is climbed via its north ridge, which is accessed from Cove Lake. [(B)(2)(a.1)] The 1,400-foot climb up the ridge is Class 2 at first and then crosses Class 3 granite blocks and boulders near the summit. The route stays on the crest for the most part. The more difficult sections are passed on the ridge's west side. USGS Boulder Chain of Lakes

Peak 11202   11,202 feet (Class 4)

This rugged summit sits 1.75 miles due east of Peak 11272 on the ridgeline that runs east from that peak. This cliffy mountain is impressive from every direction, but generally overlooked by climbers heading for the bigger peaks. The only reported route began at Shelf Lake in the Boulder Chain of Lakes drainage and ascended a rib that climbs the peak's south face to the peak's southwest ridge, which leads to the summit. The last section crosses 300 feet on a knife-edged ridge. USGS Boulder Chain of Lakes

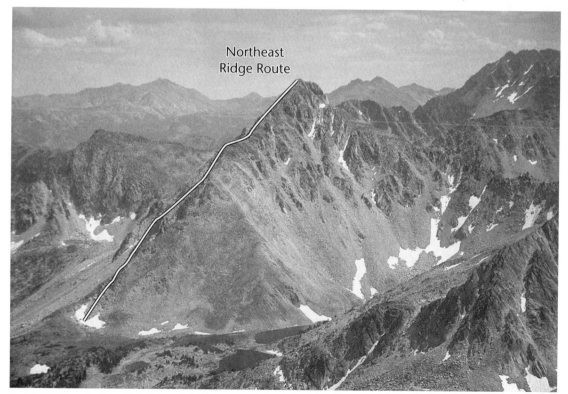

Northeast Ridge Route

Peak 11272 from Caulkens Peak. This peak's granite summit is reminiscent of the Sierra Nevada

Peak 10132   *10,132 feet (Class 2)*

This peak sits just north of Strawberry Basin and 2.2 miles northwest of Blackman Peak between Warm Springs Creek and Mountain Home Canyon. Climb the peak from the point where FST-041 [(A)(2.1)] crosses the saddle just south of Strawberry Basin by way of the connecting south ridge. This is a long, enjoyable hike from the Fourth of July Creek trailhead. USGS Washington Peak

Peak 10111   *10,111 feet (Class 3)*

This fin-shaped summit is located 1 mile north of Blackman Peak on a connecting ridgeline. There are great views of the massive Warm Springs Creek valley from the summit. The peak is best climbed via its south ridge, which is a long, interesting, mostly level ridge walk. Short Class 3 steps present no real difficulties. USGS Washington Peak

Blackman Peak   *10,307 feet (Class 2)*

Blackman Peak is situated northwest of Fourth of July Lake, 3 miles south of D. O. Lee Peak. The peak is named after George Washington Blackman, who mined in the area beginning in 1875. From the Fourth of July Lake trailhead, climb this peak from any of its three prominent ridges. FS-041 [(A)(2.1)] leaves the trailhead and contours around the peak's western slopes, providing good access to the southwest ridge. FST-219 [(A)(2)(a.1)] crosses the peak's east ridge. The peak's north and southeast ridges are also easy Class 2 routes. USGS Washington Peak

Patterson Peak   *10,872 feet (Class 2)*

Patterson Peak is a prominent pyramid-shaped summit that sits 1.8 miles southeast of Blackman Peak. Climb this peak from FST-219 [(A)(2)(a.1)] by leaving the trail where it crosses the peak's west ridge and then following the ridge 1 mile to the summit. USGS Boulder Chain of Lakes

Peak 10713   *10,713 feet (Class 2)*

This dominating summit is 0.8 mile south of Fourth of July Lake and due west of Washington Lake. Climb the northwest ridge from the mining road that runs south from the Fourth of July Lake trailhead [(A)(2)(a)] or from Washington Lake. USGS Washington Peak

Merriam Peak*   *10,920 feet (Class 3)*

Merriam Peak, which is named for Dr. John H. Merriam, founder of the Greater Sawtooth Preservation Council, is named on the latest Forest Service map, but is not yet on the USGS quad. It sits at the east end of the Serrate Ridge,

0.8 mile north of Castle Peak. Climb directly from Lake 9419 [(B)(2)(a.3)] via boulder-covered slopes. USGS Boulder Chain of Lakes

Castle Peak   *11,815 feet*

Castle Peak is unquestionably eastern Idaho's most famous landmark. Because of its distinctive color and shape, and because the peak conspicuously stands hundreds of feet above all surrounding peaks, it is easily distinguishable from most surrounding mountain ranges. The few climbers that venture into the White Cloud Peaks come to climb Castle Peak. The wedge-shaped peak is a complex maze of rock walls, talus slopes, and treacherous gullies culminating in four summit towers of almost equal height. The peak's shattered rock redefines the word "grungy." Twenty-five mountain lakes are visible from the summit, including Hell Roaring, Yellowbelly, and Alturas. Although one hiking guide correctly points out that there are several routes up the peak, none of the routes up this crumbling mountain are easy climbs. All routes encounter steep, loose rock. While talus slope routes are usually tedious but doable, Castle Peak's talus routes are in a class by themselves. They mix steepness with cliffs, talus with boulders, and present multiple route-finding difficulties. Details of the first ascent are unknown, although R. Limbert climbed the peak in the mid-1920s. The first winter ascent, which took place in December 1971, was made by R. Watters, I. Gayfield, J. Hokum, H. Hilbert, S. Schaffer, and J. Elphanson. USGS Boulder Chain of Lakes

Big Gully (Class 3). This north-side route begins at isolated Lake 9419 just northeast of the peak [(B)(2)(a.3)]. There is no trail to the lake, but there is a moderate cross-country route beginning near the junction of Chamberlain Basin and Wickiup Creek Trails. There are several exceptional camping spots at the lake.

From the lake, go due west and climb the headwall via a winding route just to the right of the waterfall. At the top of this first obstacle, the route reaches a talus-filled upper basin surrounded by the Serrate Ridge. Follow the talus slope to the south, staying close to the abrupt cliff that plunges toward Lake 9419. When the angle grows dramatically steeper, the route cuts directly to the east, winding along under several threatening towers, until the talus slope ends at the mouth of a prominent, debris-filled gully separating the north buttress from the north face.

The "big gully," a nightmare of loose rock, is no place for more than one party at a time. Climb the gully, making your own best guess about which side contains less loose rock. At the top of the gully there is a small saddle. The route goes

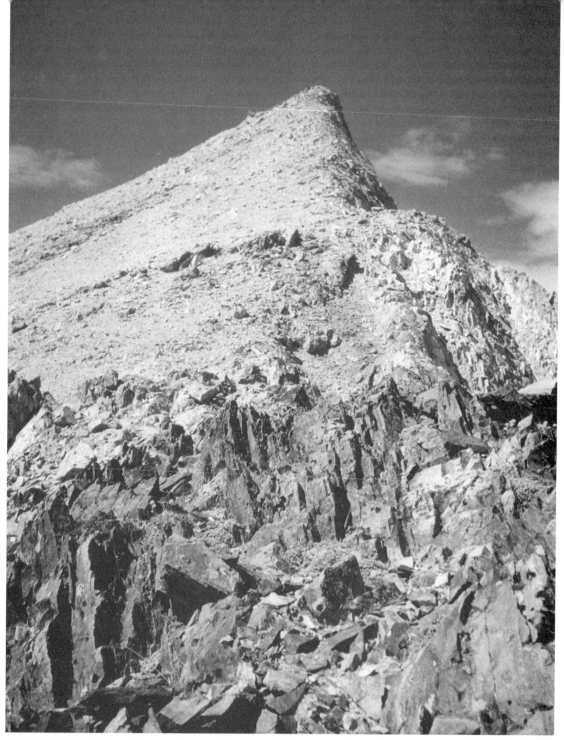

The southeast side of Peak 11202, a.k.a. Cardiac and Granite Peak. The upper reaches of this peak are composed of rubbly, unstable limestone. (Photo by Rick Baugher)

Big Gully Route

The north face of Castle Peak, with the Serrate Ridge in the foreground, viewed from Windy Devil Pass and FST-683

from this saddle onto the face, and then contours around and up to the prominent notch between the peak's two eastern summit towers another 200 feet above.

The easternmost summit is about 10 feet shorter than the other three summits, while the next summit to the west is arguably the highest of the four. From the notch, the route goes up for 40 feet along the second tower's edge and then drops down a narrow ledge and out onto the north face. The route then squeezes along the ledge, passing several climbable gullies on the way. The third gully will lead to the summit via a couple of airy moves.

From this summit (the second from east to west), scrambling over to both of the western summits is possible. There are rock cairns on three of the four, and survey markers on the westernmost summit.

Chamberlain Basin (Class 3). From the east side of Lake 9179 in Chamberlain Basin [(A)(2)(a) or (1.1)(e.1)], head due north to the base of the peak. Look for the large gully that broadly cuts the south face directly below the summit and then narrows as it nears the base of the mountain. At the base of the peak, mount the small buttress on the right-hand side and climb up across crumbly white rock until the face becomes steeper. From this point, veer to the left and climb up into the large gully one third of the way up the face. As you climb, the rock changes from crumbly talus to large boulders. Two-thirds of the way up the face, you can either continue to follow the gully up across increasingly bigger boulders, or keep to the right on steep terrain (the most direct route to the summit.)

Washington Peak   *10,519 feet (Class 2)*
Washington Peak (also named after George Washington Blackman) is located 3.5 miles south of Blackman Peak. Its summit is composed of white broken limestone. From Champion Lakes [(A)(1.1)(b) or (b.1)], climb the trail to the saddle south of the peak. From the saddle, follow a goat trail up the south ridge to the summit. The peak offers an exceptionally good view of Castle Peak. USGS Washington Peak

Croesus Peak*   *10,322 feet (Class 2)*

This peak, which is named on Forest Service maps but not on the Horton Peak quad, is located 1 mile south of Washington Peak. Croesus is a bulky peak with two summits. The lower east summit is the most spectacular of the two. Access this peak from Washington Basin [(A)(1.1)(d)]. The peak can be easily climbed via its west ridge, which is reached from either Washington Basin or Champion Lakes. From Washington Basin, follow the old mining trail [(A)(1.1)(b.1)] west out of Washington Basin until you can leave the trail and scramble to the saddle west of the peak. From Champion Lakes [(A)(1.1)(b) and (b.1)] hike to the point where the trail crosses the saddle between Champion Lakes and Washington Basin. From this pass, hike south to the top of Point 10180 and then descend its east face to the saddle below. This involves a short stretch of Class 3 climbing. From the saddle, climb the west ridge. The crux of the climb up the west ridge is a thick, nearly impregnable barrier of alpine firs. USGS Horton Peak

Peak 10081   *10,081 feet (Class 2)*

This unnamed summit is found 1.2 miles southwest of the uppermost Champion Lake and 2.6 miles northeast of Horton Peak. The peak boasts an impressive 800-foot northwest face. Climb the peak from the vicinity of Champion Lakes [(A)(1.1)(b)] by either walking the peak's east ridge from the pass south of Champion Lakes or by leaving the trail at the 8,800-foot contour and following the drainage up the peak's southern slopes. USGS Horton Peak

Peak 10181   *10,181 feet (Class 2)*

This attractive summit is 1.9 miles east of Horton Peak. It forms the highpoint on a long north/south ridgeline that divides the Champion Lakes and Pole Creek drainages from the Twin Creek drainage. Although the summit can be approached from almost any direction, the south ridge is the most economical route. The ridge can be reached cross-country from the Pole Creek/Germania Creek Road [(A)(1.1)] where the road crosses Pole Creek Summit, or by leaving the Twin Creek Trail [(A)(1.1)(a)] where it crosses the saddle that divides Twin Creek from the South Fork Champion Creek. USGS Horton Peak

Peak 10041   *10,041 feet (Class 2)*

This summit sits due east of Horton Peak and 0.5 mile north of Peak 10166. Climb the peak from Pole Creek Summit [(A)(1.1)]. USGS Horton Peak

Peak 10166   *10,166 feet (Class 2)*

This unnamed peak is located 2.5 miles southeast of Horton Peak. Its 1,200-foot northwest face is composed of brilliant white limestone. The summit is any easy scramble from any direction except the northwest. A traverse from Peak 10041 is the recommended route. Access the peak from the Pole Creek/Germania Creek Road [(A)(1.1)]. USGS Horton Peak

Horton Peak   *9,954 feet (Class 1)*

Horton Peak is 5 miles southwest of Croesus Peak on the western fringes of the White Cloud Mountains. This abandoned fire lookout site is reached by FST-106 [(A)(1)(a)], which leaves the Pole Valley Road and quickly climbs to the summit in 2.5, moderately steep miles. USGS Horton Peak

GERMANIA CREEK/EAST FORK DIVIDE

South of Germania Creek and north of the East Fork Salmon River, a major divide rises up as the last bastion of the White Cloud Mountains. Four summits, all unnamed, offer good scrambling opportunities along this 11-mile ridge. Primary access is from the Pole Creek/Germania Creek Road in the north [(A)(1.1)] and from the East Fork Salmon River Road in the south [(B)].

Peak 9988   *9,988 feet (Class 3)*

Craggy Peak 9988 sits like the Rock of Gibraltar between Germania Creek, Grand Prize, and Galena Gulches. It is located 4.2 miles southeast of Horton Peak. Climb to its summit via its southeast ridge, which can be accessed from the trails that climb up either Galena or Grand Prize Gulches. USGS Horton Peak

Peak 10488   *10,488 feet (Class 2)*

This rough summit sits 1.4 miles due west of Peak 9988 between Galena Gulch and Deer Creek. The summit can be climbed from FST-215 [(A)(1.1)(c)] in Galena Gulch or the pass at the top of the gulch. For the first route, hike up the trail for about 2 miles to a point where a large avalanche chute cuts down the mountain. Climb up the chute until it ends and then traverse toward Point 10052 (to avoid steep talus). The talus will eventually moderate and you can traverse back to the south and into the saddle between Point 10052 and the summit. From this point, follow the ridge south to the summit. To climb the peak from the pass at the top of Galena Gulch, continue on FST-215 to the pas. From the pass, hike up the ridge until you have gained about 200 feet and then traverse straight north toward the summit aiming for the saddle between it and Point 10283. The walk from this saddle to the summit is tiring, but without obstructions. USGS Horton Peak

| Peak 10621 | 10,621 feet (Class 3) |
| Peak 10705 | 10,705 feet (Class 3) |

These twin summits are located in the middle of the Germania Creek/East Fork Divide, 2 miles east of Deer Lakes. The closest trail access is via FST-112 [(A)(1.1.1)(a) or (B)(5)(b)], which can be accessed from the Pole Creek/Germania Creek Road to the north or the East Fork Salmon River Road to the east. Both summits can be climbed from the intervening saddle. The saddle can be reached from the Germania Creek Trail to the north via a trailless hike up Alta Creek, or from the East Fork Salmon River Trail to the south. If climbing to the saddle from the south, take care to avoid the cliffs between 8,400 and 8,800 feet in elevation by bypassing them on either their western or eastern ends. USGS Galena Peak

| Peak 10405 | 10,405 feet (Class 3) |

The southeasternmost White Cloud summit is one of my favorites. It crowns the eastern end of the Germania Creek/East Fork Divide. Talk about views! This summit has them in all directions, including the best view, bar none, of Castle Peak. The peak's lower northern summit evidently served as a fire lookout at one time. The remnants of a well-made trail can be found on the last half of the route to the lower summit. To reach the summit, hike FST-114 [(B)(5)(a)] from Bowery Creek GS to the pass east of the summit. Leave the trail at the pass east of the summit and follow the ridge. Keep your eyes open for the old trail. It will become more obvious above tree line. The trail ends on the top of Point 10000. From this point, descend to the saddle to the southwest and then climb out of the saddle and up the ridge to the summit. USGS Galena Peak

APPROACHES TO
THE WHITE CLOUD MOUNTAINS

There are two primary approach roads to the White Clouds. The first is ID-75, which traverses the west and north sides of the range; the second is the East Fork Salmon River Road, which flanks the range's east side from ID-75 south to the Bowery GS.

(A) ID-75 APPROACHES

ID-75 leads north from Ketchum over Galena Summit to Stanley before turning east and running to Challis. This wide, paved road accesses all the major secondary roads leading into the western and northern stretches of the White Clouds.

(1) FS-194, Pole Valley Road. This road parallels ID-75 along the base of the White Cloud Mountains for roughly 8 miles between Champion and Pole Creeks. Access to the road's northern end is from ID-75 16.5 miles south of Stanley (where the highway crosses Champion Creek). Access to its southern end is from ID-75 24 miles south of Stanley just beyond the Smiley Creek Lodge.

(a) FST-106, Horton Lookout Trail. This trail begins as a dirt road that branches off FS-194 just north of the point where it crosses Taylor Creek. Turn onto the dirt road and follow it until its end (about 0.75 mile). The trail runs to the summit of Horton Peak in 2.5 miles and 2,700 feet of elevation gain.

(1.1) FS-197, Pole Creek/Germania Creek Road. This road leaves the Pole Valley Road 2.4 miles east of ID-75. Pole Creek Summit is 6.8 miles from the Pole Valley Road junction. The road up Pole Creek is rough from the start and its condition deteriorates as the miles go by and it fords the creek several times. From the pass, the road drops into the Germania Creek Basin and ends 3.5 miles from the summit at Three Cabins Creek. (Note: A mining road continues from this point into Washington Basin and gives access to Washington Peak. See [(A)(1.1)(d)], below.) A 4WD is recommended.

(a) FST-107, Twin Creek Trail. This trail leaves the Pole Creek/Germania Creek Road just before it crosses Twin Creek. Turn off the road and follow a side road for 0.25 mile to the trailhead. The trail follows Twin Creek north to a saddle in just over 2 miles. It then drops to the South Fork Champion Creek.

(b) FST-105, Champion Lakes Trail. This trail leaves the road 1.5 miles east of Pole Creek Summit and follows a stream for a short distance before climbing out of the drainage and crossing a ridge. From the top of the ridge, the trail descends to Champion Lakes in another 2.5 miles. From the first Champion Lake, the trail runs northwest down Champion Creek to the Stanley Valley. (Note that, although the trail eventually leads to the Stanley Valley, there is no public access to the trail's western end because it dead-ends on private property.)

(b.1) FST-126, Washington Basin Trail. FST-126 begins at the southernmost Champion Lake and proceeds east over a pass and into Washington Basin in 1.5 miles.

(c) FST-215, Galena Gulch Trail. Access this trail just west of the point where Galena Gulch enters Germania Creek. This seldom-hiked trail with a relatively good tread climbs up Galena Gulch to a pass in 4.5 miles. Once across the pass, it descends to the South Fork East Fork Salmon River and FST-112 [(A)(1.1) (a) or (B)(5)(b)]. The tread is difficult to follow in places.

(d) FS-197, Washington Basin Trail. This route begins

at the point where the Germania Creek Road reaches Three Cabins Creek. The road beyond this point is more of a trail than a road—do not attempt to drive to Washington Basin, which is 5 miles away. The basin itself is a narrow valley filled with relics of the White Cloud mining era. Some land in the basin is privately owned. See [(A)(1.1)(b.1)].

(e) FST-047, East Side Trail. Access this trail from Germania Creek. From the trailhead on FS-197, follow FST-111 east down Germania Creek for 1.25 miles to a junction with FST-109 at the confluence of Washington Creek. Follow FST-109 north up Washington Creek for another mile to the junction that marks the start of FST-047 [(B)(2)(a)]. From this point, FST-047 can be followed north across the eastern front of the range to Boulder Creek.

(e.1) FST-110, Chamberlain Basin Trail. Access this trail where FST-047 crosses Chamberlain Creek. This short trail leads west to the uppermost Chamberlain Lake.

(1.1.1) Grand Prize Gulch Trailhead. This trailhead is signed. Turn off the Pole Creek/Germania Creek Road and follow a rough road a short distance down toward Pole Creek. The road is closed before the road reaches the creek.

(a) FST-112, Grand Prize Gulch/East Fork Salmon River Trail. This trail begins as an old mining road. After fording Pole Creek, it runs downstream to the west. Keep a lookout for a sharp left. Take the left and follow the road uphill. After 3 miles it crosses a pass and then descends into the South Fork East Fork Salmon River drainage [(B)(5)(b)]. Not far below the pass, it intersects with FST-108—which crosses over Gladiator Pass in the Boulder Mountains—and then FST-215—which leads back to the Pole Creek/Germania Creek Road via Galena Gulch [(A)(1.1)(c)].

(2) FS-209, Fourth of July Creek Road. To access this road, turn east off ID-75 just past the turnoff for the Forest Service Work Center turn on the east side of the highway. The road, which has been improved recently, crosses the broad alluvial fan formed, over the eons, by Fourth of July Creek, to the base of the mountains, and runs a total of 9 miles to a trailhead. A 4WD is recommended.

(a) FST-109, Fourth of July Lake Trail. This trail begins by leading 1 mile to Fourth of July Lake, which is at 9,300 feet elevation. This route is a major gateway to Chamberlain Basin. Just below the lake, FST-219 [(A)(2)(a.1)] takes off to the north, leading to Ants Basin, and FST-671 [(A)(2)(a.1.1)] leads into the Warm Springs Creek drainage. From Fourth of July Lake, FST-109 continues south to Washington Lake and a junction with FST-047 [(A)(1.1)(e)] in roughly 3 miles.

(a.1) FST-219, Ant Basin Trail. This trail acts as a connector between the Fourth of July Creek and the Warm Springs Creek drainages [(A)(2)(a.1.1). It is the shortest route into upper Warm Springs Creek. The trail leaves FST-109 at Fourth of July Lake and runs over the ridge between Blackman and Patterson Peaks to FST-671 in 2 miles.

(a.1.1) FST-671, Warm Springs Creek Trail. There are several other ways to access Warm Springs Creek, but this is the shortest approach for climbers to the high peaks at the drainage's alpine end. This trail follows Warm Springs Creek 20 miles from its confluence with the Salmon River to a high pass on the main White Cloud crest between Born Lakes and the Boulder Chain of Lakes. At the pass, it joins FST-683 [(B)(2)(a.2)], which leads east to the Little Boulder Chain of Lakes area. In addition to access from the Fourth of July Creek area, you can reach this trail from ID-75 near the Robinson Bar CG, from the Casino Lake Trail [(A)(3)(a)], and from the Rough Creek Trail [(A)(4)(a)]. Because this trail crosses Warm Springs Creek several times, its lower end is not easy to negotiate until the water level drops late in summer.

(a.1.1.1) Iron Basin/Slate Creek Trail. This trail, which is seldom maintained, leaves FST-671 and Warm Springs Creek due south of Watson Peak and works its way up to Iron Basin and OCalkens Lake. From the lake, it descends along Slate Creek to FS-666 [(A)(5)(c)] in 3 miles. Although no longer maintained, it is the primary approach to the summits known specifically as the White Cloud Peaks. Snow often remains in Iron Basin and Slate Creek until late summer; consequently, high water makes travel in this area difficult until at least mid-July.

(2.1) FS-041, Strawberry Basin Road. This road, which begins at the end of the Fourth of July Creek Road, runs north along the western side of Blackman Peak, and ends after several miles on a ridgeline between Warm Springs Creek and Mountain Home Canyon. The road is closed to vehicles and is a great trail.

(2.2) FS-053, Phyllis Lake Road. This road runs south from the Fourth of July Creek trailhead toward Phyllis Lake. A 4WD is required.

(3) FS-212, Boundary Creek Road. This gravel road leaves ID-75 at a signed junction 6 miles south of Stanley. When it forks, take the left fork and follow it to the trailhead in about 1 mile.

(a) FST-103 and FST-616, Casino Lake Trail. FST-103 leaves the Boundary Creek trailhead and proceeds to Casino Lakes in 4.5 miles, crossing a steep divide on the way. The Casino Lake area gives access to a remote section of the range, including Big Casino Creek, Garland Lakes, Rough Lake, Lookout Mountain, Warm Springs Creek, and FST-671 [(A)(2)(a.1.1.1).

(4) FS-626, Rough Creek Road. From Stanley, follow ID-75 toward Challis for 6 miles and turn south. This steep road, which is 4 miles long, follows Rough Creek to a trailhead. A 4WD is recommended.

(a) FST-647, Rough Creek Trail. This well-maintained trail provides the best access to the region around Lookout

Mountain. From its trailhead, it reaches FST-616 [(A)(3)(a)] in just under 4 miles.

(5) **FS-666, Slate Creek Road.** This road leaves ID-75 20 miles east of Stanley. There is a sign at the turnoff. The road follows the Salmon River west before turning up Slate Creek. It is 8 miles from the highway to the trailhead.

(a) **Livingston Creek Trail.** Livingston Creek flows into Slate Creek 6 miles up the Slate Creek Road. Just past this confluence, there is a sign for Crater Lake. The Livingston Creek Trail leaves from this point and ends at the lake in 4 miles.

(b) **Hoodoo Lake Trail.** This trail begins at the end of the Slate Creek Road and runs via a winding route to Hoodoo Lake in 1.5 miles. An old mining road, the route passes several abandoned digs along the way.

(c) **Slate Creek/Iron Basin Trail.** This trail is no longer maintained beyond OCalkens Lake. The Slate Creek Road is gated at an old mine. Park at this point and follow the road through the mining works until it forks. Take the left fork and cross Hoodoo Creek. The beginning of the trail is difficult to find—look for it cutting up the hillside 25 yards from Hoodoo Creek. See [(A)(2) (a.1.1.1)] for an alternative access to Iron Basin.

(B) EAST FORK SALMON RIVER APPROACHES

The East Fork Salmon River Road, which leaves ID-75 38.6 miles east of Stanley (17.4 miles west of Challis), is paved for much of its distance. The unpaved portions of the road vary in quality and a 4WD is recommended. This is a long, narrow road and it takes time to drive its entire length.

(1) **Jimmy Smith Lake Road.** This foothill lake is located 1 mile west of the main road. Turn off the East Fork Salmon River Road at a signed junction 13.6 miles from ID-75. The trailhead is reached after a short drive.

(a) **FST-677 Corral Creek/Sullivan Lake Trail.** From the Jimmy Smith Lake trailhead, this trail climbs quickly to the lake and then follows the northeast shoreline to Corral Creek. (FST-678, Big Lake Creek Trail, leaves the route at the northernmost point of Jimmy Smith Lake.) From the lake, the route climbs to a saddle southwest of Potaman Peak in 4 miles and then descends to Sullivan Lake in another 2 miles. As you climb toward the saddle from the east, the trail disappears in a large meadow with a cabin. Follow the meadow uphill to an aspen grove where the track becomes visible again.

(a.1) **FST-247, Potaman Peak Trail.** This trail to the summit of Potaman Peak leaves the Corral Creek Trail from a broad saddle. In 1991 much of its tread was no longer visible, but it is still a relatively easy route to follow. From the saddle, follow the fence line north toward the peak. The ridgeline narrows as you approach the southwest face. Switchbacks climb up the talus slope below the summit. Follow the trail from this point until it

disappears at a steep talus slope with trees at its top west of the summit. From the top of this slope, turn right and climb fairly easy rock to the summit.

(2) **FS-667, Big Boulder Creek Road.** Turn off the East Fork Salmon River Road onto this road at the well-marked junction 17.8 miles from ID-75. Livingston Mill, a semi-active mining camp, is 4 miles to the west. There is a large, well-marked trailhead with plenty of parking just below the camp.

(a) **FST-047, East Side Trail.** This trail is the major north/south approach route on the east side of the White Cloud Mountains. From the trailhead, the trail continues over a divide to Frog Lake in 5 miles. From the trailhead, it is 1.5 miles to FST-683 [(B) (2)(a.1)], which leads to Boulder Chain of Lakes, and another 6 miles to Little Boulder Creek Trail [(B)(2)(a.2)] and another divide crossing. It is an additional 3.5 miles to Chamberlain Creek and FST-110 [(A)(1.1)(e.1)]. It is a total of about 14.5 miles to Germania Creek. See [(A)(1.1)].

(a.1) **FST-680 and FST-601, Big Boulder Creek Trail.** FST-680 leaves FST-047 roughly 1.5 miles south of the trailhead and leads to the Big Boulder Chain of Lakes. The trail forks in 2 miles, with FST-680 leading to Island Lake and FST-601 leading to Walker and the many other Boulder Lakes. Traveling cross-country from Island Lake to the upper basin is possible.

(a.2) **FST-683, Little Boulder Creek Trail.** The upper portions of this trail passes spectacular examples of glacially carved lakes. The trail then climbs over two passes (one is the main divide) and connects with FST-671 [(A)(2)(a.1.1)], which leads down into Warm Springs Creek and a connecting trail that leads to Fourth of July Creek [(A)(2)] on the west side of the range.

(a.3) **Lake 9419 Cross-Country Route.** This route leads to the north side of Castle Peak. It leaves FST-047 where it intersects with FST-684 and contours northeast through the trees. Once out of the trees, look for a path running north across a talus slope. Follow this path to Lake 9419.

(3) **Little Boulder Creek Trailhead.** Three miles south of the turn for the Big Boulder Creek Road or 19.8 miles from ID-75, there is a transfer camp for Little Boulder Creek. The trailhead itself is 0.3 mile farther south on the road.

(a) **FST-682, Little Boulder Creek Trail.** This trail leaves the East Fork Salmon River Road where it crosses Boulder Creek at a signed trailhead and follows the creek west to FST-047 [(B) (2)(a)] in 6.5 miles.

(4) **Germania Creek Trailhead.** This trail begins along the East Fork Salmon River Road, 23.2 miles south of ID-75.

(a) **FST-111, Germania Creek Trail.** This trail offers a good alternative route to both Chamberlain and Washington Basins. From the trailhead, the trail runs 5 miles to a junction with FST-110, which leads northwest to Washington Basin. The

THE BOULDER MOUNTAINS

trail continues past the junction for 5 miles to Germania Creek Road [(A)(1.1)].

(5) Bowery Creek GS. The East Fork Salmon River Road ends at the Bowery Creek GS 24.5 miles from ID-75.

(a) FST-114, East Fork/Germania Creek Trail. This trail links the East Fork Salmon River and Germania Creek. It begins at the Bowery Creek GS. Park at the trailhead and walk to the GS across the river. The trail begins behind the GS. This steep but well-maintained trail crosses over the divide 2.2 miles from the GS.

(b) FST-112, East Fork Salmon River Trail/Grand Prize Gulch Trail. This trail follows the East Fork Salmon and then the South Fork East Fork Salmon west for 12 miles to the Grand Prize Gulch trailhead [(A)(1.1.1)(a)]. It is open to motorcycles and is well marked.

2

THE BOULDER MOUNTAINS

While the Boulder Mountains are best known for their multi-colored southern escarpment, which rises abruptly along ID-75 just north of Ketchum, the range stretches north from Ketchum for more than 50 miles to Challis. The western boundary of the Boulders is flanked by the White Cloud Mountains and the East Fork Salmon River in the north, and ID-75 between Ketchum and Galena Summit in the south. Its northern boundary is delineated by the main Salmon River. In the east, US-93 between Challis and Thousand Springs Valley bounds the Boulders. Finally, the Big Lost River and Pioneer Mountains flank the range's southern boundary. The Boulders comprise four major divides: the Northern Divide, the Sheep Divide, the East Fork Salmon/North Fork Big Lost Divide, and the Boulder Front.

The range is composed of granite, Challis Volcanics material, and highly metamorphosed rocks that have been extensively shattered and faulted. The impressive southern front of the Boulder is composed of three layers of material. The top layer is made up of andesite and dacite, which were deposited by the Challis Volcanics around 60 million years

ago; the middle layer is pink granite, which was intruded roughly 50 million years ago. The bottom layer is the oldest and is mainly composed of light-colored limestones and quartzites. The intrusion of igneous rock into the Boulder's sedimentary rocks formed minerals, which were exploited in the late 1800s. At one time Boulder City, now a ghost town, was Idaho's highest town at 10,000 feet.

The Boulder Mountains terrain varies considerably as one moves from Ketchum north to Challis. The Boulder Front, along ID-75, is the highest and most rugged of the range's four divides. The effects of Pleistocene glaciation are readily visible in the divide's many cirques and glacially carved valleys. The range's highest point, 11,714-foot Ryan Peak, is found along this escarpment. Moving north, the Boulder Mountains lose elevation and become more rounded. The northern peaks sit in the rain shadow of the White Cloud and Salmon River Mountains and consequently there are few trees. Only on the highest eastern slopes of appropriately named Lone Pine Peak are there any significant stands of timber. The northern peaks were also closer to the center of the Challis Volcanics eruptions and are covered by deeper deposits of volcanic rock than in the south.

The SNRA and the Sawtooth National Forest manage the southern sections of the Boulder Mountains. Both encourage recreational use of the mountains and have developed and maintained a good trail system. The northern sections of the Boulders are administered by the BLM, which emphasizes cattle grazing as the primary use of the range and maintains no hiking trails.

Overall, Boulder Mountain roads, trailheads, and trails leave a lot to be desired. A 4WD, while not a necessity on the primary approaches, will improve your chances of getting to your destination. There are many designated trails in the southern portion of the range, but few in the north. Fortunately, the northern peaks are conducive to cross-country travel. Hiking within the range, both on- and off-trail, is rewarding and seldom crowded.

Although there is stiff competition for the honor, the Boulder Mountains win the prize for being Idaho's most rotten mountains. Even rock that appears solid will crumble in your hands. Climbing is generally limited to Class 2 or Class 3 nontechnical routes because of the poor condition of the rock. Even scrambling in the Boulders can be difficult because of the loose rock and impossible talus slopes. However, the views from these high peaks are often ample reward for the high price one must pay to reach a summit.

The growing popularity of cross-country and backcountry skiing (and the proximity to Ketchum) has brought many skiers to the Boulders in recent years. Track skiing is available in several places. The Galena Touring Center, located 30 miles north of Ketchum on ID-75, is a major ski-touring center. Those who prefer to break trail will find good access to the Boulders' open slopes. The area east of Galena Summit, with its many challenging open slopes, is the most popular area. Avalanche danger can be extreme in this country.

THE NORTHERN BOULDER DIVIDE

The northernmost section of the Boulder Mountains forms a long northwest/southeast divide that parallels US-93 south of Challis. This divide encompasses high rolling range land and two named summits: Lone Pine Peak and Anderson Peak. Primary access is from the main highway.

Lone Pine Peak   *9,658 feet (Class 2)*

Lone Pine Peak is a big hulking mountain located just 11 miles due south of Challis. It forms the northernmost terminus of the Boulder Mountains. Access the peak from the Spar Canyon Road [(D)(1)] via a side road that leads to a saddle west of the peak. From the saddle, a jeep road leads toward the peak, eventually ending on the next summit south of the main summit. Walk the jeep road to its end, and then hike north along the summit ridge to the summit, passing through some thick forest on the way. Wild horses are often spotted on this hike and a horse skull sits on top of the summit block, which is reached after a short scramble. T. M. Bannon visited the summit in 1915. USGS Lone Pine Peak

Anderson Peak   *9,339 feet (Class 2)*

Anderson Peak is 12 miles southeast of Lone Pine Peak. Its summit is a 2-mile walk from where the Dry Gulch Road [(D)(2)] crosses a saddle at the head of the gulch. From the saddle, follow the 4WD road west to a fence line. Park and follow the ridge north to the summit. The ridge walk to the summit offers exceptional views of the Lost River Range and crosses spectacular wildflower displays early in the summer. T. M. Bannon visited the summit in 1915. USGS Horse Basin

THE SHEEP DIVIDE

The Sheep Divide is 12 miles long. It forms a high ridgeline between the East Fork Salmon River to the west and Herd Creek to the east. Three worthy summits, clustered together midway along the divide, are worthy destinations. Primary access is from the East Fork Salmon River Road.

Sheep Mountain   *10,915 feet (Class 2)*

T. M. Bannon called this peak Redwings when he climbed it in 1915. The Forest Service operated a fire lookout on the peak from 1935 into the 1950s. Sheep Mountain—which is inaptly named, because its slopes are home to a large mountain goat herd rather than bighorn sheep—is found 21 miles southeast of Lone Pine Peak and 1 mile north of Bowery Peak. This peak is the northernmost summit on the Sheep Divide. Because private property blocks the most direct route, the best approach is via Bowery Creek and FST-244 [(C)(2)(a)]. Take the trail east for 3.5 miles until it crosses the North Fork Bowery Creek. From this point, follow the north fork until roughly 9,200 feet elevation. Leave the creek bottom, climb up the slopes to the north for a couple of hundred feet and then turn east and head directly toward the summit of Bowery Peak. At roughly 10,000 feet, turn northeast, aiming for the saddle north of Bowery. From this saddle follow the ridgeline north to the summit. USGS Bowery Peak

Bowery Peak   *10,861 feet (Class 2)*

Bowery is located roughly 1 mile due south of Sheep Mountain. Access the peak from the East Fork Salmon River Road and the Bowery Creek Trail [(C)(2)(a)]. Follow the trail until it crosses the North Fork Bowery Creek at the base of Peak 10883's southwest ridge. Follow the north fork northeast toward the summit. At 9,200 feet leave the creek bottom, climb to the north and then due east up the ill-defined talus rib that climbs to the summit. The summit also can be reached from both Sheep Mountain and Peak 10883 via the connecting ridges. USGS Bowery Peak

Peak 10883   *10,883 feet (Class 2)*

This unnamed summit is located 0.8 mile south of Bowery Peak on the high ridgeline that begins on Sheep Mountain to the north. Climb the peak by its southwest ridge from Bowery Creek and FS-224 [(C)(2)(a)]. From FS-120 and the East Fork Salmon River it is 3.5 miles to the base of the ridge. The ridge itself is steep, but the footing is good most of the way. The north ridge to Bowery Peak is an easy Class 2 walk, much of it along goat trails.

EAST FORK/NORTH FORK DIVIDE

This long divide wiggles its way southwest from Jerry Peak for roughly 20 miles until it joins the Boulder Front near Ryan Peak. In the process, it divides the East Fork Salmon River from the North Fork Big Lost River. Primary access is from the East Fork Salmon River Road to the north and the Trail Creek Road to the south.

Jerry Peak   *10,015 feet (Class 2)*

Jerry Peak, another peak climbed by T. M. Bannon in 1915, is located 20 miles south of Lone Pine Peak and 12 miles east of Sheep Mountain. Access this peak from Herd Lake [(C)(1)], which is 3.5 miles northeast of the summit. Above the lake, Lake Creek flows down off the western slopes of Jerry Peak. Two ridges flank the drainage, both of which can be hiked to the summit. However, the easiest route is to follow the closed road west from Herd Lake to a BLM CG on a saddle just west of Point 9534 on the USGS map. From the CG, hike to Point 9534 and then follow the long connecting ridgeline south to the summit, a distance of about 6 miles. This is very open country; many variations will lead to the summit of Jerry Peak from almost any direction. USGS Jerry Peak

Peak 9977   *9,977 feet (Class 2)*

This grass-covered summit sits 2 miles southwest of Jerry Peak and 3.2 miles south of Herd Lake. It can be climbed by crossing over from Jerry Peak or by following Lake Creek southeast from Herd Lake [(C)(1)] to the base of its north ridge. If you follow this route, stay on the side slope above the creek to avoid difficult brush. USGS Herd Lake

Herd Peak   *9,860 feet (Class 2)*

Herd Peak is located 7 miles southwest of Jerry Peak. Its summit is a long, 3.5-mile hike via FST-051 [(B)(2)(a)], which crosses its northern slopes just below the summit. T. M. Bannon visited the summit in 1915. USGS Herd Peak

Peak 10552   *10,552 feet (Class 2)*

This peak, designated the Meridian triangulation station on the Meridian Peak quad, is 1.6 miles northwest of Meridian Peak. Access the summit from Meridian Peak via the connecting divide or from Hunter Creek summit [(B)(2)(c)] to the west by following the connecting ridgeline. USGS Meridian Peak

Meridian Peak   *10,400+ feet (Class 2)*

Meridian Peak is an L-shaped mountain with three summits. It is situated 5 miles southwest of Herd Peak and 5.5 miles northeast of Ryan Peak. The USGS has identified the middle summit as Meridian Peak; however, the true summit is the northernmost point, which is 100 feet higher. Climb this peak from FST-050 [(B)(2)(c)] by hiking the trail north for roughly 1 mile. Leave the trail and hike up a small drainage to the

peak's southeast ridge. Once out of the trees, follow the ridge up to Point 10285 and then follow the connecting ridge to the north summit. Total distance is 2.5 miles from the road's end. USGS Meridian Peak

Griswold Peak*   *11,057 feet (Class 2)*

This, the final peak on the East Fork/North Fork Divide, is located 2 miles southwest of Hunter Creek summit and 3 miles north of Ryan Peak. Climb the peak from Hunter Creek [(B)(2)(c)]. Hike up Hunter Creek to the first drainage, entering from the northwest (roughly 8,200 feet). Follow the drainage to the ridge crest and then follow the East Fork/North Fork Divide southwest to the summit. This peak is named for William T. Griswold (1860–1932), who headed the USGS Topographic Branch Idaho Section from 1889 to 1895. First ascent: probably R. Baugher in 1994. USGS Ryan Peak

THE BOULDER FRONT

The Boulder Front rises dramatically above ID-75 north of Ketchum/Sun Valley. The divide traverses from northwest

Griswold Peak (Photo by Rick Baugher)

to southeast for 26 miles. It is a rugged, high, and mostly trailless divide. In the north, this divide begins at Pole Creek summit, the arbitrary dividing point for the White Cloud Peaks and the Boulder Mountains, and then runs south to Trail Creek summit, the dividing point between the Boulder and Pioneer Mountains. Primary access is from ID-75, the Pole Creek/Germania Creek Road, and the Trail Creek Road.

| Peak 10126 | 10,126 feet (Class 3) |
| Peak 10243 | 10,243 feet (Class 2) |

These are the northernmost summits on the Boulder Front. They are located 5 miles northwest of Galena Summit and are best climbed in one trip. The route to the summit begins at the Galena Lodge on ID-75. From the lodge, follow the Gladiator Creek Road north for 1.5 miles and park. FST-108 [(A)(2)(a)] begins at this point and leads to Gladiator Pass on the top of the Boulder Front in roughly 2 miles. Leave the trail at the pass and climb up Peak 10243's east ridge. To reach Peak 10126, hike the connecting ridgeline that drops steeply off to the north. USGS Horton Peak

The Cross*   *9,225 feet (Class 2)*
The Cross is a small summit found 0.5 mile north of Galena Summit and ID-75. Unnamed on the quad, this peak is named for a wooden cross that once stood on its summit. (The peak is identified as the Galena triangulation station on the USGS map.) The summit is a short, easy walk from Galena Summit via the ridgeline [(A)(1)], which is also a popular ski ascent. From the summit, several open slopes descend to ID-75. The short ski up, combined with the long ski down, makes this an excellent run when there is no avalanche danger. USGS Horton Peak

Avalanche Peak*   *9,433 feet (Class 2)*
Avalanche Peak, another summit without an official name, is 0.5 mile due north of the Cross. Access this peak from Galena Summit [(A)(1)]. Like the Cross, it is a popular ski destination when snow conditions are stable. USGS Horton Peak

Galena Peak   *11,153 feet (Class 2)*
Galena Peak, a big talus pile with a rotten northeast face, is the northernmost Boulder peak to reach above 11,000 feet. It is 3 miles east of the Galena Lodge on ID-75. Its summit offers great views of the South Fork East Fork Salmon River, the Smoky Mountains, the Sawtooths, the Soldier Mountains, the Lost River Range, and the Pioneer Mountains.

Two routes are suggested. The first climbs the peak's west ridge from Senate Creek. From ID-75, take the Senate Creek Road [(A)(3)] northeast to the base of the west ridge at a little over 7,800 feet. Park and climb directly up the slopes to the east. Gain the west ridge and follow it to the summit. The second route begins at Cherry Creek [(A)(4)]. Follow the Cherry Creek Road for 1.8 miles after leaving ID-75. The road becomes too difficult for autos at this point and a large pile of mining tailings are visible across the creek. Park and follow the road upstream through the trees. The road enters a clearing and vanishes. Stay close to the edge of the trees and continue up the valley. After several hundred yards, the slopes to the north become passable. Climb due north to Galena's southwest ridge, passing mine diggings at roughly 9,200 feet and gaining the ridge at 10,200 feet. Follow the ridge to the summit. Bypass a set of black cliffs on their northwest side. USGS Galena Peak

Cerro Ciento*   *11,154 feet (Class 2)*
Cerro Ciento is located 2.5 miles southeast of Galena Peak on the same connecting ridgeline. The climb is a very long hike from the end of the Spring Creek Road [(A)(5)]. Drive the Spring Creek Road to the high bench above and north of the creek. Once at the top of the bench, you will find a junction with a second road, which leads northeast. Park here (unless you have a 4WD) and hike this second road until it eventually veers sharply to the north. Leave the road at this point and hike east through the forest, paralleling Spring Creek. Continue hiking along the upper edge of the Spring Creek bench to roughly 8,000 feet. From this point, traversing into Spring Creek is possible without losing much elevation. Once in the creek bottom, follow its steep course up to the pass just north of the peak and 2,600 feet above. The last 400 feet are on terribly loose talus. Once at the pass, follow the ridgeline to the summit. (Note: You will need both the Galena and Easley Hot Springs quads and a Sawtooth National Forest map to complete this climb. The road system shown on the USGS maps is inaccurate.) USGS Easley Hot Springs

Easley Peak   *11,108 feet (Class 2)*
Easley Peak sits 0.5 mile south of Cerro Ciento. Climb the peak by traversing the ridgeline from Cerro Ciento. The peak also can be climbed via its southwest ridge; start from ID-75 where it crosses Prairie Creek [(A)(6)]. This route involves an elevation gain of more than 4,100 feet. (Note: The King Creek Road shown on the USGS quad is no longer open to vehicles.) First ascent: E. T. Perkins and W. Griswold in 1895. USGS Easley Hot Springs

Peak 11240+   *11,240 feet+ (Class 3)*

This impressive, unnamed summit towers over the Silver Lakes cirque. It sits squarely on the Boulder Front 1.3 miles east of Easley Peak and 0.9 mile west of Silver Peak. This peak is steep on all sides. The summit is reached only after a 4,400-foot climb, most of which is over steep, loose talus. Climb to the summit via the unnamed drainage that leads from ID-75 to the peak's west side. Leave ID-75 at the Prairie Creek picnic area [(A)(6)]. Drop down to the Wood River, ford the creek and then hike directly toward the drainage's mouth. The drainage climbs northeast and then swings to the southeast. The best footing is on the north side of the bottom. Keep going to the saddle on the southwest ridge. The southwest ridge is a steep, but obstacle-free, 500-foot climb.

Silver Peak   *11,112 feet*

Silver Peak is found 2 miles east of Easley Peak, directly west of Boulder City. The best access to this peak is from the Silver Creek Lake basin. Leave ID-75 on Silver Creek Road [(A)(7)] and follow the road to its end. From the road's end, hike to the lake basin just west of the peak. USGS Easley Hot Springs

South Ridge (Class 3). From Silver Lake, walk due east and climb a talus ramp that leads to the top of the south ridge at 10,800 feet. There are trees on the lower 200 feet of this section of the route and then nothing but loose rock and lupine for the next 800 feet. Climb up the south ridge to the summit block, which is a broken mass of Challis Volcanics debris. As you climb up the ridge, stay on its west side occasionally using goat paths. Although the summit block looks ominous, it is only moderately difficult to climb.

Peak 11041 (Boulder Basin Peak)   *11,041 feet*

This unnamed peak found 0.5 mile north of Boulder Peak is often called Silver Peak, though the real Silver Peak lies more than a mile to the west. The summit is located directly west of Boulder City. USGS Easley Hot Springs

Northwest Ridge (Class 3). This ridge is an easy goal for those who can make the 4WD approach to Boulder City [(A)

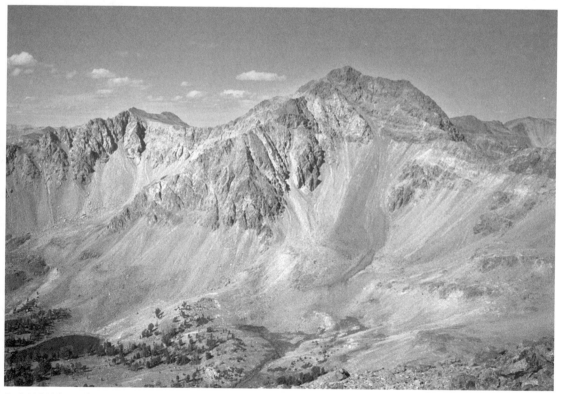

Peak 11240 from Silver Peak

(8)(a)]. Getting to Boulder City is the crux of this route. From the point where the Boulder City Road forks just east of the ruins, take the right fork and hike due west toward the ridge top. Once out of the trees, this route climbs to the saddle between Point 10723 and Peak 11041. Climb northwest until the headwall becomes steeper, and then turn due west, working your way along the peak's northeast slope until you can gain the northwest ridge. Take the ridge to the summit.

West Face/South Ridge (Class 3). From the end of FS-184 [(A)(8.1)], follow the drainage north until reaching a meadow at 10,000 feet. From this point, it is possible to climb directly up to the peak's south ridge at 10,900 feet. The footing is loose, but passable. The south ridge is passable both up and down from this point and it is possible to traverse over to Boulder Peak. See Boulder Peak's Northwest Ridge route, below.

Boulder Peak   *10,981 feet*
Boulder Peak juts out impressively into the Big Wood River Valley, 1 mile southeast of Silver Peak. Because of its position, Boulder Peak is the most prominent Boulder Mountains summit above ID-75. It is also one of the most decayed piles of rubble in the range. Nevertheless, it harbors three excellent routes. First ascent: E. T. Perkins and W. Griswold in 1895. USGS Easley Hot Springs

North Couloir (Class 3). Directly above Boulder City [(A)(8)(a)], a steep couloir leads to the top of the peak's east ridge. The couloir is often filled with snow until late summer, which makes for good footing while the snow lasts. Several people have made spring ski descents of this couloir. From the top of the couloir, follow the ridge west to the summit. Take an ice axe.

South Ridge (Class 3). This is a classic scrambling ridge blocked by big towers on its lower end and well defined as it reaches the summit. The best access is via FS-184 [(A)(8.1)]. From the end of the road, climb up to the northeast, through forest to the top of the south ridge at 9,300 feet. Turn north and climb the ridge, staying slightly below the crest on the ridge's west side until reaching the first tower. Pass this tower along its west side to reach a gully that climbs between the first and second towers. Climb the gully, and then skirt the second tower on its east side aiming toward a second gully. To enter this gully, drop down 10 feet and work across the tower's face on a ledge system for approximately 200 feet. When the ledges turn a corner, it is possible to climb into the gully and then up to the top of the ridge east of the second tower. The ridge is now free of obstacles. Endurance will

see you to the top, where you will find a large stone peace symbol and a register.

Northwest Ridge (Class 4). This ridge runs to Peak 11041, 0.7 mile to the north. In the process, the route crosses Boulder Peak's lower northern summit. For the most part the ridge is Class 3, but one small Class 4 step will stop many scramblers. Access this route from the saddle between Peak 11041 and Boulder's 10,838-foot north summit. See the West Face/South Ridge route description for Peak 11041 to reach this saddle.

Peak 11458   *11,458 feet (Class 3-4)*
This peak, one of Idaho's most impressive, is little known and seldom climbed. It sits at the head of the East Fork Salmon River 1.6 miles northwest of Glassford Peak. Its jagged summit, broken walls, and vertical north face are its major attractions. The only known route ascends its north ridge. From the Bowery GS [(C)(4)(a)], hike up the East Fork Salmon River Trail for 1 mile to the point where the trail crosses a small drainage that descends from the peak's north ridge. Follow this drainage up to the ridge summit 3,000 feet above. Once on the ridge, follow it south toward Point 11,341, which is bypassed on its steep east side. From the saddle on the point's south side, continue up the ridge to the summit. USGS Ryan Peak

Glassford Peak   *11,602 feet (Class 2)*
Glassford, a beautiful peak of red rocks and crumbling ribs, is the striking, pyramid-shaped peak that rises north of Ketchum. The peak was named for Thomas Glassford, a railroad conductor popular with Ketchum residents in the 1890s. Although easily viewed from town, it is a long way off. It is located 5.5 miles northeast of Silver Peak and 3.5 miles west of Ryan Peak.

Climb this peak from the saddle southwest of the summit. This route is extremely strenuous, but avoids the rotten rock that plagues the peak's steeper walls. The saddle can be reached from both the east and the west. Both are equally demanding approaches. From the west, the saddle is reached from the North Fork Big Wood River [(A)(9)(a)]. Follow the trail up the drainage until it ends at around 8,000 feet. From this point, gain 3,000 feet by climbing due north to the high point just south of Glassford Peak. Once on the ridge top, traverse north to the saddle just south of the Glassford summit by staying on the west side of the ridge top.

To approach the saddle from the east side, begin by making the long drive up the East Fork Salmon River Road and then FS-063 [(C)(3)], which climbs up West Pass Creek. Follow the road to where it is closed. Continue on foot until you reach the trailhead for West Pass [(C)(3)(a)]. Leave the road at this point and hike down to the creek. The farther west you go before crossing the creek, the more difficult the terrain, so cross the creek right away and stay on the north side as you follow the creek up to the saddle southwest of the summit. There are a lot of good elk trails 300 to 400 feet above the valley floor. From the saddle, the route goes directly up the peak's west ridge without significant obstacles. First ascent: E. T. Perkins and W. Griswold in 1894. USGS Ryan Peak

Ryan Peak   *11,714 feet*

Although it is well hidden from the Big Wood River Valley, this, the highest Boulder Mountains peak, is a popular destination for local climbers. The fragile pile of rock that forms this decaying summit is found 15 miles north of Ketchum. The mountain was named for Mike Ryan, an early Wood River Teamster. First ascent: E. T. Perkins and W. Griswold in 1894. USGS Ryan Peak

South Ridge (Class 2). This route is approached from the trail to West Pass [(A)(9)(a) and (b)]. From the pass southwest of the summit, the route climbs directly up to the top of the south ridge and then follows the ridge to the summit. From the trailhead, it is a 12-mile round trip that gains and then loses nearly 5,000 feet.

East Ridge (Class 2). The summit also can be reached from North Fork Lake to the northeast [(B)(2)]. Follow the drainage up to the small lake above North Fork Lake. Turn south and climb to the ridge top between Ryan and Point 11415. Follow the east ridge to the summit.

Kent Peak   *11,664 feet*

This summit is named for Kent Easton Lake, a 1950s mountaineering enthusiast who tragically died of diabetes in 1959. Kent is an extremely rugged peak. Its north face possesses a permanent snowfield, complete with a bergschrund. The summit is found 0.8 mile southeast of Ryan Peak. USGS Ryan Peak

Northwest Ridge (Class 3-4). Traversing this ridge from the saddle south of Ryan Peak is possible; access the route from FST-115 [(A)(9)(b)]. The route clambers up and down along the ridge crest and the southwest-facing slopes. Although you must avoid or climb over many towers of extremely rotten rock, the route is feasible for those with good route-finding abilities.

South Ridge (Class 3). Take the same trail [(A)(9)(b)]

Peak 11458 from Peak 10405 in the White Clouds

South Ridge route: West Pass to Ryan Peak's summit

as for Ryan Peak, but leave it at the 9,200-foot contour and climb up to the peak's south ridge, which leads directly to the summit.

Perkins Peak*   *11,220+ feet (Class 3)*

This peak, located 1 mile southeast of Kent Peak on the main crest, is named after Edmund Taylor Perkins (1864–1921), a USGS topographical engineer who surveyed in Idaho between 1889 and 1897. Perkins was responsible for the topography on Idaho's first USGS topo maps, including the Hailey and Sawtooth quads. R. Baugher reports that the peak is best climbed from the North Fork Big Lost River Road [(B)(2)]. From the road, bushwhack to the Kent/Perkins saddle. From the saddle climb the northwest ridge to the summit. First ascent: R. Baugher in 1994. USGS Ryan Peak

Peak 10680   *10,680 feet (Class 2)*

This unnamed but appealing peak 1.25 miles southwest of Kent Peak has a large, cone-shaped summit. The summit can be climbed from the saddle between it and Kent Peak, and from its northern side [(A)(9)(b)]. USGS Ryan Peak

Basils Peak*   *10,414 feet (Class 2)*

Basils Peak is 2 miles due east of Boulder Peak. It is unnamed on the USGS map. Drive 9.5 miles north from Ketchum on

ID-75 and park at the Wood River CG. Cross the highway and gain the ridge that meets the highway between Konrad Creek and Goat Creek. Follow the treeless ridge to Point 9829, then turn west and hike to Point 9935. The ridge plunging down to the west from Point 9829 is an alternative but less-appealing ascent route. From Point 9935, the route goes up the crumbling ridge to the northwest to the summit. Stay on the south side of the ridge to avoid the towers that block the way. The route is roughly 4 miles one-way with a 4,000-foot elevation gain. USGS Amber Lake

Rock Roll Peak*   *10,458 feet (Class 2)*

Rock Roll Peak is the high point along the west side of Trail Creek, 8 miles southeast of Kent Peak. This peak has excellent views of the surrounding countryside and the Pioneer Mountains. Climb the south ridge from the saddle. Access to the south ridge is possible from either Trail Creek (two alternatives) or Lake Creek. For the first Trail Creek route, drive north from Ketchum on Trail Creek Road for 5.4 miles and turn left at the Antelope Creek sign. Park above Trail Creek and drop down to the creek, which you must wade across (difficult before late summer). A poorly maintained, unofficial trail climbs up Antelope Creek toward Point 9557. From this point, drop down 500 feet into the saddle at the base of the peak's the south ridge. This is a long hike with a hefty elevation gain. For the second Trail Creek route, continue driving up Trail Creek Road, cross Trail Creek Summit, and turn left on FS-140, Park Creek Road. Drive to the FST-124 trailhead [(B)(1)(b)]. Follow the trail south to the peak's south ridge and then ascend the ridge. For the Lake Creek access, drive north from Ketchum to Lake Creek, and then drive to the FST-125 [(A)(10)(a)] trailhead. Follow the trail, built partly on an old mining road, to a point below the saddle where you can leave the trail and climb to the south ridge. Follow the south ridge to the summit. USGS Rock Roll Canyon

Peak 10598	10,598 feet (Class 2-3)
Peak 10566	10,566 feet (Class 2)

These twin peaks are at the southern end of the Boulder Mountains in the Trail Creek drainage. Upper Trail Creek and its west fork surround the peaks. Climb Peak 10598 from the point where FST-126 crosses its northwest ridge [(B)(1)(a)]. The ridge is Class 2 until a Class 3 cliff band is reached near the summit. These cliffs can be avoided by dropping down the peak's southwestern slopes for roughly 100 feet to access an easy gully that leads to the summit. To reach Peak 10566, descend to the intervening saddle on Class 2 slopes and then climb its southwest ridge. The top of the ridge is blocked by towers, which can be skirted on their west side. USGS Rock Roll Canyon

Mystery Peak*   10,785 feet

This incisor-shaped peak's summit block is a craggy pinnacle of Challis Volcanics rock that rises 500 feet above the connecting ridges. It is isolated, off-the-beaten-track, and mostly unknown. Mystery Peak sits at the eastern end of the Boulder Front. From its tiny summit there is a spectacular view encompassing the Pioneers (especially Devils Bedstead East and Goat Mountain), the White Clouds, the Lost Rivers, the White Knobs, and the Boulders. By any measure, this is an exceptional peak. USGS Meridian Peak

South East Face (Class 3). The southeast face forms a steep talus ramp that is the least precipitous side of the summit block. To reach the face, you must first hike to the saddle south of the peak. This hike starts at the end of the road in Miller Canyon [(B)(2)(b)]. Hike south upstream for about 0.5 mile until you reach a stream that descends from the southeast. Cross the stream and either follow it up to the saddle or climb the ridge just to the south up and over Point 10500. From the saddle, climb up the peak's south ridge to the cliffs above. At the base of the cliffs, contour to the northeast and out onto the southeast face. Start up this slope until encountering steep slabs. At this point, look for a low angle ledge that cuts up to the north. Follow this ledge until it ends on the northeast face. Climb back to the south until a second north-trending ledge is reached. Follow this ledge

The impressive north face of Kent Peak, viewed from Ryan Peak

Perkins Peak (right) and Kent Peak, from the east (Photo by Rick Baugher)

north to a small gully with a chockstone. From this point, climb up the remaining slabs to the summit.

APPROACHES TO THE BOULDER MOUNTAINS

The Boulder Mountains cover a large, diverse section of Idaho. Access is as varied as the terrain. In the southwest, Ketchum, ID-75, and Trail Creek Road are the primary access routes. In the north, Challis, ID-93, and the East Fork Salmon River Road are the primary access routes.

(A) ID-75 APPROACHES

The section of ID-75 that traverses the southern edge of the Boulder Mountains between Ketchum and Galena Summit is a good paved highway that provides primary access to many of the range's most important peaks.

(1) Galena Summit. Galena Summit is an 8,700-foot pass separating the Boulder and Smoky Mountains. You can find good spots to park (which are plowed during the winter) on both sides of the pass.

(2) FS-189, Gladiator Creek Area. A dirt road leads up Gladiator Creek from the Galena Lodge 30 miles north of Ketchum. At the road's end, FST-108, a steep and seldom-used trail, leads up to the top of the Boulder Front. A 4WD is recommended.

(a) FST-108, Gladiator Pass Trail. This trail, which is faint in spots, climbs to the top of the Boulder Front between Peak 10243 and Peak 10185 in 2.5 steep miles. From the divide, it descends to the West Fork East Fork Salmon River and FST-112 [(C)(4)(a)] in 0.6 mile.

(3) FS-186, Senate Creek Road. This road leaves ID-75 150 yards south of the Galena Lodge and climbs up Senate Creek for 2 miles. A 4WD is recommended.

(4) Cherry Creek Road. This road leaves ID-75 about 1 mile south of the Galena Lodge and follows Cherry Creek north for about 1.5 miles. Do not confuse this road with the road just to the west up the North Fork Cherry Creek.

(5) FS-186, Spring Creek Road. This road leaves ID-75 20 miles north of Ketchum. This route runs 0.8 mile along the creek bottom then turns sharply and climbs up the bench north of the creek. In another 0.8 mile, the road reaches a junction on top of the bench. The main road turns north and drops off the ridge toward Cherry Creek, while the Spring Creek Road runs north up the bench another 1 mile to a wide spot where parking is possible. A 4WD is recommended.

(6) Prairie Creek Picnic Area Access. This picnic area is located along ID-75 18 miles north of Ketchum on the east side of the road. There is plenty of room to park. This is the only access to Peak 11240+. At one time, a bridge across Wood River led to the trailless country on the other side, but the bridge is gone. If it has not been replaced, fording the river is the only way across. Beware of high water.

(7) FS-174, Silver Creek Road. This road leaves ID-75 15.8 miles north of the stoplight in Ketchum. Turn right (northeast), and follow the road across the river on a good bridge. After crossing the bridge, the road turns upriver for a short distance. Go right when the road forks and follow the Silver Creek drainage to a second major fork. Go right again and follow the road, which quickly climbs high up onto the flanks of the Boulders and eventually ends at around 8,400 feet. The road is about 3 miles long. A 4WD is recommended.

(a) Silver Creek Trail. From the end of the road, head uphill on an unofficial trail toward the obvious opening in the mountains. Silver Lake and several small ponds are found in the high cirque.

(8) FS-158, Boulder Basin 4WD Road. This extremely rugged road leads 6 steep miles into Boulder Basin at 9,200 feet. Driving this road requires considerable 4WD driving experience. Many 4WDs have broken down on this road. Many people hike the road rather than risk the drive. Take ID-75 north from Ketchum for 13 miles and follow the signed dirt road for 0.5 mile until it forks. Take the right fork, cross the creek, and follow the road upstream and into the mountains. In roughly 2 miles, the road reaches a steep, pitted grade that has stopped many off-roaders.

(a) FST-184 and FST-113, Boulder Basin to East Fork Trail. This poorly maintained trail climbs north out of Boulder Basin and then drops into the basin east of Silver Peak, where it follows the East Fork South Fork Salmon River north to Bowery GS [(C)(4)(a.1)].

(8.1) FS-184, Boulder Peak Access. Just after leaving ID-75, the Boulder Creek Road forks. Go left and follow this road to its end along the West Fork Boulder Creek in 4 miles. A 4WD is recommended.

(9) FS-146, North Fork Wood River. Turn off ID-75 at the SNRA headquarters building. A good dirt road leads from the headquarters for 5.5 miles to the road's end at a small camping area. A 4WD is recommended for the last mile.

(a) FST-115 and FST-128, North Fork Big Wood River Trail. This trail continues up the drainage for 4.5 miles before crossing a pass west of Glassford Peak. The trail is continually swept by avalanches during the winter, receives little maintenance, and can be hard, if not impossible, to follow at its upper end.

(b) FST-115, West Pass Trail. This trail leaves the North

Mystery Peak

Fork Trail 1.5 miles from the trailhead. The junction is in a small clearing and can be difficult to find. Look for several rock cairns in a sagebrush-filled clearing that marks the trail's start. If you are unable to find the start, hike 50 yards past the canyon opening and then hike northeast uphill until you find the trail. Despite the lack of a sign at its beginning, this is a good trail. It leads to the top of 10,400-foot West Pass, which is approximately 5 miles from the trailhead. From the pass, the trail makes its way down toward the East Fork Salmon River [(C)(3)(a)].

(c) **FST-129, West Fork Big Wood River Area.** This trail leads up the West Fork to near Window Lake. A side trail leads up to Amber Lakes.

(10) FS-142, Lake Creek Road. Lake Creek Road leaves ID-75 just north of Ketchum at a well-signed junction. Turn north off the highway and follow the road through a housing development to its end in about 5 miles. A 4WD is recommended.

(a) **FST-125/124, Lake Creek/Cold Canyon Trail.** This trail was reconstructed in the late 1970s. It begins by following an old mining road for 2 miles. The new trail forks off at a signed junction and climbs up switchbacks to the ridge above. Once on the ridge, the trail runs north to Cold Canyon [(B)(1)(b)] along the south slopes of Rock Roll Peak.

(B) TRAIL CREEK ROAD APPROACHES

Trail Creek Road leaves the center of Ketchum and continues east through Sun Valley, eventually crossing Trail Creek Summit in 12.2 miles and then drops down into the Big Lost River drainage. Turn northeast off ID-75 toward Sun Valley in the center of Ketchum. The road is paved up to the base of the pass.

(1) FS-140, Park Creek Road. This road is 14 miles east of Ketchum. It runs up the east flank of the Boulders and gives access to FST-124 and FST-126. Turn off Trail Creek Summit Road 0.8 mile east of Trail Creek summit. The road is in good condition when dry.

(a) **FST-126, Trail Creek Loop.** This enjoyable trail loops around Peaks 10598 and 10566, following Trail Creek and its west fork. The tread is sketchy in places, but follows the general route shown on the map. The two prongs of the trail join at a 10,100-foot pass northwest of Peak 10598.

(b) **FST-124/125, Cold Canyon/Lake Creek Trail.** This trail leaves the Park Creek Road at a signed trailhead and runs south, climbing up the eastern and southern slopes of Rock Roll Peak to join FST-125 [(A)(10)(a)] on the south side of the mountain.

(2) FS-128, North Fork Big Lost River Road. This road leaves the Trail Creek Road 9 miles northeast of Trail Creek Summit and heads west into the more remote sections of the Boulders. Several seldom-used trails and several high cirques can be reached from the road. A 4WD is recommended.

(a) **FST-051, Toolbox Creek Trail.** This trail is accessed 6.5 miles from the beginning of FS-128. Turn on the road that heads up Toolbox Creek and park after 100 yards. The trail runs due north up Toolbox Creek to the East Fork/North Fork Divide, and then follows the divide north toward Herd Peak. A sign at the trailhead states: 6 MERIDIAN CREEK, 7 E. FORK HERD CREEK. After passing by Herd Peak, the trail continues to follow the divide toward Lake Basin.

(b) **Miller Canyon/Mystery Peak Access.** Leave FS-128 roughly 2.4 miles past Toolbox Creek or 8.9 miles from the beginning of FS-128 on a road that descends down and crosses the North Fork. In 0.1 mile, take the road immediately to the left, which crosses Miller Creek and then begins an ascent up Miller Canyon for 0.2 mile. Follow the road as far as possible and park. From the end of the road continue hiking up the canyon, staying on the east side of the creek. At about 8,000 feet, a stream flows into Miller Creek. Leave the creek bottom at this time and follow either this new stream or the ridge on your right south to the high country above. Both routes are Class 2.

(c) **FST-050, Hunter Creek/East Pass Creek Trail.** This trail leaves the end of FS-128 12.2 miles from its beginning and proceeds north up Hunter Creek, crosses a divide, and drops down into East Pass Creek, where it is designated FST-188 [(C)(1)(a)]. The sign at the trailhead states: 5 E. PASS CREEK, 5 MERIDIAN CREEK.

(C) EAST FORK SALMON RIVER APPROACHES

The East Fork Salmon River Road, which leaves ID-75 38.6 miles east of Stanley (17.4 miles west of Challis), is paved for part of its distance. The last mile is in poor condition. A 4WD is recommended.

(1) FS-148, Herd Lake Road. Access this road from the East Fork Road at a signed junction 9.1 miles south of ID-75. Follow the road southeast for 9.5 miles, to a point where it is closed by the BLM. From here, the road can be used as a trail. It continues to a CG in a saddle at 9,000 feet.

(a) **FST-188, East Pass Creek Trail.** FST-188 leaves the Herd Creek Road where East Pass Creek flows into Herd Creek. From this point, it runs southwest until it connects with FST-050 [(B)(2)(c)], which leads across Hunter Creek Summit and into the North Fork Big Lost River.

(2) Bowery Creek Trailhead. This East Fork Road trailhead is found 24.5 miles south of ID-75. A short road drops steeply down to the east and the beginning of the trail.

(a) **FST-186, Bowery Creek/Hunter Creek Summit Trail.** This trail follows Bowery Creek east for several miles and then turns south to cross the East Fork/North Fork Divide at Hunter Creek Summit. From this pass, it drops down to the North Fork Big Lost River [(B)(2)(c)].

(3) FS-063, West Pass Road. This road leaves the East Fork

3

Road 30.25 mile south of ID-75. It starts as a good road but soon deteriorates. The trailhead for West Pass is 3.6 miles from the beginning of the road. The end of the road is in 7 miles, but the Forest Service recently blocked the road 2.5 miles from its start.

(a) **FST-115, West Pass Trail.** This trail climbs over high West Pass and then drops down to the North Fork Wood River [(A)(9)(b)] in 5 miles.

(4) **Bowery GS Access.** This GS is 31 miles south of ID-75 at the end of the East Fork Salmon River Road.

(a) **FST-112, East Fork Salmon River Trail.** This trail runs up the East Fork for 8 long miles to a junction with FST-108 [(A)(2)(a)], which leads over Gladiator Pass. It is a long, hot route.

(a.1) **FST-113, South Fork East Fork to Boulder City Trail.** Unfortunately, most people never consider hiking this fine, but remote route that leads to Boulder City. The trail leaves the East Fork Trail roughly 4 miles from the Bowery GS and then runs south to Boulder City [(A)(8)(a)] in another 8 miles.

(D) NORTHERN BOULDER MOUNTAIN APPROACHES

ID-75 follows the northern section of the range between the East Fork Salmon River and Challis. US-93 follows the eastern side of the range from Challis south toward Mackay. This area is crisscrossed by many roads that vary in quality from good gravel to almost-impossible jeep trails. The primary approach is the Spar Canyon Road, which runs across the range from the East Fork Salmon River Road to US-93. This gravel road is passable to sedans when it is dry. From this road and the two paved highways, almost every side canyon contains a road. Traveling this area requires a well-prepared vehicle and plenty of extra water.

(1) **Lone Pine Peak Access.** Besides USGS maps, you will need the newest edition of the Challis National Forest map to approach Lone Pine Peak. The Spar Canyon Road is the primary access to Lone Pine Peak. Access the road from US-93 by driving 17.1 miles south from Challis and then turning west at a well-signed junction. To approach from the East Fork Salmon River Road, follow that road south from ID-75 for 4.1 miles. To access Lone Pine Peak, take the Spar Canyon Road west from US-93 for 7 miles. The road crosses under high-tension power lines at this point. Look for a road signed for Bradshaw Basin that runs off to the north. Follow it to a fork in 0.85 miles. Go right. After 2 miles, the road reaches a cattle trough. Park at this point.

(2) **Anderson Peak Access.** This access route leaves US-93 18.2 miles south of the US-93/ID-75. Turn west onto the road at an intersection signed for the Dry Gulch and Broken Wagon Roads. Go across a cattleguard and then turn left on the Dry Gulch Road. This road crosses a pass in 7.3 miles. At the pass, a sign points west to Horse Basin. A 4WD is required from this point. Follow the new road toward Horse Basin for 1.3 miles and park.

THE PIONEER MOUNTAINS

By almost any measure, the Pioneer Mountains are Idaho's premier mountain range. Its peaks are high and wild. The rock is good. The scenic vistas are terrific. The lakes are pristine. The range stretches from west to east between Ketchum and Arco, covering a distance of nearly 50 miles. At its widest, the range is nearly 25 miles wide. The range is bounded by the Big Wood River and ID-75 in the west and the Snake River Plain in the south, while the Boulder Mountains, Copper Basin, the White Knob Mountains, and Antelope Creek flank its ragged northwest-to-southeast boundary. A wide band of foothills protects its southern escarpment, while its northern peaks impressively tower above remote Copper Basin.

The Pioneer Mountains have a northwest-to-southwest trending crest that begins on Trail Creek Summit east of Ketchum and runs in a long arch to Timbered Dome west of Arco. Geologically, the range has a granitic foundation that was intruded into schists and quartzite at approximately the same time as the Idaho Batholith was forming farther north. Pioneer granite covers roughly 25 square miles and is exposed on the eastern side of the crest. The western slopes are covered with sedimentary and metamorphic overburden that is quite broken in places. The range's highest summit, 12,009-foot Hyndman Peak, is made up of a massive pile of quartzite on a granite base. As a substance for climbing, the Pioneer rock varies in quality. The granite forms many impressive north faces, but only a few peaks have granite clear to their summits. Though the upper portions of the major faces are composed of highly shattered and weathered metamorphic rock, technical routes have been pushed up most of the faces.

The Pioneers' Pleistocene glaciers cut many spectacular U-shaped valleys and cirques and left behind dozens of jagged peaks. Wildhorse Canyon, on the north side of the range, is the largest of these U-shaped valleys. The twin cirques at its southern terminus are walled by soaring vertical rock walls of Goat Mountain, Hyndman Peak, Old Hyndman Peak, Big Basin Peak, and Brockey Peak. Dozens of high mountain lakes dot the post glacial landscape, providing pleasant base camps.

Prospectors discovered mineral deposits at the base of the Pioneers in 1864 igniting a mining boom that peaked between 1880 and 1887. The miners called the Pioneers the

Wood River Mountains. The USGS arrived in 1889 and during the next six years mapped the northwest section of the range, creating the 30-minute Hailey quadrangle. This quad remained the standard until it was replaced with 7.5-minute quads in 1967. One other interesting tidbit: in 1953 the noted dendrochronologist Edmund Schulman discovered the oldest known living limber pine in the range—age 1,650 years.

The Pioneer Mountains are managed by the Sawtooth National Forest on the southwest side of the crest and the Challis National Forest on the northeast side. Twenty years ago, the Forest Service proposed wilderness designation for 65,972 acres in the Pioneers. Congress has yet to act upon this proposal. Fortunately, the Pioneers' wilderness attributes have not deteriorated significantly over the years.

Climbing and hiking opportunities abound. The Pioneer trail system has improved over the years, but is fragmented, making it difficult to link valleys together into a long backpack trip. During the 1950s and 1960s, the northwest end of the range saw extensive use by skiers associated with Sun Valley. The resort's Pioneer Cabin served as a base camp and it is likely that most, if not all, of the peaks near the cabin were ascended during those winters. Technical climbing in the Pioneers began with ascents of the north faces of Hyndman and Old Hyndman Peaks in the 1970s, but many untested granite walls and challenging ridges are still waiting for first ascents.

There are many trailheads in the Pioneers. While good gravel roads lead to several, most trailheads are reached by roads best traveled by 4WD vehicles. Although Forest Service maps show an extensive trail system within the range, trail conditions vary from good to poor and in a few cases the trails have disappeared altogether. Cross-country travel can be difficult because of the prevalence of cliffs and walls.

TRAIL CREEK SUMMIT TO
THE ANGELS PERCH

This section covers Pioneer peaks along the main crest from Trail Creek Summit to the Angels Perch a distance of 18 miles as the crow flies. Access to this section is varied and utilizes Copper Basin, Trail Creek, and ID-75 trailheads.

Proctor Mountain   7,798 feet (Class 3)
This is an excellent early season conditioning hike. Proctor Mountain stands just east of the Sun Valley Lodge. From Trail Creek Cabin, take the Proctor Mountain Trail [(A)(1)(a)] until just east of the summit. Leave the trail, hike due east across

the meadow and into the trees to the base of a rocky wall. Scramble up the wall through a short gully to the summit. USGS Sun Valley

Phi Kappa Mountain   10,516 feet (Class 2)
Peak 10585   10,585 feet (Class 2)
These are the first major summits along the northwest end of the Pioneer crest. Phi Kappa Mountain is located 2.75 miles east of Trail Creek Pass; Peak 10585 is 0.75 mile northwest of it. Climb these peaks from the Summit Creek Trail [(A)(3)(a)]. Hike up the drainage to the southeast ridge of Phi Kappa Mountain. Follow the ridge to Phi Kappa's summit. From the summit of Phi Kappa, follow the connecting ridge northwest to Peak 10885. The route to these summits is scenic and the view is particularly worthwhile for those wishing to get a good view of the Devils Bedstead East before attempting to climb it. USGS Phi Kappa Mountain

Devils Bedstead West   11,051 feet
This is the first named summit directly on the crest west of Trail Creek Summit. It is located 2 miles southeast of Phi Kappa Mountain. There is some confusion about which Pioneer peak is really the Devils Bedstead. The USGS quad and the latest Forest Service maps for the Challis National Forest mark this peak on the main divide, while the newest Sawtooth National Forest map shows Peak 11865, above Washington Lake, as the Devils Bedstead. This is the peak that surveyors Griswold and Perkins named the Devils Bedstead. For our purposes, the USGS-named peak will be known as the Devils Bedstead West; the peak identified by the Forest Service will be known as the Devils Bedstead East. USGS Phi Kappa Mountain

West Ridge (Class 3). The shortest approach is from Trail Creek Summit via FST-053 [(A)(3)(a)]. From the alpine saddle at the top of Summit Creek, traverse the ridgeline over to the saddle just west of the peak. Although the climb is relatively steep, the presence of numerous goat trails makes it an easy walk. From the second saddle, the route works up the ridge on solid rock to the summit. The first winter ascent was by L. Stur, R. Kiesel, B. Gorton, and B. Bachman.

South Rib (Class 3). This route climbs up a gully that descends from the summit to Wilson Creek. The base of the route can be reached from FST-123 [(A)(2)(b)]. Take the trail from the Corral Creek trailhead up a ridge, cross the saddle, and drop down into Wilson Creek. As soon as possible, contour north into the headwaters of Wilson Creek. Cross the drainage and climb the rib on its northwest side to the west ridge at 10,400 feet. Follow the west ridge to the summit.

Devils Bedstead East*　　　　　　　　*11,865 feet*

This spectacular peak sits 1.5 miles northeast of the Devils Bedstead West and 0.25 mile west of Washington Lake. It is truly a forbidding peak, with sheer walls on two sides and really steep walls on the other two. The approach is long, the rock broken, and the routes challenging. This is unquestionably one of Idaho's top ten summits. USGS Phi Kappa Mountain

Northeast Ridge (Class 3-4). Access this route from Wildhorse Canyon at Wildhorse CG. From the CG, begin the approach on the Boulder Lake Trail, FST-057 [(C)(1)(a) and (a.1)]. Follow this route to the small unnamed lake between the 9,800- and 10,000-foot contours on the USGS quad. From the lake, climb west through the wall above the lake and onto the 10,600-foot saddle on the peak's northern ridge. The ridge above the saddle is direct but steep, rugged but stable, and in places, exposed. A sharp step just below a false summit is the crux of the climb.

Northwest Face (Class 3). From the saddle on the northeast ridge (see description above), contour across the mountain and onto the northwest face. Work your way into the major gully that cuts the face. Follow the gully, crossing large blocks, to the ridgeline above the sharp step that blocks the northeast ridge and then ascend the ridge to the top.

Salzburger Spitzl*　　　　　　　*11,600+ feet (Class 2)*

This peak is positioned 1.5 miles southeast of the Devils Bedstead West and 1 mile north of Handwerk Peak. It was named by Florian Haemmerle, long-time manager of Pioneer Cabin for Sun Valley Resort, to honor three Austrian friends who died while serving as members of the U.S. 10th Mountain Division in World War II. Climb from the North Fork Hyndman Creek via its southern slopes [(B)(2)(a.1)] or from Pioneer Cabin [(A)(1)(a)] via the connecting ridge.

Goat Mountain*　　　　　　　　　*11,913 feet*

This summit, the second highest Pioneer peak, is 2.25 miles southeast of the Devils Bedstead West. For many years, a

The Boulder Creek approach to the towering Devils Bedstead East, which dominates the drainage's skyline (Photo by Dana Hansen)

Salzburger Spitzl (left) and twin-summited Handwerk Peak

sign stood atop the Sun Valley ski runs identifying this peak and incorrectly giving its elevation as more than 12,000 feet. The peak has twin summits; the northernmost summit is the highest. Some climbers call the northern summit Kane Peak, but there is insufficient vertical relief between the two summits for them to constitute two mountains. USGS Phi Kappa Mountain

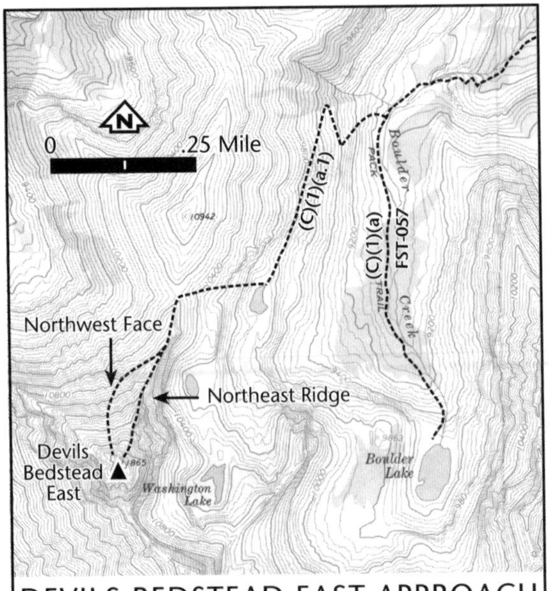

South Slopes (Class 3). The summit can be reached from the upper reaches of the North Fork Hyndman Creek via its southeastern slopes [(B)(2)(a.1)]. Follow the unnamed drainage leading into the basin south of Handwerk Peak until its walls grows considerably steeper at about 10,000 feet. From this point, the route climbs a boulder field, heading directly toward the large, distinct granite fin (known as Florians Nudl) on Goat's south ridge to a shelf 400 feet above. From the shelf, turn directly north and climb to the lower south summit on relatively stable material. From the top of the south summit, drop down the ridgeline to the saddle between the south and north summits. Keep on the east side of the ridge as much as possible by working the ledges. Once in the saddle, climb the ridge directly to the summit. There is some exposure on the traverse between the two summits, making this a difficult Class 3 climb.

Other Routes. R. Brooks, B. Troutner, and H. Bowron climbed the east face in 1991 and called the peak Kane Peak. No details of the ascent are known. K. Swigert and B. Rosso climbed the northeast ridge and rated it 5.8. Again, the details are not known.

Peak 11516 (Abel Peak)   *11,516 feet (Class 3)*
This challenging, unnamed peak, which sits between the Devils Bedstead East and Goat Mountain just east of Kane Lake, was ignored for years. The 600-foot vertical north face

DEVILS BEDSTEAD EAST APPROACH

(map, with labels:)
0 .25 Mile
Northwest Face
Northeast Ridge
Devils Bedstead East
Washington Lake
Boulder Lake
(C)(1)(a.1)
(C)(1)(a)
FST-057
Boulder Creek

246

just north of the summit is unclimbed. Access the peak from Kane Lake [(A)(4)(a)]. The route from the lake proceeds up a boulder-strewn, glacially scoured gully to the saddle south of the peak, and then climbs the south ridge to the summit. R. Baugher used this route to make the first ascent in 1994. USGS Phi Kappa Mountain

Handwerk Peak   10,840 feet

Handwerk Peak is found at the end of Goat Mountain's southeast ridge and directly north of Pioneer Cabin. While not one of the highest peaks in the range, this double-summit moun-

tain is one of the most interesting. Its unique "twin fangs" shape is breathtaking when viewed from Pioneer Cabin. The west summit may be about 10 feet shorter than the more rugged east summit. There is no practical route between the two summits. The peak is named after Ted Handwerk, who was killed while serving in Italy during World War II. USGS Phi Kappa Mountain

West Summit (Class 2). From the 9,200-foot contour in the unnamed basin [(B)(2)(a.1)] south of the peak, climb up to the west ridge through steep and loose talus. Once on the ridge, stay on its top and head east to the summit past two

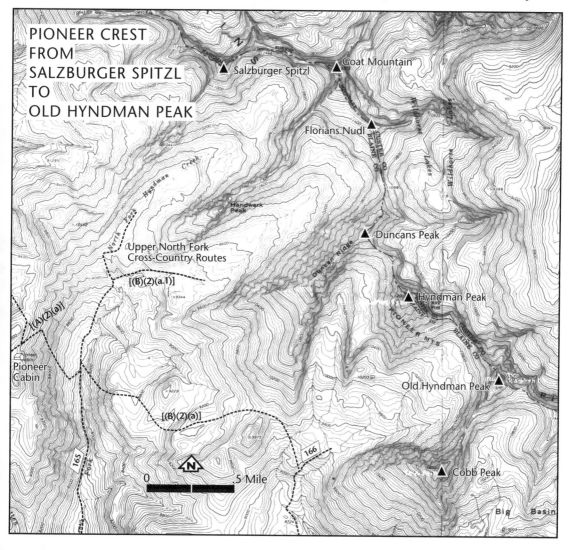

PIONEER CREST FROM SALZBURGER SPITZL TO OLD HYNDMAN PEAK

small cliffs on the south side of the ridge. A Class 4 descent leads down into the saddle between the east and west summits, but there is no reported route up the east summit from the saddle.

East Summit (Class 3-4). From the 9,800-foot contour in the unnamed basin south of the peak [(B)(2)(a.1)], climb up the ridgeline just east of the east summit. From this point, the route climbs up to the summit in a fairly direct manner, keeping on the north side of the ridge in two difficult spots.

Johnstone Peak   *9,949 feet (Class 2)*

Johnstone Peak is a popular destination for locals. When you experience its view, you will know why. The summit is situated 7 miles east of Ketchum and 5 miles southwest of Handwerk Peak. Multiple trails lead toward the summit dome. The most scenic approach is via the Pioneer Cabin Trail, FST-122 [(A)(2)(a)]. Follow it to its junction with FST-121, turn right and follow FST-121 until it crosses a saddle on the peak's northeast ridge. Follow this ridge for 1.25 miles to the summit.

FST-121 also can be accessed from Trail Creek Cabin [(A)(1)(a)]. After a long hike, the trail crosses a saddle on the peak's south side. From this point, follow the southwest ridge to the summit. The south ridge also can be approached from Parker and Bear Gulches.

A trailless route climbs the peak via its northwest ridge.

Drive up the Corral Creek Road [(A)(1)] for 1.5 miles, and turn onto the dirt road in Uncle Johns Gulch. Drive the road until it becomes too rough, then park. Hike up the road until it ends, and then continue to the saddle at the top of the gulch. From the saddle, follow the northwest ridge to the summit. USGS Hyndman Peak

Duncans Peak*   *11,755 feet (Class 3-4)*

This peak, which sits 1.1 miles due west of Handwerk Peak, is not officially named on the USGS map, but is instead identified as Duncan Ridge. The true summit is on the north end of the ridge. The peak is named for former Sun Valley resident Jonathan Duncan, who died in World War II. The peak has reportedly been climbed from two, and possibly three, directions. Access the Duncan Peak/Hyndman Peak saddle from the North Fork Hyndman Creek [(B)(2)(b)].

From the saddle at 11,340 feet, scramble northwest along the main crest until you reach the cliffy summit block. Scramble to your right on a ramp that climbs the headwall above Wildhorse Canyon. After gaining roughly 500 feet, the ramp ends 50 feet below the ridgeline. Climb up to the ridge top on good rock with good holds. The summit is a few yards beyond. Rick Baugher reports that though this route is not apparent from the saddle, "it is easy Class 3 when dry." USGS Phi Kappa Mountain

Johnstone Peak, from the Pioneer Cabin Trail

Hyndman Peak   *12,009 feet (Class 2)*

The ninth highest Idaho summit is located 0.6 mile southeast of Duncan Peak. It was named after Maj. William Hyndman, a Civil War veteran. It ranks third after Mount Borah and Thompson Peak in the Sawtooths on most climbers' wish lists. Hyndman, Cobb Peak, and Old Hyndman Peak are the impressive triumvirate of high peaks viewed from ID-75 when approaching Ketchum from both the north and south. Access this peak from the west via Hyndman Creek or from the east via Wildhorse Creek. It is not clear who recorded the first ascent. E. T. Perkins and W. Griswold climbed Hyndman sometime between 1889 and 1895 and Judge George A. McLeod, of Hailey, climbed the peak during this same time period. The first reported winter ascent was made by L. Stur and others in the early 1960s, although the details of the climb are unknown. R. Waters, J. Lowry, D. McBride, and J. Elphanson climbed the peak in December of 1992 via the east ridge. USGS Hyndman Peak

East Ridge (Class 2). Access this route from North Fork Hyndman Creek Road [(B)(2)(b)]. The east ridge is a steep but straightforward scramble once you get to the saddle between Hyndman and Old Hyndman Peaks. Reaching the saddle involves a scenic, 5-mile-approach hike. From the saddle, follow the ridge to the summit, staying on the south side of the ridge.

North Ridge (Class 3-4). Access this ridge from Wildhorse Canyon [(C)(1)]. Avoid obstacles by dropping onto the west side of the ridge. The first known ascent was made by the Idaho Alpine Club's B. Echo, C. Caldwell, and W. Sherman in 1957.

Other Routes. Hyndman has undoubtedly been climbed by other routes. Basil Service reports that a California group climbed the formidable north face in 1986, but no details are known about this climb.

Cobb Peak   *11,650 feet*

Cobb Peak is a beautiful rock horn that sits 1.25 miles south of Hyndman Peak. Its big south face dominates the entire Hyndman Creek drainage. It is believed that the peak was named for Calvin Cobb (1853–1928) who was the editor and publisher of the Idaho Statesman for nearly forty years. William McIntyre, of Twin Falls, climbed the peak in 1958, which is the earliest reported ascent. USGS Hyndman Peak

West Ridge (Class 3). This ridge is a classic mixture of

The heart of the northern Pioneer Mountains (left to right): Cobb Peak, Hyndman Peak, and Old Hyndman Peak

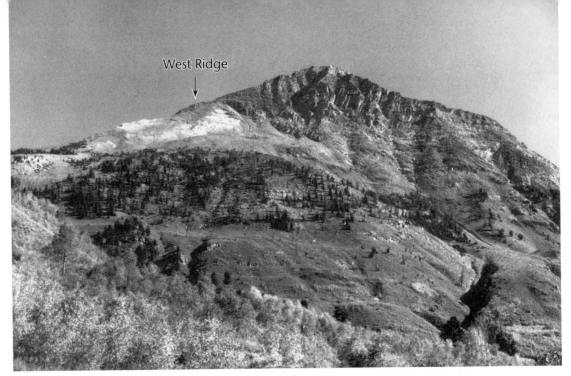

West Ridge

The massive south face of Cobb Peak rises over 3,400 feet in just under 1 mile.

talus-stepping, boulder-hopping, wall-climbing, and route-finding problems with considerable exposure thrown in for good measure. It is a great adventure. Access the west ridge from the unnamed drainage that separates Hyndman and Cobb Peaks [(B)(2)(b)]. From the point where the creek crosses the 9,440-foot contour on the USGS quad, look for a talus-covered rib that leads to the ridge top. The ridge is a walk-up except for the last 400 feet, where it turns into a series of rock walls and rotten gullies. While a variety of routes lead over this portion of the ridge to the summit, they all involve sustained Class 3 climbing and difficult route-finding problems. Stay on the south side of the ridge and be prepared to drop as much as 100 feet below the ridge crest to avoid technical climbing.

East Face (Class 3-4). This route begins in Big Basin [(B)(2)(b.2)]. The face is composed of broken ledges and slabs. Several routes are feasible. Keeping on the north side of the face is best.

North Face (II, Snow Climb). The north face of Cobb is cut by one major couloir that runs from left to right from the base of the face to the west ridge. The route is approximately 1,000 feet and varies greatly depending upon snow conditions. Access the face via Big Basin [(B)(2)(b.2)]. The first ascent was believed to be by B. Rosso. Mark Webber, in the May 1999 issue of *Rock and Ice*, reported a variation he called

the Vertical Perceptions Couloir. According to Webber, this route climbs the north couloir for one pitch and then exits to climb a line to the left of the main couloir.

Old Hyndman Peak   *11,775 feet*

Old Hyndman is located on the main Pioneer crest 1 mile southwest of Hyndman Peak. This Matterhorn-shaped summit—which is nearly vertical on every side—beckons climbers from every direction and especially when viewed from the mouth of Wildhorse Canyon. Its East Face/East Ridge route is a classic scramble reminiscent of climbs in Glacier National Park. Its nearly 3,000-foot north face is overhanging for the last 300 feet and is one of the most challenging walls in Idaho. USGS Grays Peak

East Ridge/East Face (Class 3). Access to the east face is from Hyndman Creek and Big Basin [(B)(2)(b.2)]. While the actual east face is only a little more than 300 feet high, it is located at the highest point on the mountain and is very steep. The face appears as a technical-climbing problem until you climb high enough to learn its secret. Follow the Big Basin drainage past Lake 10241 to the saddle between the peak and Point 11442. From the saddle, the route starts up the east ridge until the ridge merges into the base of the east face. From this point, you will learn the secret of the face: an eroded, black-rock dike. This dike runs up the face from southwest to northeast creating a break in the face. From the point where the east ridge ends, move into the gully at the bottom of the face and climb to the base of the dike. Once in the eroded path of the dike, the route becomes a protected staircase that leads to a point just below and south of the summit. Scramble from this point to the summit.

East Ridge/Southeast Face (Class 3). From the base of the east face (see description above) traverse southwest around the base of the large buttress that divides the east face from the southeast face. Once around the buttress, climb a steep gully to the notch above and then follow the south ridge the short distance to the summit.

Northeast Face (Class 5). This route begins in Wildhorse Canyon [(C)(1)] and climbs an obvious, southeast-slanting, ice and snow couloir on 45- to 50-degree slopes for 900 feet. At this point, the route cants to 60 degrees for a pitch that leads to a short, steep rock pitch at the top of the couloir. The route then climbs north for 1,200 feet to a steep section of loose rock roughly 150 feet below the top. Climb directly to the top from here. First ascent: B. March, N. Fujita, J. Leitch, and H. Hilbert in 1975. At least one other group has climbed this face.

Big Basin Peak*   *11,510 feet (Class 3)*
This peak is located 1 mile due east of Old Hyndman. It is yet another of the impressive peaks that form the south wall of Wildhorse Canyon. Climb the peak from Big Basin [(B)(2)(b.2)] via its west ridge, which can be climbed from the Old Hyndman/Point 11442 saddle. USGS Hyndman Peak

Peak 11210 (McIntyre Peak)   *11,210 feet (Class 3)*
This mountain, which is located 1.7 miles southeast of Old Hyndman, forms the Big Basin/East Fork Hyndman Divide. The best way to ascend this peak is to hike up the East Fork Wood River [(B)(1)(a)] past the Mascot Mine. At 8,300 feet, scramble west up a rubble-filled draw and then climb the peak's south slopes to the Class 3 southeast ridge. R. Baugher found paper shards dating from the 1950s and naming the peak McIntyre Peak on the summit in 1998. To climb the peak from Big Basin [(B)(2)(b.2)], climb to the saddle north of the peak and then follow the north ridge to the summit. USGS Grays Peak

Jacqueline Peak*   *11,027 feet (Class 3)*
This peak is a little over 1 mile southwest of McIntyre Peak. The two peaks are separated by a rugged knife-edge ridge and a common 10,600-foot saddle. W. A. McIntyre climbed the peak in 1958 and named it after his wife. He reported that he was the second person to climb the peak and left a register. By 1998 fewer than a dozen climbers had followed his foot steps. Climb the peak from the 10,000-foot saddle on the peak's west/southwest ridge. USGS Grays Peak

Old Hyndman's east face showing the black dike cutting upward from left to right

Angels Perch*   *11,687 feet (Class 2)*

This remote summit is the highest point along the east wall of Wildhorse Canyon on the divide that splits Wildhorse from Fall Creek. Angel Lake is the closest landmark 0.75 mile to the west. Climb the peak via its blocky, granite east ridge that is accessed south of Angel Lake. Getting to the lake is the crux of the climb. There are two options: Fall Creek or Moose Lake. Upper Fall Creek [(C)(2)(a.3)] is cluttered with downfall and is a difficult, but passable hike. Follow the creek until just east of the peak and then climb straight up aiming toward a point just south of the lake. From Moose Lake [(C)(2)(a.2)], climb to Lake 9455 and then hike southeast toward Point 10820. From the saddle west of Point 10820, it is an easy descent to the lake. Once at the lake, the east ridge is a straightforward scramble. USGS Standhope Peak

GRAYS PEAK DIVIDE

This 7-mile-long divide, which runs south from the main crest at Peak 11305 past Grays Peak, divides the East Fork Hyndman Creek and the Little Wood River drainages. Primary access is from Hyndman Creek.

Peak 11305 (The Box)   *11,305 feet (Class 3-4)*

This unnamed peak is the junction point for the main Pioneer crest and Grays Peak Divide. It is located 1.8 miles due east of Old Hyndman Peak. Two routes have been used to reach the peak's pointed summit. One follows the south ridge from Johnstone Pass [(B)(1)(a)]. It is the most direct route, but involves climbing around several difficult (potentially Class 5) obstacles along the way. Rick Baugher described the following alternative route.

Descend from Johnstone Pass to Box Lake. From the lake, hike north cross-country into the upper reaches of Box Canyon. The route angles northwest from this point accross Class 3 terrain to the main crest 200 feet below the summit. The summit is blocked by a 25-foot limestone cliff. Baugher climbed "a solid-looking, high-angle dihedral slab with good handholds." From the top of the cliff, the scramble moderates. Baugher's descent left the summit via the peak's southwest rib. He aimed for a "string of trees lower down on the rib." The base of the rib is blocked by cliffs. Baugher found a good granite gully through the cliffs and descended talus to the trail below Johnstone Pass. USGS Grays Peak

Peak 10805   *10,805 feet (Class 2)*

This peak is located 2.5 miles north of Grays Peak on the Grays Peak Divide. The summit is best climbed from PK Pass

[(B)(1)(c)] which is 0.8 mile to the south. From the pass, hike due north to the summit ridge, traverse around Point 10460, and continue to the summit. USGS Grays Peak

Grays Peak   *10,563 feet (Class 2)*

Grays Peak is located almost 5 miles south of Old Hyndman and the main Pioneer crest. Climb via the west ridge from Federal Gulch CG or from the saddle south of the peak, which is crossed by the Federal Gulch Trail, FST-169 [(B)(1)(b)]. USGS Grays Peak

Brocky Peak*   *11,839 feet*

This terrific summit is on the main crest 3.5 miles east/ northeast of Old Hyndman. It is a remote summit not easily approached from any direction. The summit is guarded by steep walls on every side. USGS Standhope Peak

Box Canyon (Class 3). Climb the peak from Upper Box Canyon Lake. Leave FST-175 [(B)(1)(a)] and hike around the ridge to the east and into the next drainage, losing 400 feet

Brocky Peak: Starting in the foreground, the knife-edged south ridge climbs and connects with the face. (Photo by Rick Baugher)

along the way. Continue to the top of the ridgeline to the northeast, aiming for a point north of Point 10695. Once on the ridge, turn north and make a long traverse to the summit.

Wildhorse (Class 4-5). Hike up the left fork of Wildhorse Creek [(C)(1)] into the cirque at 9,000 feet. Turn east, then northeast aiming for Point 11387 on the main crest. At this point, the peak's full grandeur and climbing problems become apparent. Following the ridge toward the summit involves traversing the jagged, Class 4 to Class 5 south ridge for 0.25 mile. To avoid this section of the ridge, descend to a tarn in the Little Wood drainage just south of Point 11387, and then re-ascend the left side of Brocky's south face to the ridge. This involves Class 3 to Class 4 climbing. Once back on the ridge you are just south of the summit. C. Ferguson and D. Ferguson made the first direct ascent of the ridge in 1994. R. Baugher made the first ascent of the upper south face on the same day.

THE STAR HOPE/BIG BLACK DOME DIVIDE

This is a major north/south divide that runs north from the main crest in a squiggly line for roughly 6 miles. It has knock-your-socks-off scenery and good trails. All of its summits are great climbs. Primary access is from Copper Basin. The peaks on the divide are listed from north to south.

Big Black Dome   *11,353 feet (Class 2)*
Big Black Dome is a hulking summit that dominates the view west from Copper Basin. The summit is located north of the main Pioneer crest, 1.75 miles north of Pyramid Peak. Follow FST-059 [(C)(3.1)(a)] west from FS-138 for about 2 miles to where the trail crosses the peak's east ridge. Leave the trail and climb the ridge to the summit. The middle portion of this broad ridge is a jumble of loose talus and the footing is poor. The view from the summit is nothing short of fantastic. USGS Big Black Dome

Pyramid Peak   *11,628 feet (Class 2)*
Pyramid is a ragged summit found due north of Bellas Lakes. The summit is protected on three sides by very steep walls and is best climbed from Bellas Lakes via the east ridge. According to Rick Baugher, the key to successfully climbing this peak is to understand that it does not resemble a pyramid. When approaching by way of Bellas Lakes, the awesome pyramid you see in front of you is the east face of Altair Peak. Pyramid Peak is 1 mile to the east. From the end of the Bellas Lake Trail [(C)(3)(a)] at the first lake, bushwhack to Point 10513. From this point, you can view the entire south face. The easiest route up the face follows the decomposed granite gullies and ledges

on the face's right-hand side. In 1997, Baugher found only five names in the register left by B. Lilley and G. MacLeod in 1990. C. Ferguson and L. Fatkin traversed the Class 4 Pyramid/Altair ridge. USGS Big Black Dome

Pegasus Peak*   *11,736 feet (Class 3)*
This superb summit is located 2 miles south/southwest of Big Black Dome and due west of Pyramid Peak. Its western face is a steep crumbling conglomeration of talus and short walls. The only reported climb began in the Left Fork Fall Creek [(C)(3.1)(a) or (2)(a.1)]. After rounding the base of Point 10910, head west up a draw. After passing some house-sized boulders, scramble up the gently sloping east ridge. First ascent: C. Ferguson and R. Baugher in 1994. USGS Standhope Peak

Altair Peak*   *11,825 feet (Class 3)*
The ridges leading south from Pegasus Peak and Pyramid Peak join at the summit of Altair. It is amazing that this Pioneer giant is officially unnamed. It should be on every peak baggers list. The peak's massive east face is one of Idaho's best and its southwest ridge is a classic scramble. Altair Peak is located 1.1 miles northeast of Standhope Peak. Climb the peak via its southwest ridge from the pass between Surprise Valley and Betty Lake [(C)(3)(b) or (2)(a)]. From the point where the trail crosses the pass, the way to the base of the ridge is blocked by a wall. Bypass this wall on its south side via a ledge system and a short down-climb. Once on the ridge, avoid obstacles by climbing around them on their south sides. USGS Standhope Peak

Standhope Peak   *11,878 feet*
This picturesque mountain is located at the head of Surprise Valley, 2.25 miles east of the Angels Perch and directly west of Altair Peak. It offers enjoyable Class 3 climbing via several routes. Although there are no reports of winter ascents, the north face would provide an exciting spring snow climb. T. M. Bannon made the first known ascent in 1915. USGS Standhope Peak

North Ridge (Class 3). Climb from the high, unnamed lake in Surprise Valley [(C)(2)(a) or (2)(a)]. From the lake, climb up to the saddle on the mountain's north ridge. Follow the ridge to the summit. The route occasionally crosses the ridge from side to side to avoid walls and to bypass several notches along the way.

Northeast Ridge (Class 3). Access this ridge by following the trail to the saddle between Betty Lake and Surprise Valley [(C)(3)(b)]. From the saddle, the route goes up the

Altair Peak (11,825) feet from the Betty Lake/Goat Lake Saddle

ridge on rotten rock, passing occasional towers that add to the difficulty.

Southeast Ridge (Class 3). Follow the trail to the saddle between Goat and Betty Lakes [(C)(3)(b.1)]. The route to the summit up the southeast ridge climbs 1,000 feet in 0.4 mile without any major difficulties.

Southwest Ridge (Class 2). Begin the climb from the saddle between Standhope Peak and Peak 11887. While this is the easiest route to the summit, reaching the saddle is a long strenuous endeavor. From Goat Lake [(C)(3)(b.1)], take the trail toward Betty Lake. Leave the trail at the last switchback before the saddle between the lakes and contour to the west into the cirque aiming for the Peak 11887/Standhope Peak saddle. Stay as high as possible on the Standhope Peak side of the cirque to avoid the loosest rock. Once at the saddle, the ridge offers a direct, uneventful route to the top.

Peak 11887   *11,887 feet*

This glorious rampart's summit ridge, which is a rooster comb of granite towers and blocks, is one of Idaho's most impregnable mountains. It is located 0.75 mile directly south of Standhope Peak and towers over Goat Lake. The peak's east face offers several potential solid lines for technical routes, but no technical climbing has been reported to date. USGS Standhope Peak

North Ridge (Class 3-4). The north ridge is accessed from Goat Lake [(C)(3)(b.1)]. Leave the trail between Goat and Betty Lakes at the last switchback before the saddle between the lakes and contour to the west into the cirque aiming for the Peak 11887/Standhope Peak saddle. Stay as high as possible on the Standhope Peak side of the cirque to avoid the loosest rock. From the saddle, the north ridge is studded with obstacles. The first obstacle is a tower. Climb over it via a broad crack. Above this tower, stay on the east side of the ridge until the route is blocked by vertical granite walls. Climb through a notch and back to the west side of the ridge. There are several options from this point. Eventually, you will reach a notch near the summit tower. Descend to the notch and then continue a short distance out onto the northwest face where a moderate-angle rock wall leads up to the tiny summit. Climb this wall on small ledges to the top.

Ascending the north ridge of Peak 11887

THE MAIN CREST FROM
GLIDE MOUNTAIN TO ERR PEAK

Glide Mountain   *10,265 feet (Class 2)*
South of the point where the Big Black Dome/Standhope Divide joins the Pioneer crest, the crest drops below 10,000 feet for several miles. Glide Mountain is the first named summit to once again rise above 10,000 feet after this uncharacteristic dip. It is located just east of the main crest and 4.5 miles southeast of Standhope Peak. Climb Glide Mountain from either Copper Basin via the Star Hope Creek Road and its east slopes [(C)(3.3)] or from FST-176 and the mountain's west ridge [(E)(1)(a)]. USGS Star Hope Mine

Peak 10444   *10,444 feet (Class 3)*
Peak 10444 sits on the divide between Star Hope Creek and Muldoon Canyon, north of the main crest. Glide Mountain is 2.4 miles to the north. The two large glaciers that cut the Star Hope and Muldoon Canyons left a long, narrow spine of rock crowned by this high peak. Access the peak from the roads in either canyon [(C)(3.3) or (3.4)]. From the west, climb via its west ridge. From the east, ascend to the saddle south of the peak and then follow the south ridge north to the top. USGS Star Hope Mine

Peak 10400+   *10,400+ feet (Class 3)*
Moving south along the crest from Glide Mountain, this unnamed, pyramid-shaped peak is located 2.5 miles to the south. The summit is reached after a short scramble via its southwest ridge. Hike FST-176 [(E)(1)(a) or (C)(3.2)(a)] to the base of the ridge at 8,200 feet. Follow the ridge to the summit. USGS Star Hope Mine

Mandolin Peak   *9,189 feet (Class 2)*
Mandolin Peak is located west of the main crest and 2 miles north of Swede Peak. Take FST-170 for 2 miles from its beginning at the end of FS-130, and then leave the trail and hike up the 200 feet to the summit [(E)(1.3)(a)]. Early in the summer, elk are often spotted grazing on the peak's western slopes. USGS Star Hope Mine

Swede Peak   *8,480 feet (Class 2)*
Swede Peak, located west of the main crest and 4 miles north of the Garfield GS, sits at the head of several small drainages. This peak is a short walk from the end of FS-130 via FST-179. USGS Star Hope Mine

Garfield Mountain   *8,700 feet (Class 3)*
The north end of this peak is called Garfield Mountain and the south end is called Bell Rock. Whatever you call it, it is located 2.5 miles south/southeast of Swede Peak. The peak has a dacite volcanic neck which offers several Class 4 and 5 route possibilities. A Class 3 route climbs up the southeast side of the summit block. In 1994, R. Baugher found a summit register with two names and a $1 bill on the summit. Access the peak from the end of FS-130 [(E)(1.3)(a)]. USGS Muldoon

Drummond Peak   *10,525 feet (Class 3)*

The next true summit along the crest south of Peak 10400+ is best accessed from Little Copper Creek via the road to the Drummond Mine [(E)(1)(b)]. Hike along the road to the highest point at more than 9,400 feet and then scramble directly east to the summit. USGS Star Hope Mine

Antares Peak*   *10,651 feet (Class 3)*

Three big peaks stand over the headwaters of Garfield Canyon; only one, Scorpion Peak, is named. This peak is the highest of the three and unofficially named for the brightest star in the Scorpion constellation. It is an enticing summit when viewed from the Garfield GS. The peak is an enjoyable scramble up its south ridge, which is accessed from Garfield Canyon, FS-228 [(E)(1.2)]. Drive up Garfield Canyon and park at the first switchback. Cross the stream and hike to the base of the south ridge. Hike directly up the ridge ignoring the mining road that switches back to 8,800 feet. Expect great views on the summit. USGS Star Hope Mine

Peak 10650   *10,650 feet (Class 3)*

The second peak above Garfield Canyon from west to east, this summit is located 0.9 mile east of Antares Peak. The most enjoyable route up the summit climbs the south face from Garfield Canyon [(E)(1.2)]. Park at the ruins of a mining operation and then hike east up the canyon bottom until you are below the south face. Follow the small drainage that cuts the face until you can gain the south ridge at roughly 10,400 feet. The peak also can be climbed from Muldoon Canyon [(C)(3.4)]. Follow the left fork of the canyon until you are east of the summit, then hike to the saddle north of the peak and climb the northeast ridge. The summit ridge between this peak and Scorpion Peak is passable. USGS Star Hope Mine

Peak 10613   *10,613 feet (Class 3)*

This rocky horn, a remnant of the large glacier that carved Muldoon Canyon, sits in the middle of the canyon 2 miles due north of Scorpion Mountain. It is a grand spot to survey this seldom visited region. Climb the peak via its south ridge, which is accessible from either fork of Muldoon Canyon [(C)(3.4)]. USGS Star Hope Mine

Scorpion Peak   *10,545 feet (Class 3)*

T. M. Bannon used this summit as a triangulation station in 1915. It is likely that either T. M. Bannon or a miner made the first ascent. Scorpion Peak is located 7.5 miles southeast of Glide Mountain at the source of Garfield and Muldoon Creeks.

The best route to the summit follows the Garfield Canyon road [(E)(1.2)]. Leave the road at its first switchback and follow the drainage up to a spring located northwest of the summit. From this point, climb a rib to the ridgeline between Scorpion Peak and the next summit to the north. Follow the summit ridge directly to the summit. USGS Star Hope Mine

Peak 10480+   *10,480+ feet (Class 3)*

Continuing east along the main Pioneer crest, this summit rises 1,200 feet above Fishpole Lake. The only reported route ascends the peak's south slopes from Argosy Creek. Unfortunately, private property blocks access into the creek making the approach a little more difficult. Follow FS-126 [(E)(1)] until you cross the Sawtooth National Forest boundary. Park at that point and then contour around the intervening ridge into upper Argosy Creek. Follow the drainage to the saddle south of the summit and climb to the top from the saddle. USGS Smiley Mountain

Pion Peak*   *10,680 feet (Class 3)*

The next peak south of Peak 10480+ was climbed by T. M. Bannon in 1915 and named Pion. For some reason Bannon's chosen name did not make it onto the newer maps. Rick Baugher suggests climbing the peak via the saddle on its north ridge, which is accessed from Argosy Creek (see the Peak 10480+ write-up). USGS Smiley Mountain/Trail Creek

Err Peak*   *10,744 feet (Class 3)*

This peak is 0.5 mile south of Pion Peak and the southernmost of the alpine Pioneer peaks. Rick Baugher recommends climbing Err via the connecting ridge from Pion Peak. First ascent: R. Baugher in 1994. USGS Trail Creek

THE SMILEY LOBE

This complicated ridge system stretches 10 miles north from the main Pioneer crest near Scorpion Mountain. Four miles from its start in the south, it splits into two ridges that embrace the multiple-lake Lake Creek Basin. Primary access to these peaks is from Copper Basin to the north and from Antelope Creek to the south. Other than Smiley Peak, few ascents of these terrific peaks take place. The Lobe's peaks are listed from north to south.

Copper Basin Knob   *10,784 feet (Class 3)*

Located at the north end of the eastern fork of the Smiley Lobe, this peak is a major landmark above Copper Basin.

Reach the summit from Lake Creek via the saddle on the west side of the peak. From where FS-138 crosses Lake Creek, follow the Lake Creek Trail [(C)(3)(d)] east for roughly 2 miles. At this point, leave the trail and bushwhack up the steep slope to the saddle between the summit and Point 10225, and then follow the ridge east to the summit. USGS Copper Basin Knob

Peak 10995   *10,995 feet (Class 2)*
Peak 11151   *11,151 feet (Class 2)*
These twin summits are the next two summits south of Copper Basin Knob on the eastern fork of the Smiley Divide. Climb both summits from Round Lake in the Lake Creek Basin [(C)(3)(d)]. From the lake, hike to the saddle between the peaks. From the saddle, it is an easy hike to both summits. USGS Smiley Mountain

Smiley Mountain   *11,508 feet*
Smiley Mountain, a large dome-shaped summit, dominates the entire eastern end of the range. It is the highest point along the Smiley Lobe. It is located 4 miles southeast of Copper Basin Knob. T. M. Bannon climbed the peak in 1915 and claimed to have taken horses to the top. USGS Smiley Mountain

North Ridge (Class 2). Climb this route from Lake Creek by going due east around Round Lake toward Point 10806. Follow the upper bowl to the south and gain the peak's broad north ridge. Follow the ridge to Point 11179 and then on to the summit [(C)(3)(d)].

South Ridge (Class 2). The south ridge is the most popular route on Smiley Mountain. Because of its southern exposure and the relatively low elevation of its approach, climbing the ridge in early May is possible—even in heavy snow years. From the Antelope Creek Road [(D)(1)], turn onto FS-221 just past Iron Bog CG. Follow FS-221 to a large, sagebrush-filled clearing from which the upper slopes of Smiley Mountain are clearly visible. The elevation at this point is roughly 8,000 feet. Park here and climb due north up a gully for a little more than 400 feet to a large level clearing. From this clearing, a second gully leads up through the forest to the treeless slopes above. Stay on the east side of the gully, topping out on the peak's southeast ridge. Follow this ridge up to the top of the south ridge, which leads to the summit.

Peak 11039 (Atlas Peak)   *11,039 feet (Class 3)*
This peak is the northernmost summit on the west fork of the Smiley Lobe that divides Muldoon Canyon and Lake Creek. The elevation is taken from the old 15-minute USGS Muldoon Canyon map. Its impressive west face rises directly above Big

Lake. Climb the peak via its north ridge. From the Muldoon Canyon Road [(C)(3.4)], take the narrow 4WD road toward Green Lake. Rick Baugher describes the route this way: "At roughly 9,000 feet, leave the road and contour northeast into the next drainage. From this drainage, scramble northeast up a gully and face to the peak's twin summit and an abandoned triangulation station." First ascent: probably a USGS survey crew. USGS Smiley Mountain

Peak 11258 (Alcyon Peak)   *11,258 feet (Class 3-4)*
This ragged summit has a 2-mile summit ridge with seven points rising above 11,000 feet. It forms the junction of the western and eastern forks of the Smiley Lobe. Its middle summit is the highest. The elevation is taken from the old 15-minute USGS quad. Rick Baugher's ascent climbed the peak from the west starting in Muldoon Canyon [(C)(3.4)]. Hike to Green Lake and then work your way southeast to the high saddle west of the peak. Climb east and then north to the summit. To climb the peak from the east, start in Iron Bog Creek. Hike up its right fork [(D)(1.1)(a)]. At 8,800 feet, bushwhack north up an unnamed drainage to the small lake at 10,100 feet (north/northeast of Brockie Lake). From the lake, climb north or northeast to the summit. First ascent: R. Baugher in 1993. USGS Muldoon Canyon map. USGS Smiley Mountain

Peak 10920   *10,920 feet (Class 3)*
This peak is located south of Brockie Lake between Muldoon Canyon and the Right Fork Antelope Creek. The only known route ascends the west face from Muldoon Canyon [(D)(1) (a)]. Climb the face via the rib that descends from the summit ridge just north of the peak. USGS Smiley Mountain

Peak 10800   *10,800+ feet (Class 3)*
This unnamed summit sits at the head of Antelope Creek between its right and left forks and directly north of Iron Bog Lake. Rick Baugher climbed the peak via its southeast ridge from Iron Bog Lake [(D)(1)(a)]. USGS Smiley Mountain

Blizzard Mountain   *9,313 feet (Class 2)*
Catching the southwesterly winds roaring up the Snake River Plain, the leeward side of Blizzard Mountain holds snow for most of the year. Private property prevents good access to this peak. The surest way to reach the summit involves taking the Old Arco-Hailey Wagon Road to Cottonwood Creek and the defunct Paymaster Mine at the south base of the peak. From this point, you can follow either a ridge or a gully northwest

to the summit. T. M. Bannon climbed the peak in 1915. According to Rick Baugher, the early season bloom of arrowleaf balsamroot on these slopes is legendary. USGS Blizzard Peak North/Blizzard Peak South

APPROACHES TO THE PIONEER MOUNTAINS

(A) TRAIL CREEK ROAD ACCESS POINTS

Trail Creek Road travels northeast from downtown Ketchum over Trail Creek Summit (where the Boulder and Pioneer Mountains meet) and then drops down into the upper reaches of the Big Lost River drainage where it links with the road leading into Copper Basin [(C)]. It is paved to the base of the pass and then is gravel for the remaining distance. Several good access points are available from this road, which is accessed either from ID-75 in the west or US-93 in the east.

(1) **Trail Creek Cabin.** Trail Creek Cabin, an exclusive restaurant owned by the Sun Valley Company, is located along the Trail Creek Road just past the resort. The junction is signed. The restaurant's parking lot is open to use by hikers. From the parking lot, head west on a road that swings around the cabin and then crosses Trail Creek on a bridge to reach the trailhead.

(a) **Proctor Mountain Trail.** From the trailhead, follow the road upstream for several hundred yards to the Proctor Mountain Trail junction. This good trail begins by switching back up the hillside to a ridge top above Trail Creek. It eventually reaches a junction with FST-121 [(A)(2)(a)]. Go left at this junction and continue toward Proctor Mountain. As an alternative, follow the road south from the trailhead to a junction with a trail that climbs up a drainage to join the Proctor Mountain Trail.

(2) **FS-137, Corral Creek Road.** Drive 4 miles east of Ketchum on Trail Creek Road. Turn right onto the Corral Creek Road and drive 4 more miles on a good gravel road to its end and a trailhead.

(a) **FST-122, FST-121, Pioneer Cabin Trail.** This 4-mile trail is well marked and maintained. The trail runs to Pioneer Cabin on an extremely scenic saddle. From the cabin, the trail continues down into the North Fork Hyndman Creek where it joins FST-165 [(B)(2)(a)]. The rodent-infested cabin is open to the public on a first-come, first-served basis.

(a.1) **Pioneer Cabin/Corral Creek Trail.** This cutoff trail runs from Pioneer Cabin north to Corral Creek, where it joins FST-123 [(A)(2)(b)]. The trail is difficult to follow in places and is not shown on the Hyndman Peak USGS quad. Its beginning is marked by a sign at Pioneer Cabin.

(a.2) **FST-165, North Fork Trail.** This trail descends from Pioneer Cabin into the North Fork Hyndman Creek [(B)(2)(a)].

(b) **FST-123, Corral Creek Ridge Trail.** This trail leaves the trailhead and climbs the ridge between Corral and Long Gulch Canyons to the top of a small subsidiary peak just south of the main divide. It then drops down into seldom-visited Wilson Creek. The trail eventually joins up with the Trail Creek Road. About 1.5 miles from the trailhead, an old trail (without a designated number on the Forest Service maps) [(A)(2)(a.1)] heads east toward Pioneer Cabin. This trail is difficult to follow in places.

(3) **Trail Creek Summit Area.** Trail Creek Summit is 12 miles east of Ketchum on the Trail Creek Road. Park on the south side of the road near a snow measurement marker.

(a) **FST-053, Summit Creek Trail.** This good trail follows tiny Summit Creek up from the pass to a high alpine valley with a large meadow. The route continues through the meadow to a saddle in 4 miles. From this point, dropping cross-country into Kane Lake and the valley below is possible via a seldom-used trail that eventually joins FST-066 [(A)(4)(a)].

(4) **FS-134, Kane Creek Road.** From Ketchum, take Trail Creek Road 21 miles to reach Kane Creek Road. Turn right and drive up the creek for 3.5 miles to the Kane Lake trailhead.

(a) **FST-066, Kane Lake Trail.** This 4-mile trail takes you to the 9,300-foot lake at the foot of the Devils Bedstead West.

(B) ID-75 ACCESS POINTS

This highway, which connects Shoshone and Challis, Idaho, is the primary approach to the Sun Valley/Ketchum area.

(1) **FS-118, East Fork Wood River Road.** Turn east off ID-75 onto this road 4 miles south of Ketchum and drive toward the mountains. The road is paved to the Triumph Mine site and then is gravel and dirt for its remaining distance. One mile above the Triumph Mine, the road forks. The left-hand fork goes to the North Fork Hyndman Creek [(B)(2)], the right fork (straight ahead) ascends the East Fork Big Wood River toward Johnstone Pass. Beyond this fork, the right fork can be ugly and may require 4WD capability. The left-hand fork has been improved and autos can usually make it to its end.

(a) **FST-175, Johnstone Pass Trail.** Keep right when the East Fork Road forks above the Triumph Mine and follow this rugged road to its end at more than 8,000 feet. There is enough parking for several vehicles at this point. The trail leaves the parking area and heads up the north side of the creek. After 2 miles, the trail crosses the creek and switches back up an unstable slope of deteriorated granite to 10,000-foot Johnstone Pass in just over 3.5 miles. This trail washed out during a thunderstorm in 1984 and has not yet been rebuilt. From the pass, the trail descends to Upper Box Canyon Lake and eventually all the way to the bottom of the Little Wood River Canyon. By following a topo map, you can reach Windy Lakes via a cross-country traverse from Upper

Box Canyon Lake. From the lake, traverse around the ridge to the east, cross the unnamed drainage and climb over the ridge to the west of Windy Lake, just north of Point 10695.

(b) FST-169, Federal Gulch Trail. FST-169 leaves FS-118 at the Federal Gulch CG and climbs to a pass southwest of Greys Peak in 3 steep miles. From the pass, the trail continues east and descends into the Little Wood River Canyon.

(c) FST-174, PK Pass Trail. This trail leaves the road 0.5 mile south of its end. Its starts out climbing up an avalanche chute and may be difficult to find after a hard winter. Once on the trail, you will find it climbs 1,300 feet to PK Pass. From the pass, the trail descends into the Little Wood River drainage.

(2) FS-203, North Fork Hyndman Creek Road. Take the left fork where the East Fork Wood River Road divides above the Triumph Mine. Three miles beyond the fork, the road crosses Hyndman Creek on a bridge and then climbs up the hillside, continuing for 2 more miles to meet the North Fork Hyndman Creek where it abruptly ends at a locked gate.

(a) FST-165, North Fork Creek Loop Trail. FST-165 provides access to Pioneer Cabin and the upper North Fork Basin. The trail, recently improved, runs to a point just below Pioneer Cabin where it forks. One fork, FST-121 climbs up to Pioneer Cabin [(A)(2)(a)]. The other loops back to Hyndman Creek (see [(B)(2)(b)], below). From the junction below Pioneer Cabin, it is possible to gain access to the trailless basins below Goat Mountain [(B)(2)(a.1)].

(a.1) Upper North Fork Basin Cross-Country Routes. The routes into the upper basin begin where FST-165 turns sharply and begins its climb out of the North Fork Hyndman Creek drainage toward Pioneer Cabin. From this turn, follow a game trail that parallels the creek up the valley, keeping west of the creek, and head toward the white cliffs at the head of the drainage. Hike up through an obvious gully that splits the cliffs to a shelf above the cliffs, and then follow the creek upstream to a crossing near the base of Handwerk Peak. From this point, game trails lead into the basins south and north of Handwerk Peak. Follow the unnamed drainage on the south side of Handwerk Peak to the east to reach Handwerk, Goat, and Duncan Peaks. To reach Salzburger Spitzl, follow the North Fork Hyndman Creek into the basin north of Handwerk.

(b) FST-165, Hyndman Creek Trail/Hyndman Peak Access. This trail starts at the end of FS-203, behind the locked gate. The trail follows an old road, fording the North Fork Hyndman Creek, then continues for 3 more miles to the base of Cobb Peak. From the old road's end, FST-165 [(B)(2)(b.1)] climbs up the hillside. The trail soon reaches a flat, where a surprisingly good sheepherder's trail can be found leading upstream into the meadows below Hyndman Peak.

(b.1) FST-165, Hyndman Cutoff Trail. This seldom-maintained trail is difficult to follow for its entire distance between Hyndman Creek and the North Fork Hyndman Creek [(B)(2)(a)]. It is an enjoyable, expert hike that allows hikers to loop-hike the two drainages.

(b.2) Big Basin Trails. Near the base of Cobb Peak, a faint and easily missed old mining road departs the Hyndman Creek Trail and leads to the south. It quickly fords the creek (difficult in high water) and then turns up the hillside to an old mine. Follow this road, which is designated as FST-166, to a point at which you can strike east and contour cross-country into the valley holding Cobb Lakes. The lakes are 3 miles from the beginning of FST-166, behind Cobb Peak and below Old Hyndman Peak.

(C) COPPER BASIN ACCESS POINTS

The Copper Basin Road leaves the Trail Creek Road 22 miles east of Ketchum and follows the East Fork Big Lost River into magnificent, windswept Copper Basin. From Copper Basin, several other roads break out to the south, east, and north. FS-135 leads over Antelope Summit to the east and eventually reaches US-93 via Antelope Creek [(E)]. Antelope Summit is the dividing point between the Pioneer and White Knob Mountains.

(1) FS-138, Wildhorse Canyon Road. This road leaves the Copper Basin Road 2.5 miles south of its junction with the Trail Creek Road and proceeds up dramatic Wildhorse Canyon. The road is in good condition to Wildhorse CG. A 4WD is required beyond the CG.

(a) FST-057, Boulder Lake Trail. This trail leaves the Wildhorse Creek Road just before the Wildhorse CG. The trail runs up Boulder Creek to the lake in 3.5 miles. There is no bridge and the stream crossing will be difficult during high water. Once across the creek and through the willows, look for a sign marking the beginning of the trail.

(a.1) Unnamed Lake Trail. This enigma of a trail leads to the unnamed lake 0.7 mile northwest of Boulder Lake. Look for this lake between the 9,800- and 10,000-foot contour lines on the Phi Kappa Mountain USGS quad. This Forest Service trail is not shown on any recent map. While its beginning is unmarked, old signs can be found along its route, and some maintenance has taken place in recent years. Look for the trail junction in a sagebrush-filled clearing at the point where the Boulder Lake Trail crosses the 8,960-foot contour on the USGS quad. Two rock cairns mark the start of the trail. From its tenuous beginning, the trail switches back up the open slopes above and then turns due south to make a direct ascent to the unnamed lake. In a stand of stunted pines, you will find trail signs and a junction for another trail that leads northwest to Kane Creek. Keep left at this junction. The trail is generally well marked, with one or two minor exceptions. When you reach the lake, you may notice a sign identifying it as Washington Lake.

(2) Fall Creek Trailhead. The trailhead is located a little more than 2 miles south of the Wildhorse GS, or about 3.5 miles south from the beginning of the Wildhorse Canyon Road. This road, which once continued east for 3 miles, now ends in 0.5 mile. At this point, the Forest Service has installed a good foot bridge across Fall Creek to mark the beginning of the Fall Creek Trail system.

(a) FST-045, Fall Creek/Surprise Valley/Broad Canyon Trail. From the end of the road, trails reach up the left, main, and right forks of Fall Creek. FST-045 continues past the Moose Lakes junction and leads to Surprise Valley and Surprise Lake, and then continues across a ridge to Betty Lake and the Broad Canyon trailhead [(C)(3)(b)].

(a.1) FST-059, Left Fork Trail. This trail runs due east to FS-138 [(C)(3.1)(a)] in 9 miles. Although little used, it provides access to several big peaks.

(a.2) FST-068, Moose Lake Trail. The Moose Lakes are reached after a long, 1-mile hike up FST-068 from the junction with FST-045. This trail is heavily used by horse packers.

(a.3) Upper Fall Creek Trail. An unmaintained trail continues up Fall Creek for some distance. It is a difficult journey thanks to heavy downfall. Nevertheless, upper Fall Creek is a special place and you may find it worth the effort.

(3) FS-138, Copper Basin Loop Road. This road leaves the main Copper Basin Road 13 miles from its junction with the Trail Creek Road. Turn south at the sign announcing Star Hope Canyon. The road creeps more than 10 miles south toward Glide Mountain before turning north and returning to the Copper Basin Road.

(a) FST-060, Bellas Lake Trail. This trail starts 5 miles south of the beginning of FS-138 and leads to Bellas Lakes near Pyramid Peak in 3 miles. Look for the trailhead at the Bellas Canyon CG.

(b) FST-061, Broad Canyon Trail. Access FST-061, 8 miles from the beginning of FS-138. This trail leads to Betty Lake and the Standhope Peak area in 4.5 miles. From the lake, the trail continues to Surprise Valley [(C)(2)(a)].

(b.1) Goat Lake/Betty Lake Trail. This trail leaves FST-061 roughly 1 mile before Betty Lake. It quickly climbs to Baptie Lake and then continues to Goat Lake. From Goat Lake, the trail switchbacks up the ridge to the north, crosses a divide and drops down to Betty Lake. Although not shown on many maps, the trail is in excellent shape.

(c) FST-062, Bear Canyon Trail. Access this trail from FS-138 at the Star Hope CG. This good trail runs due west to join FST-176 [(E)(1)(a)], which leads north to the Little Wood River and south to the Garfield GS.

(d) FST-064, Lake Creek Trail. Take FS-138 to the Lake Creek CG. The trail leaves from this point and proceeds to several lakes in the upper basin. This trail is open to ORVs

(3.1) FS-472, Ramey Creek Road. This road departs the Copper Basin Loop Road a couple of miles south of FS-135. From its beginning, it makes a rugged climb to the southwest toward Ramey Creek. Just before reaching Ramey Creek, a road forks off to the west. This road is designated FST-059. A 4WD is required.

(a) FST-059, Left Fork Trail. FST-059 leads from FS-138 east to FS-136 [(C)(2)(a.1)] in a little over 9 miles. The trail, which begins as a primitive road designated FS-472, passes over the rugged northern slopes of Big Black Dome on its way west. The tread is nonexistent in places.

(3.2) Bear Creek Trail Access. This trail leaves from a marked trailhead at the southern terminus of the Copper Basin Loop Road.

(a) FST-062, Bear Creek Trail. This trail climbs up Bear Creek. In 1.5 miles it intersects with FST-043. Going right at this junction will lead to Broad Canyon [(C)(3)(b)]. Going left will lead to the Copper Creek Trail [(E)(1)(a)].

(3.3) FS-508, Star Hope Road. This road leaves the Loop Road just east of its southern terminus and follows Star Hope Creek south for 4 miles.

(a) FST-063, Star Hope Mine Trail. This short trail leads to the mine at the base of Peak 10444 in about 1 mile.

(3.4) FS-510, Muldoon Canyon Road. This road runs south through this beautiful U-shaped valley for 4.1 miles. Near its southern terminus, FS-511 splits off and climbs to Green Lake.

(a) FST-065, Muldoon Canyon/Iron Bog Lake Trail. From the end of the Muldoon Canyon Road, this trail runs due south and then east to cross the Smiley Lobe in 4.4 miles. From the saddle, the trail descends to Iron Bog Lake and then to its eastern trailhead [(D)(1)(a)].

(D) ANTELOPE CREEK ROAD

A combination of county and Forest Service roads traverse Antelope Creek, climb over Antelope Pass and then drop into Copper Basin [(C)]. Turn off US-93 10.5 mile north of Arco and follow the Antelope Creek Road west into the mountains. At the Antelope GS, FS-135 heads north up Bear Creek and Cherry Creek, then reaches windswept Antelope Pass. The stretch of this road that climbs to Antelope Pass is narrow, winding, rutted, and can be very slick after rain. A 4WD is recommended.

(1) FS-137/221, Iron Bog Creek Road. From the GS, continue following the creek toward Iron Bog CG 23.5 miles from US-93. Roughly 1 mile past the CG, the road forks. A 4WD is recommended.

(a) FST-065, Iron Bog Lake/Muldoon Canyon Trail. Take the left-hand fork for 3.8 miles to the trailhead. This trail begins climbing immediately uphill toward Iron Bog Lake in 1.3 miles and then continues west, climbing 400 feet to cross the Smiley Lobe, and drops into Muldoon Canyon [(C)(3.4)(a)].

(a.1) FST-122, Fishpole Lake Trail. This trail makes a quick traverse to the south to Fishpole Lake. Look for the start of the trail below Iron Bog Lake along its outlet stream.

(1.1) FS-137/220, Brockie Lake Access. Follow the Iron Bog Road into the Right Fork Iron Bog Creek to the road's end. A 4WD is recommended.

(a) FST-221, Brockie Lake Trail. Brockie Lake is 2 miles from the end of the road on this surprisingly good trail.

(E) US-20/93 ACCESS POINTS

This major east/west highway system connects with ID-75 south of Ketchum, runs east to Carey and US-93, and then continues to Arco.

(1) Garfield GS Access. Leave US-93 on the east end of Carey on the road signed for Little Wood River Reservoir 11. This junction is 1.1 miles east of the US-93/ID-20 junction. Keep right at a fork in 9 miles. At the next junction in 6.3 miles, go left. The next junction is 2.1 miles ahead. There are two ranch houses at this junction. Turn right. (Going left will eventually take you to Bellevue.) You are now on FS-125. In 3 miles you will reach the junction for FS-126 that goes up Muldoon Creek. Continue straight ahead, passing Garfield CG and the GS in 9.5 and 9.7 miles respectively. The road continues up Copper Creek for roughly 2 miles to the trailhead for FST-176.

(a) FST-176, Copper Creek Trail. This trail runs north, eventually climbing across the Pioneer crest. It provides direct access to Glide Mountain and the upper reaches of the Little Wood River, as well as connecting with FST-062, the Bear Canyon Trail [(C)(3.2)(a)], in Copper Basin.

(b) Little Copper Creek Mine Road. This route, which begins at the end of FS-135, continues up Little Copper Creek to the Drummond Mine at 9,200 feet. Drive it as far as you safely can, and then hike up the remaining distance.

(1.1) Muldoon Creek Road. This road leaves FS-135 and runs east to Muldoon Creek, then follows the creek north for a couple of miles.

(1.2) FS-228, Garfield Canyon Road. FS-228, which goes up Garfield Canyon, begins just past Garfield GS. This road, built by miners, climbs up Garfield Canyon to an old mining camp in 2.5 miles. The road does continue up the slopes of Peak 10651, but is very rough from this point. A 4WD is required.

(1.3) FS-130, Mormon Hill Road. FS-130 leaves FS-135 0.75 mile past Garfield GS. FS-130 is a rough road that usually requires a 4WD.

(a) FST-160/179, Mandolin Peak Trail. From the trailhead, this trail runs west for about 1 mile to a junction. FST-179 leads straight ahead to the Little Wood River. Take this

trail to climb Swede Peak. Go right to access Mandolin Peak. This trail eventually intersects with FST-160 [(E)(1)(a)] north of Mandolin Peak.

4

THE WHITE KNOB MOUNTAINS

The White Knob Mountains are a compact group of sedimentary peaks located west of Mackay. The range's west-to-east-trending crest is about 30 miles in length and 10 miles in width. The East Fork Big Lost River and the Big Lost River almost completely encircle the White Knob Mountains, forming the range's southern, western, northern, and eastern boundaries. Antelope Creek completes the circle along the range's southern boundary as it flows east from Antelope Pass to the Big Lost River.

Geologists believe that the range was originally uplifted by forces associated with the creation of the Idaho Batholith. The range is primarily composed of limestone intruded by granite 50 million years ago and capped in places by Challis Volcanics deposits. The granitic intrusions created ore veins and the eastern end of the range was mined extensively. Remnants of this mining activity can be found in the canyons above Mackay. Four peaks reach above 11,000 feet and three other named peaks are higher than 10,000 feet. Shelly Peak, at 11,278 feet, is the highest White Knob peak. The White Knobs are in the rain shadow of the Pioneer Mountains and consequently are dry and mostly treeless.

The range is administered by the Challis National Forest and the BLM, which also administers a large section of the range surrounding Sheep Mountain on the range's eastern end. Mining activity has taken place in the area just west of Mackay; currently, cattle grazing and sheep grazing are the primary uses.

Recreational use of the range is limited, not because the White Knobs are unattractive, but rather because few people know about the scenic quality of these massive peaks. Although there are only three maintained hiking trails in the range, the terrain is open and conducive to cross-country travel. The major peaks are windswept rock piles that present attractive Class 2 and 3 goals to weekend scramblers. Because the range's valuable ore veins occurred at higher elevations, prospectors probably climbed most of the peaks by 1880. Vehicle access to these mountains can only be rated as poor. 4WDs are recommended everywhere, and required in some places. The primary approaches begin at Arco, Mackay, or Ketchum.

Wildhorse Peak   9,938 feet (Class 1)

This peak, which is at the western end of the White Knobs, is an excellent vantage point to view the surrounding country. A 1935-vintage fire lookout structure still sits on the summit. Access the peak via the Wildhorse Lookout Trail [(B)(1.1)(a)]. USGS Harry Canyon

Peak 9938   9,988 feet (Class 2)

This attractive peak is 1.2 miles west of Porphyry Peak. The summit is easily reached by hiking the connecting ridgeline from Porphyry Peak or from Castle Creek to the south. Park along the Copper Basin Road [(B)(1)] where Castle Creek flows into the East Fork Big Lost River, wade the river (difficult until mid-September), and follow Castle Creek up to Castle Rock. From this point, take the left fork of Castle Creek to the peak's south ridge and then follow the ridge up to the summit. Note: A radio repeater station is situated midway along the ridgeline between this peak and Porphyry Peak; it is reached via a road from the north. USGS Porphyry Peak

Porphyry Peak   10,012 feet (Class 2)

Porphyry Peak, the northern and westernmost of the range's 10,000-foot peaks, is a puzzle of different volcanic rocks, including andesite lava flows, ash flows, and intrusions of dacite. These volcanic rock types were deposited by the Challis Volcanics over a limestone base. The view of the Lost River Range from Porphyry's summit is awesome. T. M. Bannon climbed the peak in 1901. To approach the peak from the Copper Basin Road [(B)(1)], drive to the point where Castle Creek flows into the East Fork Big Lost River. From the road, wade the East Fork Big Lost (a dangerous undertaking until late September) and hike up Castle Creek until you are at approximately 8,000 feet. Turn east and climb out of the drainage to the peak's south ridge. Once on the ridge, climb directly to the summit. R. Baugher suggests avoiding the treacherous crossing and approaching the peak from the north via FS-489. This route requires a 4WD. USGS Porphyry Peak

Castle Rock   8,781 feet (Class 3)

Castle Rock is located 2.2 miles southwest of Porphyry Peak; it is also accessed from FS-135 [(B)(1)] and Castle Creek. Hike up Castle Creek until the drainage forks at roughly 7,500 feet. Follow the left-hand drainage past the base of Castle Rock until you can climb to the ridge on the rock's north side. Take the ridge to the summit. USGS Porphyry Peak

Mackay Peak   10,273 feet (Class 2)

Mackay Peak is located 4 miles west of Mackay. Both the town and the mountain were named for Clarence Mackay, an owner of the White Knob Copper Company. Many old mine shafts are still found on the eastern slopes of this peak, which is the northernmost summit on an impressive north/south ridgeline that extends 8 miles south to Antelope Pass. The Mackay summit ridge has three summits and many granite outcroppings. The southeasternmost summit is the highest, but just barely. Climb this granite peak by following the mining roads that lead from FS-207 [(A)(3)] in Río Grande Canyon to the peak's north ridge. Once on the ridge, climb roughly 1 mile south to the southern—and highest—summit. Bypass the lower northern and middle summits on their northeastern sides. T. M. Bannon climbed the peak in 1901. USGS Mackay Reservoir

White Knob Mountain   10,835 feet (Class 2)

White Knob Mountain is 2.2 miles southwest of Mackay Peak. The true summit is southwest of the White Knob label on the USGS quad. The peak has three summits: South White Knob at 10,805 feet; Middle White Knob at 10,835 feet; and North White Knob at 10,529 feet. The north summit is the peak visible from the valley. The mountain can be climbed from the ridgeline that connects it with Mackay Peak by working up its northeast face, or from the Mammoth Canyon Jeep Trail, which is reached from the Alder Creek Road [(A)(2)]. USGS Mackay Reservoir

Peak 10201   10,201 feet (Class 3)

This unnamed, twin-summited peak is adorned with several granite outcroppings. It is located 1.7 miles south of Mackay Peak. Its northern summit is the highest by a few feet. Climb the peak via its south ridge from Alder Creek [(A)(2)]. USGS Shelly Mountain

Cabin Mountain   11,224 feet

Cabin Mountain is situated 10 miles southeast of Porphyry Peak, between the Cabin and Corral Creek drainages. It has

Castle Rock (left) and Porphyry Peak anchor the western end of the White Knob Mountains.

two summits that are nearly a mile apart. The southernmost is the highest, but both are worthwhile goals. The peak can be climbed from almost any direction. Based on approach considerations, climb it from either its northwest ridge, which rises out of Corral Creek [(B)(2.1)(a)], or via the ridge that connects Cabin Mountain with Lime Mountain. USGS Copper Basin Knob

Northwest Ridge (Class 3). To climb the peak via its northwest ridge, follow the Corral Creek Road [(B)(2.1)] to its end, park, and hike southeast across the sagebrush flat toward the ridge. Climb up the steep side of the ridge through mixed areas of trees and talus. This ridge joins the north ridge at the mountain's northernmost summit. The ridge traverse to the south summit is strenuous with a short Class 3 stretch around a wall.

Northeast Rib (Class 2). This rib rises between the two lakes in upper Corral Creek. Take the Corral Creek Trail [(B)(2.1)(a)] to the highest lake. From the lake, hike due west to the base of the rib, which climbs steeply to the summit.

East Ridge (Class 2). The east ridge connects with Lime Mountain. From the intervening saddle, the ridge is a steep haul but without obstacles.

Lime Mountain   *11,179 feet*

Lime Mountain, which is not made of limestone, is located 2.5 miles southwest of White Knob Peak and 0.8 mile due east of Cabin Mountain. Access this peak from the pass at the head of Corral Creek and Stewart Canyon [(A)(2)(a) or (B)(2.1)(a)]. USGS Shelly Mountain

Northeast Ridge (Class 3). Several towers make the northwest ridge difficult to follow from the point where it is crossed by a trail [(A)(2)(a) or (B)(2.1)(a)]. The most economical route climbs a gully from upper Corral Creek Lake to a notch on the ridge top on the west side of the second tower. From this point, pass obstacles on the south side of the ridge.

West Ridge (Class 2). The west ridge begins in the Cabin Mountain/Lime Mountain saddle. It is a broad, sloped plateau without obstacles.

South Ridge (Class 2). This ridge begins in the Redbird Mountain/Lime Mountain saddle. It is a long walk.

Redbird Mountain   *11,273 feet (Class 2)*

This summit sits just 1 mile southeast of Lime Mountain and 0.75 mile north of Shelly Mountain. The summit is reached by a steep scramble from either its east, south, or north ridges.

The ridge walk from either Lime Mountain or Shelly Mountain is the easiest way to climb this peak. To climb the east ridge, take FS-144 [(A)(2)] up Alder Creek to Sawmill Canyon, and then follow the old jeep trail up to its end. From this point, climb north to the steep east ridge and follow it to the summit. USGS Shelly Mountain

Shelly Mountain   *11,278 feet (Class 2)*
The highest White Knob summit is found 4.5 miles north of Antelope Pass and 0.75 mile south of Redbird Mountain. The peak can be climbed from Antelope Pass [(B)(1)] by following the ridgeline across Lupine Mountain and then traversing the connecting ridge that leads to its southwest slopes. This is a long, 5-mile, up-and-down walk that includes an ascent of Lupine Mountain, which is directly on the route. The ridge crossing to and from Redbird Mountain is Class 2. T. M. Bannon climbed the peak in 1915. USGS Shelly Mountain

Lupine Mountain   *9,554 feet (Class 2)*
Lupine Mountain is located 2 miles southwest of Shelly Mountain and 3 ridge miles north of Antelope Pass. Climb via the broad ridgeline from Antelope Pass, which can be reached from Copper Basin [(B)(1)] or Antelope Creek [(A)(1)]. T. M. Bannon climbed the peak in 1915. USGS Shelly Mountain

Sheep Mountain   *9,649 feet (Class 2)*
Sheep Mountain is located 8.5 miles east of Lupine Mountain. It is the distinctive-looking, jagged summit to the north of the Antelope Creek Road. From the Antelope Creek Road, take a rugged dirt road across BLM land up the right fork of Waddoups Canyon [(A)(1.1)] until you reach a saddle just north of Point 7521 on the USGS quad. From the saddle, climb due north toward Point 8907. At 8,500 feet, contour around the side of the point to the saddle on its west side. From the saddle, climb the peak's southeast ridge to the summit. USGS Big Blind Canyon

APPROACHES TO THE WHITE KNOB MOUNTAINS

(A) EAST SIDE ACCESS ROUTES
Primary approach on the east side of the range is via US-93 from Arco north to the Big Lost River Road north of Mackay. The approaches below are listed from south to north.
(1) Antelope Creek Road. This is the primary approach cor-

ridor along the southern portion of the White Knob Mountains. A combination of county and Forest Service roads known as Antelope Creek Road lead up Antelope Creek, over Antelope Pass, and into Copper Basin [(B)(1)]. Turn off US-93 9 miles north of Arco. Several primitive roads leave the main road and head north into the eastern end of the range. At the end of Antelope Valley, FS-135 heads north up Bear Creek and Cherry Creek to Antelope Pass. The section of road that climbs to Antelope Pass is narrow, winding, rutted, and can be very slick after rain.

(1.1) Waddoups Road. This road leaves Antelope Creek at a signed junction midway between US-93 and the Antelope GS. In Township Section 14 on the USGS quad, the road forks. Though not shown on the Challis National Forest map, the right fork is a good road. Turn right on this fork and follow it past a set of water troughs to a saddle just north of Point 7521. A 4WD is recommended.

(2) FS-144, Alder Creek Road. This important access route has been closed where it crosses private property. Hopefully, by the time you read this, the Forest Service will have reached an agreement with the land owner. If the road is still closed, approach Alder Creek from Río Grande Canyon [(A)(3.1)]. Access this road just south of Mackay by turning off US-93 23.9 miles north of Arco or 2.5 miles south of Mackay. Follow the county road south for 6.8 miles to Alder Creek, and then turn southwest on Alder Creek Road. In another 2 miles there is a wire gate near an old ranch. This is the point where the road is closed as this book goes to press. Once the road reaches the national forest boundary, it deteriorates quickly and a 4WD is recommended.

(a) FST-070, White Knob Divide Trail. FST-070 leaves FS-144 12.4 miles from US-93 and leads west from Alder Creek at Stewart Canyon and quickly crosses the ridgeline just north of Lime Mountain. It then drops down to Corral Creek [(B)(2.1)(a)].

(b) FST-069, Sawmill Canyon Trail. This trail begins where Sawmill Creek empties into Alder Creek (11.5 miles from US-93). The trail, an old mining road, leads west for roughly 3 miles to the base of Redbird Mountain.

(3) FS-207, Río Grande Canyon Road. This road, which is accessed directly from Mackay, continues west into Río Grande Canyon. Drive southwest on Mackay's main street, leave town, and quickly cross the Big Lost River. In 2.4 miles you will pass a junction for FST-144 [(A)(3.1)], which provides an alternative route to Alder Creek. The road crosses another road in 2 more miles—go straight. The road continues up and eventually dies out on the north shoulder of Mackay Peak in 6.7 miles. A 4WD is required for the upper stretches of this route.

(3.1) Río Grande/Alder Creek Cutoff Road. This road leaves the Río Grande Canyon Road at a signed junction and provides an alternative route into Alder Creek. It is in surprisingly good shape, but does cross extremely rugged country. A 4WD and courage are required.

(B) COPPER BASIN ACCESS.

To reach this route from Ketchum, take Trail Creek Road east from ID-75 and the center of town. The Copper Basin Road leaves the Trail Creek Road 22 miles east of Ketchum (or 10.3 miles east of Trail Creek Summit), or 19 miles west of US-93. The road follows East Fork Big Lost River into Copper Basin. Once in Copper Basin the road leads east over Antelope Pass and eventually reaches US-93 via Antelope Creek [(A)(1)], the dividing point between the Pioneer and White Knob Mountains.

(1) FS-135, Copper Basin Road. This is a good gravel road until it reaches the turn for Wildhorse Canyon and the Copper Basin GS. After this point, conditions vary from year to year. A 4WD is recommended.

(1.1) FS-497, Wildhorse Lookout Access. This short road is 3.4 miles from the Trail Creek Road. Turn north and follow the road to the East Fork Big Lost River.

(a) Wildhorse Lookout Trail. This trail leaves the trailhead and crosses the river on a bridge. The trail climbs 2,600 feet in 4.2 miles with a good tread most of the way.

(1.2) Castle Creek Access. This access point is due south of unmistakable Castle Rock and just west of the Rosenkrance Ranch entrance. I'm sorry to report that I forgot to measure the distance. There is a parking area along the road.

(2) FS-142, Burma Road. FS-142 leaves the Copper Basin Road 17.3 miles from its western end, climbs north over the crest of the White Knob Mountains, and then descends toward the Mackay Fish Hatchery. To reach the Burma Road from Mackay, drive north on US-93 for 9.3 miles. Turn west onto a paved road and follow it for 2.6 miles to a junction. Take the paved road to the left and then go left again in another 1.2 miles. The Burma Road is now visible climbing up the mountain slope dead ahead. The Corral Creek summit at 8,728 feet is another 8, steep miles. A 4WD is recommended.

(2.1) FS-519, Corral Creek Road. Follow the Burma Road north from the Copper Basin Road for 4 miles. Turn right (east) and drive the short distance to the trailhead if you are going to hike up Corral Creek. If you are planning to climb the northwest ridge of Cabin Mountain, continue up the road until its end.

(a) FST-070 Corral Creek Trail. This trail climbs up Corral Creek to a high pass at 10,000 feet in 6.5 miles. The lake just below the pass is a good campsite. From the pass, the trail descends to Alder Creek [(A)(2)(a)].

5

THE LOST RIVER RANGE

The Lost River Range stretches 70 miles from northwest to southeast between Challis and Arco. The Big Lost River Valley and Salmon River flank the range on the west, and the Little Lost and Pahsimeroi Rivers border its east side. The range contains not only the highest point in Idaho, 12,662-foot Borah Peak, but also seven of the state's nine 12,000-foot peaks. While the entire range is designated as the Lost River Range, the northern reaches are also identified as the Pahsimeroi Mountains and two eastern subsidiary ridges are known as the Hawley Mountains and the Donkey Hills.

The Lost River Range is a textbook example of an active fault block mountain range. The range began to form 65 to 50 million years ago with most of current features developing over the last 7 million years. The mechanism that created the range was a stretching of the earth's crust that allowed the Lost River block to rise in relation to the valley floors. This impressive escarpment is steepest on its western side, but impressive when viewed from either side. On the west side, the range rises precipitously for 5,000 feet without foothills. The last earthquake to strike this massive fault block was a 7.3 magnitude shock in 1983. It raised the range roughly 6 feet in relation to the Big Lost River Valley.

Because of this intense vertical relief, the west side has only small, barren basins to catch water and no lakes. The east side rises more gradually, with many foothills and glacially carved basins that hold a few alpine lakes and many permanent streams. The Pass Creek Canyon on the west side of the range is one of the most striking gorges in the state. The heart of the gorge is more than a mile in length and 2,000 feet in depth.

The Lost River Range is administered in part by the Salmon-Challis National Forest and in part by the BLM. The Forest Service generally controls the high peaks and the BLM controls the foothills; however, the entire Hawley Mountains group is administered by the BLM.

Because of its remoteness and spectacular scenery, the Forest Service recommended 119,864 acres in the central Lost River Range for wilderness designation. Unfortunately, the proposal, which is twenty years old, has not become law. Fortunately, the range has retained its pristine nature during this period and is still worthy of inclusion in the wilderness system. While hikers will find only a few trails in the Lost River Range, those trails cross exceptionally beautiful country. Since a 4WD is necessary to approach most of the trailheads, the trails see little use. Experienced cross-country hikers can traverse many of the range's trailless regions. The going is as difficult as it is rewarding.

Although climbers come from all over the west to scale Borah because of its "highest peak" status, most of the other peaks in the range are seldom climbed. Technical climbing is gaining popularity on the massive north faces of the highest peaks and winter mountaineering is also gaining in popularity. Climbing the mostly limestone peaks is a tremendous experience, and the Lost River peaks are among the most demanding in the state. Above-average driving ability, route-finding skills, climbing expertise, and perseverance are needed to test this range—which, except for the standard route on Borah Peak, is not for beginners.

Lost River road approaches are difficult and usually require a lot of time and a 4WD vehicle. The range can be reached from Idaho Falls by taking US-20 to Arco. The Challis National Forest map combined with USGS quads should allow a good route-finder to locate all of the access routes.

THE PAHSIMEROI RANGE

The northern end of the Lost River Range, from Challis south to Doublespring Pass, is known as the Pahsimeroi Range. There is no physical reason for this distinction. If the southern portion of the range sees little use, the Pahsimeroi Range sees even less. Yet, the Pahsimeroi peaks are challenging, rewarding, and remote. Dickey Peak, which reaches 11,140 feet, is the highest summit north of Doublesprings Pass. A host of other peaks reach above 10,000 feet.

Peak 10615   *10,615 feet (Class 2-3)*
This big, dome-shaped, unnamed summit is 1.25 miles northwest of McGowan Peak on the main crest. Moving south from Challis, it is the first peak to rise above 10,000 feet. Climb the peak by its north ridge—accessed via FST-112, the Lime Creek Road, which leads east from US-93 to the top of the Lost River crest (4WD recommended). R. Baugher reports that the hike along the north ridge gives the amateur geologist an opportunity to study the contact line between Challis Volcanics deposits and Paleozoic limestone. The Lime Creek

Road leaves US-93 and proceeds up Lime Creek to the crest at 8,600 feet. The summit is 2.6 miles to the south. All but a short stretch of the route is Class 2. Close to the summit, the ridge narrows to create a short Class 3 pitch. First ascent: R. Baugher in 1996. USGS Grouse Creek Mountain

Grouse Creek Mountain   *11,085 feet (Class 2)*
This peak, located east of the main crest and directly south of Sheep Pen Basin, is the fourth highest point in the Lost River Range north of Doublespring Pass. Three routes are suggested. The first climbs the mountain from Mill Creek. Hike toward Sheep Pen Basin from the east along Mill Creek [(A)(8)(a)]. At the 8,000-foot contour, leave the trail and hike up the steep slopes to Point 10383. From this point, the route runs directly to the peak's northeast ridge. The second route begins in Dead Cat Canyon. This road eventually leads west and then north to a ridgeline at 7,700 feet. From this point, hike up the broad ridge though open forest to the open tundra meadow above. The third alternative begins in the east fork of Christian Gulch and FS-274 [(C)(4)(a)]. Hike up the canyon into the cirque due south of Grouse Creek Mountain and climb the steep talus slopes to the ridgeline above. Once on the ridge it is a long walk to the summit. USGS Grouse Creek Mountain

McGowan Peak*   *10,716 feet*
McGowan Peak is a USGS triangulation station with a great view. It is the highest of three central Idaho peaks named for the McGowans. According to R. Baugher, the McGowans were ranchers, storekeepers, innkeepers, postmistresses, county commissioners, and guides from Challis to Stanley. The peak, located 3 miles southwest of Grouse Creek Peak, is identified as the McGowan VAMB station on the USGS quad. The peak is composed of Challis Volcanics rocks overlying older sedimentary rocks, a formation typical of the Lost River Range's northern peaks. The primary problem in climbing the peak is the loose rock. Approaches are fairly easy from both the east and the west. USGS Grouse Creek Mountain

East Ridge (Class 3). From the east, approach on FST-086, which runs up Grouse Creek [(A)(8)(a)]. From the 8,400-foot contour, leave the trail and climb up the drainage that goes into the basin southeast of the peak. Although several options exist from this point, the recommended route leaves the basin at roughly the 9,200-foot contour, runs up to the peak's east ridge, and then follows the ridge to the summit.

West Ridge (Class 3). The western approach is from the McGowan Creek Road, which leaves US-93 north of

Willow Creek Summit. The west ridge can be climbed from the saddle between the peak and Point 9330. The saddle is reached from either McGowan Creek [(B)(1)(a)] or the next drainage to the south. From the saddle, the west ridge is an 1,800-foot slog over loose rock with two easily climbed walls along the way.

South Ridge (Class 3). This route begins in the unnamed drainage southwest of the summit. This is the next drainage north of Gooseberry Creek. Follow a faint logging road into the canyon and hike to the saddle on the southwest spur ridge. From the saddle, continue north up the spur toward the south ridge, which is the main crest. The steeper pitches are straightforward and pass through limestone towers near the summit. First ascent: R. Baugher in 1993

Gooseberry Peak*　　　　　　　　　　*11,090+ feet*
This imposing, unofficially named summit sits at the head of Gooseberry Creek on the main crest 2.75 miles southeast of McGowan Peak. Its summit presents a challenging prize for scramblers. First ascent: probably T. Lopez and D. Hanson in 1991. USGS Grouse Creek Mountain

East Buttress/South Ridge (Class 3). The peak is climbed via its east buttress and south ridge from Christian Gulch [(C)(4)(a)]. Approach the buttress from the lake at 8,700 feet. The buttress descends directly toward the lake. Skirt around the face that hangs above the lake to the south side of the buttress and start up. The buttress is steep in places, but the footing is generally good. At the top of the buttress, cross over to the south ridge, which is the main crest. Climb up the ridge, staying either on its top or on the west side until roughly 10,900 feet, where a rock tower blocks the ridge. Bypass the tower on the west by crossing out onto the west face on loose talus toward a small rib about 200 feet away. Climb up this rib to the base of the tower. Follow its base around and up to the left to the ridge top. A false summit is now visible. The route once again follows the south ridge to a notch below the false summit. Drop off the ridge on the west for 30 feet, cross into the notch and then climb up to the false summit. The route from the false summit to the true summit is straightforward. The peak's northeast ridge may be passable from the saddle at the top of Grouse Creek.

Southwest Canyon/South Ridge (Class 3). This route begins in the unnamed drainage southwest of the peak. This is the next drainage south of Gooseberry Creek. From the canyon's mouth, bushwhack northeast until it is possible to climb north to the saddle on the peak's southwest spur at 9,600 feet. Follow the spur to the crest/south ridge and

then continue as described above in the East Buttress/South Ridge write-up.

Trinity Peak*　　　　　　　*11,050 feet (Class 3)*
This peak is located on the ridgeline that connects Grouse Creek Mountain with the main crest that is the divide between Grouse Creek and Christian Gulch. The name is a take-off on Christian Gulch and the fact that the peak's summit is made up of three equal high points. Ascend from the east fork of Christian Gulch [(C)(4)(a)] via the southeast ridge. Gain the ridge from the area just east of the pond at 9,520 feet. The ridgelines between this summit, Grouse Creek Mountain, and Peak 11010 are also passable. First ascent: probably R. Baugher in 1993. USGS Grouse Creek Mountain

Peak 11010 (Hope Peak)*　　　　　*11,010 (Class 3)*
This peak's southwest and northwest faces are striped by rock bedding planes, making it one of the most picturesque Lost River summits. Its summit ridge splits two forks of Christian Gulch and is 1 mile long. Like many of the Lost River peaks, it is not visible from a main road. The summit is 3 miles south of Grouse Creek Mountain and 3 miles southeast of McGowan Peak. The best approach to the summit is via the east ridge, which is accessed from the end of the roadway in the north fork of Christian Gulch [(C)(4)(a)]. First ascent: probably R. Baugher in 1993. USGS Grouse Creek Mountain

Peak 10757 (Metaxy Peak)*　　　*10,757 feet (Class 3)*
This unofficially named summit is the next peak south from Gooseberry Peak on the main crest. This peak is best climbed in conjunction with assents of Gooseberry Peak or Peak 10749 by the connecting ridgelines. First ascent: probably R. Baugher in 1993. USGS Grouse Creek Mountain

Peak 10749 (Pahsimeroi Pyramid)*　　　*10,749 feet*
This is another attractive, but unnamed summit. From US-93 it appears as an almost-symmetrical, pyramid-shaped summit. The peak is located on the main crest 4.25 miles southeast of McGowan Peak. The peak undoubtedly can be climbed via a steep talus slosh from the west, but the best routes begin in Christian Gulch to the east [(C)(4)(a)]. USGS Grouse Creek Mountain

South Face (Class 2). This route begins at the unnamed lake at 8,700 feet in Christian Gulch [(C)(4)(a)]. From the lake, hike due south toward the stunning cirque at the base of Petros Peak. Once in the cirque climb the steep, narrow gully that cuts the south face. If there is snow in the gully, an ice axe is recommended. Pass through the gully's bottleneck and then left, and work toward the ridgeline. Follow the ridge to the summit.

North Ridge (Class 2). The north ridge can be accessed from the east or the west. Both approaches involve climbing steep, endless talus. From the unnamed lake at 8,700 feet in Christian Gulch, hike west southwest to the cirque between the peak and Petros Peak. Once in the cirque, aim for the lowest point of the saddle north of the peak. Once at the saddle, climb the north ridge to the summit.

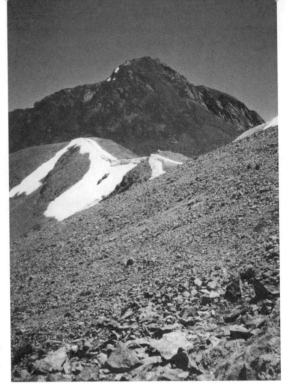

Corner Shot Peak (Photo by Rick Baugher)

Petros Peak*   *11,050 feet (Class 3)*

Unofficially, it is named for Saint Peter in keeping with the Christian Gulch theme. This peak is directly southeast of Peak 10749 on the main crest. The peak's 1,600-foot north face is nearly vertical limestone. Approach the peak from US-93 via FS-228 [(B)(2)] or FS-228A [(B)(3)]. Park at the point where the road crosses below the broad gully due west of the summit. Hike east into the gully and follow its left fork up the steep talus. When the footing gets really bad, climb to the top of the rib to the south. Climb directly up the rib toward the summit. A couple of small steps on the rib are easily bypassed. R. Baugher reports that the next gully to the south provides an equally good line of ascent and reaches the crest 0.3 mile south of the summit. Look for the "very best exposure of horn coral fossils" along the broad crest south of the summit. USGS Grouse Creek Mountain

Pavlos Peak*   *11,109 feet (Class 3)*

This summit is located 1 mile east of Petros Peak. The two peaks are separated by a broad saddle. Access the peak from Christian Gulch [(C)(4)(a)] to the east. Both the east and west ridges have been climbed. R. Baugher reports that the east ridge is a "pleasant trailless hike with some stair stepping near the top." First ascent: R. Baugher in 1993. USGS Grouse Creek Mountain

Peak 10730 (Straight Shot Peak)   *10,730 feet (Class 3)*

This pup tent-shaped summit is located on the main crest 1.3 miles south of Pavlos Peak and 2.5 miles north of Dickey Peak. The peak has been climbed from Arentson Gulch [(B)(4)] via its southwest slopes and from the Doublespring Pass Road [(C)]. From Doublespring Pass Road, park at the base of the drainage that leads directly west to the summit. This is just south of the junction with Horseheaven Pass Road. Climb the headwall just south of the summit. First ascent: probably R. Baugher and C. Furguson in 1995. USGS Grouse Creek Mountain

Peak 10925 (Corner Shot Peak)   *10,925 feet (Class 3)*

This unnamed summit is found on the main crest 1 mile southeast of Peak 10730. It sits at the top of Arentson Gulch [(B)(4)]. Climb from the gulch to the crest north of the summit and then follow the northwest slopes to the summit. A short, exposed knife edge is encountered just before the summit. First ascent: probably R. Baugher in 1994. USGS Grouse Creek Mountain

Dickey Peak   *11,141 feet (Class 2)*

T. M. Bannon established a triangulation station on Dickey Peak in 1914. Located 9.5 miles southeast of McGowan Peak and 2 miles east of Doublespring Pass, the peak is the highest point in the Pahsimeroi Mountains subrange. It is a beautiful peak with a pyramid-shaped summit formed by its three main ridges. Approach this peak from the Arentson Gulch Road [(B)(4)]. From Arentson Gulch Road, follow a two-track road not shown on the USGS quad east to a water tank that is shown on the USGS quad, and park. From the water tank, climb east up the steep slopes, skirting stands of mountain mahogany and keeping midway between the drainages to the north and south. Although the ridge is steep, it has no obstacles. At 10,600 feet, the summit will come into view. Stay on the top or the southwest side of the remaining ridge and avoid the cornices overhanging the north face. The peak also has been climbed from Doublespring Pass. USGS Dickey Peak

Peak 10420   *10,420 feet (Class 2)*

This peak is located east of the main crest between Christian Gulch to the north and Doublespring Creek to the south. Rick Baugher suggests climbing the peak from the Doublespring Pass Road [(C)] just north of its junction with the Horseheaven Pass Road. Scramble northeast up a gully to the ridge top above. Once on the ridge, hike west to the summit. USGS Doublespring

DOUBLESPRING PASS TO MOUNT BREITENBACH

Between Doublespring Pass and Pass Creek Summit the mountains are higher than any other spot in Idaho. Not only are seven of Idaho's nine 12,000 peaks in this group, but dozens of other summits fall just short of that benchmark.

Peak 11611 (Doublespring Peak)   *11,611 feet*

This peak is the first major summit south of Doublesprings Pass, which is 2.5 miles to the northwest. Its western face is formed by a complicated series of cliffs. The peak has a 0.5-miles-long summit ridge with the highest point at its east end. USGS Borah Peak

Northwest Ridge (Class 4). Climb the peak from the Doublesprings Pass Road [(C)]. Leave the Doublesprings Pass Road about 0.3 mile east of the pass. Hike southeast toward Buck Creek and then ascend the ridge that climbs above the west side of Buck Creek to Point 11038. The route is Class 2 until this point. Just beyond Point 11038, there is a short Class 4 cleft that requires considerable care to cross. This route leads to the summit in 3 miles and 3,400 feet of elevation gain. First ascent: probably R. Baugher in 1991.

Cayuse Canyon/Northeast Ridge (Class 2). This trail leaves the Horseheaven Pass Road [(C)(3)] at the mouth of Cayuse Canyon. Follow the canyon southwest into the mountains to the spot where it splits. Continue along the

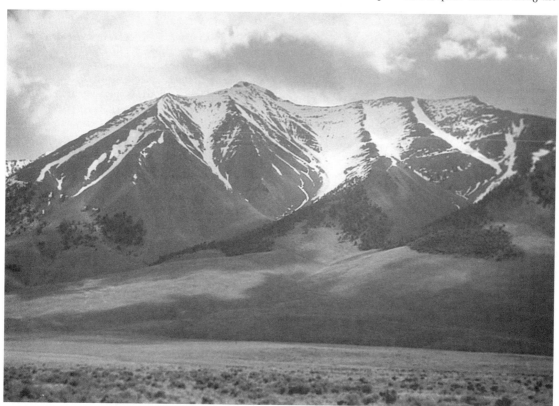

Dickey Peak

right-hand fork to the 10,460-foot saddle between the summit and Point 10878. Climb the ridge to the summit. First ascent: probably R. Baugher in 1991.

Peak 11473 (Horseshoe Mountain)   *11,473 feet (Class 3)*

This summit is located 1.2 miles south of Peak 11611 and 0.8 mile north of Al West Peak. It has an impressive east face and a complicated west face. R. Baugher placed a cairn, register, and horseshoe on the summit in 1993. The best access is from the Doublesprings Pass Road [(C)]. Climb the peak from the point where the Doublesprings Pass Road [(C)(3)] crosses the 7,400-foot contour south of the pass. From the road, head directly east toward the ridgeline north of Point 10982. Once on the ridgeline, follow it over Point 10982 and on to the summit. The peak also can be climbed from the Horseheaven Pass area via its very long east ridge. First ascent: probably R. Baugher in 1993. USGS Borah Peak

Horseshoe Mountain (Photo by Rick Baugher)

Al West Peak*   *11,310 feet (Class 3)*

This peak is located 2.9 miles north of Mount Borah. Al West (1872–1954) homesteaded at the base of this peak. T. M. Bannon used West's home, known as "Dickey Red Roof House," for triangulation in 1914. Al West was known for his willingness to give route directions to early climbers of Borah Peak and for his 1893 exploit of riding a horse from Idaho to the Chicago World's Fair. Access the peak from Rock Creek [(C)(1)]. From Rock Creek, climb to the saddle between Rock Creek and Mahogany Creek. Follow the peak's southeast ridge to the summit. The crux is between 9,800 and 10,100 feet. First ascent: R. Baugher in 1993. USGS Borah Peak

Peak 11828 (Mountaineer Peak)   *11,828 feet*

This beautiful summit is often overlooked by climbers because of its proximity to Mount Borah. Nevertheless, it is a worthy goal. It is located 1.5 miles northeast of Mount Borah on the ridgeline that divides Mahogany Creek from the East Fork Pahsimeroi River. USGS Borah Peak

North Ridge (Class 3). Access the north ridge from the saddle at 9,482 feet that is north of Point 11715. Access is from either Rock Creek [(C)(1)] or Mahogany Creek [(C)(3.1)]. The north ridge is an easy climb to Point 11715. Follow the connecting ridge east to the true summit. First ascent: probably R. Baugher in 1993.

East Side (Class 3-4). Access this route from the West Fork Pahsimeroi River Road [(C)(3.1)]. Leave the road where it crosses Rock Creek. Follow Rock Creek southwest until roughly 9,400 feet. From this point, climb due north toward the rib that descends from the south end of the peak's summit ridge. Climb this rib to the summit.

Borah Peak (a.k.a. Mount Borah)   *12,655 feet*

Borah Peak, Idaho's highest peak, is usually called Mount Borah by Idahoans. It was named for Senator William Borah and its early history is recounted in the Mountaineering History section of this book. It is located 8 miles southeast of Dickey Peak. Borah is a complex and attractive mountain with relatively good rock. Even if it were not Idaho's highest, it would be on my top ten list for best climbs in Idaho. Even the standard route is arduous and mentally demanding.

Thanks to its "highest peak" status, many attempt to climb it each year, mostly by the southwest ridge route. Borah has been climbed during every month of the year. The late Chuck Ferguson climbed the peak twenty-five times between 1979 and 1998. There have been three fatalities on the peak. This is a low number considering the number of inexperienced

Borah Peak, Idaho's highest summit

climbers who attempt Borah. The climbers who died were experienced, but tempted fate by challenging adverse snow conditions. In November of 1977, two Idaho Falls climbers were swept away and killed by an avalanche on the Southwest Ridge route. In the spring of 1987, a Boise climber died after losing control of his glissade and going over a cliff. First ascent: probably T. M. Bannon in 1912. USGS Borah Peak

Southwest Ridge (II-III, Class 3). This is the standard route to the summit. Although many inexperienced people climb this route each year, do not underestimate its potential difficulties. The route climbs more than 5,400 feet in less than 4.5 miles and there are many spots from which you can fall significant distances. When the route is covered with snow, it is best left to experienced mountaineers. From the parking area at the end of Mount Borah Road [(B)(6)] at roughly 7,200 feet, follow the well-worn two-track course through the sagebrush-covered slopes and into the drainage above and to your left. After 0.5 mile the trail crosses the gully and begins to climb up a steep side gully. After a long mile, the route tops out on a small saddle at 8,600 feet (east of Point 8714). The trail now zigzags due east, climbing steeply toward Point 10632. As you leave the timber, the ridge becomes more defined and easier to follow. The route continues up the southwest-trending ridge toward the main crest at Point

11898. The final 300 feet leading to the main crest is known as Chickenout Ridge. Chickenout Ridge climaxes in a narrow, knife-edged col just before the main crest. Although the route is well marked, many people are reluctant to cross the lower, rocky-ribbed section of Chickenout, which can be treacherous if topped by snow or ice. The final snow ridge is crossed by first down-climbing a 20-foot pitch and then carefully kicking steps in the snow. While an ice axe is recommended, there is often a wide trail across the snow made by other climbers.

Once across Chickenout, a good trail follows the ridge the west side of Point 11898 to the saddle on its north side. From the saddle, the ridge can either be climbed directly or by following a fair trail on the ridge's west side through broken rock bands and talus to the summit. The trail crosses over lots of loose rock, which can be exhausting. Take plenty of water and expect the ascent to take between 3 and 12 hours, depending on your party's abilities.

North Face Routes
Bob Boyles and Bob Moseley provided the following information on the north face and its routes.

The unsurpassed north face of Borah rises more than 2,000 feet from the top of the Rock Creek drainage. The

Borah Peak: The standard route climbs the southwest ridge above Chickenout. (Photo by E.V. Echeverria)

face, especially when covered with snow, looks more like it belongs in the Canadian Rockies than in Idaho. The first ascent was probably made by H. Hilbert and G. Grady in 1971, and the first winter ascent was by F. Florence, A. Troutner, B. Boyles, and M. Weber in February 1977. The north face can be reached by following Rock Creek [(C)(1)] from the Doublesprings Pass Road.

Follow the road into the canyon to the diversion dam and park. Cross Rock Creek at the diversion dam and continue all the way up into the cirque on the south side of the creek. It's about 3 miles to where the forest starts to thin and the north face looms above. If you're lucky, you'll be able to find the old pack trail that went up Rock Creek and headed over the pass into the Pahsimeroi Valley. It's nice to follow, but it's tedious to find—just stay relatively high on the slope above the creek

and you'll run into it. Do not go up the creek bottom! When you leave tree line below the north face you'll be presented with a 200-foot rock band that guards the cirque below the face. Negotiate this to the left of center and continue up the talus, moraines, and scree for about 2,000 feet to the base of the face. Campsites above the steep rock band mentioned above are sparse and running water may be unavailable during late summer and fall when the face above freezes for the season. Most of this face is a snow climb during the summer season. From late summer through fall, the ice fields above the moraine are bare and this face is a straightforward, but technically challenging climb. During the late season two ice tools and ice screws are recommended. Winter ascents or ascents done during unsettled snow conditions are risky owing to the extreme avalanche danger.

(1) Standard (Snow Climb). The standard line up the face begins at about 11,000 feet. Depending on how low the snow slopes extend below the face, you have about 1,500 feet of climbing to the summit, all on snow and ice. There are several variations on the left side of the face, up through narrow defiles in the cliffs, but the most common and aesthetic route lies in the middle of the face. It's an obvious, wide couloir with only a few cliff bands at the bottom. This central couloir takes you high onto the face and abruptly ends at the high, tilting cliff bands of the summit ridge. The climbing is mostly 45 degrees, possibly a little steeper near the top, and it's usually a snow slope that's a cruise when frozen. Be aware, however, that during some summers this face can be hard alpine ice from bottom to top.

Work your way up the couloir, angling to the left until you get below the summit cliff bands. From here there is a broad, tilting snow band that runs left along the base of the cliffs almost to the east ridge. Follow the ledge, shooting for a narrow couloir that leads to within a few feet of the summit. This couloir is not obvious from below and is also not obvious while on the traverse. It's nearly at the end of the snow-covered ledge. Early on the traverse you'll pass a large, obvious couloir that leads to a dead end. Keep traversing. The summit couloir is always ice, 50+ degrees, and is about 1.5 rope lengths long. Plan on a belay in the couloir if you're roped. Don't be surprised if the summit crowd gathers around the head of the couloir, wondering what all the commotion is down this hole. It'll probably be the belayer cursing about getting creamed by big dinner plates of ice.

There are two ways to get down from the summit. You can head off down the east ridge back to camp, but this involves tricky down-climbing and a few rappels. A much easier,

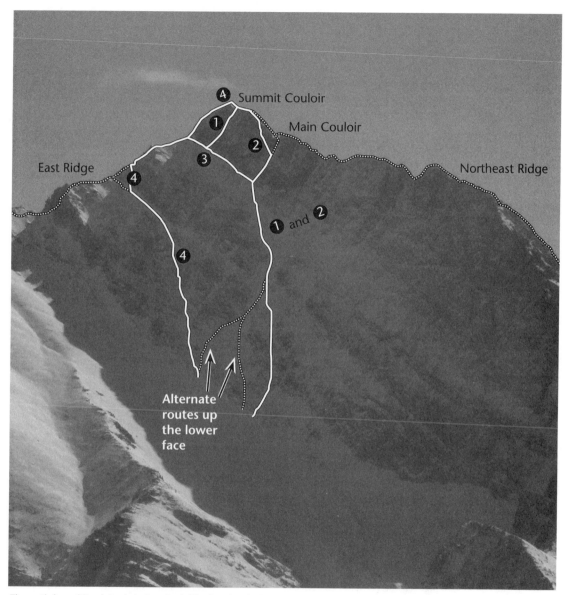

East Ridge

Summit Couloir

Main Couloir

Northeast Ridge

Alternate
routes up
the lower
face

The north face of Borah Peak. 1: Standard. (The line described as the standard route cobbles together parts of several routes.); 2: North Face Direct; 3: North Face Traverse (final route to summit not visible); 4. Lower Gully. (Photo by John Platt; route drawing by Bob Boyles)

quicker, and more direct descent is to go light and carry all your gear up and over the top. Descend the normal route, leaving the trail at a small saddle in the woods just before the last drop to the south into the drainage. Angle off to the north through the forest, then into some open sagebrush, dropping right onto Rock Creek.

(2) **Direct North Face (II, 5.7).** This route was climbed by Mike Weber and Bob Boyles in October 1976. The first winter ascent was made over 2 days by Boyles, Weber, Frank Florence, and Art Troutner on January 7 and 8, 1977 (see route (1) for approach information). This route followed a direct line up 1,500 feet of 50-degree ice to the headwall that leads to the large gully that splits the upper face above. One pitch up this gully, the route turns straight up the steep rock that leads directly to the summit. Boyles' party descended the northeast ridge down the steep rock to the uppermost gully of the north face. This 1,000-foot gully angles more than 60 degrees at its top and required front pointing in crampons for the entire length of the descent.

(3) **North Face Traverse (II, 5.4).** This route was climbed by Curt Olson and Bob Boyles in October 1979. Boyles describes the route as follows: Traverse below the summit pyramid as in route (1), past the snow couloir to a V-shaped gully on the northeast ridge. One pitch of moderate rock climbing up the V-notch gully leads to a short scramble up loose rock directly to the summit. During wetter seasons, the short steep gully that ends 20 feet below the summit can be climbed. The descent was made down the Southwest Ridge.

(4) **North Face, Lower Gully (II, 5.5).** This route was climbed by Curt Olson, Bob Boyles, and Mike Weber in September 1992. This route follows the lowermost gully on the left side of the face through the steep rock bands for approximately five pitches on mixed terrain and joins the northeast ridge below the steep rock that leads to the summit pyramid above. Climb the summit pyramid using route (1) or (3) finish.

East Face (II, 5.2). Climb the face from the notch on the northeast ridge (between the summit and Point 12247). Climb to the notch from Rock Creek [(C)(1)], which is just to the north. The crux of the climb is the first 90-foot pitch out of the notch. The angle decreases and the holds improve above this pitch. First ascent: L. Dye and W. Boyer in 1962.

Sacajawea Peak*   11,936 feet
This is the first major summit south of Borah Peak. It is located 1.1 miles south of that peak on the main Lost River crest. Sacajawea has a ragged, rectangular summit block that culminates in a tiny summit platform. Its north face is expansive, complicated, and probably unclimbed. Although it is mostly ignored by Borah Peak climbers, it is an outstanding objective for mountaineers. Its various lines offer a lot of potential for ambitious technical climbers. USGS Elkhorn Creek

Northwest Ridge (II, Class 4). This route begins at the Borah Peak access [(B)(6)]. Follow the route description for Borah's Southwest Ridge route to the main divide at the false summit marked 11898 on the USGS map. From this point, follow the ridgeline south to Sacajawea's northwest ridge. The ridgeline involves several short pitches of Class 4 climbing. First ascent: Proably L. Dye in 1962.

South Ridge (II, Class 3-4). This ridge can be accessed from Merriam Lake [(C)(3.1)(b)] to the east or Cedar Creek to the west. Both routes from the valleys to the ridge top are long and steep. Once on the south ridge—the main crest—the route climbs to the summit, staying on the top or its west side. First ascent: Proably L. Dye in 1962.

Peak 11367 (Mount Morrison)   11,367 feet
This unnamed summit is located west of the main Lost River crest 1.2 miles west of Mount Idaho. R. Baugher suggests that because the peak has an excellent view of Borah Peak, it should be named after Lee Morrison, the USGS surveyor who determined that Borah is Idaho's highest summit. This peak offers exceptional views of the crest from Mount Borah to Leatherman Peak and should not be overlooked. USGS Elkhorn Creek

West Ridge (Class 3). Climb the peak by following the West Ridge/Southwest Face route on Mount Idaho to the saddle at 10,760 feet. Turn west and follow the ridge to the summit.

West Gully (Class 3). This route begins along US-93 west of the major gully that splits the peak's west face. The rubble-filled gully is best climbed when filled with stable snow. As the gully opens, the rock changes from quartzite to slabby, loose limestone. First ascent: R. Baugher in 1993.

Mount Idaho*   12,065 feet
Mount Idaho is located 1.5 miles northeast of Pass Lake and 2 miles south of Borah Peak on the main crest of the Lost River Range. This stunning, pyramid-shaped peak is the seventh highest summit in the state and especially impressive when viewed from Merrian Lake or Borah Peak. It is a complex mountain with four big faces and four classic ridges. The peak is also known as Elkhorn Peak, but since at least eight other Idaho peaks use the word "elk" in their name, Mount Idaho will be used in this guidebook. USGS Elkhorn Creek

North Ridge (II, Class 4). The peak's north ridge can be gained from Merriam Lake [(C)(3.1)(b)] or by descending from the Sacajawea summit. Both routes involve short pitches of Class 4 climbing on rotten rock. First ascent: L. Dye.

North Face (Ice Climb). The following information was provided by Bob Moseley. It is believed that Duane Monte pioneered this route. There is a narrow couloir that snakes up the center of the north face. It's the only couloir that reaches the summit with continuous snow. There are several couloirs on either side that dead-end high on the face. Approach the base of the climb via Merriam Lake in the West Fork Pahsimeroi drainage. Continue up above the lake into the head of the cirque and swing around below the north face.

This is a straightforward climb. You enter the couloir at 10,800 feet, head straight up for about 1,000 vertical feet, then arc right for 300 vertical feet to the summit. The couloir is mostly continuous snow, but you probably will encounter about 50 feet of ice just above the corner as you begin to swing right. At about 45 degrees, this is the steepest part of the couloir. Although snow and ice can last all season in parts of the couloir, there are some years when the steep spot melts out completely by mid-summer. The rock under the ice probably is not conducive to safe climbing. Late in the year, the couloir may be hard alpine ice from top to bottom.

There's at least one variation to this route. When snow conditions were right in the mid-90s, Duane Monte exited the couloir to the right mid-way up the straight section and worked his way up a gully to the summit.

Down-climbing the route is the quickest descent. Be prepared to set anchors for a rappel or a belay if you're not comfortable down-climbing the ice section. The other option is to head over the summit and down the middle of the northwest face, eventually traversing below some cliff bands to a saddle between Cedar Creek and Merriam Lake Basin. You actually have to walk the ridge a distance to the north before finding a slope you can walk down into the basin. The slope directly below the pass is a cliff.

West Ridge/Southwest Face (II, Class 3). This classic Lost River route is accessed from US-93 at Elkhorn Creek [(B)(7)]. From the end of the road, follow Elkhorn Creek to 9,200 feet where it splits into two creeks. Start up the left-hand fork to the north for a short distance and then ascend the rib that splits the two forks, climbing toward Point 11060. At 10,500 feet look for a small game trail that traverses northeast to the saddle between Point 11060 and Mount Idaho. From the saddle, follow the ridge east toward the peak. Three towers block this ridge. Climb over the first on very broken rock. Pass the second on the north and the third on the south. The ridge merges with the steep west ridge at this point. From its base the ridge rises more than 1,000 feet in 0.3 mile. The route on the ridge stays near the crest for the first 300 feet and then

follows a moderately sloping ledge system southeast onto the southwest face to a prominent, talus-filled gully that climbs directly to the summit.

Southwest Face Direct (Class 3-4). To reach the face, follow the main fork of Elkhorn Creek [(B)(7)] past the ridge described in the West Ridge/Southwest Face route to the base of the face. This lower face is a gully system that offers several potential routes. First ascent: D. Millsap and others in 1963.

Peak 11967   11,967 feet

This impressive, but seldom-climbed summit is 0.8 mile south of Mount Idaho. Its jagged summit ridge has two summits and hangs over an impressive north face. The peak is climbed by its western slopes, which can be approached from either Elkhorn Creek [(B)(7)] or Sawmill Gulch [(B)(8)]. Both routes involve long, tedious approaches, but are well worth the effort. USGS Elkhorn Creek

West Slopes (Class 3). From the Elkhorn access, hike up Elkhorn Creek until you reach a spot corresponding with the 8,200-foot contour line on your USGS map. Climb to Point 9887, turn northeast and follow the peak's broad western slopes up to the summit cap at roughly 11,400 feet. From this point, the route stays mostly on the ridgeline, with a couple of detours onto the north slopes.

South Ridge (Class 3). This route is a classic mixture of hiking, route-finding, scrambling, and step climbing. The route leaves the Sawmill Gulch Road at roughly 7,880 feet. At this point, a mining road leaves the main road and runs northeast up a steep slope toward Point 8267. Once on top of the saddle at 8,300 feet, begin climbing due north. At 9,000 feet contour into a canyon that forms the south fork of Vance Canyon. Aim to drop into the canyon at 9,200 feet. Point 9957 is now visible. Climb up a canyon to 9,400 feet and then climb due west to the saddle north of Point 9957. You are now on the peak's south ridge, which is a straightforward climb after the complicated approach. You will encounter a couple sets of Class 3 cliffs about midway up the ridge before arriving at the lower south summit. From the south summit, climb north to the true summit.

White Cap Peak*   11,899 feet (Class 2)

White Cap Peak is also known as Mount Obsession. I will defer to evidence that early homesteaders call the peak White Cap because of its bright white quartzite and long-lasting snowfields. No matter what name is applied, it is a great climb. The peak is located just west of Leatherman Pass and

Summit of Peak 11967 from the peak's south summit

0.5 mile west of Leatherman Peak. An impressive, steep-sided summit when viewed from almost any angle, it rises almost 2,000 feet above Pass Lake. The first winter ascent was via the west ridge by W. March and R. Albano in 1975. USGS Elkhorn Creek.

West Ridge (Class 2-3). Although W. March rated this route Class 4 during his winter ascent, the route is not difficult. It begins at Leatherman Pass [(C)(3.1)(a.1) or (B)(8)(a)] and runs up the peak's west ridge over loose talus and rocky fins to the summit. The route is straightforward with no obstacles other than loose rock.

South Ridge (Class 3). Access this ridge from Sawmill Gulch [(B)(8)(a)] and follow it directly to the summit over talus and boulders. The only obstacle is a steep boulder field below Point 11045. The south ridge also can be accessed from Sawmill Pass at the top of the gulch. From this picturesque pass, several lines lead up to the ridge top above across Class 3 slopes.

Leatherman Peak   *12,228 feet*

This peak, named after Henry Leatherman, a nineteenth-century teamster who is buried within sight of the peak, is the second highest mountain in the state. It is located 4.5 miles southeast of Borah Peak. When viewed from ID-93, the summit is much more ostentatious than Mount Borah

because its steep west face is closer to the road. Unlike Borah, finding solid rock on Leatherman Peak is impossible. It is a 12,000-foot tower of crumbling rock. USGS Leatherman Peak

West Ridge (Class 3). Reach the west ridge from Leatherman Pass [(B)(8)(a)], which can be reached from the Pahsimeroi, Sawmill Gulch, and Lone Cedar Creek drainages. The climb from the pass gains more than 1,600 feet over steep talus-covered slopes, over and around several fractured rock towers. Climbing without dislodging rock is difficult. W. March and R. Albano made the first winter ascent in 1975 via the west ridge and rated the climb 5.3. This party descended via the east ridge.

Southwest Face (Class 3-4). Access is from Sawmill Gulch [(B)(8)(a)] or Lone Cedar Creek [(B)(9)]. From Sawmill Pass, you must descend into Lone Cedar Creek. From the creek bottom it is a long, talus-filled climb to the saddle between Leatherman Creek and Bad Rock Peak. From the saddle, climb up and across the face and aim for a point 100 feet below the summit. From this point, climb straight up on rotten Class 4 rock to the top. First ascent: L. Dye in 1962.

Bad Rock Peak*   *11,953 feet (Class 3)*

Early settlers identified Leatherman, Bad Rock, and Mount Church as the Three Sisters. This peak's skull-shaped summit is the next peak south of Leatherman Peak on the main Lost River crest. The summit is a ragged crown that bars scramblers from all but one direction. This is a classic Idaho climb: hard to get to, extensive talus on the lower slopes, and rotten cliffs around the summit.

The summit is reached via a short chimney through the cliffs. The only practical route to the summit climbs the peak's northwest ridge from the saddle between Leatherman and Bad Rock. The saddle is reached from the upper reaches of the Lone Cedar Creek drainage via a long slosh up a steep talus slope. The headwaters of Upper Cedar Creek can be approached from Sawmill Gulch [(B)(8)(a)], Lone Cedar Creek, [(B)(9)] or Pass Lake [(C)(3.1)(a)], with Sawmill Gulch the most direct route. From the saddle, follow the straightforward northwest ridge to the cliffs below the summit to a steep chimney that leads up though the cliffs to the summit. The southwest ridge, which rises up between the Bad Rock/Church saddle, is blocked by steep cliffs and is Class 5 terrain. Access to the saddle is from Lone Cedar Creek. First ascent: probably R. Baugher in 1993. USGS Leatherman Peak

Mount Church*   12,200+ feet (Class 3)
This peak, unnamed on the USGS quad, is the third highest peak in Idaho. The knuckle-shaped summit is located 1.5 miles southeast of Leatherman Peak. This is a very impres-

sive and complex mountain that looks different from every direction. The peak was probably first climbed in the 1920s. A rock cairn on the summit is graced with two summit registers and an axe handle that has been on the summit for many years. The peak is unofficially named for the late Idaho senator Frank Church. USGS Leatherman Peak

East Ridge (Class 3). The east ridge is mostly a scramble except for two short steps that involve easy climbing—reaching the east ridge is the difficult proposition. Reaching the peak from either the east or west sides of the range first involves climbing nearly to the summit of Donaldson Peak. From the west, drive to the base of Jones Creek [(B)(10)] and then hike up the creek bottom to the base of Donaldson Peak and the 8,440 contour line. Turn west and follow the side drainage to the saddle just west of this peak. From the saddle, contour around and up to the small pond in the cirque between the two peaks. Climb due east toward the large gully. To avoid Class 4 climbing in the gully, work around the base of the cliff to the east and climb a series of talus-filled ramps to the ridgeline just west of Donaldson Peak. It is less than 10 minutes to the top of Donaldson from this point—so before continuing to Mount Church, you might as well follow the ridge south to the top of Donaldson. From the east side of the range, make your approach via the East Fork Pahsimeroi River [(C)(3.2)(b)]. Follow the drainage up to its upper basin

Bad Rock Peak from Upper Cedar Creek

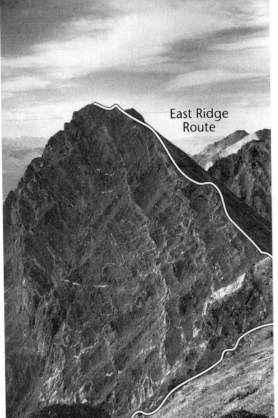

East Ridge
Route

Mount Church from the summit of Donaldson Peak

and Lake 9682. From Lake 9682, climb the steep slopes to Donaldson Peak's northeast ridge. Climb over Donaldson's summit and then follow the ridgeline north to Church.

North Rib (Class 3). Mount Church's steep north face moderates as it turns to the northeast. At this breaking point in the face, a system of ribs descends from the west end of the summit ridge toward Lake 9682 [(C)(3.2)(b)]. The rib system can be ascended by those with advanced route-finding abilities to the summit.

Northeast Face (Snow Climb). This route is recommended only when stable snow conditions are present. In an average snow year, the northeast face holds snow late into the summer. This snow rarely forms into ice, but climbers should be prepared for that possibility. The approach is via the East Fork Pahsimeroi River [(C)(3.2)(b)]. Begin at Lake 9682 northeast of the summit and climb the 35- to 50-degree snowfield directly toward the summit. As you near the summit, there are several places where you can access the east ridge. To avoid loose rock, take the ridge and follow it to the summit.

Donaldson Peak   *12,023 feet*

Although the name has yet to appear on the USGS quad, this peak, the eighth highest in Idaho, is officially named after the late chief of the Idaho Supreme Court, Chief Justice Charles Russell Donaldson. The summit is located on the main crest, 0.7 mile east of Mount Church and 1.25 miles west of Mount Breitenbach. The peak is a beautiful summit with an extremely precipitous southwest ridge and south face. The first ascent of the peak is unknown, but the first winter ascent was by W. March and R. Albano in 1975 via the west face and south ridge. They rated the climb 5.3. USGS Leatherman Peak

West Ridge (Class 3). For approach directions, refer to the East Ridge route description for Mount Church. Once you gain the main Lost River crest, it is an easy walk up the east ridge of Donaldson to the summit. The route stays on the ridge's north side for the first section, then crosses to the south side for the last short approach to the summit.

East Cirque/North Ridge (Class 3). The rather bland cirque on the east side of the peak also has been climbed and is reportedly Class 3. Access the cirque from Jones Creek [(B)(10)]. Follow the creek north from its mouth until roughly 10,000 feet then cut back to the west into the bottom of the cirque. Climb directly to the top of the ridge above and then follow the north ridge to the summit.

No Regret Peak*   *11,972 feet (Class 3)*

The main Lost River Range divide turns abruptly east on the summit of Donaldson Peak and runs east for 0.8 mile to the summit of No Regret Peak, where it once again turns southeast and runs for 0.75 mile to Mount Breitenbach. The only known approach to the summit is via its southwest ridge. Either follow the ridge over from Donaldson Peak or climb to the ridgeline from Lake 9682, which is northwest of the peak [(C)(3.2)(b)]. The ridge between No Regret and Breitenbach is broken by steep cliffs and would involve Class 5 climbing and at least two rappels. USGS Leatherman Peak

Mount Breitenbach   *12,140 feet*

The fifth highest point in Idaho is a massive summit that rests on the main crest at the heads of the Pahsimeroi River and Dry Creek. The peak was named for Jake Breitenbach, who died during the 1963 American Everest Expedition. Idaho mountaineer Lyman Dye, who learned his mountaineering skills from Jake in the Tetons in the early 1960s, successfully petitioned the governor of Idaho and the USGS to adopt the name. The peak, while not prominent when viewed from

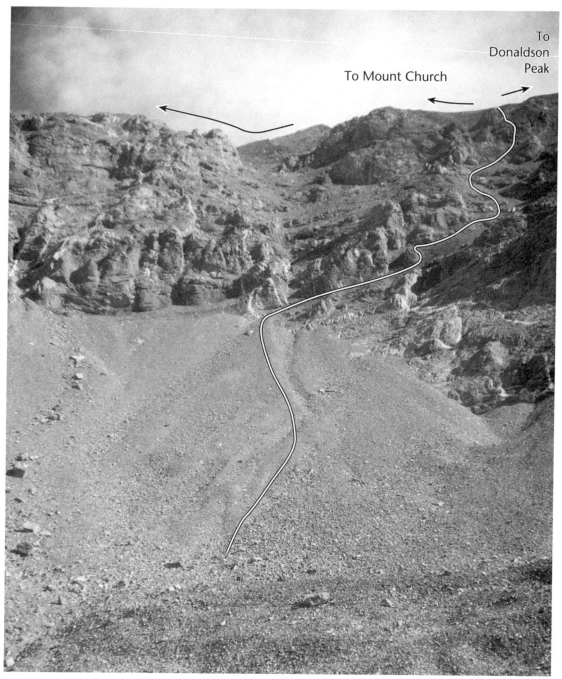

To Donaldson Peak

To Mount Church

The view from the pond: the west side approach to Mount Church's east ridge and Donaldson's west ridge climbs up this cirque.

US-93, is the most complex of Idaho's 12,000-foot summits. Though its immense north face rises nearly 3,000 feet above the headwaters of the East Fork Pahsimeroi River, it is hidden from view by intervening peaks. First ascent: probably W. Boyer in the early 1960s. USGS Leatherman Peak

South Ridge (Class 3). The easiest route to the summit is from Pete Creek [(B)(11)]. Hike up the creek to the peak's southern slopes. At 10,400 feet climb toward the saddle to the northwest at 11,400 feet. From the saddle, climb the east flange of the south ridge. Once on the ridge, follow it to the summit. Though not as difficult as the other routes, this is an extremely long and tiring route. A variation of this route climbs straight up the south face to the south ridge with little difficulty.

West Face (Class 3). The west face is accessed from Jones Creek [(B)(10)]. Follow Jones Creek until it reaches an upper cirque at about 10,200 feet. Jones creek flows year around and you must bypass three waterfalls between the 8,500- and 10,200-foot elevations. This route will be difficult during high water. From this point, the route runs northeast through an easy cliff band. A second set of cliffs is climbed via a gully that leads to the peak's west ridge about 0.1 mile west of the summit.

North Face Grand Chockstone (III, Class 5.8 A1). The first ascent of this impressive face was reported in the *American Alpine Journal* by B. Boyles, M. Weber, and C. Olson in 1982. The party used direct aid to overcome the crux. The second climb followed the first line except for one important variation, which eliminated the need for aid. (See route line at right.) The north face is reached from Dry Creek [(A)(6.1)(a)] or the East Fork Pahsimeroi [(C)(3.1)(a)].

The following information was provided by Bob Moseley. Grand Chockstone is located on the east side of the face of the north face. The route climbs an incised couloir that reaches the summit ridge between the summit and the shallow saddle to the east. There is a gigantic chockstone in this chimney that is obvious at certain angles—there is snow behind it, which sets it off nicely. It is not the obvious couloir on the left side of the face that ends below an enormous, ugly, limestone headwall. The climb starts on the snow fan directly below the summit that ends at a big headwall halfway up the face. Note: The lower end of this fan melts by mid-July uncovering loose cliff bands that make access to the climb either impossible or at least unpleasant.

Start the climb by traversing up and left near the top of the snowfield, aiming for a point below the headwall and above some small rock bands that interrupt this snowfield. This takes you to a short gully that angles up and left (may be

mixed snow and rock). Cross over the top of a short spur and descend to a snowfield, the first of two hanging snowfields that lie directly below the chockstone couloir. The route now climbs straight toward the top. Climb the first snowfield until it ends at a cliff band. Climb the cliff band (mostly easy, low-angle, climbing, except one interesting 5.6 move) to the second snowfield. Climb straight up this snowfield for several hundred feet to the headwall above. The chockstone couloir ends in a short, 25- to 30-foot, overhanging gully at the upper-right-hand corner of this snowfield. Set up a belay about 30 feet or so to the left of the gully. Climb up the cliff band (5.7 or 5.8), then right, and then around the corner to reach the base of the upper couloir, which should be filled with snow. The rock on the cliff band is relatively solid with good protection, but setting anchors once in the couloir can be problematic without snow anchors. Boyles, Weber, and Olson climbed the overhanging waterfall to the right of this line using aid.

From this point, climb straight up the snow-filled couloir toward the house-sized chockstone that soon comes into view. The bottom of the chockstone is 15 to 20 feet off the snow and is easy to climb under. The couloir eventually widens at the top to a broad snowfield below the summit ridge. The summit is a short distance to the west. The climb is best done in June, but may be possible in early July if it has been a cool spring or high snow year. The lower snowfield is essential to getting on the climb. If you wait too late and it is gone, it is very difficult to traverse the grungy buttress.

Northeast Ridge (Class 4). Duane Monte and Kevin Sweigert descended the northeast ridge to Breitenbach Pass. The route bypasses a ridgeline buttress by moving onto the north face. B. Moseley reports the ridge was tedious and required some tricky climbing over steep rock and snow.

East Face (Class 3). Follow the Dry Creek drainage to its uppermost reaches [(A)(3)]. Turn east and climb into the east-facing cirque. Once within the cirque, climb the slopes to the northeast and gain the east summit. From the east summit, walk to the true summit.

MOUNT CORRUPTION TO BREITENBACH DIVIDE

This major divide leaves the main crest at Mount Breitenbach and then runs east and then north, paralleling the main crest for several miles. The five summits on the divide are among the most challenging Lost River summits. They are described from north to south. Primary access is from the Horseheaven Pass Road in the north or Dry Creek in the south.

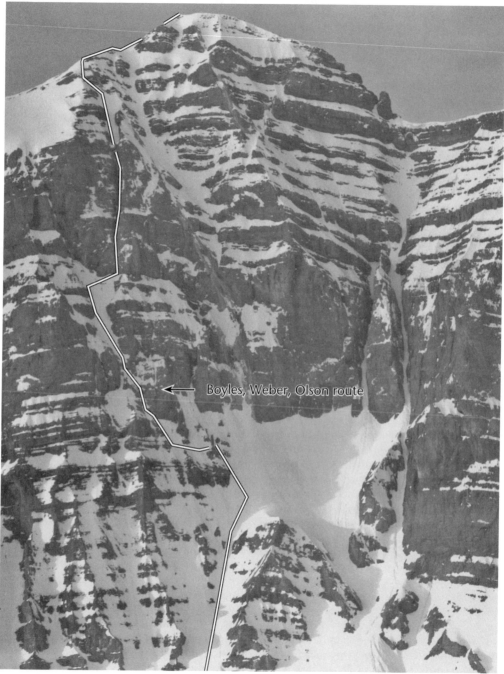

Boyles, Weber, Olson route

The north face of Mount Breitenbach, showing the Boyles, Weber, Olson route. The Monte, Sweigert variation follows the same line with the exception of the detour around the Grand Chockstone. (Photo by Wes Collins; route drawing by Bob Boyles)

Mount Corruption from Peak 11857

Mount Corruption*   11,857 feet

Mount Corruption is located east of the main divide, 3 miles north of Mount Breitenbach. The peak's position on a subsidiary ridge makes this isolated summit seem even bigger than it is. The name is derived from the peak's broken rock walls. Both routes described below begin in the East Fork Pahsimeroi [(C)(3.2)(a)]. First ascent: probably R. Baugher in 1992. USGS Leatherman Peak

Northwest Gully/North Ridge (Class 4). This is a challenging, enjoyable climb. A major gully cuts the peak's northeast quadrant. The bottom of the gully is blocked by a series of forested cliffs. Park south of opening of the gully at roughly 8,200 feet. Climb north toward the opening of the gully, aiming for a point just below the northern end of the big cliffs above. Good ledges lead around the base of the cliffs and into the gully. Once in the gully, zigzag back and forth to avoid rock walls. As the gully opens, the terrain moderates. Angle up toward the north ridge staying in the trees for better footing until the trees die out at 10,800 feet. Continue to the ridge top. Once on the ridge, the route stays close to the crest except for two short steps. The route up the first step is on its west side. The route for the second step is on its east side. This second step involves climbing a 20-foot, Class 4 crack and is the crux. Beyond the step, the route moderates. First ascent: T. Lopez and D. Hanson in 1992.

Southwest Face (Class 3). This route climbs the main gully up the southwest face. It crosses solid, steep limestone. First ascent: R. Baugher in 1992.

Peak 11200+ (Apex Peak)   11,200 feet (Class 2)

Apex Peak divides the east and west forks of Burnt Creek. It is located 1.5 miles east of Mount Corruption and 1.2 miles north of Peak 11509 (Cleft Peak). The summit is accessible from both forks of Burnt Creek. Rick Baugher recommends climbing the peak from Peak 10149 (East Burnt Peak) and the intervening saddle. USGS Leatherman Peak.

Peak 10149 (East Burnt Peak)   10,149 feet (Class 2)

This peak, which sits on the west side of Dry Creek 1.6 miles northeast of Peak 11200+ (Apex Peak), is formed from the remnants of an ancient volcano, according to Rick Baugher. It is easily approached from Dry Creek [(A)(6.1)(a)] via its eastern slopes. USGS Massacre Mountain.

Peak 11509 (Cleft Peak)   11,509 feet (Class 3)

This summit, located 1.7 miles southeast of Mount Corruption on the ridge that connects Corruption and Mount Breitenbach, is an imposing block of deteriorated rock just east of the main crest. A big, somewhat isolated summit, it dominates the Burnt and Dry Creek drainages. It can be approached from the West Fork Burnt Creek [(A)(6.2)] and Dry Creek [(A)(6.1 alt.)(a)], or from the East Fork Pahsimeroi River drainage and FST-090 [(C)(3.2)(a)].

If approached from the east fork, leave the trail where it crosses the 8,800-foot contour and climb north to the saddle at 10,600 feet north of the peak. The climb up the ridge to the summit crossses extremely loose talus to reach the point where the ridge swings to the east. It is recommended that the route be climbed while this portion is still covered by snow. If approaching from Burnt Creek, drive up the canyon until the road becomes impassable, then hike up the spectacular valley to the saddle north of the peak. First ascent: R. Baugher in 1992. USGS Leatherman Peak

Peak 11280+   *11,280+ feet (Rating unknown)*
This complicated tower, the southernmost summit on the Corruption/Breitenbach divide, is probably unclimbed. It is located 1.5 miles northeast of Mount Breitenbach. It is the steepest, most rotten looking summit in the entire range. Access the base of the peak from Breitenbach Pass [(A)(6.1) (a) or (C)(3.2)(a)]. USGS Leatherman Peak

LOST RIVER MOUNTAIN TO PASS CREEK SUMMIT

Lost River Mountain*   *12,078 feet*
This peak, the sixth highest summit in Idaho, is located on the main Lost River crest 1.8 miles southeast of Mount Breitenbach. The peak has a long north/south summit ridge with two summits, both of which reach above 12,000 feet. The southern summit is slightly higher than the more difficult northern summit. USGS Leatherman Peak

South Face Super Gully (II, Class 3). Access this route from Upper Cedar Creek [(B)(12.1)]. The route climbs the large, spectacular, southeast-facing gully that cuts the peak's southeast face. Start the climb from the end of the road by climbing directly toward Point 8881. At 8,600 feet, traverse north across a gully to a large rib, which you can follow northeast to the base of a gully. Because of terrible loose rock and rockfall, this route is best climbed before the snow melts (assuming that avalanche conditions are not present). The Super Gully is a bowling alley and the rockfall can be deadly. Plan your climb so that you are up and down the gully before it thaws out. Once you are on the summit ridge, it is an easy (although exposed) walk to the summit.

South Towers (III, Snow Climb). Though not as steep as the Super Gully, this route still crosses some 45-degree terrain and passes frozen icefalls during winter conditions. It

offers a good alternative when the Super Gully is filled with loose snow. The route begins at Point 8881 and climbs a line east of the Super Gully. Use the same approach directions as for the Super Gully. From Point 8881, you can see a huge snow-filled gully that drops from the summit. This gully winds its way through snow and ice ledges and between huge pinnacles of gravel conglomerate. Just to the east there is a large rib leading up into some spectacular decomposing rock towers. This route tops out on the summit ridge at the same spot as the Super Gully. First ascent: Rob Hart and Greg Yoder in 1999.

North Ridge (II, Class 3-4). This ridge divides the two forks of Dry Creek. Hike up the left-hand or easternmost fork of Dry Creek [(A)(6.1)(a)] to the headwall to the west of the ridge. Once out of the trees, the route encounters a lower wall between 9,600 and 10,000 feet. Bypass the wall on its right-hand (west) side. Above the wall, climb to the base of the next wall, which begins at 10,600 feet. A gully-rib system climbs directly up toward Lost River's lower northern summit. Follow this gully up until it is possible to cut back south to the saddle between the peak's two summits. Once on the ridge, follow the ridge to either summit. This route gets steeper and more rugged as it nears the northern summit. The route is one of the most challenging scrambles in the range.

Peak 11930 (Far Away Mountain)   *11,930 feet (Class 3)*
Rick Baugher notes that "this is possibly the hardest peak in the range to reach." It is located 1.5 miles east of Lost River Mountain and 1.9 miles west/northwest of Castle Mountain. Climb the peak from the upper left fork of Dry Creek [(A)(6.1.1)(a)] via its broad east face. This route is best done as an overnighter. First ascent: R. Baugher in 1993. USGS Massacre Mountain

Ferguson Peak*   *11,509 feet*
This peak is named for Chuck Ferguson (1940–1998) who made the first ascent in 1978 and climbed extensively in the range and throughout Idaho. Ferguson Peak is a spectacular helmet-shaped mountain when viewed from Dry Creek. It has a precipitous east face that rises above Swauger Lakes, which are 1.1 miles northeast of the peak. USGS Massacre Mountain

Southeast Ridge (Class 3-4). This route starts from the Swauger Lake Trail [(A)(6.1.1)(c)]. Leave the trail at Swauger Lake and hike due south toward the saddle at 10,240 feet. From the saddle, climb due west to the south ridge that is 700 feet above. A long, 1.7-mile ridge crossing leads to the summit. First ascent: C. Ferguson in 1978.

Southwest Gully (Class 3). Access this route from the upper left fork of Dry Creek [(A)(6.1.1)(a)]. The gully climbs the southwest face to the peak's southeast ridge. It tops out south of the summit. First ascent: R. Baugher in 1993.

Peak 10297   10,297 feet (Class 2)

This unnamed summit is located just northeast of Swauger Lakes and 2.8 miles north of Peak 11509. It is easily climbed from the Swauger Lakes Trail, but can be approached from almost any direction. Its summit is an excellent viewpoint for the Lost River crest and the southern half the Lemhi Range. To reach the summit, leave the lake and hike directly toward the peak's south ridge. Once on the ridge, follow it to the summit [(A)(6.1.1)(c) or (A)(6.1)(a)]. USGS Massacre Mountain

Massacre Mountain   10,924 feet

Massacre is a massive mountain with a long summit ridge separating its northern and southern summits by more than 1.5 miles. The southern summit is the highest point, but both summits are worthy goals. The long and strenuous ridge walk between the two summits is especially rewarding. USGS Massacre Mountain

North Summit (Class 2). The north summit, which rises 10,824 feet, can be reached by climbing up the peak's west slopes from Long Lost Creek [(A)(6.1.1)]. Leave Long Lost Creek where the 8,040-foot contour line crosses Dry Creek. Cross the creek and climb up the intermittent creek drainage that flows into Long Lost Creek from the east. Once the drainage angles steeper, leave it and gain the ridgeline to the south, which climbs to the summit. For those interested in making a ski ascent of the mountain, a second, longer route utilizes the Buck Springs Road [(A)(6.1 alt.)]. This road provides access to the broad saddle north of the summit. From this saddle, the route climbs through the trees at the base of Point 10382 via steep, but open slopes. Once Point 10382 is gained, the route follows the ridgeline south over Point 10416 and makes a final climb up to the summit.

South Summit (Class 2). Climb the highest Massacre summit from Long Lost Creek [(A)(6.1.1)(a) and (b)] by following FST-194 and FST-092 to the 8,800-foot contour on the USGS map. From this point, leave the trail and climb through the trees to the north and the summit's west ridge. Once on the ridge, follow it directly to the summit.

Peak 11477 (The Moat)   11,477 feet (Class 3)

This rugged peak is located 1.1 miles northwest of Castle Peak. It flanks the Upper Cedar Creek/Long Lost Pass (a.k.a. Backdrop Pass) on the north. Access the pass from either the Upper Cedar Creek [(B)(12)(a)] or Long Lost Creek [(A)(6.1.1)(a)]. From the pass, climb southeast up the ridge to the summit. Just above the pass, there is a deposit of blue chitinous

brachiopod fossils. First ascent: R. Baugher in 1993. USGS Massacre Mountain

Castle Peak   10,957 feet (Class 2)

The point named Castle Peak on the Massacre Mountain USGS quad forms a walled promontory south of the deep, U-shaped pass that separates Upper Cedar Creek from Long Lost Creek. The summit, which is impressive from most sides, is not a separate peak but actually a spur of a higher summit, USGS Peak, which is located just to the south. The peak is best climbed from the pass, which is accessed from either Upper Cedar Creek [(B)(12)(a)] or Long Lost Creek [(A)(6.1.1)(a)]. There are no obstacles from the pass to the summit. USGS Massacre Mountain

USGS Peak*   11,982 feet

This beautiful peak, which displays its sedimentary layering on a grand scale, is named to honor the United States Geological Survey. It is located 1.3 miles south of Castle Peak and is identified as the McCaleb triangulation station on the USGS quad. USGS Massacre Mountain

Lower Cedar Creek (II, Class 3). While this is the standard route to the summit, it is a difficult cross-country journey that requires a lot of stamina. Hike up Lower Cedar Creek [(B)(13)(a)] to the base of a large gully beginning around 8,600 feet. This gully runs up to the northwest almost directly to the summit. Follow this gully up, avoiding the cliffs on its south side, into the upper cirque and find the easier Class 3 cliffs that allow you to climb the peak's south ridge. Once on the south ridge, follow it to the summit. USGS Massacre Mountain

North Face (Snow Climb). The north face of USGS should be on every mountaineer's list. Although not an extreme climb, it offers a classic line with excellent scenery. Snow conditions are usually good until mid-August. The face is accessed from the east at the end of the Long Lost Creek Road [(A)(6.1.1)(a.1)]. From the base of the face, the route ascends by climbing an east-facing snow slope for roughly 200 feet to the base of a cliff. Traverse right to a series of loose rock steps. Climb the steps to a level talus field above. Climb to the base of the midsection of the face at 11,000 feet. From this point, several snow chutes lead directly to the summit ridge 900 feet above. Once on the ridge, climb west to the summit. Bypass the intervening towers on their north side. An ice axe and crampons are essential. First ascent: T. Lopez and D. Hanson in 1995. USGS Massacre Mountain

Shadow Lake Peak*   11,401 feet (Class 2)

This large, pyramid-shaped peak, is located 1.7 miles northeast

North Face
Route

The north face of USGS Peak, which sits between Shadow Lake Peak and Mount McCaleb, is one of the Lost River Range's most remote and interesting summits.

of Castle Peak and towers over the head of Dry Creek. It is unnamed on the USGS quad. Climb the peak by its southeast ridge from Shadow Lake [(A)(6.1.1)(b)]. The route, a long scramble, crosses long stretches of loose talus. The views from the summit are nothing short of spectacular. USGS Massacre Mountain

Ross Peak*   11,724 feet (Class 3)
This peak is unofficially named for USGS geologist Clyde P. Ross (1891–1965) who wrote at least forty-five scientific papers on Idaho geology, including *Geology of the Borah Peak Quadrangle* in 1945. This is another Lost River peak that few people ever view. Its 1,400-foot west and north faces are not visible from the valley. This peak can be climbed by traversing the connecting ridge from Peak 11240, or from a cross-country trip up Wet Creek [(D)(4)(a.1)] to the west, or from Long Lost Creek [(A)(6.1.1)(a.1)]. First ascent probably R. Baugher in 1993. USGS Massacre Mountain

Peak 11240   11,240 feet (Class 3)
As you approach from the east side of the range on the Pass Creek Summit Road [(D)], two stunning pyramid-shaped peaks dominate the Lost River crest to the west. Peak 11240

is the northernmost of the two peaks. It is located 1.3 miles southeast of Shadow Lake. The easiest access to its summit is up its east ridge, which is accessed from the West Side Crest Trail [(D)(4)(a)]. The hike up the ridge is straightforward and without complications. The peak's east ridge is also easy to climb from the saddle between it and Ross Peak at the head of Wet Creek [(D)(4)(a.1)]. USGS Massacre Mountain

Triple Peak*   11,332 feet (Class 4)
This jagged summit sits at the head of three drainages: Long Lost Creek, Lower Cedar Creek, and Wet Creek, and 1.4 miles east of USGS Peak. Glacial action in three adjoining cirques has left an encrusted summit ridge that is the most rugged summit in the range. Reach the saddle north of the peak from Peak 11240 or Wet Creek [(D)(4)(a.1)] to the west or from Long Lost Creek to the west [(A)(6.1.1)(a.1)]. Note that the trail on both sides of the pass is difficult to find in places but a fair tread can be located most of the way. Triple Peak has three summits; the middle summit is the highest point. From the pass hike northeast up the ridge to the base of the west tower. From this point, traverse east, scrambling over boulders and talus for about 150 feet to the base of a steep, slippery, debris-filled gully. Climb the gully—carefully as the

route crosses loose talus and hard ledges covered with loose rock. At the top of the gully, the route climbs a 12-foot-high wall which brings you to a keyhole. Climb through it. (To the north and above the keyhole there is an open book. This feature leads to the top of the West Tower and is a short 75-foot 5.7 climb up unstable rock. First ascent B. Wright and T. Lopez July 2001.) From the keyhole the route to the true summit works across the unstable, intervening ground to the base of the open book. To the left of this point, a ledge system above a cliff leads north along the base of the West Tower's north face to a 25-foot-high wall of dirt and debris. Edge across to the ledges and climb the dirt wall which is not as bad as it looks. At the top, a wide ledge traverses the remaining section of the West Tower's north face and leads into the intervening gap. From the gap the route ends with a short a walk across talus and boulders. First ascent T. Lopez & B. Wright July 2003. USGS Massacre Mountain

Hidden Peak*   11,308 feet (Class 2)
This is the next peak south from Peak 11332 and is 0.7 mile north of Wet Peak. The summit is reached via the peak's broad east ridge. Approach the ridge from the Pass Creek Road FST-092 [(D)(4)(b) or (D)(3)(b)]. The peak's south ridge

is Class 3 and it is possible to reach Wet Peak via this ridge. USGS Massacre Mountain

Octoberfest Peak*   10,800+ feet (Class 2)
This is the second large pyramid summit towering above Wet Creek. Its summit is climbed from FST-092 [(D)(4)(b) or (D)(3)(b)] via its south ridge. Leave the trail and follow an unnamed drainage to the south ridge at roughly 10,320 feet. Turn north and climb the ridge to the summit. The route up the ridge is steep, but without technical difficulties. USGS Massacre Mountain

Warren Mountain   9,469 (Class 3)
Warren Mountain is located 1.6 miles southwest of Pass Creek Summit. The easiest route to the summit follows the peak's southwest ridge from the point where FST-092 crosses the ridge [(D)(4)(b)]. USGS Warren Mountain

Little Mac*   11,071 feet (Class 2)
This often overlooked summit is 0.6 mile west of Mount McCaleb. The small summit sits above the peak's 1,200-foot north face. Approach the peak from Mackay via the Lower Cedar Creek Road [(B)(13)(a)]. When the road forks, turn

Mount McCaleb's unclimbed south face, a complex series of towers, faces, and gullies, has seen little climbing activity.

left and follow the roadway along the Cedar Creek irrigation ditch. Climb to the saddle between Little Mac and Mount McCaleb. From the saddle, it is a 400-foot scramble to the summit. USGS Mackay

Mount McCaleb   11,682 feet

This domineering peak is named after Jesse McCaleb, a teamster who was killed in a confrontation with Native Americans in 1878. The peak's impressive south face, visible from US-93, is identified by a highway sign along the road just south of Mackay. The elevation given on the map is not for the summit, but for the USGS triangulation station, which was established by T. M. Bannon in 1914 on a point south of the true summit. First ascent: probably T. M. Bannon in 1914. USGS Mackay

West Ridge (II, Class 3). Approach the peak from Mackay via the Lower Cedar Creek Road [(B)(13)(a)]. When the road forks, turn left and follow the roadway along the Cedar Creek irrigation ditch. Leave the road due south of the summit and climb the north/south gully to the west ridge. Follow the ridge to the summit.

East Face (Class 4). Approach via the Lower Cedar Creek Road [(B)(13)(a)] and Lower Cedar Creek. Continue up the drainage until it is possible to traverse to the base of the first major gully, which cuts the peak's east face. Follow this steep gully, which is very brushy at first, up to the base of the face. The route on the face follows an obvious couloir and involves several pitches of moderate Class 4 climbing. The couloir holds significant amounts of snow and ice into late June. First ascent: L. Dye and A. Barnes.

East Ridge (Class 3-4). Use the same approach as listed for the East Face route. Instead of crossing to the face, continue to the east ridge. As you follow the ridge toward the summit, it melds into the northeast side of the east face. The last 100 feet are quite steep. Early-summer climbs will require an ice axe to cut through the summit cornice. First ascent: T. Lopez and D. Lopez in 1987.

Wet Peak*   11,309 feet (Class 3)
South Wet Peak*   11,138 feet (Class 3)

Wet Peak is a double-summited peak located 3 miles due east of Mount McCaleb. It is identified on the USGS quad as the Wet triangulation station. The peak's summit ridge is 0.6 mile long. The peak is accessed from Bear Creek Lake [(D)(3)(a) or (A)(2)]. From Bear Lake, climb due north up the narrowing gully to a hidden upper basin northwest of the summit at 10,000 feet. Once in the basin, turn southeast and climb toward the summit of Point 11138. Once on the long summit ridge turn northwest and follow the broad ridge to the summit. The up-

per basin also can be reached from Wet Creek [(D)(4)(a.1)] or by dropping off the south ridge of Peak 10800. USGS Mackay

Sheephead Peak*   11,276 feet (Class 2-3)

This summit is located between Wet Peak and Invisible Mountain on the main Lost River crest. The name was first used by USGS geologist J. B. Umpleby on a 1916 sketch map of the region. It is remote from all access routes, but is easily climbed via the connecting ridge with Invisible Mountain. First ascent: probably R. Baugher in 1992. USGS Mackay

Invisible Mountain   11,330 feet (Class 3)

Invisible Mountain, a vastly unappreciated summit, is located 2.25 miles southeast of Wet Peak. The peak's most impressive feature, its 2,000-foot north face, towers over Methodist Creek that is seldom, if ever, visited and thus, this peak is truly invisible. The peak is climbed via its long south ridge from Mahogany Gulch [(B)(14)]. Hike up the jeep trail that leads into the gully until it ends at roughly 6,600 feet. Cross the creek and start up the south ridge, which is steep and brushy. Weave in and out of the thickets of mountain mahogany. Keep on the west side of the ridge crest after passing 8,000 feet. At 9,000 feet the ridge swings to the northeast and then back to the northwest at 10,000 feet. At 10,800 feet you will find a large cairn. Just past the cairn is a short Class 3 section of ridge. Once past the short climbing pitch, the summit is 500 feet above. This is a tiring route climbing 4,600 feet. Take plenty of water. First ascent: T. M. Bannon in 1914. USGS Mackay

THE HAWLEY MOUNTAINS

The Hawley Mountains are a subrange of the Lost River Range formed by a ridgeline that parallels the main Lost River crest. Located east of the main crest in the Little Lost River Valley, this subsidiary ridge is roughly 10 miles long. Hawley Mountain, at 9,752 feet, is its highest point. The entire subrange is administered by the BLM, which studied it in 1982 for possible inclusion under the Wilderness Act. Unfortunately, it is doubtful that the area will ever receive wilderness designation.

Hawley Mountain   9,752 feet

Although not a high mountain by Lost River Range standards, Hawley Mountain dominates the Little Lost River Valley, because it sits away from the main crest almost in the center of the valley. The peak, used by T. M. Bannon for a 1914 triangulation station, sits 22 miles due east of Mount Idaho and 5 miles southwest of Clyde. The name honors the Hawley family, who settled in the valley around 1880. By the start of World War I, they were the largest single supplier of horses to the U.S. Army. Their pride was their Clydesdale horses, which is how Clyde, Idaho, got its name. USGS Hawley Mountain

Northwest Ridge (Class 2). This route leaves from the point where the Pass Creek Summit Road [(D)(5)] crosses Wet Creek. Climb the steep bluffs above Wet Creek until you reach the high rolling ridge that climbs to the west. Follow the ridge to the lower tree line, and then work your way up through the forest. From tree line, the route works up the large, unstable talus slopes to the summit.

Northeast Ridge (Class 2). This route is shorter, but requires a 4WD. Starting from the Pass Creek Summit Road [(D)(5)], drive east for 200 yards and take the first road south that climbs up the steep bank. At the top of the bank, the road forks; keep to the right and follow the road to its end. This will bring you to a water trough close to the lower tree line. Park here and hike to the Douglas fir stand to your left. Cross into the forest and climb until you reach the ridge top. From here, follow the ridge until it brings you to tree line. From tree line, climb across the talus and block-covered slope to the main east ridge. From this point, take the east ridge to the summit.

PASS CREEK SUMMIT SOUTH TO KING MOUNTAIN

After Pass Creek Summit, the Lost River Range takes a hard turn to the south. Few climbers are knowledgeable of the Lost River Range south of Pass Creek Summit. This is their loss. The range's southern end is filled with impressive summits and pristine canyons.

Sunset Peak   10,693 feet (Class 2)

This peak, which forms the headwaters of three major drainages, is perhaps the most important southern summit. Although a dominant summit, the pyramid-shaped peak is not easily spotted from the valley floor. Situated 7 miles east of Invisible Mountain, it can be reached from almost any direction, but only the southern approach via Elbow Canyon is short enough to be practical [(D)(1)]. Follow the Mud Lake Road into the mountains until it forks and take the left (north) fork. When the road ends, continue up the drainage to the peak's west face. Climb up to the west ridge and follow it to the summit. First known ascent: T. M. Bannon in 1914. USGS Sunset Peak

Sunrise Peak*   10,618 feet (Class 2-3)

When viewed from US-93 this peak's west face appears as a rugged series of golden cliffs. The summit is located 1.2 miles southeast of Sunset Peak. Climb the peak from Van Dorn Can-

yon [(A)(4)]. From the end of the road, climb the avalanche chute to the ridge top above and then follow the ridgeline south to the summit. The peak also can be climbed from Elbow Canyon [(D)(1)]. Follow the canyon due east until past the cliffs at 8,300 feet. Turn north and climb to Point 10441. Follow the ridgeline north to the summit. USGS Sunset Peak

Peak 11081 (North Twin)   11,081 feet

This beautiful summit with a massive, striped eastern face is the tallest Lost River summit south of Pass Creek Summit. It is located on the main Lost River crest 3.5 miles south of Sunset Peak, at the head of the Cabin Fork Canyon. First ascent: probably R. Baugher in 1988. USGS Sunset Peak

West Face (Class 3). The west face is accessed from Elbow Canyon [(D)(1)]. From the end of the road, follow the canyon until it forks at 7,800 feet. Turn south and climb toward the saddle between Point 10286 and the summit. From the saddle, the route climbs directly to the summit. First ascent: R. Baugher.

East Side Routes (Class 3). Access the peak's two eastside routes from Cabin Fork [(A)(3)]. From the end of the road, hike upstream to the 8,200-foot contour. From this point, you can climb due west up the peak's west ridge or traverse into the cirque southeast of the summit. Once in the cirque climb to the saddle between this peak and its southern twin. From the saddle, climb up the south ridge, bypassing a tower on the east, until it is possible to reach the top of the ridge again.

Peak 11070 (South Twin)   11,070 feet

This stunning peak is located 0.8 mile south of Peak 11081. USGS Sunset Peak

North Ridge (Class 3). Climb the peak from the saddle to its north, which is approached from the east and Cabin Fork Canyon [(A)(3)]. Please refer to the East Side route under Peak 11081 (North Twin) for more details.

Southeast Gully (Class 3). Access this route from Cabin Fork [(A)(3)]. Cabin Fork forks at 7,200 feet. Take the drainage that leaves the main canyon and follow it southeast until roughly 8,000 feet. The route now angles up and almost due west. Aim for a point at the base of the gully, 400 feet above and west of the small tarn shown on the USGS quad. From this point, it is possible to climb the southeast gully northwest toward the summit ridge. The summit ridge is blocked at one point. Drop off the ridge and then ascend back to the ridge on a rib and slab system. First ascent: R. Baugher.

Jaggle Peak*   10,772 feet (Class 2)

Jaggle Peak is identified on the USGS quad as a triangulation station. It is located 6 miles south of Sunset Peak. The summit forms one of the many seldom-visited high points in the southern stretches of the Lost River Range. Approach from the Little Lost River Valley via Cabin Fork Creek [(A)(3)]. Follow the drainage to the north face of the peak, then turn west and climb to the saddle north of the summit. From the saddle, follow the ridgeline to the summit. USGS Sunset Peak

Peak 10571   *10,571 (Class 3)*
This chisel-shaped summit is located 0.9 mile east of Jaggle Peak. Climb the peak from Cedarville Canyon [(A)(2)]. Follow the canyon to a point at 8,800 feet, which is due south between the summit and Point 10493. Climb north to the saddle and then follow the ridge northwest to the summit. First ascent: probably R. Baugher in 1992. USGS Sunset Peak

Peak 10601 (Ramshorn Peak)   *10,601 feet (Class 3)*
This summit, named after a roadhouse bar in Darlington, is located 1.7 miles south of Jaggle Peak on the main Lost River crest. Climb the peak from Ramshorn Canyon [(B)(16)(a)]. From the end of the road ascend the canyon to the crest. Go north, staying as close to the crest as possible until you reach the summit. Coral fossils are found in upper Ramshorn Canyon. First ascent: R. Baugher in 1992. USGS Ramshorn Canyon

King Mountain   *10,760 feet (Class 3)*
This peak is named after James King, who settled below the peak in 1886. King Mountain, the last major summit along the Lost River crest, is a big mountain with three summits along its 2-mile summit ridge. T. M. Bannon climbed the peak in 1914. The USGS quad identifies the 10,612-foot middle summit as King Mountain, but the true summit is 1.1 miles to the northeast. The peak sits 8.5 miles south of Jaggle Peak. The peak's western slopes are a popular launching point for hang gliders.

Although the peak can be approached from any number of directions, it is best approached from the west and the road in King Canyon [(B)(17)]. This steep, 4WD road leads to the hang glider launching site near Point 7888. From Point 7888, follow the ill-defined ridgeline east/northeast toward the middle summit. This ridge or rib climbs through a stunted forest and across talus but presents no difficulties until roughly 200 feet below the middle summit where it reaches a cliff system. Climb the Class 3 cliffs to the middle summit. From the summit it is a long, up-and-down walk to the true summit along the summit ridge. USGS Ramshorn Canyon

APPROACHES TO THE LOST RIVER RANGE

(A) EAST SIDE APPROACHES
Just south of Arco, ID-33 leaves US-20 and runs east to Howe. At Howe, take the Pahsimeroi Highway north through the Little Lost and Pahsimeroi River Valleys. Most of the Little Lost Valley is managed by the BLM and is open to the public. From Howe to Clyde, the alluvial fans that stretch down from the mountains are crisscrossed by both gravel and primitive roads, which lead up to the bottoms of almost every Lost River canyon. Unfortunately, over the years many access routes have been closed by private landowners. The roads are listed from south to north.

(1) FS-125, Arco Pass Road. This route leaves the Pahsimeroi Highway just north of Howe and leads to Arco over Arco Pass. See [(E)], below.

(2) FS-124, Cedarville Canyon Road. Turn west off the Pahsimeroi Highway at a signed junction just north of Howe. In 0.7 mile the road crosses the Little Lost River and in 1.4 miles the road forks. Take the left fork, which leads directly to Cedarville Canyon. A 4WD is recommended.

(3) FS-446, Cabin Fork Road. This road is accessed from the Cedarville Canyon Road. The road splits off and heads to the northwest up the Cabin Fork. The road is passable for several miles. A 4WD is recommended.

(4) FS-431, Van Dorn Canyon Road. Access this road 24.3 miles north of Howe. Make a sharp left turn off the Pahsimeroi Highway. The road runs due south paralleling the highway for 0.8 mile and then turns due west. Cross the cattleguard and follow the road between two private pastures for 1.1 miles. Turn left (south). At 2.6 miles from the highway, the road meets the junction for FST-278, which runs to Hawley Pass. Continue south for another 0.3 mile and turn right onto FST-431. Continue straight ahead to reach Van Dorn Canyon. The road is not exactly routed as shown on the Forest Service or USGS maps. It eventually ends at 8,000 feet below an avalanche chute. Take a 4WD and an axe.

(5) FS-122, Pass Creek Summit Road. This road leaves the Pahsimeroi Highway 28 miles north of Howe at Clyde and follows Wet Creek into the mountains to Pass Creek Summit. The road crosses the range at Pass Creek Summit and drops down to Mackay in 39 miles. See [(D)], below.

(6) Pass Creek/Doublespring Connector Road. This road runs more than 30 miles from between Pass Creek Summit Road and the Doublespring Pass Road. It provides access to most of the east side canyons between Doublespring Pass and Pass Creek Summit. To reach this road from the south, take the Pass Creek Summit Road [(D)] west from Clyde. In 4 miles the road crosses Wet Creek. Just after the crossing, the road climbs a gravel bench to a junction. Go right at the junction; in 1 mile the road arrives at a second junction. Go right again and then quickly left at a junction for a two-track road that follows the course of an underground water pipe. This two-track road continues on toward Dry Creek. Shortly after rounding Taylor Mountain you will meet another junction. Go straight ahead for Dry Creek access [(A)(6.1)]. Go right to continue toward Doublesprings Road on the road now signed as FS-114 [(A) (6.2)]. Immediately after the turn, you must ford Dry Creek and later the road fords Burnt Creek. A 4WD is an absolute necessity. From the crossing of Burnt Creek the road continues toward the Doublespring Pass Road, crossing the Pahsimeroi drainage and then Horseheaven Pass [(C)(3)].

(6.1) FS-118, Dry Creek Road. From the junction described above, take this road west to the small check dam that is used to fill the underground pipeline. At this point, take the road that climbs up the south side of the canyon and then follow it into the upper sections of Dry Creek. The road gets a little rugged after passing the ruins of the Dry Creek Dam (the collapse of which is responsible for the ravaged condition of the Dry Creek drainage) and a 4WD is required. After descending to the creek bottom past the dam, the road fords Long Lost Creek and forks. The right fork continues a short way up Dry Creek to a washout. The left fork heads up Long Lost Creek [(A)(6.1.1)] for several rugged miles. A 4WD is rcommended.

(6.1 alt.) Dry Creek Cutoff Road. An alternative route into Dry Creek follows the Dry Creek Cutoff Road across BLM land to the mouth of Dry Creek. Access the cutoff from the Pass Creek Summit Road 6.3 miles west of Clyde where the road crosses a cattleguard soon after. Turn right and immediately cross a second cattleguard. Follow the relatively smooth two-track road into a narrow gulch. This road provides an alternative route into the upper reaches of Dry Creek as well as accessing the remote Buck Springs drainage. **Buck Springs Road.** This rough 4WD road should only be driven when it is thoroughly dried out. The road leaves the Dry Creek Cutoff Road 5.8 miles from the Pass Creek Summit Road and then descends to Buck Creek at a meadow with an old cabin. From the meadow, the road climbs up the drainage and eventually splits. Take the right fork and continue to follow it for a total of 4.5 miles to the saddle below the north peak of Massacre Mountain where it ends. A 4WD is required.

(a) **FST-240, Dry Creek Trails.** Keep to the right when the road forks after crossing Long Lost Creek. Just before the road crosses Dry Creek, a short road turns off to the left. Follow this road until it ends and you will find an unofficial but heavily used trail that leads upstream and eventually to Copper and Swauger

Lakes [(A)(6.1.1)(c)]. This route was created by motorcycles, but is suitable for hiking. To reach FST-091 from the road's end you must cross Dry Creek, which is difficult during high water. Once across the creek, follow the road to its end. The trail follows the west side of the creek to the Swauger Lake junction and then continues over Breitenbach Pass and into the Pahsimeroi drainage [(C)(3.2)(a)]

(6.1.1) FS-434, Long Lost Creek Road. From the point where this road leaves Dry Creek, it crosses Dry Creek twice and traverses a boggy meadow before ending on a sagebrush-covered bench in about 4 miles. A 4WD is required.

(a) **FST-194, Long Lost Creek Trail.** From the end of FS-434, FST-194 heads up the canyon. Once upon a time the trail crossed the divide and dropped into Upper Cedar Creek [(B) (12)(a)]. Unfortunately, this trail is not maintained and no longer climbs over the pass.

(a.1) **USGS North Face Cross-Country Route.** After the junction for FST-092 (see below), the trail stays on the west side of Long Lost Creek and climbs toward a meadow at the base of the headwall that climbs up to the Lower Cedar/Long Lost Pass. The tread is good in places and nonexistent in others. From the meadow, the stream turns southeast and the trail enters a grove of trees. Stay on the southwest side of the creek. At approximately 8,900 feet, the route climbs out of the trees. Cross the creek to its southeast side and begin to angle up the steep slope to climb above the cliffs blocking the canyon ahead. Once you are above the first waterfall, continue upstream past a second waterfall. Cross back over to the southwest side of the creek and follow the creek upstream to the first tributary that enters from the west at 9,200 feet. Ascend this tributary on its south side into a spectacular cirque below the north face of USGS Peak. To reach the base of the north face, stay on the east side of the cirque.

(b) **FST-092, Shadow Lake/East Side Crest Trail.** This trail turns off FST-194 1 mile from the road's end and leads to FS-539 near Pass Creek Summit [(D)(4)(a)] many miles to the south. Shadow Lake is the first stop on the trail. It is located in a grandiose box canyon below Shadow Lake Peak. From the area of the lake, the trail climbs a pass and leads into the Big Creek drainage.

(c) **FST-091, Swauger Lake Trail.** This trail leaves the Long Lost Creek Road 0.9 mile before its end. A sign at the trailhead suggests that it is 2 miles to Swauger Lake and 22 miles to the Sawmill Gulch trailhead [(B)(8)(a)] on the west side of the range. This is a steep, scenic route with a good tread.

(6.2) Burnt Creek Canyon Roads. These roads leave the Doublespring Pass/Pass Creek Summit Connector Road [(A) (6.1)] roughly 4.5 miles north of Dry Creek. Two different roads

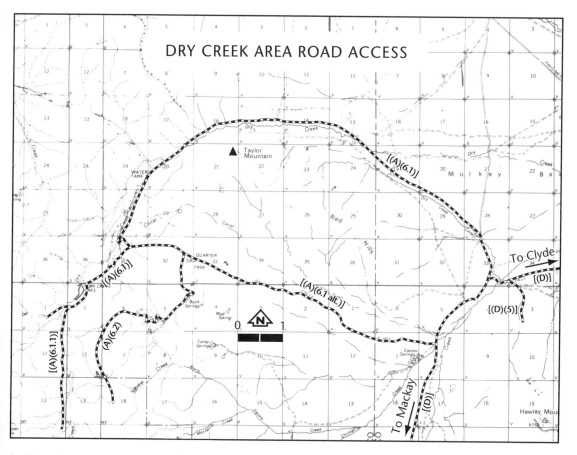

DRY CREEK AREA ROAD ACCESS

lead south into Burnt Creek. Althought the northernmost road requires fording Burnt Creek, it is the recommended choice. These roads lead nearly 6 miles into the drainage. A 4WD is recommended. Burnt Creek is a beautiful open drainage that can be crossed by determined hikers. For climbs of Peak 11509, follow game trails high above the south side of the creek when the canyon narrows to a gorge.

(7) **FS-116, Doublespring Pass Road.** See [(C)], below.

(8) **FS-112, Grouse Creek/Mill Creek Road.** Access to this road is found north of the village of May. After entering the mountains, the road forks. The right fork climbs Grouse Creek, where it ends at a trailhead for FST-086. The left fork goes a short distance up Mill Creek. A livestock trail leads up this drainage to Sheep Pen Basin at the base of Grouse Creek Mountain.

(a) **FST-086, Grouse Creek Trail.** This trail is no longer shown on the newest Challis National Forest map. The trail, which is still passable, begins at the end of FS-112 and runs

south for 6 miles to a small lake that sits between Grouse Creek Mountain and McGowan Peak.

(B) WEST SIDE APPROACHES

US-93 runs north and south between Arco and Challis, on the west side of the range. The following roads are listed from north to south.

(1) **South Fork McGowan Creek Road.** This road leaves the east side of US-93 13.3 miles south of the ID-75/US-93 junction and crosses through a gate in the fence onto a good two-track road. Drive east and to a junction in 1.3 miles and turn left onto the road that runs south. (If you go straight ahead at this junction, you will arrive at the mouth of McGowan Creek Canyon, which is an alternative route to McGowan Peak.) In 0.7 mile veer to your left and follow this road 1.7 miles to the mouth of the next canyon south of McGowan Creek. Two roads lead south from this route toward the FS-288, Gooseberry Creek Road [(B) (2)]. A 4WD is recommended.

(a) South Fork McGowan Creek Cross-Country Route. While there is no maintained trail in the canyon, cross-country travel is possible. Roughly 1 mile from the mouth of the canyon, the canyon turns to the north and quickly climbs to a saddle between Point 9304 and McGowan Peak.

(2) FS-228, Gooseberry Creek Road. This signed road leaves US-93 14.5 miles south of the US-97/ID-75 junction or 1.2 miles south of the McGowan Creek Road. Turn east off the highway and proceed toward the mountains. In 1.1 miles the road goes through a gate and in 5.5 miles it meets FS-228A, the Sheep Creek Road [(B)(3)]. In another 0.1 mile a road forks off to the left and provides access to Peak 10731. At 6.4 miles the road crosses below the mouth of a steep gully, which provides access to Pahsimeroi Pyramid. The road ends in another 0.2 mile on a high saddle. A 4WD is recommended.

(3) FS-228A, Sheep Creek Road. This road provides an alternative access point to the Pahsimeroi crest. Access the road 18.2 miles south of the US-93/ID-75 junction (or 3.7 miles south of the Gooseberry Creek Road. This road crosses Sheep Creek and can be difficult in wet conditions. It leads directly up Sheep Creek for about 2 miles, crosses the creek and climbs up a bench to the north to join the Gooseberry Creek Road [(B)(2)]. A 4WD is recommended.

(4) Arentson Gulch Road. This road leaves US-93 26.7 miles south of Challis or 4.7 miles north of the US-93/Doublespring Pass Road junction [(C)]. From the highway, drive due east 0.5 mile, turn left (north), and go through a gate in a fence. Drive 1 mile to reach the access for Dickey Peak. The road continues north into Arentson Gulch. A 4WD is recommended.

(5) FS-116, Doublespring Pass Road. See [(C)], below.

(6) FS-279, Mount Borah Trailhead. Access this trailhead from US-93 18 miles north of Mackay, or 1.8 miles south of the Doublespring Pass Road turn, or 4.5 miles north of the US-93/Big Lost River Road junction. The road is signed and well maintained.

(7) Elkhorn Creek. Access up Elkhorn Creek begins at US-93 15.9 miles north of Mackay or 0.35 miles south of where the Big Lost River Road runs east toward Ketchum. Turn east off the highway and drive through the gate. The road leads a short distance from the highway before it ends.

(8) FS-411, Sawmill Gulch Road. This route leaves US-93 13.1 miles north of Mackay. This road climbs the gulch much farther than acknowledged by the Forest Service map. It was evidently extended by mining interests. It becomes impassable for even 4WDs after 2.7 miles, but continues with a good tread for hikers. At the first switchback, look for a trailhead in the trees. A 4WD is required.

(a) FST-089, Sawmill Pass/Pass Creek Trail. This little-known and little-used hiking trail crosses Sawmill Pass in 2 miles, Leatherman Pass in 3 miles, and then leads to Pass Lake and the east side trailhead in the Pahsimeroi drainage [(C)(3.1)(a.1)]. The trail is well maintained but somewhat faint as it climbs from Sawmill Pass to Leatherman Pass.

(9) Lone Cedar Creek Access. This road leaves US-93 11 miles north of Mackay and runs roughly 2 miles northeast at the base of the mountains. From the road's end, it is possible to bushwhack up the drainage to Leatherman Pass, which is 3.5 difficult miles farther. In the lower reaches of the drainage, keep on the east side of the creek as much as possible and head for the giant pinnacle at 8,500 feet. Pass the pinnacle on its east side. Soon after the pinnacle, the trees begin to thin out and the going is less difficult. Expert cross-country skills are needed for this access route.

(10) Jones Creek. This road leaves US-93 10 miles north of Mackay. Turn off the highway, go through the cattleguard and follow the road toward the base of the mountains. In 2.1 miles, turn east on an obvious road. Follow this road for 0.4 mile and then turn once again toward the mountains. The main road goes to Jones Creek, where it ends. To reach Pete Creek, park just before the road ends and follow the base of the mountains. A 4WD is recommended.

(11) Pete Creek Road. This road leaves US-93 8.4 miles north of Mackay. It provides good access to the mouths of both Pete and Jones Creeks. A 4WD is recommended.

(12) FS-127, Upper Cedar Creek Road. This road leaves US-93 6.1 miles north of Mackay and runs northeast for 4 miles. The road starts as a broad gravel road, but narrows considerably after it crosses through a fence line onto private property. Follow the road past an abandoned house to a second gate. Pass through this gate and you will soon encounter a broad irrigation ditch, which will be difficult to cross without a 4WD. Once past the ditch, the road leads directly to the mouth of Upper Cedar Creek. A 4WD is recommended.

(a) FST-194, Upper Cedar Creek Trail. Once upon a time, a Forest Service trail ran up Cedar Creek, crossed over the Lost River crest, and dropped into Long Lost Creek [(A)(6.1.1)(a)]. Parts of this trail still exist, but those venturing into this country should have good cross-country travel skills, because the trail has been mostly obliterated by floods and rock slides. This drainage can only be traversed in the fall when the water level in the creek has dropped.

(12.1) Lost River Mountain Access. Cross the irrigation ditch described [(B)(12)] and turn sharply left to follow the road that parallels the ditch for 0.1 mile. Turn right and follow the 4WD road until it ends at the point where the 7,480-foot contour crosses the intermittent stream that drains the south face of Lost River Mountain.

(13) Lower Cedar Creek Road. Access this road directly from Mackay. From the center of town, drive east on the Bench Road for 1.85 miles, turn left toward the mountains, and follow the primitive two-track road due north to a fork in 0.9 mile. Go right at this fork, which leads around a private field. In roughly 3 miles, the road drops into the Lower Cedar Creek drainage and ends. A half mile before the end of the Cedar Creek Road, look for a road that forks very sharply to your left. Follow this road, which climbs the bench to the west. Once on the bench, the road follows the irrigation ditch to gain access to the west side of Mount McCaleb.

(a) Lower Cedar Creek Cross-Country Route. At the end of the Lower Cedar Creek Road you must immediately wade a wide, deep canal. From the far bank, walk 25 feet to your right and climb up the slope for roughly another 25 feet to an abandoned canal. Follow the course of this canal into the canyon until it ends near a stream-gauging device. From this point, the route goes upstream following a dilapidated, steel-wrapped wooden pipe. The stream bottom is extremely difficult going in places—impossible during high water—and crosses some of the wildest terrain in the state. Expert cross-country skills are essential.

(14) FS-498, Mahogany Gulch Road. Access this road from Mackay via the Bench Road; see [(B)(13)], above. Turn left onto this road 2 miles from Mackay. After 1.4 miles, the road forks. The right fork leads to Mahogany Gulch. The left fork climbs up a gravel bench. Go right to access Invisible Peak's southeast ridge. Go left to access the southwest ridge. A 4WD is required.

(15) FS-122, Pass Creek Summit Road. See [(D)], below.

(16) FS-276, Ramshorn Canyon Road. Leave US-93 at Darlington on a good gravel road that meets a second road at 2.9 miles. Turn right (south) and drive 1.7 miles to FS-276. This road heads directly toward Ramshorn Canyon in about 4.2 miles. A 4WD is recommended.

(a) Ramshorn Canyon Trail. From the end of the road, this trail leads a couple of miles up the canyon and then ends abruptly. From the end of the trail, it is possible to access the crest via a long cross-country walk near Peak 10601.

(17) King Mountain Launch Site. This road provides access to the King Mountain hang glider launch site. It also provides great access for climbing King Mountain. The launch site is approached from US-93 by turning east at Moore. Drive east nearly 2 miles to the gravel road that parallels US-93 along the base of the Lost River Range. Turn left (north) on this road and follow it for 1.25 miles to an intersection and a small gravel pit. Turn east and follow the road toward the mountain. The launch site road turns off to the left and continues steeply uphill. Although the road has been improved, a 4WD is recommended.

(18) FS-125, Arco Pass Road. See [(E)], below.

(C) DOUBLESPRINGS PASS ROAD ACCESS

This road crosses the Lost River crest at Doublesprings Pass and connects the Big Lost River Valley with the Pahsimeroi Valley. From the west, access the road from US-93 31.4 miles south of the US-93/ID-75 junction or 45.8 miles north of Arco. In the east, access the road from Goldberg. At Goldberg, the Pahsimeroi Highway splits with each fork following its side of the valley northward. Take the west-side fork to the signed junction for the Doublespring Pass Road. The road is usually passable for passenger vehicles, but a 4WD is recommended for all approaches off of this road. The approaches are listed from west to east.

(1) Rock Creek. Leave the Doublesprings Pass Road by turning right at the earthquake information center roughly 2.8 miles from US-93. A dirt road leads to a small irrigation works at Rock Creek in 1.6 miles. This point also can be reached from the Mount Borah trailhead [(B)(6)]. A 4WD is recommended.

(2) Dickey Peak East Side Access. This access point leaves the Doublesprings Road 4.2 miles from US-93 and ends at a spring in about 0.6 mile.

(3) Horseheaven Pass Road/Upper Pahsimeroi Access. This route begins by following FS-117 east from the Doublesprings Pass Road 9.5 miles from US-93 at a signed junction. The route deteriorates in several spots and is quite rugged in the upper forks of the Pahsimeroi drainage. After 0.3 mile the road forks. Keep right. A second fork is encountered in another 1.9 miles. Keep left. The road crosses Horseheaven Pass after 6.1 miles, passes FS-312 at 7.2 miles, FS-311 at 7.8 miles, and FS-310 at 9.6 miles before descending into Mahogany Creek at 10 miles. From Mahogany Creek, take the road that climbs up and over a sage-covered divide to the east, cross the divide, and descend into the Pahsimeroi drainage. At 13.9 miles, the road forks with FS-267 [(C)(3.1)], which follows the West Fork Pahsimeroi River and FS-118 [(C)(3.2)], which follows the East Fork Pahsimeroi River. A 4WD is recommended.

(3.1) FS-267, West Fork Pahsimeroi Road. Continue up the West Fork on this road, which deteriorates with every mile. A 4WD is required.

(a) FST-089, Leatherman Pass Trail. If you can get to the trailhead, this is a super trail that leads to Pass Lake and Leatherman Pass, as well as Sawmill Gulch [(B)(8)(a)] on the west side of the range. It is also the best approach to Leatherman Peak and Mount Idaho. The trail, which is in good shape, runs to Leatherman Pass in 4.1 miles.

(a.1) FST-198, Pass Lake Trail. This trail leads from FST-089 to Pass Lake in about 1 mile. The trail's tread is only so-so, but the route is easy to follow.

(b) FST-197, Merriam Lake Trail. This trail leaves FST-089 just past the trailhead and runs to the lake in 1.9 miles.

(3.2) FS-118, East Fork Pahsimeroi Road. Take the left fork 13.9 miles from the Doublespring Pass Road and follow this slow road across the West Fork Pahsimeroi River. The road forks at 1.6 miles. Take the right fork and continue for 3.5 hard miles to the trailhead for FST-090. A 4WD is required.

(a) FST-090, Breitenbach Pass Trail. This trail is overlooked by many but provides access to a lot of Lost River backcountry, including the high basins below Leatherman Peak, Bad Rock Peak, Mount Church, Donaldson Peak, and Mount Breitenbach. It is part of the trail system known as the East Side Crest Trail. It climbs out of the East Fork Pahsimeroi River, crosses 10,000-foot Breitenbach Pass at 4.4 miles and links up with Dry Creek [(A)(6.1.1)(a)]. The Forest Service is slowly upgrading this trail, but it is only a faint route over the pass and into Dry Creek.

(b) Lake 9682 Cross-Country Route. To access Lake 9682, hike up the Breitenbach Pass Trail roughly 0.5 mile from the trailhead to where the drainage splits into two forks. Leave the trail and contour due south into the right-hand fork. The route follows the meeting place between the talus and the trees. Once past a waterfall, the route contours into the stream. This is a challenging, but rewarding route for those with advanced route-finding skills.

(4) FS-115, 272, 274, and 426, Christian Gulch Roads. Access these roads from the Doublesprings Pass Road 13.6 miles from US-93. FS-115 is the main road. FS-272 forks off to the left after 1.6 miles and ends in 0.5 mile at the beginning of the south fork of Christian Gulch. At 3.7 miles, FS-115 intersects with FS-426. Take the left-hand fork and FS-426 (which ends in 1.5 miles) to reach the middle fork and the high country along the crest. FS-115 continues to the east fork of the gulch. A 4WD is recommended for all of these roads and is required for FS-426.

(a) Christian Gulch Cross-Country Routes. Although trailless, all three forks of Christian Gulch are passable to experienced cross-country hikers. The middle fork, which is accessed from FS-426, is the most alpine of these canyons and the east fork is the most impressive. The middle fork contains two lakes and several beautiful cirques. The east fork has two ponds that dry up by mid-July when finding water becomes a problem. The hiking, while strenuous, is not difficult.

(D) FS-122, PASS CREEK SUMMIT ROAD

This road crosses the Lost River Range between Mackay and Clyde. On the west side of the range, it leaves US-93 0.5 mile north of Leslie, which is 18 miles north of Arco. The road enters Pass Creek Canyon in 4.8 miles and climbs through its rugged gorge. The road also can be accessed from Mackay via the Bench Road, which leaves town from the center of Mackay. On the east side of the range, leave the Pahsimeroi Highway at Clyde, which is 27.7 miles north of Howe.

(1) FS-273, Elbow Canyon Road. This signed road leaves the east side of the Pass Creek Summit Road shortly before the mouth of Pass Creek Canyon and runs into Elbow Canyon. A 4WD is recommended.

(2) Mud Lake Road. This road leaves Pass Creek 8.3 miles from US-93 or just south of Bear Creek Road. The road is closed to cars and trucks, but open to motorcycles. It climbs up to the crest of the range near Sunset Peak in 3 miles.

(3) FS-430, Bear Creek Road. Follow the Pass Creek Summit Road for 8.7 miles from US-93 to a small, signed road that leads west up Bear Creek for almost 2 miles. Go left at the only fork. A 4WD is recommended.

(a) FST-093, Bear Creek Trail. This trail leads 2.8 miles from the end of the Bear Creek Road to Bear Creek Lake. In 1.5 miles it reaches a trail junction with FST-092 [(D)(4)(b)]. From the junction, it is roughly 1.3 miles to the lake. Bear Creek Lake is the shortest, though not necessarily the easiest, access to Wet Peak and provides passable access to Invisible Peak.

(b) FST-092, Bear Lake to Girls Camp Road Trail. This trail leads to the Girls Camp Road trailhead in 2.5 miles, crossing a saddle between Warren Mountain and Peak 10800. Also see FST-092 [(D)(4)(b)], Bear Lake to Girls Camp Road Trail.

(4) FS-539, Girls Camp Road. This road is accessed at Pass Creek Summit 12.2 miles from US-93. From the pass, the road runs uphill and west to a group campsite and then a signed, gated trailhead in 2 miles.

(a) FST-092, East Side Crest Trail. This is the beginning of an outstanding trail system that leads north along the east side of the Lost River crest to the East Fork Pahsimeroi River [(C)(3.2)(a)]. It leaves the trailhead and drops downhill into a meadow before climbing to a saddle northeast of Peak 11240 and then dropping down into Big Creek. From Big Creek it climbs up steeply and crosses over the ridgeline south of Massacre Mountain and drops into Shadow Lake [(A)(6.1.1)(b)].

(a.1) Upper Wet Creek Cross-Country Route. Old Forest Service maps show a trail leaving the East Side Crest Trail and running up Wet Creek toward Nolan Lake. The trail is no longer there. Nevertheless, traversing Wet Creek is a worthwhile, but difficult proposition. The upper reaches of Wet Creek are as wild a location as you will find. The bottom of Wet Creek is cluttered with downed timber and staying above the creek on its north side is best for the first mile. Advanced cross-country skills are needed to enter this area.

(b) FST-092, Bear Lake to Girls Camp Road Trail. This trail begins as an old roadway a short distance from the FST-092 trailhead. It leads to Bear Creek Lake and the Bear Creek Road trailhead in 4 miles, crossing a saddle between Warren Mountain and Peak 10800 on the way. Also see [(D)(4.3)(b)].

(5) Hawley Mountain Access. From the Pahsimeroi Highway at Clyde, an old townsite and a BLM GS, the Pass Creek Summit Road runs due west for 4 miles and then jogs sharply to the right to cross Wet Creek. Two roads are visible just before the jog. The first cuts sharply back to the east and climbs a gravel bench. This road leads to the Northeast Ridge route for Hawley Mountain. The second road follows the south side of Wet Creek and provides access to the Northwest Ridge route.

(E) ARCO PASS ROAD ACCESS

This is the southernmost route across the Lost River Range. It provides access to the largely untouched southern portion of the range. The road is accessed in the west from US-20/US-26 in Arco by turning west off the highway 0.3 mile south of its junction with US-93. Cross the railroad tracks and jog to your right. In another 0.3 mile, turn left and follow this route for 1.3 miles to the beginning of FST-125, the Arco Pass Road. The first portion of the route crosses private property and you will soon arrive at a ranch. Make a sharp right at the ranch, drive 1 mile, and make another sharp right. Go through the gate and follow the road 2.5 miles to a set of corrals. The road forks at this point. The left fork goes over Beaverland Pass to the King Mountain access [(B)(17)]. The right fork goes northeast over Arco Pass.

There are several options for accessing the road from the Pahsimeroi Highway. The best east side access leaves the Pahsimeroi Highway 3 miles north of Howe. Turn west off the highway and follow this road west to access FS-125 in roughly 5 miles. Turn onto FS-125 and follow it south to Arco Pass. There are many roads in this area, but the main road is obvious. Don't forget your maps. A 4WD is recommended.

6

THE LEMHI RANGE

The Lemhi Range is a quintessential linear mountain chain that runs from Salmon in a southeasterly direction for 100 miles to the Snake River Plain. It varies in width from 10 to 15 miles. The Pahsimeroi and Little Lost River Valleys border the range on its western side, and the Lemhi and Birch Creek Valleys parallel its eastern side. The range was named Lemhi in 1917 (Lemhi is a corruption of Limhi from the Book of Mormon). Signs of Native American habitation dating from 8,000 years ago can be found along the base of the range, but their name for the range is lost in time.

The Lemhis are a basin and range fault block composed of limestone, quartzite, and related sedimentary deposits. Glaciation along the crest has carved the rock at will. While many peaks are nothing more than incredible piles of talus, others are solid blocks that present impressive faces to the valleys below. The range's crest consistently rises more than 4,000 feet above the broad alluvial valleys that flank it, staying above 10,000 feet in elevation. The range is broadest in the north with high peaks, remote valleys, and dozens of mountain lakes. The central Lemhis, which are narrower, steeper, drier, and higher than the northern peaks, include the range's most impressive peaks: 12,197-foot Diamond Peak and 11,618-foot Bell Mountain. The southern end of the Lemhi Range, south of Saddle Mountain, is a semi-desert region characterized by deep canyons and massive cliffs. The two most impressive of these canyons are Box and East Canyons. Box Canyon is a winding canyon that shelters several important archeological sites and some impressive cliffs. East Canyon, north of Box Canyon, is most noted for its tremendous limestone cliffs, the largest of which is capped by a large natural bridge. Both canyons were used extensively by prehistoric inhabitants; more than eighteen archeological sites have been identified in and around the canyons.

The Lemhi Range is studded with challenging summits, most of which are inexplicably unnamed. For example, not one of the eleven fine peaks on the Fallert Springs USGS quad is named. Rick Baugher may have captured the range's character best when he wrote:

> There are not many places like the Lemhi Range left. Its fragile alpine life zone grows more than two hundred types of plants. Some, such as the Arctic poppy, face extinction. The windswept land above 10,000 feet is home to maybe four hundred of Idaho's best climbers, Oreamnos americanus, the mountain goat. Even as late as 1998, a few of its peaks have yet to be climbed. It is a special place.

The foothills and lower slopes of the Lemhi Range are administered in the north by the BLM. Two national forests share the backbone of the range. The Salmon-Challis National Forest manages the entire northernmost 25 miles and the western side of the crest south to the Snake River Plain; the Targhee National Forest administers the southern half of the Lemhis east of the crest.

Hiking opportunities abound in the northern part of

the range where an extensive trail system offers excellent backpacking opportunities. The southern part of the range has few trails, but is suitable for rugged cross-country travel. Recreational use of the range is limited, because few Lemhi Range trailheads are accessible without a 4WD.

Climbing opportunities within the range generally fall within the Class 2 to 4 categories, with most of the routes rated Class 3. The broken condition of the rock limits technical climbing. Winter mountaineering involves long approaches up to the base of the mountains. While snowfall is not excessive on the alluvial fans, the wind blows the snow into drifts that prevent vehicle access and leave much of the ground bare and unsuitable for skiing. Only a few winter ascents have been recorded, although others have undoubtedly occurred.

Primary access to the Lemhi Range is via ID-28 on the eastern side of the range, and via US-93 and the Pahsimeroi Highway on the western side. ID-33 runs along the range's southern fringes and connects ID-28 and the Pahsimeroi Highway. The crest of the Lemhi Range is so rugged that no roads cross it. While the quantity of roads that approach the range is amazing, their quality varies greatly, both from road to road and from year to year. A 4WD or a trail bike can be invaluable in this country. Gas is hard to find, start with a full tank.

THE LEMHI CREST FROM SALMON TO GUNSIGHT PEAK

The northernmost sections of the Lemhi Range contain thick spruce, pine, and fir forests. Access is limited by private property and only a few peaks see regular ascents. Primary access is from ID-28 in the east and US-93 in the west.

Sal Mountain   *9,592 feet (Class 1)*

This big peak rises just 11 miles south of Salmon. It dominates the view in all directions as it divides the Salmon River and Lemhi Valleys. Historically, the mountain has been a busy place. T. M. Bannon set a triangulation station on the summit in 1912 and the Forest Service built a standard 10-by-10-foot fire lookout (which is still standing) on its summit in 1926. A trail leads part way to the summit [(A)(11)]. Take the Withington Creek Road to its end and then follow the trail to the workings of the early 1900s Harmony copper mine. From here, bushwhack up the east face to the main crest through a stunted limber pine forest to the summit. USGS Sal Mountain

Poison Peak   *9,364 feet (Class 2)*
Watson Peak   *8,671 feet (Class 2)*

From Sal Peak south to Lem Peak, a distance of 16 miles, the Lemhi crest drops down into a series of rolling, forested ridges. The only two named peaks in this section are Poison and Watson, which are found next to each other 8 miles south of Sal Mountain. These two peaks are most frequently climbed from US-93 on the west side of the range via FST-103 [(B)(1)(a)]. Leave the trail where it crosses the saddle between the peaks and hike the easy ridges east to Watson or west to Poison. USGS Poison Peak.

Peak 10327 (McNutt Peak)   *10,327 feet (Class 2)*

The northernmost Lemhi peak to reach above 10,000 feet is a big, tri-summited, horseshoe-shaped peak located 3.1 miles north of Lem Peak. Basin Lake, Lake 9134, and the northernmost Bear Valley Lakes are found on its lower slopes. It is an easy climb from the northernmost Bear Valley Lake [(A)(10.2)(a)]. Take the trail to the lake. From the lake, climb directly north to the summit ridge and then walk due north along the ridge to the summit. USGS Lem Peak

Tendoy Peak*   *10,720 feet (Class 3)*

This peak is named in honor of the legendary Shoshone chief who was raised in the Lemhi Valley and is buried at the base of the mountain. The peak rises precipitously directly west of the largest Bear Valley Lake [(A)(10.2)(a)] and has impressive north and east faces of more than 1,000 feet. The summit is reached from the lake via its east ridge. Climb to the ridgeline directly north of the lake at 10,200 feet, then turn east and follow the ever narrowing east ridge to the summit. Rick Baugher describes a Class 2 traverse from Peak 10327 (McNutt Peak) as a straightforward talus walk. USGS Allison Creek

Peak 10456   *10,456 feet*

This Peak, sometimes called Little Lem Peak, sits at the head of the Bear Creek drainage and just north of Lem Peak. Its most impressive feature is a 900-foot face that drops into the largest of the Bear Valley Lakes [(A)(10.2)(a)]. USGS Lem Peak

South Ridge (Class 3). The straightforward south ridge leads to the summit in 0.6 mile and slightly more than 300 feet from Lem Pass, which is reached by FST-179 [(A)(10.2) (a) or (B)(2)(a)].

Northeast Face (II, 5.7). The peak's north face tops out at just over 10,200 feet. This route climbs a chimney and crack system that splits the face to its top. The first ascent was made in 1990 by P. Lang, J. Meyer-Tyson, and S. Tyson. Lang reports that the climb was six pitches on hard quartzite. According to Lang "the crux…comes at the slight overhang on the fifth pitch." From the top of the face, follow the peak's northeast ridge to the summit. (AAJ 1990 at 177)

Lem Peak   10,985 feet

This impressive mountain is the jagged highpoint for the northern Lemhis. It is located 16 miles south of Sal Mountain and 7 miles north of May Mountain, the next Lemhi summit to approach 11,000 feet in height. Lem Peak has four ridges, all of which are climbable, but it is usually climbed by its northwest ridge because of access considerations. USGS Lem Peak

Northwest Ridge Route (Class 3). The standard route to the summit begins on Lem Pass to the northwest. This pass cannot be reached via an old mining road up Allison Creek [(B)(2)(a)] on the west side because private land blocks public access. This situation may change over the years—check with the Forest Service. Consequently, access is via the Bear Valley Lake Trail on the east side [(A)(10.2)(a)]. The ridge is a relatively short scramble of 800 feet over loose, broken, and sometimes steep slopes. Stay on the ridge top when possible and bypass obstacles on the ridge's east side.

Peak 10775 (Buck Lakes Peak)   10,775 feet (Class 3)

This is the first of three challenging, unnamed summits that rise between Lem Peak and Long Mountain on a lonely stretch of the Lemhi crest. Its summit, which is 1 mile south of Lem Peak, towers over the Buck Creek drainage to the east. The closest trail access if from Buck Lakes [(A)(10.2)(a.1)]. The peak's northwest and eastern faces both rise impressively almost 1,000 feet. Climb the peak via its northern ridge. Take the trail to the first Buck Lake and then follow the inlet stream up into the cirque below Lem Peak, where you will find two more lakes and two small tarns. Once in the cirque, hike to the highest tarn at just under 9,600 feet. From this point, scramble up to the main crest to the west. Once on the crest, climb south to the summit. USGS Lem Peak

Peak 10744   10,744 feet (Class 3)

This peak sits on the main crest, 1 mile south/southeast of Peak 10775. Cow Creek is to the west and Wright Creek to the east. Its summit is the highest point on a complicated 2-mile ridgeline that runs along the main crest. Although the summit undoubtedly could be climbed from three drainages, the only reported climb traversed the connecting ridgeline from Peak 10775 to the north. USGS Lem Peak

Peak 10550   10,550 feet (Class 3)

This remote, pup-tent-shaped summit is 4 miles south of Lem Peak and 1 mile north of Long Mountain on the main crest. The peak's east side is protected by a cliff band. There is no easy approach to this isolated summit. The only reported climb followed the peak's south ridge, which was traversed from Long Mountain. USGS May Mountain

Peak 10487   10,487 feet (Class 2)

This summit is located 3 miles due south of Lem Peak and well west of the main crest on the ridgeline that divides the Morgan Creek and Cow Creek drainages. Based on access considerations, the peak is most often climbed via its west ridge by way of a long, 3-mile, ridge walk from FST-243 [(C)(1)(a.1)]. Leave the trail where it crosses the Cow Creek/Morgan Creek divide at 7,200 feet. Then follow the ridge due east and then north to Red Point and then to Point 10211, where the trees give way to the Lemhi high country. The last 300 feet of elevation gain and the summit requires another mile of hiking. USGS May Mountain

Long Mountain   10,728 feet (Class 2-3)

Long Mountain, a complicated L-shaped mountain, is found 5 miles south of Lem Peak on the main crest. Its true summit is just east of the main crest and not the 10,696-foot point shown on the USGS quad. USGS May Mountain

East Ridge (Class 2). The east ridge is approached from Kadletz Creek and FST-180 [(A)(10.2.1)(a)]. The trail crosses the east ridge 1.2 miles east of the summit at 8,080 feet. From the trail, ford Kadletz Creek and climb a long-lasting snowfield to the summit. First ascent: R. Baugher in 1997.

West Side (Class 3). Approach the peak from the Pahsimeroi Valley via FST-071 [(C)(1)(a)], which runs northeast up the North Fork Morgan Creek. When the trail ends, continue cross-country to the top of the drainage. From a point 0.5 mile below the small lake at the top of the drainage, climb up to the large, northwest-facing shelf that leads to the peak's south ridge and then follow the ridge to the summit.

Peak 10466+   10,466+ feet (Class 3)

This multi-pointed summit rises between the east and north forks of Morgan Creek between Long Mountain and May Mountain. Its complicated, mile-long summit ridge has four points that rise above 10,400 feet. Although it is difficult to tell when you are on the different summits, the USGS identifies the westernmost summit as the highest. To reach the summit, follow FST-017 [(C)(1)(b)] until the East Fork Morgan Creek splits at roughly 6,600 feet in elevation. Leave the trail and climb up the trailless fork toward the northeast. At roughly 8,600 feet in elevation, climb out of the drainage and up a gully directly toward the summit ridge. At roughly 9,800 feet veer to the northwest and aim for a point northeast of the summit. USGS May Mountain

May Mountain   10,971 feet (Class 3-4)

At May Mountain, the Lemhi crest reaches a high point just short of 11,000 feet. The crest does not exceed May Mountain's height until it reaches the slopes of Big Creek Peak, more than 20 miles to the south. May Mountain, a sharp, blocky summit, sits 2.5 miles due south of Long Mountain, square on the Lemhi crest. This peak was identified on the 1918 Salmon National Forest map and the 1965 Challis National Forest map as Hi Peak. The first ascent was probably by T. M. Bannon, who used the summit for mapping around 1913. USGS surveyor W. H. Chapman occupied the summit in 1956 and left this route description:

Horse pack east up Morgan Creek Trail about 4 miles…up steep hill to bench…to main ridge NE up ridge to end of timber and end of horse travel. Backpack up ridge to highest point and station. Horse packing time is about 4 hours and backpacking time is about 1 hour.

The recommended route to the summit begins along the East Fork Morgan Creek and FST-071 [(C)(1)(b)]. It is an interesting and challenging scramble. Leave the trail where it crosses the East Fork Morgan Creek/Tater Creek saddle southwest of the summit (and just east of Point 8140 on the USGS quad). Work your way northwest through the trees to the Lemhi crest 0.8 mile south of the summit. Follow this ridge north to the base of the summit pyramid and begin your climb on its western side, just below the ridge crest. The route climbs up the ridge for roughly 500 feet on loose talus and disintegrating ledges until a Class 4 wall in a V-shaped alcove blocks further progress. From this point, there are two options.

The first option climbs the Class 4 wall. Start on the wall's south side and traverse to your left around a boulder into the

May Mountain's south face

center of the wall. The moves on the wall involve considerable exposure and loose holds. From this point, climb straight up above the wall to a sloping ramp, which can be easily followed to the right and the top of the summit ridge. Follow the ridge the remaining distance to the summit.

The second option begins at the base of the Class 4 wall and follows a ledge south to the ridge crest and a notch. Cross through the notch and descend to a debris-covered ramp, which can be followed up the east side of the ridge under overhanging cliffs to a steep 50-foot-high mud and rock filled gully. Carefully climb the gully, which is slippery and subject to rock fall. At its top, turn left and climb up for 15 feet to the top of the summit ridge. Climbing the south ridge involves a 10-mile round trip with 4,500 feet of elevation gain. Set aside plenty of time and carry extra water. USGS May Mountain

Mogg Mountain   *10,573 feet (Class 2)*
After rising to almost 11,000 feet on May Mountain, the Lemhi crest gradually descends and curves to the east without any true summits until Mogg Mountain, which sits 6.5 miles almost due east of May Mountain. The peak was named to honor Frederick W. Mogg, who lived in the Lemhi Valley in the early 1900s. Climb to the summit via the west ridge, which is reached from Morse Creek on the peak's west side [(C)(2)(a)] or from Carol Creek on the east [(A)(10.3)(b)]. USGS Mogg Mountain

Mill Mountain   *10,793 feet (Class 2)*
Mill Mountain is found east of the crest on a subsidiary ridge, 2.5 miles northeast of Mogg Mountain. It is the most prominent Lemhi peak viewable from ID-28 in the upper Lemhi Valley. The peak is climbed from the east. From the end of the East Fork Road [(A)(10.3.1)] contour around the ridgeline to the north and into Little Mill Creek. Follow this drainage up to the peak's southeast ridge. Climb to the ridgeline and follow the ridge to the summit. USGS Mogg Mountain

Buffalo Skull Peak*   *10,735 feet (Class 3)*
This high peak is located on the main crest 1.1 miles south of Mogg Mountain and directly south of Buffalo Skull Lake. Its cone-shaped summit is the highest point on the Lemhi crest between May Mountain and Yellow Peak. Rick Baugher reports that the summit is reachable from Mill Lake

Mill Mountain (Photo by Rick Baugher)

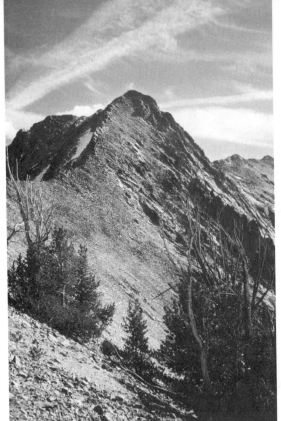

Buffalo Skull Peak (Photo by Rick Baugher)

Peak 10688 (The Wedge)   *10,699 feet (Class 2)*

This big, wedge-shaped peak is just southeast of Mill Lake and east of Peak 10569. Rick Baugher suggests climbing the peak from Mill Lake [(A)(10.3.1)(a)] in the east by heading south to gain the peak's west/southwest ridge. D. Rice also visited this summit in 1975. USGS Mogg Mountain

Gothic Peak*   *10,487 feet (Class 3)*

This peak overlooks deep Everson Lake [(A)(9.1.1)(a)] on the main crest 4.8 miles southeast of Mogg Mountain. The summit is the highest point of a rugged series of cathedral-like quartzite towers and cliffs that drop down into the Stroud Creek drainage. Rick Baugher's suggestion is to hike from Dairy or Everson Lakes southwest up the cirque to the main crest and then follow the crest north to the summit across the broad, plateau-like slope. USGS Yellow Peak/Patterson/Stroud Creek/Mogg Mountain

Patterson Peak*   *10,602 feet (Class 3)*

This peak is a big hulking summit that forms the highest point on the crest east of Patterson. The peak is best ascended by its south ridge, which is accessed from the saddle 1 mile south of the summit. This saddle is accessed from the east by FST-185 [(A)(9.1)(a)]. Leave the trail where it crosses the divide and hike due north along the winding ridge. USGS Yellow Peak

Annies Peak*   *10,288 feet (Class 2)*

This summit is directly south of Patterson Peak. Rick Baugher's route climbs to the summit via the peak's north ridge, which is accessed from FST-185 [(A)(9.1)(a)] in the saddle just to the north. Leave the trail where it crosses the divide and hike due south on the west side of the ridge. USGS Yellow Peak

[(A)(10.3.1)(a)] by a circuitous route. From the lake, hike northwest to the saddle above. From the saddle, contour west across the obvious line until the slope on your left moderates and a small bowl opens up. Climb south up the bowl to the ridge. Take the ridge west to the summit. Carry an ice axe. USGS Mogg Mountain

Peak 10569 (The Ledge)   *10,569 feet (Class 3)*

This peak is located 2.5 miles south of Mogg Mountain on the main Lemhi crest. Climb the peak from Mill Lake [(A)(10.3.1)(a)] in the east or Fall Creek [(C)(3)(a)] in the west. From Mill Lake, approach via a northeast-trending snow gully or the east ridge. There is a report of an ascent from Mill Lake via the southeast face. There are conflicting claims regarding the rating on the face. To climb the peak from Fall Creek, leave the trail directly west of the saddle on the peak's south ridge, climb to the saddle and then follow the ridge and ledges to the summit. A cairn and register dated 8/6/75 were the product of Douglas Rice and probably document the peak's first ascent. USGS Mogg Mountain

THE PATTERSON DIVIDE

The Patterson Divide parallels the Lemhi crest on its western side. The divide, which forms a long north/south-trending ridge, is capped by two worthy summits and splits Falls Creek and Patterson Creek.

Peak 10383   *10,383 feet (Class 2)*

This peak is the northernmost of the two summits on the Patterson Divide. The peak is climbed via its north ridge. Access the north ridge where FST-072 [(C)(2)(a.1) or (3)(a)] crosses the ridge and then hike due south to the summit which is 0.6 mile and 400 feet above. Expect great views of the main crest to the east. USGS Patterson

Peak 10535   *10,535 feet (Class 3)*
This is the highest point on the Patterson Divide. Climb the peak via its north ridge from Patterson Creek [(C)(2)(a.1)/(a.2) or (C)(3)(a)]. Leave the trail at roughly 7,200 feet and follow the drainage west to two small tarns at 9,600 feet. From the lakes, climb to the saddle to the northwest. From the saddle follow the ridge south to the summit. USGS Patterson

THE MAIN LEMHI CREST FROM GUNSIGHT PEAK TO ROCKY PEAK

Gunsight Peak   *10,835 feet (Class 2)*
Gunsight Peak sits on a subsidiary ridge just east of the main crest and 5 miles north of Yellow Peak. The name reportedly was given to this peak because, when viewed from Leadore, a notch in its summit looks like the rear "sight" of a rifle. Climb this peak from the highest lake in the North Fork Little Timber Creek drainage. From the lake, scramble due north to the ridge top and follow the ridge to the summit [(A)(8.1)(a)]. First ascent: attributed to "David RT and JR" in 1881. USGS Yellow Peak

Ray Lode Peak*   *10,723 feet (Class 2)*
This summit, named for the mine high on its side, is located 2 miles southwest of Gunsight Peak. The summit can be reached from three directions: (1) by traversing the ridge connecting the peak with Gunsight Peak; (2) by utilizing a mining road to reach the north ridge from Big Eightmile Creek [(A)(9.1)]; or (3) via the peak's south slopes from the point where FST-183 crosses the saddle south of the peak [(C)].

    The Gunsight Peak/Ray Lode Peak ridge traverse is straightforward. Use the Gunsight Peak write-up to reach the ridge. The mining road is accurately shown on the USGS quad. Follow the road to its end and then follow the straightforward ridge north to the summit. The southern route is not as easy to find but still presents few difficulties. The quad shows FST-183 dividing at the upper end of Big Eightmile Creek with one trail heading over the divide and into Devils Basin and Big Creek, and one fork crossing the divide into the Lake Fork drainage. A third trail (unmapped by the USGS but shown on some Forest Service maps) splits off this trail and climbs up to the divide just south of this peak. This trail then swings due south and crosses the crest and drops into the top of the Lake Creek drainage at a small lake. Leave the trail in the first saddle and climb the peak's southern slopes to the summit. USGS Yellow Peak

Peak 10540   *10,540 feet (Class 2)*
This peak, which overlooks Yellow Lake, a popular fishing hole, sits at the divide of four drainages: Lake Fork Big Creek, Big Eightmile Creek, North Fork Little Timber Creek, and Middle Fork Little Timber Creek. It is located almost 2 miles due south of Gunsight Peak. Climb the peak via its north or west ridges from FST-183 [(A)(9.1)(a) or (C)(4)(b)]. USGS Yellow Peak

Big Eightmile Peak*   *10,601 feet (Class 2)*
Big Eightmile Peak offers an excellent vantage point to view this high, wild section of the Lemhi crest. It is found at the head of Big Eightmile Creek to the north and Big Creek to the south and is almost surrounded by 10,000-foot summits. It is located 3.1 miles northwest of Yellow Peak. Poorly maintained trails cross both its northwest and northeast ridges [(A)(9.1)(a)]. Climb to the summit from either ridge. USGS Yellow Mountain

Peak 10507 (Slate Roof Peak)   *10,507 feet (Class 2-3)*
This peak is located just south of Yellow Lake at the head of Lake Fork North Fork Big Creek. A poorly maintained trail crosses its east ridge (main crest) [(A)(8.2)(a.1)]. R. Baugher notes the scramble to the top from this pass is straightforward. USGS Yellow Peak

Peak 10343 (West Rocky Peak)   *10,343 feet (Class 2)*
This peak is located 1.6 miles northeast of Yellow Peak and due west of Rocky Peak. Scramble to the top from the pass to the southwest [(A)(8.2)(a), (a.1), or (a.3)]. USGS Yellow Peak

Rocky Peak   *10,555 feet (Class 2)*
Rocky Peak, which sits 2.5 miles northeast of Yellow Peak, has a big, broad summit plateau between two summits of almost equal height. The easternmost summit is the highest and offers a sweeping vista of the Lemhi Valley to the northeast. The easiest route to the summit follows the ridgeline that connects the peak with the main crest. Follow this ridge east from near where FST-184 [(A)(8.3)(a.2)] crosses the main Lemhi crest. From the trail, hike due north to gain the crest at Point 10343. Turn east and follow the ridgeline 1.7 miles to the summit. USGS Sheephorn Peak

THE BIG CREEK DIVIDE

The Big Creek Divide sits west of the main Lemhi crest. It is a north/south-trending ridge that divides the Pahsimeroi Valley from Big Creek. There are two true summits on the divide.

Peak 10882 (Basin Peak)   *10,882 feet (Class 3)*

This big, seldom-climbed summit is the northernmost summit on the Big Creek Divide. It is located 1.9 miles north of Inyo Peak. While the summit can be approached from almost any direction, the two most efficient routes to the summit are (1) a traverse of the peak's south ridge from Inyo Peak; or (2) a climb of the peak's northeast ridge from the main crest. To reach the northeast ridge you must first access the crest. Four primary routes are available. Access from the west utilizes either Patterson Creek and FST-074 [(C)(3)(b)] or the North Fork Big Creek and FST-075 [(C)(4)(b)]. East side access is via either Big Eightmile and FST-183 [(A)(9.1)(b)] or the Middle Fork Little Timber Creek and FST-187 [(A)(8.2)(a)]. These routes provide access to hike the seldom-if-ever-maintained FST-075, which follows the top of the Lemhi crest for 3 miles. Access the crest trail using one of these routes and then follow the divide (either north or south) to the peak's northeast ridge. Once on the ridge, it is a long, but not too difficult walk to the summit. USGS Yellow Peak

Inyo Peak   *10,611 feet (Class 2)*

Inyo, the second Big Creek Divide peak, sits 5 miles west of Yellow Peak and the main Lemhi crest. It is designated as the Inyo triangulation station on the Patterson USGS quad. Although this peak can be climbed from any direction, it is most easily reached from Big Creek [(C)(4)(a)]. Follow Big Creek north until directly east of the summit. At this point, a small tributary of Big Creek flows down into the main stream. Leave the trail at this point and follow the tributary up toward the peak. From the upper slopes, gain Inyo's east ridge at a point just after the ridge turns south. Continue up the east ridge to the summit. USGS Yellow Peak

THE MAIN LEMHI CREST FROM YELLOW PEAK TO SHEEP MOUNTAIN

Yellow Peak   *10,968 feet (Class 2)*

The Lemhi Range is wider east of Leadore than at any other point. Yellow Peak is at the center of this a large, roadless area at the head of three major drainages. The peak's location, pyramidal shape, and distinctive yellow-tinted rock make it the most prominent Lemhi summit for miles. It is located 4 miles due south of Gunsight Peak. Reach the summit by any of the peak's three ridges. The north and west ridges are very open and enjoyable scrambles [(A)(8.2)(a), and (8.3) or (A) (8.3)(a) or (a.1)]. USGS Yellow Peak

Junction Peak   *10,608 feet (Class 2)*

Junction Peak, a 1913 T. M. Bannon triangulation station, is situated 1 mile southeast of Yellow Peak. Climb this peak from Yellow Pass [(A)(8.3)(a)], or by traversing the connecting ridgeline from Yellow Peak. The summit also can be reached from Big Timber Creek [(A)(8.2)(c)]. There are several springs high on the peak's west side that attract elk and mountain goat. USGS Sheephorn Peak/Yellow Peak

Sheephorn Peak   *10,665 feet (Class 3)*

Sheephorn Peak towers above Nez Perce Lake, known for its giant grayling trout. It sits 4.5 miles east of the Lemhi crest and Junction Peak. The summit can be reached via the peak's northwest slopes from Big Timber Creek [(A)(8.3)(a)]. This is a short, but arduous climb with a total distance of 2.5 miles and 3,000 feet of elevation gain. The peak also can be climbed from Nez Perce Lake [(A)(7)(a)] via its east ridge. Hike due north from the lake to the east ridge. Once on the ridge, moderate scrambling leads 800 feet to the summit. USGS Sheephorn Peak

Timber Creek Peak   *10,553 feet (Class 3)*

This seldom-visited summit sits 1.3 miles south of Sheephorn Peak on the connecting ridge. T. M. Bannon constructed a 7-foot-high cairn on the summit in 1913. Because of access considerations, the best route to the summit is from Sheephorn Creek. The route does not present any objective difficulties. USGS Iron Creek Point/Sheephorn Creek

Big Creek Peak   *11,350 feet (Class 3)*
Flatiron Mountain   *11,019 feet (Class 3)*

These two giants are on a subsidiary ridge west of the main crest and 3.5 miles south of Yellow Peak. Both peaks are good locations for sighting mountain goats. Flatiron was another summit utilized by T. M. Bannon in 1913. He named the peak Pahsimeroi after the valley it overlooks. Pahsimeroi is a Shoshone word meaning "a grove by a stream." The recommended route begins on Yellow Pass [(A)(8.2)(a.3)]. From the pass, hike southwest past the small lake just below the pass and then traverse into the 9,600-foot saddle at the top of Big Timber Creek. From the saddle, follow the ridgeline south across Point 10323 and then traverse around the west side of the next high point on the ridge. A game trail 3 feet wide and as smooth as a groomed path leads across the first part of the traverse. Unfortunately, the trail dies out before reaching the next saddle and you must traverse across steep,

The north slopes of Big Creek Peak

loose talus for the remaining distance. From the next saddle, scramble up Big Creek Peak's northwest ridge.

From the Big Creek Peak summit, drop down the southwest ridge to the saddle and then scramble up Flatiron's northwest ridge. Note that both summits can be reached by hiking up Fall Creek and then climbing to the intervening saddle. This route involves a short section of Class 3 climbing just below the saddle and difficult route-finding problems.

Big Creek Peak possesses one of the best views in the state. You can see the Beaverhead, Lost River, Pioneer, Boulder, and Salmon River mountains, as well as the Lemhi crest from Lem Peak to Diamond Peak. USGS Big Creek Peak

Peak 10256 (Smithie Peak)   *10,256 (Class 2)*
Peak 10332   *10,332 feet (Class 2)*
These two minor quartzite summits sit on the main crest just southwest of Negro Peak. Hike up Deer Creek on the old jeep road designated FST-160 [(A)(6.1)(a)] and then continue cross-

country to the saddle that separates the peak. Climb to the summits from this saddle. These peaks also can be climbed via the connecting ridge with Negro Peak. USGS Gilmore

Negro Peak   *10,571 feet (Class 2)*
This remote summit is seldom climbed. It sits 5 miles northwest of Gilmore, between Deer Creek and Negro Green Creek. Hike up Deer Creek on the old jeep road designated FST-160 [(A)(6.1)(a)]. Follow the trail until the creek splits. Leave the trail at this point and follow the North Fork Deer Creek through heavy brush up the basin to the head of the creek. Climb directly through the forest to the saddle just west of the summit. Follow the ridge northeast to the summit. The east ridge is also passable. USGS Gilmore

Portland Mountain   *10,820 (Class 2-3)*
Portland Mountain was named for the Portland Mining Company of Butte, Montana, which operated mines in the Gilmore

area. It is located 2.5 miles south of Negro Peak and 3 miles due west of Gilmore. Drive to Meadow Lake [(A)(6)] and park. Three routes are suggested. For the first, hike north to the base of the peak's south ridge, and then climb up at a slight angle to the ridge top. Follow the ridge to the summit. The second route begins at the small unnamed lake on the peak's west side (approach is via FST-160 [(A)(6.1)(a)]). From this lake, climb directly to the saddle on the peak's south ridge. Follow the ridge to the summit. The third route climbs the peak from a saddle directly west of Meadow Lake on the Lemhi crest. This saddle is reached by a recently constructed trail [(A)(6)(a)]. From the saddle hike north over Peak 10723, then northeast to Point 10666, descend into the saddle to the north, and then climb Portland Mountain's south ridge. USGS Gilmore

Peak 10723   *10,723 feet (Class 2)*
This is an easy scramble from the saddle to the south. Access the saddle from Meadow Lake via a trail [(A)(6)(a)]. Hike up the south ridge. USGS Gilmore

Gilmore Peak*   *10,748 feet (Class 3)*
This double-summited peak has a 1,400-foot north face that rises directly above Meadow Lake 2 miles south of Portland Mountain. Rick Baugher found this peak's north face gracing a copy of the 1910 Bureau of Mines annual report with a caption that reads "Gilmore Peak 11,000 feet high." From the ghost town of Gilmore, the peak rises 4,000 feet in 4.5 miles. Climb the peak from Meadow Lake [(A)(6)(a)] via the newly constructed Meadow Lake Trail, which leads to the saddle north of the summit. Once on the saddle, climb the peak's north ridge to the summit. Keep on the top of the ridge and pass obstacles on the west side. USGS Gilmore

Sheep Mountain   *10,865 feet (Class 3)*
Sheep Mountain sits 5 miles south of Portland Mountain. Climb this peak from its east side via Lemhi Union Gulch [(A)(5)]. Note the wonderfully preserved cabins high in Lemhi Union Gulch. From the mining road in the gulch, Rick Baugher climbed north to gain the east ridge, which will lead to the summit. USGS Gilmore

THE IRON DIVIDE

The 14-miles-long Iron Divide is a long northwest/southeast-trending ridgeline with three major summits: Peak 10743, Iron Creek Peak, and Bear Mountain. The divide sits west of the Lemhi main crest and is separated from the crest by the

South Fork Big Creek in the north and the Little Lost River in the south. Access the divide from the west side of the range. This seldom-visited ridge system is very popular with mountain goats.

Peak 10743   *10,743 feet (Class 3)*
This summit is the northernmost point on the Iron Divide. The easiest route to the summit is from Iron Creek Peak. Leave FST-193 [(C)(5)(a.1)] before it makes its final climb to Iron Creek Peak and follow the ridgeline northwest to the summit. The route switches between the top and south side of the ridge for its entire length. While this is the easiest route to the summit, it is still a long tiring climb. USGS Big Creek Peak

Iron Creek Peak   *10,736 feet (Class 1)*
Designated Iron Creek Point on the USGS quad, this is a true peak with exceptional views. This former fire lookout site is situated 2 miles due southeast of Peak 10743 and 10 miles due west of Sheephorn Peak. It is another excellent place to view mountain goats. A poorly maintained trail reaches the summit where the remnants of the old fire lookout are still in place. Approach on the Big Gulch Road, FS-099 [(C)(5)]. From the road's end, FST-079 leads up to the saddle between Iron Creek Point and Bear Mountain. In the saddle, a trail forks off and leads to the summit. USGS Iron Creek Point

Bear Mountain   *10,744 feet (Class 2)*
Bear Mountain is a big, dark, reddish mass of ferrous rock that sits at the head of the Little Lost River Valley, 2 miles southeast of Iron Creek Point. The summit can be reached by following the route for Iron Creek Point [(C)(5)(a)] to the saddle between the two peaks and then cutting cross country to the summit. It is 1.25 miles and about 1,000 feet of elevation gain from the saddle to the summit. USGS Moffett Springs

THE MAIN CREST FROM BIG WINDY PEAK TO SADDLE MOUNTAIN

South of Sheep Mountain, the Lemhi Range narrows down to a single ridgeline without the outriding divides found in the north. While the range is less complicated than in the north, the peaks are consistently higher and more rugged.

Big Windy Peak   *10,360+ feet (Class 1)*
This peak is located 3.5 miles south of Sheep Mountain. Its summit, which is anything but pointed, is a good example of what geologists call a peneplain (the remnants of an ancient

plain). Its summit is reached by a mining road. Although the peak has been carved up by mining roads and digs, it offers exceptional views and a relatively easy introduction to the Lemhi crest. From the Hahn town site [(A)(5)], walk or drive (the roads are in poor condition; driving is not recommended) on the mining road that climbs up Spring Mountain Canyon. This road eventually climbs onto the crest north of Big Windy at a 100-years-old cabin and then continues to the summit. The road then drops to the saddle between Big Windy and Trail Peak and climbs nearly to 10,200 feet on Trail Peak's north ridge. The summit also can be reached from the west via the mining roads and trails that climb up Squaw Creek [(C)(6)(a)] and Warm Creek [(C)(6.1)(a)]. USGS Big Windy Peak

Trail Peak   *10,533 feet (Class 2)*
This peak is 0.5 mile south of Big Windy Mountain. Its impressive north face tumbles 1,500 feet into Horseshoe Gulch in less than a 0.5 mile. Climb the peak via its north ridge. See the Big Windy write-up for access information. USGS Big Windy Peak

Mountain Inspiration*   *10,715 feet (Class 3)*
This big, twin-summited peak, which rises more than 4,000 feet from both the Little Lost River and Birch Creek Valleys, is not blessed with high access routes. Its north summit is the highest, while its southern summit, 1 mile to the southeast, is 10,693 feet high. The summits are separated by a 10,300-foot saddle. The north summit can be climbed from either side, but it is a very long climb to the summit from either side. The suggested route begins with a hike up Coal Kiln Canyon [(A)(4)]. Follow the drainage until it broadens around 8,000 feet. Then climb due north to the saddle between Points 9140 and 10546. From this saddle, a classic ridgeline climbs up to Point 10456. Once at the top of this point, follow the ridgeline west and then north to the summit. First ascent R. Baugher in 1991. USGS Big Windy Peak/Coal Kiln Canyon

Peak 10162 (Rainbow Mountain)   *10,162 feet (Class 2)*
Rainbow Mountain is located 1 mile east of the main crest. It is the big peak that towers over the Coal Kiln. Climb the peak from Mammoth or Coal Kiln Canyon [(A)(4) or (A)(4.1.1)]. Hike up either drainage to the saddle west of the peak and then ascend the west ridge. USGS Coal Kiln Canyon

Peak 10533 (Medusa)   *10,533 feet (Class 3)*
This complicated, multiple-summitted peak is the next summit south of Mount Inspiration on the main crest. It has a 3.5-mile, curving summit ridge with at least ten points

above 10,000 feet. The highest point on this long ridge rises above Mammoth Canyon on the east and Mahogany Creek on the west. Like Mount Inspiration, a climb to the summit involves a lot of trailless uphill adventure. The best access to the summit is from Meadow Creek [(C)(7)] on the west. Follow the drainage as it wraps around the north end of the summit ridge. At roughly 9,200 feet it is possible to climb to the summit ridge and then continue 1.5 miles south to the summit. USGS Coal Kiln Canyon

Peak 10490 (The Knoll)   *10,490 feet (Class 3)*
This peak sits just north of Bell Mountain on the main Lemhi crest. It is separated from Umpleby Peak by 0.6 mile and a narrow saddle. This peak has been climbed from both the east and west. From the east, approach via Mammoth Canyon [(A)(4.1.1)] and climb the north ridge. From the west, access the peak from Bassinger Canyon [(C)(7)]. Leave Bassinger Creek at 8,600 feet and climb the prominent gully that climbs due north to a saddle on the peak's west ridge. From this saddle it is a straightforward hike up the ridge to the summit. The peak reportedly can be climbed via its south ridge also, but no details of the route are known. USGS Coal Kiln Canyon

Umpleby Peak*   *10,713 feet (Class 3-4)*
This spectacular peak located between Peak 10490 and Bell Mountain presents a cliff-riddled face toward Birch Creek that resembles a ship's prow. Although Bell Mountain is 900 feet higher and lords over this peak, Umpleby is equally impressive in its own right. Its summit is protected by cliffs of varying heights on all sides and its north summit is nothing short of superb. This peak is named for Joseph B. Umpleby (1883–1967), a USGS geologist who wrote *Geology and Ore Deposits of Lemhi County* in 1913. Umpleby, who was the first to suggest Lemhi as the name of the range, collaborated with R. N. Bell. The peak has been climbed from both the east and the west sides of the crest. From the east, climb the east face from Bell Mountain Canyon [(A)(4.1.1)(a)]. In the west, access the peak from Bassinger Canyon [(C)(7)]. Hike the canyon to the base of the peaks, then climb to the saddle between Peak 10490 (The Knoll) and this peak, and climb the northwest ridge (main crest). This ridge reportedly can cause some problems with route-finding. No other details of the climb are known. First ascent R. Baugher in 1991. USGS Coal Kiln Canyon

Bell Mountain   *11,612 feet (Class 3)*
This peak, named after Robert Bell, Idaho's first state mining inspector, looks like a giant imitation of the Liberty Bell. It is

The east face of Bell Mountain, as seen from the Birch Creek Valley

7.5 miles south of Trail Peak. Its rugged summit block dominates both the Little Lost River and Birch Creek Valleys. The summit block is composed of rock that varies in composition from solid and stable to broken and loose.

The first recorded ascent was made by T. M. Bannon, probably in 1913. In 1980, an old tobacco can and several plastic bags formed a makeshift summit register. The Amy family of Howe has signed in on the register almost every year since it was placed on the mountain. L. Dye has climbed the peak from every side and pioneered the four most difficult routes on the summit block. The tiny, quartzite summit area is home to rare and endangered alpine wildflowers. Please chose your hand and footholds with care. USGS Bell Mountain

West Face (Class 3). Approach this route by driving to Bassinger Creek [(C)(7)], where you will find running water and several good campsites. The West Face route begins at about 6,400 feet and climbs south up a steep slope to the top of the west ridge through aspens and sagebrush and into Douglas firs. Once on the main ridge, take its crest up to tree

line at 10,000 feet. Traverse this skyline portion of the ridge around two rock towers to the base of the summit dome. To reach the summit, climb the middle rib on the west face of the dome. This rib is steep, but the route moves from one small shelf to another and the exposure is minimal.

Southwest Gully (Class 4). This gully is between the west face and southwest ridge; access it from Black Creek [(C)(7)]. First ascent: L. Dye, A. Barnes, and W. Boyer in 1963.

East Ridge (Class 3). Approach from ID-28 on the Charcoal Kiln Road [(A)(4)]. Hike up Bell Mountain Canyon and gain the east ridge, which leads to the summit.

Northeast Ridge (Class 4). This prominent ridge leads steeply to the summit, involving moderately difficult pitches with moderate exposure. Access is from the Charcoal Kiln Road [(A)(4)]. First ascent: L. Dye in 1963.

North Couloir (Snow Climb). This route offers an early season snow-and-ice climb of more than 700 feet on 50-degree slopes. Gain the couloir from upper Bell Mountain Creek [(A)(4.1.1)(a)]. First ascent: L. Dye in 1962.

Northwest Face (Class 4). Moderate Class 4 climbing leads to the top of this near-vertical face [(A)(4.1.1)(a) or (C) (7)]. First ascent: L. Dye, A. Barnes, and W. Boyer in 1973.

Peak 10720+ (The Clapper)   *10,720+ (Class 3)*
The next peak south of Bell Mountain on the main crest is an excellent vantage point for viewing its bigger, more compelling neighbor. Climb from Meadow Canyon [(A)(3.1)]. Follow the drainage to the saddle between Bell Mountain and this peak, and then follow the crest to the summit 500 feet above. USGS Bell Mountain

Meadow Peak*   *10,652 feet (Class 2)*
Meadow Peak presents a bold face to the Birch Creek Valley. The cliffy north face hides a gentle meadow-covered route up the peak's northeastern slopes. The hike begins near McCoy and Box Springs [(A)(4.1)]. Leave the springs and hike due south toward McCoy Canyon, cross the gully, and continue southeast to a broad ridge. Ascend this slope to 9,200 feet, then turn southwest and continue the climb to the summit. Rick Baugher recommends the excellent flower-filled alpine meadow at 10,300 feet just before the summit and the ter-rific view of Bell Mountain from the summit. USGS Coal Kiln Canyon

Incredible Hulk*   *10,858 (Class 3)*
This peak, a chunk of limestone that towers over Meadow Canyon, is located 3 miles due east of Bell Mountain and east of the Lemhi crest. Rick Baugher suggests climbing to the summit via the peak's southwest ridge, accessible from the saddle southwest of the summit, which in turn is accessed from either fork of Meadow Canyon [(A)(3.1)]. First ascent: R. Baugher in 1990. USGS Bell Mountain

Foss Mountain   *9,182 feet (Class 1)*
Foss Mountain sits 2.5 miles due south of Bell Mountain. Its summit is reached by a very rough, 4WD mining road [(C)(8)]. The road makes a good hiking route to the summit, which has great views of the Lemhi crest. USGS Bell Mountain

Rust Peak*   *10,759 (Class 2)*
Rust Peak is located 4.5 miles southeast of Bell Mountain just east of the Lemhi crest. The peak's south and west slopes are composed of rust-colored rock. Rick Baugher's route climbs

The view to the south from Meadow Peak to Incredible Hulk and Diamond Peak (Photo by Rick Baugher)

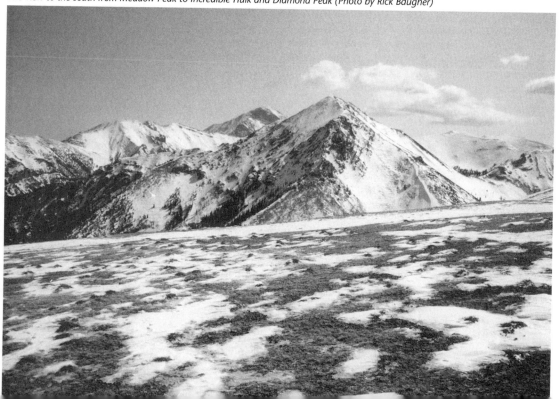

the peak from the Rocky Canyon Trail [(A)(3)(a)] by ascending to the saddle southwest of the summit and then climbing directly to the summit. USGS Diamond Peak

Lame Jake Peak*   *10,810*

This stunning peak is located east of the main crest, directly north of Diamond Peak. Its mile-long summit ridge sports three summits. The southernmost summit is the highest while the middle summit is crowned by a difficult summit block. The peak is unofficially named after a Shoban tribe medicine man who regularly passed through the Birch Creek Valley with his tribe during the spring and fall to fish in the Salmon River. USGS Diamond Peak

East Ridge (Class 3-4). Access the east ridge from the east side of the range near Kaufman Gulch [(A)(2.1)]. Once on the lower east ridge it is about 2.5 miles to the summit. The route grows steeper at 10,200 feet. Keep on the south side of the ridge to avoid the northeast face.

Southwest Ridge (Class 2). Access the ridge by ascending to the saddle southwest of the summit from either Rocky Canyon [(A)(3)(a)] or the North Fork Pass Creek [(A)(2)]. Follow the ridge north to the summit.

Big Sister*   *10,946 (Class 2)*
Little Sister*   *10,723 (Class 2)*

These two peaks are located on the west side of the crest, 4 miles northwest of Diamond Peak. Rick Baugher reports that both are excellent early season destinations. The snow usually melts off Little Sister's west ridge by late March. Snow will last longer on the connecting ridge between the two peaks. Climb Little Sister via its west ridge from Mud Spring [(C)(9)]. Climb Big Sister by the ridge connecting it with Little Sister. USGS Bell Mountain

The Brow*   *11,005 (Class 3)*

The Brow, located 1.3 miles northwest of Diamond Peak, did not become an 11,000-foot peak until the 1987 publication of the USGS Bell Mountain quad. Its north face towers above the left fork of Rocky Canyon. Follow Rick Baugher's suggestion and climb the peak via its east ridge, which is accessed from Rocky Canyon [(A)(4.3.1)(a)]. First ascent: R. Baugher in 1990. USGS Diamond Peak

Diamond Peak   *12,197 feet*

Diamond Peak, the fourth highest mountain in Idaho, is shaped like a large pyramid, and is visible from the Idaho Falls area on clear days. Because it is one of Idaho's nine 12,000-foot peaks, it is climbed by fifty to one hundred people each

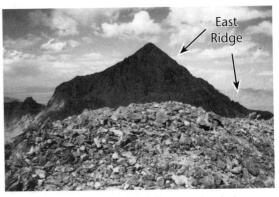

Diamond Peak from The Riddler (Photo by Rick Baugher)

year. The first known attempt on Diamond Peak was by Vernon Bailey of the U.S. Biological Survey in 1890. T. M. Bannon is credited with the first ascent, probably in 1913. Diamond is located on the main Lemhi crest 8.5 miles southeast of Bell Mountain. On its eastern side, the peak rises almost 6,000 feet directly out of the Birch Creek Valley without intervening foothills. The east ridge, though not technically difficult, is the most appealing line on the peak. The summit pyramid is a complex grouping of tilted faces and many vertical walls. USGS Diamond Peak

East Ridge (Class 3). This route climbs the prominent east ridge from the North Fork Pass Creek [(A)(2.1)]. From the end of the vehicle access, hike up to the east ridge. The ridge is broad and rounded along its lower stretches as it arcs upward. The east ridge narrows and becomes more well defined as you climb. The upper route involves moderate Class 3 climbing.

Southwest Ridge (Class 3). Access this route from the Badger Creek Road [(C)(10)]. Follow Badger Creek up to its origin on the peak's western slopes and start climbing from there. The route runs south to an east/west-trending buttress, which connects with the southwest ridge at 10,400 feet. From this point, several lines will lead to the ridge top. Once on the ridge top, follow it north to the summit.

Northwest Ridge (Class 4). This ridge rises out of the Badger Creek [(C)(10)] drainage to the main divide and then turns southeast and connects with the summit dome. The ridge is an easy scramble for most of its distance. There is one Class 4 pitch right above the prominent notch in the ridge. First ascent: L. Dye, A. Barnes, and W. Boyer in 1962.

The Riddler   *11,598 feet (Class 4)*

This beautiful summit is hidden in the shadow of Diamond Peak, which is just to the north. The elevation is not shown on the USGS Diamond Peak quad and is taken from the older Diamond Peak 15-minute quad. The summit is the southernmost high point on the new map. Long overlooked by climbers, the first ascent was made by Rick Baugher in 1990. Baugher's route is the only reported route to the summit. He says it may be his most rewarding climb. His route climbs the peak's southeast face using a series of ribs and gullies and a couloir to the upper east ridge then to the summit. It is best to avoid a direct ascent via the rotten couloir. The complex southeast face is composed by twisted and folded sedimentary rock bands. The right side of the face is cut by a major gully that climbs directly up to the peak's east ridge at roughly 10,300 feet. At the top of the gully, follow the ridge to the summit. Approach the face from the east from the Pass Creek trailhead [(A)(2)(a)]. USGS Diamond Peak/Fallert Springs

Big Boy Peak   11,402 feet (Class 2-3)
The next peak south of The Riddler on the main crest is difficult to access and should be climbed as part of an ascent of Shoshone John Peak to the south via the connecting ridge. USGS Fallert Springs

Shoshone John Peak*   11,212 (Class 3)
Named for a 300-pound Shoshone Indian who seasonally inhabited the valley at the mouth of Skull Canyon, this summit sits 2.6 miles south of Diamond Peak on the main crest. Climb via the east ridge from Middle Fork Pass Creek [(A)(2)]. R. Baugher reports that a "wonderful limestone arch" is found at the northern base of this peak. First ascent: probably R. Baugher in 1992. USGS Fallert Springs

Black and White Peak*   10,970 feet (Class 3)
The name of this peak relates to the black and white carboniferous limestone with quartz intrusions that is found here. This peak's elevation is incorrectly listed on the 1987 quad as 11,970 feet. The peak sits on the main Lemhi crest 1 mile south of Shoshone John Peak and 0.8 mile north of Little Diamond Peak. Climbing the peak involves long a cross-country walk from the Middle Fork Pass Creek [(A)(2)(a)]. Bushwhack

The Riddler's southeast face (Photo by Rick Baugher)

up the Middle Fork Pass Creek until it splits. Take the left fork toward Little Diamond Peak and then climb the broken southeast face to the summit. R. Baugher reports that a ski descent is possible in the northeast gully is possible when snow conditions are good. First ascent: probably R. Baugher in 1990. USGS Fallert Springs

Nicholson Peak*   11,051 (Class 3)

Nicholson Peak, which is named after the nearby Nicholson Sunny Bar Ranch, is located on a spur ridge 4.1 miles south of Diamond Peak and 1.3 miles west of Little Diamond Peak and the main crest. The USGS did not include an elevation for the peak on its Fallert Springs provisional quad. The elevation comes from the 1957 USGS 15-minute Diamond Peak quad. Rick Baugher suggests climbing the peak from Fowler Springs via its southwest slopes and west ridge [(C)(10.1)]. USGS Fallert Springs

Peak 10965   10,965 feet (Class 2-3)

This peak sits between Nicholson Peak and the main crest. Rick Baugher says that "the ridgeline between it and Nicholson is Class 3 and the ridgeline to Little Diamond Peak is Class 2." USGS Fallert Springs

Little Diamond Peak*   11,272 (Class 3)

Little Diamond Peak is a pyramid-shaped summit on the main crest 1.4 miles south of Diamond Peak. Rick Baugher climbed the peak via its west ridge from Bunting Canyon [(C)(10)]. Hike up Bunting Canyon to the saddle west of the summit at 10,225 feet. Turn east and climb up the west ridge. The summit also can be reached by following the crest north from the Uncle Ike/Pass Creek saddle, which will include an ascent of Swanson Peak. First ascent: probably R. Baugher in 1988. USGS Fallert Springs

Peak 10512 (Sunny Bar Peak)   10,512 feet (Class 2)

This wedge-shaped, blocky, quartzite peak is an outrider on the west side of the main crest. It sits at the head of Rocky Run Creek. Climb the peak via its long south ridge from Fallert Springs [(C)(11.1)]. USGS Fallert Springs

Swanson Peak*   10,808 (Class 2)

Swanson Peak is found on the main crest 1.2 miles south of Little Diamond Peak and 4 miles north of the Uncle Ike/Pass Creek saddle [(A)(2)(a) or (C)(11.1)(a)]. The peak is named after Dr. Earl H. Swanson, an archeologist who excavated prehistoric sites in Birch Creek in the 1960s. Climb the peak

from the main crest at the Uncle Ike/Pass Creek saddle by following the crest north and then west to the summit. USGS Fallert Springs

Bald Mountain   9,006 feet (Class 2)

Bald Mountain sits east of the main crest between Pass Creek to the north and Eightmile Canyon to the south [(A)(1)]. It offers good early and late season hiking from the Birch Creek Valley. USGS Eightmile Canyon

Peak 10045 (Marshalls Mount)   10,045 feet (Class 2)

This is the first peak south of the Uncle Ike/Pass Creek saddle. The peak is named for Marshall Bare, who ranched at Blue Dome from 1950 until his death. He is buried along Pass Creek near the base of this peak. The peak is an easy scramble from the trail across the saddle [(C)(11)(a)] or from the saddle connecting it with White Bird Peak. USGS Fallert Springs

White Bird Peak*   10,502 feet (Class 3)

This big peak, the second summit south of the Uncle Ike/Pass Creek saddle, has two large snow gullies on its northeast face which suggest a bird in flight from the Birch Creek Valley. This is why the mine at the south base of the peak is called White Bird. Access the summit from Uncle Ike Creek [(C)(11) (a)]. Follow the Uncle Ike Trail into the canyon. At roughly 7,800 feet a mining road leaves the main route and climbs to 9,600 feet on the peak's northwest slopes. From the highest point on the mining road, the summit is about 900 feet above. Work your way to the north ridge and ascend it to the summit. USGS Fallert Springs

Buckhorn Peak*   10,412 feet (Class 2)

Another summit unofficially named after an 1880s era mine. Mining claims are found to this day near the summit. This peak is located southwest of the Lemhi crest and 2 miles south of the Uncle Ike/Pass Creek saddle, and it rises above Uncle Ike Creek to the west. The summit, although imposing when viewed from the Little Lost River Valley, is easily climbed via its eastern slopes. From Uncle Ike Creek [(C)(11)] or Mormon Gulch [(C)(12)] or White Bird Peak 10502, climb to the saddle east of the peak and then follow the east slopes to the summit. USGS Fallert Springs

Peak 10475 (Dome Peak)   10,475 feet (Class 3)

This peak, which has an impressive northeast limestone face and a long narrow top, has a noticeable dome shape when viewed from the Birch Creek Valley. Rick Baugher suggests climbing the peak by traversing the connecting peak to the Uncle Ike/Pass Creek saddle [(C)(11)] or Mormon Gulch [(C)(12)]. USGS Fallert Springs

Shril Peak*   10,690 feet (Class 2)
Shril Peak is 2.3 miles north of Tyler Peak. It was an early triangulation station named after George H. Shril, the working partner in the Shril and Comstock Mining Co. Opposite of most Lemhi peaks, Shril contains a rugged south face and gentle north slopes. The Mormon Gulch Mining Road [(C)(12)] leads to the Lemhi crest north of the peak. Climb the peak by either following the road to the crest and climbing the north slopes or by climbing the peak's west ridge over Point 10604 and the connecting ridgeline. According to R. Baugher, the summit also can be reached from Eightmile Canyon [(A)(1)] by following the south fork to the saddle north of the peak. Baugher notes "the north face salient is eminently skiable in the spring." USGS Eightmile Canyon

Peak 10604   10,604 feet (Class 2)
This peak is located 1 mile west/southwest of Shril Peak. Climb to the summit via the connecting ridge between the two peaks or from the road into Mormon Gulch [(C)(12)]. First ascent: attributed to R. Anderson in 1948. USGS Fallert Springs

Tyler Peak   10,740 feet
Named after William Tyler who settled in Birch Creek Valley around 1882, this classic Idaho summit sits high above Tyler Canyon 12 miles south of Diamond Peak. From the mouth of Tyler Canyon, the peak's east side gains roughly 4,500 feet in less than 3 miles. USGS Tyler Peak

East Side (II, 5.4). Follow Tyler Canyon until you can gain the east ridgeline, which descends directly from the summit. This ridge is on the north side of Tyler Canyon [(A)(1)]. It is possible to climb the ridge without any difficulty except for the last 200 feet. The crux continues up a narrow snow gully that varies from 6 feet to 2 feet in width as it cuts through a rock band. The rock is reportedly good (remember, everything is relative) and the holds are more than adequate.

Northwest Face (Class 3). Drive as far as your 4WD vehicle will carry you on the North Creek Road [(C)(12)]. Then follow the creek bottom toward the crest to a point just north of Point 10401. Continue up the northwest slope until you are about 300 feet below the summit. At this point, cut back to the west toward the west ridge. Gain the west ridge and scramble to the summit. First ascent: B. Hammer.

West Ridge (Class 3-4). This climb ascends the west ridge directly from North Fork Creek [(C)(12)]. It is reported to be a straightforward route with no particular difficulties, but R. Baugher questions the report, noting "this is very cliffy country." Be prepared for a challenge.

Mount Hoopes*   10,728 feet (Class 2-3)
This peak, 0.7 mile south of Tyler Peak, is named for Clint Hoopes who farmed the high valley below the peak for many years. Rick Baugher climbed the peak from Bartel Canyon [(A)(1)]. At the end of the road, the canyon forks. Take the left fork and follow the drainage to roughly 8,800 feet. At this point, climb out of the drainage with short stretches of serious bushwhacking and scrambling toward Point 9882, which is directly to the north. Hike the ridgeline north from Point 9882 to Point 10580 and then follow the crest north to the summit. First ascent: R. Baugher in 1989. USGS Tyler Peak

Saddle Mountain   10,810 feet
This prominent peak, the last major summit at the south end of the Lemhi Range, is located 2.5 miles south of Tyler Peak. On most days it is visible from Idaho Falls 70 miles away. The peak has two summits, which are about 0.5 mile apart. The lower south summit is 10,248 feet high. Either summit can be reached from the west or the east. The first recorded ascent was by Vernon Bailey of the US Biological Survey in 1890. His name for the peak was Needle Peak. The peak is surrounded by cliffs and it is recommended that climbers return via their ascent route to avoid becoming entangled in unexpected cliffs. All routes on Saddle Mountain are steep, arduous, and long bushwhacks. Reaching its summit is a superior accomplishment. USGS Tyler Peak

Southeast Side (Class 2). Drive to the end of the East Canyon Road [(C)(14)], then hike up to the main crest south of the summit and follow the ridge to the summit. This is a long arduous bushwhack and scramble.

East Rib (Class 3). Access the east rib from Deer Canyon on the peak's east side [(A)(1)]. Deer Canyon is a box canyon with the east face of Saddle Mountain closing the box. The rib descends from a point just south of the summit. Climb the rib, which is initially tree-covered, to the crest. The crux is an 8-foot rock band that presents no real problems. This is a long, grueling climb that takes 10 to 12 hours round trip.

North Ridge (Class 2). This route also begins in Deer Canyon [(A)(1)]. From the end of the road, angle northwest toward Point 7922. West of this point, a ridgeline leads west to Point 9654 and then to Point 10196, which is on the north

North side of Saddle Mountain from the north (Photo by Rick Baugher)

ridge. Follow the ridge south to the summit. USGS Tyler Peak

Cedar Canyon/East Side (Class 2). This route is relatively straightforward. Follow the Cedar Canyon Road [(A)(1)] until the canyon splits. Park at this point and work up the north fork until you can gain the crest southeast of the south summit. Cross over the south summit, descend to the saddle and then climb up the southeast ridge of the higher north summit. This route, while easy to follow, is no easier than any other route on the peak.

North Gully/North Ridge (Class 3). Access this route from the Lemhi Valley via South Creek [(C)(13)]. The north gully drops off the peak's north face between the summit and Point 10196. Climb the gully until it is possible to access the north ridge.

APPROACHES TO THE LEMHI RANGE

(A) EAST SIDE APPROACHES/BLUE DOME TO SALMON

The broad alluvial fans on the east side of the range are crisscrossed by roads that are easily accessible from ID-28. While some access routes are open to automobiles, most require a 4WD and some are extremely rugged. The following roads are listed from south to north.

(1) Southern Access Points: Cedar Canyon to Eightmile Canyon. The Idaho National Engineering and Environmental Laboratory (INEEL) borders the Lemhis' southern end. There is no public access across the INEEL. Nevertheless, the labyrinth of roads between the INEEL boundary and the eastern edge of the Lemhi Range link to roads that do not cross the INEEL. Consequently, the INEEL problem is a mere inconvenience rather than a complete barrier to access.

To use these roads, take a Targhee National Forest Dubois Ranger District map and your topos. Good map-reading skills and a 4WD are recommended. The primary access roads are linked by a two-track road that parallels the base of the range for many miles and provides access to each of the southern canyons. This road can be reached from ID-28 in two primary locations. Both roads are marked with Forest Service signs.

The first approach is signed for Cedar and Bartel Canyons. Turn west off ID-28 just north of the INEEL boundary. (The land south of this road is administered by the INEEL and you could be arrested if you stray.)

The second approach, Eightmile Canyon, leaves ID-28 about

5 miles north of the INEEL boundary. This is a relatively new road that was put in as part of a canal project that diverts Birch Creek water to a hydroelectric generator. Follow the road west from the highway until you cross the dry bed of Birch Creek. Turn right and follow the road north. In 1.6 miles you will turn left on a road that leads due west to the Eightmile Canyon trailhead in another 6 miles.

There is also a third approach farther north along ID-28. Although this approach is signed, it requires a difficult ford of Birch Creek. Many vehicles have not made it across.

As you near the base of the mountains from either of these approaches, you will cross the connecting two-track road that leads to the following destinations. FS-531 runs up Cedar Canyon; FS-534 runs up Deer Canyon; FS-530 runs up Bartel Canyon; FS-540 runs up Tyler Canyon; FS-539 leads up Surrett Canyon; and FS-173 provides access to Eightmile Canyon. Only the Eightmile Canyon road has been developed in any way for recreationists.

(a) **FST-026, Eightmile Trail.** FST-026 leaves FS-173 1 mile from its end and runs up the north fork of Eightmile Creek and then north to FST-045 [(A)(2)(a)] in about 2.1 miles. This trail sees a lot of ORV use and is washed out in several places.

(2) **FS-181, Pass Creek Area.** The Pass Creek Road, FS-181, leaves ID-28 just south of Lone Pine—Lone Pine has a small store, the only gas in Birch Creek, and a motel. Although there are many roads in this area, the Pass Creek Road is the only road that is numbered. At one time the road crossed the Lemhi crest, but the Forest Service closed the road in the 1970s to prevent erosion. The main road and the feeder roads departing from it provide rugged access to the area around Diamond Peak.

(a) **FST-025 and FST-045, Pass Creek Trails.** Both trails leave the end of the FS-181 4 miles from ID-28. FST-025 runs up the South Fork Pass Creek, and FST-045 runs up the Middle Fork Pass Creek. The two trails rejoin below Pass Creek Lakes and continue across the Lemhi crest to connect with the Uncle Ike Road on the west side of the range [(C)(11)].

(2.1) **Diamond Peak/Lame Jake Access.** The area north of FS-181, Pass Creek Road is traversed by two-track and 4WD roads that are only partially shown on the Targhee National Forest map. Nevertheless, this unmapped road system provides good, though difficult, access to Diamond Peak's east ridge. Follow FS-181 east from ID-28 for almost 2 miles. Look for a two-track road leading off to the north. Follow this road up the bench and onto the flats above. Continue on this road in a northerly direction. In about a mile, veer off to the left on another road leading due west. This road, which is shown on the Diamond Peak and Blue Dome USGS quads, approaches the base of the range and then loops back to the east. At its westernmost point the road is north and

high above the North Fork Pass Creek. Look for a rough road that drops down to the south, crosses the creek, and continues south to the base of Diamond Peak's east ridge. Remember, a 4WD and off-road driving skills are required in this country and check with the Forest Service to learn current vehicular access regulations.

(3) **Rocky Canyon Road.** Access this canyon by either (1) turning off ID-28 at a point directly west of the Kaufman GS (which is east of ID-28 and marked with a sign), or (2) turning west off ID-28 7.5 miles north of Lone Pine (or 34.6 miles south of Leadore). Both roads lead to the mouth of Rocky Canyon and provide access to FST-047. A 4WD is recommended as the last portion of the road crosses steep, rugged terrain.

(a) **FST-047, Rocky Canyon Trail.** This trail begins at the westernmost point of the Rocky Canyon Road, then drops down the hill and crosses the creek. The trail's tread comes and goes as the trail climbs up the canyon about 5.5 miles.

(3.1) **Meadow Canyon Access.** Turn right off the Rocky Canyon Road at the transfer camp and follow this road north to Keg Spring.

(4) **FS-188, Coal Kilns Road Area Access Points.** This road provides access to Bell Mountain Canyon and Coal Kiln Canyon. It is located along ID-28 13.3 miles from Lone Pine (or 28.8 miles south of Leadore). Follow the road west for 5 miles to the charcoal kilns in Coal Kiln Canyon. The road to the kilns is usually well graded and suitable for passenger cars.

(4.1) **FS-541, McCoy Springs Access.** This route leaves the charcoal kiln area and runs south across the base of the range for several miles. To access McCoy Springs, drive due south for roughly 4 miles. The main road crosses a gully descending from UC Gulch. A jeep track leads southwest from FS-541 to McCoy Springs in 3 miles. A 4WD is recommended.

(4.1.1) **FS-183, Bell Mountain and Mammoth Canyon Road.** FS-183 leaves FS-541 a short distance south of the kiln area and leads into Mammoth and Bell Mountain Canyons. These two roads are not maintained often and a 4WD is recommended. Access Bell Mountain Canyon shortly after the road drops into Mammoth Canyon and access Mammoth Canyon by staying on the road.

(a) **Bell Mountain Canyon Trail.** This route starts as a jeep trail that is open to vehicles for almost 2 miles. The trail continues into the upper reaches of the canyon and then splits.

(5) **FS-296, Hahn Area Roads.** These roads are accessed from ID-28 5 bumpy miles south of the ghost town of Gilmore. From the highway, a dirt road leads 2 miles west to the old town site of Hahn (there are no buildings). From a junction at this point, the road leads to Spring Mountain Canyon and provides access to an old mining road system that continues to the top of the

Lemhi crest and Big Windy and Trail Peaks. Turning right at this junction and driving north 2 miles will bring you to a junction for Lemhi Union Gulch. Turning left on the Lemhi Union Gulch Road and driving on it for 2 more miles brings you within striking distance of Sheep Mountain.

(6) FS-002, Gilmore to Meadow Lake Campground Road. This washboard road leaves ID-28 17 miles south of Leadore, passes through the ghost town of Gilmore (many buildings are still standing) and then continues to the Meadow Lake CG at 9,000 feet. The small campground is usually busy throughout the summer. This road may not open until early July.

(a) Meadow Lake Trail. This relatively new trail leads to the Lemhi crest from Meadow Lake in 1.3 miles and 1,000 feet. The trail leaves a nature trail loop near the west end of the lake.

(6.1) FS-212, Gilmore to Deer Creek Road. From Gilmore, this nasty road can be followed approximately 4 miles north to Deer Creek. A 4WD and a map are required.

(a) FST-160, Deer Creek Trail. FST-160 leaves the end of FS-212 and runs up Deer Creek for 5 miles to a small lake on the west side of Portland Mountain.

(7) FS-212, Big Timber Creek Cutoff Road. This road leaves ID-28 6 miles south of Leadore. Follow the road west for about a mile to where it swings to the south. After another mile it swings back to the west and then south once again. In roughly 6 miles the road forks, go right. The Forest Service boundary is crossed in another 0.4 mile and Nez Perce Springs (a historic site) is at 7 miles. The road continues past this point for 0.5 mile, but is very rough and a 4WD is recommended.

(a) Nez Perce Lake Trail. The trail leaves the end of the road and climbs, steeply at first, to Nez Perce Lake at 8,900 feet in 2.5 miles.

(8) Big Timber Creek Road: Access to Big Timber Creek, North Fork, and Middle Fork Little Timber Creeks. The Timber Creek drainage is the largest drainage on the eastern side of the Lemhi crest and has miles of excellent hiking trails to explore. To reach its various roads and trails, turn west off ID-28 at the main intersection in downtown Leadore and drive west 0.9 mile to the signed Big Timber Creek Road. In another 3.5 miles the North Fork Little Timber Creek Road [(A)(8.1)] forks off to the right, while the main road continues to the left toward Timber Creek Reservoir/Middle Fork Little Timber Creek [(A)(8.2)] and Big Timber Creek [(A)(8.3)]. After another 3.3 miles the road forks, stay to the right and in 0.6 mile you will reach another junction. The road to the right leads to Timber Creek Reservoir [(A)(8.2)] and the road to the left goes to Big Timber Creek [(A)(8.3)]. A 4WD is necessary to reach the end of the road.

(8.1) FST-106, North Fork Little Timber Creek Road. This road forks off the Timber Creek Reservoir Road at a signed junc-

tion 5.5 miles from Leadore. Go right at the first fork and be prepared to ford four irrigation ditches and a creek, as well as crossing through five fences. Crossing of the North Fork Little Timber Creek requires a 4WD. This access is not maintained for recreationists. Have patience, take care at the crossings, and leave the gates as you find them.

(a) FST-627, North Fork Little Timber Creek Trail. From the end of the road, this trail leads to an unnamed lake in 3 miles with a 1,100-foot elevation gain.

(8.2) FS-172, Timber Creek Reservoir/Middle Fork Little Timber Creek Road. This road is well signed and leads to Timber Creek Reservoir 10 miles from Leadore. The road continues past the reservoir, ending in 11.1 miles at a ford. The trail begins on the other side of the creek.

(a) FST-187, Middle Fork Little Timber Creek Trail. This trail leads across the Lemhi crest to Yellow Lake in 7 miles. After crossing the crest, the trail reaches Lemhi Junction, perhaps the most important trail junction in the entire range. From this point, hikers can access the following drainages: Big Timber Creek [(A)(8.3)], the North Fork Little Timber Creek [(A)(8.1)], Big Eightmile Creek [(A)(9)], and the East Fork Patterson Creek [(C)(3)(b)].

(a.1) Yellow Lake Cut-Off. ORVs have created a shortcut that bypasses Lemhi Junction, stays high, and leads directly west to Yellow Lake. The cut-off leaves the main trail about 1.8 miles from the end of the road, continues up the Middle Fork Little Timber Creek past an unnamed lake, and then crosses the divide east of Yellow Lake.

(a.2) FST-184, Rocky Creek Trail. This trail leaves FST-187 at Lemhi Junction, continues east, crosses the crest and descends Rocky Creek to Big Timber Creek [(A)(8.3)(a.1)].

(a.3) FST-183, Yellow Pass/Big Timber Creek. This trail leaves FST-187 at Lemhi Junction and leads both north and south. The southern portion of the trail begins by descending the Park Fork Big Creek for about 1 mile through forest, then boggy forest, and then a huge meadow. At the bottom of the meadow, 1.5 miles from the Timber Creek Pass, there is a tree with five directional signs on its trunk. FST-196 [(C)(3)(b)] continues down the stream at this point and FST-183 turns south and climbs up to Yellow Pass in another 0.5 mile. At the pass, the trail begins a long descent down Big Timber Creek. FST-183 has a good tread to the pass. South of the pass, there are several small ponds with excellent camping. The northern section of the trail runs north to the Big Eightmile Creek trailhead [(A)(9.1)(b)]. Along the way it visits Yellow Lake and links up with the Yellow Lake Cut-Off [(A)(8.2)(a.1)].

(a.3.1) Falls Creek/Squirrel Creek Loop. The northern end of this trail turns off FST-183 3 miles below Yellow Pass and proceeds up Falls Creek to an unnamed and unmapped lake below Flatiron Mountain. This trail is shown on the latest Salmon National Forest map, but not on the USGS maps. The beginning of this trail is difficult to find, but once you are on it, the tread is very good. Good cross-country skills are invaluable in this area.

(8.3) FS-105, Big Timber Creek Road. From the point where this road leaves the Middle Fork Big Timber Creek, it is 4.4 miles to the trailhead. It is a rough road and a 4WD is recommended. Big Timber Creek Road is a main Lemhi thoroughfare with many trails to explore. Although it is difficult to access its trailhead from ID-28, once you are in the drainage you have easy access to a large portion of the central Lemhi Range. These trails are difficult to find in places and good route-finding skills are recommended.

(a) FST-183, Big Timber Creek/Big Eightmile Creek Trail. This trail, which sees little use, traverses the entire Big Timber Creek drainage, the upper portion of the Park Fork Big Timber Creek and a section of Big Eightmile Creek, a distance of nearly 26 miles. For more information on this route refer to the various write-ups under [(A)(8.2)], above and [(A)(9.1)] below.

(a.1) FST-184, Rocky Creek Trail. FST-184 leaves the main Big Timber Creek Trail roughly 3 miles from the trailhead. It climbs up west Rocky Creek, crosses the crest between Rocky Peak and Yellow Peak, and connects with the Middle Fork Little Timber Creek Trail [(A)(8.2)(a)] at Lemhi Junction. See [(A)(8.2)(a.2)], above.

(a.2) FST-186, Trail Creek Trail. FST-186 leaves Big Timber Creek 1.5 miles south of the Rocky Creek Trail junction and leads south up Trail Creek. It then crosses the crest at Timber Creek Pass and drops into Sawmill Canyon [(C)(6)(b)] on the west side of the range. Another trail loops up Squirrel Creek and down Falls Creek.

(a.3) FST-127, Snowbank Trail. This trail leaves Big Timber Creek 1.5 miles south of the Trail Creek Trail junction and climbs over the divide at an unnamed pass west of Timber Creek Pass. (Note that a trail leads east from this pass to Timber Creek Pass.) The trail continues to the south for 9 miles to the Iron Divide [(C)(5)(a)]. Other trails drop down toward the Sawmill Canyon Road.

(9) County Road: Big Eightmile Creek, Everson Creek, Stroud Creek, and Mill Creek Access. From Leadore, take the county road that leads west from the center of town and ID-28 toward the mountains to reach each of these drainages.

(9.1) FS-096, Big Eightmile Creek Road. This road is found 5.4 miles west of Leadore. Continue due west when the county road turns to the north (your right) to the beginning of FS-096. The pavement ends in a little over a mile and the road swings sharply to the left (south). Almost immediately, the road forks. Take the right fork (the left fork leads to Everson and Stroud Creeks (9.1.1)). Big Eightmile CG and the end of the road are 13.3 miles from Leadore.

(a) FST-185, Big Eightmile/East Fork Patterson Creek Trail. This trail continues up the closed road past the CG and crosses the Lemhi crest in 5 miles. At the crest it meets FST-075 [(C)(4)(a)], which follows the crest south toward North Fork Big Creek and FST-074, which drops down to the East Fork Patterson Creek.

(b) FST-183, Big Eightmile Creek Trail. This trail leaves the road just before the CG and leads south upstream. It divides in 5 miles. The right-hand fork climbs to the divide and joins FST-075 [(C)(4)(a)]. The left-hand fork also climbs to the divide to the southeast to join the Middle Fork Little Timber Creek Trail [(A)(8.2)(a)]. See [(A)(8.2)(a.3)] for more information.

(b.1) Blue Jay Mine Road. This road leaves the Big Eightmile Creek Road just after the road forks. Take the right fork and look for the mining road on your left. In a vehicle, this is a treacherous route, but as a trail it is a wonderful walk to 10,000 feet on Gunsight Peak's north ridge.

(9.1.1) Everson and Stroud Creek Roads. These roads fork off the Big Eightmile Road 11.4 miles from Leadore. Follow the directions for that road. It is 2 miles to Everson Creek and another 0.9 mile to Stroud Creek. A 4WD is recommended for both roads.

(a) FST-155, Everson Lake Trail. From the end of the road, if you get that far, it is 3.5 miles and 1,300 feet to the lake. This trail is an old jeep road and usually in poor condition.

(b) FST-211, Stroud Lake Trail. Stroud Lake is 3 miles and 1,200 feet from where the road becomes impassable for everything but tough 4WDs.

(9.2) FS-006, Mill Creek Road. Follow the county road west out of Leadore. The pavement ends in 10.4 miles. At 12.8 miles, turn left onto FST-006. After another 1.7 miles, go left at a junction and follow the road along Mill Creek and into the mountains. A 4WD is recommended.

(a) FST-181, Mill Lake Trail. From the end of the road it is 4 miles and 1,400 feet to the lake on a poor trail. From the lake, the trail continues to the north and into Hayden Creek [(A)(10.3.1)(a)].

(10) Lemhi Access Routes via Hayden Creek Road. Take ID-28 to a point 1 mile north of the Lemhi Post Office (27 miles south of Salmon) and turn onto paved Hayden Creek Road, which soon becomes FS-008 [(A)(10.3)]. At 3.5 miles, the road turns to gravel, and then forks. The unnumbered right fork traverses BLM lands leading up Basin Creek [(A)(10.1)]; the left fork continues south along Hayden Creek. At 8.4 miles, the road forks again. The left fork is the Bear Valley Creek Road [(A)(10.2)] and the right fork continues to follow Hayden Creek.

(10.1) Basin Creek Road. This road crosses private land. Thanks to the courtesy of the landowner, it remains open to the public. Please respect the private land.

(10.2) FS-009, Bear Valley Creek Road. Access this road from FS-008 10 miles from ID-28. Just after you pass a very narrow spot with caution signs, the Bear Valley Road winds away to your right.

(a) FST-179, Bear Valley Lake Trail. Drive 6 miles up FS-009 to its end, keeping right at Ford Creek. The trail starts at a developed trailhead and proceeds to Bear Valley Lake in 5.5 miles. From the lake, the trail continues over the Lemhi crest to join with the Allison Creek Road [(B)(2)(a)]. Look for a trail sign that indicates the way to Allison Creek and the Allison Creek Pass. The trail is sketchy in the meadow below the pass, but it is in good condition above the meadow.

(a.1) FST-081, Buck Lakes Trail. This trail leaves the Bear Valley Lake Trail roughly 2.2 miles from its trailhead and proceeds to the lowest Buck Lake in another 2 miles.

(10.2.1) FS-162, Kadletz Creek Road. This road leaves the Bear Valley Creek Road just after the road crosses Kadletz Creek and then follows the creek southwest into the mountains. It eventually turns into FST-180. A 4WD is recommended.

(a) FST-180, Hayden Creek Trail. This trail leaves from the end of the road, goes upstream, turns south, crosses a saddle on the east ridge of Long Mountain and then leads down into the headwaters of Hayden Creek [(A)(10.3)(a)]. It sees little use or maintenance.

(10.3) FS-008, Upper Hayden Creek Road. This road continues south along Hayden Creek for another 4.3 miles.

(a) FST-180, Hayden Lake Trail. This trail follows Hayden Creek north to a saddle on the east ridge of Long Mountain and then drops into Kadletz Creek [(A)(10.2.1)(a)].

(b) FST-118, Carol Creek Trail. This trail leaves FS-008 roughly 20 miles from ID-28 and runs 6 miles south across the Lemhi crest to Morse Creek [(C)(2)(a)]. This trail passes within 1.5 miles of Mogg Mountain's western slopes.

(10.3.1) FS-010, East Fork Hayden Creek Road. FS-010 leaves FS-008 just past the point where FS-008 crosses Hayden Creek at 11.5 miles from ID-28. The road follows the East Fork Hayden Creek for 4 miles and then leaves the creek, climbing out of the drainage to the north. It eventually links with FS-006, the Mill Creek Road [(A)(9.2)].

(a) FST-181, Mill Lake Trail. FST-181 leaves FS-010 where the road crosses the east fork and follows the East Fork Hayden

Creek east, past Mill Mountain, to cross the East Fork/Mill Creek divide due south of Mill Mountain. From Mill Lake, the trail runs down along Mill Creek to meet FS-006 [(A)(9)].

(11) FS-031, Withington Creek Road/Sal Mountain Access. This road leaves ID-28 roughly 8 miles south of Salmon and leads toward the Harmony Mine. From the road's end, a trail goes the remaining distance to the mine near the summit of Sal Mountain.

(B) WESTSIDE APPROACHES/SALMON TO ELLIS

You will find a relative abundance of good approach points on the west side of the Lemhis. US-93 parallels the west side of the range for 42 miles between Salmon and Ellis. The following approaches are described from north to south.

(1) FS-017, Poison Creek Road. This road provides access to several trails in the area between Poison and Watson Peaks. Take US-93 south from Salmon for 24 miles to reach this road.

(a) FST-103, Long Ridge Trail. This trail climbs up the Lemhi crest between Poison and Watson Peaks and then continues north to connect with the Warm Creek Road, which also can be used to access this area from US-93.

(2) FS-019, Allison Creek Road. This road, which stretches high up into the Lemhis and nearly reaches the crest near Lem Peak, is currently blocked by closed private property. Check with the Forest Service before using this route. If it is open to the public, take US 93 south from Salmon for roughly 34 miles to reach this road. A 4WD is recommended.

(a) FST-179, Bear Valley Lake Trail. From the end of the road, the trail climbs over Lem Pass and then drops down to Bear Valley Lake in 3.5 miles [(A)(10.2)(a)].

(C) WEST SIDE APPROACHES/ELLIS TO HOWE

The Pahsimeroi Highway begins at US-93 42 miles south of Salmon and leads 60 miles southeast through the Pahsimeroi and Little Lost River Valleys to Howe. Much of this road is paved and the remainder is a high-quality gravel surface. The following road descriptions all leave the main thoroughfare and extend east into the mountains. The listings are from north to south.

(1) FS-093, Morgan Creek Road. This road begins 7.2 miles south of US-93 junction. Turn off the Pahsimeroi Highway at a signed junction next to a private field. The road runs north and northeast to the mouth of Morgan Creek, crosses the creek in a stand of cottonwood trees, and then continues into the canyon. Three miles from the highway, the road forks just below a large fenced meadow. Go left and follow the road around this private land. The road eventually recrosses Morgan Creek and ends shortly thereafter. A 4WD is required.

(a) FST-071, North Fork Morgan Creek Trail. FST-071

leaves the end of FS-093 and follows the North Fork Morgan Creek toward Long Mountain. This poor trail completely dies out about 3 miles from the base of the peak, but it is possible to follow the drainage cross-country to the Lemhi crest.

(a.1) FST-243, Cow Creek/Morgan Creek Trail. This trail leaves FST-071 roughly 0.5 mile north of its trailhead. It leads to Cow Creek, the next major drainage to the north. A divide saddle is reached in 2 miles. This saddle is the jump-off point for climbing Peak 10487.

(b) FST-071, East Fork Morgan Creek Trail. This trail, which has the same trail number as the North Fork Morgan Creek Trail described above, leaves FS-093 just after it crosses Morgan Creek for the second time and runs east for 7.5 miles to the Morse Creek Road. This trail is rarely maintained; its beginning is difficult to locate and it is hard to follow between the 7,000- and 7,600-foot contours on the USGS quad. FST-071 is a beautiful walk and provides the closest trail approach to May Mountain.

(2) FS-094, Morse Creek Road. This road leaves the Pahsimeroi Highway 10.3 miles south of US-93 at a small cemetery near the village of May, and heads due west into the mountains.

(a) FST-072-118, Carol Creek Trail. This trail leaves the end of the Morse Creek Road, crosses the Lemhi crest west of Mogg Mountain, and then descends into Carol Creek [(A)(10.3)(b)].

(a.1) FST-072, Morse Creek/Falls Creek/Patterson Creek Trail. This route traverses the west side of the crest between Morse Creek and Patterson Creek in about 9 miles. It leaves FST-072/118 2.8 miles from the end of the Morse Creek Road. Once at Patterson Creek, it follows that creek south to the end of the Patterson Creek Road [(C)(3)(a)].

(3) FS-096, Patterson Creek Road. This road is located 12.8 miles south of May (23.1 miles from US-93). The road turns off the main road at the former village of Patterson and leads past an old tungsten mine and through a large canyon. The upper reaches of the road are passable by 4WD only.

(a) FST-072, Morse Creek/Fall Creek/Patterson Creek Trail. See [(C)(2)(a.1)], above.

(b) FST-074, East Fork Patterson Creek/Devils Basin Trail. This trail leaves the end of FS-096 and climbs to the top of the Lemhi crest, where it forks. One trail descends to the North Fork Big Eightmile Creek [(A)(10.3.1)(a)]; the other, poorly defined trail, FST-075, follows the crest south toward Yellow Peak, where it connects with many other trails. See [(C)(4)(b)], below. These trails do not receive much use and require strong route-finding skills.

(4) FS-097, Big Creek Area Road. This road turns off the Pahsimeroi Highway 6 miles south of Patterson (30.2 miles south of US-93). The road, which ends at a Forest Service CG, provides access to a large, roadless area dominated by Big Creek Peak.

(a) FST-075, North Fork Big Creek Trail. This trail follows the North Fork Big Creek north for 5 miles, then connects with FST-074 [(C)(3)(b)], which climbs to the Lemhi crest near Devils Basin. The trail then follows the crest north and intersects with FST-074 [(C)(3)(b) and (A)(10.3.1)(a)].

(a.1) FST-196, Park Fork Trail. This trail leaves FST-075 and climbs up Park Fork Creek to connect with the many trails in the Yellow Peak area. See the trail write-ups under [(A)(8.2)] and [(A)(8.3)].

(b) FST-109, South Fork Big Creek/Devils Basin Trail. FST-109 leaves FS-097, runs south along the north side of the Iron Divide, crosses a saddle just east of Iron Creek Point, and then heads into the upper Little Lost River drainage. In the Little Lost drainage it hooks up with FST-076, the Snowbank Trail, and other trails in the Iron Creek Point vicinity.

(5) FS-099, Big Gulch Road. This road leaves the Pahsimeroi Highway just north of Summit Reservoir. The road, which is signed, dead-ends after 4 miles.

(a) FST-079, Iron Divide Trail. From the end of FS-099, this trail continues up to the top of the Iron Divide in 2.25 miles. From the saddle, the trail continues to the north where it links with FST-109 [(C)(4)(C)] and other trails.

(a.1) FST-193, Iron Creek Point Trail. This short trail leaves FST-079 at the top of the Iron Divide north of Bear Mountain. The tread disappears in places, but the route is not too difficult to follow.

(6) FS-101, Sawmill Canyon Road. The Sawmill Canyon Road is a major gravel artery that leaves the Pahsimeroi Highway at a signed junction roughly 9 miles north of the Clyde schoolhouse. The road heads due west into the Challis National Forest to the headwaters of the Little Lost River. There is an extensive trail system in the upper regions, as well as logging and mining operations.

(a) FST-082, Mill Lake. This is a popular hike on the range's west side. The trail leaves the Sawmill Canyon Road 2 miles north of the Fairview GS just after the road crosses Mill Creek. Turn east and drive the short distance to the road's end at 7,200 feet. Mill Lake is 2.5 miles away, with 1,200 feet of elevation gain.

(b) FST-137, Timber Pass Trail. This trail leads to Timber Creek Pass and then down into Big Timber Creek [(A)(8.3)(a.3)]. It provides quick access to a large section of roadless country.

(c) Other Trails. On the west side of the road, FST-078 and FST-076 provide good access to Iron Creek Point and Bear Mountain [(C)(5)(a)].

(6.1) FS-449, Warm Creek Road. Look for this road where Sawmill Canyon comes up against the edge of the Lemhis. Turn south and follow the road to the mouth of Warm Creek in a little more than a mile.

(a) Warm Creek Trail. This trail follows Warm Creek northeasterly to the Lemhi crest between Big Windy and Trail Peaks in about 4.5 miles and 2,600 feet, depending upon where you park. It is an excellent way to see the crest.

(6.2) FS-102, Squaw Creek Road. This road leaves the Sawmill Canyon Road just past the Fairview GS and then runs northwest toward the crest. Mining roads at its end eventually lead to the Lemhi crest just north of Big Windy Peak, where it connects with an east side route [(A)(5)].

(7) Bell Mountain Area Roads. These roads are not maintained. A 4WD is recommended. The best approach to this area leaves the Pahsimeroi Highway 5.8 miles north of Clyde, where the road crosses the broad alluvial fan that descends out of the Lost River Range. At this point, you will notice an extensive set of sheep pens to the east. Take the road leading down to the pens (0.7 mile), drive through a wire gate, then quickly turn right. The road crosses a bridge over the Little Lost River. In this general area, you will find roads leading up to almost every canyon in this stretch of the Lemhis. Meadow Creek is almost due north. Bell Mountain is accessed by going up Bell Mountain Creek (a.k.a. Bassinger Canyon), which is dead ahead, or Black Creek, which is the next canyon to the south.

(8) FST-126, Deep Creek/Foss Mountain Road. Cross the Little Lost River at Clyde by driving across the bridge that leads to the BLM CG. From this point, drive north, paralleling the Little Lost River, and pass through a gate. You will find this road after about 1 mile. It leads up Deep Creek to the base of the Lemhis in 3.5 miles. The road then enters a gulch and runs to the summit of Foss Mountain at 9,182 feet. This road, built by miners, absolutely requires a 4WD, but I recommend using it as a trail.

(9) FS-404, Mud Spring Access. Turn off the Pahsimeroi Highway at Clyde, cross the river on the bridge, and drive directly east toward Cedar Run and Mud Spring about 3 miles ahead.

(10) Badger Creek Road. Leave the Pahsimeroi Highway 4.8 miles south of Clyde (23.2 miles north of Howe). The road begins where a gravel road forks off the highway at a small gravel pit. Turn into the gravel pit and follow a two-track road that leaves the back side of the gravel pit and continues due east along a fence line for 5 miles to the mouth of Badger Creek, where you will find several old mines and good access to the west side of Diamond Peak. A 4WD is recommended.

(10.1) FST-435, Fowler Springs Access. Access this road from the mouth of Badger Creek Canyon. Drive south for 3 miles and then turn hard left at a junction. Follow this road to the spring in a little more than 1 mile. A 4WD is recommended.

(11) Uncle Ike Road. This road, which is now closed to vehicles in its upper reaches, is located 13.6 miles north of Howe. Turn east off the highway and cross through a wire gate. The road is rough in its last mile and fords Uncle Ike Creek. A 4WD is recommended. The road is closed at the mouth of Uncle Ike Canyon. The closed portion of the road leads to the Lemhi crest and eventually to the east side of the range [(A)(1)(a) or (A)(2)(a)].

(a) FST-045, Pass Creek Lakes Trail. FST-045 leaves the Uncle Ike Road 8 miles from the Pahsimeroi Highway and runs across the Lemhi crest to the Pass Creek Road in 7.5 miles. See [(A)(2)(a)], above.

(11.1) Fallert Springs Access. This access route leaves the Uncle Ike Road about a mile before the Forest Service boundary. Turn left and follow the road across Uncle Ike Creek to the first road leading back to the base of the range. The road is just as it is shown on the USGS maps. A 4WD route heads upstream after the springs. Use it as a trail.

(12) North Fork Creek Road. This route begins as a good gravel road that leads up to the base of the Lemhis. The turnoff is 12.8 miles north of Howe, just south of the Uncle Ike Road turnoff. At the top of the alluvial fan there is a small ranch and a fork in the road. Beyond the ranch, the left fork into the canyon is very rough and requires a 4WD. It leads to an old mine and eventually gets within striking distance of Tyler Peak about 3 miles from the ranch. From this point, it leaves North Fork Creek and works its way across the steep slopes to Mormon Gulch in another 4 miles. An even more difficult road continues up Mormon Gulch to the crest just north of Shril Peak.

(13) South Creek Road. This road leaves the Pahsimeroi Highway north of Howe at a signed junction. It leads several miles into the range and provides access to Saddle Mountain.

(14) Southern Tip Roads. Access the southern end of the range, which is managed by the BLM, via Howe on dirt roads. Drive north of Howe on the Pahsimeroi Highway for 3 miles and turn right on the road to Bernice. Drive through Bernice and then turn left in 1 mile. In another mile, this road will bring you to BLM land and roads that lead into Black, Barrel, and East Canyons. All three of these canyons provide interesting hikes in the spring before it gets too hot.

7

THE BEAVERHEAD MOUNTAINS

by Tom Lopez and Rick Baugher

The Beaverhead Mountains form the Idaho/Montana border and the Continental Divide for nearly 200 miles, from Chief Joseph Pass and Montana-43 north of Salmon, to Monida Pass and I-15 north of Dubois. Many maps still call this range the Bitterroot Mountains. The Beaverhead crest is graced with pristine glacial cirques, massive limestone cliffs, knife-edged ridges, and dozens of imposing summits. It has, for the most part, a single spine and only two significant subsidiary ridges. This crest is above 8,000 feet for almost its entire length and is highlighted by two high, rugged segments: one near Salmon and one at the range's southern terminus.

In the north, at Chief Joseph Pass, the Beaverheads barely reach tree line, but the divide gains in stature farther south. The first high segment begins at Pyramid Peak. From Pyramid Peak to Center Mountain, Pleistocene glaciers cut dozens of cirques and left impressive rock horns and high ridges. A dozen peaks reach above 10,000 feet, including six within Idaho. While Montana's Homer Youngs Peak, at 10,621 feet, is the highest summit in this group, 10,362-foot Freeman Peak is the most impressive summit in the group.

South of Salmon, the divide is somewhat lower in elevation and rolling in nature. Signs of prehistoric habitation have been found throughout the Beaverheads. For thousands of years Native Americans crossed the range's broad passes in search of game, horses, and buffalo. Lewis and Clark crossed into Idaho on August 12, 1805, near Lemhi Pass, 7,373 feet. More recently, miners built a railroad line over Bannock Pass to serve Salmon and the now abandoned town of Gilmore. Although this middle section is lower in stature, many impressive peaks reach above 10,000 feet.

Many miles to the south, the crest again rises dramatically to its highest point on 11,393-foot Scott Peak. The Scott group includes fourteen peaks higher than 10,000 feet (three above 11,000 feet), the Italian Peak roadless area, and some of the least-visited terrain in the nation. The Scott group is higher and drier than the Salmon group, because it sits in the rain shadow created by the ranges to the west, including the Lemhi and Lost River Ranges.

The Beaverheads also spread out in this area, encompassing more than the single crest that characterizes the range farther north. At Scott Peak, the main Beaverhead crest splits into three divides. The first of these divides is the Continental Divide, which turns sharply north, running to 7,600-foot Bannock Pass, and then turns again, running due east toward Monida Pass. Although this stretch of the Continental Divide geologically resembles the Centennial Mountains, which begin on the eastern side of Monida Pass, the mapmakers have included it as part of the Beaverheads. The two southern divides, which radiate south from Scott Peak, contain a number of archeological sites, big canyons, and high summits.

In addition to the early habitation by Native Americans, trappers, miners, and surveyors played a significant part in the exploration of the Beaverhead Mountains. Trappers penetrated the range well before 1840, miners were active by the 1860s, and the surveyors explored the entire crest while marking the state boundary between 1904 and 1906. During this survey, iron mile markers were placed along the Beaverhead crest for its entire distance. Many of the mile markers are still in place today. Undoubtedly, the surveyors climbed most if not all of the Beaverhead peaks during this survey.

The Beaverheads, like the Lost River and Lemhi Ranges, were formed by fault blocking, which fractured, lifted, and piled Precambrian era metamorphic rocks, Paleozoic era limestone, and granites into a long, narrow mountain chain. The Challis Volcanics event covered part of the Beaverhead Mountains 50 million years ago with pale rhyolite ashes. Perhaps the most interesting geological feature in the Beaverheads is rock made up of compressed gravel welded together into a distinctive rock mottle. While the Montana side of the divide is cluttered by exceptionally fine mountain lakes, only a few lakes are found on the drier, Idaho side of the border.

The Salmon-Challis National Forest manages the north sections of the range on the Idaho side, while the Beaverhead National Forest manages the Montana side of the range. The BLM manages the range's lower slopes and is, in places, responsible for the range right up to the crest. The southern sections of the range are administered by the Targhee National Forest.

In 1978, Congress mandated that a Continental Divide National Scenic Trail (CDT) be constructed along the continental divide between Canada and Mexico. Although little money has been allocated for this project over the years, the trail route is identified and the entire Idaho portion of the route can be followed. The trail stays on the Montana side of the border for most of its distance.

Climbers and hikers are, for the most part, unaware of the scenic and wilderness values found in the Beaverhead Mountains. While the areas around Freeman Peak in the north and the Italian Peaks in the south offer the best alpine climbing opportunities, all of the peaks listed below are worthwhile and rewarding goals. The popularity of the Beaverheads is increasing as more people discover the 300,000 roadless acres around the Italian Peaks and the CDT. Historically the range's trail system was small and infrequently maintained. The Congressional mandate creating the CDT has led to improvements to trails and access roads. Additionally, the open terrain and large vistas make cross-country travel enjoyable.

CHIEF JOSEPH PASS TO THE ITALIAN PEAKS

At 7,264-foot Chief Joseph Pass, the Beaverhead Mountains and Montana's Pintlar Range merge into a geographically and geologically confusing mess. The Beaverhead Mountains emerge from this mess to run south as a narrow crest. Primary access to this stretch of the Beaverheads is via US-93 and ID-28.

Perce Peak   8,266 feet (Class 1)

Perce Peak, located 7.5 miles southeast of Lost Trail Pass, is a worthwhile destination. Although not truly an alpine peak, many of its slopes are open and there are wonderful vistas of both Montana and Idaho from the summit. FST-124 leads to the summit from the Gibbonsville Road [(A)(1)(a)] in 6 miles with a 4,000-foot elevation gain. The CDT also provides good access to the peak. USGS Big Hole Pass

Sheep Mountain   9,858 feet (Class 2)

Sheep Mountain, the first truly alpine Beaverhead summit, sits 9.5 miles southeast of Perce Peak. T. M. Bannon used the peak for a triangulation station in 1913. The peak can be accessed from the Beaverhead National Forest in Montana. Take the Gibbsonville Road [(A)(1)] over Big Hole Pass. About 0.5 mile below the pass on the Montana side, a 4WD road runs due south to the border. The CDT drops off the crest at this point. Do not follow it. Instead, follow the actual divide east and then south to the summit, which is 5 miles away. The only other reported route on the Idaho side of the border follows the Continental Divide north from Pyramid Peak. USGS Shewag Lake

Pyramid Peak   9,616 (Class 3)

Pyramid Peak sits on the Continental Divide 2.2 miles southwest of Sheep Mountain above a lake-filled cirque on the Montana side of the border. A 22-year-old fur trapper named

Angus Ferris crossed over the Beaverheads at Pyramid Peak on August 26, 1832. He wrote of this adventure in his book *Life in the Rocky Mountains*, recounted in the Mountaineering History section of this book. Climb the peak from FST-129 [(A)(2)(a)]. USGS Shewag Lake.

Ajax Peak   10,028 feet (Class 2)

Ajax Peak is located 10 miles due south of Sheep Mountain. Though the peak's south ridge is an easy scramble, it is difficult to approach the peak from Idaho. Instead, approach the peak from Montana via the Big Swamp Creek Trail, which leads to Ajax Lake [(D)(3)(a)]. From the lake, climb due west to the top of the south ridge. USGS Homer Youngs Peak

Copperhead Peak   10,060 feet (Class 2)

This peak sits west of the Continental Divide and 1.5 miles south of Ajax Peak. From the end of the road [(A)(3.1.1)], the route contours up and into the Golway drainage to the north. Keep as high as possible and aim for the tiny pond in the upper drainage. Just below the pond, work up the steep southeast ridge and boulder field to the summit. If you make it to the end of the road, you will find the climb up the southeast ridge anticlimactic. USGS Homer Youngs Peak

Freeman Peak   10,273 feet

This eye-catching rock dominates the Salmon skyline. Geologist J. B. Umpleby's 1913 geologic map identified this peak as Fremont Peak. The peak sits just west of the Continental Divide above Freeman Creek, 2.5 miles south of Copperhead Peak. The peak has been climbed via its three major ridges and during the winter. The northeast and southeast ridges are the most accessible and the most difficult routes. The summit is crowned by a giant cairn and offers spectacular views of the surrounding country. USGS Homer Youngs Peak

East Face/Ridge (Class 3). From the end of the road, follow the trail up Freeman Creek [(A)(3.1)(a)] to the vicinity of the Ore Cash Mine. (Remnants of the mining operation are still visible above the trail.) From this point, a faint trail descends from the road to the creek. Take this trail down to the creek, cross it, and then climb up into the boulder field that drops out of the peak's east face cirque. Climb into the cirque, hugging its right side. Look for a prominent gully at the top of the cirque that leads up toward the ridge south of the summit, which is not yet visible. To reach this gully, hug the bottom of the east face. Climb the gully—which has fair footing, but a lot of loose rock—until a point roughly 200 feet below the ridge top. Climb out onto the east face and ascend a series of short cliffs toward the summit. This route involves

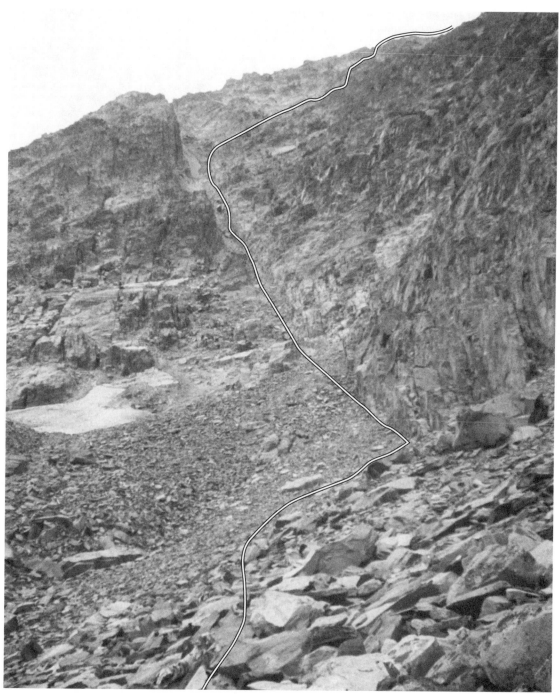

East Face/Ridge route through the east face cirque on Freeman Peak

sustained Class 3 climbing and route-finding difficulties. The cirque contains snow late into the summer and the route can be very slippery when wet or icy.

Monument Peak   *10,323 feet*

Monument Peak, also known as McGarvey Peak, is situated 1 mile south of Freeman Peak on the Continental Divide. It is a rugged peak that is not easily climbed. USGS Homer Youngs Peak

North Ridge (Class 3). To climb this peak by its north ridge, ascend Freeman Creek [(A)(3.1)(a)] until the old mining road ends and a trail begins. Follow the trail to the pass east of Freeman Peak. From the saddle, cross into Montana, descend about 100 feet, and then work the obvious ledges back to the west, traversing around the impressive cirque that holds upper Miner Lake. This route eventually leads to the saddle between Freeman Peak's southeast flank and Monument Peak. Climb the boulder-strewn north ridge to the summit.

South Ridge (Class 3). From the end of the Mail Truck Road [(B)(2.1)] at 9,200 feet on the divide between South Kirtley and Geertson Creeks, scramble north along the divide to the main crest at roughly 10,160 feet. Note that you are almost at the top of the North Doublet at this point. Now follow the crest north by down-climbing Class 3 ledges to a saddle at 9,550 feet. From here, it is a straightforward, Class 2 hike up the crest to the summit. First ascent: R. Baugher.

North Doublet*   *10,390 feet*
South Doublet*   *10,365 feet*

These unnamed summits, which have been identified as both Monument Peak and El Dorado Peak in the past, are the most impressive summits in the northern stretches of the Beaverhead Mountains. Both summits have east faces that drop almost 1,200 vertical feet into Montana. They are located 1 mile south of Monument Peak. The route between the summits involves a rappel and technical climbing. No one has reported making this traverse. USGS Homer Youngs Peak/Bohannon Spring

North Doublet/North Ridge (Class 3). The north ridge connects with Monument Peak and is passable, but takes a while to traverse. However, the best way to approach and climb the peak is via the Mail Truck Road [(B)(2.1)]. From the end of the road, follow the ridgeline north to the crest at 10,160 feet and then follow the ridge to the summit. First ascent: R. Baugher in 1998.

South Doublet/North Ridge (Class 3). Because Geertson Creek is closed to public access, use the Mail Truck Road to reach this peak. From the end of the road, drop down into

The North and South Doublets (Photo by Rick Baugher)

the Geertson drainage. From this drainage, climb the chute that leads to the saddle between the peaks and then climb South Doublet's north ridge.

Center Mountain   *10,362 feet*
Peak 10056 (Skytop Peak)   *10,056 feet*

Climbing these two peaks together is best, because of access considerations. Center Mountain is 3 miles east of Monument Peak. Peak 10056 is 2 miles southeast of Center Mountain on a remote stretch of the Continental Divide. USGS Bohannon Spring/Goldstone Pass

Geertson Creek Route (Class 3). Unfortunately, the best route up Center Mountain is now closed to the public. This situation could change. Check with the BLM. If you are fortunate enough to get permission to ascend Geertson Creek [(B)(2)(a)], hike to Geertson Lake. From the lake, hike directly to the north ridge and follow it to the summit.

Whimpey Creek Route (Class 2). This is a long route. Begin by turning off ID-28 at Bohannon Creek. Follow the road upstream. At 5,000 feet, Bohannon Creek forks. Take the road that twists up to the east and then crosses over to West Fork Whimpey Creek. This road is better suited for walking and is *not* recommended for 4WDs. The road continues on to the Continental Divide. To ascend Center Mountain and

Center Mountain from the North Doublet (Photo by Rick Baugher)

Skytop Peak, leave the road at about 9,000 feet (which is about 1 mile short of the divide) and hike due north to the top of the divide at mile marker 482. Follow the divide north, passing several mile markers that read 478. Evidently, the surveyors either got confused or used this area to correct an error. Skytop Peak's summit is reached at mile marker 478.15 after an uneventful walk. From Skytop, continue heading north along the divide toward Center Mountain. Interestingly, at the next high point, 10049, there are ten or more small cairns placed randomly around the crest. It is possible that these cairns could be ceremonial placements in conjunction with Native American vision quests. Please do not disturb them. The route along the crest passes a succession of cirques with lakes on the Montana side. From a saddle at 9,500 feet, either climb up the persistent snow ramps or the rock outcroppings to the summit of Center Mountain.

Goldstone Mountain   9,909 feet (Class 2)
This peak's summit sits just west of the Continental Divide, 8 miles southeast of Center Mountain. T. M. Bannon ascended the peak in 1913. His name for the Beaverhead Mountains was the Continental Divide Range. Its summit ridge is reached by FST-111 [(D)(1)(a) or (B)(3.1)(a)], which follows the divide from Goldstone Pass to the north. From the pass, follow the

CDT south over Point 9735. Leave the trail after another 0.6 mile and follow the spur ridge west to the summit. USGS Goldstone Mountain

Goat Mountain   9,924 feet (Class 2)
This large, twin-summited mountain's reddish summit ridge runs southwest from the Continental Divide between Paterson and Big Eightmile Creeks. T. M. Bannon, who climbed the peak in 1913 and used the west peak as a triangulation station, named the two summits East Peak and West Peak. A later USGS survey by Walter Helm changed the name to Goat Mountain. It is believed that this summit was described by Sgt. Patrick Goss of the Corps of Discovery. On August 19, 1805, he wrote "About 5 miles south of us we saw snow on top of a mountain, and in the morning there was a severe white frost...." Two routes are suggested. For the first route, access the summit from the CDT, which is accessed from FST-195 and Eightmile Creek [(B)(4)(a)]. Once on the divide follow it west to the peak's summit ridge. The second route climbs the peak's south ridge from the Maryland Mine. USGS Goat Mountain.

Elk Mountain*   10,153 feet (Class 1)
Yet another Elk Mountain stands about 8 miles east/southeast of Bannock Pass and ID-29. Follow the CDT south from the pass to the summit at mile 536. At this summit, a major spur ridge heads north from the crest into Montana. USGS Deadman Pass

Horse Prairie Peak   10,194 feet (Class 2)
Horse Prairie Peak is a long mile south of Elk Mountain. The common saddle between the peaks drops to 9,740 feet. T. M. Bannon named this peak in 1913. The name was first used by Lewis and Clark to identify the valley in Montana north of the peak. Climb the peak via its west ridge, which is accessed from Hall Creek [(B)(5.1)(a)] USGS Deadman Pass

Bear Peak   9,595 feet (Class 2)
This peak was used as a triangulation station in 1956. Climb to the summit from the CDT, which can be accessed from Big Bear Creek [(B)(6.4)(a)]. USGS Tepee Mountain

Peak 10067 (Bull Peak)   10,067 feet (Class 2)
This is the prominent peak visible to the south/southeast from Leadore. Access the peak from Big Bear Creek [(B)(6.4)]. A mining road climbs out of the creek bottom to 8,000 feet on the peak's eastern slopes. Follow the road and then climb the east slopes to the summit. USGS Powderhorn Gulch

Conical Top Peak*   *10,125 feet (Class 3)*

This peak sits 3.3 miles northwest of Baldy Mountain on a subsidiary ridge that runs west from the Continental Divide. This peak, with its splendid, splintered quartzite summit, was named by USGS surveyor Walter Helm in 1950. Helm described the peak as "a prominent, conical-topped peak." The summit can be reached via the connecting ridge with Bull Peak to the west, or via its southwest ridge by taking the Dry Canyon Trail, FST-188 [(B)(6.3)(b)], to the saddle 1 mile southeast of the summit. USGS Reservoir Creek/ Powderhorn Gulch.

Baldy Mountain   *10,773 feet (Class 2)*

Baldy Mountain is a big mountain with two summits rising above 10,700 feet. Its summit ridge is more than 3 miles long and its massive north face drops rapidly into Montana. The peak is located 11 mile south of Horse Prairie Peak directly on the Continental Divide at mile 553. Climb this peak via its northwest ridge by taking Dry Canyon Trail, FST-188, [(B) (6.3)(b)] to a saddle 2.5 miles northeast of the summit. Follow the ridgeline southeast to the summit. The peak also can be climbed from Powderhorn Gulch and FST-222 [(B)(6.3)(a)]. Follow FST-222 until it crosses the peak's west ridge, which leads to the summit. USGS Morrison Lake

Mount Carpenter*   *10,680 feet (Class 2)*

Mount Carpenter is found at mile 557, 4.5 miles south of Baldy Mountain and directly on the Continental Divide. The name is suggested to honor Howard Carpenter, who surveyed the Idaho/Montana border from 1904 to 1906. Start the approach to this peak in the Clear Creek [(B)(6.2)] drainage. Follow the road that runs east toward Poison Creek. From the saddle above, start up the peak's west ridge, climb over Point 10126, and then continue southeast to the summit. USGS Morrison Lake

Cottonwood Mountain   *11,024 feet (Class 2)*

Cottonwood Mountain, which is 10 miles south of Baldy Mountain, is a big dome-shaped pile of rubble with excellent views into Montana. It is identified as the Cottonwood triangulation station on the USGS quad. The peak can be climbed from almost any line of attack, but access considerations dictate that the peak be climbed from Eighteenmile Creek [(B)(6.1)]. From the end of the road, climb up the easy slopes to the summit. The Cottonwood Mountain/ Eighteenmile Peak ridge is another alternative and allows a relatively easy climb of both peaks in one day. USGS Cottonwood Creek

Eighteenmile Peak   *11,141 feet*

Eighteenmile Peak, which is the highest summit surrounding the Eighteenmile Creek cirque, is a rugged mountain with a rugged quartzite summit block capping its steep talus slopes. It sits 1.5 miles south of Cottonwood Mountain and 1 mile east of Jump Peak. This peak dominates the view from ID-28 south of Leadore. In 1978, there was a register on the summit with only a few names. USGS Eighteenmile Peak

South Ridge/Southwest Face (Class 3). This route begins

The summit of Baldy Mountain

in the Eighteenmile Peak/Jump Peak saddle, which is easily reached from Eighteenmile Creek [(B)(6.1)] and begins by climbing up the south ridge. This ridge tops out west of the summit. From this point, the summit ridge is Class 2 until the summit block, which is Class 3 and can be climbed by two routes.

The first route begins at the point where the south ridge reaches the summit ridge. From here, climb east along the summit ridge utilizing the top and both sides to avoid the Class 4 obstacles that litter the route. The summit block itself is climbed via a series of short, steep walls on the block's southwest side. While the route will test your route-finding skills, exposure is minimal if you chose the correct path. The second route begins roughly 100 feet below the top of the south ridge. From this point, contour northeast into a prominent gully that cuts the lower portion of the southwest face. Climb this gully until you reach the steeper portions of the face, which brings you to the same series of short, steep walls utilized by the first alternative.

Northwest Ridge (Class 3). This ridge connects Eighteenmile Peak with Cottonwood Peak to the north. The ridge is reached from Eighteenmile Creek [(B)(6.1)] by climbing due east from the end of the road on Class 2 terrain. To climb the Class 3 summit block, refer to the South Ridge/Southwest Face route description above.

Jump Peak   10,941 feet (Class 3)

Jump Peak is the third prominent peak surrounding the upper Eighteenmile Creek cirque. It sits 2 miles south of Cottonwood Peak and 1 mile west of the Continental Divide. [(B)(6.1)]. USGS Cottonwood Creek

West Ridge (Class 2). This route begins in Eighteenmile Creek [(B)(6.1)] where the road ends at 8,300 feet. From the starting point, climb directly south to Point 9975 and the west ridge. This ridge presents no problems as it leads to the summit in 3 miles with a 2,500-foot elevation gain.

North Rib (Class 3). This route begins in the saddle between Jump Peak and Eighteenmile Peak. Reach the saddle by following Eighteenmile Creek southeast from the end of the road [(B)(6.1)]. The route from the saddle presents some moderate route-finding problems. The north rib climbs steeply from the saddle. The middle section of the rib is composed of vertical rock cliffs that are impassable. From the pass, climb to the base of cliffs and then contour out onto the rib's east face to the base of a rock wall that is sparsely covered with small pine trees and broken by two rubble filled gullies. Climb the first gully to the top of the peak's easternmost summit and then follow the summit ridge west to the true summit.

Dianes Peak*   10,404 feet (Class 2)

This is one of four interesting summits that surrounds the head of Willow Creek. Its summit is 5.5 miles south of Eighteenmile Peak. The peak is locally named after Diane Palmer (1946–1947), who is buried at her ranching family's cemetery in the Birch Creek Valley. Scramble to the summit from Willow Creek [(B)(7.2)(a)] via the peak's south or western slopes. USGS Eighteenmile Peak

Edelman Peak*   10,201 feet (Class 2)

This summit is 2 miles southwest of Dianes Peak on the south side of Willow Creek. The peak's north side contains a glacial cirque. The peak is named after prospector Henry Eidelman (1857–1944). The spelling on the map is incorrect. The peak can be climbed from almost any direction, but the most direct route goes up the southwest side from the valley [(B)(7)]. Also consider climbing it from FST-057/FST-081 [(B)(7.1)(a) or (B)(7.2)(a)] where it crosses the divide between Italian Canyon and Willow Creek. USGS Eighteenmile Peak

Peak 10100+ (Reentrant Peak)   10,100+ feet (Class 2)

This obscure summit forms a reentrant angle toward Montana's hidden corner or cul-de-sac. Archeologists found a "napped" obsidian point from the Beaverhead period near the summit, suggesting that Native American hunters visited the summit sometime between 1450 and 950 B.C. Climb the peak from Willow Creek [(B)(7.2)(a)] by climbing to the saddle west of the peak and following the ridgeline east to the summit. USGS Eighteenmile Peak

Peak 10340   10,340 feet (Class 2)

The fourth and final summit surrounding upper Willow Creek is a conical-shaped peak just north of the Italian Peaks at milepost 575.221. Climb to its summit via its west ridge, which is accessed from FST-057/FST-081 [(B)(7.1)(a) or (B)(7.2)(a)]. USGS Eighteenmile Peak

Peak 10776 (Tuscany Peak)   10,776 feet (Class 3)

This ragged jumble of broken rock is located 1.2 miles northwest of Italian Peak. Access the summit from the divide between Italian Canyon [(B)(7.1)(a)] and Scott Canyon [(B)(8)(a)]. From the divide, contour northwest toward the saddle between this peak and Italian Peak. Once at the saddle climb the divide to the summit. USGS Scott Peak

Italian Peak   10,998 feet

Italian Peak has two summits and while it is unclear which is higher, it appears that the eastern summit is the highest. The

The western summit of Italian Peak

summit and descends to the notch that separates the two summits staying, for the most part, on the southwest side of the ridge during the descent. From the notch, continue to descend to the southeast to a talus-covered shelf that circles the base of the east summit. Once on the shelf, stay close to the upper wall on a goat path. Eventually, this shelf turns a corner and a steep, 60-foot chimney on a wall directly east of the corner comes into view. This chimney is the crux of the climb. Stay in the chimney for the first 30 feet and then climb out onto the face to your right for the last 30 feet. Excessive loose rock precludes the effective use of a rope for protection. Once above the chimney, look up and due north to locate a gully. Climb the intervening and treacherous talus slope to the base of this Class 3 gully. Carefully check your handholds in the gully as most will be loose. Once above the gully, it is a short stroll to the summit. A USGS Idaho/Montana boundary mile marker is located slightly below and to the east of the summit.

THE SOUTHWESTERN DIVIDE

Near mile 578 in an area of limestone arêtes and towers, the state of Montana reaches its southernmost point. Here, the Beaverhead Mountains abruptly change direction and head northeast, while two subsidiary divides run southwest and southeast toward the Snake River Plain. This divide runs due south from the Continental Divide to Gallagher Peak, a distance of 14 miles. Birch Creek is on its west and Crooked Creek and Nicholia Canyon are on its eastern side.

Peak 11292 (Huhs Horn)   *11,292 feet (Class 3)*
It has been suggested that this peak be named for Oscar Huh, a Penn State geologist who explored and studied the geology of this area in the 1950s and 1960s and named its limestone formations. This summit sits 0.7 mile due west of Scott Peak. It is protected on three sides by steep cliffs. The only suggested route to the summit is via a traverse from Scott Peak. First ascent: probably R. Baugher in 1998. USGS Scott Peak

Dead Horse Summit*   *10,120+ feet (Class 2)*
This peak sits 5 miles due south of the Continental Divide and 6 miles due south of Peak 11292. The summit is immediately east of the Mahogany triangulation station and there is a Forest Service radio facility on its top. The summit is covered with horse bones and there is a Native American ceremonial structure utilizing blanched horse bones near the summit. The

peak sits 9 miles southeast of Eighteenmile Peak and marks the southernmost point of the Continental Divide in Idaho. For scramblers, this is a good news/bad news peak for many reasons. The good news is that the lower east summit is only Class 2. The bad news is that the slightly higher west summit is Class 4 if climbed via the connecting ridge between the summits. More bad news, the highly fractured rock leading to the eastern summit is not conducive to technical climbing. Some more good news, both summits provide excellent views of one of the most remote sections of the Continental Divide. Both routes are accessed via the peak's southwest ridge, which divides Italian Canyon [(B)(7.1)(a)] from Scott Canyon [(B)(8)(a)]. USGS Scott Peak

West Summit (Class 2). More bad news, the route up the southwest ridge to the east summit involves a long climb over terribly rotten and agonizing talus. It must be the most unforgiving talus in the state. There is a little good news, however—the climb is only Class 2 and straightforward. If you persevere, you will arrive on the summit.

East Summit (Class 4). This route begins on the west

peak can be climbed from almost any direction, but access considerations dictate that you climb the peak from its west side via Mahogany Gulch [(B)(9)]. USGS Scott Peak

Copper Mountain   *10,303 feet (Class 2)*
Copper Mountain sits 12 miles due south of Scott Peak. Climb this peak via its west ridge. The west ridge can be accessed from either Skull Canyon [(B)(10)] or from Long Canyon. An old mining road can be followed between the two canyons to the saddle on the west ridge. From this point, it is an easy walk to the top. Look for Mississippian era brachiopod fossils on the summit. USGS Copper Mountain

Gallagher Peak   *9,877 feet (Class 2)*
This peak's double summit is located 2 miles east of Copper Mountain. The peak can be climbed easily—if you are in good shape—from the summit of Copper Mountain, from Blue Canyon [(C)(1.2)], or from Gallagher Canyon [(C)(1.1)]. USGS Copper Mountain

THE SOUTHEASTERN DIVIDE

This is the second southern Beaverhead divide. It runs in a southeasterly direction for 12 miles from Italian Peak and is home to Scott Peak, the highest Beaverhead summit. Crooked Creek flows along its southwestern flank and the North Fork Webber and Medicine Lodge Creeks along its northeastern flank.

Scott Peak   *11,393 feet (Class 3)*
Scott Peak, the highest Beaverhead peak, sits 2 miles southeast of Italian Peak and just south of the Idaho/Montana border. It is named after Winfield Scott (1848–1915) a teamster and a miner who was the first permanent settler in the Birch Creek Valley. Take the road up Scott Canyon [(B)(8)(a)] to 7,700 feet where there is a locked gate. Then continue on the trail up Scott Canyon. From the Scott/Crooked Creek divide, contour northeast into the uppermost Crooked Creek Canyon. At 10,200 feet in an amphitheater surrounded by cliff bands, look east/northeast for a break in the cliff. Pick your way up this face, utilizing this break. Given the difficulty of climbing the face, you will be happy to find a gentle summit ridge above. USGS Scott Peak

Webber Peak   *11,223 feet (Class 2)*
Although named on the map, this peak is not a true summit, but an extension of Scott Peak's south ridge. USGS Scott Peak

Heart Mountain   *10,422 feet (Class 2)*
Heart Mountain sits 4 miles southeast of Webber Peak between Crooked Creek and Myers Creek. The easiest approach is from Myers Creek. Follow the Crooked Creek Road north until it forks. Take the left fork past the Ellis Ranch to Myers Creek. Follow the road up Myers Creek until it turns into a trail [(C)(2.1.1)(a)]. Follow this trail north to the top of the 9,200-foot Grouse Canyon/Webber Creek divide on the north side of the peak. Climb the ridge from the point where the trail begins to descend into Webber Creek—a distance of 0.75 mile with 1,200 feet of elevation gain. USGS Heart Mountain

Black Mountain   *8,860 feet (Class 2)*
Black Mountain is located 4.5 miles southeast of Heart Mountain and just west of Antelope Lakes. Climb the southeast slopes from Antelope Lakes. Access the lakes via the Crooked Creek Road system [(C)(2.1)]. USGS Heart Mountain

ITALIAN PEAKS TO MONIDA PASS

At Italian Peak, the Beaverhead crest turns northeast and runs to Bannack Pass (not to be confused with Bannock Pass crossed by ID-29 farther north). At Bannack Pass it turns again and runs east to Monida Pass and I-15. This section of the range is perhaps the most rugged section of the Beaverheads. Between the many towers and cliffs you will find the limestone contorted into chevron folds and spectacular breach anticlines.

Fritz Peak   *9,738 feet (Class 3)*
Fritz Peak is located 4.2 miles south of the Continental Divide and northeast of Scott Peak, and 4 miles north of Heart Mountain. Climb the peak from Webber Creek [(C)(3.1)] via its southeast ridge, which is accessed at roughly the 7,200-foot contour. From the road, hike the grassy slopes northeast into the forest above and on to the summit. USGS Fritz Peak/Deadman Lake

Red Conglomerate Peak   *10,240+ feet (Class 2)*
Red Conglomerate Peak is the easternmost Beaverhead Peak to reach above 10,000 feet. It is located 15 miles northeast of Scott Peak, at the head of Irving Creek. The USGS triangulation station was located on the peak's lower north summit directly on the Continental Divide. The true summit is 50 feet higher and 0.25 mile to the south. The best ascent route follows Irving Creek [(C)(3.2)] and Red Canyon to its upper reaches. Continue toward the divide and then follow the

peak's west ridge to the summit. Other routes surely exist on this peak, but none have been reported. USGS Edie Creek

Cobble Mountain*   *9,996 feet (Class 3)*
This entire mountain is a cobble heap from a massive 60-million-year-old river that flowed east. This cobble formation is known as the Beaverhead Formation. The peak's summit is 1 mile southeast of Red Conglomerate Peak. The CDT touches its northern flank. From the East Fork Irving Creek [(C)(3.2)] hike up the peak's 2-mile south ridge. The high point is a detached volcanic knob that involves a short, exposed, Class 3 stretch on unstable rock. USGS Edie Creek

APPROACHES TO
THE BEAVERHEAD MOUNTAINS

(A) US-93 ACCESS POINTS

US-93 winds north out of Salmon and crosses Lost Trail Pass into Montana. At the pass, ID-43 cuts over to Chief Joseph Pass and leads east into Montana. The following approach points begin at Lost Trail Pass and are located successively to the south along the highway.

(1) FS-079, Gibbonsville Road. This road leaves US-93 11 miles north of North Fork (32 miles north of Salmon), and climbs up and over the crest at Big Hole Pass on its way to Wisdom, Montana. The pavement ends 0.8 mile from the highway

(a) FST-124, Perce Peak Trail. This trail begins just east of the confluence of Threemile Creek and Dohlonega Creek 4.4 miles east of US-93 and 0.1 mile east of FS-80. This is a steep, well-maintained trail that climbs up the ridge between Threemile Creek and the west fork of Dahlonega Creek for about 6 miles to Perce Peak and the Idaho/Montana border.

(2) FS-071, Fourth of July Creek Road. This road leaves US-93 roughly 4 miles south of North Fork at a signed junction. The road eventually leads to Stein Mountain after climbing out of Fourth of July and Blacktail Creeks. Look for FST-129 on your right at the point where the road swings west toward Stein Mountain.

(a) FST-129, South Fork Trail. This trail leaves FS-071 and runs east for 1.5 miles before swinging north and descending into the South Fork Sheep Creek. To access Pyramid Peak, leave the trail before descending.

(3) FS-069, Carmen Creek Roads. Four miles north of Salmon, turn onto the Carmen Creek Road. Drive west until the road forks in 4.1 miles. The left fork follows Carmen Creek and eventually reaches FST-138, which climbs up to the crest and crosses into Montana. The right fork leads up Freeman Creek [(A)(3.1)].

(3.1) Freeman Creek Road. Take the right fork described above along Freeman Creek. After a couple of miles, the road forks. Go left (east). The left fork climbs up Freeman Creek to a second fork that provides access to Copperhead Peak. See [(A) (3.1.1)], below. Continue straight at this second fork for a short distance to a small camping spot along the creek. Although the mining road continues up Freeman Creek beyond this point, it quickly deteriorates and it is advisable to start your climb at this point.

(a) FST-033, Freeman Creek Trail. This trail, an old mining road, leads to the Ore Cash Mine and then to the Continental Divide behind Freeman Peak in 4.5 miles. From the divide, the trail drops into Montana and Miner Lakes.

(3.1.1) Copperhead Peak Access. From the junction on the Freeman Creek Road described above this road leads north and then climbs east up the ridge that separates Freeman Creek and Golway Creek. The USGS Homer Youngs Peak quad shows only the main road and not the several roads that branch off it. At roughly the 6,600-foot contour on the map, a road forks left and heads toward the northeast. This road eventually leads into Golway Gulch and ends at 6,800 feet due south of Copperhead Peak. A 4WD is recommended.

(B) ID-28 ACCESS POINTS

This state highway follows the Beaverheads south from Salmon through the Lemhi and Birch Creek Valleys to a junction with ID-22 in 109 miles. The following entries begin in Salmon.

(1) Kirtley Creek Road Access. To access Kirtley Creek, drive southeast on ID-28 for 0.5 mile from the ID-28/US-93 junction and turn left (north) onto this road. The road quickly turns southeast to parallel ID-28. The Kirtley Creek Road leaves the county road 2.2 miles from ID-28 and follows the creek east toward the base of Monument Peak. It ends in 4.8 miles at a gravel pit. This road crosses private property and may not be open to the public. Check with the BLM before using it.

(2) Geertson Creek Road. Note that this road is now closed by a private landowner. It may be possible to secure permission to use it. Check with the BLM's Salmon office. To access this road, turn left (east) off ID-28 7 miles east of Salmon and follow the road to its end in 7.5 miles.

(a) Geertson Lake Trail. This trail leaves the end of the road and climbs to Geertson Lake in 4.5 miles. Although not maintained by the BLM, the trail is in descent condition.

(2.1) Mail Truck Road. Because the Geertson Creek Road is closed, this route, suitable only for foot travel and ORVs, is recommended to access the Continental Divide peaks between Monument Peak and Center Mountain. Start up Geertson Creek Road and turn left several hundred feet before the locked gate on this steep, eroded, and overgrown track. After twenty-four switchbacks, the road ends on a narrow ridge at 9,200 feet. The remains of a large mail truck are found at this point. This truck was last used 50 years ago to deliver supplies to miners working in the upper basin.

(3) FS-185 to Lemhi Pass. This good gravel road goes up Spring Creek and Pattee Creek to the crest and then follows the Idaho side of the border south to Lemhi Pass. When dry and recently graded, it is passable to passenger cars. The Agency Creek Road, FS-013, provides an alternative route to Lemhi Pass from Tendoy. This route meets FS-185 just below the pass. From the pass, a road and trail system leads south to Bannock Pass.

(3.1) FS-184, Continental Divide Road. This road leaves FS-185 at the upper end of Pattee Creek and then follows the divide 4 miles north to its end. A 4WD is recommended.

(a) FST-111, Continental Divide Trail. From the end of FS-184 this section of the CDT follows the divide north to Goldstone Pass [(D)(1)(a)] in about 9.5 miles.

(4) FS-303, Cedar Gulch/Eightmile Creek Road. This trail leaves the county road that parallels ID-28 between Tendoy and Leadore. Access this road at Leadore or from ID-28 by turning east 7 miles north of Leadore. FS-303 runs northwest up Cedar Gulch and then crosses southeast into Eightmile Creek where it ends at the Commodore Mine. A 4WD is recommended.

(a) FST-195, Eightmile Creek Trail. This trail climbs up Eightmile Creek to the Continental Divide in 5 miles where it meets the CDT. To reach Goat Mountain, follow the CDT north for roughly 2.5 miles.

(5) ID-29 to Railroad Canyon/Bannock Pass. This paved and gravel road leads from ID-28 at Leadore into Montana at Bannock Pass. During the winter, this road is usually plowed and open.

(5.1) FS-130, Cruikshank Road. This road leaves ID-29 several miles below Bannock Pass and leads up Cruikshank Creek, and then up Horse Prairie Peak.

(a) FST-191, Hall Creek Trail. FST-191 begins at the road's end and proceeds south, paralleling the range for 4.5 miles to Reservoir Creek.

(6) Lemhi River Road. This road runs between ID-29 and Gilmore Summit on the east side of ID-28. Its southern terminus is accessed 38.1 miles north of the INEEL boundary or 2.1 miles north of Gilmore Summit. Its northern terminus leaves ID-29 just east of Leadore. The road also can be accessed from ID-28 midway between Leadore and the Gilmore Summit. This road, which leads to the headwaters of the Lemhi River, is the primary access route to the Beaverhead crest between Bannock Pass and Jump Peak. Use it to reach Eighteenmile Creek Road [(B)(6.1)], Clear Creek Road [(B)(6.2)], Powderhorn Gulch Road [(B)(6.3)], and Hawley Creek Road [(B)(6.4)].

(6.1) Eighteenmile Creek Road. This is not an easy access route to describe and private property may present a problem. From the south end of the Lemhi River Road, drive for roughly 5 miles. Turn right and follow this road east along the northern boundary of a private field and then southeast for a total of 4.6 miles. At this point, you have arrived on private property and a confusing intersection. One road leads due south between two buck-and-pole fences to a crossing of an irrigation ditch. A second road begins behind a gate to your left and runs due east, also across private property. Take the latter road if you have received permission from the owner. After 0.8 mile, the road crosses an irrigation canal and then reaches a white house in another 0.6 mile. From this point, the road climbs up a hill to the right (south) and passes through a gate in another 0.7 mile. After 0.3 mile, a road heads east up Pass Creek and continues straight south for another 0.3 mile to cross Eighteenmile Creek. The road now continues along the creek to its end 2.2 miles from the last crossing. From the crossing, be prepared for rough travel to the road's end. A 4WD is required.

(6.2) Clear Creek Road. Access this road from the Upper Lemhi Road 2.5 miles north of the Eighteenmile Creek junction or, if traveling south on ID-28, directly from ID-28, 12.9 miles north of Gilmore Summit. Follow the road uphill and then across the flats to a junction in 2 miles. Turn right, cross Eighteenmile Creek on a bridge, and continue east into the Clear Creek drainage. A 4WD is recommended.

(6.3) Powderhorn Gulch Road. This road can be accessed from several directions including from ID-29 [(B)(5)] to the north or Clear Creek Road [(B)(6.2)] to the south. Access from either road is straightforward and well mapped on the Salmon National Forest map. If you take the Lemhi River Road [(B)(6)], continue north for 11.3 miles to the junction. If approaching from ID-29, leave ID-29 just east of Leadore after crossing the Lemhi River. The junction is signed for Powderhorn Gulch, Perk Canyon, and Dry Canyon. Turn east onto the road, cross a cattleguard, and then go through a gate at 1.4 miles. In another 0.3 mile, a road leads to the left up Perk Canyon. Continue straight ahead for another 0.3 mile to the Powderhorn Gulch junction. A 4WD is required beyond this point to reach the road's ends in 0.7 mile.

(a) FST-222, Powderhorn Gulch Trail. This trail, which begins as a closed road, leads up Powderhorn Gulch, then turns south and leads to Tenmile Creek, a total of 6 miles.

(b) FST-188, Dry Creek Trail. This trail begins as a road that leaves the Powderhorn Gulch Road 2 miles from ID-28. A 4WD is required to get from the junction to a gate that closes the route to vehicles in 0.7 mile. The trail is relatively good condition and climbs to a saddle in 2.5 miles

(6.4) FST-275, Hawley Creek Roads. This road can be accessed from the Lemhi River Road at two points. Either route leads toward the point where Hawley Creek spills out of the mountains. About 1 mile beyond the National Forest boundary, the road forks. The left fork follows Reservoir Creek to FST-192. The right fork becomes FS-177 and follows Big Bear Creek southeast to trailheads for FST-190 and FST-189.

(a) **FST-190, Bear Creek to CDT.** This trail leads to the CDT on a fair tread.

(7) **FS-189, Nicholia Area Roads.** The road to Nicholia is 24.2 miles north of the INEEL boundary on ID-28. This road begins as a good gravel road that runs northeast to a junction in about 3 miles. From this junction, roads lead both north and south. Going north will take you to FS-189 [(B)(7.2)] and going south leads to both FS-174 [(B)(7.1)], which traverses Italian Canyon, and FS-190 [(B)(8)], which climbs up Scott Canyon.

(7.1) **FS-174, Italian Canyon Road.** Access this road from Nicholia in the north by driving south on the road that parallels the base of the range for 2 miles or from the Scott Canyon Road to the south. The road enters Italian Canyon and ends after about 1.5 miles.

(a) **FST-057, Italian Canyon Trail.** This trail leaves the end of FS-174 and climbs 1 mile up the canyon to join FST-081 [(B)(7.2)(a)]. This trail is used by motorcycles and is in fair condition.

(7.2) **FS-189, Willow Creek Road.** Access this road from Nicholia Road. Drive west across private property for a little more than 1 mile and turn north on FS-189. FS-189 leads north and then east into Willow Canyon to a trailhead in 5.5 miles. Mr. Newman, the ranch owner, is now gating the road in the fall. Please exercise courtesy as you pass through his property. A 4WD is recommended.

(a) **FST-081, Willow Creek to Crooked Creek Trail.** This trail is 14 miles long and crosses four drainages: Willow Creek, Italian Canyon, Scott Canyon, and Crooked Creek. The northern section of the trail traverses Willow Creek, crosses a saddle, and drops into Italian Canyon to meet FST-057 [(B)(7.1)(a)]. The trail then climbs again toward the southeast to a second saddle just west of the Italian Peaks. It then continues downhill into Scott Canyon and FS-058 [(B)(8)(a)] and then climbs southwest toward a third saddle and Crooked Creek. The trail is open to motorcycles and is in fair to poor condition.

(8) **FS-190, Scott Canyon Road.** This road is accessed from ID-28 19.5 miles north of the INEEL boundary or from Nicholia. Do not confuse this road with the Scott Butte Road 2.6 miles north of the INEEL boundary. From the signed junction on ID-28, drive northeast for roughly 10 miles to a trailhead. From Nicholia, drive south for another 2.2 miles past Italian Canyon on the two-track road that parallels the base of the

mountains. The road ends at a locked gate at 7,700 feet. A 4WD is recommended.

(a) **FST-058, Scott Canyon Trail.** FST-058 leaves FS-190 and climbs up Scott Canyon to join FST-081 [(C)(2.1)(a)] in a quick 2 miles.

(9) **Kaufman Picnic Area Access.** The Kaufman picnic area is located at a signed intersection along ID-28. To reach Mahogany Gulch from the picnic area, follow the main road east past the picnic area along the drainage to the junction with FS-538. Turn left on FS-538 and follow it for a little over 1 mile to the junction that climbs up into Mahogany Gulch. Turn right and follow the road to its end. A 4WD is recommended.

(10) **FS-298, Skull Canyon Road.** This road is signed and leaves the old town site of Blue Dome (no buildings remain). The road is open to the public, but looks to be private because it goes right through a ranch yard and a closed gate. A 4WD is required.

(11) **FS-176, Long Canyon Roads.** Access these roads 8.2 miles north of the INEEL boundary. Turn east off the highway and drive toward the mountains. As you approach the base of the mountains, you can access three separate canyons.

(C) ID-22 ACCESS POINTS

This state highway runs west from its junction with ID-28 to I-15 and Dubois. The roads below are listed from west to east.

(1) **FS-202, Chandler Canyon Road.** This road leaves ID-22 10 miles northeast of its junction with ID-28 and runs north into the southern tip of the Beaverhead range. A 4WD recommended.

(1.1) **FS-201, Gallagher Canyon Road.** The road begins 6.25 miles north of ID-22 and proceeds west up Gallagher Canyon for 3 increasingly rough miles. A 4WD is recommended.

(1.2) **FS-203, Blue Canyon Road.** The road begins a couple of miles north of the Gallagher Canyon Road and then leads west up Blue Canyon for 2 more miles. A 4WD is recommended.

(2) **FS-192, Antelope Lakes Road.** This road leaves ID-22 13 miles northeast of its junction with ID-28 (1.5 miles southwest of Lidy Hot Springs) and runs north along the eastern edge of the Beaverhead range for 20 miles to a junction with FS-196 [(C) (3.1)]. It connects with a road system that accesses most of the Beaverheads' southeastern canyons. Some of these roads are passable for autos, but most require a 4WD.

(2.1) **FS-178, Crooked Creek Road.** This road forks off FS-192 8 miles from ID-22 and runs northwest up Crooked Creek for 8 miles. A 4WD is recommended.

(a) **FST-081, Willow Creek/Crooked Creek Trail.** This trail leaves the end of FS-178 and proceeds northwest. See [(B) (8)(a)], above.

(2.1.1) **FS-191, Myers Creek Road.** This road leaves FS-178

5 miles from its beginning and ends 3 miles up the drainage.

(a) FST-113, Myers Creek Trail. FST-113 leaves the end of FS-191 and climbs up the drainage and over the saddle on the east slopes of Heart Mountain to connect with FST-111 in the Webber Creek drainage in 5.5 miles.

(3) FS-280, Medicine Lodge Road. This road leaves ID-22 6 miles west of I-15 and continues 34 miles to the northwest to cross the Continental Divide and enter Montana.

(3.1) FS-196, Webber Creek Road. This road can be accessed from either FS-192 or FS-280. The road follows Webber Creek westward into the Beaverhead Range and ends at the Webber Creek CG.

(a) FST-111, Webber Creek Trail. FST-111 leaves from the end of FS-196 and follows the Webber Creek drainage west to the Continental Divide in 8 miles. It then drops down into the Divide Creek drainage. It connects with FS-280 in another 6 miles.

(3.2) FS-187, Irving Creek Road. This road leaves the Medicine Lodge Road and follows Irving Creek northeast for 4.5 miles. A 4WD is recommended.

(D) MONTANA ACCESS

Only a few of the Beaverhead access points from Montana are included in this book. Many other roads and trails traverse the eastern side of the range. Several of these routes can be used to climb Beaverhead peaks.

(1) Goldstone Pass. To reach this pass, begin either in Leadore or in Dillon, Montana. From Leadore, take ID-29 over Bannock Pass. Roughly 14 miles north of the pass there is a junction with a national forest access sign. To reach this junction from Dillion, drive south on I-15 for 19 miles and exit at the Clark Reservoir exit. Drive west on Montana 234 (signed for Grant, Montana, and for Salmon, Idaho), for 20 miles to a junction and turn north. Continue to the next junction, and then turn right onto FS-181. After 18 miles the road passes Reservoir Lake and CG. The road continues north to a signed junction for Goldstone Pass. A 4WD is recommended.

(a) Continental Divide Trail. This section of the CDT leads south to FS-184 [(B)(3.1)(a)] near Lemhi Pass and then northward until it drops into the trenched canyons on the Montana side of the border.

(2) Pioneer Lake Access. This access begins 1 mile south of Jackson, Montana, on US-278. Turn right and follow the road south and then west to Van Houten Lake CG. From the campground, continue straight ahead for 1.5 miles along the Bloody Dick Road to a trailhead on Janke Creek.

(a) Pioneer Lake Road. The trail, which begins as a 4WD road, follows Janke Creek for 0.4 mile to a junction. From here,

head north, descending downhill to the Pioneer Creek Trail. The trail now follows Pioneer Creek to Pioneer Lake in 7 miles. The Continental Divide and other lakes in the area can be accessed from this lake.

(3) Ajax Lake Access. This access begins near Jackson, Montana, south of Montana Highway 43 and Wisdom, Montana. Because of the narrow ranch roads and changeable conditions west of Jackson, it is best to ask for updated directions in Jackson.

(a) Big Swamp Creek Trail. This trail climbs up Big Swamp Creek to Ajax Lake below Ajax Peak. It is about 6 miles from the trailhead to the lake.

8

THE CENTENNIAL MOUNTAINS

The Centennial Mountains begin where the Beaverhead range ends at Monida Pass. The Centennials form both the Continental Divide and the Idaho/Montana border for 62 miles, from Monida Pass at I-15 to Red Rock Pass west of Yellowstone National Park. The range is 12 miles wide in places. In the west, the range begins as a series of high rolling ridges that gradually gain in elevation to the east. On its eastern end, the range climbs abruptly out of the forested Island Park Caldera to form a high rugged crest that reaches its highest elevation at 10,203 feet on Mount Jefferson.

The Centennial Mountains are unusual because their east/west orientation is contrary to the predominant basin and range fault blocking that dissected southern and eastern Idaho into a series of north/south-trending mountain ranges. Geologists have speculated that the range formed in this contrary matter because the Yellowstone hot spot heated and raised this section of the earth's crust. As the hot spot moves east, the Centennials will probably sink and be sliced up by basin and range faults.

The Idaho portions of this range are administered by the Targhee National Forest and the BLM. Most of the Montana side of the range is administered by the BLM and, in a small area, by the Beaverhead National Forest. This escarpment is both a big game corridor to and from the Yellowstone ecosystem and an important north/south flyway for raptors, upland game birds, and waterfowl. Black bears are common at higher elevations. Thanks to its importance as wildlife habitat, a large chunk of the range is under consideration for designation as wilderness. The management agencies have made wildlife habitat protection a priority.

Climbers and hikers often overlook this beautiful corner of eastern Idaho in favor of the more rugged ranges to the west. This is their loss. The range has many acres suitable for wilderness designation, many worthwhile summits, several quaint lake basins, and miles of open ridgeline suitable for cross-country travel. On the Idaho side, most summits are easy scrambles or hikes. Climbing options are all in the Class 1 to Class 3 categories. The CDT will eventually traverse the entire Centennial escarpment. The range's trail system is widely disbursed, providing many day-hiking opportunities and a few overnight destinations. The Centennial Range's roads are plentiful, but quality varies considerably.

Signal Mountain   8,534 feet (Class 2)

This prominent basalt peak, visible for many miles along I-15, is located 6 miles northeast of Spencer. It was named by the men building the Utah-Northern Railroad. Rick Baugher recommends ascending its southern slopes from FS-477 [(A) (1)]. USGS Paul Reservoir NE

Lookout Point   8,716 feet (Class 2)

This peak sits 3 miles due east of Signal Mountain. Approach the peak from the end of FS-477 and Lone Pine Pass [(A)(1)(a)] and climb its southern slopes. USGS Lookout Point

Big Table Mountain   9,220+ feet (Class 1)

This flat-topped peak is located on the Continental Divide in a roadless area 11.5 miles northwest of Kilgore. Its broad, ill-defined summit forms a major chunk of the divide between state line mileposts 640.099 and 646. The actual high point is at the east end of this basalt tabletop at milepost 646. On the Idaho side of the divide, the summit can be reached by hiking up either the Bear Gulch Trail, FST-008 [(A)(2.1.1)(a)], or the Big Table Mountain Trail, FST-009 [(A)(2.2)(a)]. Both trails are readily accessible from Kilgore via good gravel roads. On the Montana side of the divide, the Price Peet Road leads to Pete Creek Divide; from this saddle, FST-004, the CDT, follows the crest east to the summit. Once on the tabletop, the grassy fields resemble a moor. The CDT is marked with posts. USGS Big Table Mountain/Winslow Creek

Baldy Mountain   9,889 feet (Class 2)

Baldy Mountain is the most impressive summit at the western end of the Centennial Range. It is found 8 miles east of Big Table Mountain directly on the Continental Divide. The peak has a north/south-trending summit ridge with its highest point at the north end just inside Montana. Climb the peak either by following the ridgeline north from Slide Mountain, or by following the Ching Creek drainage from a point just south of Hancock Lake [(A)(2.2.1)(a)] to its highest point. From this point, gain the west ridge. USGS Slide Mountain

Slide Mountain   9,805 feet (Class 2)

Slide Mountain was named because a huge landslide took out its southwest side. The unstable remains of the slide of white rhyolite is visible for many miles. The peak is directly on the Continental Divide, 1.5 miles southeast of Baldy Mountain. Take FST-039 [(A)(2.2.1)(a)] to Aldous and Hancock Lakes. From the southeast end of Aldous Lake, bushwhack northeast up a ridge—an 800-foot vertical climb—to the divide at milepost 655.926. Continue north along the divide to the summit. USGS Slide Mountain

Dry Creek Peak   8,200+ feet (Class 2)

This small summit is located just south of the Continental Divide above Dry Creek, 3.75 miles southeast of Slide Mountain. The summit is reached by hiking up FST-007/FST-171 [(A)(4)(a)] to the peak's south ridge, and then by following that ridge to the top. USGS Slide Mountain

Taylor Mountain   9,855 feet (Class 2)

Taylor has an impressive north face that descends quickly down into Montana. Its southern slopes, clear to the summit, were mined for phosphate in the mid-1950s. The summit is reached after a great ridge walk from where FS-042 [(A)(5)] reaches the Continental Divide 4 miles to the east. According to Rick Baugher, the peak also can be reached by a road that climbs to the divide just west of its summit from Montana or via its southern slopes. USGS Upper Red Rock Lake

Reas Peak   9,371 feet (Class 2)

Reas Peak sits on the Continental Divide 14 miles east of Dry Creek Peak and 1.6 miles due south of Mount Jefferson. Climb this peak from the Yale/Kilgore Road via FS-048 [(A)(6)] at Blue Creek. Head west on foot to gain the broad south ridge. This area is closed to vehicles. Follow the road until you reach the peak's upper slopes. Reas is best known for its wide-open southern slope, which is excellent for March and early April cross-country skiing. USGS Mount Jefferson

Mount Jefferson

Mount Jefferson *10,203 feet (Class 2)*

Jefferson, the highest peak in the Centennial Range, is located 1.6 miles due north of Reas Peak. (The Continental Divide doubles back on itself—both Mount Jefferson and Reas Peak sit on the divide, with Montana's Hell Roaring Creek in-between. It is a very impressive summit when viewed from Island Park. Jefferson is frequently climbed from a trailhead on the Sawtelle Peak Road [(B)(1)(a)]. From the trailhead, hike west for 2.3 miles. Leave the trail where it turns north and climb Jefferson's east ridge, a broad, easy-to-follow ramp to the summit. USGS Mount Jefferson

Red Rock Mountain *9,512 feet (Class 3-4)*

Red Rock Mountain is 0.9 mile north of Mount Jefferson, to which it is connected by a snaking, jagged ridge. This peak can be climbed from Mount Jefferson via this ridge. However, the descent to the saddle between the two peaks involves Class 3 to Class 4 climbing in two places. Although there is only minimal exposure, some will want to turn back. To climb the peak via this route from Jefferson's summit, descend to the west, going over a subsidiary peak along the way. Continue down and north until reaching the saddle between the two peaks. Ascend Red Rock Mountain's south ridge without any difficulty. R. Baugher reports that a Class 2 approach is possible from the Montana side. Ascend Cole Creek to the

Red Rock/Jefferson saddle, and then climb the saddle to the summit. USGS Mount Jefferson

Sawtelle Peak *9,902 feet*

This peak was named for Gilman Sawtelle, who settled at Henry's Lake in the late 1860s. The first known ascent was by the A. D. Wilson topographic party in 1878. The peak, home to a Federal Aviation Administration radar station, sits just 3 miles east of Mount Jefferson. The radar dome on top of this imposing peak is plainly visible from the surrounding valleys. A good roadway [(B)] is kept open to the public throughout most of the summer. The sweeping view from the nearly 10,000-foot summit includes large parts of Idaho, Montana, and Wyoming. Beware, grizzly bears den on the peak's northeast slopes. USGS Sawtelle Peak

APPROACHES TO THE CENTENNIAL MOUNTAINS

(A) THE YALE/KILGORE ROAD ACCESS POINTS

This road, an early route for the migratory Nez Perce tribe, is the primary approach route to the Centennial range. Take I-15 to the Spencer exit to reach the west end of this road; take US-20/ US-191, which runs between Idaho Falls and West Yellowstone,

Montana, to reach the road's eastern end. From this road, any number of side roads lead into the Centennials. The following roads are listed from west to east.

(1) FS-477, Threemile Creek Road. This road leaves the Yale/Kilgore Road roughly 2 miles east of I-15 and follows Threemile Creek northeast into the Centennials. The road eventually ends south of Lone Pine Pass. A 4WD is recommended.

(a) FST-175/FST-005, Lookout Point Access. Use these trails to access the slopes of Lookout Point. From the end of the road, the trail quickly climbs to Lone Pine Pass in 1 mile. FST-175 continues north while FST-005 heads east, mostly on a ridge top to a point just west of Lookout Point's summit. FST-005 then turns due south and descends to a Forest Service road.

(2) Kilgore Access Roads. Kilgore is a village located just north of the Yale/Kilgore Road. Gas and food is available. From Kilgore, three roads extend into the western end of the range.

(2.1) FS-006, West Camas Creek/Porcupine Pass Road. This road leads up West Camas Creek to Porcupine Pass, and then continues west to I-15. To reach this road, drive north from the Kilgore Post Office and turn left when the road ends. Drive west for 2.2 miles, turn right and drive 0.8 mile, then turn left and you are on FS-006. Nine miles from Kilgore, the road crosses West Camas Creek. At this point, FS-006 continues upstream while FS-019 forks off and extends downstream.

(2.1.1) FS-019, Bear Gulch Road. This road leaves FS-006 just after it crosses West Camas Creek. FS-019 begins by running southeast along West Camas Creek, and then crosses over to Bear Gulch. Once in Bear Gulch, it continues north to a developed trailhead with parking for ten cars.

(a) FST-008, Bear Gulch Trail. This trail follows Bear Gulch north and connects with FST-009, the Big Table Mountain Trail [(A)(2.2)(a)] in 2 miles.

(2.2) East Camas Creek/Cotton Wood Creek Roads. From the Kilgore Post Office, drive north. Turn left at the T-intersection at the north edge of town, then turn right at the next intersection and follow this gravel road north until it forks. The fork is the beginning of FS-026, a loop road that begins and ends here. Three major side roads and several trails are accessed from this road system. Only one trailhead has been developed.

(a) FST-009, Big Table Mountain Trail. This trail begins at Hirschi Flat. From the junction described above, take the left fork north for 3 miles and then turn left (west) onto a short feeder road. The road ends in 0.1 mile; find the trail on the south side of the road. The trail quickly crosses East Camas Creek and works its way south to Larkspur Creek. In 3 miles, the trail meets the Bear Gulch Trail [(A)(2.1.1)(a)] and then continues uphill to the Continental Divide and Big Table Mountain.

(b) FST-004, Spruce Creek Trail. This is an alternate route to the area around Big Table Mountain. Take the west fork of FS-026 to the point where the road turns due east. FS-023 begins here and runs north. At this point, find FST-004 along the banks of Spruce Creek. Follow the trail up the drainage until it reaches the Continental Divide. The trail runs east and then west along the divide, providing many miles of excellent high ridge walking.

(2.2.1) FS-027, Aldous Lake Trailhead Road. Drive out of Kilgore on FS-026. When the road divides, take the right (east) fork and continue for 2.3 miles to a junction with FS-027. Turn right here and follow this road for 7 miles to the Aldous Lake trailhead.

(a) Aldous/Hancock Lakes Trail. This short trail leads to Aldous and Hancock Lakes in 1.3 and 2.3 miles respectively.

(b) FST-171. This trailhead is found 0.25 mile south of the end of FS-027. See [(A)(4)(a)] for further details.

(4) Dry Creek Trailhead. This trailhead is located east of Kilgore on Dry Creek. To reach it, drive the Yale/Kilgore Road to a point 8 miles east of Kilgore and turn north. The trailhead is a short distance up the creek.

(a) FST-007/FST-171, Dry Creek Trails. Follow Dry Creek directly to the Continental Divide. Roughly 1.5 miles north of the trailhead, FST-007 intersects with FST-171. FST-171 leads due west, climbs over a ridge above Moose Creek, and then descends to Ching Creek, where it joins FST-014. From this junction, FST-171 continues west to a trailhead on FS-027 [(A)(2.2.1)].

(5) FS-042, Keg Springs Road. Turn north on this road located at the signed Clark County/Freemont County line east of Kilgore and 14.1 miles west of US-20. This road runs north for 4.9 miles to a gate at 8,100 feet. A 4WD is recommended. A trail runs east to Blair Lake on the Montana side of the border.

(6) FS-048, Blue Creek Road. This road is found along the Yale/Kilgore Road, 6 miles east of US-20. The road, which follows Blue Creek north, is connected to several other logging roads not shown on the maps and closed to all vehicles. This is the best winter approach to Reas Peak.

(B) US-20 ACCESS POINTS

This highway travels between Idaho Falls and West Yellowstone, Montana.

(1) FS-024, Sawtelle Peak Road. This road leads to the summit of Sawtelle Peak from US-20. Turn east off US-20 8 miles north of Mack's Inn or 32 miles north of Ashton and follow the gravel road to a radar facility on the summit. Passenger cars can negotiate the road, but be aware that it is steep—the descent will be hard on the brakes of cars with automatic transmissions. The Rock Basin Trail leaves this road 11.9 miles from US-20 or 1.5 miles below the top of Sawtelle Peak.

(a) FST-165, Rock Basin Trail. This trail leaves the trailhead and descends for a short distance before starting uphill. Follow it for 2.3 miles until it turns sharply north and drops off the Continental Divide. This turn is the starting point for climbing Mount Jefferson and Red Rock Mountain. If you continue on, the trail will take you to Lake Marie in Montana.

9

HENRYS LAKE MOUNTAINS

The Henrys Lake Mountains, a small arc-shaped range, form the Continental Divide and the Idaho/Montana border for roughly 40 miles. The range begins at Red Rock Pass in the west (where the Centennial Mountains end) and arcs around to Reas Pass, elevation 6,941 feet, and the Yellowstone Plateau in the east. North Targhee Peak, at more than 10,440 feet, is the highest Idaho Henrys Lake Mountains peak, while the highest of all the Henrys Lake peaks is Peak 10609, which lies north of the Continental Divide in Montana.

The Henrys Lake Mountains are a mixture of Paleozoic sedimentary rocks and volcanic materials, including rhyolite and basalt with some Precambrian metamorphic rocks thrown in for good measure. The range, which was forced up with the uplifting of the Rocky Mountains, has been shaped most recently by glaciation and the nearby Henrys Fork and Island Park Calderas and the collapsed volcanoes that preceded them. One of these volcanoes covered more than 6,000 square miles of Idaho and Montana with red-hot ash and other materials. The resulting terrain, which is steep and abrupt in places, forms a transition zone between the drier mountains to the west and the wetter mountains to the east.

The range, administered by the Targhee National Forest in Idaho and by the Gallatin National Forest in Montana, is managed as prime grizzly bear habitat. The bears found in the Henrys Lake Mountains are of two varieties—endemic and transplanted. The transplanted bears are "troubled bears"—that is, bears that are unafraid of humans. They are captured

in Yellowstone National Park and "paroled" in the Henrys Lake range. A word of warning: Strictly observe all bear-country precautions. The Forest Service has recommended roughly 30,000 acres in the range for wilderness designation.

Exceptional access (by Idaho standards) leads into these mountains via US-20 and ID-87. Several Forest Service roads provide secondary access from the paved highways. Although there are few trails into the Henrys Lake Mountains, access to the peaks is adequate and much of the higher terrain is above tree line. This small group has good hiking and climbing opportunities. The trail system has one excellent loop that leads to the range's two mountain lakes. Its peaks are reached by nontechnical routes and are well worth the effort. Off-trail, cross-country skiing is exceptional with parking available all winter at US-20 on Targhee Pass.

Pup Peak*   *8,568 feet (Class 3)*
This peak sits directly on the Continental Divide 4 miles west of Henrys Lake. Park at the base of Schoolhouse Canyon and follow the jeep trail west to the divide. Once on the divide, follow it south and then west to the summit. The route is blocked by a 20-foot, Class 3 ledge and gully near the summit. First winter ascent: R. Baugher in 1997. USGS Hidden Bench Lake

Black Mountain   *10,237 feet (Class 3)*
Black Mountain, which is situated 3 miles due east of Raynolds Pass directly on the Continental Divide, has a vertical north face and an L-shaped summit ridge that is almost 1.5 miles long. Climb from either the east or the west via the Continental Divide. The shortest route begins on Raynolds Pass [(A)] and follows the divide east to the summit in 3 miles. To approach the peak from the east, use FST-027 [(B)(1)(b)], which runs up Dry Fork. USGS Targhee Peak

Targhee Peak   *10,280 feet*
This peak, a beautiful mixture of trees, cliffs, and meadows with a boulder-strewn summit, is located 1.5 miles northeast of Black Mountain and just east of the Continental Divide. It can be climbed via several routes. USGS Targhee Creek

West Ridge (Class 2). Take the Targhee Creek Trail [(B)(1)(a)] to the point where it crosses the west ridge, and follow the ridge to the top.

East Ridge (Class 2). Take FST-027 [(B)(1)(a)] to the point where it crosses to the south side of Targhee Creek for the second time. Climb up through the trees to the broad ridge and follow it to the summit.

Targhee Peak

West Fork Cliffs (Class 3). Follow the Targhee Creek Trail [(B)(1)(a)] to the point where the creek forks. Leave the trail and head up the west fork. Look around and find a good game trail that leads up the valley. The game trail eventually reaches open terrain and you can see the large sedimentary cliffs that tower over the valley—if a grizzly doesn't get you first. The route goes up the large gully that splits the cliff. Route-finding is straightforward. From the top of the cliff, take the east ridge to the summit.

North Targhee Peak*   *10,400+ feet (Class 3).*
The highest Idaho peak in the Henrys Lake Mountains is found on the Continental Divide 1.1 miles north of Targhee Peak. North Targhee is composed of light-colored Paleozoic limestone carved into impressive cliffs. Access the divide via Targhee Creek [(B)(1)(a)]. A shorter approach to the divide is

possible from Montana via a new trail up Mile Creek. Once on the divide, follow it north to the summit. USGS Earthquake Lake/Hebgen Dam

Bald Peak   *10,180 feet (Class 3)*
Bald Peak presents a bold, nearly vertical 800-foot face on both its north and east sides and is protected in places by bands of limestone cliffs. It is 2 miles due east of Targhee Peak. Climb this peak from FST-027 [(B)(1)(a)] by leaving the trail just below Clark Lake and traversing due east and up to the summit—a steep but straightforward approach. This peak undoubtedly could be climbed from almost any direction. The first ascent is credited to G. Bechler in 1872. Bechler published a sketch map of the area, naming this peak and others in the Centennial Mountains. USGS Targhee Pass

Lionhead Peak   *9,574 feet (Class 2)*

This minor summit is distinctive when viewed from Montana. The summit is located 1.25 miles east of Bald Mountain. Approach the summit from FST-027 [(B)(1)(a)]. Leave the trail where it crosses the East Fork Targhee Creek and follow this drainage due north for 2 miles. At roughly 8,800 feet, climb northeast to the ridge, then follow the ridgeline east to the summit. USGS Targhee Pass

APPROACHES TO THE HENRYS LAKE MOUNTAINS

(A) ID-87 ACCESS POINTS

This highway runs between US-20 and the Idaho/Montana border at Raynolds Pass. The only access point of interest is at Raynolds Pass, where there is good parking, access to Black Mountain, and open slopes for skiing.

(B) US-20 ACCESS POINTS

This major north/south highway runs between Idaho Falls and West Yellowstone.

(1) Targhee Creek Trailhead. This trailhead can be reached by driving 2 miles north from the US-20/ID-87 junction to a signed turn for the Targhee Creek Road. Turn left and follow this road west into the mountains to the Targhee Creek trailhead in 2.5 miles. Keep right at the only junction along this route.

(a) FST-027, Targhee Creek Trail. This trail climbs up Targhee Creek to the lake basin north of Targhee Peak. From the lake basin, a poorly maintained trail climbs up to the Continental Divide near Point 10130 west of Targhee Peak. From the divide, the trail drops into the saddle between the peaks and connects with the Dry Fork Trail.

(b) Dry Fork Trail. This trail begins as a logging road that turns off the Targhee Creek road just below the Targhee Creek trailhead. Follow the logging road until it turns into a trail. The trail, not shown on the Targhee Pass USGS quad, works its way up Dry Fork until it crosses the ridge above the West Fork Targhee Creek just east of two small ponds, which are shown on the quad. From the ponds, the trail eventually leads to the Continental Divide where it joins the Targhee Creek Trail.

(2) Targhee Pass. At 7,072 feet, this pass offers the highest highway access point to the Henrys Lake Mountains crest. This pass is a popular destination for cross-country skiers. The ski terrain at the higher elevations is suitable for advanced intermediates, while lower slopes are fine for beginners. From the pass, the western slopes are moderate and interspersed by forest and meadow. This route can be followed through alternating open and forested slopes to the crest.

THE BIG HOLE MOUNTAINS AND THE SNAKE RIVER RANGE

These mountains are located east of Idaho Falls and north of the Snake River. Although designated as two separate ranges by the USGS mapmakers, the Big Hole and Snake River ranges are physically and geologically the same group of mountains. ID-31 divides the groups. The Big Hole Mountains encompass the peaks west of the highway, the Snake River Range encompass those to the east.

These mountains form a tangled web of ridges, streams, aspen thickets, and meadows that rise out of the Snake River Plain. They gradually gain elevation from west to east. Piney Peak, at 9,019 feet, is the highest point in the Big Hole group; Mount Baird, at 10,042 feet, is the highest point in the Snake River Range.

Geologically, the range has a limestone foundation and is part of the Overthrust Belt. Over the centuries, the tilted limestone formations have proved to be very unstable, resulting in massive slope failures. Blowout Canyon, located at the eastern end of the range, is a spectacular example of what happens when a lot of rock moves downhill rapidly. Although the extraordinary landslide that ravaged this canyon took place in prehistoric times, the canyon is still filled with rubble and debris that make it look like it just recently came roaring down the mountain. Upper Palisades Lake is also the result of a slide, which dammed up the canyon. There are many high cirques evidencing Pleistocene glaciation. An interesting feature is the presence of the largest coal deposit in Idaho in the northwest end of the range.

The Targhee National Forest administers most of the range; cattle and sheep grazing are the main commercial uses. Much of this terrain is still in a semi-wilderness condition with two large roadless areas, one of 40,000 acres surrounding Garns Peak in the Big Holes and one of 200,000 acres in the Snake River Range. Since the earliest settlers arrived, these mountains have been celebrated big game country. When hiking at lower elevations in the Snake River Range, it is almost impossible to avoid seeing moose, and the slopes around Mount Baird are thick with mountain goats. The range is threatened by those who want to explore for oil within its boundaries. So far, drilling activity has not taken place.

These mountains contain an extensive trail system accessed by a better-than-average road system. Trail conditions vary, but most trails are passable. There are few foot bridges so many streams must be waded. The lower elevations are often cluttered with brush and aspen thickets, which makes cross-country travel difficult, while the high country is composed of bare ridges ideally suited for walking. Big Hole and Snake River Peaks fall into the Class 1 to Class 3 range—often the crux of a climb will be working your way through the low-level brush to get to the base of a climb.

BIG HOLE PEAKS

Garns Mountain   *9,016 feet (Class 2)*
Garns Mountain, found 12 miles south of Driggs, is a big bald mountain with the remains of an old fire lookout on the summit. The summit can be approached by several different trails. The most direct approach is via FST-056, the Elk Flat Trail [(C)(1)(a)], a well-maintained tread that passes through Elk Flat, a pleasing high-altitude meadow on the peak's eastern flanks. USGS Garns Mountain

Prospect Peak   *8,023 feet (Class 2)*
Prospect Peak is 4.2 miles southwest of Garns Mountain. Take FST-068, the Big Burns Creek Trail [(A)(1)(b)], northeast up Burns and Beartrap Canyons to the point where the trail crosses over the peak's north ridge in roughly 5.5 miles. Leave this little-used trail and walk south to the summit. USGS Temple Peak

Twin Peaks   *7,761 feet (Class 2)*
Twin Peaks is situated 3 miles southwest of Prospect Peak. Although this peak offers a good view of the Snake River Plain, finding a human footprint on this summit would be about as likely as finding one on the moon. Hike up the Burns Canyon Trail [(A)(1)(b)] for 2 miles and then hike up the steep, forested east ridge of the peak. The high point is at the northwest end of the summit ridge, 1.5 miles away. USGS Temple Peak

Piney Peak   *9,019 feet (Class 2)*
The highest point in the Big Hole Mountains can be approached most directly by the Black Canyon Trail, FST-073 [(A)(1)(c)], or from the West Pine Creek Trail, FST-078 [(B)(1)(a)]. Both trails provide access to the peak's south slopes, from which it is an easy 400-foot scramble to the summit. USGS Garns Mountain

Red Mountain   *8,715 feet (Class 1)*
Red Mountain is the prominent summit seen from the Teton Valley as you drive toward Pine Creek Summit from Victor. It is located 4 miles southeast of Garns Mountain. Several trails converge near the summit. The Big Hole Crest Trail [(B)(2)(b)] is the recommended approach during the summer. From Pine Creek Summit, it is roughly 6 miles to the point where the trail crosses over the peak's northwest ridge. Leave the trail at this point and hike southeast for 0.25 mile to the summit. Winter ski ascents are best made by following Patterson Creek. Be warned—high avalanche conditions can exist. USGS Garns Mountain

Liars Peak   *8,689 feet (Class 2)*
Chicken Peak   *8,250 feet (Class 2)*
Black Mountain   *8,796 feet (Class 2)*
These three summits are located on a ridge that extends south from Garns Mountain. A connecting trail, which has several different number designations, runs from north to south past each of these peaks. The shortest approach is from FST-078 [(B)(1)(a)], which runs up West Pine Creek from ID-31. However, you can approach the divide that contains these peaks from the several other trails. Climb Black Peak by leaving FST-078 on the peak's north slope and climbing the last 1,000 feet to the summit over steep, forested ground. Climb Chicken Peak by leaving the trail on the peak's east side and climbing 150 feet to the summit. The northernmost of these three summits, Liars Peak, is 300 feet higher than the point where the trail crosses its southeast ridge. To climb it, leave the trail and hike up the southeast ridge. USGS Garns Mountain/Stouts Mountain

Stouts Mountain   *8,620 feet (Class 2)*
Stouts Mountain overlooks the mouth of Pine Creek and is readily visible from US-26. Climb to the summit from ID-31 [(B)(1)] via the peak's south ridge. Rick Baugher warns climbers to be prepared for tough bushwhacking through mountain mahogany. USGS Stouts Mountain

SNAKE RIVER RANGE

Fourth of July Peak   *7,496 feet (Class 1)*
Fourth of July Peak is located 4.5 miles southeast of where ID-31 crosses Pine Creek Pass. From Pine Creek Pass, take FST-084 [(B)(2)(a)] to the summit. It is roughly 0.75 mile to the summit from the trailhead at Rainey Creek. USGS Fourth of July Peak

Oliver Peak   *9,004 feet (Class 2)*

This peak, the northeasternmost Snake River summit, is found 5.5 miles southeast of Victor. FST-049 [(C)(2)(a)] passes within a short distance of its summit. Follow the trail until it passes the peak's southeast slopes. Leave the trail at this point and hike uphill for roughly 600 feet to the summit. USGS Victor

Thompson Peak   *9,481 feet (Class 2)*

Thompson Peak sits 4 miles almost due south of Fourth of July Peak on the high north/south divide that separates Rainey Creek from Palisades Creek. Take FST-089, the Rainey Creek Trail [(A)(2)(a)], northeast to Dry Elk Canyon. Follow FST-091 [(A)(2)(a.2)] up Dry Elk Canyon to FST-091 [(A)(2)(a.2.1)]. Follow this trail to the peak's southeast or north ridges and scramble up to the summit, which is a little more than 600 feet above the trail. USGS Thompson Peak

Atkinson Peak   *9,366 feet (Class 2)*

Atkinson Peak is located 1.75 miles southwest of Thompson Peak on the same divide. Approach this peak via Rainey Creek [(A)(2)(a)] or Palisades Creek [(A)(3)(a)]. From either of these routes, take FST-092 [(A)(2)(a.1) or (A)(3)(a.1)] to the peak's south ridge. Scramble up the ridge 800 feet to the summit. USGS Thompson Peak

Palisades Peak   *9,778 feet (Class 2)*

Palisades Peak is located in the upper Palisades Creek drainage, just north of Upper Palisades Lake and 4.4 miles south/southeast of Atkinson Peak. Approach the summit from FST-097 [(A)(6)(a)], which crosses the saddle east of the peak. From the saddle, hike 0.5 mile due west to the summit. USGS Palisades Peak

Little Palisades Peak   *9,707 feet (Class 2)*

Little Palisades is located just east of Palisades Peak and is also accessed from FST-097 [(A)(3)(b)], which crosses the peak's southern slopes. From the trail, follow the south ridge to the summit. USGS Palisades Peak

Baldy Mountain   *9,835 feet (Class 2)*

Baldy Mountain is the very prominent peak that rises east of the village of Swan Valley. It is located 4.5 miles southwest of Atkinson Peak and 4.5 miles north of Irwin. The best route to the summit is a trailless scramble of almost 5,000 vertical feet up the south ridge from a starting point near Palisades Creek CG [(A)(3)(a.1)]. Rick Baugher notes that though the national forest map shows a trail to the summit, any vestige of the trail on the Rainey Creek side was wiped out by a fire in the early 1980s. The old route is clogged by snags and deadfall. A 100-foot meteorite crater is found at the west base of this peak. The impact is thought to have occurred around 1600. USGS Thompson Peak

Sheep Mountain   *9,680 feet (Class 2)*

Sheep Mountain sits between Palisades Creek and Sheep Creek, 4 miles southeast of Baldy Mountain. Climb this peak via its east ridge from the point where FST-096 [(A)(4)(a)] crosses the ridge 1.5 miles east of the summit. USGS Thompson Peak

Sheep Creek Peak   *9,950 feet (Class 2)*

Sheep Creek Peak is found 2 miles southeast of Sheep Mountain, between Sheep Creek and Little Elk Creek. Climb this peak from Sheep Creek via FST-096 [(A)(4)(a)], which crosses its west ridge, or from FST-151 [(A)(5)(a)], which provides access to the peak's north ridge. Both routes are roughly 2.5 miles in length. Neither ridge presents any objective difficulty. USGS Palisades Dam

Mount Baird   *10,025 feet (Class 3)*

The highest Snake River Range peak is situated on the high ridge that divides Big Elk and Little Elk Creeks. Baird was named for Spencer Baird, a secretary of the Smithsonian Institution and a benefactor of the Hayden Survey. Its summit is reached via Little Elk Creek Trail [(A)(3)(b)]. Take the trail to the saddle west of the peak. The summit is visible from the trail as you approach the saddle. Climb the peak via its north ridge, a rewarding scramble on unstable terrain. The crux is a short gully just below the summit. The view north to the Grand Tetons is memorable. The first ascent was by the Hayden Survey, probably O. St. John, in 1877. USGS Mount Baird

Elkhorn Peak   *9,988 feet (Class 2)*

Elkhorn Peak sits 0.5 mile south of Mount Baird. It can be climbed from Mount Baird by traversing down Baird's south ridge to a saddle and then climbing up Elkhorn's north ridge. The summit also can be reached via a steep gully that climbs out of Little Elk Creek to the saddle north of the peak. USGS Mount Baird

Needle Peak   *9,449 feet (Class 3)*

Needle Peak sits 3 miles southeast of Elkhorn Peak just west of the Idaho/Wyoming border. The USGS has attached the

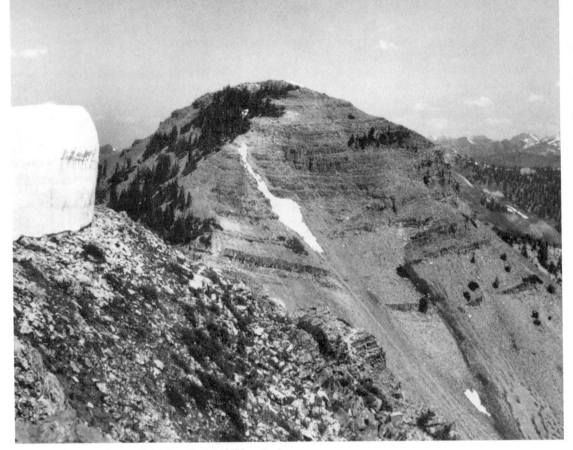

The chiseled summit of Mount Baird, from the top of Elkhorn Peak

name Needle Peak to a high point on the peak's north ridge. The true summit is designated by elevation number 9449. The peak is climbed from Quaker Flat, which can be reached from either the Blowout Canyon Trail [(A)(7)(a)] or from Big Elk Creek via FST-108 [(A)(6)(b)]. At the top of Quaker Flat, a sign high up on a tree trunk marks the trail to the summit. The trail is no longer maintained and the ascent from this point is a serious bushwhack. Follow the ridge 0.5 mile east to the summit. USGS Mount Baird

Mount Richards*　　　　　　　*9,660+ feet (Class 2)*
According to Rick Baugher, this peak, which is half in Idaho and half in Wyoming, is named after Alonzo Richards who surveyed this portion of the Idaho/Wyoming border in 1874. Mount Richards is 2 miles south of Needle Peak. Climb the peak from Blowout Canyon [(A)(7)(a)]. Hike up the trail until its junction with the Quaker Flat Trail. Follow the left-hand trail toward Spaulding Basin until reaching a saddle above Spring Run. From this point, scramble toward Point 8496 and then east toward the summit. USGS Mount Baird

APPROACHES TO THE BIG HOLE MOUNTAINS AND THE SNAKE RIVER RANGE

(A) US-26 ACCESS POINTS

US-26 runs east from Idaho Falls through Swan Valley and on to Alpine Junction in Wyoming. The following approach points are described from west to east.

(1) Heise/Kelly Canyon Road. This road begins 13.7 miles east of Idaho Falls at a signed junction. From this point, it is roughly 8 miles to the Kelly Canyon Ski Area. This road forks just before it enters Kelly Canyon. The right fork, FS-206 (a dirt road), leads east along the Snake River to Wolverine Creek, Big Burns Creek, and Black Canyon. The left fork, FS-218/FS-217, leads to the ski area and then continues into the mountains before rejoining FS-206 along the Snake River.

(a) FST-082, Wolverine Creek Trail. There are two major routes up Wolverine Creek. Neither are well-maintained, but both offer a good deal of solitude and are especially pleasant for early-season day hikes. The east fork of Wolverine Canyon features unique, 40-foot-high rock "tepees." Look for these formations roughly 1 mile into the valley in a stand of aspen on the west side of the trail.

(b) FST-068, Big Burns Creek Trail. This trail is located along the Snake River roughly 14.3 miles east of Heise. Turn north off FS-206 and follow a bumpy road 0.5 mile to the trailhead. The trail accesses the entire Big Hole backcountry. The trail is maintained in reasonably good shape.

(b.1) FST-071, Little Burns Canyon Trail. This trail leaves FST-068 3 miles northeast of its trailhead and proceeds east to connect with FST-073 [(A)(1)(c)] just west of Chicken Peak.

(c) FST-073, Black Canyon Trail. This trail starts in the next major canyon east of Big Burns Creek. Access it by following FS-206 east for another 1.4 miles from Big Burns Creek . FST-073 links with the Little Burns Canyon Trail, FST-071 (described above), before continuing north to a junction with FST-072.

(2) FS-257, Rainey Creek Road. This road leaves US-26 just east of Swan Valley and works its way 5 miles northeast into the Rainey Creek Canyon to a developed trailhead. This road also can be reached from US-26, where a road leaves the hamlet of Irwin and proceeds due north to the mouth of Rainey Creek.

(a) FST-089, Rainey Creek Trail. FST-089 begins as a closed road at the end of FS-257 and follows Rainey Creek north to FST-253 [(B)(2)(a)] at the top of the Snake River crest. As with most trails in these mountains, be prepared to wade. Rainey Creek is closed to all entry during some springs to protect wildlife.

(a.1) FST-092, Cross Divide Trail. This trail leaves FST-089 2 miles northeast of its trailhead, then continues due east to the Palisades Creek drainage, crossing the divide between Atkinson Peak and Baldy Mountain in 6.5 scenic miles.

(a.2) FST-092, Dry Elk Canyon Trail. This trail leaves FST-089 at the confluence of the north and south forks of Rainey Creek and runs east to a junction with FST-091 [(A)(2)(a.2.1)] just south of Thompson Peak.

(a.2.1) FST-091, Thompson Divide Trail. This trail follows the Thompson Peak divide north from FST-092 to FST-050 [(B)(2)(a)].

(3) FS-255, Palisades Creek Access. Take US-26 52 miles east of Idaho Falls or 10 miles east of Swan Valley to Irwin and the Palisades Creek Road. FS-255 quickly leads up the road to a trailhead and campground.

(a) FST-084, Palisades Creek Trail. This trail gains roughly 600 feet in its first 4 miles, bringing the hiker to Lower Palisades Lake. There are a few camping spaces at the lake's southern end, along with pit toilets. The trail continues along the western side of the lake up the canyon toward Upper Palisades Lake. The farther upstream you go, the more wild the country. Expect more than twenty difficult fords of the creek in high water.

(a.1) FST-092, Cross Divide Trail. See [(A)(2)(a.1)], above.

(a.1.2) FST-091, Thompson Divide Trail. See [(A)(2)(a.2.1)], above.

(b) FST-099/FST-118/FST-097, Palisades Peak Loop Trail. These trails form a 12-mile loop through the Snake River Range high country. Begin this loop by leaving the Palisade Creek Trail 1.5 miles north of Lower Palisades Lake and hiking east to Upper Palisades Lake. Just above the lake, the trail forks into three routes. Stay left at these route junctions and follow the trail north to a saddle between Palisades and Little Palisades Peaks. From this point, the trail descends northwest to rejoin Palisades Creek.

(c) FST-102. This trail leaves the Palisades Creek Trail just south of Lower Palisades Lake and crosses east over a divide to Sheep Creek. See [(A)(4)(a)], below.

(4) FS-260, Sheep Creek Access. This road is 3 miles east of Palisades Creek. The road stretches a short distance into the mountains and then turns into a seldom-used trail.

(a) FST-096/FST-102. This trail climbs out of Sheep Creek, crosses a divide east of Sheep Mountain, and then drops into the Palisades drainage.

(5) FS-268, Little Elk Creek Access. Take US-26 2.5 miles east of Palisades Dam and turn left on the good gravel road that leaves the highway just west of where a causeway leads across the reservoir. Follow this road to its end.

(a) FST-151, Little Elk Creek Trail. This steep, but well-maintained trail runs up Little Elk Creek to a pass just east of Mount Baird in just over 3 miles. At the pass, the trail forks. FST-099 descends Waterfall Canyon to Upper Palisades Lake, [(A)(3)(b)]. FST-104 leads to several side trails that head east into Wyoming and north to the far side of Palisades Peak.

(6) Big Elk Creek Access. Take US-26 4.5 miles east of Palisades Dam and turn onto the gravel road that leads up Big Elk Creek. Follow the road to its end in 2.4 miles at a YMCA camp.

(a) FST-097, Big Elk Creek Trail. This trail leaves the trailhead and ascends Big Elk Creek into Wyoming. In Wyoming, two feeder trails can be taken back into Idaho.

(b) FST-108, Quaker Flat Trail. This trail, which is not shown the Mount Baird USGS quad, leaves the trailhead and goes around a Boy Scout camp and then up a draw to the saddle between Big Elk Creek and Booth Canyon. At the saddle, the trail divides. The right fork descends Booth Canyon to US-26. The main trail, which is not well marked, cuts up the north side hill and then continues to Quaker Flat and Blowout Canyon, [(A)(7)(a)].

(7) FS-271, Blowout Canyon Road. This road leaves US-26 about 5 miles east of Palisades Dam at a signed junction. The road is 2 miles long and passable to autos.

(a) Blowout Canyon Trail. This trail climbs up the canyon and over the rubble of a rock slide. Just 1.1 miles up the canyon, the trail forks. The right fork goes into Wyoming, and the left fork, FST-108, leads to Quaker Flat [(A)(6)(b)]. Quaker Flat is a beautiful high-altitude meadow. Take the left fork toward Quaker Flat and Needle Peak. Another steep mile brings you to the top of Quaker Flat. The left fork of the trail descends to Booth Canyon and Big Elk Creek [(A)(6)(a)]. The right fork—shown on the USGS quad but not on the Forest Service map—is the Needle Peak Trail. It passes along the south side of Needle Peak before dropping into Wyoming.

(B) ID-31 ACCESS POINTS

This road leaves US-26 at Swan Valley and leads northeast to Victor in 21 miles, crossing the mountains at Pine Creek Pass.

(1) Pine Creek Access. Take ID-31 from Swan Valley north toward Driggs for 9.2 miles. Turn onto the Pine Creek Road and follow it to its end in 0.5 mile.

(a) FST-078, West Pine Creek Pass. This trail leaves ID-31 at a signed trailhead about 4 miles northeast of where the highway enters the mountains. The trail runs northwest up West Pine Creek to Trail Canyon. It then climbs up Trail Canyon and joins FST-072 [(A)(1)(c)] in 5 miles.

(b) FST-050, Pine Creek Trail. This trail leaves from ID-31 where North Fork Pine Creek flows into Pine Creek. (Look for a turn with a sign announcing an organizational camp.) The trail follows the North Fork Pine east to Elk Flat in 12 miles. Over its course, this trail encounters a good cross-section of Big Hole terrain. It eventually joins up with the central Big Hole trail system.

(2) Pine Creek Summit Area. This pass, crossed by ID-31, is on the Big Hole/Snake River crest. When snow conditions are stable, good cross-country skiing is available on both the east and west sides of the highway.

(a) Snake River Range Crest Trail. From Pine Creek summit, follow the gravel road east to its end. FST-050 leaves the end of the road, follows the crest over Fourth of July Peak, and then continues to the Big Elk drainage.

(b) FST-053, Big Hole Crest Trail. This seldom-used trail begins on Pine Creek Summit and quickly climbs west to the ridge top above. From here, the trail follows the undulating ridge west and eventually connects with the central trail system [(A)(1)(a)].

(C) ID-33 ACCESS POINTS

From Driggs, a county road leads directly west for 12 miles to Horseshoe and Mahogany Canyons.

(1) Horseshoe Canyon and Mahogany Canyon Access. Both canyons contain trails that lead into Big Hole backcountry near Garns Peak. The Mahogany Canyon trail system is the preferred route.

(a) Central Big Hole Trail System. From the Horseshoe Canyon trailhead, FST-056, the Elk Flat Trail continues south to the top of the Horseshoe drainage where it connects with the central trail system. This system includes trails that connect with every other trailhead listed in this section.

(2) Oliver Peak Access. Take ID-33 south from Victor for 3.5 miles and turn onto the road signed for the Mike Harris CG. Just before the CG, turn left on the road that parallels Trail Creek and follow it for another 0.5 mile to a junction where the trail begins. A 4WD is recommended.

(a) FST-049, Micksell Canyon Trail. This trail leaves the junction described above to the right and follows a jeep track for a short distance before narrowing to a trail. It makes a 1,600-foot climb up to a ridgeline that runs from northwest to southeast. It is about 3.8 miles to the jump-off point for climbing Oliver.

SOUTHERN IDAHO

From the Snake River South to the Utah and Nevada Borders

1

THE OWYHEE MOUNTAINS

The Owyhee Mountains are the home of cowboys, miners, and quasi-feudal estates. The range has also been described as "the land the environmentalist forgot." Resource exploitation has dominated the range's human history. For every hiker, there are probably one hundred motorcyclists, 4WD enthusiasts, and miners. Cattle are everywhere and NO TRESPASSING signs are more common than directional signs. In short, these mountains have many problems. Yet, the Owyhee Mountains have many excellent qualities, too. The country is still primitive. The hiking season is long. The views are expansive. With a little loving care by land managers, the purchase of a few easements, and the publishing of a good map, the range would become a very popular destination for hikers.

The range extends from the Oregon border eastward for 50 miles across southwestern Idaho. This range is bounded by the Oregon border in the west, the Nevada border in the south, the Snake River in the north, and the barren plains of central Idaho in the east. Owyhee was the name originally used by Captain Cook for the Hawaiian Islands. It was attached to these mountains after several Hawaiian trappers vanished in the area in 1818. The name Silver City Range is sometimes used to identify the mountains that surround Silver City, and the southeastern extension of the range is often called the Ruby Mountains.

The Owyhee Mountains were forced up by the Owyhee Batholith 40 million years ago. Some geologists believe that Owyhee granite is part of the Idaho Batholith, isolated from the main batholith by the passage of the Yellowstone hotspot. Much of the range's granite is covered by Miocene rhyolite that erupted as a result of a meteorite impact 17 million

Sherman Peak is characteristic of southern Idaho's mountains.

343

years ago. The range is surrounded by the younger volcanic rocks of the Snake River Plain, and is still covered in places by extensive deposits of older sedimentary rock. Where Owyhee granite has been exposed to the surface, it has formed impressive outcroppings and an occasional dome. However, the granite is somewhat soft and has been plastered with various water-deposited materials, which gives it a poor climbing surface. Hayden Peak, at 8,403 feet, is the range's highest peak.

The formation of the batholith created zones of extensive mineralization, which were discovered during the Civil War. Soon after the discovery, Silver City was established. Today, the town does not have a single permanent resident—but midsummer finds the Silver City area thronged with sightseers and ORV enthusiasts who congregate around the town like an encampment of modern-day gypsies. This area's popularity with the off-roaders significantly detracts from the quality of the superb recreation opportunities available.

The entire range is administered by the BLM. While recreational use of the Owyhees is the current rage, the more traditional consumptive uses of mining and grazing still dictate the pulse of Owyhee life. Mining has historically dominated human use of the range, and while it has ebbed and flowed in importance over the years, it is currently on the upswing. De Lamar Mountain is the site of the world's largest open-pit silver mine as well as smaller-scale prospecting operations, all with the blessing of lackadaisical federal mining laws.

There are no officially maintained hiking trails within the range, but many trails and old mining roads do exist. Be forewarned: The entire range receives heavy use by off-road

This unnamed granite dome near Silver City is one of the many granite outcroppings that can be found throughout the Owyhee Mountains.

vehicles. If you go hiking in the range on a summer weekend, the noise around Silver City can be very annoying. Climbing is limited to Class 1 and Class 2 ascents, but this chapter only scratches the surface of hiking and climbing opportunities in the Owyhees. The real joy of the Owyhee Mountains is not in its summits, but in its lower-elevation canyons and its vast southern stretches, which are still in a wilderness condition. See Sheldon Bluestein's *Exploring Idaho's High Desert* at www.hikeidaho.com for information on several enjoyable Owyhee hikes.

Rooster Comb Peak   6,390 feet (Class 2-3)
Rooster Comb Peak is located at the headwaters of Succor and Crane Creeks. It has a rock rib on its top that is very distinctive when viewed from the north. The peak is Class 2 when approached from the east, west, or north. Climb Rooster Comb from the north [(A)(1)]. From the parking area by the corrals, wade across the steam and follow the road west for about 100 yards to a gate. Continue along the road until you reach a small drainage descending from the east. Climb this drainage to the base of the summit block. From this point, pick the easiest route and climb to the summit through thick brush. USGS Rooster Comb Peak

War Eagle Mountain   8,051 feet (Class 2)
War Eagle Mountain sits 1.5 miles southeast of Silver City. It is the northernmost of the four big peaks—War Eagle, Turntable Mountain, Hayden Peak, and Quicksilver—that form the northern escarpment easily viewable from Boise. The summit of this peak, reached by a 4WD road, is covered with radio towers. The summit also can be reached on foot from Silver City via its juniper-covered western slopes [(A)(2)(a.1)]. Watch out for snakes! USGS Cinnabar Mountain

Turntable Mountain   8,122 feet (Class 2)
Turntable Mountain sits just southeast of War Eagle Mountain and northwest of Hayden Peak. The same 4WD road that gives access to War Eagle runs past the summit only 200 vertical feet below [(A)(2)(a.1)]. USGS Cinnabar Mountain

Hayden Peak   8,403 feet (Class 2)
The USGS map identifies Cinnabar Mountain's highest point as Hayden Peak. The highest point in the Owyhees is a long, but easy walk from Silver City. It is located 2 miles southeast of War Eagle Mountain. Reach the peak directly from the Silver City Road by turning south on the Linehan Flat Road located midway between New York summit and Jordan Creek. Follow this jeep trail south to the saddle between Hayden and War Eagle peaks in roughly 6 miles. From the saddle, another jeep trail leads nearly to the summit [(A)(2)(a)]. USGS Cinnabar Mountain

Quicksilver Mountain   8,082 feet (Class 2)
Quicksilver Mountain is the southernmost of the range's big four peaks. It has three summits and is located 2 miles southeast of Hayden Peak. Quicksilver is about as wild of peak as you can find in the Owyhees. It is a pleasant hike in the early summer with a terrific view of the Snake River Plain and the Boise Mountains to the north. Because of access problems, the best approach is from the south from the Boulder Creek/Silver City Road [(A)(3.1)]. Park where the road crosses the saddle between Bridge Creek and North Boulder Creek. A jeep trail runs north from this point. Follow this road north until the 7,400-foot contour and then climb directly to the highest summit that is 0.8 mile and 800 feet above. USGS Cinnabar Mountain

Rough Mountain   7,090 feet (Class 2)
Rough Mountain is located at the southeast end of the Owyhees. While not a big mountain, it does rise more than 2,000 feet above the surrounding, desolate country. Climb the peak from the Mud Flat Road [(A)(4.1)]. Leave the Mud Flat Road where it crosses Juniper Creek and follow the two-track course upsteam. This road eventually leads to Half Moon Pass. Park at the pass and then hike southwest to the summit 0.8 mile away. USGS Rough Mountain

APPROACHES TO THE OWYHEE MOUNTAINS

OWYHEE MOUNTAIN ACCESS
Primary access is via several major highways: I-84 runs to the north of the range, US-95 cuts along the western border, and state highways ID-78 and ID-51 run along the eastern fringes of the range. Besides the major paved highways, Owyhee County maintains several unpaved roads. Although rough and winding, they do provide access to almost every corner of these mountains. Within the range, an extensive system of primitive roads and abandoned mining roads makes the Owyhees easily accessible to 4WDs, motorcycles, mountain bikes, horses, and hikers. The internal Owyhee roads are often open between April and November. Be forewarned that many roads cross private property and are closed to the public.

(A) ID-78 ACCESS ROUTES
ID-78 runs along the northern edge of the range from

Quicksilver Mountain's north side

Marsing in the northwest to Murphy (and ID-45) in the middle and Bruneau in the southeast.

(1) **Reynolds/Rooster Comb Peak Access.** From the ID-45/ID-78 intersection take ID-78 north for 1.1 mile to the Reynolds Creek Road. Turn left on this paved road. The pavement ends in 9.5 miles. At 13.7 miles you will reach Reynolds and a junction for Hill Road. Turn left on Hill Road. After another 1.4 miles, two roads go off to the right. Turn on the second. After another 3.7 miles you will reach yet another junction, go right again. After 0.9 mile you will reach a gate. Go left this time and follow this road due south for 1.4 miles to a set of corrals. This is the starting point for Rooster Comb Peak.

(2) **Murphy/Silver City Road Access.** Drive south from I-84 at Nampa on ID-78 to Murphy. Just south of Murphy, a well-signed dirt road leads south and crosses over New York summit into the heart of the Owyhees. This winding, narrow road can be crowded on summer weekends, so be prepared for oncoming traffic on your side of the road. From the beginning of the road, it is 18 miles to Silver City, 21 miles to Dewey, 25 miles to De Lamar [(B)(1)], and 53 miles to Jordan Valley, Oregon.

(a) **Jordan Creek Area.** Although there are no designated trails within the Owyhees, the old mining roads allow you to penetrate the brushy lower slopes and reach the relatively open upper slopes where no trails are needed. Within the Silver City area, the Jordan Creek drainage acts as a major conduit that can be used to reach locations throughout the drainage. South of Silver City, the road quickly dwindles down to a jeep trail. The jeep trail follows the creek south and eventually climbs to the top of the drainage in 3.5 miles. At this point, it joins a two-track road that leads east to the War Eagle Mountain/Hayden Peak area and west to several destinations.

(a.1) **War Eagle Mountain Jeep Trails.** This area begins 0.25 mile south of Silver City at a ford of Jordan Creek. Cross the creek and follow the well-worn jeep trail southeast and then due east to a saddle south of War Eagle Mountain where it joins the Linehan Flat Road.

(2.1) **Linehan Flat Road.** This road is reached from the Silver City Road, midway between New York summit and Jordan Creek. The road continues south for 3 miles to where it joins a jeep trail leading up from Silver City [(A)(1)(a.1)]. After this junction, the road continues south for another mile to a second junction. From this point, the left fork goes southeast to Pickett Creek saddle.

(a) **Hayden Peak Jeep Trail.** This primitive road leaves the Linehan Flat Road on the northeast side of Hayden Peak and climbs to the summit of Hayden Peak in 1.5 miles. It is recommended that you walk this jeep trail.

(3) **Oreana/Triangle Access.** From Murphy, drive southeast on ID-78 for 13.3 miles. Turn south on the paved road signed

for Oreana, which is 2.25 miles to the south. Turn left onto the Triangle Road. After 13.8 miles from ID-78, the road crosses Toy Pass. In another 3.9 miles this road intersects with the Boulder Creek/Silver City Road. From this junction the road continues south to Spencer Reservoir and a major junction. The road south toward Triangle is closed to the public in about 1.5 miles. The road heading west provides access to a large chunk of the range, but may be closed by private land owners.

(3.1) **Boulder Creek/Silver City Road.** Follow this road west to Silver City in 19 miles. Keep left at 0.2 mile, then turn right after 1.2 miles. At 2.2 miles, go left. A 4WD is required.

(4) **Mud Flat Road.** Access this road near Grand View. Follow ID-78 south from Grand View and then bear right onto the Shoofly Road. Shoofly then intersects with Poison Creek Road, go right and follow Poison Creek Road southwest to a junction with Castle Creek Road. Keep left and you are now on the Mud Flat Road. Continue southwest until it crosses Juniper Creek.

(4.1) **Juniper Creek/Half Moon Pass Road.** This road leaves the Mud Flat Road and climbs to Half Moon Pass. A 4WD is required.

(B) US-95 ACCESS

US-95 runs south from I-84 to Jordan Valley, Oregon, and beyond. It passes many roads that lead into the Owyhees. Only one is listed in this guidebook.

(1) **De Lamar Silver Mine Road.** Take US-95 south toward Jordan Valley, Oregon. Near Shearville, two routes lead east into the Silver City area. Both dirt roads are more than 30 miles long. The road to the De Lamar Silver Mine is kept open to the mine throughout the winter.

2

THE GOOSE CREEK MOUNTAINS

This group of mountains located south of Twin Falls and southwest of Burley is also known as the South Hills and the Cassia Mountains. These mountains stretch roughly 25 miles from north to south and 20 miles from east to west, forming

a group of complicated ridges and peaks—8,050-foot Monument Peak is the highest summit. One of the most prominent features of the Goose Creek Mountains is a long north/south ridgeline known as Deadline Ridge, which runs from Grand View Peak south into Utah. The range has a sedimentary foundation covered by thick deposits of rhyolite.

The Goose Creek Mountains are administered by the Sawtooth National Forest, which maintains an extensive road system within its boundaries. Primary access begins either from Twin Falls or from Oakley. Beyond the primary approaches, scores of roadways offer secondary access to almost every drainage within the range.

Although almost every valley and basin is penetrated by a road, there is only one designated hiking trail within the range. Nevertheless, the range has many open ridges conducive to cross-country travel. The range includes nineteen named summits ranging in elevation from 7,100 to 8,000 feet. While hikers and climbers may be put off by the many roads within the range, these roads are perfect for mountain bike excursions and allow for many quick ascents.

Monument Peak   *8,050 feet (Class 1)*

Monument Peak is 18 miles southwest of Oakley in the central part of the Goose Creek Mountains. Take FS-515 south to the Porcupine CG. Turn onto FS-538 and follow it to FS-671. Follow FS-671 for 1 mile and then turn east on the short dirt road that leads to the summit. USGS Trapper Peak

APPROACHES TO THE GOOSE CREEK MOUNTAINS

(A) TWIN FALLS ACCESS

Twin Falls, one of Idaho's largest cities, is reached via I-84 and US-93. All necessary services are available.

(1) **FS-515, Rock Creek Canyon Road.** To access this road, which leads south from Twin Falls into the Sawtooth National Forest (where it becomes FS-515), drive to the Magic Mountain Ski Area. This road continues past the ski area and links up with FS-500 [(B)(1)].

(B) OAKLEY ACCESS

The village of Oakley is reached from I-84 and Burley by taking ID-27 south from Burley for 26.5 miles. Food and gas are available in Oakley.

(1) **FS-500, Cottonwood Creek Road.** This road runs from downtown Oakley due west into the Goose Creek Mountains and eventually links with FST-515 south of Rock Creek CG [(A)(1)].

3

THE ALBION RANGE

The Albion Range extends 25 miles north from the Idaho/Utah border to a point just southeast of Burley. The range varies in width from 10 to 25 miles and includes a parallel southwestern ridgeline named Middle Mountain, and an eastern ridgeline known as the Malta Range. On the main Albion crest, Cache Peak reaches an elevation of 10,339 feet, making it not only the highest Albion peak, but also the highest point in Idaho south of the Snake River.

The main Albion crest is composed of two large, rolling ridges separated by a low saddle. In the north, Mount Harrison reaches 9,265 feet and in the south Cache Peak is the high point. The largest glacial cirque in southern Idaho is nestled in the northeast slopes of this mountain. It holds several mountain lakes, which is rare in the mostly dry mountains of southern Idaho.

The geology of the range is complicated and not yet fully understood. Basin and range faulting has lifted Paleozoic sedimentary rocks as well as very old Precambrian rocks.

From a climber's perspective, the range is highlighted by the 40-square-mile Cassia Batholith, which pushed up into the earth's crust some 28 million years ago. This batholith's granite, exposed at the southern end of the range, is popularly known as the City of Rocks. The City is a rock-climbing Mecca, with an assortment of towers, spires, and faces of hard, clean, and readily accessible granite. The variety of routes, both established and unclimbed, is unlimited. Most routes present one-to-two-pitch problems with routes rated as high as 5.14. Several rock-climbing guides to the City of Rocks have been published over the last fifteen years and access [(A)(3)] is excellent.

Most of the Albion Range is managed by the Sawtooth National Forest. Many sections along the range's foothills are managed by the BLM. In 1988, Congress declared the City of Rocks a Natural Reserve. The reserve is cooperatively managed by the National Park Service and the Idaho Department of Parks and Recreation. The reserve's management has improved facilities and increased the protection, but it also has led to decreases in the freedom once enjoyed by climbers. Overall, the tradeoff has worked well.

The Albion Range has an extensive road system and a small trail system. Beyond the City of Rocks, recreational use of the glacial cirque below Cache Peak is high, but the rest of the area sees little use by hikers. The terrain is open and the

The City of Rocks, with Graham Peak in the background

spectacular vistas make it well worth your time to explore cross-country. Road access is relatively good.

THE MALTA RANGE

The Idaho Encyclopedia identified the barren ridge that lies in the afternoon shadow of the Albion Range as the Malta Range. The USGS has since identified this ridge as the Cotterrel Mountains in the north and the Jim Sage Mountains in the south. This subrange, which is visible from I-84, looks like a high desert plateau and is a rugged piece of real estate dominated by junipers, rocky cliffs, and ragged, red-tinted rock outcroppings. In the east, this escarpment rises precipitously above the town of Malta and the Raft River. On the west, the range merges into the Albion Range. The Jim Sage Mountains reach an elevation of 8,046 feet on a mountain top sometimes identified as Elba Peak. This area is administered by the BLM and the state of Idaho. [(A)(4)].

THE ALBION RANGE

Mount Harrison   *9,265 feet (Class 2)*

Mount Harrison, named after President Benjamin Harrison, is located 16 miles southeast of Burley. The peak, which sports a fire lookout, has an excellent view of the Snake River Plain and, on clear days, the mountains of central Idaho. To reach the summit from the northeast, hike or mountain bike up FS-549 [(A)(1)] from Cleveland Lake. For a more interesting and rewarding trip to the top of this peak, follow the ridgeline north from FS-548 and Elba Pass [(A)(2)]. This journey covers roughly 7 undulating miles (14 miles round trip) of the Albion crest. USGS Mount Harrison

Mount Independence   *9,950 feet (Class 2-3)*

Mount Independence, located 7 miles due south of Mount Harrison and 10 miles southeast of Oakley, is a somewhat pointed peak that rises out of the rolling crest and towers over the Independence Lakes cirque. Its east face, the most precipitous wall in southern Idaho, drops 900 feet in less than 0.25 mile. The summit can be approached from almost any direction. USGS Cache Peak

South Ridge (Class 2-3). This route leads up from the Independence Lakes [(A)(2.1)(a)] to the saddle between Cache Peak and Mount Independence. Hike to a point midway between the upper two Independence Lakes and look for a gully that splits the lower east end of the east face. This gully leads up to a point roughly 100 feet above the saddle. Climb to the south ridge and then hike up to the summit.

If you run into any sections along the ridge that are beyond your abilities, move off the crest and onto the western slopes, which are much easier.

North Slopes (Class 2). Mount Independence also can be climbed from almost anywhere along the Rangers Trail, FST-012 [(A)(2.1)(a)]. Hike FST-012 east from the trailhead until it enters a large meadow (the second clearing on the USGS quad). Leave the trail and hike due north. This route is filled with brush in its lower stretches, but despite this inconvenience, it does lead to the summit in only 2 miles.

Cache Peak   *10,339 feet*

The highest Albion Range summit sits 1.1 mile southeast of Mount Independence. Cache Peak, like Mount Independence, can be approached from almost any direction. Because of approach considerations, however, it is best climbed from the Independence Lakes. The first known ascent was by Fred Clark of the Wheeler Survey in 1877. USGS Cache Peak

Northwest Ridge (Class 2). From the saddle between Cache Peak and Mount Independence, the northwest ridge of Cache Peak provides a 0.5-mile route to the summit. (To reach the saddle, follow the South Ridge route for Mount Independence.) While there are no real obstacles along the peak's northwest ridge, the trees are clumped so close together that progress is often difficult. The higher you get on this route, the easier the journey.

South Slopes (Class 2). The peak's broad southern slopes can be reached from the Rangers Trail [(A)(2.1)(a) or (A)(3.1) (a)] from any number of points.

Graham Peak   *8,867 feet (Class 3)*

Graham Peak is located 5.5 miles southwest of Cache Peak, due north of the City of Rocks. This peak is accessed from FS-562 [(A)(3.1)], which follows the Albion crest north and passes along Graham's western slopes to within 200 feet of the summit. At the northwest end of the summit, an old road can be followed almost to the top of the peak. USGS Almo

APPROACHES TO THE ALBION RANGE

(A) ALBION RANGE ACCESS

ID-27 and ID-77 are on the range's west and east sides, respectively. A combination of county and Forest Service roads traverse the southern part of the range between Oakley, City of Rocks, Almo, and Elba.

(1) FS-549, Cleveland Lake Road. This road leads to Cleveland Lake and Harrison Peak in the northern section of the range.

Dome-shaped Cache Peak, the highest Albion Range peak, from Mount Independence.

To reach FS-549, take ID-77 south from Albion for 4.5 miles and turn west. This road is signed for the Pommerel Ski Area.

(2) **FS-548, Elba to Oakley Road.** This road connects Elba and Oakley, crossing the range at Elba Pass. The road is easily found in either village. This road is steep, narrow, and can be difficult to drive when wet. A 4WD is not absolutely required, but is highly recommended.

(2.1) **FS-562, Pot Holes Road.** At Elba Pass, take FS-562 south toward the Pot Holes. Drive past the Pot Holes and turn onto a rough road. This road eventually merges into FS-728, which leads into the Dry Creek drainage and the trailhead for FST-012 at 4.7 miles from the pass.

(a) **FST-012, Rangers Trail.** This trail, which circles Cache Peak, begins in Dry Creek from a well-developed trailhead at 7,000 feet. From the trailhead, the Rangers Trail runs east and then south around the fringes of Mount Independence. After 2 miles, it intersects with the Independence Lakes Trail, FST-035, which continues due west to the lakes. From this junction, the Rangers Trail is signed but difficult to follow as it continues its course around Cache Peak.

(3) **City of Rocks Access.** To visit the City of Rocks, drive along I-84 to the Malta-Sublett exit, roughly 32 miles north of the Utah border. Drive west from the exit through the villages of Malta, Elba, and Almo on a good paved road. From just south

of Almo, you take a good gravel road another 6 miles until you reach the City of Rocks.

(3.1) FS-562, Graham Peak Access. FS-562 is accessed just east of the City of Rocks. Follow the main road through the City to the west, cross over a low saddle, and immediately look for FS-562, which leaves the main road in a large meadow. This road runs 3 miles north along the west side of the Albion crest to the northern slopes of Graham Peak. After passing Graham Peak, the road continues north and follows a ridgeline to upper Aspen Creek where there is an undeveloped trailhead for the Rangers Trail, FST-012 [(A)(2.1)(a)]. A 4WD is recommended.

(a) FST-012, Rangers Trail. See [(A)(2.1)(a)], above.

(4) Malta Range Access. Roads penetrate into many parts of the Malta Range. Primary approach is via two state highways. ID-77 follows the west and south sides and ID-81 follows the east side. There are no hiking trails.

4

THE BLACK PINE MOUNTAINS

The Black Pine Mountains are located just north of the Utah border and west of I-84. Geographically the range, which is 17 miles in length and 7 miles in width, is the most distinctly defined mountain range in Idaho. It is surrounded by wide, flat valleys, and rises steeply on all sides. Geologically, the range is a textbook example of a Great Basin mountain range. The fault block, which forms the entire range, rises to 9,395 feet on Black Peak and is surrounded on all sides by broad alluvial fans.

The Black Pine Mountains are managed by the Sawtooth National Forest and are seldom visited by climbers or hikers. A mining company has operated an open-pit gold mine on the range's eastern side since 1990. While the severe mining abuses of the past have not reoccurred, the aesthetic impact of the mine cannot be erased. Since so few knew about this range, there was little public participation into the permit process.

Hikers should place this isolated escarpment on their lists

of places to visit. This tiny mountain range offers exceptionally good hiking opportunities that are truly away from the crowds. While the Black Pine peaks are only Class 2 climbs, the view of the Great Salt Lake from the southern end of the range alone is worth the price of admission. Road access to the range is good, but remote. Be fully prepared for any contingency.

Black Peak*   *9,395 feet (Class 2)*

Black Peak, identified on the USGS quad as the Black triangulation station, is the highest of the Black Pine summits. It is located at the north end of the range between Pole Canyon to the east and Little Eightmile Canyon to the west. The USGS survey marker is found on a point about 10 feet lower than the true summit. Black Peak can be climbed from almost any direction, but because of approach considerations, it is suggested that you climb it from either Pole Canyon or from Black Pine Peak. The traverse over from Black Pine Peak involves roughly 1.25 miles of scenic ridge-walking across easy terrain. USGS Sandrock Canyon/Sweetzer Canyon

Black Pine Peak   *9,385 feet (Class 2)*

Black Pine Peak is 1.25 miles south of Black Peak. Climb this summit from Kelsaw Canyon [(A)(3.1)(a)] or Pole Canyon [(A)(1.1)(a)], which are linked by FST-018. Follow the trail to the south side of War Eagle Peak. Leave the trail at this point, climb over War Eagle Peak and then traverse the connecting ridgeline to Black Pine Peak. Total distance from the trail is about 1.5 miles with an 800-foot elevation gain. USGS Black Pine Peak

War Eagle Peak   *8,720 feet (Class 2)*

War Eagle Peak is a very minor summit. Actually, it is only a bump on the south ridge of Black Pine Peak. Access the peak via its south slopes from FST-018 [(A)(1.1)(a)] or [(A)(3.1)(a)]. USGS Black Pine Peak

Black Pine Cone   *8,008 feet (Class 2)*

Black Pine Cone is, as might be expected, a cone-shaped summit located 3 miles southeast of War Eagle Peak and just east of Black Pine Canyon. Climb from either Mineral Gulch [(A)(1.2)] or Black Pine Canyon [(A)(2)]. USGS Black Pine Peak

Gunnell Peak*   *8,316 feet (Class 2)*

Gunnell Peak is identified as the Gunnel triangulation station on the USGS quad. It sits 2.5 miles southwest of War Eagle Peak and provides the best Idaho view of Great Salt Lake. Climb to the summit of this peak via its northern slopes

The windswept crest of the Black Pine Mountains is nearly uniform in height as it runs from north to south.

from Kelsaw Canyon [(A)(3.1)]. This route follows the peak's partially forested northeast ridge, which climbs to the summit in 1 mile with an elevation gain of 2,300 feet. USGS Strevell/ Black Pine Peak

APPROACHES TO THE BLACK PINE MOUNTAINS

(A) BLACK PINE MOUNTAIN ACCESS

Primary approach to this range is via ID-81 on the west side, I-84 on its east side, and Utah-42 along the range's southern slopes.

(1) FS-187, East Side Road. This road parallels the Black Pines' east side. To access this road, exit I-84 at the Juniper exit (13 miles north of the Utah border) and drive to the west side of the freeway. The dirt road immediately turns south, leading to the southern end of the range in 13 miles.

(1.1) FS-761, Pole Canyon Road. This road leaves FS-587 0.5 mile south of I-84 and proceeds due west into Pole Canyon, ending in 9 miles. A 4WD is recommended.

(a) FST-018, East/West Divide Trail. FST-018 begins in Pole Canyon 0.5 mile before the end of FS-761 and continues up Pole Creek to climb onto the ridge east of the creek. The trail then follows the ridge up to the crest south of War Eagle Peak and ultimately descends into Kelsaw Canyon [(A)(3.1)].

(1.2) FS-198, Mineral Gulch Road. Access this road by taking FS-587 south from I-84 for 4 miles. The road proceeds west up Mineral Gulch for 4 miles. A 4WD is recommended.

(2) Utah Highway 42, Curlew Junction and Black Pine Canyon. Take Utah Highway 42 west from I-84 for 15 miles to Curlew Junction. FS-586 leaves the highway at this point and heads 10 miles north across the Idaho border to Black Pine Canyon.

(3) ID-81, West Side Canyons. The canyons on the western slopes of the Black Pine Mountains are situated 13 miles south of Malta by turning east from ID-81 onto FS-588. This dirt road proceeds east toward the range. After 4.2 miles, the road reaches a junction where FS-767 leads northeast to Eighteenmile and West Canyons. At 5.2 miles, FS-588 makes a 90-degree turn and runs due south to rejoin ID-81 in another 7 miles.

(3.1) FS-589, Kelsaw Canyon Road. This is the most important access road on the west side of the Black Pine Mountains. The road leaves FS-588 just over 5 miles north of ID-81. A 4WD is recommended.

(a) FST-018, East/West Divide Trail. This trail is in poor condition on the west side of the range and difficult to follow after 1 mile. Consider this a cross-country route for now, and write the Forest Service and ask them to fix it [(A)(1.1)(a)].

5

THE SUBLETT MOUNTAINS

The Sublett Mountains are named after trapper William Sublette who passed through Idaho in the early 1800s. The range extends from the Snake River Plain south almost to Snowville on the Idaho/Utah border. From the surrounding valleys, the range resembles a low grouping of rugged hills. The highest point in the range is an unnamed summit that reaches 7,492 feet—7,464-foot Cedar Creek Peak is the highest named summit. The Subletts are yet another product of basin and range faulting. Most of the range's rock is sedimentary, but younger volcanic rocks are found on the surface in places.

The Sawtooth National Forest administers the northern sections of the range, and the BLM administers the southern expanses. While both agencies maintain extensive road networks within the range, there is only one designated hiking trail. Because the Subletts are mostly open, their grass- and sage-covered ridges provide good cross-country hiking opportunities. The range thaws out earlier than most Idaho mountain ranges, and in many years it is possible to hike this country by mid-May. All Sublett peaks are rated Class 2; the ability to navigate by map and compass is the only real requirement.

Cedar Creek Peak   *7,464 feet (Class 2)*
Cedar Creek Peak is located at the northern end of the Sublett Range between North and South Helgar Canyons. The best approach to this peak is from North Helgar Canyon [(A)(1)] via the Spring Canyon drainage. It is roughly 1.5 uneventful miles from the road to the top of Spring Canyon (and Point 7442 on the USGS quad). Once on the summit ridge of Cedar Creek Peak, hike north 0.5 mile to the summit. USGS Sublett

APPROACHES TO THE SUBLETT MOUNTAINS

(A) SUBLETT MOUNTAIN ACCESS

Primary approach to the Sublett Range is via I-84 on the range's western flanks and ID-37 on its eastern side. There are only two approach routes listed below. The range is covered with roads, however, and those with 4WDs can access almost every nook and cranny of these mountains.

(1) **Helgar Canyon Access.** Turn off I-84 at the first exit south of its junction with I-86. Proceed west for 15 miles to where the road forks. The left fork leads to North Helgar Canyon; the right fork leads to South Helgar Canyon. These are good gravel roads, usually passable in dry conditions for two-wheel-drive vehicles. Spring Canyon, the jumping-off point for Cedar Creek Peak, is 8 miles southeast of the junction for North and South Helgar Canyons.

(2) **Sublett Reservoir Access.** Leave I-84 at the Malta-Sublett exit and drive east toward the mountains. After passing through the village of Sublett, the road passes Sublett Reservoir and then forks. The left fork, FS-564, creeps north up Lake Fork Creek; the right fork, FS-578, goes east and northeast up Sublett Creek. Both roads cross saddles and join the Helgar Canyon road [(A)(1)].

6

THE DEEP CREEK MOUNTAINS

The Deep Creek Mountains form a rolling, unbroken escarpment that begins near American Falls and runs south for 30 miles toward Holbrook. Arbon Valley flanks the range on the east; Rockland Valley on the west. Deep Creek Peak is the highest point in the range at 8,748 feet. The range includes several long, well-developed canyons, including Knox Canyon.

Some geologists speculate that the crest of the Deep Creek Mountains is an ancient peneplain (the surface of a former flat plain), which was uplifted roughly 40 million years ago. This ancient surface has been repeatedly eroded, leaving only the crest as a remnant of the high plain that once existed here.

Others speculate that the Deep Creek Mountains were part of the Lost River Range, and that the creation of the Snake River Plain separated the two 18 million years ago. R. Baugher's field observations appear to confirm this hypothesis. He notes that Bannock Peak is similar in structure and appearance to Lost River peaks and that fossils found around Howe Peak and on Deep Creek Peak are a close match.

The BLM administers much of the Deep Creek Mountains. The state of Idaho also controls portions of the range, and the Fort Hall Indian Reservation controls the northern end of the range, including the summit of Bannock Peak. Although the range is without hiking trails, the mostly treeless terrain is suitable for cross-country hiking. Water, although not plentiful, is found in several canyons and at a few springs. Road access is adequate. The best maps available for approach routes are the BLM's Pocatello and Malad City land status maps.

Bannock Peak   *8,263 feet*

With its classic pyramid shape, Bannock Peak is the most impressive of the Deep Creek Mountains peaks. It sits at the north end of the range 14 miles southeast of American Falls in the southwest corner of the Fort Hall Indian Reservation. Access to this peak is across the reservation; permission must be secured by writing or calling the reservation before attempting the peak. Reportedly, permission is seldom granted. (See Addresses in the appendices.) USGS Bannock Peak

Deep Creek Peak   *8,748 feet (Class 2)*

Deep Creek Peak is 9 miles south of Bannock Peak, east of the main Deep Creek crest. The highest point in the range rises steeply from the valley floor—a good conditioning climb in late spring. This peak can be climbed from almost any direction. Two routes are suggested. The longest route begins at the Knox Canyon Road [(A)(2.1)] and ascends the peak's western slopes. This is a steep, but easy hike. The second route begins at the point where the Knox Canyon Road [(A)(2.1)] and Big Canyon Road [(A)(1.1)] join on the peak's west ridge. From this point, it is a 2.5-mile ridge walk to the summit. The first reported ascent was made by Fred Clark and other members of the Wheeler Survey in 1877. USGS Deep Creek Peak

Deep Creek Peak, the highest Deep Creek summit

APPROACHES TO THE DEEP CREEK MOUNTAINS

(A) DEEP CREEK MOUNTAINS ACCESS

Primary approach is via ID-31, which traverses Rockland Valley on the range's west side, or via Arbon Valley Road, which parallels the range on the east.

(1) ID-37 Access Points. ID-37 is a good paved highway that runs through the Rockland Valley providing primary access to all westside approaches to the Deep Creek Mountains (only one is listed in this guide).

(1.1) Big Canyon Road. This road is accessed from ID-37 19.5 miles south of I-86. This good gravel road, which is signed, runs due east to the top of the Deep Creek crest in 9.5 miles. In dry conditions, this road does not require a 4WD.

(2) Arbon Valley Road. This paved secondary road runs the entire length of the Arbon Valley. Access this road and the east side of the Deep Creek range by taking exit 52 off I-86 and following the Arbon Valley south.

(2.1) Knox Canyon Road. This road leaves the Arbon Valley Road 27.25 miles south of I-86 at a signed junction. It leads up into the Deep Creek range to a divide above Knox, Bull, and Big Canyons. Roads descend from the pass through both Big [(A)(1.1)] and Bull Canyons.

7

THE BANNOCK RANGE

This range begins just west of Pocatello. Its main crest stretches southeast for 65 miles, ending near Weston and the Utah border. Geographically, besides the main crest, this upland encompasses a group of small escarpments—the North Promontory Range, the Blue Springs Hills, the Samaria Mountains, and the Malad Range—that are loosely tied to the Bannock crest.

The main Bannock Range crest is broken into three distinct high sections linked together by low passes. In the north, near Pocatello, the range reaches an elevation of 8,710

feet on Scout Mountain and 8,733 feet at Old Tom Mountain and then loses elevation as it runs south, dropping to 5,468 feet at Garden Creek Gap. It then rises again, this time to more than 9,000 feet on Elkhorn Peak, before descending to Malad Summit, 5,615 feet. At Malad Summit, the crest splits. The Blue Springs Hills, Samaria Mountains, and the North Promontory Range trail off to the southwest. The main crest curves to the east and then to the southeast before climbing to the summit of the highest point in the range, Oxford Peak at 9,282 feet. The extreme southern end of the range is anchored by Old Baldy Peak at 8,356 feet. The Malad Range is attached to the west side of the main crest.

The Bannock Range is composed of several blocks raised along basin and range faults and is composed for the most part of Paleozoic sedimentary rock. Some undated Precambrian rock is found on Scout Mountain. The Bannock peaks are high, but rolling in nature with few prominent faces and cirques.

The main Bannock Range crest is administered by the Caribou National Forest. The BLM controls the North Promontory Range and the Samaria Mountains. Hiking opportunities abound. The Forest Service maintains several good hiking trails throughout its portion of the range and the BLM lands are open and suitable for cross-country hiking. Climbing opportunities on the peaks are limited to Class 1 and 2 excursions. Rock climbers have placed a number of challenging technical climbing routes on the cliffs at Garden Creek Gap.

A good portion of the land surrounding these mountains is privately owned, so access quality varies. Primary access is from I-15, which parallels the range for almost its entire length and crosses it at Malad Summit. US-91 provides access to east-side approaches in the southern end of the range. In the Pocatello area, paved roads lead to many locations, and trails are reasonably well maintained. The southwestern sections of the range see few hikers, and the roads are not developed for passenger cars. Additionally, county roads cross Garden Creek Gap and Mink Creek Summit west of Pocatello. Unfortunately, many Bannock Range trails are open to motorcycles.

NORTHERN PEAKS: KINPORT PEAK TO ELKHORN MOUNTAIN

Kinport Peak   *7,222 feet (Class 2)*
Kinport Peak sits 4 miles southeast of Pocatello. Although it has a road to its summit, it makes a good early season conditioning hike. Climb this peak from downtown Pocatello by taking Lincoln Road southwest to the Pocatello Greenbelt trailhead and a parking area near a Mormon church [(A)(1)].

Follow the trail, which will take you about half of the distance to the summit, and then continue cross-country until you cross the road to the summit. Continue on the road to the summit in a total of 2.5 miles. The road continues to Wild Mountain, 7,160+ feet, which is 1 mile to the southeast. USGS Pocatello South

Slate Mountain   6,980 feet (Class 2)

This peak, found 4.5 miles south of Kinport Peak, loses its snow cover early, making the summit a good place for spring hiking. Follow the West Fork Trail [(A)(2)(a)] until you reach several beaver dams in roughly 2.5 miles. From this point, the summit is due east. Hike up the peak's west ridge from the beaver dams to the summit. USGS Pocatello South

Scout Mountain   8,710 feet (Class 2)

Scout Mountain is 6.5 miles south of Slate Mountain. Because of its proximity to Pocatello, it is probably the most popular summit in southeast Idaho. This peak can be reached from the Scout Mountain CG [(A)(2.1)]. At the south edge of the picnic area, a hiking trail leads off to the south. Follow the trail for 200 yards, until it breaks out of the aspens. Start toward a saddle on the mountain's north shoulder. The route is steep and crosses some talus. From this saddle, it is an easy walk to the summit. Another route to the summit follows the Crestline Cycle Trail. This trail is heavily used by motorcycles later in the day and on weekends. Avoid the motorcycles by hiking or biking this trail on weekday mornings. The trail is accessed from the Scout Mountain CG road midway between the campground and the Bannock Highway. (Note: A road leads to the summit from the opposite side of the mountain.) USGS Scout Mountain

Old Tom Mountain   8,733 feet (Class 2)

Old Tom Mountain, which sits 3 miles south of Scott Mountain is one of the prominent peaks visible from I-15 south of Pocatello. R. Baugher suggests that Old Tom was a pesky mountain lion. Climb the peak via its west ridge from Garden Creek Gap. The first ascent was probably by the Hayden Survey in the 1870s. USGS Hawkins/Scout Mountain

Wakley Peak   8,801 feet (Class 2)

Wakley Peak is 5 miles northwest of Malad Summit and 4.5 miles north of Elkhorn Mountain. Surveyors found Wakley interesting because it is positioned on the Columbia/Great Basin Divide. Wakley was named Fontaine Peak by the Wheeler Survey, which made the first ascent, and T. M. Bannon identified it as Elkhorn. Reach the peak by hiking north on the Wright Creek National Recreation Trail, FST-130 [(B)(2)(c)]. Follow the trail north for 5 miles until the trail crosses the peak's southwest ridge. Climb to the summit via this ridge. R. Baugher and C. Ferguson ascended the north ridge in February 1995. USGS Wakley Peak

Elkhorn Mountain   9,095 feet (Class 2)

The first recorded ascent of this southern Idaho landmark was by Henry Gannett and A. D. Wilson in 1878. The peak is 5.25 miles due west of Malad Summit and was called West Malade Peak by Gannett and Wilson, who built the 8-foot high cairn that still sits on the summit. The highest point, which is formed by a narrow promontory on the mountain's 4.5-mile summit ridge, is known as Elkhorn Peak. The peak can be climbed by either its north ridge or its eastern slopes. Access to the north ridge is via FST-133 [(B)(2)(a)]; access to the eastern slopes is via FST-134 [(B)(2)(b)]. The recommended route is FST-133, which leads to the Bannock Range divide 1.5 miles north of the peak. From this point, follow the ridgeline south to the summit in 1 mile with a 1,000-foot elevation gain. USGS Elkhorn Peak

SOUTHERN PEAKS: OXFORD PEAK TO OLD BALDY PEAK

Oxford Peak   9,282 feet (Class 1 or 2)

Oxford Peak, the highest point in the Bannock Range, sits east of Malad Summit and 4 miles west of the village of Oxford. H. Gannett and A. D. Wilson climbed this peak in 1878 and called it East Malade Peak. Surveyors returned in 1897 (Welker of the US Coast and Geodetic Survey) and in 1915 (T. M. Bannon). Likewise, most of the 50 to 75 yearly climbers are returnees. Its summit is reached by a trail that approaches from the south. This trail can be approached from several trailheads, all of which are shown on the Caribou National Forest map. The summit also could be reached by scrambling up from the trail on its east and west sides. The following approach offers a good Class 2 route to the summit. Start your journey in Oxford and follow Oxford Creek Road west toward Rockslide Canyon [(B)(4)(a)]. This road is gated after roughly 3 miles. From the gate, take the Forest Service trail west for 1 mile to the Oxford Ridge Trail [(B)(1)(a.1)]. Hike north on this trail for 0.5 mile to the Gooseberry drainage. From this point, it is possible to leave the trail and climb southwest directly toward the ridge top and Point 8416, which is about 1,000 feet above. Once on the ridgeline, climb Oxford Peak's north ridge to the summit in another 0.75 mile and another 800-feet of elevation gain. USGS Oxford Peak

Elkhorn Mountain: The Hayden Survey's giant cairn still sits on the summit. (Photo by Rick Baugher)

Weston Peak   *8,165 feet (Class 2)*

Weston Peak is situated 7 miles south of Oxford Peak and 4 miles southwest of Clifton. The summit is easily reached from FST-122 [(B)(3)(a.1)], which passes along its southern and western slopes. Climb the peak from the trail by ascending either its north or south ridges. Both ridges gain roughly 500 feet of elevation from the trail. USGS Clifton

Old Baldy Peak   *8,356 feet (Class 2)*

Darn near every Idaho mountain range has a peak with the word "bald" in its name, and the Bannock Range is no exception. This Old Baldy Peak is 1 mile due south of Weston Peak. Ascend the peak's north ridge from the point where FST-191 [(B)(3)(a)] crosses the ridge. Total distance up the ridge is about 0.5 mile with a 700-foot elevation gain. The first recorded ascent was by Gannett and Wilson in 1878. USGS Clifton

THE MALAD RANGE

The Malad Range is tucked into the western slopes of the Bannock Range just east of I-15. The southern end of the range extends into Utah, where it reaches well above 8,000 feet in elevation. The highest Idaho point is an unnamed 6,995-foot summit. The Malad Range is geologically similar to the Bannock Range and is also administered by the Caribou National Forest. [(C)]

THE SAMARIA MOUNTAINS

The Samaria Mountains are located on the Idaho/Utah border just west of I-15. The range's high point is on Samaria Mountain, which is 7,795 feet tall. The first Mormon settlers in this area adopted the name, which has its origins in Palestine. The Samaria Mountains are linked to the Bannock Range via a long spur ridge known as the Blue Spring Hills, which run north for nearly 30 miles to connect the two ranges. The range is administered by the BLM. [(D)]

THE NORTH PROMONTORY RANGE

The North Promontory Range is an extension of the Bannock Range and, like the Samaria Mountains, is connected to the Bannock Range by the Blue Spring Hills. The range, which is also known as the North Hansel Range, is located south of Holbrook and just west of the Samaria Mountains. Only 12 miles of this range are on the Idaho side of the Idaho/Utah border. Its highest point, north of the border, is an unnamed

6,986-foot summit. From Holbrook, these mountains look like a series of dry, broken hills with few trees other than junipers. The range is administered by the BLM. Limited access is available via dirt roads that leave ID-37 from the Holbrook area. [(E)]

APPROACHES TO
THE BANNOCK RANGE

(A) POCATELLO AREA ACCESS POINTS

Pocatello is reached by both I-15 and I-86. It is a college town with all necessary services, including outdoor equipment stores.

(1) Lincoln Road South/City Creek Road. Access this road from downtown Pocatello. The road leaves town as Lincoln Road South, runs west uphill onto Pocatello's south bench, becomes City Creek Road, and proceeds southwest up City Creek. It is paved for 2 miles and then turns into dirt, deteriorating rapidly as it climbs into the mountains.

(2) Bannock Highway Access Points. Bannock Highway leaves the south end of Pocatello, crosses Mink Creek Summit on the range's crest, and then descends to the Arbon Valley Road on the range's eastern flanks. This paved highway provides access to several hiking areas and, in the winter, to a state-run Park and Ski trail system.

(a) West Fork Trail. Take the Bannock Highway for 11.7 miles to the West Fork Trail turnoff. Turn right just past the Pocatello water system intake structure on the left. The trail is well maintained and closed to motorized vehicles.

(2.1) FS-001, East Fork Mink Creek Road. Take the Bannock Highway southwest from Pocatello for 10 miles and turn at a signed junction onto the East Fork Mink Creek Road, which leads to Scout Mountain CG.

(B) MAIN BANNOCK RANGE ACCESS POINTS

Access to the Bannock Range south of Pocatello is a complex subject. This write-up includes only limited information designed to get you to the peaks listed in the guide. If you have time, you can find miles of interesting country to explore.

(1) FS-047, Cherry Creek Road. This road is accessed from I-15 at Malad Summit or at Downey. The road that connects these two locations provides two different access points for Cherry Creek. Once on the Cherry Creek Road, follow it south for 5 miles to the Cherry Creek CG. The road is closed by a gate just past the campground.

(a) FST-181, Left Fork Trail. FST-181 leaves the end of FS-047 just beyond the Cherry Creek CG and follows the Left Fork Cherry Creek east for 2 miles, where it meets FST-119/FST-189.

(a.1) FST-119/FST-189, Oxford Ridge Trail. This is the premier trail in this part of the Bannock Range. It begins in the north near Red Rock Pass and runs south for more than 12 miles along the east side of the crest. The southern end of the trail traverses windswept Oxford Ridge. This trail intersects with seven trails and three roads and eventually ends at FS-045 west of Clifton [(B)(5)(a)].

(2) FS-041, Mill Creek/Summit Guard Station Access. This road begins at the Malad Summit exit off I-15 and leads west to the GS in a little more than 1 mile. There are many trails in this area besides the three listed below.

(a) FST-133, Elkhorn Mountain Trail. This trail is accessed at the end of FS-041. The trail follows Mill Creek west to its headwaters, crosses over Elkhorn Mountain, and then descends west along Indian Mill Creek to FST-129.

(b) FST-134, Kents Canyon Trail. FST-134 leaves the end of FS-041 and continues 2 miles due south to the Bannock Range crest, then descends Kents Canyon to FST-129 in another 3 miles.

(c) FST-130, Wright Creek National Recreational Trail. This trail leaves the Mill Creek Road 0.2 mile before the Summit CG. From the road, it runs northwest to the crest south of Wakley Peak and then north along the crest.

(3) FS-038, Deep Creek/Weston Creek Road. This road is accessed from the Malad area via either I-15 or the old highway that parallels it. Take the Malad exit and drive east on this road, which runs between the Bannock Range and its Malad subrange, toward Weston.

(a) FST-191, Old Baldy/Weston Peak Trail. Access this trail just south of Weston Creek Reservoir. This old jeep trail leaves FS-038, runs northeast past the western slopes of Baldy Peak, and then joins FST-122 just south of Weston Peak.

(a.1) FST-122, Weston Peak Trail. This trail is accessed by FST-191, which connects with it roughly midway between its two ends. The trail also can be accessed via FST-231, which begins near the Forest Service's Deep Creek administrative site.

(4) FS-230, Oxford Creek Road. This road is accessed from the village of Oxford. Oxford is on the east side of the range just south of Red Rock Pass on US-91. Follow the signs from the highway to the village. This road leaves the county highway just north of the village, continues northeast along Oxford Creek for 2 miles and then climbs due west toward Rockslide Canyon for another 0.5 mile, where it is closed by a gate.

(a) Rockslide Canyon Cutoff Trail. This trail begins at the gate on the Oxford Creek Road and climbs up Rockslide Canyon for nearly 1 mile to join with FST-119 [(A)(1)(a.1)] just east of Oxford Peak.

(5) Clifton Access. Clifton is found along ID-23, north of

Dayton and south of Oxford. From downtown Clifton, follow the signs to the cemetery (100 Street South). This road becomes FS-045, which leads to the Davis Basin trailhead in 6.9 miles.

(a) **FST-189/FST-119, Oxford Ridge/Peak Trail**. This trail takes a mile to reach the top of the ridge and a total of 4 miles to reach the junction of FST-119, which leads north toward Cherry Creek [(B)(1)(a.1)]. From the junction it is 2 miles to the summit.

(C) MALAD RANGE ACCESS

This range is accessed from Malad via the old highway that parallels the freeway, or from FS-038, which begins at I-15 just north of Malad. FS-038 follows Deep Creek and then Weston Creek along the eastern side of this subrange. From either of these roads, many roads lead into the mountains.

(D) SAMARIA MOUNTAIN ACCESS

To approach this small mountain range, you will need the BLM Malad City land status map. The roads shown on that map are accurate. The only recommended approach route into this group is via the North Canyon Road, which is on the range's southern edge. This road, which can be approached by any number of roads from both Idaho and Utah, connects with most of the range. The Gardner Canyon Road is a more direct route into the range, but requires a 4WD. (All of these roads require a 4WD when wet.) While there are no hiking trails, the open nature of the terrain makes for good hiking on the ridgelines.

(E) NORTH PROMONTORY RANGE ACCESS

This small group of mountains is shown on the BLM Malad City land status map. All of the roads on the map are open to the public. All will require a 4WD when they are wet.

8

THE PORTNEUF RANGE

The Portneuf Range, which begins east of Blackfoot and extends southeast for 60 miles, is broken by the Portneuf River, which cuts through it at Lava Hot Springs. The northern section of the range begins along the Blackfoot River

and gradually climbs up to the summits of North and South Putnam Mountains. Moving south, the crest undulates, reaching its highest elevation southeast of Pocatello on 9,278-foot Bonneville Peak. After being broken by the Portneuf River, the range again climbs steeply, reaching high points at Sedgwick Peak, Baldy Mountain, and Cottonwood Peak. Sedgwick Peak, at 9,167 feet, is the highest point in the southern section, and the second highest point in the Portneuf Range. The range encompasses two minor subranges, the Pocatello Range and the Fish Creek Range. The Pocatello Range consists of a group of low peaks just east of Pocatello that are connected to the western slopes of the main Portneuf crest. Chinks Peak, at 6,791 feet, is the highest Pocatello Range summit. The Fish Creek Range is centered just east of Lava Hot Springs. This small but rugged subrange is about 21 miles in length and 6 miles in width. Petticoat Peak is the highest peak in the subrange at 8,033 feet.

Geologically, these mountains are composed of sedimentary and volcanic formations. Volcanic ash has been deposited in places over underlying layers of limestone, dolomite, shale, and quartzite. The eastern slopes contain thick stands of Douglas fir, lodgepole, and limber pine. The drier western slopes of the range are covered by juniper and other mountain shrubs.

The Portneuf Range is administered by the Fort Hall Indian Reservation in the north, the Caribou National Forest in the central sections, and the State of Idaho and the BLM in the south. The BLM manages the Pocatello and Fish Creek subranges. Much of the southern Portneuf Range is private land.

The Forest Service has gradually improved hiking opportunities in the Pocatello area, but because of low use, much of the remaining range is ignored by government planners. Many Portneuf peaks make enjoyable day hikes and scrambles. Portneuf peaks are nontechnical, but tower over the surrounding valleys and offer exceptional views. The walk to the top of any of these peaks will be strenuous. Also of note is the public yurt system operated by the Idaho State University Outdoor Program and the City of Pocatello. There are four yurts in the Portneuf Range and each is near superb backcountry skiing.

The quality of vehicular access points varies considerably throughout the range. Overall, there are plenty of roads and only a few trails. Primary access is from Pocatello via I-15, and from US-30, which runs east from I-15 to the town of Lava Hot Springs. The southern section around Sedgwick Peak is administered by the state of Idaho and has no hiking trails, but plenty of roads.

South Putnam Mountain   *8,949 feet (Class 2)*

South Putnam Mountain is 15 miles due east of Pocatello at the north end of the range. It is inside the Fort Hall Indian Reservation and permission must be secured before attempting the ascent (see Addresses in the appendices). The southern slopes of this peak are outstanding intermediate telemarking terrain when conditions are safe. The peak is rated Class 2 via the south ridge, which can be reached from McNabb Creek [(A)(1.1)(a)] or Inman Pass [(A)(1.2)] in the west or Toponce Creek [(B)(2)(a)] in the southwest.

R. Watters reports that "the McNabb Creek trailhead is the jumping off point for the McNabb Yurt which is an great base camp for winter ascents. To ascend the peak via this route, climb to the ridge top, cut across Buckskin Basin and follow the south ridge to the summit." The next best approach is to follow the Inman Road to Inman Pass. From the pass, follow the ridgelines north to the summit. On clear days, most of the region is visible from the summit, including the Pioneers to the northwest and the Tetons to the northeast. USGS South Putnam Mountain

Bonneville Peak   *9,271 feet (Class 2)*
Snow Peak   *9,132 feet (Class 2)*

Bonneville Peak is the highest point in the Portneuf Range. The peak can be climbed from almost any direction. Many people climb it from the Pebble Creek Ski Area by following the ski runs up toward the ridgeline. Another route, recommended as more aesthetically pleasing, involves a long ridge walk and an ascent of 9,132-foot Snow Peak. Drive to the Robbers Roost trailhead [(A)(3)(a)] and then hike FST-073 east to the Portneuf divide. From the divide, hike the Class 2 ridgeline north to Snow Peak, which is roughly 1.5 miles away. Descend that peak's north ridge toward Bonneville Peak, which is 1 mile to the north. If a car is left at the Pebble Creek trailhead, a descent to that point would save reclimbing Snow Peak. It is a 15-mile round trip—with no reliable

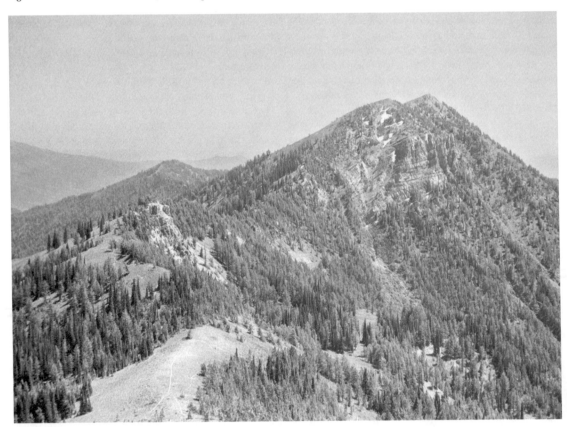

Haystack Mountain from the north

water—to climb both peaks from the Robbers Roost trailhead. Alternative access to these peaks begins on the east side of the range [(B)(1)(a)]. USGS Bonneville Peak

Haystack Mountain   *9,033 feet (Class 2)*
Haystack Mountain, an impressive summit when viewed from the saddle to the north, is the large, rounded summit 3 miles south of Snow Peak. Climb to the summit from the pass between Snow Peak and Haystack Mountain. Leave FST-073 at the saddle and hike the north ridgeline, staying on the east side of the ridge, south to the summit less than 1 mile away [(A)(3)(a) or (B)(1)(a)]. R. Watters suggests climbing the peak from the east. This approach begins at Big Springs CG on the east side of the range. Follow the east-trending ridge from the campground to the Haystack Mountain/Snow Peak saddle. USGS Haystack Mountain

Petticoat Peak   *8,033 feet (Class 2)*
Petticoat Peak, the only named summit in the Fish Creek Range, is 4 miles northeast of Lava Hot Springs. Its summit is an easy Class 2 scramble from the roads on its west and north slopes. Climb the southeast ridge from US-30 where the highway crosses the Fish Creek divide just east of Soda Springs [(C)(1)]. Most of the range is administered by the BLM. USGS Soda Springs

APPROACHES TO THE PORTNEUF RANGE

(A) POCATELLO AREA ACCESS
Primary approach to Pocatello is via I-15 and I-86. All essential services are available in town.

(1) Rapid Creek Road. This road is the main artery used to access the McNabb Creek Road and Inman Creek Road. To reach the Rapid Creek Road, drive south from Pocatello on I-15 to the Inkom exit (15 miles south of I-86). From the stop sign at the end of the exit, turn right and drive 50 yards, then turn left. Follow this road until you reach a stop sign. Turn left again, and you are on the Rapid Creek Road. The road goes under the interstate and then north. It is 5 miles to the Webb Creek Road and 4.2 miles to the Inman Creek Road. A 4WD is recommended.

(1.1) McNabb Creek Road. From the Inkom exit on I-15, drive north up the Rapid Creek drainage toward the north. One mile after the road makes a turn to the west, the road forks. Take the right fork and follow it north for slightly more than a mile to the McNabb Creek Road. Turn onto this road and follow it up the McNabb Creek drainage until its ends. This road provides access to the Webb Creek Yurt and is usually in good shape.

(a) FST-080, McNabb Creek Trail. This trail climbs up McNabb Creek. About 1.5 miles from the trailhead it crosses a ridge and then drops down into the next unnamed drainage to the north. The trail crosses this unnamed drainage and eventually reaches the top of the Webb Creek drainage and the Webb Creek Yurt. From this point, the trail descends down Webb Creek, but it is not well maintained and not recommended. East of the yurt, FST-083 [(B)(2)(a)] continues to the east, crosses the Portneuf crest south of South Putnam Mountain, and then descends Toponce Creek.

(1.2) FS-018, Inman Creek Road. To reach FS-018, exit I-15 at Inkom and drive up along Rapid Creek to Inman Creek. FS-018 follows the Inman Creek drainage and crosses the Portneuf divide to join with FS-013, which descends along the North Fork Pebble Creek to the Big Springs CG. A 4WD is recommended.

(2) FS-210, Green Canyon Road. Access this road from the Inkom exit on I-15. Drive west from the freeway for a little more than 1 mile and then follow the road south for a long mile to Green Canyon. The road turns east and climbs up to the Pebble Creek Ski Area.

(a) FST-072, Boundary Trail. This trail forms a 36-mile loop, which circles Bonneville Peak, Snow Peak, and Haystack Mountain. There are several other ways to approach this trail, but none is on a better road. Access this trail just after the road crosses the national forest boundary.

(3) FS-035, Robbers Roost Road. Take I-15 to the Inkom exit. Exit and drive south through Inkom and under the freeway on US-91/US-191 for 7 miles to reach FS-035. Turn east onto FS-035 and drive 2.3 miles to its end.

(a) FST-073, Robbers Roost Creek Trail. From the road's end, it is 5 miles to the Portneuf divide between Haystack and Snow Peaks. The trail begins in the creek bottom and then climbs out of the trees to the steep, dry ridges above. From the divide, FST-073 and FST-074 both descend east to the Big Springs area on Pebble Creek. The trails vary in quality, but are passable.

(B) EAST SIDE ACCESS
The following approach routes begin in Lava Hot Springs, a small resort town on US-30. Originally, US-30 left Lava Hot Springs and proceeded around the northern end of the Fish Creek Range on its journey to Soda Springs. The highway now runs straight across the Fish Creek Range just south of Petticoat Peak and proceeds directly east to Soda Springs. The old highway is called US-30N in the following write-ups.

(1) FS-036, Pebble Creek Road. From Lava Hot Springs,

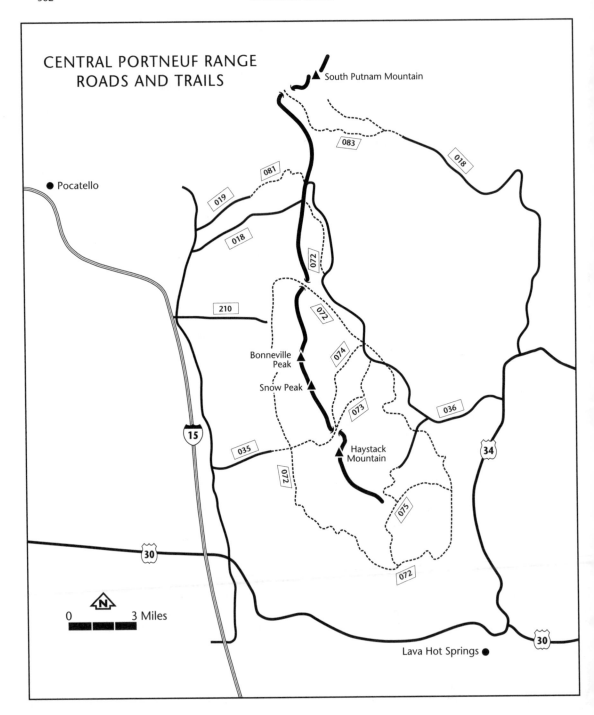

CENTRAL PORTNEUF RANGE
ROADS AND TRAILS

South Putnam Mountain

083

018

081

019

Pocatello

018

072

210

072

074

Bonneville
Peak

073

036

Snow Peak

35

34

072

Haystack
Mountain

15

075

072

30

072

N

0   3 Miles

30

Lava Hot Springs

follow US-30N north for 8 miles. Turn west on FS-036 and follow it to the Big Springs CG.

(a) **Big Springs Area Trails.** FST-072, FST-073, and FST-074 all can be reached from the Big Springs area. See [(A)(3) (a)], above, for more details.

(2) **FS-018, Toponce Creek Road.** Take US-30N north from Lava Hot Springs for 9 miles to the point where the highway makes a sweeping turn to the east. Turn left off the highway and follow the gravel road that leads north up the Portneuf River. This road leads to Toponce Creek in roughly 5 miles. Turn west on FS-018 and follow the road to its end.

(a) **FST-083, Buckskin Trail.** This primitive trail stretches from the end of the Toponce Creek Road up the Middle Fork Toponce Creek to the Portneuf divide south of South Putnam Mountain.

(C) SOUTHERN PORTNEUF RANGE ACCESS

Primary approach to the southern sections of the Portneuf Range is via US-30.

(1) **Fish Creek Range Access.** The Fish Creek Range is surrounded by US-30N and US-30. US-30 crosses this range 3 miles southeast of Petticoat Peak. A second road leaves US-30N just north of Lava Hot Springs and proceeds northeast up Hadley Canyon to cross the range north of Petticoat Peak. Though its upper reaches are a crude jeep trail, it provides the best access to Petticoat Peak.

9

THE BLACKFOOT MOUNTAINS

The Blackfoot Mountains and two subranges, the Chesterfield and Ninety Percent Ranges, form a group of barren ridges that trend from northwest to southeast for more than 50 miles between Idaho Falls and Soda Springs. The range's western slopes climb roughly 2,400 feet above the Snake River, but the eastern slopes rise only 600 feet above the Willow Creek and Blackfoot River drainages. Taylor Mountain at 7,404 feet and Blackfoot Peak at 7,550 feet are the range's highest points.

Wolverine Canyon, a scenic gorge on the western slope of the range, offers some rock climbing opportunities on impressive cliffs and weird rock formations.

Much of this land is privately owned. There is no national forest land, but the BLM and the state of Idaho control some large tracts in this upland. Private land often blocks access to public land and complicates access considerations. For example, the summit of Taylor Mountain is owned by the public, but it's surrounded by private land.

Access is via the numerous county and BLM roads that penetrate the entire range. There are no maintained trails within these mountains. Because of the low elevations, the Blackfoot Mountains are usually free of snow a month earlier than more lofty mountains. Opportunities for early season cross-country hikes and ascents are plentiful.

Taylor Mountain   *7,404 feet (Class 2)*

Taylor Mountain was named for James Madison Taylor who in 1865 built a bridge over the Snake River at the future site of Idaho Falls. The earliest known ascent was by O. St. John of the Hayden Survey in 1877. The peak sits southeast of Idaho Falls and 12 miles east of Firth. At one time, a small ski area operated on its slopes. The summit is publicly owned, but the surrounding land is private. If you are interested in visiting the summit, contact the BLM's Idaho Falls office to learn the status of public access to the peak. Aesthetically, the best route to the summit is from Wolverine Canyon [(A) (1)]. USGS Wolverine

Blackfoot Peak   *7,550 feet (Class 2)*

Blackfoot Peak, the highest point in the Blackfoot Mountains, is located on Blue Ridge east of Blackfoot and 8.5 miles south of Taylor Mountain. The summit is on BLM land and can be climbed from any direction; but because the peak is surrounded by private land, approaching it is difficult. As with Taylor Mountain, discuss your approach route with the BLM beforehand. USGS Poison Creek

THE CHESTERFIELD RANGE

The Chesterfield Range, an extension of the Blackfoot Mountains, is located between the Blackfoot River and the Portneuf River. This minor escarpment is roughly 30 miles in length and is composed of a series of parallel ridges with no prominent peaks. Elevations reach above 7,000 feet on Reservoir Mountain, which is on the west shore of Blackfoot Reservoir.

Reservoir Mountain   *7,141 feet (Class 2)*

Reservoir Mountain, which served as a USGS triangulation station in 1914, is located on the west shore of Blackfoot Reservoir. It is an easy climb from the road along the reservoir's west shore via the peak's east slopes [(A)(1.1)] or [(B)(1)]. The mountain is entirely owned by the state of Idaho, so access is no problem. USGS Reservoir Mountain

NINETY PERCENT RANGE

The Ninety Percent Range is the southernmost extension of the Blackfoot Mountains. It extends southeast from the Chesterfield Range to Soda Springs. The smallest mountain range in Idaho, it is roughly 7 miles long and 3 miles wide. The highest point, 6,851 feet in altitude, is unnamed. Most of this mountain group is privately owned, though the BLM administers a few acres.

APPROACHES TO THE BLACKFOOT MOUNTAINS

(A) WEST SIDE ACCESS

Primary approach is from Idaho Falls and US-91, which parallels I-15 between Idaho Falls and Blackfoot. Beyond the primary routes, these mountains are crisscrossed by washboard gravel roads, most of which are closed during the winter.

(1) **Wolverine Canyon Road.** This road starts south of Firth and traverses the range south of Taylor Mountain at a pass known locally as the Double W before eventually meeting the Bone Road south of Bone. This road also splits and follows the Blackfoot River along the southern portion of the range.

(1.1) **Blackfoot Reservoir Road.** This well-maintained gravel road leaves the Wolverine Canyon Road just before it enters the canyon and then runs east to Blackfoot Reservoir.

(B) EAST SIDE ACCESS

Access for the eastern side of the Blackfoot Mountains begins along US-30 in Soda Springs.

(1) **Chesterfield Range Access.** The Chesterfield Range is covered with roads. The main public road follows along the west side of Blackfoot Reservoir from Soda Springs. It is advisable to use a BLM land status map on visits to this area, because the public and private lands are difficult to differentiate.

(2) **Ninety Percent Range Access.** Access this range directly from Soda Springs via several dirt roads that leave from the town site. There is very little public land to visit in this area.

If you want to visit this area, contact the BLM for up-to-date access information.

10

THE BEAR RIVER RANGE

The Bear River Range is a northern extension of Utah's Wasatch Range. The Idaho portion of the range is 43 miles long and more than 20 miles wide with many points reaching above 9,000 feet. The name is derived from the Bear River, which loops around the range on its east, north, and west sides. Sherman Peak is the highest point in the Bear River Range, reaching an elevation of 9,682 feet.

For the most part, the Bear River crest is rolling, with large rounded summits nipped by Pleistocene glaciation. Much of the range is composed of limestone, which has eroded to form sinkholes, ponds, disappearing streams, and many subsurface caves. Lower slopes are covered with thick forests and its higher reaches are home to abundant blooms of wildflowers.

The Caribou National Forest administers the range. While only one section of the range is managed as roadless land, the 40,000-plus area west of St. Charles encompasses several high lakes and a stretch of the crest with several summits reaching above 9,000 feet. Although the range is crisscrossed by roads, there are several excellent trails for hikers. Foremost among Bear River Range trails is the High Line National Recreation Trail that follows the range's crest for more than 50 miles from north to south. The major peaks in the range offer hikers and peak baggers interesting nontechnical climbing goals. All are rated as Class 2 climbs.

US-30 and US-89 provide primary access to the east side of the range; ID-34 is the primary access route on the west side. ID-36 crosses the range between Preston and Montpelier. Two other roads cross the range, one north of ID-36 and one south of ID-36. Only a few of the many roads and trails in the range are covered below.

Soda Peak   *8,921 feet (Class 2)*

This summit sits 8.5 miles due south of Soda Springs near the northern terminus of the High Line Trail that runs along its eastern slopes. The shortest route to the summit begins near Camp Ho-Nok to the east. Follow either FST-348 or FST-330 [(A)(1.1)(a) or (b)] to the High Line Trail and then scramble to the summit from that trail. USGS Soda Springs

Sherman Peak   *9,682 feet (Class 1)*

Sherman Peak, the highest Bear River Range peak, is a large twin-summited mountain with a broad north/south summit ridge. It is found 12 miles south of Soda Springs. The Hayden Survey called this Soda Peak. The Wheeler Survey renamed it after Gen. William T. Sherman of Civil War fame. The summit has a register in an old Forest Service communication box. The peak can be reached from either the north or the south via FST-317, the Sherman Peak Trail [(A)(1)(a)]. It is roughly 3 miles to the summit via the trail from the northern trailhead and 1.2 miles from the southern trailhead. USGS North Canyon

Paris Peak   *9,575 feet (Class 2)*

Paris Peak is situated 18 miles due south of Sherman Peak and just north of Bloomington Creek. The peak is accessed via FS-409, the Bloomington Creek Road. Follow this road west from Bloomington until it reaches the confluence of the North Fork, Middle Fork, and South Fork Bloomington Creeks. From this point, FST-453, an old road, follows the North Fork Bloomington [(A)(2)(a)]. After 1 mile, this route switches back out of the creek bottom and begins a climb up the south slopes of Paris Peak. The former jeep trail ends on the north side of the peak at 8,800 feet. To climb this peak, leave the road at its end and climb the peak's north ridge, or leave the road at the point where it crosses the peak's broad south ridge and hike that ridge to the summit. Neither ridge presents any objective problems. USGS Paris Peak

Bloomington Peak   *9,311 feet (Class 2)*

Bloomington Peak sits at the head of the Bloomington Canyon, 3 miles southwest of Paris Peak. Bloomington

The south summit of Sherman Peak from the north summit

Peak's north face is as steep and rugged as Bear River Range peaks get. Climb to the summit from almost any direction. The north ridge, from Middle Fork Bloomington Creek, is recommended as the most enjoyable ascent route [(A)(2.1)]. USGS Paris Peak

Saint Charles Mountain*   **9,245 feet (Class 2)**
This unofficially named mountain rises directly south of Bloomington Lake and 2 miles southeast of Bloomington Peak. The peak is a tri-summited mass, with the middle summit the most impressive point. The peak can be climbed from the High Line Trail [(A)(2)(b.1)], which intersects the western ridge, or from Bloomington Lake [(A)(2)(b)]. The route from the lake is more challenging, bordering on a Class 3 climb. From the lake, the route circles the lake's east shore and climbs up the sloping terrace above the sedimentary cliffs that rise out of the lake. Above the cliffs are three gullies. All three will lead to the upper slopes on the middle summit without significant difficulties. From the ridgeline, follow the crest east to the highest summit. USGS Paris Peak

Cub Peak   **9,216 feet (Class 1)**
This peak, identified as the Cub Peak triangulation station, is 4 miles south Bloomington Peak. The High Line Trail crosses close to its summit [(A)(3)(a)]. USGS Egan Basin

Wilderness Peak*   **9,460 feet (Class 2)**
Wilderness Peak is the high point of Andrew Nymon Mountain. The names are taken from the latest Caribou National Forest maps and do not show up on the USGS quad. Wilderness Peak is the high point on a long north/south-trending ridgeline. It is found 9 miles south of Bloomington Peak and directly west of Gibson Lakes. Climb the peak from the uppermost Gibson Lake [(A)(4)]. From the lake, ascend to Point 8966, which is on a spur ridge. Follow the spur from Point 8966 to the summit ridge and then hike that ridge south to the summit. USGS Mapleton

APPROACHES TO THE BEAR RIVER RANGE

(A) US-30 ACCESS POINTS
This two-lane highway is the main travel route between Soda Springs and Utah, on the range's western side.
(1) FS-425, Eightmile Creek Road. This road is accessed from downtown Soda Springs. The road runs due south into

the mountains to Cold Springs CG in about 12 miles and then continues south, eventually connecting other Forest Service roads, which link with ID-36. Drive 9.4 miles south of town to where the road reaches a junction, turn to the right. At 12.4 miles from town the road arrives at the FST-317 trailhead at Mill Creek.
(a) FST-317, Sherman Peak Trail. Access this trail from FS-425 12.4 miles south of Soda Springs or 0.4 mile south of Cold Springs CG. The trail runs from the road up Mill Fork Creek for nearly 2 miles and then begins an ascent of Sherman Peak, which is reached after 3.5 miles. This trail, which is not well-maintained, continues to the south off the summit to join up with FS-403, the Skinner Canyon Road in 1.2 miles.
(1.1) FS-475, Wilson Creek Road. This road leaves FS-425 roughly 0.5 mile north of the Eightmile GS. The road quickly forks. The right fork leads up the North Fork Wilson Creek; the left fork leads up the South Fork Wilson Creek past Camp Ho-Nok.
(a) FST-348, North Fork Wilson Creek Trail. This trail leads to the High Line Trail in 2.1 miles. The High Line Trail is below the east side of the crest at this point and runs south from here to a junction with FST-330 [(A)(1.1)(b)] roughly 1 mile to the south.
(b) FST-330, South Fork Wilson Creek Trail. This trail follows the South Fork Wilson Creek west to the High Line Trail in roughly 2.5 miles. The junction is due east of the summit of Soda Peak.
(2) FS-409, Bloomington Creek Road. Access this road from US-89 in Bloomington and take it west into the mountains. The road eventually divides into three routes. The south fork goes to the Bloomington Lake trailhead. The middle fork goes to the area north of Bloomington Peak; the north fork provides access to the Paris Peak area. A 4WD is recommended along the upper reaches of this road system.
(a) FST-453, Paris Peak Trail. This trail leaves FS-409 at the confluence of the north and middle forks of Bloomington Creek and climbs to 8,800 feet on the north side of Paris Peak in 3.5 miles. This trail is an old road now closed to all but hikers, horses, and motorcycles.
(b) Bloomington Lake Trail. Take the South Fork of the Bloomington Creek Road until it splits at Telegraph Park. Go left at this fork for roughly 1 mile. The road ends just below the lakes.
(b.1) High Line Trail Access. The South Fork Bloomington Creek Road also provides access to the High Line Trail, which follows the Bear River Range crest from north to south for more than 45 miles. Although the trail does not cross any major summits along its route, it is the premier ridge walk in southeastern Idaho. The trail crosses alpine meadows and hovers around the 9,000-foot contour for almost its entire distance.

(2.1) FS-456, Middle Fork Bloomington Creek Road. This road follows the Middle Fork Bloomington west for 2.5 miles. Passenger cars are not recommended.

(3) FS-412, Saint Charles Canyon Road. This paved road leaves US-89 just north of St. Charles and runs west to Minnetonka Cave.

(a) FST-318/FST-319, North Fork St. Charles Creek Trails. These trails leave from a trailhead at 7,100 feet. Turn off FS-412 just past the Big Creek picnic area and 7 miles from US-89. Follow FS-716 the short distance to the trailhead. The trail stands out on FST-318 and follows the North Fork Saint Charles Creek northwest for about 2 miles to a junction. From the junction, FST-319 leads west to Snowslide Lake and then south to the High Line Trail in 2.6 miles. FST-319 continues following the North Fork St. Charles to the High Line Trail north of Cub Peak.

(4) Wilderness Peak Access. Access to Wilderness Peak begins in St. Charles. Leave town on FS-411, which climbs Green Canyon, crosses a divide, and drops into Denver Creek where it intersects with FS-415. Turn right on FS-415 and follow it northwest to Banish Pass at 8,500 feet and the trailhead for the High Line Trail. Continue west of the pass to a junction with FS-406. Turn south on this road and follow it to FS-450. Turn right (west) and follow FS-450 to Gibson Lakes. A 4WD is recommended.

11

THE PEALE MOUNTAINS

East of the Bear River Range, a tangled web of geologically related ridges and peaks fills Idaho's easternmost corner. The name Peale Mountains was suggested by USGS geologist/geographer George Mansfield (1875–1948) in 1927 to honor Hayden Survey geologist A. C. Peale (1849–1913), who had conducted field work in the area in 1877. Mansfield extensively explored this corner of Idaho and in 1927 published his findings in *Geography, Geology, and Mineral Resources of Part of Southeastern Idaho*. In this treatise, he contended that this corner of Idaho was actually one mountain group rather than many. Although the USGS adopted separate names for each individual ridge, this book uses Mansfield's designation.

The primary USGS subdivisions of the Peale Mountains are the Schmid Ridge, the Grays Range, the Aspen Range, Dry Ridge, the Pruess Range, and the Wooley Range. These ridges occupy an area roughly 65 miles in length and 25 miles in width. Meade Peak is the highest point in the Peale Mountains.

Geologically, the ranges that make up the Peale Mountains are associated with the basin and range faulting and the Overthrust Belt. The block faulting is not as pronounced as in ranges farther west. The range receives little more than 24 inches of precipitation per year and consequently is somewhat dry in appearance. Large stands of pine and fir are interspersed with thick aspen groves, while thick brush fills many creek bottoms. The high ridges are bare of trees. Valley-to-summit elevation differences can be substantial, and sections of the range are quite rugged.

The majority of the Peale Mountains are administered by the Caribou National Forest. The BLM controls scattered tracks throughout the area. Mining and grazing have traditionally dominated the economic uses of these mountains. Large chemical companies hold the mineral rights to extensive deposits of phosphates found throughout the range and several large open-pit mining operations are causing significant environmental deterioration in some localized areas.

The area is lightly used by hikers for two reasons. First, there are few trails and these are not well maintained. Second, most people overlook the charm of the Peale Mountains in favor of more famous destinations nearby. This is unfortunate, because the Peale Mountains encompass stretches of untouched and almost pristine terrain. While cross-country travel can be difficult due to brushy conditions, many open slopes exist and some peaks reach well above treeline.

Make it your business to visit the range. The scenery is exceptional, access is adequate and, above all, the range needs friends. Hike the range and tell the Forest Service to consider your interests the next time they make a planning decision. At this time, mining and grazing interests are the only groups that make demands on the Forest Service. You can change that!

THE GRAYS RANGE

This Peale Mountains subrange forms the northernmost extension of the Peale Mountains. This group rises south of Grays Lake and extends southeast for roughly 10 miles. The range contains two named peaks: Lanes Butte at 8,320 feet, and Henry Peak at more than 8,300 feet. Although no one has reported summiting Lanes Butte, it is likely that many people have ambled across its summit. This subrange is administered by the Caribou National Forest.

Henry Peak*   *8,300+ feet (Class 2)*
Henry Peak sits 7 miles due east of Blackfoot Reservoir; it is the northernmost Peale Mountains peak covered by this guide. The Lander Emigrant Road, built by the government in the late 1850s, passed along the north base of this peak named after Henry Schmid. Schmid established the Henry Store in the 1880s. The mercantile is still in operation today. R. Baugher suggests climbing this peak from FS-191, which follows Gravel Creek [(A)(1)] on the peak's eastern slopes. Hike to the top from the end of FS-191. USGS Wayan West

THE WOOLEY RANGE

The Wooley Range is located east of Blackfoot Reservoir and due south of the Grays Range. It is the smallest of the Peale Mountains subranges, extending only 7 miles from northwest to southeast. The range's highest point—unnamed—reaches 7,800 feet. USGS Lower Valley and Upper Valley

THE WEBSTER RANGE

This Peale Mountains subrange forms the eastern edge of these mountains. The range stretches 25 miles from north to south along the Idaho/Wyoming border. Draney Peak, at 9,131 feet, is the highest point in this group. Draney Peak overlooks the Smoky Canyon phosphate mine; the summit is only recommended for those who wish to view the mining operations from a great height.

Diamond Peak   *8,697 feet (Class 2)*
Diamond Peak, the second highest peak in the Webster Range, is 10 miles west of Auburn, Wyoming. The summit is reached from Stump Creek to the east. From the road's end, follow FST-016 [(A)(2)(a)] up the Horse Creek drainage to the base of the peak's east ridge. From there, you can hike cross-country up the east ridge to the summit. A second option is to continue on the trail until it intersects with another trail, which leads off to the north. From this junction, hike north to the top of the peak's west ridge and then follow the ridge to the top. USGS Diamond Flat

THE ASPEN RANGE

The Aspen Range forms the westernmost section of the Peale Mountains. This subrange extends south from the Blackfoot River for 23 miles, ending at the range's highest point, 8,554-foot Harrington Peak. Sulphur Peak, 8,302 feet, is the only other named peak in the range. Its lower slopes are the site of an active phosphate mine and an ascent of the peak is not recommended. The range is administered by the BLM in the north and by the Caribou National Forest at its southern end. The north end contains many private land holdings.

Harrington Peak   *8,554 feet (Class 2)*
Harrington Peak is the highest Aspen Range peak. It is 8 miles northeast of Georgetown. The summit can be reached from the left fork of Georgetown Canyon by following the peak's southeast ridge north from Summit View CG [(A)(4)]. It is about 3.5 cross-country miles to the summit. USGS Harrington Peak

THE PRUESS RANGE

The Pruess Range forms the southern end of the Peale Mountains. This group is roughly 25 miles from north to south and 12 miles from east to west. The range was named for William Pruess, a topographer in John C. Freemont's 1842 expedition. It has three peaks worth climbing.

Hawks Peak   *9,079 feet (Class 2)*
This peak is located directly above the Georgetown Canyon Road [(A)(3)] due east of Snowdrift Mountain. The summit is a very steep Class 2 scramble from the road via its south ridge. USGS Harrington Peak

Snowdrift Mountain   *9,577 feet (Class 1)*
Snowdrift Mountain is not a true summit, but instead is the name given for the ridge that contains Meade Peak. The high point designated as Snowdrift Mountain is situated east of Georgetown. The high point is reached after an enjoyable, Class 1 hike via the Snowdrift Mountain Trail [(A)(3)(a)]. It is roughly 4.5 miles to the summit from the Georgetown saddle. The peak is a broad, high ridge with a north/south orientation. Water that falls onto the mountain's western slopes flows into the Great Basin; water from its eastern slopes flows into the Columbia Basin via the Salt and Snake Rivers. The views from the top are terrific! USGS Snowdrift Mountain

Meade Peak   *9,957 feet (Class 3)*

Meade Peak is the highest point in the Peale Mountains, and the second highest Idaho peak south of the Snake River. The first ascent was recorded by Henry Gannet in 1887. The peak, which is 7 miles east of Georgetown, was named for Gen. George C. Meade of Civil War fame. The summit can be reached from two directions. The first approach follows the Snowdrift Mountain Trail [(A)(3)(a)] to Meade Basin—a long, but enjoyable 7-mile hike. The second approach leaves the Georgetown Canyon Road just before the national forest boundary and proceeds up the right fork of the canyon [(A)(5)] until the road ends. From the road's end, you must go cross-country up to the ridgeline south of the peak and then cross into Meade Basin. The peak is a walk-up via its north ridge or east slopes. The south ridge and west slopes are Class 3 scrambles on rotten rock. R. Baugher reports that only a couple of climbing parties visit the summit each year. USGS Meade Peak

APPROACHES TO THE PEALE MOUNTAINS

(A) PEALE MOUNTAIN ACCESS POINTS

The primary approaches to these mountains begin along US-30 in the west; US-89, which traverses the southern and eastern reaches; and ID-34, which provides access in the north. Many secondary and Forest Service roads access all parts of the range from these primary roads.

(1) **Henrys Peak Access.** This route begins along ID-34 at Wayan. Turn south off the highway and drive south nearly 1 mile to a second junction, where you turn right. In just over another mile, turn left and drive south along Gravel Creek until the road ends.

(2) **Diamond Peak Access.** Begin along US-89 4 miles north of Alton, Wyoming. Turn west off the highway and drive to Auburn, where the road jogs to the south for 0.5 mile. Turn west again on Stump Creek Road and follow it for about 5 miles to the Stump Creek GS.

(a) **FST-016, Horse Creek Trail.** This trail begins near the Stump Creek GS and runs due west up the drainage for 5 miles to a four-trail junction. Diamond Peak is just north of the trail near its western end.

(3) **FS-102, Georgetown Canyon Road.** This major approach leads to the center of the Peale Mountains. Access this road from US-30 at Georgetown. The road leads due east into the mountains. Just over 2 miles from US-30, a left turn leads north into the Left Fork Georgetown Canyon. The main road continues to Georgetown saddle and then drops down into Diamond Creek. The Diamond Creek Road eventually connects with ID-34 many miles to the north. Georgetown Canyon was the sight of a phosphate mine; its remnants are still visible today.

(a) **Snowdrift Mountain Trail.** From the Georgetown saddle, a good trail leads up the ridgeline to the south, crosses over Snowdrift Mountain, then drops into Meade Basin on the east side of Meade Peak. After steeply climbing for the first mile, the trail emerges on the top of the Snowdrift Mountain ridge, where there is open hiking with spectacular views of the Bear River area and the Salt River Range in Wyoming. It is 7 miles to the basin from the Georgetown saddle.

(4) **FS-095, Left Fork of Georgetown Canyon Road.** This road leads north from the Georgetown Canyon Road between the Aspen Range and Schmid Ridge. Dozens of roads depart from this road.

(5) **FS-225, Right Fork of Georgetown Canyon Road.** This road leaves FS-102 just west of the national forest boundary and runs up the canyon for 3 miles. A 4WD is recommended.

12

THE CARIBOU RANGE

The Caribou Range, which was named by Orestes St. John way back in 1879, is located just south of the Snake River on the Idaho/Wyoming border. Palisades Reservoir and the Snake River form the Caribou's northern boundary. The Salt River in Wyoming forms the eastern boundary; the Peale Mountains are on the southern boundary; and Blackfoot Reservoir and Grays Lake frame the western boundary.

The Caribou Range encompasses an area more than 60 miles in length and 20 miles in width and reaches 9,805 feet on Caribou Mountain. The northern end of the range is composed of parallel ridges that rise and fall in wavelike succession, while the central portion of the range contains all the major summits. The Caribou landscape is interspersed with rolling meadows, dense stands of pines and fir trees, and compact quaking aspen groves. The geologic history is written in sedimentary rocks, which have been intruded by igneous rock. These intrusions produced gold deposits, and the area was mined beginning in the 1870s. In addition, there are phosphate deposits just waiting to be exploited. The range is officially part of the Caribou National Forest, but is managed in a large part by the Targhee National Forest.

Climbing opportunities are limited to Class 1 and Class 2 hikes up dome-shaped summits. Hiking use of the range is minimal; a pity, because these mountains are among the most picturesque in the state. Access is better than average and the trail system, while not heavily used, is extensive. Primary road access to the Caribou Range is from US-26 in Idaho, US-89 in Wyoming, and ID-34 between Freedom, Wyoming, and Wayan. All other access points are reached by secondary Forest Service roads.

Red Peak   *8,720+ feet (Class I)*

Red Peak, the northernmost Caribou peak covered in this guidebook, is 6 miles due west of the Palisades Dam. The summit is reached by the Red Ridge Trail from Long Gulch [(A)(1.1)(a)]. The peak can be approached from several other directions, but these routes are much longer. USGS Red Ridge

Big Elk Mountain   *9,476 feet (Class 1)*
Little Elk Mountain   *8,760+ feet (Class 1)*

Big Elk and Little Elk Mountains are roughly 7.5 miles south of Red Peak. These two summits are separated by a snaking, up-and-down ridgeline about 3 miles long. Trails lead to the summits of these two peaks from four directions. From the McCoy Creek Road, take FST-003 [(B)(1)(b)] up Box Canyon to the summit. The shortest route is via FST-153 [(A)(2.1)(a)]. Follow FS-063 to its end and then take the seldom-used trail east to the summit of Big Elk. Another alternative is to follow FST-041 [(B)(1)(d)] up Wolverine Canyon to the saddle east of Little Elk, and then follow the ridge trail east to Big Elk or west to Little Elk. The fourth alternative begins at the Bear

Caribou Range from Mount Baird

Creek trailhead and utilizes FST-164 [(A)(2)(b)], which follows Muddy and Currant Creeks to the summit of Big Elk. The grown-over terraces near the summit of Big Elk bear evidence of coal prospecting, which occurred in this area early in the twentieth century. USGS Big Elk Mountain

Poker Peak   8,720 feet (Class 2)
Poker Peak is 4 miles east of Big Elk Mountain, 6 miles south of the Palisades Dam. Just south of the Currant Creek GS, FST-035 [(A)(2)(c)] climbs up Pine Creek and traverses nearly to the summit. From the trail, it is an easy walk to the summit. USGS Poker Peak

Caribou Mountain   9,803 feet
Caribou Mountain is situated 5 miles east of Bald Mountain. It is a unique-looking summit, with windswept upper ridges and small glacial cirques nestled into its northern and eastern slopes. The summit ridge is almost 1 mile long and has two high points—the southern summit is 9,586 feet; the northern, 9,803 feet. The mountain can be climbed from the west or the east. In the early days, this mountain was known as Mount Pisgah. The name was changed when Jesse "Caribou Jack" Fairchilds was killed by a grizzly bear in 1881. Soon after, his friends built a cairn and left a note in a tin can telling Caribou Jack's story. USGS Caribou Mountain

West Side (Class 2). From FS-119, follow the old jeep trail [(B)(2.1)] (best accomplished on foot) that climbs up the North Fork Eagle Creek to the Evergreen Mine at 8,400 feet. From the mine, gain the ridgeline above by hiking due south to Point 8732. Once at this point, follow the ridgeline northeast to the peak's lower southern summit, and then follow the summit ridge north to the north summit. Total distance from the mine is 1.5 miles with a 1,200-foot elevation gain. The peak's south slopes can be climbed from the mine, but that route is steeper.

Northeast Ridge (Class 2). The east side route climbs the peak's northeast ridge from the trail that cuts across it at 8,400 feet. This trail can be assessed from Caribou City or McCoy Creek [(B)(1.1) or (B)(1)(a)]. The northeast ridge provides straightforward access to the summit ridge as it climbs 1,200 feet in 0.6 mile. Once on the summit ridge, turn northeast and follow the ridge the last 0.3 mile to the north summit.

Monte Cristo Mine (Class 2). From the Monte Cristo Mine [(B)(1.2)] climb due east until you reach the top of the ridge that descends from the summit in an arc that includes Point 9642. Follow this ridge on its long arcing journey to the summit over talus and the occasional boulder field.

Old Baldy   8,325 feet (Class 1)
Bald Mountain   8,488 feet (Class 1)
Old Baldy and Bald Mountain are on a large northwest/southwest-trending ridgeline 8 miles south of Poker Peak. These two peaks are separated by 1 mile of ridge. Use FST-109 [(B)(1)(c)] from the McCoy Creek Road to reach the summits of both peaks. USGS Tincup Mountain

Black Mountain   8,920 feet (Class 1-2)
Black Mountain sits 4.5 miles east of Bald Mountain on the next parallel ridgeline. Black Mountain is formed by a ridge and has three high points, all of which reach above 8,900 feet. This mountain is reached via FST-004 [(B)(1)(a)], which leads along the ridge almost to the top of all three summits. There is a large communications facility on the summit. USGS Etna

Tincup Mountain   8,184 feet (Class 2)
Tincup Mountain is situated 6.5 miles southeast of Caribou Mountain and just north of the Pinebar CG. Take FST-009 to FST-110 [(B)(2)(a)]. Follow FST-110 north for 1 mile and then (after a junction) southeast for 0.8 mile. At this point, a trail leads down the Tin Cup ridge toward the summit. USGS Tincup Mountain

APPROACHES TO THE CARIBOU RANGE

(A) US-26 ACCESS POINTS
This highway runs between Idaho Falls and Alpine Junction, Wyoming. The roads below are listed from west to east.

(1) FS-058, Snake River Road. This good gravel road follows the south side of the Snake River between the point where US-26 crosses to the north side of the river west of Swan Valley and east of Palisades Dam.

(1.1) FS-059, Long Gulch Road. This road leaves FS-058 at its midpoint and ascends Long Gulch to an organizational camp and a trailhead in about 3 miles.

(a) FST-035, Red Ridge Trail. This trail leaves the end of the Long Gulch Road and climbs up to the top of Red Ridge in 2 miles. Once on the ridge, the trail continues southeast, just past the summit of Red Peak, and eventually leads to Palisades Dam in about 9 miles.

(2) FS-058, Bear Creek Road. This road leaves US-26 at the Palisades Dam, crosses the dam and proceeds along the reservoir, then turns up Elk Creek and down Jensen Creek, where it meets the McCoy Creek Road, FS-087 [(B)(1)]. When dry, this road is passable to passenger cars.

(a) **FST-031, Bear Creek Trail System.** This trail system begins just south of the Bear Creek arm of the Palisades Reservoir at a large trailhead. Bear Creek is the heart of an extensive roadless area. Although the trails do not lead to any major peaks, the drainage offers exceptional hiking opportunities. Several loop trips can be put together from the trailhead.

(b) **FST-044, Big Elk Peak Trail.** FST-044 is accessed from FST-031 just 1 mile west of its trailhead. The trail begins by following Muddy Creek and then climbs to the ridgeline between Muddy and Currant Creeks. After 3 miles, the trail reaches the north ridge of Big Elk, where it turns south and continues to that peak's summit in another mile. In this vicinity, it intersects with FST-153, which traverses the ridgeline between Big Elk and Little Elk Mountains.

(c) **FST-035, Poker Peak Trail.** This trail leaves FS-058 where it crosses Pine Creek. The trail climbs east to the Poker Peak ridgeline. Once on the ridge, the trail turns south and leads to the eastern slopes of Poker Peak in 3.5 miles. One mile south of the peak, the trail intersects with several other trails that provide access to the roadless area between the Bear Creek Road and Palisades Reservoir.

(2.1) **FS-063, West Fork Elk Creek Road.** This road is accessed from FS-058 a little more than 2 miles south of where FS-058 leaves Bear Creek. This road runs up the West Fork Elk Creek for 4 miles. It is a primitive road and a 4WD is recommended.

(a) **FST-153, Elk Mountain Trail.** This trail begins east of Big Elk Mountain at the end of FS-063 and proceeds west to a junction with FST-044 just south of the Big Elk Mountain summit. From this point, the trail continues west along a ridgeline and intersects with FST-041 in roughly 2 miles. After this junction, the trail continues west to Little Elk Mountain and ends at FS-159 in another 3 miles.

(B) US-89 ACCESS POINTS

US-89, between Alpine Junction and Afton, Wyoming, provides access to the western edge of the Caribou Range. It is a wide two-lane highway. The following roads are listed from north to south.

(1) **FS-087, McCoy Creek Road.** To reach this road, take US-89 south from Alpine, Wyoming, for 8 miles and turn east. This road eventually traverses the range and ends at Grays Lake.

(a) **FST-004, Black Mountain Trail.** Follow the McCoy Creek Road south from Palisades Reservoir for 4 miles. The trailhead is on the east side of the road. This trail traverses the major north/south ridgeline that has Black Mountain as its high point.

(b) **FST-003, Canyon Creek Trail.** This trail leaves FS-087 a little over 6 miles west of the McCoy Creek CG and follows Canyon Creek northwest to Big Elk Mountain in 6.5 miles.

(c) **FST-109, Bald Mountain Trail.** This trail leaves FS-087 near the Bald Mountain GS and quickly climbs a ridgeline. It then runs south to Old Baldy Peak in 3 miles and Bald Mountain in another mile.

(d) **FST-164, Wolverine Creek Trail.** This trailhead is located between the Bald Mountain and Caribou Basin guard stations. Turn north on FS-164, which quickly leads to the trailhead. The trail immediately crosses Clear Creek and then leads north to a ridgeline south of Wolverine Creek. The trail then follows the ridge northwest to the saddle between Big Elk and Little Elk Mountains.

(1.1) **FS-165 Caribou City Access.** FS-165 leaves FS-087 west of the Bald Mountain GS and leads south to Caribou City in about 3 miles. A 4WD is recommended.

(1.2) **Caribou Mountain Western Access.** FS-188, a rocky, seldom-used road, leaves FS-087 at the site of Keenan City just west of the Caribou Basin GS and leads south up Barnes Creek toward Caribou Mountain. Near the headwaters of Barnes Creek, a 4WD road leaves FS-188 and runs south to a mine on Caribou Mountain's northeastern slope. This jeep trail reaches the mountain's northeast ridge in 2 miles. It is suggested that you hike this road to reach the northwest ridge. From the point where the jeep road leaves FS-188, the route turns southwest toward the Monte Cristo Mine. At the mine, the road designation changes to FS-118. FS-118 continues south to a county road and the Grays Lake National Wildlife Refuge. A 4WD is recommended.

(2) **ID-34, Tin Cup Highway.** ID-34 crosses the range between Freedom, Wyoming, and Wayan. This road is well maintained, but far from a major access route.

(a) **FST-009/FS-010, Tincup Mountain Trail.** This trail leaves ID-34 1.5 miles west of Pinebar CG and heads north to the ridgeline west of Tincup Mountain. From this point, the trail connects with a series of lonesome trails that traverse the roadless area between Black Mountain and Caribou Mountain.

(2.1) **Evergreen Mine Access.** Leave ID-34 and Grays Lake 2.5 miles northwest of Wayan by turning onto the county road that parallels the eastern shore of Grays Lake. Shortly after this road crosses Eagle Creek, turn east onto FS-119, which ends in a mile. From this point, a jeep road leads northeast up the North Fork Eagle Creek to the Evergreen Mine in 3.2 miles. The jeep trail requires a 4WD.

APPENDIX A

IDAHO PEAKS 10,000 FEET OR HIGHER

PEAK	RANGE	ELEVATION	USGS QUAD	LOCATION
1. Borah Peak*	Lost River	12,655	Borah Peak	
2. Leatherman Peak	Lost River	12,230	Leatherman Peak	
3. Mount Church	Lost River	12,200+	Leatherman Peak	(2 miles W of Mount Brietenbach/1.5 Miles SW of Leatherman Peak)
4. Diamond Peak*	Lemhi	12,197	Diamond Peak	
5. Mount Brietenbach	Lost River	12,140	Leatherman Peak	
6. Lost Rivers Mountain	Lost River	12,078	Leatherman Peak	(1.75 miles SE of Mount Brietenbach)
7. Mount Idaho	Lost River	12,065	Elkhorn Creek	(1.5 NE of Pass Lake)
8. Donaldson Peak	Lost River	12,023	Leatherman Peak	(1.25 miles W of Mount Britenbach)
9. Hyndman Peak*	Pioneer	12,009	Hyndman Peak	
10. Peak 11990	Lost River	11,990	Leatherman Peak	(0.25 mile N of Leatherman Peak)
11. USGS Peak	Lost River	11,982	Massacre Mountain	(McCaleb triangulation station)
12. No Regret Peak	Lost River	11,972	Leatherman Peak	(0.75 mile NE of Mount Brietenbach)
13. Peak 11967	Lost River	11,967	Elkhorn Creek	(0.9 mile S of Mount Idaho)
14. Bad Rock Peak	Lost River	11,953	Leatherman Peak	(0.5 mile SE of Leatherman Peak)
15. Sacajawea Peak	Lost River	11,936	Elkhorn Creek	(1 mile S of Mount Borah)
16. Peak 11930	Lost River	11,930	Massacre Mountain	(1.5 miles E of Lost River Mountain)
17. Goat Mountain	Pioneer	11,913	Phi Kappa Mountain	(2.25 miles SE of the Devils Bedstead)
18. White Cap Peak	Lost River	11,899	Elkhorn Creek	(0.5 mile W of Leatherman Peak)
19. Peak 11887	Pioneer	11,887	Standhope Peak	(0.75 mile S of Standhope Peak)
20. Standhope Peak	Pioneer	11,878	Standhope Peak	
21. Devils Bedstead East	Pioneer	11,865	Phi Kappa Mountain	(0.25 mile W of Washington Lake)
22. Mount Corruption	Lost River	11,857	Leatherman Peak	(3 miles N of Mount Brietenbach)
23. Brocky Peak	Pioneer	11,839	Standhope Peak	(2.5 miles SW of Standhope Peak)
24. Peak 11828	Lost River	11,828	Borah Peak	(1.6 miles NE of Borah Peak)
25. Altair Peak	Pioneer	11,825	Standhope Peak	(1 mile NE of Standhope Peak)
26. Castle Peak*	White Cloud	11,815	Boulder Chain of Lakes	
27. Old Hyndman Peak	Pioneer	11,775	Grays Peak	
28. Duncans Peak	Pioneer	11,755	Phi Kappa Mountain	(High point on Duncan Ridge)
29. Pegasus Peak	Pioneer	11,736	Standhope Peak	
30. Ross Peak	Lost River	11,724	Massacre Mountain	(Due S of Shadow Lake)
31. Ryan Peak*	Boulder	11,714	Ryan Peak	
32. The Angels Perch	Pioneer	11,687	Standhope Peak	(0.75 W of Angel Lake)
33. Mount McCaleb	Lost River	11,682	Mackay	
34. Kent Peak	Boulder	11,664	Ryan Peak	
35. Cobb Peak	Pioneer	11,650	Hyndman Peak	
36. Pyramid Peak	Pioneer	11,628	Copper Basin	
37. Bell Mountain	Lemhi	11,612	Diamond Peak	(1.5 miles SE of Devils Bedstead West)
38. Peak 11611	Lost River	11,611	Borah Peak	(2.5 miles SE of Doublespring Pass)

39. Glassford Peak	Boulder	11,602	Ryan Peak	
40. Salzburger Spitzl	Pioneer	11,600+	Phi Kappa Mountain	
41. The Riddler	Lemhi	11,598	Diamond Peak	(1.25 miles S of Diamond Peak)
42. Big Basin Peak	Pioneer	11,510	Grays Peak	(0.9 mile E of Old Hyndman)
43. Peak 11509	Lost River	11,509	Leatherman Peak	(1.8 miles SE of Mount Corruption)
44. Ferguson Peak	Lost River	11,509	Massacre Mountain	(1.3 miles W of Swauger Lakes)
45. Smiley Mountain	Pioneer	11,508	Smiley Mountain	
46. Caulkens Peak	White Cloud	11,500+	Boulder Chain	(Caulkens triangulation station)
47. Peak 11485	Boulder	11,485	Ryan Peak	(1.6 miles N/NW of Glassford Peak)
48. Peak 11477	Lost River	11,477	Massacre Mountain	(0.9 mile NW of Castle Peak)
49. Peak 11473	Lost River	11,473	Borah Peak	(3.7 miles N/NE of Borah Peak)
50. Big Boy Peak	Lemhi	11,402	Fallert Springs	(Due S of The Riddler)
51. Shadow Lake Peak	Lost River	11,401	Massacre Mountain	
52. Scott Peak*	Beaverhead	11,393	Scott Peak	
53. Peak 11367	Lost River	11,367	Elkhorn Creek	(1.2 miles W of Mount Idaho)
54. Big Black Dome	Pioneer	11,353	Big Black Dome	
55. Big Creek Peak	Lemhi	11,350	Big Creek Peak	
56. D.O. Lee Peak	White Cloud	11,342	Washington Peak	(0.5 mile W of Cirque Lake)
57. Triple Peak	Lost River	11,332	Massacre Mountain	(0.8 mile W of Nolan Lake)
58. Invisible Peak	Lost River	11,330	Mackay	
59. Al West Peak	Lost River	11,310	Borah Peak	(2.9 miles NE of Borah Peak)
60. Wet Peak	Lost River	11,309	Mackay	
61. Hidden Peak	Lost River	11,308	Massacre Mountain	(0.6 mile N of Wet Peak)
62. Peak 11305	Pioneer	11,305	Grays Peak	(1.8 miles E of Old Hyndman)
63. Peak 11302	White Cloud	11,302	Boulder Chain	(2 miles N of Patterson Peak)
64. Peak 11292	Beaverhead	11,292	Scott Peak	(0.7 mile W of Scott Peak)
65. Peak 11280	Lost River	11,280	Leatherman Peak	(1.5 miles NE of Mount Brietenbach)
66. Shelly Mountain*	White Knob	11,278	Shelly Mountain	
67. Sheephead Peak	Lost River	11,276	Mackay	(1 mile NW of Invisible Mountain)
68. Redbird Mountain	White Knob	11,273	Shelly Mountain	
69. Little Diamond Peak	Lemhi	11,272	Fallert Springs	(1.4 miles S of Diamond Peak)
70. Peak 11272	White Cloud	11,272	Boulder Chain of Lakes	(0.75 mile S of Cove Lake)
71. WCP-9	White Cloud	11,263	Washington Peak	(0.9 mile SE of Ocalkens Lake)
72. Peak 11258	Pioneer	11,258	Smiley Mountain	(1.7 miles W of Smiley Mountain)
73. Peak 11240+	Lost River	11,240+	Massacre Mountain	(2 miles S/SE of Massacre Mountain)
74. Peak 11240+	Boulder	11,240+	Easley Hot Springs	(1 mile W of Silver Peak)
75. Cabin Mountain	White Knob	11,224	Copper Basin	
76. Perkins Peak	Boulder	11,220	Ryan Peak	(1 mile SE of Kent Peak)
77. Shoshone John Peak	Lemhi	11,212	Fallert Springs	(2.6 miles S of Diamond Peak)
78. Peak 11210	Pioneer	11,210	Grays Peak	(1.7 miles SE of Old Hyndman)
79. Peak 11202	White Cloud	11,202	Boulder Chain of Lakes	(1.5 miles W of Frog Lake)
80. Peak 11200 (Apex Peak)	Lost River	11,200	Leatherman PK	
81. Lime Mountain	White Knob	11,179	Shelly Mountain	
82. Cerro Ciento	Boulder	11,154	Easley Hot Springs	
83. Galena Peak	Boulder	11,153	Galena Peak	
84. Peak 11151	Pioneer	11,151	Smiley Mountain	(2.1 miles N of Smiley Mountain)
85. Eighteenmile Peak	Beaverhead	11,141	Scott Peak	
86. Dickey Peak	Lost River	11,141	Dickey Peak	
87. South Wet Peak	Lost River	11,138	Mackay	(3 miles E of Mount McCaleb)
88. Silver Peak	Boulder	11,112	Easley Hot Springs	
89. Pavlos Peak	Lost River	11,109	Grouse Creek Mountain	(1 mile SE of Petros Peak)
90. Easley Peak	Boulder	11,108	Easley Hot Springs	
91. WCP-10	White Cloud	11,102	Boulder Chain of Lakes	(0.5 mile E of Caulkens triangulation station)

92.	Gooseberry Peak	Lost River	11,090	Grouse Creek Mountain	(2.75 miles SE of McGowan Peak)
93.	Grouse Creek Mountain	Lost River	11,085	Grouse Creek Mountain	
94.	Peak 11081	Lost River	11,081	Sunset Peak	(North Twin: 2.5 miles N of Jaggle Peak)
95.	Peak 11080+	Lost River	11,080+	Leatherman Peak	(Due S of Peak 11509)
96.	Little Mac	Lost River	11,071	Mackay	(0.6 mile W. Mount McCaleb)
97.	Peak 11070	Lost River	11,070	Sunset Peak	(South Twin: 1.6 miles N of Jaggle Peak)
98.	Griswold Peak	Boulder	11,057	Ryan Peak	(3 miles N of Ryan Peak)
99.	Devils Bedstead W.	Pioneer	11,051	Phi Kappa Mountain	
100.	Nicholson Peak	Lemhi	11,051	Fallert Springs	(1.3 miles S/SW of Diamond Peak)
101.	Petros Peak	Lost River	11,050	Grouse Creek Mountain	(Due S of Peak 10731)
102.	Trinity Peak	Lost River	11,050	Grouse Creek Mountain	(Grouse Creek/Christian Gulch Divide)
103.	Peak 11041	Boulder	11,041	Easley Hot Springs	(0.7 mile N/NW of Boulder Peak)
104.	Atlas Peak	Pioneer	11,039	Smiley Mountain	(0.6 mile W of Big Lake)
105.	Jacqueline Peak	Pioneer	11,027	Grays Peak	(1.8 miles SE of Old Hyndman)
106.	Cottonwood Mountain	Beaverhead	11,024	Cottonwood Creek	
107.	Flatiron Peak	Lemhi	11,019	Big Creek Peak	
108.	Peak 11010	Lost River	11,010	Grouse Creek Mountain	(3 miles S of Grouse Creek Mountain)
109.	The Brow	Lemhi	11,005	Diamond Peak	(1.3 miles NW of Diamond Peak)
110.	Italian Peak	Beaverhead	10,998	Scott Peak	
111.	Peak 10995	Pioneer	10,995	Smiley Mountain	(Due S of Copper Basin Knob)
112.	Lem Peak	Lemhi	10,985	Lem Peak	
113.	Boulder Peak	Boulder	10,981	Easley Hot Springs	
114.	May Mountain	Lemhi	10,971	May Mountain	
115.	Yellow Peak	Lemhi	10,968	Patterson	
116.	Black and White Peak	Lemhi	10,970	Fallert Springs	(0.8 mile N of Little Diamond Peak)
117.	Peak 10965	Lemhi	10,965	Fallert Springs	(Between Nicholson Peak and the Lemhi crest)
118.	Castle Peak	Lost River	10,957	Massacre Mountain	
119.	Big Sister	Lemhi	10,946	Bell Mountain	(3 miles NW of Diamond Peak)
120.	Jump Peak	Beaverhead	10,941	Cottonwood Creek	
121.	Peak 10925	Lost River	10,925	Grouse Creek Mountain	(Head of Arentson Gulch)
122.	Massacre Mountain	Lost River	10,924	Massacre Mountain	
123.	Merriam Peak	White Cloud	10,920	Boulder Chain of Lakes	(0.5 mile N of Castle Peak)
124.	Peak 10920	Pioneer	10,920	Smiley Mountain	(S of Brockie Lake)
125.	Sheep Mountain	Boulder	10,915	Bowery Peak	
126.	Peak 10883	Boulder	10,883	Bowery Peak	(0.7 mile S of Bowery Peak)
127.	Peak 10882	Lemhi	10,882	Yellow Peak	(1.5 miles SW of Devils Basin)
128.	Patterson Mountain	White Cloud	10,872	Boulder Chain of Lakes	
129.	Sheep Mountain	Lemhi	10,865	Gilmore	
130.	Bowery Peak	Boulder	10,861	Sheep Mountain	
131.	Incredible Hulk	Lemhi	10,858	Bell Mountain	(3 miles E/SE of Bell Mountain)
132.	Handwerk Peak	Pioneer	10,840	Phi Kappa Mountain	
133.	Gunsight Peak	Lemhi	10,835	Patterson	
134.	White Knob Mountain	White Knob	10,835	Shelly Mountain	(2 miles N of Redbird Mountain)
135.	Portland Mountain	Lemhi	10,820	Gilmore	
136.	Saddle Mountain	Lemhi	10,810	Tyler Peak	
137.	Lame Jake Peak	Lemhi	10,810	Diamond Peak	(2 miles N of Diamond Peak)
138.	Swanson Peak	Lemhi	10,808	Fallert Springs	(4 miles N of Uncle Ike/Pass Creek saddle)
139.	Peak 10805	Pioneer	10,805	Grays Peak	(1.5 miles S of Upper Box Canyon Lake)
140.	Octoberfest Peak	Lost River	10,800+	Massacre Mountain	(0.9 mile N of Bear Creek Lake)
141.	Peak 10800+	Pioneer	10,800+	Smiley Mountain	(Head of Antelope Creek)
142.	Mill Mountain	Lemhi	10,793	Patterson	
143.	Peak 10790	Lemhi	10,790	Fallert Springs	(1 mile S of Shoshone Jake Peak)
144.	Mystery Peak	Boulder	10,785	Meridian Peak	(5 miles N Trail Creek Summit/Rock Roll Canyon quad)

145.	Copper Basin Knob	Pioneer	10,784	Copper Basin	
146.	WCP-7	White Cloud	10,777	Washington Peak	(0.7 mile E of Ocaulkens Lake)
147.	Peak 10776	Beaverhead	10,776	Scott Peak	(1.2 miles NW of Italian Peak)
148.	Peak 10775	Lemhi	10,775	Lem Peak	(1 mile S of Lem Peak)
149.	Baldy Mountain	Beaverhead	10,773	Morrison Lake	
150.	Jaggle Peak	Lost River	10,772	Sunset Peak	
151.	King Mountain	Lost River	10,760	Ramshorn Canyon	
152.	Rust Peak	Lemhi	10,759	Diamond Peak	(4.5 miles SE of Bell Mountain)
153.	Peak 10757	Lost River	10,757	Grouse Creek Mountain	(Due S of Gooseberry Peak)
154.	Thompson Peak*	Sawtooth	10,751	Stanley Lake	
155.	Peak 10749	Lost River	10,749	Grouse Creek Mountain	(4.25 miles SE of McGown Peak)
156.	Gilmore Peak	Lemhi	10,748	Gilmore	(1.1 mile S of Mogg Mountain)
157.	Bear Mountain	Lemhi	10,744	Moffet Springs	
158.	Err Peak	Pioneer	10,744	Trail Creek	(Due E of Scorpion Peak)
159.	Peak 10744	Lemhi	10,744	Lem Peak	(2 miles S/SE of Lem Peak)
160.	Peak 10743	Lemhi	10,743	Iron Creek Point	(2 miles NE of Iron Creek Point)
161.	Peak 10743	Lemhi	10,743	Big Creek Peak	(Iron Divide)
162.	Tyler Peak	Lemhi	10,740	Tyler Peak	
163.	Iron Creek Point	Lemhi	10,736	Iron Creek Point	
164.	Buffalo Skull Peak	Lemhi	10,735	Mogg Mountain	(1.1 mile S of Mogg Mountain)
165.	Peak 10730	Lost River	10,730	Grouse Creek Mountain	(2.5 miles N of Dickey Peak)
166.	Long Mountain	Lemhi	10,728	May Mountain	
167.	Mount Hoopes	Lemhi	10,728	Tyler Peak	(0.7 mile S of Tyler Peak)
168.	Peak 10723	Lemhi	10,723	Yellow Peak	(1.9 miles SW of Gunsight Peak)
169.	Little Sister	Lemhi	10,723	Bell Mountain	(3 miles NW of Diamond Peak)
170.	Tendoy Peak	Lemhi	10,720	Allison Creek	(Due W of Bear Valley Lakes)
171.	Mount Cramer	Sawtooth	10,716	Mount Cramer	
172.	McGowan Peak	Lost River	10,716	Grouse Creek Mountain	(McGowan Vamb Site)
173.	Mount Inspiration	Lemhi	10,715	Big Windy Peak	(S of Trail Peak)
174.	Umpleby Peak	Lemhi	10,713	Coal Kiln Canyon	(N of Bell Mountain)
175.	Peak 10713	White Cloud	10,713	Washington Peak	(0.9 mile S/SW of Fourth of July Lake)
176.	Peak 10705	White Cloud	10,705	Galena Peak	(2 miles E of Deer Lakes)
177.	Decker Peak	Sawtooth	10,704	Mount Cramer	
178.	Sunset Peak	Lost River	10,693	Sunset Peak	
179.	Shril Peak	Lemhi	10,690	Eightmile Canyon	(2.3 miles N of Tyler Peak)
180.	Peak 10688	Lemhi	10,688	Mogg Mountain	(SE of Mill Lake)
181.	Mickeys Spire	Sawtooth	10,680	Stanley Lake	(0.4 mile SE of Tompson Peak)
182.	Mount Carpenter	Beaverhead	10,680	Cottonwood Creek	(10 miles south of Baldy Mountain)
183.	Peak 10680	Boulder	10,680	Ryan Peak	(1.8 miles S of Ryan Peak)
184.	Pioneer Peak	Pioneer	10,680	Smiley Mountain	(0.5 mile S of Peak 10480)
185.	Sheephorn Peak	Lemhi	10,665	Sheephorn Peak	
186.	Meadow Peak	Lemhi	10,652	Coal Kiln Canyon	(Due E of Bell Mountain)
187.	Snowyside Peak	Sawtooth	10,651	Snowyside Peak	
188.	Antares Peak	Pioneer	10,651	Star Hope Mine	(1.5 miles NE of Scorpion Peak)
189.	Peak 10650	Pioneer	10,650	Star Hope Mine	(1.2 miles N of Scorpion Peak)
190.	Williams Peak	Sawtooth	10,635	Stanley Lake	
191.	Peak 10621	White Cloud	10,621	Galena Peak	(2 miles E of Deer Lakes)
192.	Sunrise Peak	Lost River	10,618	Sunset Peak	(1.1 miles SE of Sunset Peak)
193.	Peak 10615	Lost River	10,615	Grouse Creek Mountain	(1.25 miles NW of McGowan Peak)
194.	Peak 10613	Pioneer	10,613	Star Hope Mine	(2 miles N of Scorpion Peak)
195.	Inyo Peak	Lemhi	10,611	Yellow Peak	
196.	Junction Peak	Lemhi	10,608	Yellow Peak	
197.	Peak 10604	Lemhi	10,604	Fallert Springs	(1 mile W/SW of Shril Peak)

198.	Patterson Peak	Lemhi	10,602	Yellow Peak	(1.85 miles S of Everson Lake)
199.	Big Eightmile Peak	Lemhi	10,601	Yellow Peak	(Due W of Devils Basin)
200.	Peak 10601	Lost River	10,601	Ramshorn Canyon	(1.7 miles S of Jaggle Peak)
201.	Peak 10598	Boulder	10,598	Rock Roll Canyon	(4 miles NW of Trail Creek Summit)
202.	WCP-5	White Cloud	10,597	Robinson Bar	(0.9 mile SE of Swimm Lake)
203.	Mount Carter	Sawtooth	10,590	Stanley Lake	(0.3 mile W of Thompson Peak)
204.	WCP-3	White Cloud	10,588	Robinson Bar	(0.5 mile NE of Swimm Lake)
205.	Peak 10585	Pioneer	10,585	Phi Kappa Mountain	(0.8 mile NW of Phi Kappa Mountain)
206.	Elk Peak	Sawtooth	10,582	Warbonnet Peak	
207.	Mogg Mountain	Lemhi	10,573	Mogg Mountain	
208.	Negro Peak	Lemhi	10,571	Gilmore	
209.	Peak 10571	Lost River	10,571	Sunset Peak	(0.9 mile E of Jaggle Peak)
210.	Peak 10569	Lemhi	10,569	Mogg Mountain	(2.5 miles S of Mogg Mountain)
211.	Peak 10566	Boulder	10,566	Rock Roll Canyon	(0.5 miles E of Peak 10598)
212.	Grays Peak	Pioneer	10,563	Grays Peak	
213.	WCP-8	White Cloud	10,557	Washington Peak	(1.25 miles South of Ocalkens Lake)
214.	Rocky Peak	Lemhi	10,555	Sheephorn Peak	
215.	Timber Creek Peak	Lemhi	10,553	Iron Creek Point	
216.	Peak 10552	Boulder	10,552	Meridian Peak	(1.6 miles NW of Meridian Peak)
217.	Peak 10550	Lemhi	10,550	May Mountain	(1 mile NW of Long Mountain)
218.	Scorpion Mountain	Pioneer	10,545	Muldoon Canyon	
219.	Peak 10540	Lemhi	10,540	Yellow Peak	(2 miles S of Gunsight Peak)
220.	Peak 10533	Lemhi	10,533	Patterson	(Patterson Divide)
221.	Trail Peak	Lemhi	10,533	Gilmore	
222.	Peak 10533	Lemhi	10,533	Coal Kiln Canyon	
223.	Drummond Peak	Pioneer	10,525	Star Hope Mine	(0.4 mile E of Drummond Mine)
224.	Washington Peak	White Cloud	10,519	Washington Peak	
225.	Phi Kappa Mountain	Pioneer	10,516	Phi Kappa Mountain	
226.	Peak 10512	Lemhi	10,512	Fallert Springs	(Head of Rock Run Creek)
227.	Peak 10507	Lemhi	10,507	Yellow Peak	(W of Yellow Lake)
228.	Peak 10488	Boulder	10,488	Horton Peak	(0.6 mile N of Deer Lakes)
229.	Peak 10487	Lemhi	10,487	May Mountain	(2 miles W of Long Mountain)
230.	Gothic Peak	Lemhi	10,487	Yellow Peak	(4.8 miles SE of Mogg Mountain)
231.	Peak 10480+	Pioneer	10,480+	Smiley Mountain	(1.2 miles E of Scorpion Mountain)
232.	Mount Sevy	Sawtooth	10,480	Mount Cramer	(0.5 mile W of Finger of Fate)
233.	Peak 10475	Lemhi	10,475	Fallert Springs	
234.	Horstmann Peak	Sawtooth	10,470	Warbonnet Peak	
235.	Peak 10466	Lemhi	10,466	May Mountain	(1.3 miles NW of May Mountain)
236.	Peak 10466	Boulder	10,466	Ryan Peak	(2.4 miles W of Kent Peak)
237.	Sheephorn Peak	Lemhi	10,465	Sheephorn Peak	
238.	Rock Roll Peak	Boulder	10,458	Rock Roll Canyon	(Above Rock and Roll Canyon)
239.	Peak 10456	Lemhi	10,456	Lem Peak	(Due N of Lem Peak)
240.	Watson Peak	White Cloud	10,453	Robinson Bar	
241.	WCP-4	White Cloud	10,450	Robinson Bar	(0.6 mile N of Watson Peak)
242.	Peak 10448	Boulder	10,448	Horton Peak	(N of Deer Lakes)
243.	Peak 10444	Pioneer	10,444	Star Hope Mine	(2.2 miles E/SE of Glide Mountain)
244.	Saivers Peak*	Smoky	10,441	Galena	(0.5 mile E of Bromingham Peak)
245.	Heart Mountain	Beaverhead	10,422	Heart Mountain	
246.	Peak 10420	Lost River	10,420	Doublespring	(Christian Gulch/Doublespring Divide)
247.	Basils Peak	Boulder	10,414	Amber Lakes	(Directly W of Amber Lakes)
248.	Buckhorn Peak	Lemhi	10,412	Fallert Springs	(2 miles S of Uncle Ike/Pass Creek saddle)
249.	Peak 10405	White Cloud	10,405	Galena Peak	(1.7 miles W of Bowery GS)
250.	Dianes Peak	Beaverhead	10,404	Eighteenmile Creek	(5.5 miles S of Eighteenmile Creek)

251.	White Mountain*	Salmon River	10,400+	Twin Peaks	
252.	North Targhee Peak*	Henrys Lake	10,400+	Earthquake Lake	(1.1 mile N of Targhee Peak)
253.	Meridian Peak	Boulder	10,400+	Meridian Peak	
254.	Peak 10400	Pioneer	10,400+	Star Hope Mine	(2.4 miles S of Glide Mountain)
255.	North Doublet	Beaverhead	10,390	Homer Youngs Peak	(1.1 miles S/SE of Monument Peak)
256.	Mount Limbert	Sawtooth	10,385	Stanley Lake	(1 mile SW of Thompson Peak)
257.	Peak 10383	Lemhi	10,383	Patterson	(Patterson Divide)
258.	South Doublet	Beaverhead	10,365	Homer Youngs Peak	(1 mile S of Monument Peak)
259.	Center Mountain	Beaverhead	10,362	Bohannon Spring	
260.	Big Windy Peak	Lemhi	10,360	Big Windy Peak	
261.	WCP-1	White Cloud	10,353	Robinson Bar	(0.7 mile W of Hoodoo Lake)
262.	Braxon Peak	Sawtooth	10,353	Mount Cramer	
263.	Peak 10343	Lemhi	10,343	Yellow Peak	(1.6 miles NE of Yellow Peak)
264.	South Twin Peak	Salmon River	10,340	Twin Peaks	
265.	Peak 10340	Beaverhead	10,340	Eighteenmile Cr	(Above Willow Creek)
266.	Cache Peak*	Albion	10,339	Independence Mountain	
267.	Norton Peak	Smoky	10,336	Galena	
268.	Peak 10332	Lemhi	10,332	Gilmore	(SW of Negro Peak)
269.	Peak 10330	Sawtooth	10,330	Stanley Lake	(0.6 mile NW of Baron Peak)
270.	The General	Salmon River	10,329	Mount Jordan	(General triangulation station)
271.	Mount Iowa	Sawtooth	10,327	Mount Cramer	(0.75 mile N of Braxon Peak)
272.	Peak 10327	Lemhi	10,327	Lem Peak	(3.1 mile N of Lem Peak)
273.	Mounument Peak	Beaverhead	10,323	Homer Youngs Peak	
274.	Croesus Peak	White Cloud	10,322	Horton Peak	(1 mile S of Washington Peak)
275.	Merrit Peak	Sawtooth	10,312	Stanley Lake	(1 mile S of Goat Lake)
276.	Bald Mountain	Salmon River	10,313	Bald Mountain	
277.	Blackman Peak	White Cloud	10,307	Washington Peak	
278.	Copper Mountain	Beaverhead	10,303	Copper Mountain	
279.	Baron Peak	Sawtooth	10,297	Warbonnet Peak	
280.	Peak 10297	Lost River	10,297	Massacre Mountain	(0.7 mile NE of Swauger Lakes)
281.	Annies Peak	Lemhi	10,288	Yellow Peak	(Due S of Patterson Peak)
282.	Targhee Peak	Henrys Lake	10,280	Henrys Lake	
283.	Mackay Peak	White Knob	10,273	Mackay	
284.	Freeman Peak	Beaverhead	10,273	Homer Youngs Peak	
285.	WCP-2	White Cloud	10,271	Robinson Bar	(0.6 mile NW of Swimm Lake)
286.	Perfect Peak	Sawtooth	10,269	Snowyside Peak	(1.7 miles SE of Snowyside Peak)
287.	Glide Mountain	Pioneer	10,265	Star Hope Mine	(0.5 mile NE of Ocalkens Lake)
288.	WCP-6	White Cloud	10,256	Robinson Bar	(0.5 mile NE of Ocalkins Lake)
289.	Peak 10256	Lemhi	10,256	Gilmore	(SW of Negro Peak)
290.	Peak 10243	Boulder	10,243	Horton Peak	(3 miles NW of Galena Peak)
291.	Red Conglomerate Peak	Beaverhead	10,240+	Edie Creek	
292.	Packrat Peak	Sawtooth	10,240+	Warbonnet Peak	
293.	Black Mountain	Henrys Lake	10,237	Henrys Lake	
294.	Bromaghin Peak	Smoky	10,225	Galena	
295.	Vienna Peak	Sawtooth	10,224	Frenchman Creek	(Vienna triangulation station)
296.	Redfish Peak	Sawtooth	10,212	Mount Cramer	(2 miles W of Decker Peak)
297.	Payette Peak	Sawtooth	10,211	Snowyside Mountain	
298.	Cirque Lake Peak	Sawtooth	10,210	Warbonnet	(Directly E of Warbonnet Peak)
299.	Parks Peak	Sawtooth	10,208	Snowyside Mountain	
300.	Edelman Peak	Beaverhead	10,201	Eighteenmile Creek	(2 miles SW of Dianes Peak)
301.	Peak 10201	White Knob	10,201	Shelly Mountain	(2.8 miles NE of Redbird Mountain)
302.	Peak 10200+	Sawtooth	10,200+	Mount Cramer	(0.5 mile W of Saddleback Lakes)
303.	Warbonnet Peak	Sawtooth	10,200+	Warbonnet Peak	

304. Heyburn Mountain	Sawtooth	10,200+	Mount Cramer	
305. Mount Jefferson*	Centenial	10,203	Mount Jefferson Lakes	
306. North Twin Peak	Salmon River	10,196	Twin Peaks	
307. Horse Prairie Peak	Beaverhead	10,194	Deadman Pass	
308. Mount Regan	Sawtooth	10,190	Stanley Lake	
309. Peak 10181	White Cloud	10,181	Horton Peak	(1.9 miles E/NE of Horton Peak)
310. Bald Peak (Lionhead)	Henrys Lake	10,180	Henrys Lake	
311. Baker Peak	Smoky	10,174	Baker Peak	
312. Peak 10166	White Cloud	10,166	Horton Peak	(2.5 miles SE of Horton Peak)
313. Peak 10162	Lemhi	10,162	Coal Kiln Canyon	
314. Mount Underhill	Sawtooths	10,160	Warbonnet Peak	(0.5 mile S of Packrat Peak)
315. Elk Mountain	Beaverhead	10,153	Deadman Pass	(8 miles E/SE of Bannock Pass)
316. Peak 10149	Lost River Range	10,149	Massacre Mountain	
317. Peak 10149	Pioneer	10,149	Smiley Mountain	(Directly above Iron Bog Lake)
318. Prairie Creek Peak	Smoky	10,138	Baker Peak	(1.5 miles SW of Norton Peak)
319. Peak 10137	Smoky	10,137	Baker Peak	(0.9 mile SE of Baker Peak)
320. Peak 10132	White Cloud	10,132	Washington Peak	(2.2 miles NW of Blackman Peak)
321. Peak 10129	Sawtooth	10,129	Marshall Peak	(E of Eureka Gulch)
322. Peak 10127	Sawtooth	10,127	Snowyside Peak	(1.2 miles S of McDonald Peak)
323. Peak 10126	Boulder	10,126	Horton Peak	(2.2 miles NW of Govenors Punchbowl)
324. Imogene Peak	Sawtooth	10,125	Snowyside Mountain	
325. Conical Top Peak	Beaverhead	10,125	Reservoir Peak	(3.3 miles NW of Baldy Peak)
326. Two Point Mountain*	Boise	10,124	Newman Peak	
327. Dead Horse Summit	Beaverhead	10,120	Scott Peak	
328. Peak 10111	White Cloud	10,111	Washington Peak	(1.1 miles N of Blackman Peak)
329. Titus Peak	Smoky	10,110	Galena	(0.5 mile E of Bromingham Peak.)
330. Peak 10100	Beaverhead	10,100	Eighteenmile Peak	(Above Willow Creek)
331. Peak 10099	Smoky	10,099	Baker Peak	(0.5 mile W of Baker Lake)
332. Smoky Dome*	Soldier	10,095	Smoky Dome	
333. Mount Mcguire*	Big Horn Crags	10,082	Mount Mcguire	
334. Peak 10081	White Cloud	10,081	Horton Peak	(2 miles E/NE of Horton Peak Lookout)
335. Monte Verita	Sawtooth	10,080	Warbonnet Peak	
336. Mayan Temple	Sawtooth	10,080+	Warbonnet Peak	(Directly W of Packrat Peak)
337. Reward Peak	Sawtooth	10,074	Warbonnet Peak	
338. Mcdonald Peak	Sawtooth	10,068	Snowyside Peak	
339. Peak 10067	Beaverhead	10,067	Powderhorn Gulch	(S of Bannock Pass)
340. Mount Jordan	Salmon River	10,063	Mount Jordan	
341. Copperhead Peak	Beaverhead	10,060	Homer Youngs Peak	
342. Peak 10056	Beaverhead	10,056	Bohannon Spring	(2 miles SE of Center Mountain)
343. Glens Peak	Sawtooth	10,053	Mount Everly	
344. Peak 10052	Sawtooth	10,052	Snowyside Peak	(1 mile NE of Snowyside Peak)
345. Big Peak	Smoky	10,047	Baker Peak	
346. Tohobit Peak	Sawtooth	10,046	Warbonnett Peak	
347. Peak 10045	Lemhi	10,045	Fallert Springs	(Due S of Uncle Ike/Pass Creek saddle)
348. Peak 10041	White Cloud	10,041	Horton Peak	(2.1 miles E/SE of Horton Peak)
349. Ajax Peak	Beaverhead	10,028	Homer Youngs Peak	
350. Peak 10027	Sawtooth	10,027	Snowyside Peak	(Due S of McDonald Peak)
351. Mount Baird*	Snake River	10,025	Mount Baird	
352. Jerry Peak	Boulder	10,015	Jerry Peak	
353. Prophyry Peak	White Knob	10,012	Copper Basin	
354. Mount Loening*	Salmon River	10,012	Knapp Lakes	
355. Peak 10006	Salmon River	10,006	Mount Jordan	(1.1 miles SW of The General)

APPENDIX B

HIGHEST PEAKS IN EACH IDAHO MOUNTAIN RANGE OR SUBRANGE

RANGE	PEAK	ELEVATION	USGS QUAD
Albion	Cache Peak	10,339	Independence Mountain
Aspen	Harrington Peak	8,554	Harrington Peak
Bannock	Oxford Peak	9,282	Oxford Peak
Bear River	Sherman Peak	9,682	North Canyon
Beaverhead	Scott Peak	11,393	Scott Peak
Big Hole	Piney Peak	9,019	Garns Mountain
Bighorn Crags	Mount McGuire	10,082	Mount McGuire
Bitterroot	Peak 9439	9,439	Mount Jerusalem
Blackfoot	Blackfoot Mountain	7,550	Poison Creek
Black Pine	Black Peak	9,395	Strevel
Boise	Two Point Mountain	10,124	Newman Peak
Boulder	Ryan Peak	11,714	Ryan Peak
Caribou	Caribou Mountain	9,803	Caribou Mountain
Centenial	Mount Jefferson	10,196	Upper Red Rocks
Chesterfield	Reservoir Mountain	7,143	Henry's Lake
Chilco	Chilco Mountain	5,685	Bayview
Clearwater	Stripe Mountain	9,001	Stripe Mountain
Coeur D'Alene	Grizzly Mountain	5,960	Kellog
Cotterrel	Peak 7718	7,718	Idahome
Craigs	Craigs Mountain	5,341	Frye Point
Cuddy	Cuddy Mountain	7,867	Copperfield
Danskin	Danskin Peak	6,694	Danskin Peak
Deep Creek	Deep Creek Peak	8,748	Deep Creek Peak
Fish Creek	Petticoat Peak	8,033	Bancroft
Goose Creek	Monument Peak	8,050	Trapper Peak
Grass	Granite Mountain	8,478	Hazzard
Grays	Lanes Butte	8,320	Lanes Creek
Hawley	Hawley Mountain	9,752	Hawley Mountain
Henrys Lake	North Targhee Peak	10,280	Henrys Lake
Hitt	Sturgill Peak	7,589	Sturghill Peak
Hoodoo	Bald Mountain	5,344	Emida
Jim Sage	Elba Peak	8,046	Elba
Lemhi	Diamond Peak	12,197	Diamond Peak
Lick Creek	Nick Peak	9,064	Fitsum Peak
Little Goat	Black Dome Peak	6,412	Boehls Butte
Lost River	Borah Peak	12,662	Borah Peak
Malad	Peak 6995	6,695	Henderson Creek
Moose	Moose Creek Butte	6,937	Moose Mountain
Ninety Percent	Peak 6851	6,851	Soda Springs

380

North Fork	East Mountain	7,752	Boiling Springs
North Hansel	Peak 6986	6,986	Co-Op Spring
Owyhee	Hayden Peak	8,403	Triangle
Pahsimeroi	Dickey Peak	11,141	Dickey Peak
Palouse	Moscow Mountain	4,983	Moscow Mountain
Pioneer	Hyndman Peak	12,078	Hyndman Peak
Pocatello	Chinks Mountain	6,791	Inkom
Portneuf	Mount Bonneville	9,271	Bonneville Peak
Preuss	Meade Peak	9,953	Meade Peak
Purcell	Goat Mountain	6,673	Line Point
Saint Joe	Latour Peak	6,408	Saint Joe
Salmon River	White Mountain	10,400	Twin Peaks
Samaria	Samaria Peak	7,795	Samaria
Sawtooth	Tompson Peak	10,776	Stanley Lake
Schmid	Peak 7923	7,293	Lanes Creek
Selkirk	Parker Peak	7,670	Pyramid Peak
Selway Crags	Fenn Mountain	8,021	Fenn Mountain
Seven Devils	He Devil	9,393	He Devil
Sheep	Eagle Point	5,709	Sheep Mountain
Shoshone	Bennet Peak	6,209	Taylor Peak
Silver City	Hayden Peak	8,403	Triangle
Smoky	Saviers Peak	10,441	Galena
Snake River	Mount Baird	10,025	Mount Baird
Soldier	Smoky Dome	10,095	Fairfield
SubletT	Peak 7492	7,492	Sublet Trough
Tango Peaks	Mount Loening	10,012	Knapp Lakes
Webster	Draney Peak	9,131	Stewart Flat
West	Snowbank Mountain	8,322	Smiths Ferry
White Cloud	Castle Peak	11,775	Boulder Chain of Lakes
White Knob	Shelly Mountain	11,278	Mackay
Williams	Williams Peak	7,501	Cayuse Junction
Wooley	Peak 7800	7,800	Lanes Creek
Yellowjacket	Middle Fork Peak	9,127	Aparejo Point

APPENDIX C

TENTATIVE LIST OF IDAHO FIRST ASCENTS OF PEAKS AND MAJOR FORMATIONS

* Only a peak's first ascent and first winter ascents are listed. First ascents by other routes are listed with route descriptions in the main text. Many first ascents were probably completed by persons who are no longer living and the information is lost forever. However, the author welcomes any pertinent information regarding first ascents.

PEAK	RANGE	SEASON AND YEAR	PARTY
Al West Peak	Lost River	Summer 1993	R. Baugher
Annas Pinnacle	Sawtooth	Summer 1948	Iowa Mountaineers
Arrowhead	Sawtooth	Summer ?	G. Webster/J. Beaupre
Bald Peak	Henrys Lake	Summer 1872	Hayden Survey: Gustavas Bechler
Baron Peak	Sawtooth	Summer 1934	R. and M. Underhill/D. Williams
Black and White Peak	Lost River	Summer 1990	R. Baugher
Bell Mountain	Lemhi	Summer 1913	T. M. Bannon
Big Baron Spire	Sawtooth	Summer 1949	F. Beckey/J. Schwabland/P. Schoening
Black Aiguille	Sawtooth	Summer 1960	H. Gmosser/R. Harris/Iowa Mountaineers
Borah Peak	Lost River	Summer 1912	T. M. Bannon
		Winter 1971	F. Florence
Boulder Peak	Boulder	Summer 1895	E. T. Perkins and W. Griswold
Braxon Peak	Sawtooth	Summer	Unknown
		Winter 1975	W. Cove/L. Adkins
Breakfast Tower	Sawtooth	Summer 1961	E. Bjornstad/D. Davis
The Brow	Lemhi	Summer 1990	R. Baugher
Cabin Creek Peak	Salmon River	Summer 1988	P. Bellamy/D. Lopez/T. Lopez
Cache Peak	Albion	Summer 1877	Wheeler Survey/Fred Clark
Caribou	Caribou	Summer 1877	Hayden Survey
Castle Peak	White Cloud	Summer ?	T. M. Bannon
		Winter 1971	R. Watters/I. Gayfield/J. Hokum/H. Hilbert/S. Schaffer/J. Elphinston
Cathedral Rock	Bighorn Creek		
	N. Summit	Summer 1924	U.S. Forest Service
	S. Summit	Summer 1955	L. Hales/P. Schoening
Chimney Rock	Selkirk	Summer 1934	J. Carey/M. Chamberlain/F. Thieme/B. Ward
		Winter 1973	C. Kopczynski/W. Parks
The Chisel	Bighorn Creek	Summer 1955	L. Hales/P. Schoening
Chockstone Peak	Sawtooth	Summer 1960	Iowa Mountaineers
Cirque Lake Peak	Sawtooth	Summer 1954	Seattle Mountaineers
Cleft Peak	Lost River	Summer 1992	R. Baugher
Cobb Peak	Pioneer	Summer ?	Unknown
		Winter 1971	R. Watters/J. Lowry/R. Albano/D. Mcbride/J. Elphinston
Damocles	Sawtooth	Summer 1961	F. Beckey/S. Marts
Deep Creek Peak	Deep Creek	Summer 1877	Wheeler Survey/Fred Clark
Desert Tower	Sawtooth	Summer 1961	D. Davis

Devils Bedstead West	Pioneer	Summer ?	Unknown
		Winter ?	L. Stur/R. Kiesel/B. Gorton/B. Bachman
Devils Throne	Seven Devils	Summer 1938	A. H. Marshall
Devils Tooth	Seven Devils	Summer 1963	D. Eastman/J. Angel
Diamond Peak	Lemhi	Summer 1913	T. M. Bannon
Dinner Tower	Sawtooth	Summer 1961	E. Bjornstad/D. Davis/S. Marts
Donaldson Peak	Lost River	Summer ?	Unknown
		Winter 1975	W. March/R. Albano
Duncans Peak	Pioneers	Summer ?	Unknown
		Winter 1957	C. Caldwell/D. Millsap/B. Echo
Eagle Perch	Sawtooth	Summer 1960	H. Gmosser/Iowa Mountaineers
Easley Peak	Boulders	Summer 1895	USGS: W. Griswold, E. Perkins
East Lions Head	Selkirk	Summer 1960s	N. McAvoy and others
Ed-Da-How Spire	Sawtooth	Summer 1973	L. Dye/Spring/Howard/Taylor/Bravance
Mount Limbert	Sawtooth	Summer 1948	Iowa Mountaineers
Eighteenmile Peak	Beaverhead	Summer 1900s	Howard Carpenter
El Capitan	Sawtooth	Summer 1935	R. and M. Underhill/D. Williams
Elephants Perch	Sawtooth	Summer 1960	Iowa Mountaineers
Elkhorn Peak	Bannock	Summer 1878	Hayden Survey: H. Gannett/A. Wilson
Elk Peak	Sawtooth	Summer 1934	R. Underhill/D. Williams
El Pima	Sawtooth	Summer 1947	F. Beckey/J. Schwabland/P. Schoening
Err Peak	Pioneer	Summer 1994	R. Baugher
Finger of Fate	Sawtooth	Summer 1958	L. Stur/J. Fuller
Fishhook Spire	Sawtooth	Summer 1960	R. Maynard/F. Chappel/Iowa Mountaineers
Flat Iron	Lemhi	Summer 1913	T. M. Bannon
Flatrock Needle	Sawtooth	Summer 1960	H. Gmosser/B. Echo/D. Millsap/C. Brown
Ferguson Peak	Lost River	Summer 1978	C. Ferguson
Galena Peak	Boulder	Summer 1890s	W. Griswold, E. Perkins
Glassford Peak	Boulder	Summer 1894	E. T. Perkins/W. Griswold
Goat Perch	Sawtooth	Summer 1960	H. Carter/Iowa Mountaineers
Goblin	Seven Devils	Summer 1935	A. H. Marshall/E. Hughes
Gooseberry Peak	Lost River	Summer 1991	D. Lopez, T. Lopez
Grand Aigille	Sawtooth	Summer 1946	J. Hieb/W. Grande/R. Widrig/W. Graham Mathews
Grand Mogul	Sawtooth	Summer 1948	F. Beckey/J. Fuller
Graves Peak	Bitterroot	Summer 1897	Joseph Lippencott
Gunsight Peak	Lemhi	Summer 1881	David R. T. and J.R.
He Devil	Seven Devils	Before 1938	B. Savage/C. Brown/H. Barton/J.Ratcliff
Hope Peak	Lost River	Summer 1993	R. Baugher
Horstmann Peak	Sawtooth	Summer 1934	R. and M. Underhill/D. Williams
Hyndman Peak	Pioneer	Summer 1890s	W. Griswold/E. Perkins or G A. McLeod
		Winter ?	L. Stur and others
Incredible Hulk	Lemhi	Summer 1990	R. Baugher
Knuckle Peak	Bighorn Creek	Summer 1955	L. Hales/P. Schoening
La Fiama	Sawtooth	Summer 1962	F. Beckey/S. Marts/D. Davis
Leaning Tower of Pisa	Sawtooth	Summer 1961	F. Beckey/D. Davis/S. Marts
Leatherman Peak	Lost River	Summer 1910s	T. M. Bannon
		Winter 1975	W. March/R. Albano
Le Bec d'Aigle	Sawtooth	Summer 1954	H. Carter/G. Constan
Lem Peak	Lemhi	Summer 1910s	T. M. Bannon
Litner Peak	Bighorn Creek	Summer 1955	L. Hales/P. Schoening
Lunch Tower	Sawtooth	Summer 1961	E. Bjorstad/D. Davis
May Mountain	Lemhi	Summer 1913	T. M. Bannon

Peak	Range	Date	Party
McGown Peak	Sawtooth	Summer 1934	R. and M. Underhill
Meade Peak	Peale	Summer 1887	Hayden Survey: H. Gannett
Metaxy	Lost River	1991	R. Baugher
Mickeys Spire	Sawtooth	Summer 1934	R. and M. Underhill
Mount Baird	Snake River	Summer 1877	O. St. John
Mount Belial	Seven Devils	Summer 1943	A. H. Marshall
Mount Bush	Sawtooth	Summer 1948	Iowa Mountaineers
Mount Carter	Sawtooth	Summer 1948	Iowa Mountaineers
Mount Ebert	Sawtooth	Summer 1957	Iowa Mountaineers
Mount Heyburn	Sawtooth		
	W. Summit	Summer 1935	R. and M. Underhill/D. Williams
		Winter 1975	W. Cove/L. Adkins
	E. Summit	Summer 1927	B. Limbert
Mount Hoopes	Lemhi	Summer 1989	R. Baugher
Mount Inspiration	Lemhi	Summer 1991	R. Baugher
Mount McCaleb	Lost River	1914	T. M. Bannon
Mount McGuire	Bighorn Crags	Summer 1912	T. M. Bannon
Mount Obsession	Lost River	Summer ?	Unknown
		Winter 1975	W. March/R. Albano
Mount Orge	Seven Devils	Before 1940	Unknown
Mount Regan	Sawtooth	Summer 1934	R. and M. Underhill/D. Williams
		Winter 1971	R. Sargent/J. Leonard/N Garrison/B. Weaver
Mount Underhill	Sawtooth	Summer 1935	R. and M. Underhill/D. Williams
North Doublet	Beaverhead	Summer 1998	R. Baugher
North Raker	Sawtooth	Summer 1934	R. and M. Underhill
Old Tom Mountain	Bannock	Summer 1870s	Hayden Survey
Oxford Peak	Bannock	Summer 1878	Hayden Survey
Packrat Peak	Sawtooth	Summer 1935	R. and M. Underhill/D. Williams
Painted Peak	Seven Devils	Summer 1963	Mazama Club
Parks Peak	Sawtooth	Summer 1960	D. Miller/T. Robertson/H. Wendling
Pavlos	Lost River	Summer 1993	R. Baugher
Peak 10569	Lemhi	Summer 1975	D. Rice
Peak 10601 (Ramshorn Peak)	Lost River	Summer 1996	R. Baugher
Peak 10604	Lemhi	Summer 1948	R. Anderson
Peak 10688	Lemhi	Summer 1975	D. Rice
Peak 10970 (Black and White)	Lemhi	1998	R. Baugher
Peak 11039 (Atlas)	Pioneer	Summer 1990	R. Baugher
Peak 11070 (South Twin)	Lost River	Summer1990	R. Bauger
Peak 11081 (North Twin)	Lost River	Summer 1988	R. Baugher
Peak 11258 (Alcyon Peak)	Pioneer	Summer 1993	R. Baugher
Peak 11292 (Huhs Horn)	Beaverhead	Summer 1998	R. Baugher
Peak 11367 (Morrison Mt.)	Lost River	Summer 1993	R.Baugher
Peak 11473 (Hoseshoe Mt.)	Lost River	Summer 1993	R. Baugher
Peak 11477	Lost River	Summer 1993	R. Baugher
Peak 11516 (Abel Peak)	Pioneer	Summer 1994	R. Baugher
Peak 10533 (Medusa)	Lemhi	Summer 1991	R. Baugher
Peak 10571	Lost River	Summer 1992	R. Baugher
Peak 10601	Lost River	Summer 1992	R. Baugher
Peak 11887	Pioneer	Summer 1993	R. Baugher
Peak 11930 (Far Away Mts.)	Lost River	Summer 1993	R. Baugher
Pegasus	Pioneer	Summer 1994	R. Baugher
Pyramid Peak	Beaverhead	Summer 1840s	Warren Ferris

Quartzite Peak	Sawtooth	Summer 1960	H. Gmosser/W. Joura/Iowa Mountaineers
Ramskull Peak	Bighorn Crags	Summer 1955	L. Hales/P. Schoening
Red Bluff Peak	Sawtooth	Summer 1960	G. Vendor/E. Vendor
Redfish Peak	Sawtooth	Summer 1948	Iowa Mountaineers
Reward Peak	Sawtooth	Summer 1925	Unknown
Riddler, The	Lemhi	Summer 1990	R. Baugher
Ross Peak	Lost River	Summer 1993	R. Baugher
Rothorn Spire	Sawtooth	Summer 1973	L. Dye/Spring/Howard/Taylor/Bravance
Rotten Monolith	Sawtooth	Summer 1961	F. Beckey/L. Stur
Ryan Peak	Boulder	Summer 1894	E. T. Perkins/W. Griswold
Saddle Mountain	Lemhi	Summer 1890	V. Bailey
Salzburger Spitzl	Pioneer	Summer ?	Unknown
		Winter ?	C. Caldwell/D. Millsap/B. Echo
Sawtelle	Centennial	Summer 1870s	Hayden Survey
Schwartz Pinnacle	Sawtooth	Summer 1948	Iowa Mountaineers
Scorpion Peak	Pioneer	Summer 1915	T. M. Bannon
She Devil	Seven Devils	Summer 1940	A. H. Marshall
Sherman Peak	Bear River	Summer 1877	Hayden Survey
Shoshone John Peak	Lemhi	Summer 1992	R. Baugher
Silicon Tower	Sawtooth	Summer 1961	H. T. Carter
Sleeping Deer	Salmon River	Summer 1879	Sheepeater Tribe
Smiley Mountain	Pioneer	Summer ?	T. M. Bannon
		Winter 1957	C. Caldwell/D. Millsap/B. Echo
Smokey Dome	Soldier	Summer 1895	USGS: W. Griswold, E. Perkins
Snowyside Peak	Sawtooth	Summer 1890s	USGS: W. Griswold, E. Perkins
South Raker	Sawtooth	Summer 1949	F. Beckey/P. Schoening
Spire #3	Bighorn Crags	Summer 1963	B. Hammer/Idaho Alpine Club
Spire #4	Bighorn Crags	Summer 1963	B. Hammer/Idaho Alpine Club
Splinter Tower	Sawtooth	Summer 1948	J. Holden/J. Schwabland
Split Tooth	Sawtooth	Summer 1960	B. Echo and Idaho Alpine Club
Standhope Peak	Pioneer	Summer ?	T. M. Bannon
Steeple Tower	Sawtooth	Summer 1948	F. Beckey/H. King
Taylor Mountain	Blackfoot Mountains	Summer 1877	Hayden Survey: O. St. John
Thimble Tower	Sawtooth	Summer 1948	F. Beckey/H. King
Thompson Peak	Sawtooth	Summer 1934	R.and M. Underhill/D. Williams
Tilted Slab	Sawtooth	Summer 1971	L. Dye
Timber Peak	Lemhi	Summer 1913	T. M. Bannon
Twin Imp	Seven Devils		
	N. Summit	Summer 1963	Mazama Club
	S. Summit	Summer 1938	A. H. Marshall
Tower of Babel	Seven Devils	Summer 1939	A. H. Marshall
Umpleby Peak	Lehmi	Summer 1991	R. Baugher
Wakley Peak	Bannock	Summer 1870s	Wheeler Survey
Warbonnet Peak	Sawtooth	Summer 1947	P. Petzoldt/J. Speck/C. Wilson/B. Adams/C. Fish/B. Merrian
West Lions Head	Selkirk	Summer 1960s	N. McAvoy
White Cap Peak	Lost River	Summer	Unknown
		Winter	W. March/R. Albano
Williams Peak	Sawtooth	Summer 1934	R. and M.Underhill/D. Williams

APPENDIX D

ADDRESSES

GUIDE SERVICES

Sawtooth Mountain Guides
P.O. Box 18
Stanely, Idaho 83278
(208) 774-3324
www.sawtoothguides.com
e-mail: getaway@sawtoothguides.com

FOREST SERVICE ADDRESSES

Bitterroot National Forest
1801 North First St.
Hamilton, Montana 59840
(406) 363-7100
fs.usda.gov/bitterroot/
    Bitterroot Mountains
    Clearwater Mountains

Boise National Forest
1249 S. Vinnell Way, Suite 200
Boise, Idaho 83709
(208) 373-4100
fs.usda.gov/boise/
    Boise Mountains
    Salmon River Mountains
    West Mountains
    Danskin Mountains

Caribou-Targhee National Forest
1405 Hollipark Dr.
Idaho Falls, Idaho 83401
(208) 524-7500
    Bannock Range
    Beaverhead Mountains
    Caribou Mountains
    Centennial Range
    Henrys Lake Range

Lemhi Range
Malad Range
Peale Mountains
Portneuf Range

Challis Salmon National Forest
1206 So. Challis St.
Salmon, Idaho 83467
(208) 756-5100
www.fs.fed.us/r4/sc/
    Beaverhead Range
    Bighorn Crags
    Bitterroot Mountains
    Boulder Mountains
    Lemhi Range
    Lost River Range
    Salmon River Mountains
    White Cloud Peaks
    Yellowjacket Mountains

Clearwater National Forest
12730 Highway 12
Orofino, Idaho 83544
(208) 476-4541
www.fs.fed.us/r1/clearwater/
    Clearwater Mountains

Hells Canyon National Recreation Area
P.O. Box 832
Riggins, Idaho 83549
(208) 628-3916
fs.usda.gov/hellscanyon/index.htm
    Seven Devils Mountains

Lolo National Forest
Fort Missoula—Bldg. 24
Missoula, Montana 59804
(406) 329-3750
fs.usda.gov/lolo
    Bitterroot Mountains

Nez Perce National Forest
104 Airport Road
Grangeville, Idaho 83530
(208) 983-1950
fs.usda.gov/nezperce
    Clearwater Mountains
    Seven Devils Mountains
    Cuddy Mountains
    Hitt Mountains

Idaho Panhandle National Forests
3815 Schreiber Way
Coeur D'Alene, Idaho 83815
(208) 765-7223
fs.usda.gov/ipnf
    Bitterroot Mountains
    Cabinet Mountains
    Chilco Mountains
    Coeur d'Alene Mountains
    Purcell Range
    Saint Joe Mountains
    Selkirk Range

Payette National Forest
800 West Lakeside Avenue
McCall, Idaho 83638
(208) 634-0700
fs.usda.gov/payette/
    Cuddy Mountains
    Hitt Mountains
    Lick Creek Range
    Salmon River Mountains
    Seven Devils Mountains
    West Mountains

Sawtooth National Forest
2647 Kimberly Road East
Twin Falls, Idaho 83301
(208) 737-3200
fs.usda.gov/sawtooth/
    Albion Range

    Black Pine Range
    Boulder Mountains
    Goose Creek Mountains
    Pioneer Mountains
    Smoky Mountains
    Soldier Mountains
    Sublette Range

Sawtooth National Recreation Area
Headquarters Office
Star Route
Ketchum, Idaho 83340
(208) 726-8291
    Boulder Mountains
    Sawtooth Range
    Smoky Mountains
    White Cloud Peaks

BUREAU OF LAND MANAGEMENT
Idaho State Office
1387 South Vinnell Way
Boise, Idaho 83709
(208) 373-4000
www.blm.gov/id/st/en.html

STATE OF IDAHO
Priest Lake State Forest
Idaho Department of Lands
314 Indian Creek Park Rd.
Coolin, Idaho 83821
(208) 443-2200
http://parksandrecreation.idaho.gov/parks/priestlake.aspx

APPENDIX E

SELECTED REFERENCES

GENERAL INTEREST

Conley, Cort. *Idaho for the Curious*. Cambridge, Idaho: Backeddy Books, 1981.

Federal Writers Project. *The Idaho Encyclopedia*. Caldwell, Idaho: Caxton Printers, 1938.

State of Idaho. *Idaho Almanac*. Boise, Idaho: 1977.

HIKING

Bluestein, Sheldon. *Exploring Idaho's High Desert*. Available online at *www.hikeidaho.com*

———. *Trails of the Frank Church–River of No Return Wilderness*. Edmonds, Washington: Signpost Books, 1987.

Fuller, Margaret. *Trails of the Sawtooth and White Cloud Mountains*. 2d ed. Edmonds, Washington: Signpost Books, 1989.

Fuller, Margaret and Painter, Jerry. *Trails of Eastern Idaho*. Trail Guide Books, 1998.

Landers, Rich and Dolphin, Ida Rowe. *100 Hikes in the Inland Northwest*. Seattle, Washington. The Mountaineers Books, 1992.

Maughan, Ralph and , Jackie Johnson. *The Hikers Guide to Idaho*. Billings and Helena, Montana: Falcon Press Publishing Company, 1990.

CLIMBING GUIDES

Bingham, Dave. *City of Rocks, A Climber's Guide*. 2d ed. Ketchurn, Idaho: Self-Published, 1988.

Caffrey, Pat. *Climber's Guide to Montana*. Missoula, Montana: Mountain Press Publishing Company, 1986.

Green, Randall. *Idaho Rock*. Seattle, Washington: The Mountaineers Books, 1988.

CROSS-COUNTRY SKIING

Watters, Ron. *Winter Tales and Trails*. Moscow, Idaho: Great Rift Press, 1998.

GEOLOGY

Alt, David and Hyndman, Donald. *Roadside Geology of Idaho*. Missoula, Montana: Mountain Press Publishing Company, 1989.

Maley, Terry. *Exploring Idaho Geology*. Boise, Idaho: Mineral Land Publications, 1987.

INDEX

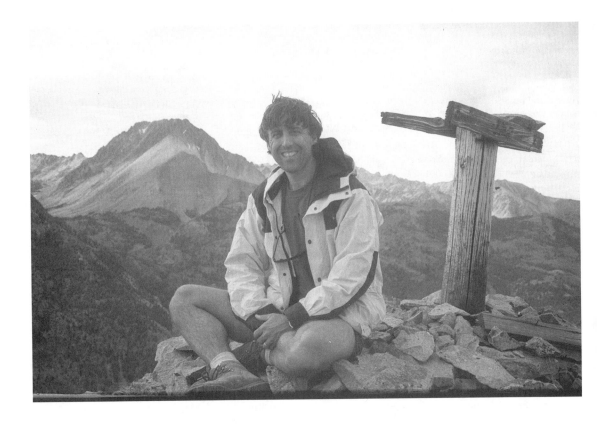

ABOUT THE AUTHOR

Tom Lopez climbed his first Idaho peak in 1972 and started to collect information for a climbing guide in 1978. During this time, he has lived and climbed out of Boise, Idaho Falls, Moscow, Shoshone, and Salmon. He has also climbed extensively across the United States, including several first ascents in Alaska, and trips to Bolivia, Mexico, and New Zealand. He prefers searching for hidden places others have missed or overlooked, "there is nothing better than finding a challenging route on an attractive peak, far from roads and trails." Fortunately, he notes, "Idaho is full of such opportunities."

THE MOUNTAINEERS, founded in 1906, is a nonprofit outdoor activity and conservation club, whose mission is "to explore, study, preserve, and enjoy the natural beauty of the outdoors...." Based in Seattle, Washington, the club is now one of the largest such organizations in the United States, with seven branches throughout Washington State.

The Mountaineers sponsors both classes and year-round outdoor activities in the Pacific Northwest, which include hiking, mountain climbing, ski-touring, snowshoeing, bicycling, camping, kayaking and canoeing, nature study, sailing, and adventure travel. The club's conservation division supports environmental causes through educational activities, sponsoring legislation, and presenting informational programs. All club activities are led by skilled, experienced volunteers, who are dedicated to promoting safe and responsible enjoyment and preservation of the outdoors.

If you would like to participate in these organized outdoor activities or the club's programs, consider a membership in The Mountaineers. For information and an application, write or call The Mountaineers, 7700 Sand Point Way NE, Seattle, Washington 98115; 206-521-6001.

The Mountaineers Books, an active, nonprofit publishing program of the club, produces guidebooks, instructional texts, historical works, natural history guides, and works on environmental conservation. All books produced by The Mountaineers are aimed at fulfilling the club's mission.

Send or call for our catalog of more than 500 outdoor titles:

The Mountaineers Books
1001 SW Klickitat Way, Suite 201
Seattle, WA 98134
800-553-4453
mbooks@mountaineers.org
www.mountaineersbooks.org

The Mountaineers Books is proud to be a corporate sponsor of the Leave No Trace Center for Outdoor Ethics, whose mission is to promote and inspire responsible outdoor recreation through education, research, and partnerships. The Leave No Trace program is focused specifically on human-powered (nonmotorized) recreation.

Leave No Trace strives to educate visitors about the nature of their recreational impacts, as well as offer techniques to prevent and minimize such impacts. Leave No Trace is best understood as an educational and ethical program, not as a set of rules and regulations.

For more information, visit www.lnt.org or call (800) 332-4100.

OTHER TITLES YOU MIGHT ENJOY FROM
THE MOUNTAINEERS BOOKS

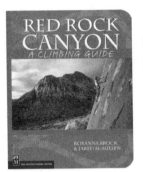
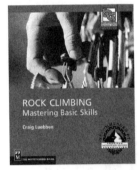
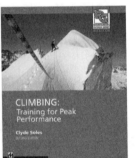